THE TIMES
THE SUNDAY TIMES

Good University Guide

2014

John O'Leary

With

Dr Nicki Horseman

IN ASSOCIATION WITH

milkround

D0566489

C 2 000 004 822063

Published in 2013 by Times Books

HarperCollins Publishers
Westerhill Road
Bishopbriggs
Glasgow G64 2QT
www.harpercollins.co.uk

First published in 1993 by Times Books. Twentieth edition 2013

ISBN 978-0-00-752813-4

Dr Nicki Horseman was the lead consultant for UoE Consulting Ltd, which has compiled the main university league table and the individual subject tables for this guide on behalf of *The Times, The Sunday Times* and HarperCollins.

Please see chapters 4 and 5 for a full explanation of the sources of data used in the ranking tables. The data providers do not necessarily agree with the data aggregations or manipulations appearing in this book and are also not responsible for any inference or conclusions thereby derived.

Project editor: Christopher Riches
Design, editorial and additional research: Edenside Computing Services Ltd

Printed and bound in Great Britain by Clays Ltd, St Ives plc.

MIX
Paper from
responsible sources
FSC www.fsc.org **FSC™ C007454**

FSC is a non-profit international organisation established to promote the responsible
management of the world's forests. Products carrying the FSC label are
independently certified to assure customers that they come from forests that are
managed to meet social, economic and ecological needs of present and future generations.

Find out more about HarperCollins and the environment at:
www.harpercollins.co.uk/green

Contents

About the Author

John O'Leary is a freelance journalist and education consultant. He was the Editor of *The Times Higher Education Supplement* from 2002 to 2007 and was previously Education Editor of The Times, having joined the paper in 1990 as Higher Education Correspondent. He has been writing on higher education for more than 30 years and is a member of the executive board of the QS World University Rankings. He is the author of *Higher Education in England*, published in 2009 by the Higher Education Funding Council for England. He has a degree in politics from the University of Sheffield.

Acknowledgements

We would like to thank the many individuals who have helped with this edition of *The Times and Sunday Times Good University Guide*, particularly Greg Hurst, Education Editor of *The Times*, Alastair McCall, Editor of *The Sunday Times* University Guide, and Dr Nicki Horseman, the lead consultant for UoE Consulting Ltd, which has compiled the main university league table and the individual subject tables for this guide on behalf of *The Times*, *The Sunday Times* and HarperCollins Publishers; to the members of *The Times Good University Guide* Advisory Group for their time and expertise: Patrick Kennedy, Consultant, Collective Intelligence Ltd; Dr Alison Powell, Business Intelligence Officer, Cardiff University; Tom Wright, Senior Planning Manager, Northumbria University; Tom Wale, Senior Planning Officer, Loughborough University; Christine Couper, Head of Planning and Statistics, University of Greenwich; Aaron Morrison, Principal Planning Officer at De Montfort University; Josie Lewis-Gibbs, Planning Officer, Imperial College, London; James McLaren and Rebecca Hobbs of HESA for their technical advice; Martin Ince, Mary Bowers, Kaya Burgess and Sue O'Leary for their contributions to the book.

We also wish to thank the publishers of the QS World University Rankings, the Academic Ranking of World Universities and *Times Higher Education* for permission to reproduce some of their main league tables, and all the university staff who assisted in providing information for this edition.

How to Use This Book

The Times and Sunday Times Good University Guide 2014 will help you to select the subject and university of your choice and to guide you through the whole process of getting to university. The answers to the questions below will help you to get the most out of the information we offer.

How do I choose a course?
» The first half of chapter 1 provides advice on what you should consider when choosing a subject area and relevant courses within that subject.
» The tables near the beginning of chapter 2 give details of the employment prospects for all major subjects.
» Chapter 5 provides details for 64 different subject areas (as listed on page 68).
» For each subject there is a league table that provides our assessment of the ranking of all universities offering courses in the particular subject area.
» For each subject we also provide some background information, details of employment prospects and selected websites where you can find out more about the subject.
» Specific advice for international students is given in chapter 12.

How do I choose a university?
» The second half of chapter 1 provides advice on choosing a university.
» If you are considering studying abroad, chapter 3 provides guidance and practical information.
» Central is the main *Times and Sunday Times* league table on pages 60–64. This ranks the universities by assessing their quality not just according to student satisfaction (drawn from the National Student Survey) but also through seven other factors, including research quality, the spending on services and facilities, and graduate employment prospects. This table gives an indication of the overall performance of each university.
» The second half of the book contains two pages on each university, giving a general overview of the institution as well as data on student numbers, how to contact the university, the accommodation provided by the university, and the fees and financial support for 2014–15, wherever possible. Note that details for support for 2014–15 had not been released for some institutions when this book went to print in September 2013.
» In addition, chapter 10 provides information on sport and sporting facilities across all the universities.
» For those considering Oxford or Cambridge, details of admission processes and of all the colleges can be found in chapter 13.
» Specific advice for international students is given in chapter 12.

How do I apply?
» Chapter 6 outlines the application procedure for university entry.
» It starts by advising you on how to complete the UCAS application, and then takes you through the process that we hope will lead to your university place for autumn 2014.
» Specific information about applying to Oxford and Cambridge is given in chapter 13.

Can I afford it?

» Chapters 7 and 8 outline the costs of studying at university (including the payment of fees) as well as sources of funds (including student loans, grants and bursaries).

» Chapter 9 provides advice on where to live while you are there.

» Accommodation charges for 2013–14 for each university are given in the university profiles in chapter 14. Figures for 2014–15 were not available when this book was printed.

How will university enhance my career?

» The employment prospects and average starting salaries for the main subject groups are given in chapter 2.

» Universities are now doing more to increase the employability of their graduates. Some examples are given in chapter 2 – and check whether your chosen universities provide similar services.

How do I find out more?

» In each university profile (chapter 14) contact details are given (including email addresses and websites), so you can obtain more information on any university you are interested in.

» At the end of each chapter, a selection of useful websites is given.

» A further listing at the back of the book provides contact details for higher education institutions that are not covered elsewhere within the book.

» *The Times and Sunday Times Good University Guide* website at **www.thetimes.co.uk/gooduniversityguide** or **www.thesundaytimes.co.uk/gooduniversityguide** will keep you up to date with developments throughout the year and contains further information and online tables.

Introduction

The merger of *The Times* and *Sunday Times* university guides begins a new chapter in the ranking of higher education institutions in the UK. The two guides had 35 editions between them and, in their new form, will provide the most comprehensive and authoritative assessments of undergraduate education at UK universities. But in many ways it is business as usual. Not only are the rankings in this book compiled on the same basis as those in last year's *Times Good University Guide* but, by a quirk of fate, the results have an echo of the first edition, over 20 years ago. In 1993, Oxford and Cambridge tied for first place in the only dead heat for that position in the *Guide*'s history. This year, only one point in 1,000 separates the two ancient rivals, effectively repeating that initial result. Indeed, the 2014 *Guide* underlines the enduring stability of the leading universities: while they may be in a different order, seven of the top ten are common to both tables.

Cambridge is fractionally ahead of Oxford for the first time in more than a decade, but of greater significance is the widening gap between the two universities and the rest of the higher education system. More than 100 points now separate Oxford from the London School of Economics in third place. The first edition of the *Guide* predicted the development of a new pecking order in an era of growing competition between universities, many of which had just acquired that title. There certainly has been no shortage of competition – now more intense than ever – but the old guard retains its allure.

Age is no guarantee of future success, however. Some long-established institutions were left with empty places in 2012, the first year of £9,000 fees in England, and many good judges expect to see university mergers or even closures in the years ahead. Now that fees account for a much larger proportion of a university's income, institutions will not be able to afford continuing under-recruitment. The demand for higher education places has recovered in 2013 – school leavers, if not yet aspiring mature students, appear resigned to paying higher fees. But that demand is not evenly spread, either between subjects or institutions. Some universities are already closing courses and shedding staff in response to the changes.

Anyone hoping to embark on a degree in 2013 will therefore need to tread carefully and muster as much comparative information as possible before making their choices. This *Guide* is intended as a starting point, a tool to help navigate the statistical minefield that will face applicants, as universities present their performance in the best possible light. There is a chapter on the impact of the fee changes, as well as one focusing on all-important employment issues along with the usual ranking of universities and 64 subject tables, including, for the first time, tables for physiotherapy and radiology.

No one can be sure that the volume or pattern of applications this year will be repeated in 2014, not least because the Universities and Colleges Admissions Service (UCAS) has refused to disclose the level of applications to individual institutions for the first time. The fact that such key information is being denied to prospective students during the application season, after more than a decade of regular updates, speaks volumes about the nervousness of universities as they adapt to the new system. The organisation is concerned that applicants may draw unwarranted conclusions about the vulnerability of courses they might be considering if the demand for places at particular universities is dropping. Such is the volatility of the demand for different subjects that those courses might be thriving even at a university that is struggling in other areas. Despite ministers' promises of more information to guide applicants' decision making, UCAS's response is not to publish applications by subject, but to keep the figures secret until after the deadline for applications has passed.

What UCAS has published is the shift in demand for different subject areas at a national level, and this confirms that £9,000 fees are having a predictable impact on choices of course. Applications by 18 year-olds for courses in the physical sciences and maths are now 15 per cent higher than in 2010, the last year considered unaffected by the prospect or reality of higher fees, whereas they are 36 per cent down in non-European languages and approaching 17 per cent down in European languages. Engineering is 8 per cent up, while architecture, building and planning is still 22 per cent down. There have been exceptions like anthropology, which has seen big increases in demand in spite of the new fees, but the trend is towards subjects that students think will lead to jobs and away from those that are seen as more risky. The employment tables in Chapter 2 show that these impressions are not always correct – architecture was among the top 20 subjects for positive destinations in 2012, for example – but the trend may still affect the number of courses that remain available. It is noticeable that degrees both in languages and architecture take longer than the standard three-year degree in England, Wales and Northern Ireland, so it may be the extra debts that students will incur are an additional influence in these subjects.

Perceived employment prospects have always had an influence on students' choices of degree – career advancement is the most common motivation of those opting for higher education, after all. It is not surprising, therefore, that higher fees have accelerated an existing trend. But the best economists in the land struggle to predict labour market conditions three or more years ahead and, with most graduate jobs open to graduates of any discipline, it would be a shame to abandon a subject that captures your interest on the basis of informed guesswork. There may well be strong demand for graduates in Chinese Studies in four years' time and talented linguists are not confined to jobs that demand translation skills.

Just as it may be unwise to second-guess employment prospects, the same goes for the competition for places in different subjects. Universities may close or reduce the intake to courses that have low numbers of applicants while some of the more selective institutions may make more places available, especially to candidates who achieve ABB or better at A level since they are no longer restricted in the numbers they can recruit at this level. Bristol and University College London each took hundreds more students than usual in 2012, and Exeter has done the same in 2013. Some may announce similar plans for 2014, but applicants are best advised to go for the courses and universities that meet their requirements, rather than trying to play the system.

Neither are fee levels likely to play a great part in applicants' choices of university – other than in Scotland and Northern Ireland, where there are big financial incentives to study at a home university. The continuing absence of fees north of the border has been particularly influential in dissuading Scottish students from studying elsewhere. But there has been little evidence that candidates have been swayed by differences of a few hundred pounds in the fees charged by universities in England. Even those differences are diminishing: only 20 universities will charge less than £9,000 for any of their degrees in 2014–15. In any case, applicants know that they have up to 30 years to repay their loans and graduates will all pay the same proportion of their salary (9 per cent) once they pass the threshold of £21,000 a year. Some will repay for a lot longer than others, but that will depend more on salary levels than any marginal differences in the size of loans.

One certainty for 2014 is that competition at the most popular universities, particularly in the most popular subjects, will remain stiff. A growing number of jobs require a degree and international comparisons continue to show that the UK is one of the countries where the career earnings of graduates outstrip those of less-qualified workers by the largest margin. Inevitably, that gap will be reduced as graduates are required to pay higher loans following the introduction of £9,000 fees. But the Organisation for Economic Cooperation and Development believes that the extra repayments will merely dent and certainly not wipe out a graduate premium that amounts to more than £100,000 over the average career. This figure is far from uniform, however, even within the same university, and graduates who attended the leading institutions can expect to earn more, on average, than others. Even when the demand for places dropped in 2012, there were between five and six applications (not applicants) to the place across the whole higher education system. The figure was almost double that at the most popular universities.

In theory, winning a place should be slightly easier in 2014. There will be fewer 18 year-olds in the population and there is no sign of mature students applying in the same numbers as they did before the fees went up. It will take more of an economic recovery than the UK has seen so far to persuade people in their twenties and thirties to give up jobs, if they have them, and take on much higher levels of debt to try higher education. Universities will be anxious to fill as many places as they can without endangering quality. There should again be more choice for those who achieve at least ABB at A level or the equivalent because, as in 2013, universities will be allowed to recruit as many such students as they wish – although many of the top universities do not wish to increase the size of their intakes and may not be able to do so anyway because of the they have no room to expand. There will still be more qualified candidates than places on the most popular courses and it may be even more important to make the right "insurance" choice. Growing numbers of well-qualified students have been left without a place in recent years because they have applied only to high-demand courses, and then have not been interested in the options available in Clearing. It saves a wasted year and a considerable amount of money to secure an offer from a university with lower entrance requirements than your first-choice institutions.

For those who do not reach the ABB threshold in 2014, it will be even more important to be realistic about your choices. Universities in England will still be restricted in the number of places they can offer to such students. It was this, rather than any inability to attract enough students that led to empty places even at some Russell Group universities in 2012. The entry grades quoted in the subject tables are a good guide to levels of competition, but they include AS levels and multiple entries at A level, so most candidates with ABB at A level will score considerably more than 320 points overall. The standard offers for each course appear on the UCAS website and on universities' own sites.

Candidates with better grades than they expected may also find more options available in the Adjustment Period that runs for five days after results have been published. Although only 1,329 students found places this way in 2012, the numbers rose in 2013 with the lifting of recruitment restrictions and may continue rising as the system becomes better known. Universities at the very top of the table may still be full, but there should be more opportunities to "trade up" if your grades are better than your highest offer.

The level of demand for places in 2014 and beyond remains shrouded in uncertainty, however, despite this year's recovery. The 18 year-olds who have applied for places in the two years since the fees went up were already on track for higher education before the Government imposed higher charges. Sixth-formers and college students who are weighing up their options in the coming months will be the first to have embarked on A levels or other qualifications in the full knowledge of what a degree would cost. With some of the leading employers expanding their recruitment at 18, the Government funding many more apprenticeships and economic recovery promising higher levels of employment, many may try to avoid the undoubtedly high costs of higher education.

This year's tables

Unlike most of the rankings that have sprung up in recent years, this *Guide* has remained as consistent as possible in the methods used to compare universities. A change of name will not alter that philosophy. The indicators and weightings used in the overall ranking of universities are the same as last year. One marginal change in the institutional and subject tables flows from the recategorisation of graduate jobs by the Higher Education Statistics Agency, which has led to the use of a single year's employment figures rather than the usual two. That, together with considerable increases in student satisfaction at many universities, has produced more movement than usual in universities' positions. Even a modest increase in satisfaction has not been enough to prevent some universities falling behind their rivals.

The other change is presentational. Universities' research scores are shown as a percentage of the estimated maximum score that they could have achieved if every eligible academic had been entered for the 2008 Research Assessment Exercise and all their work had been considered world-leading. Even the very best departments were not likely to come close to 100 per cent, but the new format has been adopted as a more accessible way to present the outcomes.

There four more universities than last year in the main League Table because the Government has reduced the minimum number of students required for university status and also awarded the title to more institutions in the private sector. In total, 13 university colleges and private institutions have become universities, but only seven appear in the main table because the new Norwich University of the Arts and the Royal Agricultural University were considered too specialised to be compared usefully with more mainstream universities. The new arrivals from the 'public' sector are the University of St Mark and St John, Arts University Bournemouth, Bishop Grosseteste, Falmouth, Harper Adams, Leeds Trinity and Newman universities.

University College Birmingham, which was also awarded university status, chose not to release date for use in league tables because it believed that its high proportion of further education students would place it at a disadvantage. The new University of South Wales and the University of Wales, Trinity St David have also opted out of league tables after recent mergers, and both Liverpool Hope and Wolverhampton universities continue to refuse to release data. Wolverhampton says on its website that measures of its quality are available elsewhere – as they are, if you know where to look. But the way in which it quotes existing measures may help to explain why readers value the independent nature of guides such as this. Wolverhampton says, quite accurately, that it is among the top universities in the National Student Survey for the quality of its learning resources and access to specialist equipment, but it neglects to mention that it was only just in the top 100 universities in the 2013 survey for overall satisfaction.

Three private colleges have also been awarded university status since the last *Guide* appeared, joining Buckingham in a fledgling private university sector. They are BPP University, Regent's University and the University of Law, none of which will qualify for inclusion in our tables in the immediate future because they do not feature in official assessments of research or student satisfaction.

The leadership of the main table has changed for the first time since 2002, with Cambridge finishing a single point ahead of Oxford. The gap is too small to be statistically significant, although Cambridge is dominant in the 64 subject tables, leading 34 of them to Oxford's ten. The two ancient universities are now well ahead of their rivals, although 16 others head at least one of the subject tables. Scores are close in many other parts of the main table, emphasising how competitive the modern higher education system has become. Three universities tie for 52nd place, for example, with one university only one point ahead of them and another three points behind.

In Scotland, St Andrews remains the leading university, having moved up to fourth place overall, while Cardiff retains a clear in Wales and Queen's, Belfast is the long-established leader in Northern Ireland. Several universities have made strong progress in the upper reaches of the table. Surrey has moved up 14 places to equal 12th, Birmingham eight places to 16th and East Anglia 11 places to 17th. Coventry is up ten places to 45th with the third-highest satisfaction rating at any university and becomes the highest-placed post-1992 university in the history of the *Guide*. Coventry has gone up 32 places in two years, but even that feat is eclipsed by Northampton, which is up 40 places this year alone, with big improvements on every measure.

2014 *Guide* Award Winners

University of the Year:	**Birmingham**
Runner-up:	**Leicester**
Shortlisted:	**Coventry**
	St Andrews
	Surrey
Modern University:	**Coventry**
Scottish University:	**St Andrews**
Welsh University:	**Cardiff**

There is one other important new development in this year's *Guide*, with Birmingham being named as the first University of the Year in the new, merged publication. Leicester is the runner-up from a shortlist that included Coventry, St Andrews and Surrey. Coventry is Modern University of the Year, while St Andrews and Cardiff take the awards for Scotland and Wales respectively. The awards were a well-established feature of the *Sunday Times* University Guide and take account of league table positions and other achievements during the year. Birmingham has made significant progress both in our league table and the QS World University Rankings this year, as well as introducing a radical change in admissions by offering unconditional places to more than 1,000 students who were predicted at least three As at A level.

A 20-year view

School-leavers who enter higher education in 2014 were not born when our first league table was published and most will never have heard of polytechnics, even if they attend a university that once carried that title. But it was the award of university status to the 34 polytechnics, 21 years ago, that was the inspiration for the first edition of *The Times Good University Guide*. The original poly, the Polytechnic of Central London, had become the University of Westminster, Bristol Polytechnic was now the University of the West of England and – most mysteriously of all – Leicester Polytechnic had morphed into De Montfort University. The new *Guide* charted the lineage of the new universities and offered the first-ever comparison of institutional performance in UK higher education.

The university establishment did not welcome the initiative. The vice-chancellors described the table as "wrong in principle, flawed in execution and constructed upon data which are not uniform, are ill-defined and in places demonstrably false." The league table has changed considerably since then, although Oxford and Cambridge still reign supreme. While consistency has been a priority for the *Guide* throughout its 20 years, only six of the original 14 measures have survived. Some of the current components – notably the National Student Survey – did not exist in 1992, while others have been modified or dropped at the behest of the expert group of planning officers from different types of universities that meets annually to review the methodology and make recommendations for the future.

While ranking is hardly popular with academics, the relationship with universities has changed radically, and this *Guide* is quoted on numerous university websites. As Professor David Eastwood, now vice-chancellor of the University of Birmingham, said in launching an official report on university league tables that he commissioned as Chief Executive of the Higher Education Funding Council for England: "We deplore league tables one day and deploy them the next."

Most universities have had their ups and downs over the 20 years, although Oxford and Cambridge have tended to pull away from the rest. Both have benefited from the introduction of student satisfaction ratings and from the extra credit given to the top research grades – the two measures that carry an extra weighting in our table. They also have famously high entry standards, much the largest proportions of first and upper-second class degrees and consistently good scores on every other measure. Several other famous names have been among the chasing pack throughout. The London School of Economics, Imperial

---

Top ten then and now

1993		This year	
=1	Cambridge	1	Cambridge
=1	Oxford	2	Oxford
3	Imperial College	3	London School of Economics
4	University College London	4	St Andrews
=5	London School of Economics	5	Imperial College
=5	Edinburgh	6	Durham
=5	London*	7	Bath
=8	Warwick	8	Exeter
=8	York	9	University College London
10	Bath	10	Warwick

Note: The University of London's colleges that were not listed separately had their own ranking in the early editions.

College and University College London have seldom been out of the top five, while Warwick and, in recent years, Durham and St Andrews have all been fixtures in the top ten.

There have been spectacular rises, however. Exeter, for example, was 36th in the inaugural table and only one place better off in the 2003 *Guide*, but is now enjoying its third year in the top ten. Lancaster has slipped out of the top ten, but is still 25 places better off than it was in 1993. Even more impressively, Lincoln was only five places off the bottom of the table six years ago. Since then, it has moved 50 places up the table and into the top half, cementing a position among the highest-placed universities to be established in the last 20 years. Northampton is only two places behind, after jumping an unprecedented 40 places in a single year.

So what of the former polytechnics, which unwittingly sparked the whole ranking process? They harboured the strongest objections at the outset because they argued that their open-access mission was not reflected in the criteria by which they were being judged. Nevertheless, many commentators expected them to make their mark on the table, as they embraced a research culture and were able to compete for resources with the older universities on a more equal footing.

However, most of the 'new' universities are yet to catch the older institutions in our table. Coventry has reached the highest-ever position for a former poly this year, benefiting from outstanding student satisfaction ratings and good scores on the other measures to finish 45th. That places it above almost a dozen of the 60 older universities that featured in the first *Guide*. Robert Gordon and Oxford Brookes are well established in the top half of the table, which also includes Chester, Arts University Bournemouth (in its first year in the table), Portsmouth, Lincoln, Winchester, Northampton and West of England.

A few of the older universities have become detached from the rest in our table, notably Salford, which is only just in the top 100 this year. But most of the former polytechnics have not made the progress in league table terms that was predicted when they became universities. They still feel that the inclusion of research grades and entry standards, in particular, place them at a disadvantage while they focus on widening participation in higher education. But they do also produce lower scores, on average, for student satisfaction and graduate employment.

Higher education has changed enormously in the 20 years since this book was first published. The number of universities has increased by another third and the full-time student population has rocketed. Individual institutions are almost unrecognisable from their 1993 forms. Greenwich, for example, had less than 8,500 students then, compared with more than 18,500 now. Manchester Metropolitan, the largest of the former polys, had little more than 10,000 full-time students in 1993, compared with almost 28,000 last year. The diversity of UK higher education is celebrated as one of its greatest strengths, and the modern universities are neither encouraged nor anxious to compete with the older foundations on some of the measures in our table.

The next 20 years may see another transformation in the higher education landscape, with the private sector competing strongly with established universities in some fields and distance learning becoming more popular as there is greater investment in Massive Open Online Courses (MOOCs) and the cost of full-time degrees rises. There may, indeed, be university closures and mergers, although they have been predicted before and seldom come about. Universities are among the most enduring of the UK's institutions, and will take some shifting.

Why university?

Particularly if the UK economy continues its modest recovery, more young people will be tempted to write off higher education, once the cost of living has been added to the growing fees burden and the attractions of university life balanced against loss of potential earnings. There are plenty of self-made millionaires who still swear by the University of Life as the only training ground for success. Yet even by narrow financial criteria it would be rash to dismiss higher education. With so many more competing for jobs, a degree will never again be an automatic passport to a fast-track career. But graduates' financial prospects remain much brighter than school leavers', as are their prospects in other important areas, such as health.

Even for those who cannot or do not wish to afford three or more years of full-time education after leaving school, university remains a possibility. The modular courses adopted by most universities enable students to work through a degree at their own pace, dropping out for a time if necessary, or switching to part-time attendance. Distance learning is another option, and advances in information technology now mean that some nominally full-time courses are delivered mainly online.

For many – perhaps most – students, the university experience is not what it was in their parents' day. There is more assessment, more crowding, more pressure to get the best possible degree while also finding gainful employment for at least part of the year. The proportion of students achieving first-class degrees has risen significantly, while an upper second (rather than the previously ubiquitous 2:2) has become the norm. Research shows that the classification has a real impact in the labour market.

Most graduates do not regret their decision to go to university, however. Students from all over the world flock to British universities, and they offer a valuable resource for those on their doorstep. No league table can determine which is the right university for any candidate, but this *Guide* should provide some of the information necessary to draw up a shortlist for further investigation.

1 What and Where to Study

Higher fees at most UK universities are encouraging prospective students to think more carefully about what, where and even whether to study at degree level. That is perhaps the most positive aspect of the reforms introduced in 2012, although yet again it reduces any discussion of the value of higher education to one about money. The advantages conferred by a university education are much broader and deeper than that – graduates are healthier, happier and more engaged in civic society than those who were not lucky enough to take a degree. But it is only natural, when you may build up debts of £50,000 or more as an undergraduate, to look for a return on your investment.

Career prospects were already the number one consideration for three-quarters of those choosing a degree course even before the era of £9,000 fees. With demand for fine art and foreign languages in decline, while science and technology boom, it is already fair to assume that this proportion is rising. But it would be both sad and misguided if the likely currency of a degree in the labour market became the only criterion for selecting a course.

Your choice of university and course may influence the whole course of your life, not just your career. Many graduates end up living and working near their university; they often make their closest friends in their student days and may even meet their future partner there. So finding the right university demands serious thought and research, and this *Guide* may play an important part.

Is higher education for you?

Before you start, there is one important question to ask yourself: what do you want out of higher education? The answer will make it easier to choose where (and if) to be a student. With more than a third of school-leavers going on to university, it is easy to drift that way without much thought, opting for the subject in which you expect the best A-level grades, and looking for a university with a reasonable reputation and a good social life. Your career will look after itself – you hope.

With graduate debt soaring, however, and job prospects varying widely between subjects, now is the time to look at your own motivation. Some – though not as many as predicted – opted out of higher education in the first year of higher fees, while others appear to be rethinking their choice of course. The choices of these first cohorts were limited by the subjects they were taking, or had already taken, in the sixth-form. More may be steered towards apparently lucrative courses in future.

Love of a subject is an excellent reason for taking a degree, and one that allows you to focus almost exclusively on the search for a course that corresponds with your passions. If, however, higher education is a means to an end, you need to think about career ambitions and look carefully at employment rates for any courses you might consider. These are examined in more detail in chapter 2.

Many graduates look back on their student days as the best years of their lives, and there is nothing wrong with wanting to have a good time. Remember, though, that you will be paying for it later (literally) and there will be more studying than partying. If you have not enjoyed sixth-form or college courses, you may be better off in a job and possibly becoming one of the hundreds of thousands each year who return to education later in life.

Key reasons for going to university

To improve job opportunities	**74%**
To improve knowledge in an area of interest	**64%**
To improve salary prospects	**62%**
To obtain an additional qualification	**58%**
To specialise in a certain subject / area	**57%**
To become more independent	**48%**
Essential for my chosen profession	**47%**
To meet new people	**45%**
It's the obvious next step, it's just what you do	**40%**
To experience a different way of life	**37%**
To have a good social life	**26%**
My parents expected me to	**26%**
I didn't want to get a job straightaway	**24%**
I didn't know what else to do	**18%**
All my friends were going	**13%**
Can live at home and still go to university	**10%**

Sodexo University Lifestyle Survey 2012

Setting your priorities

With graduate unemployment at an 18-year high and the cost of going to university growing dramatically, economic considerations are sure to become even more dominant. Yet there are good reasons to believe that the right degree will still be a good investment. The latest research by London Economics for the Million Plus group of universities suggested that, on average, a degree would add £115,000 to lifetime earnings.

No one knows which subjects will be in demand when the downturn ends, but graduates will almost certainly be in a stronger position than those who choose not to invest in better qualifications. The majority of graduate jobs are not subject-specific – employers value the transferable skills that higher education confers. Rightly or wrongly, however, most employers are influenced by which university a graduate attended, so the choice of institution remains as important as ever.

Some students may cut their costs by taking a part-time course; others by enrolling on a two-year Foundation degree, which can be converted into an honours degree later. But, at a time of low employment generally, logic suggests that it would still be a false economy to dismiss higher education entirely.

Those who want to add value to their degree in the jobs market will find that growing numbers of universities are offering employment-related schemes that are considered in more detail in chapter 2. In many cases, this will involve work experience or extra activities organised by the careers service. Some universities, such as Leicester, now run certificated employability programmes, while others, such as Liverpool John Moores, have built such skills into degree programmes. Such programmes are also highlighted in chapter 2 and in the institutional profiles in chapter 14.

Narrowing down the field

Once you have decided that higher education is for you, the good news is that, as long as you start early enough, finding the right university can be relatively straightforward. Media attention focuses on the scramble for places on a relatively small proportion of courses where competition is intense, but there are plenty of places at good universities for candidates with the basic qualifications – it's just a matter of finding the one that suits you best. For older applicants, relevant work experience and demonstrable interest in a subject may be enough to win a place.

If anything, the problem is that of too much choice, although universities have reduced the number of degree combinations in anticipation of tougher financial conditions. Students prepared to move away from home will still have more than 100 universities and numerous specialist colleges to consider, most with hundreds – even thousands – of course combinations on offer. Institutions come in all shapes and sizes, so there is work to do at the outset narrowing down your options.

Deciding what you want to study may reduce the field considerably – there are only seven institutions offering veterinary medicine for example, although the total is around 100 in subjects such as law and English. By the time you have factored in personal preferences about the type or location of your ideal university, the list of possibilities may already be reduced to manageable proportions.

After that, you can take a closer look at what the courses contain and what life is really like for students. Prospectuses and university websites will give you an accurate account of course combinations, and important facts like the accommodation available to new students, but it is their job to sell the university. To get a true picture, you need more – preferably a visit not just to the university, but to the department where you would be studying. If that is not possible, there are plenty of other sources of objective information, such as the National Student Survey (which is available online, with a range of additional data about the main courses at each institution, at **http://unistats.direct.gov.uk**).

Some students' unions publish alternative prospectuses, giving a "warts and all" view of the university, and those that do not provide this service may be able to arrange a brief discussion with a current student, either by phone or email. Some alternative prospectuses and other apparently random students' views can be found at **www.realuni.com**. Your school or college may put you in contact with someone who went to a university that you are considering. Guides and collections of statistics may give you valuable information about a course or a university, but there is no substitute for personal experience.

What to study?

Most people seeking a place in higher education start by choosing a subject and a course, rather than a university. If you take a degree, you are going to spend at least three years immersed in your subject. It has to be one you will enjoy and can master – not to mention one that you are qualified to study. Many economics degrees require maths, for example, while some medical schools demand chemistry or biology. The UCAS website (**www.ucas. com**) contains course profiles, including entrance requirements, which is a good starting point, while universities' own sites contain more detailed information. In chapter 5, we describe 64 subject areas and provide league tables for each of them.

Your school subjects and the UCAS tariff

The official yardstick by which your results will be judged is the UCAS tariff, which gives a

The UCAS tariff

Tariffs for selected qualifications are given below. The full range of acceptable qualifications and their tariff values are given at **www.ucas.com/how-it-all-works/ explore-your-options/entry-requirements/tariff-tables**.

GCE AS/AS VCE	GCE AS Double Award	GCE/VCE Qualifications GCE A level/A VCE	A level with additional AS (9 units)	GCE/AVCE Double Award	Points	Scottish Qualifications Advanced Higher	Higher
				A*A*	280		
				A*A	260		
				AA	240		
				AB	220		
			A*A	BB	200		
			AA	BC	180		
			AB		170		
				CC	160		
			BB		150		
		A*	BC	CD	140		
					130	A	
	AA	A	CC	DD	120		
	AB		CD		110	B	
	BB	B		DE	100		
	BC		DD		90	C	
	CC	C	DE	EE	80		A
					72	D	
	CD				70		
					65		B
A	DD	D	EE		60		
B	DE				50		C
C	EE	E			40		
					36		D
D					30		
E					20		

UCAS tariff for the International Baccalaureate

Points for the International Baccalaureate (IB) are awarded to candidates who achieve the IB Diploma.

IB Dip.	Points	IB Dip.	Points	IB Dip.	Points	IB Dip.	Points	IB Dip.	Points
45	720	40	611	35	501	30	392	25	282
44	698	39	589	34	479	29	370	24	260
43	676	38	567	33	457	28	348		
42	654	37	545	32	435	27	326		
41	632	36	523	31	413	26	304		

score for each grade of most UK qualifications considered relevant for university entrance, as well as for the International Baccalaureate (IB). This tariff has become controversial as more subjects and types of qualifications have been included in it. Top scores in the IB, for example, earn considerably more points than the maximum for four, let alone three, A levels.

While the majority of universities use the tariff to make offers of places, many of the leading institutions prefer to stipulate the grades that they require. This allows them to specify the subjects in which particular grades must be achieved, as well as to determine which vocational qualifications are relevant to different degrees. In certain universities, some departments, but not others, will use the tariff to set offers. There has been debate within UCAS about scrapping the tariff altogether, but it will still be in place for applications for courses beginning in 2014. Course profiles on the UCAS website and/or universities' own sites should show whether offers are framed in terms of grades or tariff points. It is important to find out which, especially if you are relying on points from qualifications other than A level or Scottish Highers.

"Soft subjects"

There is a related issue for some of the top universities about the subjects studied at A level. The variety of A-level courses now available includes many subjects that they do not consider on a par with traditional academic subjects. For many years a minority of universities have refused to accept General Studies as a full A level for entrance purposes (although even some leading universities do). The growth of supposedly "soft" subjects, such as media studies and photography, has prompted a few universities to produce lists of subjects that will only be accepted alongside at least two traditional academic subjects.

The Russell Group of 24 leading universities has published an extremely useful report, called *Informed Choices,* on the post-16 qualifications preferred by its members for a wide range of degrees. Although it names media studies, art and design, photography and business studies among the vocational subjects that would normally be given this label, it does not subscribe to the notion of a single list of "soft" subjects. The report suggests you choose at most a single vocational course and primarily select from a list of "facilitating subjects",

---

"Soft Subjects"

The London School of Economics would prefer to see only one subject from this list in your mix of A-level subjects.

» Accounting
» Art and design
» Business studies (especially when combined with Economics)
» Communication studies
» Design and technology
» Drama/theatre studies (some departments)
» Home economics

» Information and communication technology
» Law
» Media studies
» Music technology (music is acceptable)
» Sports studies
» Travel and tourism

Those studying either accounting or law at A level "should not be put off applying to the LSE, as, depending on their overall academic profile, they may be made an offer". General studies and critical thinking A levels will only be considered as fourth A-level subjects and will not therefore be accepted as part of a conditional offer.

Admissions tests

Some of the most competitive courses now have additional entrance tests. The most significant are listed below. Some universities administer their own tests; details are given at: **www.ucas.com/how-it-all-works/explore-your-options/ entry-requirements/providers-own-tests**.

Law

Law National Admissions Test (LNAT): for entry to law courses at Birmingham, Bristol, Durham, Glasgow, King's College London, Nottingham, Oxford, University College, London.
For 2014, registration opened 1 August 2013; closing date 5 October 2013 (for Oxford), 15 January 2014 (other universities).
> **www.lnat.ac.uk**

Mathematics

Mathematics Admissions Test (MAT): for entry to mathematics courses at Imperial College, London and Oxford.
Closing date for 2014 admissions is 15 October 2013.
> **www.admissionstestingservice.org/our-services/subject-specific/mat/**

Sixth Term Examination Papers (STEP): for entry to mathematics at Cambridge and Warwick (also encouraged by Bristol, Bath, Imperial College London, and Oxford).
Standard closing date for 2013 entry was 30 April 2013. Date for 2014 entry to be announced in September 2013.
> **www.stepmathematics.org.uk**

Medical subjects

BioMedical Admissions Test (BMAT): for entry to medicine, veterinary medicine and biomedical sciences at Brighton and Sussex Medical School (graduate entry), Cambridge, Imperial College London, Oxford, Royal Veterinary College, University College London.
Standard closing date for 2014 admissions is 1 October 2013.
> **www.bmat.org.uk**

Graduate Medical School Admissions Test (GAMSAT): for graduate entry to medicine and dentistry at Cardiff, Exeter, Liverpool, Nottingham, Plymouth, St. George's, University of London, Swansea. Closing date for registration is 9 August 2013.
> **www.gamsatuk.org**

Health Professions Admissions Test (HPAT-Ulster): for certain health profession courses at Ulster.
Closing date for 2014 registration is 8 January 2014, with test on 1 February 2014.
> **www.hpat-ulster.acer.edu.auk**

UK Clinical Aptitude Test (UKCAT): for entry to medical and dental schools at Aberdeen, Brighton and Sussex Medical School, Cardiff, Dundee, Durham, East Anglia, Edinburgh, Exeter, Glasgow, Hull York Medical School, Imperial College London (graduate entry), Keele, King's College London, Leeds, Leicester, Manchester, Newcastle, Nottingham, Plymouth, Queen Mary, University of London, Queen's University Belfast, Sheffield, Southampton, St Andrews, St George's, University of London, Warwick (graduate entry).
Registration for 2014 entry from 1 May to 21 September 2013; tests from 1 July to 4 October 2013.
> **www.ukcat.ac.uk**

Cambridge University

Modern and Medieval Languages Test (MML): for entry to modern and medieval languages at Cambridge, taken at Cambridge during interview process.
> **www.mml.cam.ac.uk/prospectus/undergrad/test.html**

Thinking Skills Assessment (TSA) Cambridge: mainly for computer science, economics, engineering, human, social and political sciences, land economy, natural sciences, psychological and behavioural sciences at most Cambridge colleges, taken at Cambridge during interview process. See also Mathematics and Medical subjects.
> **www.tsacambridge.org.uk**

which are required for many degrees and welcomed generally at Russell Group universities. The list comprises *maths, further maths, English, physics, biology, chemistry, geography, languages (classical and modern) and history*. In addition their guide indicates the "essential" and "useful" A-level subjects for 60 different subject areas studied at Russell Group universities.

For most courses at most universities, there are no such restrictions, as long as your main subjects or qualifications are relevant to the degree you hope to take. Nevertheless, when choosing A levels it would be wise to bear the Russell Group lists in mind if you are likely to apply to one or more of the leading universities. At the very least, it is an indication of the subjects that admissions tutors may take less seriously than the rest. Although only the London School of Economics identifies those subjects publicly (see page 19), others may adopt less formal weightings.

Vocational qualifications

The Education Department has announced that many vocational qualifications will be downgraded in school league tables from 2014. This can only add to the confusion surrounding the value placed on diplomas and other qualifications by universities. The engineering diploma has won near-universal approval from universities (for admission to engineering courses and possibly some science degrees), but some of the other diplomas are in fields that are not on the curriculum of the most selective universities. Regardless of the points awarded under the tariff, it is essential to contact universities direct to ensure that a diploma or another vocational qualification will be an acceptable qualification for your chosen degree.

Admission tests

Oxford University

Specific registration by 15 October 2013 is required for the following subject tests. Tests taken on 6 November 2013, usually at candidate's educational institution.

classics (**www.catoxford.org.uk**)

computer science, mathematics (**www.matoxford.org.uk**)

economics and management, experimental psychology, geography, philosophy, politics and economics (PPE), psychology (**www.tsaoxford.org.uk**)

engineering, materials science, physics (**patoxford.org.uk**)

English (**www.elat.org.uk**)

history (**www.hatoxford.org.uk**)

modern languages, courses including linguistics (**mlatoxford.org.uk**)

oriental studies (**www.olatoxford.org.uk**)

For law and medicine, see sections above.

For fine art, music and philosophy, there will be a test at interview in December 2013.

Full details at **www.ox.ac.uk/admissions/undergraduate_courses/applying_to_oxford/tests**

University College London

Thinking Skills Assessment (TSA) UCL: for entry to European social and political studies at University College London; the test is arranged in the interview process.

www.tsaucl.org.uk

The growing numbers of applicants with high grades at A level have encouraged the introduction of separate admission tests for some of the most oversubscribed courses. There are national tests in medicine and law that are used by some of the leading universities, while Oxford and Cambridge have their own in a number of subjects. The details are listed on pages 20–21. In all cases, the tests are used as an extra selection tool, not as a replacement for A level or other general qualifications.

Making a choice

Your A levels or Scottish Highers may have chosen themselves, but the range of subjects across the whole university system is vast. Even subjects that you have studied at school may be quite different at degree level – some academic economists actually prefer their undergraduates not to have taken A-level economics because they approach the subject so differently. Other students are disappointed because they appear to be going over old ground when they continue with a subject that they enjoyed at school. Universities now publish quite detailed syllabuses, and it is a matter of going through the fine print.

The greater difficulty comes in judging your suitability for the many subjects that are not on the school or college curriculum. Philosophy and psychology sound fascinating (and are), but you may have no idea what degrees in either subject entail – for example, the level of statistics that may be required. Forensic science may look exciting on television – more glamorous than plain chemistry – but it opens fewer doors, as the type of work portrayed in *Silent Witness* or *Raising the Dead* is very hard to find.

Academic or vocational?

There is frequent and often misleading debate about the differences between academic and vocational higher education. It is usually about the relative value of taking a degree, as opposed to a directly work-related qualification. But it also extends to higher education itself, with jibes about so-called "Mickey Mouse" degrees in areas that were not part of the higher education curriculum when most of the critics were students.

Such attitudes ignore the fact that medicine and law are both vocational subjects, as are architecture, engineering and education. They are not seen as any less academic than geography or sociology, but for some reason social work or nursing, let alone media studies

The ten most popular subjects by applications in 2013		The ten most popular subjects by acceptances in 2012	
1 Nursing	224,526	1 Nursing	23,836
2 Law	103,841	2 Law	18,026
3 Psychology	99,401	3 Design studies	17,324
4 Design studies	91,254	4 Psychology	16,174
5 Pre-clinical medicine	82,570	5 Computer science	12,565
6 Combinations within business and admin studies	73,978	6 Combinations within business and admin studies	12,265
7 Management studies	71,233	7 Management studies	11,971
8 Computer science	67,611	8 Business studies	11,864
9 Business studies	61,561	9 Social work	11,279
10 Social work	60,599	10 Sports science	10,855
UCAS 2013 (number of applicants to 30 June 2013)		UCAS 2012	

and sports science, are often looked down upon. The test of a degree should be whether it is challenging and a good preparation for working life. Both general academic and vocational degrees can do this.

Nevertheless, it would be surprising if the prospect of much higher graduate debt did not encourage more students into job-related subjects, rather than traditional academic disciplines, in the hope of improving their employment prospects. This is understandable and, if you are sure of your future career path, possibly also sensible. But much depends on what that career is – and whether you are ready to make such a long-term commitment. Some of the programmes that have attracted public ridicule, such as surf science or golf course management, may narrow graduates' options to a worrying extent, but often boast strong employment records.

As you would expect, many vocational courses are tailored to particular professions. If you choose one of these, make sure that the degree is recognised by the relevant professional body (such as the Engineering Council or one of the institutes) or you may not be able to use the skills that you acquire. Most universities are only too keen to make such recognition clear in their prospectus; if no such guarantee is published, contact the university department running the course and seek assurances.

Even where a course has professional recognition, bear in mind that a further qualification may be required to practise. Both law and medicine, for example, demand additional training to become a fully qualified solicitor, barrister or doctor. Nor is either degree an automatic passport to a job: only about half of all law graduates go into the profession and the UK is now training more medical students than the National Health Service can afford. Both law and medicine also provide a route into the profession for graduates who have taken other subjects. Law conversion courses, though not cheap, are increasingly popular, and there are a growing number of graduate-entry medical degrees.

One way to ensure that a degree is job-related is to take a "sandwich" course, which involves up to a year in business or industry. Students often end up working for the organisation which provided the placement, while others gain valuable insights into a field of employment – even if only to discount it. The drawback with such courses is that, like the year abroad that is part of most language degrees, the period away from university inevitably disrupts living arrangements and friendship groups. But most of those who take this route find that the career benefits make this a worthwhile sacrifice.

Employers' organisations calculate that more than half of all graduate jobs are open

Total number of students by subject area 2011–2012

Business and admin studies	249,955
Subjects allied to medicine	242,780
Social studies	172,420
Biological sciences	166,315
Creative arts and design	159,400
Engineering and technology	120,025
Languages	118,390
Education	107,260
Combined	93,455
Historical and philosophical studies	81,255
Computer science	76,590
Physical sciences	75,060
Law	71,800
Medicine and dentistry	46,745
Mass communications	43,850
Architecture, building and planning	43,065
Mathematical sciences	37,245
Agriculture and related subjects	17,785
Veterinary science	4,735
All Subjects	1,928,140

HESA 2013

to applicants from any subject, and recruiters for the most competitive graduate training schemes often prefer traditional academic subjects to apparently relevant vocational degrees. Newspapers, for example, often prefer a history graduate to one with a media studies degree; computing firms take a disproportionate number of classicists. A good degree classification and the right work experience are more important than the subject for most non-technical jobs. But it is hard to achieve a good result on a course that you do not enjoy, so scour prospectuses, and email or phone university departments to ensure that you know what you are letting yourself in for. Their reaction to your approach will also give you an idea of how responsive they are to their students.

Studying more than one subject

You may find that more than one subject appeals, in which case you could consider Joint Honours – degrees that combine two subjects – or even Combined Honours, which will cover several related subjects. Such courses obviously allow you to extend the scope of your studies, but they should be approached with caution. Even if the number of credits suggests a similar workload to Single Honours, covering more than one subject inevitably involves extra reading and often more essays or project work.

However, there are advantages. Many students choose a "dual" to add a vocational element to make themselves more employable – business studies with languages or engineering, for example, or media studies with English. Others want to take their studies in a particular direction, perhaps by combining history with politics, or statistics with maths. Some simply want to add a completely unrelated interest to their main subject, such as environmental science and music, or archaeology and event management – both combinations that are available at UK universities.

At most universities, however, it is not necessary to take a degree in more than one subject in order to broaden your studies. The spread of modular programmes ensures that you can take courses in related subjects without changing the basic structure of your degree. You may not be able to take an event management module in a single-honours archaeology degree, but it should be possible to study some history or a language. The number and scope of the combinations offered at many of the larger universities is extraordinary. Indeed, it has been criticised by academics who believe that "mix-and-match" degrees can leave a graduate without a rounded view of a subject. But for those who seek breadth and variety, close scrutiny of university prospectuses is a vital part of the selection process.

What type of course?

Once you have a subject, you must decide on the level and type of course. Most readers of this *Guide* will be looking for full-time degree courses, but higher education is much broader than that. You may not be able to afford the time or the money needed for a full-time commitment of three or four years at this point in your life.

Part-time courses

Tens of thousands of people each year opt for a part-time course – usually while holding down a job – to continue learning and improve their career prospects. The numbers studying this way have dropped recently, but that may change as the new funding arrangements, which give most part-time students access to loans for the first time, become better known. Under these arrangements, loans are available for students whose courses occupy between a quarter and three-quarters of the time expected on a full-time course. Repayments are on the same conditions as those for full-time courses, except that repayments will begin after three years of study even if the course has not been completed by then. The downside is that many universities have increased their fees in the knowledge that part-time students will be able to take out student loans to cover fees and employers are now less inclined to fund their employees on such courses. Nevertheless, the change should still be beneficial overall. At Birkbeck, University of London, for example, full-time fees are £9,000 a year, with part-timers paying in proportion to the number of credits they take. For the first time, students need pay nothing up front if they take out income-contingent loans.

Part-time study can be exhausting unless your employer gives you time off, but if you have the stamina for a course that will usually take twice as long as the full-time equivalent, this route should still make a degree more affordable. Part-time students tend to be highly committed to their subject, and many claim that the quality of the social life associated with their course makes up for the quantity of leisure time enjoyed by full-timers.

Distance learning

If you are confident that you can manage without regular face-to-face contact with teachers and fellow students, distance learning is an option. Courses are delivered mainly or entirely online or through correspondence, although some programmes offer a certain amount of local tuition. The process might sound daunting and impersonal, but students of the Open University (OU), all of whom are educated in this way, are among the most satisfied in the country, according to the results of the annual National Student Survey. Attending lectures or oversized seminars at a conventional university can be less personal than regular contact with your tutor at a distance. Of course, not all universities are as good at communicating with their distance-learning students as the OU, or offer such high-quality course materials, but this mode of study does give students ultimate flexibility to determine when and where they study. Distance learning is becoming increasingly popular for the delivery of professional courses, which are often needed to supplement degrees. The OU now takes students of all ages, including a growing number of school-leavers, not just mature students.

In addition, there is now the option of Massive Open Online Courses (MOOCs) provided by some of the leading UK and American universities, usually free of charge. As yet, such courses are the equivalent of a module in a degree course, rather than the entire qualification. Some are assessed formally but none is likely to be seen by employers

Subjects with highest ratio of applications to acceptances 2012		Universities with the highest application to place ratio 2012	
1 Medicine	10.6	1 Brighton and Sussex Medical School	17.8
2 Dentistry	9.8	2 Buckingham	12.4
=3 Nursing	8.9	3 London School of Economics	11.5
=3 Veterinary medicine	8.9	4 St George's, University of London	9.6
=5 Anatomy, physiology and pathology	8.7	5 Dundee	9.4
=5 Medical technology	8.7	6 Keele	8.9
7 Pharmacology, toxicology and pharmacy	7.4	7 Stirling	8.8
8 Training teachers	7.1	8 Edinburgh	8.6
9 Economics	6.9	9 St Andrews	8.4
10 Architecture	6.7	10 Liverpool	8.0

UCAS 2012 (for subjects with over 1,000 acceptances)

UCAS 2012

as the equal of a conventional degree, no matter how prestigious the university offering the course. That may change – some commentators see in MOOCs the beginning of the end of the traditional, residential university – but their main value at the moment is as a means of dipping a toe in the water of higher education. For those who are uncertain about committing to a degree, or who simply want to learn more about a subject without needing a high-status qualification, they are ideal.

Several leading UK universities will be offering MOOCs through the Futurelearn platform, run by the Open University (**http://futurelearn.com**). But the beauty of MOOCs is that they can come from all over the world. Perhaps the best-known providers are Coursera (**www.coursera.org**), which originated at Stanford University, in California, and now involves a large number of American and international universities including Edinburgh, and edX (**www.edx.org**), which numbers Harvard among its members.

Foundation degrees

Even if you are set on a full-time course, you might not want to commit yourself for three or more years. Two-year vocational Foundation degrees have become a popular route into higher education in recent years. Many other students take longer-established two-year courses, such as Higher National Diplomas or other diplomas tailored to the needs of industry or parts of the health service. Those who do well on such courses usually have the option of converting their qualification into a full degree with further study, although many are satisfied without immediately staying on for the further two or more years that completing a BA or BSc will require.

Other short courses

A number of universities are experimenting with two-year degrees, squeezing more work into an extended academic year. The so-called "third semester" makes use of the summer vacation for extra teaching, so that mature students, in particular, can reduce the length of their career break. Several universities are offering accelerated degrees as part of a pilot project initiated under the last government. But only at the University of Buckingham, the UK's only established private university, is this the dominant pattern for degree courses.

Other short courses – usually lasting a year – are designed for students who do not have the necessary qualifications to start a degree in their chosen subject. Foundation courses in art and design have been common for many years, and are the chosen preparation for a degree at leading departments, even for many students whose A levels would win them a degree place elsewhere. Access courses perform the same function in a wider range of subjects for students without A levels, or for those whose grades are either too low or in the wrong subjects to gain admission to a particular course. Entry requirements are modest, but students have to reach the same standard as regular entrants if they are to progress to a degree.

Yet more choice

No single guide can allow for personal preferences in choosing a course. You may want one of the many degrees that incorporate a year at a partner university abroad, or to try a six-month exchange on the Continent through the European Union's Erasmus Programme. Either might prove a valuable experience and add to your employability. You might prefer a January or February start to the traditional autumn start – there are plenty of opportunities for this, mainly at post-1992 universities.

In some subjects – particularly engineering and the sciences – the leading degrees may be Masters courses, taking four years rather than three (in England). In Scotland, most degree courses take four years, although those who come with A levels may apply to go straight into the second year.

Where to study

Once you have decided what to study, there are still several factors that might influence your choice of university or college. Obviously, you need to have a reasonable chance of getting in, you may want reassurance about the university's reputation, and its location will probably also be important to you. On top of that, most applicants have views about the type of institution they are looking for – big or small, old or new, urban or rural, specialist or comprehensive. You may surprise yourself by choosing somewhere that does not conform to your initial criteria, but working through your preferences is another way of narrowing down your options.

Entry standards

Unless you are a mature student or have taken a gap year, your passport to your chosen university will be a conditional offer based on your predicted grades, previous exam performance, personal statement, and school or college reference. A lucky few may get an offer that is so low that success is a foregone conclusion – because the university considers them outstanding and needs no further evidence of their potential. But at most universities, only those who already have their grades receive unconditional offers.

Supply and demand dictate whether you will receive an offer – whatever the reaction to the second year of higher fees in England, large numbers will still apply for entry in 2014. Beyond the national picture, your chances will be affected both by the university and the subject you choose. A few universities (but not many) at the top of the league tables are heavily oversubscribed in every subject; others will have areas in which they excel, but may make relatively modest demands for entry to other courses. Even in many of the leading universities, the number of applicants for each place in languages or engineering is still not high. Conversely, three As at A level will not guarantee a place on one of the top English or law degrees, but there are enough universities running courses to ensure that three Cs will put you in with a chance somewhere.

University prospectuses and the UCAS website will give you the "standard offer" for each course, but in some cases this is pitched deliberately low in order to leave admissions

Non-academic factors considered when choosing a university

Good impression from open days	53%
Friendly atmosphere	43%
Geographic location	43%
Attractive university environment	37%
Campus university	34%
Close to transport links	32%
Living away from home, but sufficiently close if support needed	29%
Active social life and good social facilities	28%
Internet research favourable to university	27%
Quality of accommodation	23%
City centre university	22%
Recommendation from friends	22%
Close to home/able to live at home	22%
Low cost of living	17%
Cost of accommodation	15%
Advice from teachers	14%
Advice from parents	12%
Good sporting facilities	12%
Opportunities for part-time jobs	9%

Sodexo University Lifestyle Survey 2012

staff extra flexibility. The standard A-level offer for medicine, for example, is often two As and a B, but nearly all successful applicants have three As or more.

The average entry scores in our subject tables give the actual points obtained by successful applicants – many of which are far above the offer made by the university, but which give an indication of the pecking order at entry. The subject tables (in chapter 5) are, naturally, a better guide than the main table (in chapter 4), where average entry scores are influenced by the range of subjects available at each university.

Location

The most obvious starting point is the country you study in. Most degrees in Scotland take four years, rather than the UK norm of three. It is possible, but not normal, for A-level candidates to go straight into the second year of a Scottish degree course. Fewer applicants than might be expected, given the savings, take this option, perhaps partly because they do not wish to join a year group where friendships are already well established. It goes without saying that four years cost more than three, especially given the loss of the year's salary you might have been earning after graduation. A later chapter will go into the details of the system, but suffice to say that students from Scotland pay no fees, while those from the rest of the UK do. Nevertheless, Edinburgh and St Andrews remain particularly popular with English students, despite charging them £9,000 a year for the full four years of a degree. The number of English students going to Scottish universities actually increased by almost a quarter in 2012 and increased again in 2013, despite the fact that there would be no savings on fees, perhaps because institutions tried harder to attract them. More than 4,000 students went north, while the numbers coming in the opposite direction dropped to 1,600.

Close to home

Far from crossing national boundaries, however, growing numbers of students choose to study near home, whether or not they continue to live with their family. This is understandable for Scots, who will save themselves tens of thousands of pounds by studying at their own fees-free universities. But many others are choosing to study close to home either to cut living costs or for personal reasons, such as family circumstances, a girlfriend or boyfriend, continuing employment or religion. Some simply want to stick with what they know.

The trend for full-time students who do go away to study, is to choose a university within

Most popular universities by degree application		Most satisfied with student union	
1 Manchester	52,780	1 Sheffield	93%
2 Nottingham	52,271	3 Leeds	90%
3 Leeds	49,389	2 Loughborough	88%
4 Manchester Metropolitan	49,327	4 Bath	86%
5 Edinburgh	46,875	=5 East Anglia	84%
6 Sheffield Hallam	41,737	=5 Keele	84%
7 Leeds Metropolitan	39,504	=7 Teesside	83%
8 Kingston	39,341	=7 Winchester	83%
9 Birmingham	38,807	=9 Cardiff	82%
10 Bristol	36,451	=9 Dundee	82%
UCAS applications 2012		National Student Survey 2013	

about two hours' travelling time. The assumption is that this is far enough to discourage parents from making unannounced visits, but close enough to allow for occasional trips home to get the washing done, have a decent meal and see friends. The leading universities recruit from all over the world, but most still have a regional core.

University or college?

This *Guide* is primarily concerned with universities, the destination of choice for the vast majority of higher education students. But there are other options – and not just for those searching for lower fees. A number of specialist higher education colleges offer a similar, or sometimes superior, quality of course in their particular fields. The subject tables in chapter 5 chart the successes of various colleges in art, agriculture, music and teacher training in particular. Some colleges of higher education are not so different from the newer universities and may acquire that status themselves in future years, as ten have in 2012–13.

The second group of colleges offering degrees are further education colleges. These are often large institutions with a wide range of courses, from A levels to vocational subjects at different levels, up to degrees in some cases. Although their numbers of higher education students have been falling in recent years, the new fee structure presents them with a fresh opportunity because they tend not to bear all the costs of a university campus. For that reason, too, they may not offer a broad student experience of the type that universities pride themselves on, but the best colleges respond well to the local labour market and offer small teaching groups and effective personal support.

FE colleges are a local resource and tend to attract mature students who cannot or do not want to travel to university. Many of their higher education students apply nowhere else. But, as competition for university places has increased, they have become more of an option for school-leavers, as well as for their own students, to continue their studies, as they always have done in Scotland. Ministers hope that they will now also become more attractive by virtue of price.

Their predominantly local, mature student populations do FE colleges no favours in comparisons with universities. But it should be noted that 16 per cent of their graduates were unemployed six months after graduation in 2011, compared with 10 per cent at universities. The average salary of 2011 FE graduates at that time was £15,000, compared with a university equivalent of £19,000. This may be why not all of the 10,000 extra places reserved for FE colleges were filled in 2012, although the total number of entrants showed a modest rise.

Both further and higher education colleges are audited by the Quality Assurance Agency and appear in the National Student Survey, where their results usually show wide variation. Some demonstrate higher levels of satisfaction among their students than most universities.

The final group of colleges that present an alternative to university has been insignificant in terms of size until recently, but may also prosper under the new fee regime. This is the private sector, seen mainly in business and law but also in some other specialist fields. The best-known currently is BPP University, which became a full university in 2013 and offers degrees, as well as shorter courses, in both law and business subjects. Like Buckingham, BPP offers two-year degrees with short vacations to maximise teaching time – a model that other private providers are likely to follow. Fees were £6,000 a year for a two-year degree in 2013.

At the other end of the cost spectrum, the New College of the Humanities took its first students in 2012. Offering economics, English, history, law and philosophy, the college is charging £18,800 a year for guaranteed small-group teaching and some big-name visiting lecturers. Up to 30 per cent of students will be offered bursaries for degree courses validated by the University of London.

Two other private institutions have been awarded university status since the last *Guide* was published. Regent's University, attractively positioned in London's Regent's Park, caters particularly for the international market with courses in business, arts and social science subjects priced at £14,200 a year in 2013. However, about half of the students at the not-for-profit university, which offers British and American degrees, are from the UK or other parts of Europe. The University of Law, as its name suggests, is more specialised. It has been operating as a college for more than 100 years and claims to be the world's leading professional law school. Law degrees, as well as professional courses, are available in London and Manchester, with fees totalling £18,000 for a two-year course.

There are also growing numbers of specialist colleges offering degrees, especially in the business sector. Greenwich School of Management, with 3,500 students on two London campuses, is probably the largest in terms of full-time students, but there are others that have forged partnerships with universities or are going it alone. The ifs School of Finance, for example, also dates back more than 100 years and now has university college status (as ifs University College) for its courses in finance and banking. Some others that rely on international students have been hit by tougher visa regulations, but the Government is keen to encourage the development of a private sector to compete with the established universities.

City universities

The most popular universities, in terms of total applications, are nearly all in big cities – generally with other major centres of population within that two-hour travelling window. For those looking for the best nightclubs, top sporting events, high-quality shopping or a varied cultural life – in other words, most young people, and especially those who live in cities already – city universities are a magnet. The big universities also, by definition, offer the widest range of subjects, although that does not mean that they necessarily have the particular course that is right for you. Nor does it mean that you will actually use the array of nightlife and shopping that looks so alluring in the prospectus, either because you cannot afford to, because student life is focused on the university, or even because you are too busy working.

The top universities for student satisfaction in the 2014 *Times and Sunday Times* table		The top universities for students going into professional jobs or studying in the 2014 *Times and Sunday Times* table	
1 Bath	87.9%	1 Imperial	89.2%
2 East Anglia	87.1%	2 Cambridge	85.1%
3 Coventry	86.9%	3 Bath	83.6%
=4 Buckingham	86.3%	4 Buckingham	83.1%
=4 St Mark and St John	86.3%	5 Durham	82.6%
=6 Cambridge	86.2%	6 King's College London	82.0%
=6 Surrey	86.2%	7 Robert Gordon	81.8%
8 Exeter	86.0%	8 Birmingham	80.8%
=9 Oxford	85.9%	9 St Andrews	80.5%
=9 St Andrews	85.9%	10 University College London	79.8%

Campus universities

City universities are the right choice for many young people, but it is worth bearing in mind that the National Student Survey shows that the highest satisfaction levels tend to be at smaller universities, often those with their own self-contained campuses. It seems that students identify more closely with institutions where there is a close-knit community and the social life is based around the students' union rather than the local nightclubs. Few UK universities are in genuinely rural locations, but some – particularly among the more recently promoted – are in relatively small towns. Several longer-established institutions in Wales and Scotland also share this type of setting, where the university dominates the town.

Importance of Open Days

The only way to be certain if this, or any other type of university, is for you is to visit. Schools often restrict the number of open days that sixth-formers can attend in term-time, but some universities offer a weekend alternative. The full calendar of events is available at **www.opendays.com** and on universities' own websites. Bear in mind, if you only attend one or two, that the event has to be badly mismanaged for a university not to seem an exciting place to someone who spends his or her days at school, or even college. Try to get a flavour of several institutions before you make your choice.

How many universities to pick?

When that time comes, of course, you will not be making one choice but five; four if you are applying for medicine, dentistry or veterinary science. (Full details of the application process are given in chapter 6.) Tens of thousands of students each year eventually go to a university that did not start out as their first choice, either because they did not get the right offer or because they changed their mind along the way. UCAS rules are such that applicants do not list universities in order of preference anyway – indeed, universities are not allowed to know where else you have applied. So do not pin all your hopes on one course; take just as much care choosing the other universities on your list.

The value of an "insurance" choice

Until recently, nearly all applicants included at least one "insurance" choice on that list – a university or college where entry grades were significantly lower than at their preferred institutions. This practice has been in decline, presumably because candidates expecting high grades think they can pick up a lower offer either in Clearing or through UCAS Extra, the service that allows applicants rejected by their original choices to apply to courses that still have vacancies after the first round of offers. However, it is easy to miscalculate and leave yourself without a place that you want. You may not like the look of the options in Clearing, leaving yourself with an unwelcome and potentially expensive year off at a time when jobs are thin on the ground.

If you are at all uncertain about your grades, including an insurance choice remains a sensible course of action – especially since entry requirements have risen in response to increased demand for places. Indeed, even if you are sure that you will match the standard offers of your chosen universities, there is no guarantee that they will make you an offer. Particularly for degrees demanding three As at A level, there may simply be too many highly qualified applicants to offer places to all of them. The main proviso for insurance choices, as with all others, is that you must be prepared to take up that place. If not, you might as well go for broke with courses with higher standard offers and take your chances in Clearing, or even retake exams if you drop grades. Thousands of applicants each year end up rejecting their only offer when they could have had a second, insurance, choice.

Reputation

The reputation of a university is something intangible, usually built up over a long period and sometimes outlasting reality. Before universities were subject to external assessment and the publication of copious statistics, reputation was rooted in the past. League tables are partly responsible for changing that, although employers are often still influenced by what they remember as the university pecking order when they were students.

The fragmentation of the British university system into groups of institutions is another factor: the Russell Group represents 24 research-intensive universities, nearly all with medical schools; the 1994 Group, a similar number of smaller research universities; and the Million+ Group containing many of the former polytechnics and newer universities. To these have been added the University Alliance, which provides a home for 23 universities, both old and new, that did not fit into the other categories. In addition, there is GuildHE, an organisation mainly for specialist colleges and the newest universities, and the Cathedrals Group, an affiliation of 16 church-based universities and colleges. The university profiles in chapter 14 give the affiliation of each university.

Many of today's applicants will barely have heard of a polytechnic, let alone be able to identify which of today's universities had that heritage, but most will know which of two universities in the same city has the higher status. While that should matter far less than the quality of a course, it would be naïve to ignore institutional reputation entirely if that is going to carry weight with a future employer. Some big firms restrict their recruitment efforts to a small group of universities (see chapter 2), and, however shortsighted that might be, it is something to bear in mind if a career in the City or a big law firm is your ambition.

Cost

Quite apart from the level of fees, the cost of studying in different parts of the UK inevitably varies. Some cities – notably London – are notoriously expensive for students and non-students alike. But even these comparisons can be complicated by the availability of part-time employment – an important factor for a growing number of students today. The 2010 NatWest survey rated London as the cheapest place in the UK to study once earning opportunities are taken into account. If you intend to take part-time employment while

---

Checklist

Choosing a subject and a place to study is a major decision. Make sure you can answer these questions:

Choosing a course

» What do I want out of higher education?
» Which subjects do I enjoy studying at school?
» Which subject or subjects do I want to study?
» Do I have the right qualifications?
» What are my career plans and does the subject and course fit these?
» Do I want to study full-time or part-time?
» Do I want to study at a university or a college?

Choosing a university

» What type of university do I wish to go to: campus, city or smaller town?
» How far is the university from home?
» Is it large or small?
» Is it specialist or general?
» Does it offer the right course?
» How much will it cost?
» Have I arranged to visit the university?

studying, check that your chosen university has a "job shop", or some other organisation to help students find reasonably paid work.

Accommodation costs listed alongside the university profiles in this *Guide* are probably the nearest proxy for a cost-of-living indicator. The *Guide* also includes a summary of the bursaries available at each university. The size of bursaries varies enormously, as do the rules governing eligibility. Scholarships are awarded for other achievements, regardless of family income.

Facilities

Universities compete for the best students not only through their courses but, increasingly, also through non-academic facilities. Accommodation is the main selling point for those living away from home, but sports facilities, libraries and computing equipment also play an important part. Even campus nightclubs have become part of the facilities race that has coincided with the introduction of top-up fees.

Many universities guarantee first-year students accommodation in halls of residence or university-owned flats. But it is as well to know what happens after that. Are there enough places for second or third-year students who want them, and if not, what is the private market like? Rents for student houses vary quite widely across the country and there have been tensions with local residents in some cities. All universities offer specialist accommodation for disabled students – and are better at providing other facilities than most public institutions. Their websites give basic information on what is provided, as well as contact points for more detailed inquiries.

Special-interest clubs and recreational facilities, as well as political activity, tend to be based in the students' union – sometimes knows as the guild of students. In some universities, the union is the focal point of social activity, while in others the attractions of the city seem to overshadow the union to the point where facilities are underused. Students' union websites are included with the information found in the university profiles (chapter 14).

Sources of information

With more than 120 universities to choose from, the Unistats and UCAS websites, as well as guides such as this one, are the obvious places to start your search for the right course. Unistats now includes figures for average salaries at course level, as well as student satisfaction ratings and some information on contact hours, although this does not distinguish between lectures and seminars. The site does not make multiple comparisons easy to carry out but it does contain a wealth of information for those who persevere. But once you have narrowed down the list of candidates, you will want to go through undergraduate prospectuses. Most are available online, where you can select the relevant sections rather than waiting for an account of every course to arrive in the post. Beware of generalised claims about the standing of the university, the quality of courses, friendly atmosphere and legendary social life. Stick, if you can, to the factual information.

If the material that the universities publish about their own qualities is less than objective, much of what you will find on the internet is equally unreliable, for different reasons. A simple search on the name of a university will turn up spurious comparisons of everything from the standard of lecturing to the attractiveness of the students. These can be seriously misleading and are usually based on anecdotal evidence, at best. Make sure that any information you may take into account comes from a reputable source and, if it conflicts with your impression, try to cross-check it with this *Guide* and the institution's own material.

Useful websites

The following websites will help you find out more about the topics discussed in this chapter. The best starting point is the UCAS website (**www.ucas.com**). On the site there's lots of information on courses, universities and the whole process of applying to university. In addition UCAS has an official presence on Facebook (**www.facebook.com/ucasonline**) and Twitter (**@UCAS_online**) and now also has a series of video guides (**www.ucas.tv**) on the process of applying, UCAS resources and comments from other students.

For statistical information which allows limited comparison between universities (and for full details of the National Student Survey), visit: **http://unistats.direct.gov.uk**

For an official listing of recognised degrees and recognised higher education institutions: **www.gov.uk/recognised-uk-degrees**

UK Course Finder: **www.ukcoursefinder.com**

For a full calendar of university and college open days: **www.opendays.com**

Students with disabilities: Disability Alliance: **www.disabilityalliance.org/personal-care-university**

University groupings
1994 Group, a group of medium and small research-intensive universities: **www.1994group.ac.uk**
GuildHE, a group of higher education colleges, specialist institutions and new universities: **www.guildhe.ac.uk**
Million+ Group, a group of newer universities: **www.millionplus.ac.uk**
Russell Group: a group of large research-intensive universities: **www.russellgroup.ac.uk**
The University Alliance, a group of old and new universities: **www.university-alliance.ac.uk**
The Cathedrals Group: an affiliation of church-based universities and colleges: **www.cathedralsgroup.org.uk**

2 Graduate Employment Prospects

The graduate labour market has been badly affected by the banking crisis and by the continuing worldwide recession, both of which have depressed graduate recruitment around the world. The 2012 *Graduates in the Labour Market* survey, published by the Office of National Statistics (ONS), showed that in the last three months of 2011, almost 19 per cent of UK graduates who had left university in the previous two years were unemployed. This is a big figure and reflects the fact that they were trying to get their working life started at the worst time in decades.

Nevertheless, most research suggests that in the long-term graduates fare much better in the labour market than those without a degree. Indeed, the salary premium enjoyed by UK graduates over those who do not go to university continues to be higher than in most of the rest of the world. Looking at employment rather than unemployment, the ONS found that 86 per cent of graduates were employed in late 2011, compared with only 72 per cent of non-graduates.

Inevitably, such surveys average out the experiences of millions of people. This chapter will begin to tease out the often contrasting prospects of graduates in different subjects and different types of institution. Research by the Higher Education Funding Council for England, for example, found that university graduates in 2011 earned a median salary after six months that was £4,000 higher than those whose degrees came from further education colleges.

According to the ONS the best-paid graduates are naturally the medics, on an average

Median wage for graduates aged 21–64 by degree subject studied (average hourly earnings, 2011)

Medicine and dentistry	£21.29
Mathematical sciences, engineering, technology and architecture	£18.92
Physical or environmental sciences	£17.74
Business	£17.30
Education	£16.97
Law	£16.95
Social studies	£16.33
Biological and agricultural sciences	£15.83
Librarianship and languages	£14.85
Medical related subjects	£14.65
Humanities	£14.63
Arts	£12.06
All graduates	**£15.18**
Non-graduates	**£8.92**

Source: Office for National Statistics Labour Force Survey

income of £21.29 per hour at the time of the survey. The least well-rewarded were the arts and humanities types, paid an hourly average of £12.06. Overall, graduates were earning an average of £15.18 an hour. That compares to £8.92 an hour for non-graduates and a UK minimum wage of £6.19 an hour from April 2013.

The news is less positive, however, when we turn to the sort of jobs that graduates are doing. In 2001, the ONS found that 73 per cent of graduates were working in jobs for which a degree was needed, and 27 per cent in lower-skill roles that did not require university. By 2011, only 64 per cent of graduates were doing work that needed a degree and 36 per cent were not. This suggests that the growing supply of graduates is outstripping the supply of graduate jobs, at least during the current economic downturn.

It should be noted that the definition of a graduate job is a controversial one. New universities in particular often claim that it fails to reflect the employment reality for their alumni. In any case, a degree is about enhancing your whole career and your view of the world, not just your first job out of college.

No one can predict the changes that may take place in the four or more years before those starting a degree in 2014 begin their careers. But anyone choosing a course now will want to know what they can do to insulate themselves against the possibility of joining the growing band of unemployed or underemployed graduates after they leave university.

The good news is that the worst may be over. Almost half of the Times Top 100 employers surveyed by High Fliers for the annual *Graduate Market* report planned to increase recruitment in 2013, while about a third intended to maintain 2012 levels. Of course, plans do not always translate into reality. The same employers recruited fewer graduates than expected 12 months earlier, but the prospects for 2013 do look rosier, with a 2.7 per cent increase in vacancies forecast.

Universities targeted by the largest number of top employers in 2012–13

1	(7)	Warwick
2	(4)	Nottingham
3	(1)	Manchester
4	(3)	Cambridge
5	(6)	Bristol
6	(8)	Durham
7	(5)	Oxford
8	(9)	Birmingham
9	(10)	Bath
10	(11)	Leeds
11	(12)	Sheffield
12	–	Imperial
13	(14)	Loughborough
14	(13)	Edinburgh
15	–	London School of Economics
16	–	University College London
17	(15)	Southampton
18	(16)	Newcastle
19	(21)	Strathclyde
20	(20)	Exeter

Last year's position in brackets
Source: *The Graduate Market in 2013*

Perhaps surprisingly, public sector employers are planning the biggest increases, together with retailers, engineering and industrial companies. Both high street and investment banking were planning more recruitment, albeit only by 0.4 per cent (eight jobs) in the case of investment banking. However, the accountancy and finance sector were anticipating lower recruitment overall, by a significant 5.9 per cent.

The High Fliers survey found that although most government departments had a recruitment freeze in place, at least on paper, public sector employers were planning to take 6 per cent more graduates in 2013 than in 2012. This amounts to 153 more jobs. The only big losers seem to be the armed forces, where recruitment targets are on the way down. However, it would be foolish to assume that we have seen the total scale of public sector job losses and recruitment cuts just yet.

Despite this optimism, High Fliers acknowledges that the overall number of graduate posts on offer is still less than in the heady days before the recession, even at the upper end of the market that it covers. That era is certainly not going to return in the immediate future, and graduates will need to do all they can to make themselves attractive to employers. They will still be in a much better position than young people without higher education, but there will be a lot of graduates chasing a more limited number of opportunities than in the past.

Subject choice and career opportunities

The tables on pages 38–41 will help you assess whether your course will pay off in career terms, at least to start with. They show both the amount you might expect to earn with a degree in a specific subject, and the odds of being in work. They reflect the experiences of those who graduated in 2012, and the picture may be less gloomy by the time you leave university. But there is no reason to believe that the pattern of success rates for specific subjects and institutions will have changed radically.

The Higher Education Statistics Agency (HESA) collects data on what graduates do straight after graduation (sometimes called graduate destinations) and on their average salaries. The results are to be treated with caution because they represent only the first six months of a graduate's career – not even that if he or she has gone on to postgraduate study – and they make no allowances for the variety of entry routes into different areas of employment. Degrees in social work can sometimes involve a placement after final exams, so people doing these courses can seem to be unemployed when they might in fact have reasonable job prospects.

The table of employment statistics does reveal some unexpected results. For example, only 67 per cent of computer science graduates are working in graduate jobs or doing further study. More traditional engineering subjects fare a little better. The table also shows that some subjects, especially sciences such as physics, chemistry and geology, have a higher expectation than others, such as art and design or hospitality, that their graduates will undertake further study. In both physics and anatomy and physiology, more than 40 per cent of graduates continued to study. Those going into art and design appreciate that it, too, has its own career peculiarities. Periods of freelance or casual work may be an occupational hazard at the start of their career, and perhaps later on as well. One less surprising result: doctors and dentists are virtually guaranteed a job if they complete a degree successfully, as are nurses. HESA found that less than one medic or dentist in 100 was unemployed six months after graduating.

We use a new classification developed by the Higher Education Statistics Agency to distinguish between "graduate-level" work and jobs that do not normally require a degree. Subjects are ranked on "positive destinations", which include postgraduate study and other forms of training, whether or not they are combined with a job. Some similar tables do not make a distinction between different types of job. These tend to give the misleading impression that all universities and subjects offer uniformly rosy employment prospects. In previous editions, we have combined two years' employment data to reduce the volatility in subjects with small numbers of graduates. This has not been possible this year, with a new categorisation, and some subject tables contain fewer universities as a result.

The second table, on pages 40–41, gives average earnings of those who graduated in

What graduates do by subject studied

Subject Area
ranked by the total of the first four columns

	Subject Area	Employed in professional job	Employed in professional job and studying	Studying	Non-professional job and studying	Non-professional job	Unemployed
1	Medicine	92%	1%	6%	0%	0%	1%
2	Dentistry	94%	3%	1%	0%	0%	1%
3	Nursing	89%	3%	1%	0%	3%	4%
4	Pharmacology and Pharmacy	75%	6%	9%	0%	4%	6%
5	Radiography	85%	1%	2%	0%	5%	6%
6	Veterinary Medicine	84%	1%	2%	0%	5%	7%
7	Physiotherapy	78%	1%	2%	0%	9%	8%
8	Chemical Engineering	57%	4%	19%	0%	7%	12%
9	Civil Engineering	61%	3%	13%	1%	9%	13%
10	Mechanical Engineering	63%	2%	12%	1%	10%	12%
11	General Engineering	63%	2%	13%	0%	10%	12%
12	Physics and Astronomy	31%	4%	40%	1%	9%	15%
13	Land and Property Management	57%	9%	8%	1%	14%	11%
14	Chemistry	34%	3%	35%	1%	14%	13%
15	Other Subjects Allied to Medicine	55%	4%	11%	2%	17%	11%
16	Education	56%	3%	11%	2%	21%	7%
17	Mathematics	40%	7%	23%	1%	15%	13%
18	Building	62%	4%	4%	1%	16%	13%
19	Electrical and Electronic Engineering	56%	3%	11%	1%	14%	15%
20	Town and Country Planning and Landscape	51%	5%	13%	2%	17%	12%
21	Economics	46%	8%	15%	2%	15%	15%
22	Anatomy and Physiology	23%	2%	41%	4%	19%	11%
23	Aeronautical and Manufacturing Engineering	54%	1%	13%	1%	14%	16%
24	Architecture	51%	5%	10%	2%	16%	15%
25	Computer Science	57%	2%	8%	1%	15%	17%
26	German	45%	3%	17%	3%	20%	13%
27	Food Science	50%	3%	12%	2%	22%	11%
28	Italian	43%	2%	19%	3%	22%	11%
29	Law	24%	5%	31%	7%	22%	11%
30	French	41%	3%	18%	3%	22%	12%
31	Materials Technology	42%	1%	21%	1%	20%	15%
32	Social Work	56%	3%	5%	2%	22%	13%
33	Geology	36%	1%	27%	1%	19%	15%
34	Theology and Religious Studies	29%	5%	27%	5%	24%	11%
35	Celtic Studies	13%	3%	44%	5%	21%	14%

What graduates do by subject studied

Subject Area ranked by the total of the first four columns	Employed in professional job	Employed in professional job and studying	Studying	Non-professional job and studying	Non-professional job	Unemployed
36 Iberian Languages	40%	4%	18%	2%	24%	13%
37 East and South Asian Studies	40%	3%	17%	3%	19%	18%
38 Librarianship and Information Management	51%	1%	8%	3%	24%	13%
39 Politics	36%	4%	20%	3%	23%	15%
40 Biological Sciences	27%	2%	30%	3%	23%	15%
41 Classics and Ancient History	28%	3%	28%	3%	26%	13%
42 Russian	35%	3%	22%	2%	17%	22%
43 Middle Eastern and African Studies	35%	5%	17%	4%	16%	24%
44 Accounting and Finance	38%	11%	9%	3%	25%	14%
45 Music	36%	4%	17%	3%	28%	13%
46 Philosophy	28%	3%	24%	4%	26%	16%
47 Geography and Environmental Sciences	33%	2%	20%	3%	27%	14%
48 Business Studies	46%	3%	6%	2%	28%	14%
49 History of Art, Architecture and Design	32%	2%	19%	4%	27%	15%
50 Sport Science	36%	4%	14%	3%	33%	10%
51 Linguistics	32%	2%	19%	4%	30%	13%
52 Anthropology	31%	2%	18%	5%	27%	17%
53 History	26%	3%	23%	4%	30%	14%
54 English	29%	3%	21%	4%	31%	13%
55 Archaeology	28%	2%	19%	4%	33%	15%
56 Psychology	26%	4%	16%	5%	36%	12%
57 Agriculture and Forestry	37%	3%	9%	3%	33%	16%
58 Art and Design	43%	1%	6%	2%	32%	16%
59 American Studies	30%	3%	14%	3%	33%	17%
60 Social Policy	28%	3%	13%	4%	36%	15%
61 Drama, Dance and Cinematics	36%	2%	7%	2%	38%	15%
62 Communication and Media Studies	39%	1%	6%	2%	36%	17%
63 Hospitality, Leisure, Recreation and Tourism	38%	1%	4%	2%	41%	14%
64 Sociology	27%	2%	12%	4%	40%	15%
Total	**44%**	**3%**	**14%**	**2%**	**24%**	**13%**

Source: HESA 2011/12 DLHE return
Data shown rounded to the nearest percentage point.

What graduates earn by subject studied

	Subject	Professional employment	Non-professional employment
1	Dentistry	£30,681	..
2	Chemical Engineering	£28,992	£16,481
3	Medicine	£28,862	..
4	General Engineering	£27,221	£17,665
5	Mechanical Engineering	£26,175	£17,542
6	Economics	£26,146	£17,343
7	Veterinary Medicine	£26,045	£18,467
8	Aeronautical and Manufacturing Engineering	£25,061	£15,882
9	Materials Technology	£24,707	£17,776
10	Electrical and Electronic Engineering	£24,506	£14,708
11	Physics and Astronomy	£24,504	£14,990
12	Mathematics	£24,438	£15,980
13	Librarianship and Information Management	£24,038	£15,900
14	Civil Engineering	£23,947	£17,445
15	Geology	£23,766	£14,320
16	Social Work	£23,294	£14,536
17	Computer Science	£23,103	£15,697
18	Russian	£22,880	£17,340
19	Nursing	£22,514	£15,417
20	Building	£22,347	£15,274
21	Radiography	£21,899	£14,615
22	Accounting and Finance	£21,811	£16,499
23	Politics	£21,655	£15,291
24	Business Studies	£21,574	£16,039
25	Physiotherapy	£21,502	£13,953
26	Chemistry	£21,187	£14,472
27	Education	£21,122	£14,053
28	Food Science	£21,009	£15,709
29	Philosophy	£20,807	£14,717
30	Land and Property Management	£20,804	£15,209
31	History	£20,759	£14,582
32	Geography and Environmental Sciences	£20,293	£14,449
33	Town and Country Planning and Landscape	£20,267	£15,604
34	German	£20,263	£15,288
35	Anatomy and Physiology	£20,133	£14,846
36	Other Subjects Allied to Medicine	£20,007	£14,555
37	Classics and Ancient History	£19,995	£14,389
38	French	£19,921	£16,090
39	East and South Asian Studies	£19,799	£16,317
40	Pharmacology and Pharmacy	£19,744	£14,243
41	Anthropology	£19,674	£15,648
42	Theology and Religious Studies	£19,648	£14,662

Subject	Professional employment	Non-professional employment
43 Biological Sciences	£19,564	£14,423
44 History of Art, Architecture and Design	£19,446	£14,962
45 Iberian Languages	£19,405	£15,406
46 Middle Eastern and African Studies	£19,363	£14,320
47 Agriculture and Forestry	£19,306	£14,853
48 Law	£19,229	£15,381
49 Hospitality, Leisure, Recreation and Tourism	£19,021	£15,285
50 Psychology	£19,006	£14,287
51 Sociology	£18,819	£14,720
52 Social Policy	£18,764	£14,428
53 Italian	£18,732	£15,490
54 Sports Science	£18,539	£14,032
55 American Studies	£18,343	£14,016
56 Linguistics	£18,120	£14,339
57 English	£18,071	£14,396
58 Art and Design	£17,996	£13,936
59 Archaeology	£17,982	£14,646
60 Architecture	£17,827	£14,000
61 Communication and Media Studies	£17,599	£14,292
62 Drama, Dance and Cinematics	£17,384	£14,107
63 Music	£16,406	£13,914
64 Celtic Studies		£15,119
Average	**£21,704**	**£14,991**

NOTE: .. indicates a suppressed mean salary based on 7 or fewer graduates
Source: HESA 2011/12DLHE return

2012, six months after leaving college. As we said above, the details of a survey such as this will change over time but the pattern overall may well remain durable. It contains interesting – and in some cases surprising – information about early career pay levels. Few would have placed social work or Librarianship and information management in the top 20 fields for graduate pay, while accounting and business studies appear in 22nd and 24th place respectively. Those positions underline the differences between starting salaries and long-term prospects in different jobs. Over time the accountants may well end up with big rewards. In future years, the data will improve as information emerges on salary levels for specific courses at each university. Incidentally, the top non-City pay for a graduate is thought to be with supermarket group Aldi. Despite its budget image, it pays graduates training to be area managers £40,000 in their first year and adds an Audi A4.

HESA also reported good news in September 2013 on the longer-term outlook for students, based on questioning those who had graduated in 2009. Of the UK graduates surveyed, 87.1 per cent were in employment, 6.7 per cent were studying full-time and only 3.2 per cent were unemployed, compared with 7.2 per cent when the same cohort was surveyed six months after graduation. The median salary of the 2009 graduates had risen from £21,000 to £27,500 over the same three and a half year period. A lucky few had seen their incomes rise by over £20,000 and 87.1 per cent had had some increase despite tricky times for the UK economy

Enhancing your employability

Universities are well aware of the difficulties in the graduate employment market and have been introducing all manner of schemes to try to give their graduates an advantage in the labour market. Many have incorporated specially designed employability modules into degree courses; some are certificating extra-curricular activities to improve their graduates' CVs; others are stepping up their efforts to provide work experience to complement degrees.

Opinion is divided on the value of such schemes. Some of the biggest employers restrict their recruitment activities to a small number of universities, believing that these institutions attract the brightest minds and that trawling more widely is not cost-effective. These companies, often big payers from the City of London and including some of the top law firms, are not likely to change their ways at a time when they are more anxious than ever to control costs. Widening the pool of universities from which they set out to recruit is costly, and unnecessary in a buyers' market like the one we see today. As before, they will expect outstanding candidates who went to other universities to come to them, either on graduation or later in their careers.

The best advice for those looking to maximise their employment opportunities (and who isn't?) must be to go for the best university you can. But most graduates do not work in the City and most students do not go to universities at the top of the league tables.

University schemes

If a university that offers extra help towards employment, it is worth considering whether its scheme is likely to work for you. Some are too new to show results in the labour market, but they may have been endorsed by big employers or introduced at an institution whose graduates already have a record of success in the jobs market. In time, these extras may turn into mandatory parts of degree study, complete with course credit.

At Liverpool John Moores University, for example, the World of Work (WoW) programme was devised with the help of the CBI, Shell, Sony, and Marks and Spencer. Taken by students in all subjects, including postgraduates, it offers classes in CV writing, interview skills, finance, entrepreneurship and negotiation skills, among many other topics. There are guest lectures and demonstrations related to the eight employment-related skills that WoW is intended to develop, and employers carry out mock interviews to assess students' strengths and weaknesses. It began as an option and is now part of all courses.

Hertfordshire is another institution which has demonstrated a sustained focus on its students' job prospects. It was arguably the first of many universities to describe itself as "business-facing". Employer groups are consulted on the curriculum and often supply guest lecturers on degree courses. Like some other universities, such as Derby, it offers career development support to graduates throughout their working life.

Other universities, such as Exeter, have taken a different tack and are helping students make the most of their voluntary and extra-curricular activities by certificating them. The Exeter Award gives credit for attendance at skills sessions and training courses, active participation in sporting and musical activities, engagement in work experience and voluntary work. The university already claimed to have more students than any other involved in voluntary activities. It believes that the award will encourage employers to take more notice of them.

The York Award is another well-established example of this type of scheme that has the involvement of organisations from the public, private and voluntary sectors. The university has found that employers value a combination of academic study, work experience and leisure interests. The scheme offers York students a framework to gain recognition for activities that are not formally recognised through the degree programme. Among the subjects on an extensive list of courses are networking, time management, counselling and understanding different cultures.

The value of work experience

As the table earlier in this chapter showed, there are big differences in the average employment prospects for different subjects. The majority of graduate jobs are open to applicants from any discipline. For these general positions, employers tend to be more impressed by a good degree from what they consider a prestigious university than by an apparently relevant qualification. Here numeracy, literacy and communications – the arts needed to function effectively in any organisation – are of vital importance.

Specialist jobs – for example in engineering or design – are a different matter. Employers may be much more knowledgeable about the quality of individual courses, and less influenced by a university's overall position in league tables, when the job relies directly on knowledge and skills acquired as a student. That goes for the likes of medicine and architecture as well as the new vocational areas such as computer games design or environmental management.

In either case, however, work experience has become increasingly important. The High Fliers survey shows that more than a third of the jobs taken by 2012 graduates went to people who had already worked in the organisation that now employs them, whether in holiday jobs or via placements or sponsored degrees. Sandwich degrees, extended programmes that include up to a year at work, have always boosted employment prospects. Graduates often end up working where they undertook their placement. And while a sandwich year will make your course longer, it will not be subject to a full year's fees.

Many conventional degrees now include shorter work placements that should offer some advantages in the labour market. Not all are arranged by the university so, unless you have an opening that you would like to pursue, that is something to establish and weigh in the balance when choosing a course. The majority of big graduate employers offer some provision of this nature, although access to it can be competitive.

If your chosen course does not include a work placement, you may want to consider arranging your own part-time or temporary employment. The majority of supposedly full-time students now take jobs during term time, as well as in vacations, to make ends meet. But such jobs can boost your CV as well as your wallet. Even working in a bar or a shop shows some experience of dealing with the public and coping with the disciplines of the workplace. Inevitably, the more prosperous cities are likely to offer more employment opportunities than rural areas or conurbations that have been hard hit in the recession.

The ultimate work-related degree is one sponsored by an employer or even taken in the workplace, something that ministers have encouraged recently. Middlesex University provides tailored programmes for Dell and Marks and Spencer, among other organisations, and has more than 1,000 students taking courses run by its Institute of Work Based Learning. Most such courses are provided for people already employed by the companies concerned, rather than as a route into the company. But they may come to be considered as an alternative to entering full-time higher education straight from school or college.

Consider part-time degrees

Another option, also favoured by ministers, is part-time study. Although enrolments fell sharply both leading up to and immediately following the 2012 increases in fees, there are now loans available for most part-time courses the first time. Employers may be willing to share the cost of taking a degree or another relevant qualification, and the chance to earn a wage while studying has obvious attractions.

Part-time study requires a high degree of commitment – knuckling down to an essay or an assignment after a hard day at work is not easy – but it does reduce the cost of higher education for those in work. Bear in mind, however, that most part-time courses take twice as long to complete as the full-time equivalent. If your earning power is linked to the qualification, it will take that much longer for you to enjoy the benefits.

Plan early for your career

Whatever type of course you choose, it is sensible to start thinking about your future career early in your time at university. There has been a growing tendency in recent years for students to convince themselves that there would be plenty of time to apply for jobs after graduation, and that they were better off focusing entirely on their degree while at university. In the current employment market, all but the most obviously brilliant graduates need to offer more than just a degree, whether it be work experience, leadership qualities demonstrated through clubs and societies, or commitment to voluntary activities. Many students finish a degree without knowing what they want to do, but a blank CV will not impress a prospective employer.

The recession had the effect of reducing the number of vacancies for graduate-level jobs while increasing the number of applications to 52 per graduate-level job in 2011, according to High Fliers. The leading employers also told High Fliers that they are not interested in applicants with no previous work experience. He may be overstating the case, but Martin Burchall, High Fliers' Managing Director, claimed that work placements and internships were now "just as important as getting a 2:1 or first-class degree".

Useful websites

Prospects, the UK's official graduate careers website:
www.prospects.ac.uk
For information on internships, graduate schemes and career advice:
www.milkround.com
HESA Longitudinal survey on graduate employment: **http://bit.ly/10KSjoz**
High Fliers: **www.highfliers.co.uk**

3 Going Abroad to University

Since fees at the majority of UK universities hit £9,000, there have been frequent predictions of a student exodus to take degree courses abroad. There is logic to the argument, especially in relation to Continental universities, where tuition costs a fraction of the amounts charged on this side of the Channel. Some European universities – especially those in the Netherlands – have mounted aggressive marketing campaigns for the growing number of courses now taught in English. Even American degrees are not out of reach: state universities can be cheaper per year than their UK counterparts, while Ivy League institutions offer generous scholarships and bursaries.

So far, however, the anticipated flood has been more of a trickle. There was an impressive 77 per cent rise in the number of Britons at Dutch universities in 2012, but they still totalled less than 1,000 of the 2.5 million UK student population. There were more than 9,000 UK students in the USA in 2011 but, despite reports of many more inquiries to US universities, this represented only a 2.7 per cent increase on the previous year.

Nevertheless, it would be surprising if high fees at home and an increasingly international graduate labour market did not encourage at least gradual growth in overseas study. It is certainly on the radar of many more sixth-formers and college students, particularly in the independent sector.

There is good reason for applicants to spread the university net more widely. Research by QS, publishers of the World University Rankings, found that 60 per cent of employers worldwide – and 42 per cent of those in the UK – gave extra weight to an international student experience when recruiting graduates. Of course, everything will depend on what and where that experience was. Harvard is going to carry more weight than the University of Lapland, which has been trying to attract British students recently. But leaving the UK to study certainly need not hold back your career or provide an inferior education.

Indeed, most students who go abroad are motivated by a desire to study at a "world-class" institution, according to a study for the Department of Business, Innovation and Skills. Often the trigger is failure to win a place at a leading UK university and being unwilling to settle for second best. Other motivations included a desire for adventure and a belief that overseas study might lead to an international career.

The question is how to judge a university that may be thousands of miles from home against more familiar names in the UK. This chapter will make some suggestions, including the use of the growing number of global rankings that are available online or in print.

It is possible to have your academic cake and eat it by going on an international exchange or work placement organised by a UK university, or even to attend a British university in another country. Nottingham University has campuses in China and Malaysia; Middlesex can offer Dubai or Mauritius, where students registered in the UK can take part or all of their degree. Other universities, such as Liverpool, also have joint ventures with overseas institutions which offer an international experience (in China, in Liverpool's case) and degrees from both universities.

In most cases, however, an overseas study experience means a foreign university. Until recently, this was usually for a postgraduate degree – and there are still strong arguments for spending your undergraduate years in the UK before going abroad for more advanced study. Older students taking more specialised programmes may get more out of an extended period overseas than those who go at 18 and, since first degrees in the UK are shorter than elsewhere, it may also be the more cost-effective option.

If cost is the main consideration, however, even the generally longer courses at Continental universities can work out cheaper than a degree in the UK. The main obstacle, apart from British students' traditional reluctance to take degrees anywhere else, concerns the language barrier. Although there are now thousands of postgraduate courses taught in English at Continental universities, first degree programmes are still much thinner on the ground. A few universities, like Maastricht in the Netherlands, have made a serious pitch for business from the UK and are offering a wide range of subjects in English. Maastricht doubled its UK intake in 2012 and now has almost 300 UK students. But most European universities teach undergraduates in the host language – and, up to now, that has always deterred UK students.

The obvious alternative lies in American, Australian and Canadian universities, all of which are keen to attract more international students. Here, cost and distance are the main obstacles. Four-year courses add considerably to the cost of affordable-looking fees, while the state of the pound has been another serious disadvantage. Add in the natural reluctance of most 18-year-olds to commit to life on the other side of the world (or even just the Atlantic), and the prospect of a dramatic increase in student emigration lessens considerably.

Where do students go to?

There is remarkably little official monitoring of how many students leave the UK, let alone where they go. But it seems that for all the economic advantages of studying in Continental Europe, the USA remains by far the most popular student destination. Most surveys put Canada, France and Germany (in that order) as the biggest attractions outside the US.

A few British students find their way to unexpected locations, like South Korea or Slovakia, but usually for family reasons or to study the language. The figures suggest that British students are more attracted to countries that are familiar or close at hand, and where they can speak English. Many are doubtless planning to stay in their adopted country after they graduate, although visa regulations may make this difficult.

Studying in Europe

More than 10,000 UK students now attend Continental European universities and colleges: UNESCO put the total at 9,764 in 2009, and it is safe to assume that more than 240 have been added since then. But international statistics pick up those whose parents emigrated or are working abroad, as well as those who actually leave the UK to take a degree. A minority are undergraduates, if only because the availability of courses taught in English is so much greater at postgraduate level.

The increased interest in Continental universities arises both from the generally low fees they charge and from the growth in the number of courses offered in English. Lund University in Sweden, for example, which is ranked in the top 100 in the world by QS and *Times Higher Education*, had more than 600 applications from the UK in 2012 – 15 per cent up on the previous year – and is adding science and business degrees to its five BA programmes taught in English. Even then, however, the undergraduate portfolio will be dwarfed by the 90 MAs taught in English.

Fees will remain low, or even non-existent, for UK students attending public universities in other EU countries because they are entitled to study there for the same fees as local residents. In the EU, you will also be able get a job while studying. Farther afield, your student visa might not allow you to take on paid work.

Undergraduates can study at a French university for £150 a year but, not surprisingly, nearly all first degrees are taught in French. Only 50 of the 775 programmes taught in English and listed on the Campus France website (**www.campusfrance.org/en**) are at the Licence (Bachelors equivalent) level – and 14 of them have some teaching in French.

Germany is much the same, despite attracting large numbers of international students. The DAAD website (**www.daad.de/en**) lists 125 undergraduate programmes taught wholly or mainly in English, but many are at private universities like Jacobs University in Bremen, which charges up to €10,000 a semester. There are cheaper alternatives in the public sector – tuition fees are "optional" for the BSc in applied chemistry at the University of Applied Sciences in Aachen – but they remain relatively scarce.

Any potential saving has to be considered with care. Despite the Bologna process – an intergovernmental agreement which means that degrees across Europe are becoming more similar in content and duration – most Continental courses are longer than their UK equivalents, adding to the cost and to your lost earnings from attending university. And, of course, you will have higher travel costs. It is harder to generalise about the cost of living. It can be lower than the UK in southern Europe, but frighteningly high in Scandinavia. You can cut down the cost of an international experience and hedge your bets about committing yourself to a full course overseas by opting instead for an exchange scheme. UK universities have exchange partners all over the world, providing opportunities for

Top 10 European countries, as destinations for UK students, 2010

1	France	2,704
2	Ireland	1,804
3	Germany	1,342
4	Spain	531
5	Czech Republic	412
6	Norway	338
7	Switzerland	336
8	Austria	318
9	Netherlands	232
10	Portugal	211

Source: UNESCO Institute for Statistics, 2010 data

Top 10 student cities in the world

1	Paris	France
2	London	United Kingdom
3	Boston	USA
4	Melbourne	Australia
5	Vienna	Austria
6	Sydney	Australia
7	Zurich	Switzerland
=8	Berlin	Germany
=8	Dublin	Ireland
10	Montreal	Canada

Source: QS Best Student Cities in the World 2012

everything from a summer school of less than a month to a full year abroad.

The most common offering is the EU's Erasmus scheme, which funds exchanges of between three months and a year, the work counting towards your degree. More than 2 million students throughout Europe have used the scheme, and there are 2,000 universities to choose from in 30 countries. Applications, which are made through universities' international offices, must be approved by the UK university as well as by the Erasmus administrators. Erasmus students do not pay any extra fees and they are eligible for grants to cover the extra expense of travelling and living in another country.

Studying in America

American universities remain the first choice of British students going abroad to take a degree, just as the UK is the first choice for Americans. Regardless of any special relationship, this is not surprising since international rankings consistently show US and UK universities to be the best in the world (as well as teaching in English).

Around half of the British students taking courses in the USA are undergraduates. Already by far the most popular student destination, the attractions of an American degree have multiplied since fees trebled in England. The Fulbright Commission, which promotes American higher education, has seen a 30 per cent increase in the number of Britons taking US university entrance exams. Even before the latest rise in UK fees, the top American universities had seen demand rise sharply: Harvard received 41 per cent more applications from the UK in 2010–11, Yale 23 per cent and Pennsylvania 50 per cent more.

The sheer depth of the US university system means that if you are thinking of studying abroad, the USA is almost bound to be on the list of possibilities. Tuition fees at Ivy League institutions are notoriously high – Harvard's were $38,891 in 2013–14 and the university put the full cost of attendance at over $60,000 a year – but generous student aid programmes ensure that most pay far less than the "sticker price". Outside the Ivy League, the fee gap for UK students is narrower, although fees at many state universities have shot up in the last three years as politicians have tried to balance the books. At Texas A&M University, for example, ranked in the top 200 in the world, international students still only paid $12,500 a year for tuition, about £8,000 at the time of writing, although the university put undergraduates' total costs at $36,000. Fees are lower than that at the State University of New York, although the university puts the total cost for those living on campus at $31,000.

The individual systems of state universities and private universities mean that there is a great variation in the financial support given to international students. Fulbright advises students considering a US degree to assess and negotiate a funding package at the same time as pursuing their application. Otherwise, they may end up with a place they cannot afford, losing valuable time in the quest for a more suitable one.

Which countries are best?

Anyone going abroad to study will be in search of a memorable all-round experience, not just a good course. In 2010 the British Council completed a detailed analysis of how well countries around the world work to attract foreign students, as well as how well-regarded the degrees they award are internationally.

The report shows that, relative to their student population, smaller countries send the most people abroad to study. Almost 11 per cent of Moroccan students are outside Morocco, and 10 per cent of Irish students are outside Ireland. The equivalent for the UK would be about 0.7 per cent, although that figure may grow. The proportion in China may be similarly low but, as it is the world's most populous country, it is much the biggest exporter of students.

The British Council report, prepared by the Economist Intelligence Unit, went on to look in detail at which countries have the most developed approach to welcoming international students. No doubt to the British Council's relief, Britain came third in the world as a destination for international students. The top place goes to Germany, with Australia second. China is in fourth place, while Malaysia, the USA, Japan, Russia, Nigeria, Brazil and India (these two in joint tenth place) complete the top eleven.

The report says that Germany is one of the few nations that does not allow public universities to increase fees for foreign students, and a German student visa lasts until a year after graduation, to help you look for a permanent job there. In Australia, universities can charge foreign students big fees, but other aspects of its system are highly rated. The quality of Australian degrees is generally regarded as high, and despite the high cost of getting there and the strength of the Australian dollar, life there costs less than in the UK once you arrive.

Many Asian countries are looking to recruit more foreign students, both as part of a broader internationalisation agenda and to compensate for falling numbers of potential students at home. Japan is a case in point. The high cost of living may put off many potential students, as may the unfamiliarity of its language, but more support is being offered to attract foreign students and more courses are being taught in English. However, as with any non-English speaking country, the language of instruction is only part of the story. You will need to know enough of the local language to manage the shops and the transport system, and, of course, to make friends and get the most out of being there.

Another option of growing interest is China. While you may not believe the whole of the story that China is about to take over the world, it has already grown massively in importance. Its university system is growing in quality, especially at the C9 group of international institutions, which have become known as the Chinese Ivy League. Familiarity with China is unlikely to be a career disadvantage for anyone in the 21st century. Some see Hong Kong, which has several world-ranked universities and a familiar feel for Britons, as the perfect alternative to mainland Chinese universities.

Will my degree be recognised?

Even in the era of globalisation, you need to bear in mind that not all degrees are equal. At one extreme is the MBA, which has an international system for accrediting courses, and a global admissions standard. But with many professional courses, study abroad is a potential hazard. To work as a doctor, engineer or lawyer in the UK, you need a qualification which the relevant professional body will recognise. It is understandable that to practise law in England, you need to have studied the English legal system. For other subjects, the issues are more to do with the quality and content of courses outside UK control.

There are ways of researching this issue in advance. One is to contact NARIC, the National Recognition Centre for the UK (**www.ecctis.co.uk/naric**). NARIC exists to examine the compatibility and acceptability of qualifications from around the world. The other approach is to ask the UK professional body in question – maybe an engineering institution, the Law Society or the General Teaching, Medical or Dental Councils – about the qualification you propose to study for.

The British Council report suggests that Australian and German degrees are the most internationally acceptable from its Top 11 countries, with Brazil at the bottom. The USA comes fifth. While it is home to the world's top universities, the USA also has many less prestigious institutions whose qualifications are less likely to be welcomed around the world.

Which are the best universities?

Going abroad to study is a big and expensive decision, and you want to get it right. Some surveys have suggested that excitement, adventure and glamour are more important to many overseas applicants than career positioning. But let's assume that you are more thoughtful in your approach. Especially if you plan to study abroad to establish yourself as an internationally mobile high-flyer, you will want to know that the university you are going to is taken seriously around the world.

At the moment there are three main systems for ranking universities on a world scale. One is run by QS (Quacquarelli Symonds), an educational research company based in London (**www.topuniversities.com**). Another is by Shanghai Ranking Consultancy, a company set up by Shanghai Jiao Tong University, in China, and is called the Academic Ranking of World Universities (ARWU) (**www.arwu.org**). These two have been joined by *Times Higher Education* (**www.timeshighereducation.co.uk**), a weekly magazine with no connection to *The Times*, which produced its own ranking for the first time in 2010, having previously published the QS version.

The QS system uses a number of measures including academic opinion, employer opinion, international orientation, research impact and staff/student ratio to create its listing, while the ARWU uses measures such as Nobel Prizes and highly cited papers, which are more related to excellence in scientific research. *The Times Higher* has added a number of measures to the QS model, including research income and a controversial global survey of teaching quality. Despite these different approaches, many universities appear in all three rankings. If you go to a university that features strongly in any of the tables, you will be at a place that is well-regarded around the world. After all, even the 200th university on any of these rankings is an elite institution in a world with more than 4,000 universities. The top 50 universities in all three rankings are listed on the following pages.

These systems tend to favour universities which are good at science and medicine. Places that specialise in the humanities and the social sciences, such as the London School of Economics, can appear in deceptively modest positions. In addition, the rankings tend to look at universities in the round, and contain only limited information on specific subjects. QS published the first 26 global subject rankings in 2011 and has since increased this to 30. One advantage of the QS ranking system is that 10 per cent of a university's possible score comes from a global survey of recruiters. So you can look at this column of the table for an idea about where the major employers like to hire. Note that the author of this *Guide* has a role in developing the QS Rankings.

Other options for overseas studies

If you decide that studying abroad for a complete degree is too much, a number of options remain open. A language degree will typically involve a year abroad, and a look at the UCAS website will show many options for studying another subject alongside your language of choice. UK universities offer degrees in information technology, science, business and even journalism with a major language such as Chinese.

Many universities offer a year abroad, either studying or in a work placement, even to those who are not taking a language. At Aston University, for example, 70 per cent of students do a year's work placement and a growing number do so abroad. China and Chile have been among recent destinations. Other universities offer the opportunity to take credit-bearing courses with partner institutions overseas. American universities are again the most popular choice. The best approach is to decide what you want to study and then see if there is a UK university that offers it as a joint degree or with a placement abroad. Be aware that employers and academics alike sometimes look askance at joint degrees. Make sure that all the universities involved are well-regarded, for example by looking at their rankings on one or other of the websites mentioned at the end of the table.

Useful websites
Prospects: studying abroad: **www.prospects.ac.uk/studying_abroad.htm**
Association of Commonwealth Universities: **www.acu.ac.uk**
Campus France: **www.campusfrance.org/en**
College Board (USA): **www.collegeboard.org**
DAAD (for Germany): **www.daad.de/en**
Education Ireland: **www.educationinireland.com/en**
Erasmus Programme (EU): **www.britishcouncil.org/erasmus**
Finaid (USA): **www.finaid.org**
Fulbright Commission: **www.fulbright.co.uk**
Study in Australia: **www.studyinaustralia.gov.au**
Study in Canada: **www.studyincanada.com**
Study Overseas: **www.studyoverseas.com**

The top 50 universities in the world in 2013 according to QS World University Ranking (QS), the Academic Ranking of World Universities (ARWU) and *Times Higher Education* (THE)

QS Rank	Institution	Country	ARWU Rank	Institution	Country	THE Rank	Institution	Country
1	Massachusetts Institute of Technology	USA	1	Harvard University	USA	1	California Institute of Technology	USA
2	Harvard University	USA	2	Stanford University	USA	2	University of Oxford	UK
3	University of Cambridge	UK	3	University of California, Berkeley	USA	3	Stanford University	USA
4	University College London	UK	4	Massachusetts Institute of Technology	USA	4	Harvard University	USA
5	Imperial College London	UK	5	University of Cambridge	UK	5	Massachusetts Institute of Technology	USA
6	University of Oxford	UK	6	California Institute of Technology	USA	6	Princeton University	USA
7	Stanford University	USA	7	Princeton University	USA	7	University of Cambridge	UK
8	Yale University	USA	8	Columbia University	USA	8	Imperial College, London	UK
9	University of Chicago	USA	9	University of Chicago	USA	9	University of California, Berkeley	USA
=10	California Institute of Technology	USA	10	University of Oxford	UK	10	University of Chicago	USA
=10	Princeton University	USA	11	Yale University	USA	11	Yale University	USA
12	ETH Zurich (Swiss Federal Institute of Technology)	Switzerland	12	University of California, Los Angeles	USA	12	ETH Zurich (Swiss Federal Institute of Technology)	Switzerland
13	University of Pennsylvania	USA	13	Cornell University	USA	13	University of California, Los Angeles	USA
14	Columbia University	USA	14	University of California, San Diego	USA	14	Columbia University	USA
15	Cornell University	USA	15	University of Pennsylvania	USA	15	University of Pennsylvania	USA
16	Johns Hopkins University	USA	16	University of Washington	USA	16	Johns Hopkins University	USA
=17	University of Edinburgh	UK	17	Johns Hopkins University	USA	17	University College London	UK
=17	University of Toronto	Canada	18	University of California, San Francisco	USA	18	Cornell University	USA
=19	École Polytechnique Fédérale de Lausanne (EPFL)	Switzerland	19	University of Wisconsin, Madison	USA	19	Northwestern University	USA

Rank	University	Country
=19	King's College London	UK
21	McGill University	Canada
22	University of Michigan	USA
23	Duke University	USA
24	National University of Singapore	Singapore
25	University of California, Berkeley	USA
26	University of Hong Kong	Hong Kong
27	Australian National University	Australia
28	École Normale Supérieure, Paris	France
29	Northwestern University	USA
30	University of Bristol	UK
31	University of Melbourne	Australia
32	University of Tokyo	Japan
33	University of Manchester	UK
34	Hong Kong University of Science and Technology	Hong Kong
=35	Kyoto University	Japan
=35	Seoul National University	S. Korea
37	University of Wisconsin, Madison	USA
38	University of Sydney	Australia
39	Chinese University of Hong Kong	Hong Kong

Rank	University	Country
20	ETH Zurich (Swiss Federal Institute of Technology)	Switzerland
=21	University of Tokyo	Japan
=21	University College London (UCL)	UK
23	University of Michigan, Ann Arbor	USA
24	Imperial College, London	UK
25	University of Illinois, Urbana-Champaign	USA
26	Kyoto University	Japan
27	New York University	USA
28	University of Toronto	Canada
29	University of Minnesota, Twin Cities	USA
30	Northwestern University	USA
31	Duke University	USA
32	Washington University in St Louis	USA
33	University of Colorado at Boulder	USA
34	Rockerfeller University	USA
35	University of California, Santa Barbara	USA
36	University of Texas at Austin	USA
37	Pierre and Marie Curie University, Paris 6	France
38	University of Maryland, College Park	USA
39	University of Paris Sud (Paris 11)	France

Rank	University	Country
20	University of Michigan	USA
21	University of Toronto	Canada
22	Carnegie Mellon University	USA
23	Duke University	USA
24	University of Washington	USA
=25	Georgia Institute of Technology	USA
=25	University of Texas at Austin	USA
27	University of Tokyo	Japan
28	University of Melbourne	Australia
29	National University of Singapore	Singapore
30	University of British Columbia	Canada
31	University of Wisconsin, Madison	USA
32	University of Edinburgh	UK
33	University of Illinois, Urbana-Champaign	US
34	McGill University	Canada
=35	University of California, Santa Barbara	USA
=35	University of Hong Kong	Hong Kong
37	Australian National University	Australia
38	University of California, San Diego	USA
39	London School of Economics	UK

The top 50 universities in the world in 2013 according to QS World University Ranking (QS), the Academic Ranking of World Universities (ARWU) and *Times Higher Education* (THE)

QS Rank	Institution	Country	ARWU Rank	Institution	Country	THE Rank	Institution	Country
40	University of California, Los Angeles	USA	40	University of British Columbia	Canada	40	École Polytechnique Fédérale de Lausanne	Switzerland
=41	École Polytechnique ParisTech	France	41	University of Manchester	UK	41	Nanyang Technological University	Singapore
=41	Nanyang Technological University	Singapore	42	University of Copenhagen	Denmark	=42	Karolinska Institute	Sweden
43	University of Queensland	Australia	42	University of North Carolina, Chapel Hill	USA	=42	University of North Carolina, Chapel Hill	USA
44	New York University	USA	44	Karolinska Institute	Sweden	=44	University of California, Davis	USA
45	University of Copenhagen	Denmark	45	University of California, Irvine	USA	=44	Washington University in St Louis	USA
46	Peking University	China	46	University of Texas Southwestern Medical Center at Dallas	USA	46	Peking University	China
47	Brown University	USA	=47	University of California, Davis	USA	47	University of Minnesota	USA
48	Tsinghua University	China	48	University of Southern California	USA	48	Ludwig-Maximilians-Universität Munich	Germany
49	University of British Columbia	Canada	49	Vanderbilt University	USA	49	University of Manchester	UK
50	Ruprecht-Karls-Universitat, Heidelberg	Germany	50	Technical University Munich	Germany	50	Pohang University of Science and Technology	S. Korea

We gratefully acknowledge permission to reproduce these three rankings. The full QS World University Rankings 2013–14 can be consulted at www.topuniversities.com, the full Academic Ranking of World Universities 2013 at www.arwu.org and the full Times Higher Education 2012–13 rankings at www.timeshighereducation.co.uk.

For information on the recognition in the UK of international degrees, visit the National Recognition Centre for the UK (NARIC): www.naric.org.uk

4 The Top Universities

Universities publish reams of statistics about themselves – more than ever now that the Government insists on greater transparency. But even some of the official attempts to provide prospective students with better information can leave the reader more confused, rather than less. Our main table has been developed over 20 years to focus on the fundamentals of undergraduate education and make meaningful comparisons in an accessible way.

What distinguishes a top university? And who is to say that one course is better than another – especially when the university system is so reluctant to make any such comparison? Critics of league tables insist that this is because every university has different priorities, and every course has a different ways of approaching a subject. Students must choose the one that suits them best. So they must. Not everyone would find the top universities to their taste, even if they were able to secure a place. But that does not mean that there are not important differences in the quality of universities and the courses they offer. These, in turn, can have a crucial bearing on future employment prospects.

The table in this chapter offers applicants and others with an interest in higher education a means to assess the standing of UK universities with undergraduate education in mind. The institutions will have their own ideas about what should go into comparisons of this type, but ours has stood the test of time because it uses the statistics that universities themselves employ to measure their own performance and combines them in a way that generations of students have found revealing.

Every element of the table has been chosen for the light it shines on the undergraduate experience and a student's future prospects. This is what distinguishes it from the international rankings of universities, which necessarily focus more on research, and produce a different order. Unlike some others, our *Guide* has placed a premium on consistency, confident that the measures are the best available for the task. Some changes have been forced upon us. Universities stopped assessing teaching quality by subject, when this was the most heavily weighted measure in the table, for example. Conversely, the arrival of the National Student Survey six years ago has enabled the student experience to be reflected in the table.

The basic information that applicants need, however, in order to judge universities and their courses does not change. A university's entry standards, staffing levels, completion rates, degree classifications and graduate employment rates are all vital pieces of intelligence for anyone deciding where to study. Research grades, while not directly involving undergraduates, bring with them considerable funds and enable a university to attract top academics.

Any of these measures can be discounted by an individual, but the package has struck a chord with readers. The ranking is the most-quoted of its type both in Britain and overseas, and has built a reputation as the most authoritative arbiter of changing fortunes in higher education. The measures used are kept under review by a group of university administrators and statisticians, which meets annually. The raw data that go into the table in this chapter and the subject tables in chapter 5 are all in the public domain and are sent to universities for checking before any scores are calculated.

Indeed, while the various official bodies concerned with higher education do not publish league tables, several produce system-wide statistics in a format that invites comparisons. The Higher Education Funding Councils' Research Assessment Exercise was one early example of this. The Higher Education Statistics Agency (HESA), which supplies most of the figures used in our tables, also publishes annual "performance indicators" on everything from completion rates to research output at each university.

Any scrutiny of league table positions is best carried out in conjunction with an examination of the relevant subject table – it is the course, after all, that will dominate your undergraduate years and influence your subsequent career. In the following chapter you will find tables for 64 subject areas.

How *The Times and Sunday Times* league table works

The table is presented in a format that displays the raw data, wherever possible. In building the table, scores for student satisfaction and research quality were weighted by 1.5; all other measures were weighted by 1. The indicators were combined using a common statistical technique known as Z-scores, to ensure that no indicator has a disproportionate effect on the overall total for each university, and the totals were transformed to a scale with 1000 for the top score.

For entry standards, student–staff ratio, good honours and graduate prospects, the score was adjusted for subject mix. For example, it is accepted that engineering, law and medicine graduates will tend to have better graduate prospects than their peers from English, psychology and sociology courses. Comparing results in the main subject groupings helps to iron out differences attributable simply to the range of degrees on offer. This subject-mix adjustment means that it is not possible to replicate the scores in the table from the published indicators because the calculation requires access to the entire dataset.

The Z-score technique makes it impossible to compare universities' total scores from one year to the next, although their relative positions in the table are comparable. Individual scores are dependent on the top performer: a university might drop from 60 per cent of the top score to 58 per cent but still have improved, depending on the relative performance of other universities.

Only where data are not available from HESA are figures sourced directly from universities. Where this is not possible scores are generated according to a university's average performance on other indicators.

The organisations providing the raw data for the tables are not involved in the process of aggregation, so are not responsible for any inferences or conclusions we have made. Every care has been taken to ensure the accuracy of the tables and accompanying information, but no responsibility can be taken for errors or omissions.

The Times and Sunday Times league table uses eight important measures of university activity, based on the most recent data available at the time of compilation:

» Student satisfaction
» Research quality
» Entry standards
» Student–staff ratio

» Services and facilities spend
» Completion
» Good honours
» Graduate prospects

Student satisfaction

This is a measure of students' views of the quality of their courses. The National Student Survey (NSS) was the source of this data. The NSS is an initiative undertaken by the Funding Councils for England, Northern Ireland and Wales. It is designed, as an element of the quality assurance for higher education, to inform prospective students and their advisers in choosing what and where to study. The survey encompasses the views of final-year students on the quality of their courses. Data from the survey published in 2013 were used.

» The National Student Survey covers six aspects of a course: teaching, assessment and feedback, academic support, organisation and management, learning resources and personal development, with an additional question gauging overall satisfaction. Students answer on a scale from 1 (bottom) to 5 (top) and the measure is the percentage of positive responses (4 and 5) in each section, averaged to produce the final score.

» The survey is based on the opinion of final-year students rather than directly assessing teaching quality. Most undergraduates have no experience of other universities, or different courses, to inform their judgements. Although all the questions relate to courses, rather than the broader student experience, some types of university – notably medium-sized campus universities – tend to do better than others.

» Scottish universities were not automatically included in the survey, although all 15 opted to take part in the 2013 survey.

Research quality

This is a measure of the quality of the research undertaken in each university. The information was sourced from the 2008 Research Assessment Exercise (RAE), a peer-review exercise used to evaluate the quality of research in UK higher education institutions undertaken by the UK Higher Education funding bodies. Additionally, academic staffing data for 2007–08 from the Higher Education Statistics Agency have been used.

» A research quality profile was given to every university department that took part. This profile used the following categories: 4* world-leading; 3* internationally excellent; 2* internationally recognised; 1* nationally recognised; and unclassified. The Funding Bodies decided to direct more funds to the very best research by applying weightings. The English, Scottish and Welsh funding councils have slightly different weightings. Those adopted by HEFCE (the funding council for England) for funding in 2012–13 are used in the tables: 4* is weighted by a factor of 3, 3* is weighted by a factor of 1. Outputs of 2* and 1* carry zero weight. This results in a maximum score of 3.

» The scores in the table are presented as a percentage of the maximum score. To achieve the maximum score all staff would need to be at the 4* world-leading level.

» Universities could choose which staff to include in the RAE, so, to factor in the depth of the research quality, each quality profile score has been multiplied by the number of staff returned in the RAE as a proportion of all eligible staff.

» Estimations of the eligible staff for each university were made drawing from publicly available data that have been quality assured by universities themselves. The eligible staff data include all staff directly responsible for teaching and research (excluding those on part-time contracts of less than 20 per cent of a full-time position as they were not eligible), with an adjustment made to remove more junior staff on research-only contracts. An adjustment has also been made to reflect patterns of staffing in those institutions which carry out further education as well as higher education. The calculations were checked against the figures published by a number of universities that declared the proportion of eligible staff entered for assessment.

Estimation was necessary because, as you will see from the note on page 65, HESA decided not to publish data on numbers of staff in university departments who were eligible to be submitted in the RAE. The proportion of staff entered by each university had been considered sufficiently important to be included in the grades used in every previous RAE to give an indication of the ethos and overall quality of departments. The methodology used in *The Times and Sunday Times* league table attempts to replicate that process as accurately as possible, given the restrictions imposed by HESA.

Entry standards

This is the average score, using the UCAS tariff (see page 18), of new students under the age of 21 who took A and AS Levels, Scottish Highers and Advanced Highers and other equivalent qualifications (eg, International Baccalaureate). It measures what new students actually achieved rather than the entry requirements suggested by the universities. The data comes from HESA for 2011–12. The original sources of data for this measure are data returns made by the universities themselves to HESA.

» Using the UCAS tariff, each student's examination results were converted to a numerical score. HESA then calculated an average for all students at the university. The results have then been adjusted to take account of the subject mix at the university.

» A score of 360 represents three As at A level. Although all of the top 38 universities in the table have entry standards of at least 360, it does not mean that everyone achieved such results – let alone that this was the standard offer. Courses will not demand more than three subjects at A level and offers are pitched accordingly. You will need to reach the entry requirements set by the university in any course description and in any offer to you, rather than the scores represented here.

Student–staff ratio

This is a measure of the average number of students to each member of the academic staff, apart from those purely engaged in research. In this measure a low score is better than a high score. The data comes from HESA for 2011–12. The original sources of data for this measure are data returns made by the universities themselves to HESA.

» The figures, as calculated by HESA, allow for variation in employment patterns at different universities. A low value means that there are a small number of students for each academic member of staff, but this does not, of course, ensure good teaching quality or contact time with academics.

» Student–staff ratios vary by subject, for example the ratio is usually low for medicine. In building the table, the score is adjusted for the subject mix taught by each university.

Services and facilities spend

The expenditure per student on staff and student facilities, including library and computing facilities. The data comes from HESA for 2010–11 and 2011–12. The original data sources for this measure are data returns made by the universities to HESA.

» This is a measure calculated by taking the expenditure on student facilities (sports, grants to student societies, careers services, health services, counselling, etc.) and library and computing facilities (books, journals, staff, central computers and computer networks, but not buildings) and dividing this by the number of full-time-equivalent students. Expenditure is averaged over two years to even out the figures (for example, a computer upgrade undertaken in a single year).

Completion

This measure gives the percentage of students expected to complete their studies (or transfer to another institution) for each university. The data comes from the HESA performance indicators, based on data for 2011–12 and earlier years.

» This measure is a projection, liable to statistical fluctuations.

Good honours

This measure is the percentage of graduates achieving a first or upper second class degree. The results have been adjusted to take account of the subject mix at the university. The data comes from HESA for 2011–12. The original sources of data for this measure are data returns made by the universities themselves to HESA.

» Four-year first degrees, such as an MChem, are treated as equivalent to a first or upper second.
» Scottish Ordinary degrees (awarded after three years of study) are excluded.
» Universities control degree classification, with some oversight from external examiners. There have been suggestions that since universities have increased the numbers of good honours degrees they award, this measure may not be as objective as it should be. However, it remains the key measure of a student's success and employability.

Graduate prospects

This measure is the percentage of the total number of graduates who take up graduate-level employment or further study. The results have been adjusted for subject mix. The data come from HESA for 2012 graduates.

» HESA surveys graduates six months after graduation to find out what they are doing and the data are based on this survey.

2014 Rank	2013 Rank	Institution	Student satisfaction (%)	Research quality (%)	Entry standards	Student–staff ratio	Services and facilities spend per student (£)	Completion (%)	Good honours (%)	Graduate prospects (%)	Total
1	2	Cambridge	86.2	45.0	610	11.6	3054	98.8	89.4	85.1	1000
2	1	Oxford	85.9	44.3	583	11.1	3490	98.4	90.9	78.3	999
3	3	London School of Economics	80.9	38.7	542	11.1	2464	97.0	81.3	77.1	892
4	6	St Andrews	85.9	28.0	524	12.6	2298	96.8	88.8	80.5	868
5	4	Imperial College	83.2	33.0	567	11.7	3041	97.0	84.6	89.2	860
6	5	Durham	83.9	29.7	510	15.1	2365	96.1	83.9	82.6	848
7	9	Bath	87.9	23.3	480	16.8	1734	96.8	82.8	83.6	814
8	10	Exeter	86.0	28.0	470	17.8	2120	97.1	83.8	77.1	810
9	7	University College London	78.5	33.0	511	10.2	2225	96.7	84.2	79.8	798
10	8	Warwick	81.5	29.0	506	14.3	2122	95.7	79.6	78.3	785
11	13	York	84.1	29.0	457	15.5	1996	95.1	78.1	73.9	776
=12	12	Lancaster	83.8	28.3	439	15.4	1684	94.7	73.0	72.7	755
=12	26	Surrey	86.2	20.3	418	16.6	2121	92.7	74.7	75.6	755
14	17	Leicester	84.0	20.0	413	12.9	2271	93.7	75.5	71.6	744
15	11	Bristol	80.0	29.7	487	14.2	2034	97.4	84.0	79.1	742
16	=24	Birmingham	81.8	24.0	444	14.8	2219	95.1	78.8	80.8	741
17	28	East Anglia	87.1	21.0	418	13.5	1813	91.3	71.6	68.7	738
=18	23	Newcastle	84.6	21.7	438	15.3	1724	94.9	78.3	79.0	726
=18	21	Sheffield	84.6	27.3	442	15.5	1574	95.3	77.5	71.7	726
20	=18	Southampton	81.8	23.0	438	13.7	1930	93.3	77.6	75.2	723
21	16	Loughborough	83.6	24.7	411	16.9	1818	93.4	73.3	75.4	722
22	14	Edinburgh	76.4	32.7	489	13.9	2185	90.7	82.6	75.3	716

23	20	Nottingham	81.9	24.0	439	14.0	1795	94.0	76.5	77.0	715
24	31	SOAS London	79.7	21.7	437	11.8	1895	87.1	80.6	66.8	713
25	15	Glasgow	83.1	24.3	477	16.4	2206	88.8	74.5	74.6	702
26	33	Manchester	81.1	28.7	457	14.8	1671	93.4	72.0	71.9	688
27	22	King's College London	76.8	23.3	467	11.7	1975	92.8	80.6	82.0	687
28	27	Royal Holloway	82.2	27.7	400	16.2	1457	93.2	73.7	63.9	685
=29	30	Leeds	83.2	22.7	428	16.8	1496	93.2	79.5	69.2	682
=29	=36	Aston	84.6	13.3	398	16.2	1632	91.1	73.5	73.6	682
=29	35	Queen's, Belfast	85.4	18.7	388	15.6	1816	91.9	71.7	74.8	682
32	=18	Sussex	82.2	25.7	407	17.1	1729	92.4	79.6	54.4	675
=33	34	Kent	82.4	17.0	380	14.6	1347	90.5	73.5	70.7	670
=33	32	Cardiff	82.3	21.0	433	14.2	1289	93.1	74.5	77.6	670
35	=24	Reading	82.3	22.7	378	15.6	1484	90.4	74.6	69.2	669
36	29	Liverpool	81.5	20.0	420	13.3	2041	91.7	72.8	71.5	667
37	38	Queen Mary, London	81.3	23.0	417	12.2	1914	89.0	68.1	69.7	656
38	42	Heriot-Watt	84.2	18.0	391	18.3	1342	84.8	69.3	77.7	641
39	40	Essex	85.4	22.7	342	16.4	1946	85.6	60.7	51.8	637
40	39	Aberdeen	81.7	20.7	443	16.4	1599	81.6	72.0	75.8	634
41	41	Buckingham	86.3		310	11.4	1720	79.5	43.9	83.1	629
42	=36	Strathclyde	79.9	16.7	465	18.3	1639	83.5	75.1	74.3	628
43	46	City	81.1	14.3	390	18.6	1952	87.2	69.9	71.0	617
44	45	Keele	85.6	12.7	356	16.5	1195	89.8	70.0	68.1	615
45	55	Coventry	86.9	2.3	294	14.6	1279	83.6	66.1	71.0	610
46	43	Brunel	83.3	17.0	357	17.5	1757	87.1	62.5	60.5	609
47	=52	Swansea	79.7	16.0	360	16.1	1477	88.2	63.8	77.5	596
48	48	Goldsmiths College	82.0	24.7	370	19.2	954	84.6	73.5	52.6	589
49	44	Dundee	81.7	15.7	396	14.4	1295	78.9	69.3	71.8	582
50	=52	Oxford Brookes	82.2	5.7	352	17.3	1387	89.4	68.9	63.6	575

2014 Rank	2013 Rank	Institution	Student satisfaction (%)	Research quality (%)	Entry standards	Student-staff ratio	Services and facilities spend per student (£)	Completion (%)	Good honours (%)	Graduate prospects (%)	Total
51	50	Stirling	80.3	13.7	374	18.3	1335	81.3	63.0	63.5	550
=52	59	Chester	82.8	1.0	296	16.3	1494	81.2	62.4	69.4	549
=52		Arts University, Bournemouth	83.6	0.3	316	19.3	653	92.4	57.8	68.7	549
=52	51	Robert Gordon	81.3	5.3	350	19.7	1216	81.9	62.5	81.8	549
55	63	Portsmouth	82.2	5.3	316	19.2	1375	87.2	67.3	63.4	546
56	56	Bangor	81.3	16.0	313	17.9	1113	84.7	60.1	64.4	545
=57	=52	Lincoln	80.8	5.0	324	19.4	1282	87.4	60.7	68.4	543
=57	=75	Winchester	83.8	4.0	307	17.7	1069	88.9	63.0	53.0	543
59	99	Northampton	83.7	1.3	299	20.0	2053	81.9	61.0	57.9	540
60	62	West of England	80.9	4.7	322	21.7	1548	84.7	69.6	68.0	535
61	=78	Nottingham Trent	81.4	4.3	321	20.0	1468	86.2	63.0	61.7	532
62	58	Northumbria	81.2	2.7	331	17.1	1429	87.2	59.3	61.8	531
63	49	Hull	83.2	11.0	344	19.8	1358	86.0	58.3	54.8	529
=64	80	York St John	84.3	1.0	301	20.9	1158	88.6	61.5	61.7	528
=64		Harper Adams	84.5	2.0	332	22.2	1158	86.2	52.3	67.2	528
66	57	Huddersfield	83.1	2.0	317	18.4	1287	80.3	60.9	67.6	527
67	=81	Bournemouth	78.3	4.3	345	21.5	1377	87.2	68.4	63.9	523
68	61	Chichester	82.1	1.7	307	18.8	1098	90.7	60.1	59.4	522
69	=73	Edge Hill	83.8	0.7	307	17.2	1360	83.7	56.9	60.7	519
70	70	Bath Spa	82.0	3.0	339	21.8	865	87.1	68.6	57.3	514
=71	83	Queen Margaret Edinburgh	78.7	3.3	332	20.5	1339	80.4	73.4	69.7	513
=71		St Mark and St John	86.3	0.3	253	20.5	954	87.2	51.7	63.7	513

=73	64	Plymouth	81.3	6.7	315	16.7	1273	86.2	61.9	57.3	512
=73	=65	Ulster	83.4	11.0	284	18.6	1429	83.1	60.3	50.7	512
=73		Newman	85.4	0.3	307	18.4	1235	78.3	56.8	60.0	512
76	69	Brighton	81.0	9.7	304	19.0	929	85.4	65.3	58.6	510
=77	=73	Sheffield Hallam	79.6	4.0	316	20.0	1376	86.5	63.1	57.8	499
=77		Falmouth	77.8	2.0	289	23.9	1916	88.0	64.4	60.2	499
=77	60	University of the Arts, London	74.3	20.3	316	22.4	1372	90.9	65.0	53.7	499
80	86	Roehampton	81.1	7.7	275	20.0	1676	83.1	59.9	53.3	498
81	=81	Glasgow Caledonian	78.9	3.0	356	21.4	1556	81.1	65.9	65.3	493
82	47	Aberystwyth	76.9	20.3	327	19.4	1186	86.5	58.5	53.9	492
83	=93	Liverpool John Moores	81.4	3.7	327	21.6	1237	83.6	68.0	55.0	489
=84	67	Bradford	79.7	10.0	311	19.4	1393	82.8	52.8	69.8	488
=84	89	Derby	83.8	1.0	288	18.8	1312	80.3	54.7	55.6	488
86	72	De Montfort	80.6	6.0	313	20.2	1214	85.2	61.4	53.0	482
87	=78	Cardiff Metropolitan	82.0	3.3	312	23.4	1243	84.4	59.1	52.0	481
88	71	Central Lancashire	81.2	3.7	298	19.0	1730	79.1	54.6	54.6	476
89	102	Manchester Metropolitan	79.3	4.3	333	19.2	1083	81.0	61.8	57.8	475
90	85	Canterbury Christ Church	80.5	1.7	273	19.5	1100	85.2	62.7	57.9	471
=91	=65	Gloucestershire	78.4	2.0	295	22.3	1299	84.4	62.6	61.1	469
=91	=75	Birmingham City	78.7	2.3	323	21.0	1483	81.9	59.1	62.4	469
93	87	Teesside	83.0	1.7	321	20.1	1233	79.1	56.0	54.1	465
94	90	Middlesex	79.7	5.0	250	23.0	2333	76.9	55.3	52.8	464
95	=97	Cumbria	81.0	0.3	253	18.6	871	82.6	65.7	59.2	462
=96	77	Sunderland	81.4	4.7	272	17.0	1355	78.4	52.6	49.6	461
=96	68	Hertfordshire	77.0	3.3	312	19.5	1628	80.1	61.6	62.4	461
98	=91	Salford	76.5	9.3	300	17.6	1202	82.4	61.4	60.0	458
99	103	University for Creative Arts	74.3	5.0	307	17.1	1860	82.1	56.3	51.2	453
100	84	Edinburgh Napier	80.4	3.0	325	23.8	1009	75.2	66.5	62.8	452

2014 rank	2013 rank	Institution	Student satisfaction (%)	Research quality (%)	Entry standards	Student–staff ratio	Services and facilities spend per student (£)	Completion (%)	Good honours (%)	Graduate prospects (%)	Total
101	=91	Greenwich	82.0	3.0	286	21.3	1396	77.3	57.3	53.1	451
102	=93	Worcester	79.2	0.3	281	23.6	1026	85.9	60.8	63.8	448
103	104	Leeds Metropolitan	79.0	2.0	278	20.7	1073	80.2	57.5	60.3	443
104		Leeds Trinity	81.9	1.7	286	23.3	1001	80.6	50.8	57.9	441
105	112	Abertay	78.1	3.0	315	24.0	1249	71.6	59.9	67.0	435
=106	=95	Westminster	76.0	5.0	327	20.8	1292	80.9	60.3	53.7	433
=106	=106	Bishop Grosseteste	81.8	0.3	247	32.9	452	91.6	58.9	66.4	433
108	100	Staffordshire	80.3	1.0	254	20.3	1249	78.8	56.3	54.5	430
109	=97	Glyndŵr	79.5	1.3	232	21.1	1683	74.1	53.9	61.2	422
110	107	Anglia Ruskin	78.2	1.7	248	20.2	1160	81.7	56.6	61.6	420
111	101	Kingston	76.2	3.3	313	20.4	1183	80.1	57.1	57.3	410
112	110	West London	78.1	2.0	234	21.6	1265	73.4	51.1	62.3	393
113	106	Buckinghamshire New	76.2	0.7	237	24.1	2159	83.1	46.4	43.7	384
114	113	Southampton Solent	74.9	0.7	282	20.5	1243	76.7	58.8	48.5	383
115	88	Bedfordshire	76.6	1.7	214	22.5	1644	79.1	50.2	53.5	378
116	114	Highlands and Islands	80.7	2.0	294	..	592	73.1	70.8	43.9	370
117	109	West of Scotland	78.2	4.7	288	21.7	1256	65.8	56.0	56.5	369
118	111	London South Bank	76.6	2.7	242	23.7	1110	76.1	53.5	56.0	353
119	115	Bolton	77.0	2.0	270	20.6	899	68.6	49.2	52.8	341
120	=116	East London	77.5	4.0	238	24.8	1118	62.9	49.0	43.8	296
121	=116	London Metropolitan	72.4	3.3	229	21.7	369	72.2	51.5	45.6	265

Notes on the Table

University College Birmingham, Liverpool Hope, South Wales, Trinity St David, University of Wales, and Wolverhampton have refused the release of data, so do not appear in this year's league table.

The following universities provided specific data as follows: London South Bank, Greenwich and De Montfort provided replacement tariff data; London South Bank used previous completion data and Manchester Metropolitan provided replacement data; Glyndŵr provided replacement good honours data; Bedfordshire, Central Lancashire, Exeter, Glyndŵr, Liverpool John Moores, Manchester Metropolitan, Northumbria and Plymouth provided student–staff ratio adjustments; Bedfordshire, Central Lancashire, De Montfort, Exeter, Liverpool John Moores, Loughborough, Manchester Metropolitan, Nottingham Trent and Queen Mary, London and provided changes to spend per student.

Statement from the Higher Education Statistics Agency (HESA) regarding the use of staffing data in looking at Research Assessment Exercise performance:

This analysis of the results of the Research Assessment Exercise 2008 makes use of contextual data supplied under contract by the Higher Education Statistics Agency (HESA). It is a contractual condition that this statement should be published in conjunction with the analysis. HESA holds no data specifying which or how many staff have been regarded by each institution as eligible for inclusion in RAE 2008, and no data on the assignment to Units of Assessment of those eligible staff not included. Further, the data that HESA does hold is not an adequate alternative basis on which to estimate eligible staff numbers, whether for an institution as a whole, or disaggregated by Units of Assessment, or by some broader subject-based grouping.

5 The Top Universities by Subject

Knowing where a university stands in the pecking order of higher education is a vital piece of information for any prospective student, but the quality of the course is what matters most – particularly in the short term. Your chosen course, rather than the character of the whole university, will determine what you get out of taking a degree and may have a big bearing on your employment prospects. As the latest Research Assessment Exercise (RAE) in 2008 confirmed, the most modest institution may have a centre of specialist excellence, and even famous universities have mediocre departments. This section offers some pointers to the leading universities in a wide range of subjects. With a number of universities reviewing the courses they will offer in the future, it is possible that not all institutions listed in a particular subject area will be running courses in 2014.

The subject tables in this *Guide* also include scores from the National Student Survey (NSS). These distil the views of final-year undergraduates on several aspects of their course, including teaching quality, assessment and feedback, and the quality of learning resources. The three other measures used are research quality, students' entry qualifications and graduate employment prospects. None of the measures are weighted.

The tables include the research grades drawn from the deliberations of expert assessors in the 2008 RAE. No data have been released on the proportion of academics entered for assessment, for example, so it has not been possible to mirror the approach adopted in the main institutional ranking (see pages 60–64). Data supplied by the Higher Education Statistics Agency (HESA) are used to calculate average entry qualifications and the employment prospects of graduates. The graduate prospects information draws a distinction between different types of employment: professional employment and non-professional employment. The tables give the percentage of "positive destinations" by adding those undertaking further study to the total in professional employment.

Many subjects, such as dentistry or sociology, have their own table, but others are grouped together in broader categories, such as "other subjects allied to medicine". For the first time the specialisms of physiotherapy and radiography are now in separate subject tables. Scores are not published where the number of students is too small for the outcome to be statistically reliable. In the NSS, a 50 per cent response rate is required from a minimum of 30 students. If there is no student satisfaction score, then to qualify for inclusion in the table a university has to have data for at least two of the other measures.

Cambridge is again the most successful university. It tops 34 of the 64 tables. Oxford has the next highest number of top places with 10, while 16 other universities also gain top spots. The subject rankings demonstrate that there are "horses for courses" in higher education. Thus the London School of Economics shares top spot in social policy with Leeds, and while Durham takes over from Loughborough in sports science, Loughborough retains a top spot in building. In their own fields, table-toppers such as Warwick in American studies and communication and media studies, Nottingham in agriculture and veterinary medicine, and Surrey in hospitality, are well-known. For the full list of all top universities, see page 200.

Research quality

This is a measure of the quality of the research undertaken in the subject area. The information was sourced from the 2008 Research Assessment Exercise (RAE), a peer-review exercise used to evaluate the quality of research in UK higher education institutions, undertaken by the UK Higher Education Funding Bodies.

For each subject, a research quality profile was given to those university departments that took part, showing how much of their research was in various quality categories. These categories were: 4* world-leading; 3* internationally excellent; 2* internationally recognised; 1* nationally recognised; and unclassified. The funding bodies decided to direct more funds to the very best research by applying weightings. The English, Scottish and Welsh funding councils have slightly different weightings. Those adopted by HEFCE (the funding council for England) for funding in 2012–13 are used in the tables: 4* is weighted by a factor of 3, 3* is weighted by a factor of 1. Outputs of 2* and 1* carry zero weight. This results in a maximum score of 3.

The scores in the table are presented as a percentage of the maximum score. To achieve the maximum score all staff would need to be at 4* world-leading level.

Staffing data to show how many of a department's academics were submitted in the RAE are not currently available. Some research ratings shown could relate to a relatively low proportion of the academic staff in the department.

Entry standards

This is the average UCAS tariff score for new students under the age of 21, based on A and AS Levels and Scottish Highers and Advanced Highers and other equivalent qualifications (including the International Baccalaureate), taken from HESA data for 2011–12. Each student's examination grades were converted to a numerical score using the UCAS tariff (see page 18 for details) and added up to give a total score. HESA then calculated an average score for each university.

Student satisfaction

This measure is taken from the National Student Survey results published in 2012 and 2013. A single year's figures are used when that is all that is available, but an average of the two years' results is used in all other cases. The score for each university represents the percentage of final-year undergraduates declaring themselves satisfied or very satisfied with their course, averaged over the seven sections of the survey (teaching, assessment and feedback, academic support, organisation and management, learning resources, personal development and overall satisfaction).

Graduate prospects

This is the percentage of graduates undertaking further study or in a professional job, in the annual survey by HESA six months after graduation. The format of the survey has changed and so only one year of data (2012 graduates) is used for these tables. A low score on this measure does not necessarily indicate unemployment – some graduates may have taken jobs that are not categorised as professional work. The averages for each subject are given close by the relevant subject table in this chapter and in a table in chapter 2 (see pages 38–41). The Education table uses a fifth measure: teaching quality, as measured by the outcomes of Ofsted inspections of teacher training courses.

The subjects listed below are covered in the tables in this chapter:

Accounting and Finance
Aeronautical and Manufacturing
   Engineering
Agriculture and Forestry
American Studies
Anatomy and Physiology
Anthropology
Archaeology
Architecture
Art and Design
Biological Sciences
Building
Business Studies
Celtic Studies
Chemical Engineering
Chemistry
Civil Engineering
Classics and Ancient History
Communication and Media Studies
Computer Science
Dentistry
Drama, Dance and Cinematics
East and South Asian Studies
Economics
Education
Electrical and Electronic Engineering
English
Food Science
French
General Engineering
Geography and Environmental Sciences
Geology
German
History

History of Art, Architecture and Design
Hospitality, Leisure, Recreation and
   Tourism
Iberian Languages
Italian
Land and Property Management
Law
Librarianship and Information Management
Linguistics
Materials Technology
Mathematics
Mechanical Engineering
Medicine
Middle Eastern and African Studies
Music
Nursing
Other Subjects Allied to Medicine
   (see page 167 for included subjects)
Pharmacology and Pharmacy
Philosophy
Physics and Astronomy
Physiotherapy
Politics
Psychology
Radiography
Russian and East European Languages
Social Policy
Social Work
Sociology
Sports Science
Theology and Religious Studies
Town and Country Planning and Landscape
Veterinary Medicine

Accounting and Finance

Accounting was not immune to the impact of higher fees in 2012, when applications and the number of students starting degrees dropped by more than 10 per cent. The much smaller finance courses fared better, maintaining the demand for places, although the competition for entry is similar in both subjects. Application rates across all business subjects had still not returned to 2011 levels when UCAS reported in 2013, but the difference was marginal and entry to courses at leading universities is expected to remain competitive in 2014. The demand for places has been growing over several years, despite the fact that the early career prospects for graduates are surprisingly meagre. While those who found graduate jobs in 2012 were just outside the top 20 for graduate salaries, averaging £21,800, the subjects were almost in the bottom 20 in the employment table. Some universities managed a healthy employment rate, but nine saw fewer than 40 per cent go straight into a professional job or onto a postgraduate course.

Bath remains the leader in accounting and finance, having taken over at the top of the table last year, although it does not lead on any single measure. Lancaster has made the most progress among the leading universities, moving up four places to third, while Loughborough has dropped seven places and out of the top ten. The best scores are again distributed through the top half of the table. Like last year, Lincoln, in 33rd place, has the most satisfied students, while Robert Gordon, in =19th, has the best employment record. The London School of Economics has the highest entry standards, while Cardiff, the leader in Wales, had the best grade in the last Research Assessment Exercise, but has fallen to =16th because of another low employment rate.

Strathclyde remains in second place and the leader in Scotland, while Robert Gordon is by far the highest-placed post-1992 university. As in many of the subject tables, higher entry scores and research grades make the difference for the old universities. Entry grades have risen again since the 2013 *Guide*: 25 universities (rather than 23) averaged at least 400 points at A level, and only two had averages below 200 points, compared with five last year.

Some of the top universities demand maths at A level, but most have no specific entry requirements beyond their standard offer. The number of graduates continuing to study after securing a professional job dropped substantially in 2012, although the numbers in that grade of employment rose. However, more than a quarter of all leavers start work in a non-graduate job and the 14 per cent unemployment rate is above average for all subjects.

Employed in professional job:	38%	Employed in non-professional job and studying:	3%
Employed in professional job and studying:	11%	Employed in non-professional job:	25%
Studying:	9%	Unemployed:	14%
Average starting professional salary:	£21,811	Average starting non-professional salary:	£16,499

» Association of Chartered Certified Accountants: **www.accaglobal.com**
» Careers in accounting: **www.careers-in-accounting.com**
» Chartered Institute of Public Finance and Accountancy: **www.cipfa.org.uk**
» Institute of Chartered Accountants: **www.icaew.co.uk**
» Institute of Chartered Accountants of Scotland: **www.icas.org.uk**
» Institute of Financial Services: **www.ifslearning.ac.uk**

Accounting and Finance

	Research quality %	Entry standards	Student satisfaction %	Graduate prospects %	Overall rating
1 Bath	43.3	487	93.0	80.8	100.0
2 Strathclyde	38.3	495	87.7	78.7	95.4
3 Lancaster	41.7	401	88.8	88.4	95.3
4 London School of Economics	43.3	522	79.3	91.4	95.1
=5 Warwick	41.7	507	81.4	82.2	93.7
=5 Leeds	36.7	461	87.5	79.7	93.7
7 Queen's, Belfast	28.3	414	90.8	86.7	92.9
8 Queen Mary, London	28.3	431	90.1		91.7
=9 Durham	28.3	404	87.7	86.0	90.6
=9 Reading	23.3	408	90.8	83.3	90.6
11 Loughborough	30.0	438	85.2	84.4	90.5
12 Glasgow	21.7	492	85.1	85.0	90.2
13 Newcastle	23.3	441	85.7	87.7	89.7
14 Exeter	25.0	458	83.1	83.4	88.5
15 City	28.3	446	83.8	76.1	88.0
=16 Cardiff	46.7	427	81.5	57.6	87.6
=16 Surrey	23.3	406	91.4	65.5	87.6
18 Manchester	38.3	450	80.9	64.6	87.1
=19 Aberdeen	20.0	474	81.7	84.1	86.9
=19 Robert Gordon	10.0	401	87.8	94.4	86.9
21 East Anglia	21.7	407	87.3	71.1	85.8
22 Kent	27.4	392	83.6	75.8	85.5
23 Heriot-Watt	21.7	382	87.6	71.1	85.1
24 Southampton	28.3	440	74.7	84.6	84.0
25 Sheffield	30.0	377	80.1	76.8	83.8
26 Bristol	25.0	461	80.0	67.0	83.7
27 Liverpool	23.3	395	83.5	70.8	83.5
28 Birmingham	31.7	403	79.1	69.7	83.4
29 Edinburgh	23.3	444	75.5	80.0	82.3
30 Bangor	31.7	317	87.2	53.8	82.0
31 Dundee	16.7	396	87.2	60.0	81.9
32 Swansea	20.0	349	83.1	75.8	81.6
33 Lincoln		321	94.7	70.9	80.9
34 Nottingham	36.7	393	70.3	76.0	80.4
35 Stirling	15.0	393	80.8	74.1	80.2
36 Salford	13.3	300	90.1	64.6	79.9
37 Aberystwyth	13.3	306	87.5	70.1	79.7
38 De Montfort	18.3	337	85.8	55.9	78.6
39 Essex	25.0	356	86.6	39.2	78.5
40 Birmingham City	11.7	293	91.8	54.9	78.4
41 Portsmouth	15.0	312	81.1	78.5	78.2
=42 Hull	18.3	321	85.8	56.7	78.1
=42 Huddersfield	10.0	330	82.7	77.1	78.1

44	Gloucestershire		279	88.3	81.5	77.5
45	Manchester Metropolitan	15.0	315	85.6	57.3	77.0
46	Coventry		299	90.2	67.6	76.8
47	Central Lancashire	13.3	314	89.1	46.8	76.6
=48	Keele	21.7	341	75.7	67.6	75.9
=48	Greenwich	10.0	285	90.1	50.3	75.9
50	Chester		306	84.5	78.6	75.7
51	Bradford	25.0	323	74.6	67.7	75.5
52	Ulster	15.0	305	82.5	58.0	74.9
=53	West of England	20.0	291	78.7	63.8	74.6
=53	Glasgow Caledonian	5.0	354	85.0	53.3	74.6
55	Winchester		291	89.0	60.0	74.4
56	Bournemouth	13.3	348	77.7	64.1	74.3
57	Nottingham Trent	13.3	324	77.7	65.4	73.7
58	Sheffield Hallam	11.7	321	78.8	62.9	73.3
59	Edinburgh Napier	5.0	317	86.0	50.5	73.2
60	Brighton	28.3	283	74.6	55.0	72.6
61	London South Bank	10.0	230	86.5	54.1	72.4
62	Brunel	21.7	337	80.3	33.8	72.2
63	Westminster	13.3	329	77.2	55.8	71.8
64	Bolton	3.3	254	85.0	60.0	71.6
65	West of Scotland	13.3	289	80.5	48.6	70.9
66	Northumbria	6.7	334	79.9	50.0	70.7
67	Leeds Metropolitan		259	88.4	44.9	70.1
68	Kingston		316	82.7	50.7	69.9
69	Southampton Solent		231	86.1	56.4	69.8
70	Northampton		253	86.8	47.9	69.5
71	Plymouth	13.3	291	80.1	40.7	69.3
72	Derby		253	88.8	39.5	69.1
73	Liverpool John Moores	1.7	317	81.4	46.9	68.9
74	Hertfordshire	15.0	303	75.7	46.4	68.7
75	Oxford Brookes		321	84.5	36.4	68.5
76	West London		202	86.7	50.0	67.9
77	Staffordshire		212	81.9	61.4	67.5
78	Sussex		378	73.0	55.6	67.3
79	Buckinghamshire New	6.7	199	85.8	39.1	67.1
80	Canterbury Christ Church		234	83.8	48.1	67.0
81	Cardiff Metropolitan		305	81.3	37.8	66.3
82	Middlesex		235	80.6	45.7	64.7
83	Edge Hill		289	80.6	32.4	64.2
84	London Metropolitan		207	82.0	33.7	62.3
85	Bedfordshire		175	77.9	50.0	61.7
86	Anglia Ruskin		210	71.4	63.2	61.6
87	East London		226	81.4	22.8	60.6

Aeronautical and Manufacturing Engineering

New employment categories used by the Higher Education Statistics Agency have had a big effect on the ranking for aeronautical and manufacturing engineering. Because intakes are relatively small at some institutions, several of the universities in last year's table do not have enough graduates to create a reliable picture of destinations. In previous editions, two years' figures have been averaged to produce a score and a single year has been used where necessary. This is not possible when the definition of a professional job has changed, and nine universities have dropped out as a result.

In fact, there was only a small decline in aeronautical courses as a consequence of increased fees, although the smaller manufacturing area was hit harder. Graduates in these branches of engineering have generally done well in the employment market. Taken together, the subjects are just outside the top 20 subjects for "positive destinations" this year, five places higher than in the 2013 *Guide*, although the 16 per cent unemployment rate is well above average. Salaries have shown even greater improvement, topping £25,000 in graduate-level jobs and moving into the top ten for all subjects.

Most of the courses in this ranking focus on aeronautical or manufacturing engineering, but it includes some with a mechanical title. To add to the confusion, manufacturing degrees often go under the rubric of production engineering (*see* General Engineering and Mechanical Engineering).

Cambridge has an even bigger lead than last year, registering the best scores for research and entry standards. Southampton has jumped nine places to second in the table, while Bristol has made almost the reverse journey to tenth. Coventry, in 23rd place, has the most satisfied students, while the University of the West of England, the leading post-1992 university, has managed a rare 100 per cent employment rate among its graduates. Strathclyde is the leader in Scotland, Swansea in Wales.

Entry grades are high at the leading universities, with Cambridge averaging more than 600 points and Southampton, Bristol, Imperial and Bath more than 500. Scores have risen since last year, but three Bs at A level was enough secure a place at about a quarter of the universities in the table. Many universities demand maths and physics at A Level, and give extra credit for further maths and/or design technology. More than half of the 2012 graduates went straight into high-level work, but there were big differences between universities. While four universities reported "positive destinations" for nine out of ten graduates, the rate dropped below 60 per cent at five others.

Universities we were unable to include this year because of insufficient data: Cardiff Metropolitan, De Montfort, Glasgow Caledonian, Glyndŵr, Liverpool John Moores, London South Bank, Ulster, West of Scotland.

Employed in professional job:	54%	Employed in non-professional job and studying:	1%
Employed in professional job and studying:	1%	Employed in non-professional job:	14%
Studying:	13%	Unemployed:	16%
Average starting professional salary:	£25,061	Average starting non-professional salary:	£15,882

» Manufacturing Institute: **www.makeit.org.uk**
» Royal Aeronautical Society: **www.aerosociety.com**
» Why Aeronautical Engineering?:
  www.science-engineering.net/aeronautical_engineering.htm

Aeronautical and Manufacturing Engineering	Research quality %	Entry standards	Student satisfaction %	Graduate prospects %	Overall rating
1 Cambridge	60.0	631	89.7	96.2	100.0
2 Southampton	30.0	519	87.5	87.8	85.3
3 Bath	25.0	511	91.0	86.4	85.0
4 Imperial College	46.7	551	82.3	71.4	84.7
5 Sheffield	45.0	438	80.8	85.0	82.9
6 Surrey	35.0	446	81.9	91.3	82.5
7 Newcastle	31.7		82.2	92.0	81.9
8 Loughborough	36.7	440	83.7	83.2	81.6
9 Leeds	39.2	412	89.7	69.1	80.8
10 Bristol	43.3	520	69.0	85.7	80.1
11 West of England	25.0	319	85.9	100.0	79.3
12 Manchester	36.7	433	84.0	66.7	77.7
13 Brunel	23.3	372	88.7	75.0	76.1
14 Nottingham	41.7	394	73.0	73.3	74.3
15 Strathclyde	26.2	469	77.4	64.5	72.6
16 Queen's, Belfast	31.7	365	81.8	63.3	72.3
17 Swansea	21.7	398	79.7	72.0	71.8
18 Staffordshire	20.0	247	84.4	85.7	71.6
19 Liverpool	35.4	398	70.2	73.0	71.4
20 Glasgow	21.7	465	67.8	78.1	70.2
21 Queen Mary, London	21.7	375	82.1	58.3	68.9
22 Hull	13.3	299	87.0		68.8
23 Coventry	7.4	283	91.6	66.7	68.3
24 Hertfordshire	26.7	316	73.6	74.5	68.2
25 City	21.7	361	80.3	57.1	67.4
26 Brighton	26.7	316	74.7		66.9
27 Aston	18.3	377	76.6	59.4	65.9
28 Salford	23.3	294	76.1	64.6	65.4
29 Bradford	20.0	297	77.1		65.1
30 Portsmouth	18.3	281	73.8	67.2	63.2
31 Manchester Metropolitan	11.7	333	81.3	41.2	60.6
32 Kingston	11.7	281	74.1	57.9	59.4
33 Sussex		329	74.2	60.0	58.5
34 Plymouth	8.3	251	75.5		58.0
35 Northampton		310	72.8	60.0	57.3
36 Sheffield Hallam	15.0	273	62.7		53.6

Agriculture and Forestry

Nottingham remains the clear leader in agriculture and forestry, with the best research record, the highest entry grades and the most satisfied students. But Newcastle, moving up from third place, has by far the best employment record and has narrowed the gap slightly at the top. Reading, which shared top place three years ago, has dropped from second to sixth, as one of several universities whose graduates struggled in the employment market. More than half of all 2012 graduates went into non-professional jobs or were unemployed six months after finishing their course. As a result, the subjects dropped into the bottom ten for positive destinations.

Only 16 institutions are left in the ranking because small cohorts of graduates left statistical gaps that prevented three more being placed. Two of those that remain – Harper Adams and the Royal Agricultural University – have received university status since the last table was published. Harper Adams, which held on to fifth position, is the highest-placed of nine post-1992 universities in the ranking. Aberystwyth jumps ahead of Bangor as the top university in Wales for these subjects, while Glasgow is Scotland's only representative, while Glasgow is Scotland's only representative. The Scotland's Rural College, one of the institutions with too little data to qualify for this table, is now the only place to take a full degree in agriculture north of the border, although Aberdeen offers forestry and plant and soil science, and Highlands and Islands provides a number of forestry courses.

There are generally low scores on all measures in these subjects: no university averages

Agriculture and Forestry	Research quality %	Entry standards	Student satisfaction %	Graduate prospects %	Overall rating
1 Nottingham	30.0	394	87.3	60.0	100.0
2 Newcastle	18.3	362	85.6	82.9	97.7
=3 Queen's, Belfast	13.3	364	83.1	52.6	88.0
=3 Glasgow	21.7	324			88.0
5 Harper Adams	8.3	338	82.1	71.5	87.9
6 Reading	21.7	361	70.9	53.8	84.8
7 West of England	18.3	323		46.9	82.5
8 Lincoln	6.7	320	73.3	66.7	80.3
9 Greenwich	13.3	331		42.1	79.6
10 Aberystwyth	21.7	265	76.3	49.4	78.7
=11 Bangor	18.3	296	68.1	53.7	76.9
=11 Royal Agricultural University	5.0	301	75.8	55.3	76.9
13 Nottingham Trent		302	78.2	54.5	76.3
14 Plymouth	3.3	328	80.0	32.0	75.5
15 Central Lancashire		291		51.3	73.1
16 Cumbria	0.0	261	74.8	33.3	66.5

Employed in professional job:	37%	Employed in non-professional job and studying:		3%
Employed in professional job and studying:	3%	Employed in non-professional job:		33%
Studying:	9%	Unemployed:		16%
Average starting professional salary:	£19,306	Average starting non-professional salary:		£14,853

400 points at entry or satisfies 90 per cent of final-year undergraduates. But it is the employment scores that cause the most concern. Only Newcastle, Harper Adams and Lincoln saw two-thirds of those completing degrees go straight into graduate-level jobs or onto postgraduate courses. The definition of a graduate job does no favours to agriculture or forestry in the employment statistics, however. Those who did get one earned an average of £19,300 – well clear of the bottom ten in the salary league.

Applications for degree courses in agriculture dropped by less than the average for all subjects when higher fees arrived in 2012, but there was a sharp decline in the already small numbers applying for forestry. With only 3.5 applications per place and half that in forestry, the level of competition is low. A quarter of those enrolling for degrees in agriculture and more than a third in forestry do so without A levels, often coming with relevant work experience. About one in seven arrives through the Clearing system.

Universities we were unable to include this year because of insufficient data: Aberdeen, Highlands and Islands, Kent, Oxford Brookes, Worcester.

» Institute of Chartered Foresters: **www.charteredforesters.org**
» Royal Agricultural Society of England: **www.rase.org.uk**
» Royal Forestry Society: **www.rfs.org.uk**
» Royal Scottish Forestry Society: **www.rsfs.org**
» Sector Skills Council for Land-Based and Environmental Industries (LANTRA): **www.lantra.co.uk**

American Studies

American studies enjoyed a surge in popularity when Barack Obama was first elected and continued in that vein until higher fees arrived in 2012. Even then, departments survived with no more than an average fall in enrolments, despite suffering a 22 per cent decline in applications – one of the biggest in any subject. Long-term concerns remain, however, because American Studies is among the bottom ten subjects for both employment and earnings. Average starting salaries for those in professional jobs had dropped by more than £1,000 since the previous survey, although the small numbers taking the subject make such figures subject to volatility year by year.

Warwick is the perennial leader and remains well clear of the field, sharing the lead for research quality and boasting much the highest entry standards. Only Hull, in ninth place, had more satisfied students, while second-placed Birmingham had the best employment record. Manchester, which was the other research star in the last assessments, is the big riser in this year's table, jumping from ninth to third. Swansea is the only university outside England to remain in the table. Dundee offers the subject in Scotland, but did not have enough graduates to qualify for a score this year.

Satisfaction levels remain high throughout the table: only two of the 19 universities failed to satisfy at least three-quarters of their final-year undergraduates. Entry scores remain relatively high, with nearly five applications for every place. Nine out of ten students taking American Studies have A levels or equivalent qualifications and there is an impressive level of firsts and 2:1s. Some universities expect English or history at A level or the equivalent. Employment levels were low at most of the universities in the table: only Birmingham and Liverpool saw more than 60 per cent of graduates go into professional work or further study.

American Studies cont

Universities we were unable to include this year because of insufficient data: Derby, Dundee, Goldsmiths College, Lancaster, Lincoln, Winchester.

Employed in professional job:	30%	Employed in non-professional job and studying: 3%
Employed in professional job and studying:	3%	Employed in non-professional job: 33%
Studying:	14%	Unemployed: 17%
Average starting professional salary:	£18,343	Average starting non-professional salary: £14,016

American Studies	Research quality %	Entry standards	Student satisfaction %	Graduate prospects %	Overall rating
1 Warwick	45.0	456	90.7		100.0
2 Birmingham	28.3	419	84.5	85.7	91.6
3 Manchester	45.0	461	78.5	54.4	90.1
4 Kent	41.7	362	90.9	50.0	88.5
5 East Anglia	30.0	431	88.5	52.2	87.6
6 Sussex	40.0	414	84.3	49.6	87.5
7 Leicester	30.0	402	88.6	56.7	87.0
8 Nottingham	31.7	402	79.0	53.9	82.3
9 Hull	25.0	357	91.7	47.6	82.2
10 Liverpool	21.7	369	74.2	81.8	80.9
11 Keele	23.3	349	85.7	54.9	80.0
12 Essex	25.0	364	79.6		77.0
13 Portsmouth	25.0	290	86.2	43.8	75.1
14 Swansea	16.7	340	71.4	52.5	69.8
15 Canterbury Christ Church		259	75.1	31.0	56.8

» British Association for American Studies: **www.baas.ac.uk**

Anatomy and Physiology

Anatomy, physiology and pathology are only just outside the 20 most popular subjects, and both applications and enrolments have increased since £9,000 fees were introduced in 2012. It is a highly competitive field, with almost nine applications for every place, although average entry scores at some of the universities towards the bottom of the table remain around 300 points. Entry grades are boosted by the fact that the subjects are often a fall-back for candidates whose real target was medical school. The ranking covers degrees in cell biology, neurosciences and pathology, as well as anatomy and physiology. Universities often demand at least two science subjects – usually biology and chemistry – although some new universities will accept just one science.

Cambridge has taken over from Oxford at the top of the table with much the highest entry standards. Oxford, which only regained the leadership last year, has the best research grades, but only two of the 28 universities in the ranking had lower levels of satisfaction among final-year undergraduates. The most satisfied students are at fourth-placed Queen's, Belfast while Huddersfield, in 16th place, has easily the best employment record and is the highest-placed post-1992 university. Dundee, which has moved up to second place, is the leading university in Scotland in this area. There is no representative from Wales since Cardiff – like Keele and Nottingham Trent – has dropped out of the table this year.

Scores in the 2013 National Student Survey were generally high, with only four universities satisfying less than 80 per cent of the final-year undergraduates. Anatomy and physiology are just outside the top 20 subjects for the proportion of graduates going straight into professional jobs or further study. More than four in ten go on to postgraduate courses. The subjects are rather lower in the earnings table, although they have moved up 11 places this year with average starting salaries of over £20,000 in professional jobs.

Universities we were unable to include this year because of insufficient data: Cardiff, Keele, Nottingham Trent.

Anatomy and Physiology	Research quality %	Entry standards	Student satisfaction %	Graduate prospects %	Overall rating
1 Cambridge	33.3	651	88.7	86.1	100.0
2 Dundee	38.3	494	86.9		94.4
3 Oxford	46.7	575	78.6	78.0	94.0
4 Queen's, Belfast	30.0	405	92.5	86.3	93.6
5 Manchester	35.0	454	86.6	75.1	90.8
6 University College London	35.1	520	78.9	80.2	89.4
7 Leeds	30.0	423	89.9	65.9	88.5
8 Newcastle	30.0	487	86.2	63.6	87.8
9 Edinburgh	28.3		87.4	66.7	87.0
10 King's College London	31.7	457	81.3	75.4	86.9
11 Loughborough	33.0	374	82.9	75.8	85.7
=12 Glasgow	28.3	487	81.5	66.9	85.2
=12 Aberdeen	16.7	460	85.1	77.2	85.2
14 Liverpool	25.0	422	88.8	58.6	84.8
15 Bristol	28.3	462	78.4	67.9	82.8
16 Huddersfield		368	86.4	93.0	81.4
17 Portsmouth	28.3	290	87.0	60.0	80.8
18 St George's	16.7	360	87.4		80.7
19 Nottingham	16.7	436	87.6	51.4	80.6
20 Leicester		422	87.8	76.4	80.5
21 Sussex	31.7	411	80.5	51.8	80.1
22 Reading	15.0	404	82.1	66.7	79.0
23 East London	16.7	312	86.1		77.6
24 Ulster		309	87.3	79.2	77.2
25 Manchester Metropolitan	15.0	308	82.5		74.0
26 Oxford Brookes	16.7	331	86.6	37.5	73.8
27 Plymouth	6.7	342	83.9	45.0	71.2
28 Westminster		284	68.9	65.1	62.8

Employed in professional job:	23%	Employed in non-professional job and studying:	4%
Employed in professional job and studying:	2%	Employed in non-professional job:	19%
Studying:	41%	Unemployed:	11%
Average starting professional salary:	£20,133	Average starting non-professional salary:	£14,846

» Anatomical Society: **www.anatsoc.org.uk**
» British Association of Clinical Anatomists: **www.liv.ac.uk/HumanAnatomy/phd/baca**
» Physiological Society: **www.physoc.org**

Anthropology

A 25 per cent increase in applications to study anthropology provided the biggest surprise in the run-up to £9,000 fees in 2012 – not least to anthropologists, who had feared for the future of the subject. The news was even better at the start of the new academic year, when for the first time more than 1,000 students started degrees – an increase of more than 50 per cent. The relatively small numbers taking anthropology make for substantial swings, but this was exceptional (and unexplained). Fewer than 700 people started degree courses in 2011, so more than 5,000 applications should have increased the competition for entry, but universities responded with more places.

Cambridge maintains its accustomed leadership in the new table, while Oxford has regained the second place it lost to the London School of Economics last year. The LSE had the top research score in the 2008 Research Assessment Exercise, when 40 per cent of its work was judged to be world-leading, but Oxford has the best employment record this year. Cambridge's high entry grades and strength across the board preserved its lead, but Brunel, in ninth place, boasts much the most satisfied students.

There are no subject-specific requirements for most degree courses, but anthropology tends to be the preserve of old universities. Roehampton is the highest-placed of a handful of post-1992 universities at the foot this year's table. St Andrews is the top university in Scotland and has moved back up to fourth in the new table, but there are no representatives from Wales this year. Employment rates have fluctuated, partly because of the small numbers taking the subject. Unemployment in the new table is above average for all subjects, but average salaries for those in professional jobs have increased by almost £1,000. Only Cambridge, Oxford and St Andrews saw three-quarters of anthropologists go straight into graduate-level employment or start postgraduate courses.

University we were unable to include this year because of insufficient data: Glasgow.

Employed in professional job:	31%	Employed in non-professional job and studying:	5%
Employed in professional job and studying:	2%	Employed in non-professional job:	27%
Studying:	18%	Unemployed:	17%
Average starting professional salary:	£19,674	Average starting non-professional salary:	£15,648

» Royal Anthropological Institute: **www.therai.org.uk**

Anthropology

	Research quality %	Entry standards	Student satisfaction %	Graduate prospects %	Overall rating
1 Cambridge	45.3	551	87.0	77.6	100.0
2 Oxford	35.0	536	89.0	79.7	97.1
3 London School of Economics	48.3	468	88.7	62.1	94.8
4 St Andrews	35.0	492	85.7	75.0	92.6
5 University College London	40.0	460	84.0	63.2	89.5
6 Manchester	30.0	429	83.8	70.1	86.2
7 SOAS London	43.3	467	81.1	48.4	86.0
8 Durham	31.7	450	82.8	61.8	85.1
9 Brunel	30.0	340	94.4	57.1	84.6
10 Sussex	35.0	407	86.6	45.6	82.5
11 Kent	27.1	379	85.1	62.6	81.9
12 Aberdeen	38.3	392	86.8	38.5	81.6
13 Edinburgh	36.7	490	65.8	63.2	80.6
14 Goldsmiths College	35.0	364	85.8	41.0	79.3
15 Queen's, Belfast	41.7	372	83.3	31.5	78.6
16 Roehampton	36.7	269	83.8	48.4	76.9
17 Liverpool John Moores	21.7	308	75.6	65.9	73.1
18 Bournemouth	18.3	331	84.4		72.6
19 Oxford Brookes	15.0	328	72.9	45.1	65.2
20 East London	20.0	291	70.4		62.1

Archaeology

Archaeology remains a niche subject with only around 500 students starting degrees each year. But, while it was not immune to the declines in applications and enrolments that hit most arts subjects with the switch to higher fees, archaeology is far more widely available than it was a decade ago. Even after losing five universities from the ranking because of low numbers, the remaining 48 represent twice the number in the 2004 *Guide*. Unlike then, almost half of the universities in the table are post-1992 institutions. Many of those attracted onto courses are mature students – often retired – who are studying the subject out of interest and not for career progression. Archaeology is in the bottom ten both for employment prospects and graduate salaries.

Oxford has extended its lead over Cambridge at the top of the table, although it does not have the top score on any single indicator. Cambridge has the highest entry standards, while third-placed Durham and Reading, in sixth, achieved the best results in the last Research Assessment Exercise. York, in fourth place, recorded the best of a high set of scores in the National Student Survey, satisfying 97 per cent of final-year undergraduates. Robert Gordon, the only post-1992 university in the top 20, has the best employment record. With 96 per cent of graduates going straight into professional jobs or further study, it is a full 16 points ahead of its nearest rival and contrasts with just 9 per cent at London Metropolitan.

Archaeology produces consistently high levels of satisfaction. Only four universities in the

Archaeology cont

ranking failed to satisfy at least 70 per cent of their students in the results published in 2013. The increase in the number of universities offering the subject has had the effect of spreading out entry scores, which now range from little more than 200 points to over 500. Applications for pure archaeology degrees lag well behind those for forensic and archaeological science, which generally require a science A level.

Universities we were unable to include this year because of insufficient data: Huddersfield, Hull, West of Scotland.

Employed in professional job:	28%	
Employed in professional job and studying:	2%	
Studying:	19%	
Average starting professional salary:	£17,982	

Employed in non-professional job and studying:	4%	
Employed in non-professional job:	33%	
Unemployed:	15%	
Average starting non-professional salary:	£14,646	

Archaeology	Research quality %	Entry standards	Student satisfaction %	Graduate prospects %	Overall rating
1 Oxford	45.0	539	89.0	80.0	100.0
2 Cambridge	40.0	551	87.0	77.6	97.5
3 Durham	48.3	473	84.6	78.9	95.7
4 York	36.7	421	97.5	77.7	95.4
5 University College London	40.0	489	96.2	59.6	94.8
6 Reading	48.3	358	93.1	51.3	88.1
7 Liverpool	38.3	443	87.1	45.8	84.7
8 Exeter	31.7	449	74.0	80.5	84.6
9 Newcastle	26.7	405	89.6	57.4	83.0
10 Nottingham	33.3	363	86.8	60.3	82.5
11 Queen's, Belfast	35.0	365	90.3	50.0	82.4
12 Birmingham	23.3	428	81.6	67.1	81.5
13 Sheffield	36.7	361	83.9	54.3	80.7
=14 Leicester	38.3	380	78.1	59.5	80.6
=14 Cardiff	28.3	384	88.1	52.0	80.6
16 Southampton	36.7	358	86.1	48.8	80.4
17 Manchester	30.0	397	89.3	37.1	78.9
18 Glasgow	23.3		90.7	50.0	78.5
19 Robert Gordon		368	81.2	96.2	77.6
20 Aberdeen	23.3	432	79.6	50.0	76.7
21 Edinburgh	33.2	417	67.4	61.9	76.2
22 Bradford	30.0	283	82.9	57.0	75.2
23 Bristol	26.7	403	69.9	60.8	74.4
24 Dundee		494	81.5	46.2	72.0
=25 Liverpool John Moores		332	87.2	65.8	71.8
=25 Keele		318	91.7	59.0	71.8
27 Kent	6.7	365	77.9	64.9	70.9
28 Winchester	6.7	305	90.2	51.4	70.8
29 Lincoln		308	83.8	71.4	70.4

30 Nottingham Trent	13.3	343	75.3	60.7	69.9
31 Bournemouth	18.3	317	77.1	50.5	68.7
32 Glasgow Caledonian		356	78.2	65.2	68.5
33 Central Lancashire	10.0	308	89.4	35.6	68.0
34 De Montfort		299	85.9	56.3	67.5
35 Swansea		387	76.2	58.1	67.4
36 Derby		303	85.4	50.0	66.0
37 Chester		269	79.4	69.0	65.9
38 West of England		262	81.8	63.2	65.4
39 Canterbury Christ Church		260	86.2	51.6	64.8
40 Coventry		296	73.8	69.5	64.6
41 Teesside		341	78.3	36.8	61.3
42 Staffordshire		277	80.8	43.0	61.0
=43 Kingston		234	89.7	31.8	60.6
=43 Anglia Ruskin		214	78.4	58.8	60.6
45 Worcester		271	80.1	40.3	59.7
46 West London		247		21.4	49.1
47 London South Bank		239	63.1	27.6	47.3
48 London Metropolitan		261	60.1	8.7	42.5

» Council for British Archaeology: **www.britarch.ac.uk**
» TORC (Training Online Resource Centre for Archaeology): **www.torc.org.uk**

Architecture

Taken together with its companion subjects of building and planning, architecture has seen one of the biggest declines in applications of any area. Even as demand was recovering in 2013, the subjects were more than 22 per cent down on 2010. Only languages have suffered a bigger drop. However, there were still approaching seven applications per place in 2012 and average entry grades increased at the leading universities. Some universities ask for art at A level, while others look for a mix of art and science subjects. Candidates may be asked to produce a portfolio of work if they have not taken an art or design-based A level.

Training in architecture is a long haul – usually seven years, in which the first degree is but one step on the way. Until recently, the graduate employment rate had been some compensation, but the recession saw unemployment shoot up and another big rise has taken the rate to 16 per cent in this edition. More than half of all architects still go straight into graduate-level jobs, but the training structure of the profession means that starting salaries are low. The £17,800 average is in the bottom four for all subjects and only £4,000 better than the figure for other employment. Nevertheless, satisfaction rates are higher after graduation than during the course itself. Three years into their careers, architects are among the least likely of all graduates to say that they wished they had taken a different degree or chosen a different profession.

Cambridge has regained first place in the table from Bath, only a year after losing it. Cambridge has the highest entry grades and is second only to University College London for research. Edinburgh, which is the top university in Scotland, also has the best employment record in the UK. Queen's, Belfast, has the most satisfied students, just ahead

Architecture cont

of Northumbria, which is the highest-placed post-1992 university and the only one in the top ten. Two-thirds of the institutions in the table are modern universities, including eight of the top 20. The Manchester School of Architecture, in 13th place, is a joint enterprise between Manchester and Manchester Metropolitan universities.

Universities we were unable to include this year because of insufficient data: Bolton, Dundee, Glasgow Caledonian.

Employed in professional job:	51%	
Employed in professional job and studying:	5%	
Studying:	10%	
Average starting professional salary:	£17,827	

Employed in non-professional job and studying:	2%
Employed in non-professional job:	16%
Unemployed:	15%
Average starting non-professional salary:	£14,000

Architecture	Research quality %	Entry standards	Student satisfaction %	Graduate prospects %	Overall rating
1 Cambridge	46.7	578	86.9	92.0	100.0
2 Bath	40.0	567	91.1	88.1	98.9
3 Sheffield	43.5	508	90.4	72.5	93.4
4 Cardiff	35.0	506	82.4	86.1	90.4
5 Newcastle	36.7	461	84.1	85.1	89.8
6 Edinburgh	40.0	498	73.8	92.6	88.8
7 Northumbria	20.0	385	92.4	85.4	86.5
8 University College London	48.3	495	71.7	78.3	86.4
9 Strathclyde	16.7	487	79.2	90.0	84.1
10 Nottingham	20.0	477	82.7		82.9
11 West of England	18.3	354	90.1	79.8	82.4
12 Liverpool	45.0	426	70.8	77.6	82.2
13 Manchester School of Architecture	24.3	465	79.9	67.9	80.3
=14 De Montfort	31.7	334	73.9	89.1	79.5
=14 Brighton	45.0	366	77.6	62.1	79.5
16 Queen's, Belfast		394	92.7	71.0	78.2
17 Robert Gordon	16.7	369	77.9	83.3	77.4
18 Sheffield Hallam	18.3	384	85.9	62.4	77.2
19 Liverpool John Moores	30.0	353	79.3	65.5	76.7
20 Central Lancashire	16.7	329	84.6	72.2	76.5
21 Westminster	33.3	379	76.5	59.1	75.6
22 Kent		437	74.6	87.8	75.0
23 Salford	38.3	310	82.3	47.1	74.2
24 Oxford Brookes		459	84.7	60.0	74.0
25 Coventry		260	87.9	80.6	73.0
26 London Metropolitan	23.3	300	74.2	76.0	72.9
27 Plymouth	25.0	333	74.6	64.1	71.9
28 Lincoln	15.0	355	70.6	77.3	71.3
29 Huddersfield		321	86.3	66.7	71.2
30 Portsmouth	3.3	352	81.7	65.6	70.8

31 Northampton		281	83.3	70.3
32 Derby		273	86.2	70.7	70.2
33 Nottingham Trent	10.0	329	75.4	69.1	69.4
34 Ulster	31.7	280	80.7	41.7	69.2
35 Kingston		362	79.6	65.5	69.1
36 Cardiff Metropolitan		273	74.9	86.7	68.6
37 Anglia Ruskin		260	79.1	75.0	67.3
38 The Arts University at Bournemouth	3.3	295	76.7	69.6	67.0
=39 Greenwich	20.0	345	77.3	37.5	65.9
=39 Leeds Metropolitan		324	79.0	59.6	65.9
41 University of the Arts, London		320	73.7	70.0	65.7
42 East London		264	82.1	45.5	61.7
43 University for Creative Arts		308	75.7	50.0	61.4
44 Birmingham City		311	67.5	60.0	59.9
45 Southampton Solent		184	76.4	61.5	59.8
46 London South Bank		253	57.9	47.6	49.9

» Design Council (now incorporating CABE): **www.designcouncil.org.uk**
» Royal Institute of British Architects: **www.architecture.com**
» Royal Incorporation of Architects in Scotland: **www.rias.org.uk**

Art and Design

Only nursing attracts more applications than art and design. But the subjects were hit hard by the switch to higher fees in 2012, when the number of students starting courses throughout the creative arts dropped by more than 5,000. Design is much the largest area, but applications fell from 110,000 to 91,000 in 2012, and the decline was even steeper in proportional terms in fine art. In spite of a recovery in 2013, applications were still 3.6 per cent lower than in 2010. Inevitably, graduates' employment prospects are seen as the root of the recruitment changes since the subjects are fixtures in the bottom ten for both earnings and graduate destinations. Artists and designers have always accepted that they are likely to have a period of self-employment early in their career while they find a way to pursue their vocation, but this may be more of a deterrent with fees or up to £9,000 a year. More than 40 per cent of all leavers go straight into graduate-level jobs, but only 6 per cent go on to take another full-time course – one of the lowest proportions for any subject.

Most courses in art and design are at post-1992 institutions – including three more specialist arts universities, created since the last *Guide* was published – but the top nine places are filled by older foundations. Oxford, the oldest of them all, where fine art is taught at the Ruskin School of Drawing, retains top place. Not surprisingly, it has the highest entry standards. Lancaster has moved up to second, fractionally ahead of University College London, where students attend the Slade School of Fine Art. Essex has the most satisfied students, while Roehampton has much the best employment score, over 15 percentage points better than its nearest rival and twice the rate at many universities. UCL shares the best research score with Kent.

Art and Design cont

Fifth-placed Glasgow is the top university in Scotland. Bangor retains the lead in Wales, although the Principality now has no universities in the top 50. The University of the West of England is the only modern university in the top ten, having moved up nine places since last year. Low entry grades and research scores count against many of the new universities and colleges, although most artists would argue that these are of less significance than in other subjects. Selection in art and design rests primarily on the quality of candidates' portfolios.

University we were unable to include this year because of insufficient data: Manchester.

Art and Design	Research quality %	Entry standards	Student satisfaction %	Graduate prospects %	Overall rating
1 Oxford	41.7	503		66.7	100.0
2 Lancaster	43.3	445	83.3	65.4	93.2
3 University College London	46.7	439	86.8	55.6	92.8
4 Newcastle	45.0	498	83.1	52.5	92.5
5 Glasgow	35.0	463	83.2		92.4
6 Goldsmiths College	37.7	467	86.0	57.7	92.3
7 Reading	45.6	357	84.7	69.0	91.1
8 Brunel	11.7	397	87.1	77.1	88.8
9 Loughborough	43.2	428	79.4	59.2	88.6
10 West of England	26.7	388	85.5	61.4	86.5
11 Leeds	36.2	414	78.9	59.1	86.0
12 Brighton	45.0	328	86.6	50.1	85.2
13 Bournemouth	33.3	336	84.4	60.8	84.8
14 Roehampton		311	81.5	95.2	84.0
15 Manchester Metropolitan	21.7	449	77.1	57.0	82.9
16 Kent	46.7	347	73.3	60.5	82.6
=17 Coventry	18.0	336	83.2	67.5	82.5
=17 Falmouth	13.3	314	85.6	70.7	82.5
19 Westminster	38.3	474	70.4	49.0	82.3
20 Kingston	10.0	468	76.0	60.9	81.7
21 Northampton	1.7	353	91.1	58.7	81.3
22 Nottingham Trent	15.0	340	81.8	65.2	80.7
23 Dundee	41.7	363	78.2	45.3	80.5
24 The Arts University at Bournemouth	3.3	317	86.9	67.0	80.0
=25 Edinburgh	23.8	400	75.2	56.3	79.8
=25 Heriot-Watt	26.7	345	66.8	79.4	79.8
27 Norwich University of the Arts	15.0	323	88.1	52.0	79.4
28 Oxford Brookes	20.0	379	83.0	42.9	78.1
=29 Robert Gordon	18.3	333	78.7	59.1	77.8
=29 Southampton	11.7	342	88.8	44.4	77.8
=29 Abertay		366	79.1	67.7	77.8
32 Teesside		352	90.6	48.3	77.7
33 Derby	11.7	318	85.4	54.2	77.6
34 University of the Arts, London	33.1	317	76.2	53.4	77.5

35 Birmingham City	40.0	385	71.0	43.6	77.1
36 Northumbria	25.0	333	75.6	56.4	77.0
37 Plymouth	25.0	305	84.2	44.2	76.6
=38 Huddersfield		329	83.0	61.0	76.1
=38 Ulster	28.3	291	85.1	40.4	76.1
=40 Bath Spa	10.0	330	79.9	57.4	75.9
=40 York St John		305	90.7	50.0	75.9
42 Cardiff Metropolitan	30.0	305	79.6	45.4	75.7
43 Chester	1.7	326	76.2	70.0	75.4
44 Sheffield Hallam	30.0	318	77.9	44.5	75.2
45 Edinburgh Napier	8.3	372	74.7	57.0	74.8
46 Lincoln	8.3	325	74.5	65.5	74.7
47 University for Creative Arts	13.3	321	79.6	51.0	74.2
48 Salford	10.0	286	83.5	51.7	74.0
49 De Montfort	18.3	323	78.0	48.0	73.8
50 Anglia Ruskin	13.3	307	85.1	40.7	73.5
51 Bangor		291	80.5	61.1	73.0
52 Middlesex	11.7	280	81.9	50.5	72.9
=53 Winchester		276	82.8	58.3	72.7
=53 Essex		220	95.4	45.3	72.7
55 Hertfordshire	26.7	303	74.7	46.1	72.5
56 Central Lancashire	5.0	272	84.0	51.7	72.3
57 Liverpool John Moores	11.7	318	80.5	42.2	71.7
58 Portsmouth	3.3	361	79.5	39.7	70.7
59 Greenwich		275	77.4	60.7	70.5
60 Cumbria	3.3	273	88.7	37.2	70.4
=61 Leeds Metropolitan	8.3	245	82.2	43.9	68.7
=61 Staffordshire	3.3	254	82.9	45.1	68.7
=61 Sunderland	16.7	266	79.9	37.8	68.7
64 Buckinghamshire New	13.3	268	79.3	39.3	68.2
=65 Hull		347	76.3	38.1	67.2
=65 Bolton	0.0	285	75.2	51.2	67.2
67 Gloucestershire	6.7	309	72.4	45.9	67.0
68 Canterbury Christ Church		273	76.3	50.0	66.8
=69 Worcester		296	76.1	44.8	66.4
=69 West London	6.7	219	82.6	40.9	66.4
71 Southampton Solent	10.0	290	72.5	36.5	64.3
72 London South Bank		246	76.4	42.1	63.4
73 Glyndŵr	1.7	225	76.6	42.3	62.8
74 East London	20.0	248	66.4	39.0	62.0
=75 London Metropolitan	3.3	274	65.7	47.5	61.5
=75 Chichester		294	70.1	38.5	61.5
77 Glasgow Caledonian		372	67.4	28.0	61.0
78 Aberystwyth		351	63.3	38.8	60.9
79 Bedfordshire		201	73.6	34.9	57.7

Art and Design cont

Employed in professional job:	43%	Employed in non-professional job and studying:	2%
Employed in professional job and studying:	1%	Employed in non-professional job:	32%
Studying:	6%	Unemployed:	16%
Average starting professional salary:	£17,996	Average starting non-professional salary:	£13,936

» Design Council: **www.designcouncil.org.u**k
» National Society for Education in Art and Design: **www.nsead.org**
» Creative Skillset: **www.creativeskillset.org**

Biological Sciences

Biology and the various more specialist degrees in the same area have held their own since the introduction of higher fees. There were small increases in both applications and enrolments in 2012, when most subjects were struggling to recruit, and the three-year period up to 2013 also saw marginal growth in applications. Biology itself, the largest of the group, had more than 30,000 applications in 2012, but zoology was more competitive, with almost six applications per place. Microbiology was tougher still and commanded higher grades. The subjects remain well ahead of chemistry and physics in the demand for places. Two-thirds of all entrants arrive with A levels or their equivalent, and more than a third go on to take postgraduate courses, either full or part-time.

The top five in the table are unchanged – for the ninth successive year in the cases of Oxford and the leader, Cambridge. Cambridge has extended its lead again with some of the highest entry grades in any subject. Despite averaging 580 points on the UCAS tariff, even Oxford's entrants are 70 points behind Cambridge's score. However, neither of the ancient universities registered the best score in the 2008 Research Assessment Exercise. That distinction was shared by Manchester and Dundee. The top scores on the other indicators went to universities further down the table: Robert Gordon, in 30th position after jumping more than 50 places, had the best employment record, while Gloucestershire had the most satisfied biologists, but only just made the top 50. Nottingham Trent is again the highest-placed modern university, just ahead of Robert Gordon. St Andrews made the most progress in the upper reaches of the table, almost reaching the top ten, but could not overhaul Glasgow as the leading university in Scotland.

Entry standards have been rising: in addition to Oxford and Cambridge, another 30 universities average at least 400 points – seven more than last year. Only one university has an average below 200 points, even though a relatively high proportion of the entrants win places through Clearing. Graduate employment prospects and starting salaries are slightly below average for all subjects. Only 22 of the 90 institutions in this year's table saw more than 70 per cent of those finishing courses go straight into graduate-level employment or go on to postgraduate study.

Universities we were unable to include this year because of insufficient data: Teesside, Ulster.

Employed in professional job:	27%	Employed in non-professional job and studying:	3%
Employed in professional job and studying:	2%	Employed in non-professional job:	23%
Studying:	30%	Unemployed:	15%
Average starting professional salary:	£19,564	Average starting non-professional salary:	£14,423

Biological Sciences

	Research quality %	Entry standards	Student satisfaction %	Graduate prospects %	Overall rating
1 Cambridge	33.3	651	88.7	86.1	100.0
2 Oxford	37.4	580	87.6	78.0	96.2
3 York	36.7	472	90.7	71.6	92.6
4 Sheffield	36.7	475	86.6	79.5	92.4
5 Imperial College	35.0	523	79.1	81.7	90.0
6 Bristol	29.0	469	89.2	70.4	89.2
7 Bath	23.3	457	89.5	77.2	89.1
=8 Lancaster	33.3	425	91.2	65.6	88.9
=8 Manchester	38.3	467	85.3	67.3	88.9
10 Glasgow	28.3	467	84.2	76.0	87.7
11 St Andrews	23.3	497	85.0	73.8	87.1
12 University College London	35.1	515	78.0	70.1	86.3
13 Surrey	33.3	419	84.6	67.8	85.7
14 King's College London	35.0	454	81.8	66.7	85.5
=15 Nottingham	28.3	412	85.8	70.0	85.2
=15 Leicester	21.7	448	87.6	68.9	85.2
17 Exeter	23.3	446	86.0	69.9	85.0
18 Birmingham	23.3	442	80.8	81.2	84.8
19 Durham	23.3	509	79.0	75.7	84.7
=20 Dundee	38.3	441	83.7	56.0	84.4
=20 Edinburgh	30.0	506	80.2	64.6	84.4
=20 East Anglia	23.3	415	90.8	60.7	84.4
=23 Newcastle	30.0	405	83.6	67.4	83.6
=23 Southampton	23.3	418	87.2	65.0	83.6
25 Aston	26.7	397	89.7	54.5	82.6
26 Cardiff	28.3	441	82.0	62.6	82.3
27 Leeds	30.0	422	81.0	63.8	81.9
28 Nottingham Trent	30.0	310	84.0	68.9	81.1
29 Royal Holloway	33.3	376	77.5	68.5	80.6
30 Robert Gordon		367	84.7	90.9	80.2
=31 Aberdeen	28.3	431	81.5	55.9	80.1
=31 Warwick	23.3	452	77.2	68.8	80.1
33 Queen's, Belfast	13.3	386	85.2	69.0	79.5
34 Liverpool	20.0	428	81.4	62.8	79.3
35 Edge Hill		274	94.2	78.0	79.2
36 Heriot-Watt	16.7	374	88.1	55.9	78.5
=37 Abertay	21.7	339	75.5	80.0	77.8
=37 Strathclyde	28.3	480	76.4	51.4	77.8

Biological Sciences cont

	Research quality %	Entry standards	Student satisfaction %	Graduate prospects %	Overall rating
39 Brunel	15.0	365	87.6	56.8	77.7
40 Sussex	24.4	405	78.9	57.8	77.2
41 Huddersfield	8.3	291	87.1	71.4	76.7
42 Coventry		287	92.1	70.4	76.6
=43 Portsmouth	25.6	309	84.3	54.4	76.5
=43 Glasgow Caledonian	13.3	399	78.4	69.8	76.5
45 Queen Mary, London	16.7	419	76.7	66.2	76.3
46 Keele	5.0	357	85.1	68.6	76.1
47 Swansea	6.7	378	77.9	75.4	75.0
48 Kent	15.0	383	78.1	63.6	74.8
49 Northampton		288	82.8	83.3	74.7
=50 Gloucestershire		290	96.4	51.9	74.5
=50 Canterbury Christ Church		252	89.6	71.9	74.5
52 Stirling	18.7	395	76.2	59.5	74.2
53 Essex	16.7	335	83.7	52.3	73.9
54 Bradford	16.7	324	79.5	62.8	73.8
55 Plymouth	14.7	360	85.9	44.3	73.4
56 West of Scotland	23.3	290	80.0	51.6	72.2
57 Hertfordshire	15.0	300	77.7	63.5	71.8
58 Kingston	11.7	266	82.7	60.3	71.7
59 Bangor	11.7	343	77.9	60.3	71.6
=60 Oxford Brookes	10.0	339	80.9	55.6	71.4
=60 Northumbria	13.3	338	77.9	58.2	71.4
=62 West of England	27.5	312	83.8	32.0	71.3
=62 Edinburgh Napier	6.7	333	81.9	57.4	71.3
=62 Liverpool John Moores	13.6	334	84.3	43.8	71.3
65 Reading	15.0	368	72.8	60.5	70.6
=66 Manchester Metropolitan	15.0	317	79.0	53.0	70.5
=66 Hull	8.3	354	82.7	47.6	70.5
68 Brighton	18.3	312	79.8	47.2	70.2
=69 Bath Spa	0.0	291	85.5		69.2
=69 East London		268	83.0	62.9	69.2
71 Roehampton	1.7	272	78.7	69.4	69.1
72 Staffordshire		259	78.7	72.2	68.9
73 Sheffield Hallam	8.3	338	77.4	54.7	68.8
74 Leeds Metropolitan		263	81.5	64.0	68.5
=75 Chester	5.0	269	82.9		68.3
=75 Bolton		234	75.0	81.4	68.3
77 Salford	15.0	274	80.3	45.0	67.8
78 Derby	5.0	310	79.7	52.5	67.7
79 Greenwich		286	81.6	57.1	67.6
80 Cardiff Metropolitan	8.3	291	74.9	60.0	67.2
81 Anglia Ruskin		258	82.8	55.6	67.0

82 Central Lancashire		321	89.7	30.0	66.6
83 Aberystwyth		327	78.0	51.1	65.5
84 Bournemouth		324	78.1	41.9	63.3
85 London South Bank	11.7	207	68.1	64.7	62.9
86 Worcester		288	78.0	43.0	62.3
87 Bedfordshire	8.3	181	77.0		61.4
88 Sunderland		234	73.5	53.3	60.6
89 Westminster		287	73.8	42.0	59.8
90 London Metropolitan	1.7	230	68.5		54.9

» Biochemical Society: **www.biochemistry.org**
» British Society for Cell Biology: **www.bscb.org**
» Society of Biology: **www.societyofbiology.org**
» Society for Experimental Biology: **www.sebiology.org**

Building

Building degrees have been struggling to recruit students since the start of the recession and yet the unemployment rate is no higher than the national average in this year's *Guide*. Against all expectations, the subject has jumped 22 places and finds itself in the top 20 for employment prospects – thanks mainly to a large rise in the proportion going straight into graduate-level jobs. Average starting salaries in such jobs are also in the top 20, albeit £2,400 lower than they were in the 2011 *Guide*. Even so, both applications and enrolments dropped by about a quarter when the fees went up in 2012 and there was only a marginal recovery in 2013.

Entry standards have always been comparatively modest, but a gradual decline in average grades has been arrested in the latest table. Third-placed Nottingham averages more than 450 points and, although University College London (UCL) is the only other institution to top 400, for the first time no university averages less than 200 points. More than half of the 31 universities in the table now average at least 300 points at entry.

Loughborough has extended its lead in an unchanged top four, although it no longer leads on any single indicator. UCL recorded the best grades in the 2008 Research Assessment Exercise, while Edinburgh Napier achieved the best score in the 2013 National Student Survey. Satisfaction rates are almost universally high: no university failed to satisfy at least two-thirds of final-year building undergraduates. Reading, in fourth place, has the best employment score, with nearly 95 per cent of leavers in graduate-level jobs or further training after six months. Heriot-Watt leads four Scottish universities in the top ten. Another of them, Glasgow Caledonian, is this year's top post-1992 university for building. Wales has no representation because the new University of South Wales has chosen not to submit data for league tables.

University we were unable to include this year because of insufficient data: Manchester.

Employed in professional job:	62%	Employed in non-professional job and studying:	1%
Employed in professional job and studying:	4%	Employed in non-professional job:	16%
Studying:	4%	Unemployed:	13%
Average starting professional salary:	£22,347	Average starting non-professional salary:	£15,274

Building	Research quality %	Entry standards	Student satisfaction %	Graduate prospects %	Overall rating
1 Loughborough	41.7	360	87.1	94.4	100.0
2 University College London	48.3	414	71.2	90.0	95.5
3 Nottingham	20.0	453	81.2		93.0
4 Reading	40.0	345	75.6	94.7	92.9
5 Heriot-Watt	26.7	364	83.8	85.1	91.7
6 Aston	18.3	383		90.9	91.0
7 Glasgow Caledonian	30.0	350	85.9	75.0	90.4
8 Robert Gordon	16.7	346	80.1	82.9	85.4
9 Edinburgh Napier	15.0	357	90.1	61.2	85.0
10 Northumbria	20.0	309	78.9	81.1	83.4
11 Nottingham Trent	10.0	292	81.5	85.0	81.9
12 Westminster	33.3	316	77.2	60.0	81.3
13 Salford	38.3	324	69.1	67.8	81.1
14 Liverpool John Moores	30.0	315	75.8	65.0	80.8
15 Plymouth	25.0	281	69.4	88.9	80.5
16 Sheffield Hallam	18.3	311	79.6	68.7	80.1
17 Brighton	13.3	304	79.8	73.7	79.7
18 Ulster	31.7	208	81.9	64.4	78.6
19 Anglia Ruskin		297	81.4	79.4	77.8
20 West of England	18.3	291	71.3	77.9	77.2
21 Oxford Brookes		296	80.5	77.3	76.7
22 Kingston		294	78.1	79.2	75.9
23 Bolton	20.0	227	77.5	70.0	75.4
24 Coventry		260	88.7	61.9	74.9
=25 Greenwich	20.0	259	72.4	67.6	73.9
=25 Central Lancashire	16.7	300	79.6	48.7	73.9
27 Leeds Metropolitan		272	76.8	68.8	71.4
28 Portsmouth		266	74.2	72.6	70.7
29 Birmingham City		284	70.5	69.0	68.9
30 London South Bank		237	68.5	63.0	63.7
31 Southampton Solent		204	71.6	60.0	62.8

» Chartered Institute of Building: **www.ciob.org.uk**

Business Studies

The various branches of business and management are among the most popular subjects in higher education. Even without the many dual or combined honours degrees that are common for both of the main areas, there were nearly 130,000 applications in 2012. But this was still 13,000 down on the previous year and, while there has been a recovery in 2013, not all the ground has been made up. Management is the more competitive field, attracting six applications for every place, compared to less than five for business studies. The subjects are the biggest recruiters in many of the new universities, but some of the most famous business schools are absent from this ranking because they do not offer undergraduate courses. Manchester Business School provides Manchester's undergraduate courses.

Oxford has taken first place back from Cambridge, which has dropped to third this year. Neither Oxford's Said Business School nor Cambridge's Judge School of Management qualify for the table, being exclusively postgraduate institutions, so both universities are assessed on courses offered by other faculties. As usual, neither of the ancient universities' undergraduates in this field responded to the National Student Survey in sufficient numbers for a satisfaction rate to be compiled. But Oxford has by far the highest entry standards in the table and Cambridge, which does not publish separate entry scores for business, achieved the best grades in the 2008 Research Assessment Exercise (RAE). Imperial College London actually produced the best RAE grades, but does not have enough undergraduates in this area to qualify for the table.

Bath has moved up to second place this year with the most satisfied students and one of the best employment scores. However, even it could not compete with the 100 per cent positive destinations recorded by Durham, in 13th place, and University College London (UCL), which did not make the top 20. UCL would have finished considerably higher if it had entered the RAE in these subjects. Even before the recession, employment scores were surprisingly varied. Overall, the subjects are only just in the top 50 for positive destinations. Average starting salaries in graduate jobs are just outside the top 20 for all subjects, at £21,574.

More than half of the institutions in one of our biggest tables are modern universities, but only Robert Gordon appears in the top 30, with Bath Spa following in 40th place. St Andrews has maintained its position as the top Scottish university, while Cardiff remains the clear the leader in Wales. Business and management filled twice as many places in Clearing as any other subject in 2012. Entrance qualifications vary widely, with four universities averaging more than 500 points and two less than 200. Scores in the National Student Survey have been improving rapidly: around 45 per cent of the institutions in the table managed to satisfy at least 80 per cent of final-year undergraduates, twice as many as last year.

Universities we were unable to include this year because of insufficient data: Dundee, Harper Adams.

Employed in professional job:	46%	Employed in non-professional job and studying:	2%
Employed in professional job and studying:	3%	Employed in non-professional job:	28%
Studying:	6%	Unemployed:	14%
Average starting professional salary:	£21,574	Average starting non-professional salary:	£16,039

Business Studies	Research quality %	Entry standards	Student satisfaction %	Graduate prospects %	Overall rating
1 Oxford	43.3	596		80.2	100.0
2 Bath	43.3	487	90.6	90.5	98.7
3 Cambridge	48.3			81.6	96.9
4 St Andrews	26.7	582	87.3	75.0	93.0
5 Lancaster	41.7	431	82.8	82.0	90.1
6 London School of Economics	43.3	512	79.5	73.0	89.7

Business Studies cont

	Research quality %	Entry standards	Student satisfaction %	Graduate prospects %	Overall rating
7 Cardiff	46.7	419	82.9	73.8	89.4
8 Leeds	36.7	440	84.1	77.2	89.0
9 Loughborough	30.0	439	83.2	88.2	88.9
10 Warwick	41.7	511	74.3	84.8	88.5
11 Exeter	30.0	454	83.1	82.3	88.2
12 Strathclyde	38.3	466	83.3	61.9	86.9
13 Durham	28.3	395	79.1	100.0	86.8
14 SOAS London	16.7	427	88.3		85.6
=15 Aston	30.0	404	83.5	73.3	84.9
=15 City	28.3	457	84.3	62.8	84.9
17 Birmingham	31.7	428	75.0	89.3	84.3
18 Leicester	28.3	377	84.7	72.2	84.0
19 Nottingham	36.7	404	78.0	74.5	83.6
=20 York	23.3	405	81.7	76.5	82.9
=20 Surrey	23.3	366	84.6	75.1	82.9
=22 University College London		455	80.7	100.0	82.7
=22 Manchester	38.3	424	76.6	68.5	82.7
24 Newcastle	23.3	426	78.0	82.6	82.6
25 Robert Gordon	16.7	375	83.0	83.6	82.2
26 Heriot-Watt	21.7	384	83.8	71.5	81.9
27 Southampton	28.3	427	74.5	80.8	81.5
28 Aberdeen	20.0	414	82.4	69.6	81.4
=29 King's College London	43.3	471	67.8	72.3	81.2
=29 Kent	25.0	364	80.5	76.8	81.2
31 Sussex	30.0	390	78.6	70.3	81.0
32 Edinburgh	23.3	467	75.9	72.5	80.9
=33 Sheffield	30.0	396	77.1	73.0	80.8
=33 East Anglia	21.7	341	83.6	73.9	80.8
35 Glasgow	25.0	457	75.7	72.0	80.7
36 Royal Holloway	28.3	382	81.1	64.4	80.6
37 Reading	23.3	388	80.1	71.2	80.3
38 Liverpool	23.3	390	81.6	63.5	79.7
39 Brunel	21.7	355	83.1	60.3	78.4
40 Bath Spa		327	89.2	74.4	78.3
41 Bristol	10.0	446	79.9		77.7
=42 Coventry	6.7	276	87.5	70.2	76.3
=42 Keele	21.7	318	79.4	67.8	76.3
=42 Buckingham		296	90.1	67.4	76.3
=45 Portsmouth	15.0	316	78.7	73.9	75.4
=45 Stirling	20.0	390	76.9	59.3	75.4
=45 Bradford	25.0	300	78.0	66.2	75.4
=45 Bournemouth	13.3	344	78.8	70.9	75.4
=49 Edinburgh Napier	5.0	325	84.6	65.3	75.0

=49 Queen's, Belfast	28.3	361	74.3	59.9	75.0
51 De Montfort	18.3	302	85.6	48.8	74.9
52 Essex	25.0	298	81.6	51.4	74.6
53 Nottingham Trent	13.3	333	77.3	71.7	74.3
54 Huddersfield	10.0	319	80.4	68.9	74.2
55 Bangor	31.7	312	77.9	48.7	74.0
=56 Northumbria	6.7	348	80.2	66.7	73.9
=56 Swansea	20.0	338	73.6	71.1	73.9
58 West of England	10.0	311	78.1	69.0	72.6
59 Sheffield Hallam	11.7	315	79.7	60.6	72.5
60 Manchester Metropolitan	15.0	320	77.8	60.3	72.3
61 Brighton	28.3	292	74.1	58.7	72.2
=62 Birmingham City	11.7	299	82.2	54.1	72.1
=62 Hull	18.3	312	81.0	46.5	72.1
64 Aberystwyth	13.3	295	81.3	54.5	72.0
65 Lincoln	6.7	304	78.0	71.3	71.9
=66 Ulster	15.0	278	85.4	40.4	71.5
=66 Central Lancashire	13.3	296	82.0	49.5	71.5
=66 Northampton	8.3	283	82.7	56.7	71.5
69 Oxford Brookes	11.7	345	76.8	57.8	71.4
70 Queen Mary, London	28.3	387	69.2	43.6	69.8
=71 Salford	22.8	297	72.1	58.4	69.7
=71 Gloucestershire	3.3	271	74.7	80.0	69.7
=71 Hertfordshire	15.0	305	76.7	52.9	69.7
74 Kingston	21.7	285	77.5	44.5	69.6
75 Liverpool John Moores	1.7	320	82.1	48.8	69.3
76 Royal Agricultural University		286	79.7	64.0	69.2
77 Teesside	11.7	288	82.1	39.2	68.8
78 York St John		271	82.6	54.8	68.6
=79 Chester		289	77.7	65.3	68.4
=79 Winchester		296	80.7	54.6	68.4
=81 Greenwich	10.0	268	82.5	37.8	67.7
=81 Middlesex	13.3	230	83.6	37.4	67.7
=83 Glasgow Caledonian	8.3	347	75.4	46.1	67.5
=83 Derby		275	82.8	47.7	67.5
=85 Westminster	13.3	326	74.0	46.7	67.3
=85 Worcester		290	77.9	58.8	67.3
=87 Plymouth	13.3	291	73.1	54.6	67.1
=87 West of Scotland	13.3	282	77.7	42.7	67.1
=89 Abertay	5.0	281	74.1	63.6	66.9
=89 Leeds Trinity		239	77.9	66.2	66.9
=89 Queen Margaret Edinburgh	1.7	293	75.3	61.9	66.9
92 Canterbury Christ Church		253	78.2	61.1	66.6
93 Sunderland		262	84.8	37.8	66.3
94 Chichester		264	81.2	47.8	66.2
95 Roehampton		226	84.1	44.0	65.8
=96 Leeds Metropolitan	6.7	270	72.8	61.2	65.7

	Research quality %	Entry standards	Student satisfaction %	Graduate prospects %	Overall rating
=96 London South Bank	10.0	233	79.4	43.6	65.7
98 Cardiff Metropolitan	3.3	295	80.6	36.5	65.6
99 West London		195	81.6	55.0	65.4
100 Edge Hill		291	79.1	41.3	64.7
101 Staffordshire	15.0	211	75.9	42.7	64.0
102 Southampton Solent		263	73.4	55.7	63.1
103 St Mary's College		267	75.5	48.2	63.0
104 Glyndŵr		211	72.1	68.2	62.9
105 University of the Arts, London		293	73.0	44.3	61.8
106 Anglia Ruskin		241	73.8	48.8	61.2
107 Buckinghamshire New	6.7	214	73.4	43.0	60.6
108 Bolton	3.3	274	74.3	26.9	59.3
109 Bedfordshire	5.0	198	72.1	36.9	57.7
110 East London		215	73.9	33.8	57.5
111 London Metropolitan	5.0	220	67.5	42.1	56.8
112 Cumbria		225	57.9	35.5	48.8

» Chartered Management Institute: **www.managers.org.uk**
» Confederation of British Industry: **www.cbi.org.uk**
» Institute of Consulting: **www.iconsulting.org.uk**

Celtic Studies

Only 150 students started full-time Celtic studies degrees in 2012, making it one of the smallest categories in the *Guide*. Indeed, there were not enough recent graduates in professional jobs at the time of the latest survey to produce an average starting salary. Only three of the eight universities in this year's table had enough graduates to compile an employment score. Applications had been rising until the switch to higher fees in 2012, when there was an 11 per cent decline. Entry grades remain relatively high, however; only one university in the table averages less than 300 points. Students seem to enjoy their courses: only Ulster (just) failed to satisfy at least 80 per cent of their final-year undergraduates.

Cambridge retains the leading position that it assumed last year, with the most satisfied students, entry grades nearly 200 points ahead of its nearest rival and by far the best results in the 2008 Research Assessment Exercise, when almost half of its submission was judged to be world-leading. Swansea has moved up five places to second with the best employment record. Third place has also changed hands, with Bangor moving up from fifth.

The ranking is split between four universities from Wales, which naturally major in Welsh, and the remaining six, which focus on Irish or Gaelic studies. Ulster has regained its lead over Queen's, Belfast as the top university in Northern Ireland. The University of the Highlands and Islands is the only representative of Scotland since both Aberdeen and Glasgow have dropped out because of low numbers.

The small numbers make for extremely volatile results from year to year. In last year's

Guide, only 5 per cent of graduates were unemployed, for example. This year the figure is 14 per cent. Yet Celtic Studies is only just in the bottom half of the employment data because 44 per cent of graduates – the largest proportion in any subject – went on to full-time postgraduate courses.

Universities we were unable to include this year because of insufficient data: Aberdeen, Glasgow, Liverpool.

Employed in professional job:	13%	Employed in non-professional job and studying:	5%
Employed in professional job and studying:	3%	Employed in non-professional job:	21%
Studying:	44%	Unemployed:	14%
Average starting professional salary:	n/a	Average starting non-professional salary:	£15,119

Celtic Studies	Research quality %	Entry Standards	Student satisfaction %	Graduate prospects %	Overall rating
1 Cambridge	55.0	612	95.3		100.0
2 Swansea	35.0	383	84.5	82.6	87.0
3 Bangor	25.0	372	94.5		86.5
4 Aberystwyth	38.3	413	87.5	74.8	84.9
5 Cardiff	28.3	441	79.9	76.7	82.6
6 Ulster	48.3	294	79.1		81.8
7 Queen's, Belfast	16.7	358	81.1		78.5
8 Highlands and Islands	8.3	324			74.7

» You can find out more about Celtic studies directly from the universities listed.

Chemical Engineering

Only dentists earn more than chemical engineering graduates, according to the latest salary survey. With average starting salaries in professional jobs only just below £30,000, this year for the first time even medicine cannot compete. Big salaries naturally depend on finding graduate-level employment, but only 7 per cent of 2012 graduates started their careers on lower-level jobs and the 12 per cent unemployment rate was below the average for all subjects. This may help to explain the continuing popularity of the subject, which has been growing for several years and saw one of the biggest increases in applications of any mainstream subject in 2012. Although it is still one of the smaller branches of engineering, applications were over 13,500.

Cambridge tops the chemical engineering table for the twelfth year in a row and has much the highest entry standards, the best employment record, and shares the top research score with second-placed Imperial College London. Both universities had 30 per cent of their work rated as world-leading in the 2008 Research Assessment Exercise. Cambridge and Imperial were both ranked by QS among the top five universities in the world for chemical engineering in 2013.

For the second year in a row, the most satisfied students were at Heriot Watt, which is also the leading university in Scotland for chemical engineering. Swansea is the only

Chemical Engineering cont

representative of Wales and London South Bank is the higher-placed of only two post-1992 universities left in the ranking.

Degree courses normally demand chemistry and maths A levels or their equivalent and often physics as well. Four out of five chemical engineers come with A levels or equivalent qualifications, and average entry grades are the highest for any engineering subject – all but 5 of the 21 universities in the table average more than 400 points at entry. This helps produce engineering's largest proportion of Firsts and 2:1s. Most courses offer industrial placements in the final year and lead to Chartered Engineer status.

» Institution of Chemical Engineers: **www.icheme.org**
» Royal Society of Chemistry: **www.rsc.org**

Chemical Engineering	Research quality %	Entry standards	Student satisfaction %	Graduate prospects %	Overall rating
1 Cambridge	48.3	652	89.7	95.0	100.0
2 Imperial College	48.3	593	91.0	87.8	96.6
3 Leeds	40.0	443	84.6	88.7	86.0
4 Heriot-Watt	31.1	407	92.3	86.4	84.8
5 Bath	25.0	465	88.8	88.4	84.2
=6 Birmingham	35.0	476	83.3	80.4	83.2
=6 Manchester	45.0	517	71.1	83.7	83.2
8 Surrey	35.0	425	82.1	85.7	82.1
=9 Loughborough	36.7	433	82.9	80.0	81.8
=9 Sheffield	28.3	437	84.8	85.8	81.8
11 Aberdeen	31.7	395	78.3	94.4	80.4
12 Edinburgh	28.3	520	73.7	82.9	79.5
13 Swansea	36.7	371	77.8	88.9	79.4
14 Newcastle	26.7	445	76.4	89.4	78.9
15 Strathclyde	16.7	492	77.7	85.7	77.5
16 Nottingham	41.7	425	66.9	82.2	76.6
17 University College London	35.0	475	71.1	71.0	75.6
18 Queen's, Belfast	18.3	406	79.9	75.0	73.0
19 London South Bank	23.3	277	80.3	67.9	68.0
20 Aston	18.3	383	76.6	60.3	67.1
21 Teesside	8.3	365	70.1	40.0	55.9

Employed in professional job:	57%	Employed in non-professional job and studying:	0%
Employed in professional job and studying:	4%	Employed in non-professional job:	7%
Studying:	19%	Unemployed:	12%
Average starting professional salary:	£28,992	Average starting non-professional salary:	£16,481

Chemistry

Chemistry's slide in popularity from the sixth form onwards has been reversed in recent years and even the arrival of £9,000 fees did not dent the number of applications or enrolments at degree level. Applications grew by 20 per cent in the five years before the new fees regime and almost reached 25,000 in 2012, when there were more five for every place. Forensic science has become an attractive alternative to the pure subject but, for many, chemistry remains the classic science. Some courses demand maths as well as chemistry, and most successful candidates for the leading universities take more than one science at A level. Forensic science is offered at about 40 institutions and covers aspects of biology, physics, mathematics and statistics, as well as chemistry.

Cambridge has extended its already substantial lead at the top of the table with the highest entry standards and the best research grades. Durham's high student satisfaction rate has helped it to overtake Oxford and take second place, but the most satisfied students of all are at Heriot Watt, where a low research grade confines the university to 14th place. The best employment record is at Aberdeen, which is even lower in the table, at 24th. There are good employment scores throughout most of the ranking, with only three universities seeing less than 60 per cent of their chemists go into professional jobs or postgraduate study. More than a third of 2012 graduates continued on full-time courses, helping the subject to 14th place in the employment table. However, despite some improvement since last year's *Guide*, the subject is still just below average for graduate starting salaries.

Chemistry is old university territory, with only one post-1992 institution, Nottingham Trent, in the top 30. Indeed, only nine modern universities remain in the table, with Sheffield Hallam and Central Lancashire making the top 40. Entry grades are high: only 4 of the 47 universities in the table average less than 300 points on the UCAS tariff and the top six all average more than 520 points. Nearly nine out of ten undergraduates have A levels or their equivalent, although entry requirements are not far above the average for all subjects.

Universities we were unable to include this year because of insufficient data: Abertay, Greenwich, West of Scotland.

Employed in professional job:	34%	Employed in non-professional job and studying:	1%
Employed in professional job and studying:	3%	Employed in non-professional job:	14%
Studying:	35%	Unemployed:	13%
Average starting professional salary:	£21,187	Average starting non-professional salary:	£14,472

Chemistry	Research quality %	Entry standards	Student satisfaction %	Graduate prospects %	Overall rating
1 Cambridge	53.3	651	88.8	86.1	100.0
2 Durham	35.0	564	88.8	87.7	93.2
3 Oxford	45.0	604	84.0	79.7	92.4
4 St Andrews	43.3	524	88.6	80.5	91.9
5 Edinburgh	43.3	537	82.6	83.5	90.2
6 Imperial College	38.3	539	82.0	87.5	89.8
7 York	35.0	494	87.3	83.5	89.1
8 Manchester	35.0	458	92.7	77.2	88.9

Chemistry cont

		Research quality %	Entry standards	Student satisfaction %	Graduate prospects %	Overall rating
9	Warwick	35.0	466	87.5	82.7	88.2
10	Nottingham	48.3	453	86.9	72.4	87.9
11	Bath	23.3	449	88.8	88.5	87.0
12	Bristol	41.7	497	83.1	74.6	86.4
13	Sheffield	33.3	455	87.3	77.4	85.8
14	Heriot-Watt	23.3	407	95.3	76.9	85.7
15	Sussex	23.3	393	91.6	85.1	85.6
16	Southampton	26.7	447	87.9	81.2	85.3
17	Surrey	33.3	429	85.9	79.3	84.8
18	Strathclyde	30.0	464	83.8	80.0	84.3
19	Liverpool	36.7	415	83.5	76.0	83.1
20	Cardiff	26.7	396	83.5	86.0	82.8
=21	Birmingham	26.7	411	84.1	81.0	82.3
=21	Bradford	28.3	292	93.6	76.7	82.3
23	Leeds	36.7	435	82.2	70.3	81.6
24	Aberdeen	16.7	437	79.1	91.3	81.0
25	Keele	23.3	353	91.5	70.5	80.4
26	Glasgow	30.0	473	75.2	78.5	80.0
27	East Anglia	21.7	425	87.9	66.3	79.4
28	Newcastle	18.3	394	83.3	81.1	79.3
=29	Aston	18.3	406	86.2		78.9
=29	Nottingham Trent	28.3	274	91.8	69.4	78.9
31	Leicester	16.7	381	88.6	72.0	78.7
32	Queen's, Belfast	18.3	362	85.9	75.0	77.9
33	Loughborough	8.3	360	84.5	83.6	77.1
34	University College London	31.7	498	73.5	61.8	75.9
35	Hull	20.0	346	85.7	67.8	75.8
36	Bangor	21.7	303	81.7	75.3	74.9
37	Reading	8.3	345	82.9	71.2	72.5
38	Sheffield Hallam	8.3	323	83.0	66.2	70.5
39	Queen Mary, London	21.0	392	83.4	44.3	70.1
40	Central Lancashire	13.3	319	88.2	50.0	69.8
41	Northumbria	13.3	324	84.5	52.9	68.9
42	Manchester Metropolitan	10.0	324	77.5	60.9	66.8
43	Brighton	18.3	327	71.9	62.0	66.5
44	Huddersfield	8.3	299	76.9	63.3	66.0
45	Plymouth	14.7	326	69.9	66.7	65.9
46	Kent		351	74.6	66.1	65.3
47	Kingston		281	76.8	68.5	64.7

» European Association for Chemical and Molecular Sciences: **www.euchems.org**
» Royal Society of Chemistry: **www.rsc.org**
» Society of Dyers and Colourists: **www.sdc.org.uk**

Civil Engineering

Imperial College was ranked as the top university in the world for civil engineering in 2013, but it remains some way behind Cambridge in our table. Cambridge has a clear lead over Imperial on student satisfaction, entry standards and graduate destinations, none of which are available in international comparisons, while it was just ahead with the best grades in the last Research Assessment Exercise. Not surprisingly, Cambridge's average of 631 points at entry and 96 per cent of graduates going straight into professional jobs or further study are also the best in the table. But Heriot-Watt, in 12th place, has the most satisfied students and is now the leading university in Scotland for civil engineering. Bath holds on to third place, while Manchester makes the most progress in the upper reaches of the table, jumping 13 places to 14th after big rises in student satisfaction and employment. Post-1992 universities make up a third of the table, with Greenwich again the highest-placed at 25th. Cardiff remains the leader in Wales.

The demand for places in civil engineering recovered to some extent in 2013, but the subject suffered more than other branches of the discipline from the move to higher fees. The number of students starting degrees in 2012 was down by almost 15 per cent on the previous year, following two years of significant growth. The latest figures show that the subject's slide down the employment and salary tables has been arrested. Civil engineering is back in the top ten for graduate destinations, having fallen to 17th last year. It is a little lower for graduates starting salaries but, at almost £24,000, these are still in the top quarter of all subjects. Almost two-thirds of all civil engineers go straight into graduate jobs and the 13 per cent unemployment rate is average for higher education. Employment scores are good almost throughout the table.

Entry scores have been rising in civil engineering, with the top 24 universities all averaging more than 350 points. Fewer than half of all undergraduates are admitted with A levels or equivalent qualifications, reflecting the large numbers of mature students who are upgrading their qualifications. Some of the top degrees in civil engineering are four-year courses leading to an MEng; others are sandwich courses incorporating a period at work. The leading departments will expect physics and maths A levels, or their equivalent.

Universities we were unable to include this year because of insufficient data: Abertay, Anglia Ruskin, Durham, Northumbria.

Employed in professional job:	61%
Employed in professional job and studying:	3%
Studying:	13%
Average starting professional salary:	£23,947

Employed in non-professional job and studying:	1%
Employed in non-professional job:	9%
Unemployed:	13%
Average starting non-professional salary:	£17,445

Civil Engineering	Research quality %	Entry standards	Student satisfaction %	Graduate prospects %	Overall rating
1 Cambridge	60.0	631	89.7	96.2	100.0
2 Imperial College	58.3	572	86.1	81.6	92.1
3 Bath	40.0	490	93.3	88.9	90.5
4 Southampton	43.3	499	82.0	96.5	88.6
5 Surrey	35.0	398	90.2	95.0	86.8

Civil Engineering cont

	Research quality %	Entry standards	Student satisfaction %	Graduate prospects %	Overall rating
6 Newcastle	43.3	419	86.0	90.4	86.1
7 Sheffield	41.7	475	86.4	83.6	85.9
8 Cardiff	46.7	437	84.1	87.4	85.8
9 Bristol	43.3	515	75.9	91.7	85.1
10 Warwick	36.7	448	87.2	84.8	84.6
11 Loughborough	31.7	424	85.5	92.1	83.9
=12 Heriot-Watt	21.7	386	93.9	90.6	83.8
=12 Swansea	55.0	373	77.7	91.1	83.8
14 Manchester	36.7	447	83.5	85.5	83.1
15 Dundee	38.3	388	85.2	83.1	81.7
16 Edinburgh	28.3	526	73.9	93.3	81.6
17 University College London	28.3	522	78.5	80.0	80.0
18 Nottingham	45.0	412	76.5	82.2	79.8
19 Exeter	25.0	440	81.2	85.3	79.2
20 Aberdeen	31.7	428	73.3	92.9	78.8
21 Leeds	25.0	430	83.8	79.7	78.5
22 Birmingham	28.3	426	74.3	85.4	76.4
23 Liverpool	32.1	380	76.1	83.8	76.1
24 Strathclyde	16.7	454	77.1	84.5	75.7
25 Greenwich	15.0	265	94.3		75.3
26 Glasgow	28.3	458	67.9	86.7	75.0
27 Queen's, Belfast	38.3	358	74.9	77.9	74.7
28 Nottingham Trent	10.0	299	86.5	86.0	73.8
29 Salford	38.3	295	77.8	74.1	72.9
30 Coventry	6.7	291	90.2	79.1	72.5
31 Brunel		385	81.8	85.7	72.2
32 Liverpool John Moores		321	92.7	71.4	71.1
33 Plymouth	25.0	296	75.5	76.7	69.7
34 West of Scotland		326	89.4	69.2	69.2
35 West of England		323	76.7	89.7	68.9
36 Kingston	11.7	262	84.1	71.6	68.0
37 Edinburgh Napier	13.3	309	76.1	75.0	67.2
38 Ulster		241	87.2	74.6	66.9
39 Glasgow Caledonian		342	73.3	80.0	65.4
40 Bradford	21.7	307	73.5	65.0	65.2
41 Brighton	13.3	305	74.7	70.0	65.1
=42 City	21.7	371	80.2	45.5	64.9
=42 Leeds Metropolitan		249	79.5	78.9	64.9
44 Portsmouth		313	72.2	79.8	63.9
45 Teesside		343	74.8	66.7	62.5
46 London South Bank	23.3	222	72.6	50.0	58.4
47 East London		237	77.1	59.4	58.1

» EngineeringUK: **www.engineeringuk.com**
» Institution of Civil Engineers: **www.ice.org.uk**
» Institution of Structural Engineers: **www.istructe.org**

Classics and Ancient History

Classics was one of the subjects that commentators expected to suffer when £9,000 fees were introduced in 2012. In fact, although applications did drop, the number of students starting degrees was almost exactly the same as the number starting in 2011. There were still more than five applications for every place in both classics and ancient history. As a result, the only university to drop out of the table is Trinity St David, which has not released data for league tables this year.

There is never much between Oxford and Cambridge in classics and ancient history, but Cambridge clinches top place this year with the highest score in the table for research while Oxford has the highest entry grades. University College London, the only new entrant to the top five, has the top employment score. Glasgow has the most satisfied students, but is restricted to tenth place as one of three universities where fewer than half of the 2012 graduates found professional work or began postgraduate courses within six months of graduating. Satisfaction levels are generally high in classics, but employment prospects are much more mixed. Classicists are often said to be favourite recruitment targets of computer companies and management consultants, but that is not obvious from the latest results. The subject is below average for employment prospects and graduate salaries.

St Andrews remains the leader in Scotland, while Swansea is the only representative of Wales. Roehampton is the only post-1992 university in the ranking. Several universities teach the subjects as part of a modular degree scheme, but not as a degree in its own right. A-level grades in classics are among the highest for any group of subjects, but most universities offering classics teach the subject from scratch, as well as to more practised students. More than a third of graduates opt for postgraduate courses, but the proportion going straight into graduate jobs is among the lowest in any subject.

Employed in professional job:	28%	Employed in non-professional job and studying:	3%
Employed in professional job and studying:	3%	Employed in non-professional job:	26%
Studying:	28%	Unemployed:	13%
Average starting professional salary:	£19,995	Average starting non-professional salary:	£14,389

Classics and Ancient History	Research quality %	Entry standards	Student satisfaction %	Graduate prospects %	Overall rating
1 Cambridge	53.3	568	91.2	81.0	100.0
2 Oxford	50.0	585	90.1	76.8	98.5
3 Durham	38.3	519	91.3	68.8	93.1
4 Exeter	40.0	480	88.7	80.2	92.4
5 University College London	41.7	485	83.9	83.9	90.7
6 Warwick	38.3	477	86.1	73.6	89.3
7 King's College London	41.7	454	84.9	61.8	86.4

Classics and Ancient History cont	Research quality %	Entry standards	Student satisfaction %	Graduate prospects %	Overall rating
8 St Andrews	30.0	491	81.5	73.9	85.4
9 Bristol	31.7	490	78.7	78.4	84.8
10 Glasgow	15.0	491	92.9	42.9	83.9
11 Nottingham	25.0	433	86.2	65.7	83.6
12 Edinburgh	21.7	483	80.6	73.5	82.8
13 Manchester	35.0	418	83.7	60.4	82.7
14 Newcastle	21.7	396	90.3	57.6	82.6
15 Birmingham	30.0	412	81.7	63.9	80.9
16 Royal Holloway	18.3	387	82.2	67.0	78.5
17 Liverpool	23.3	414	81.0	57.8	78.2
18 Reading	23.3	378	84.6	45.9	76.9
19 Swansea	11.7	356	86.3	57.1	76.7
20 Leeds	13.3	405	80.8	58.9	75.9
21 Kent	6.7	384	78.6	67.5	73.9
22 Roehampton		287	89.0	17.5	66.6

» Classical Association: **www.classicalassociation.org**
» Society for the Promotion of Roman Studies: **www.romansociety.org**

Communication and Media Studies

Taken together, journalism and media studies still attract more applications than mathematics. Students have flocked to degrees in these subjects, despite carping in mainstream media about their currency in the employment market. But the boom did not survive the switch to higher fees: applications for journalism were down by 19 per cent and media studies by 10 per cent in 2012. There were some signs of recovery in 2013, but the whole group of media subjects remained 8 per cent down since 2010, the last year considered by UCAS to have been unaffected by imminent or actual fee rises.

The division of jobs into professional and non-graduate fields of employment hits communication and media studies harder than most other subjects. Academics in the field argue that it is normal for students completing media courses to take "entry level" work that is not classified as a graduate job. Nevertheless, the subjects are in the bottom three of the employment league, with 17 per cent unemployment, and in the bottom four for graduate starting salaries.

Communication and media studies are mainly the preserve of the new universities, but older universities have been moving in and now fill the top nine places. Warwick has retained top place with the highest entry grades, the most satisfied students and one of the two top research grades. Sixty per cent of its work in film and television studies was rated as world-class in the 2008 Research Assessment Exercise. Westminster matched Warwick's research score and is again the leading post-1992 university, moving up four places to enter the top ten this year.

Student satisfaction is relatively high. No university succeeded in satisfying 90 per cent or more of its final-year undergraduates in the 2013 National Student Survey, but only one dipped fractionally below 60 per cent. Inevitably, the employment scores are lower, with Sheffield performing best. Even at East Anglia, in third place, fewer than half of the leavers went straight into graduate-level jobs or started postgraduate courses. The same was true at more than half of the institutions in the table and at Cumbria, no graduate secured professional employment – a score unprecedented in any subject table over 20 years.

Cardiff remains the top university in Wales, while Stirling is the leader in Scotland. Entry grades have continued to rise: 13 universities (compared with 9 last year) average more than 400 points, while for the first time no university drops below 200 points.

Universities we were unable to include this year because of insufficient data: Cardiff Metropolitan, Hertfordshire, Liverpool, Manchester, Strathclyde.

Employed in professional job:	39%	Employed in non-professional job and studying:	2%
Employed in professional job and studying:	1%	Employed in non-professional job:	36%
Studying:	6%	Unemployed:	17%
Average starting professional salary:	£17,599	Average starting non-professional salary:	£14,292

Communication and Media Studies	Research quality %	Entry standards	Student satisfaction %	Graduate prospects %	Overall rating
1 Warwick	70.0	484	89.2	62.9	100.0
2 Exeter	45.2	463			95.6
3 East Anglia	63.3	435	87.1	47.6	91.5
4 Sheffield	21.7	423	88.0	80.4	90.4
5 King's College London	55.0	437	83.5	55.5	89.9
6 Cardiff	55.0	407	82.0	62.2	89.1
7 Lancaster	43.3	366	85.8	69.0	88.2
8 Leeds	26.7	403	86.8	70.1	87.5
9 Southampton	38.3	429	85.8	52.5	86.6
10 Westminster	70.0	365	75.1	60.9	86.0
11 Loughborough	31.7	406	81.3	69.8	85.7
12 Queen Mary, London	40.0	397	83.1	58.9	85.4
13 Leicester	46.3	394	79.1	56.6	83.9
14 Royal Holloway	38.3	387	79.9	60.1	83.2
15 Goldsmiths College	56.7	404	79.9	37.0	82.4
16 Newcastle	23.3	399	85.7	53.8	82.3
17 Sussex	35.0	391	84.8	40.7	80.7
18 Lincoln	33.3	331	77.4	70.0	80.2
19 Bournemouth	26.7	386	72.7	65.9	78.3
20 Oxford Brookes		343	86.3	65.0	77.6
21 Nottingham Trent	40.0	337	77.1	51.0	77.3
22 Birmingham City	40.0	334	76.8	51.8	77.2
23 Kent		383	82.1	61.5	76.6
24 Stirling	30.0	405	71.0	54.9	76.5
25 West of England	30.0	327	82.5	44.3	76.1

Communication and Media Studies cont	Research quality %	Entry standards	Student satisfaction %	Graduate prospects %	Overall rating
26 Leeds Metropolitan	28.3	277	76.6	67.9	75.5
27 Surrey	13.3	388	67.7	75.0	75.2
28 Coventry	23.3	274	82.2	58.2	75.0
29 Hull	25.0	312	84.6	39.5	74.3
=30 Northumbria	23.8	325	80.4	46.2	74.0
=30 Robert Gordon		343	82.5	57.9	74.0
=32 Central Lancashire	21.7	296	77.3	60.2	73.8
=32 De Montfort	36.7	304	78.7	42.6	73.8
34 Brighton	15.0	306	85.3	43.4	73.2
35 Glasgow Caledonian	15.0	402	75.3	43.2	72.9
=36 Portsmouth	17.4	295	83.4	45.8	72.7
=36 Winchester	15.0	311	81.9	47.5	72.7
38 Bath Spa	13.3	317	80.4	50.2	72.5
39 Keele		342	81.8	52.2	72.2
40 Swansea	18.3	351	68.9	63.1	72.1
41 Huddersfield	0.0	302	83.7	55.8	72.0
42 Brunel	18.3	347	76.1	45.1	71.6
43 Chichester		263	86.8	55.1	71.4
44 St Mark and St John		230	89.1	51.9	70.2
45 Queen Margaret Edinburgh	20.0	346	79.1	30.6	70.1
46 Teesside		271	83.9	52.2	69.7
=47 City		448	65.4	54.2	69.6
=47 Canterbury Christ Church		274	82.1	55.3	69.6
49 Edinburgh Napier		353	77.6	47.2	69.4
50 York St John		273	88.0	40.6	69.2
=51 Sheffield Hallam	16.7	302	79.5	38.3	69.1
=51 Staffordshire	11.7	267	79.3	50.8	69.1
=53 Ulster	31.7	277	77.4	33.2	68.6
=53 Bradford	10.0	285	81.1	42.2	68.6
=53 Chester		273	78.9	58.3	68.6
56 Northampton		281	81.2	50.8	68.4
57 Falmouth		270	83.1	45.4	67.6
58 Kingston	10.0	317	73.3	47.2	67.3
59 West London	6.7	226	75.8	63.8	67.1
60 Sunderland	31.7	286	71.3	38.0	67.0
61 Southampton Solent		307	77.4	46.6	66.8
62 Derby	30.0	266	77.5	28.3	66.7
63 Leeds Trinity		276	83.0	40.0	66.6
64 Manchester Metropolitan	13.3	309	74.6	38.2	66.3
65 Bedfordshire	23.3	202	81.6	36.9	66.1
66 Roehampton	15.0	284	77.0	34.3	65.7
67 Bangor		275	77.0	48.9	65.5
68 Liverpool John Moores		316	74.6	43.3	65.1

69 Gloucestershire	0.0	295	74.6	47.7	65.0
70 West of Scotland	16.7	286	71.9	40.0	64.7
=71 Buckinghamshire New		251	80.4	41.7	64.4
=71 London Metropolitan	23.3	222	73.6	42.9	64.4
73 Salford	26.7	330	61.2	41.3	63.8
74 Worcester		271	74.5	45.5	63.2
=75 East London	40.0	230	71.2	26.0	63.0
=75 Middlesex	15.0	263	72.3	38.3	63.0
=77 Edge Hill		297	77.2	31.4	62.7
=77 University of the Arts, London		300	64.0	60.7	62.7
79 Aberystwyth		298	73.6	38.8	62.6
80 Bolton		287	79.7	26.1	62.3
81 Anglia Ruskin		237	82.8	29.6	62.1
=82 St Mary's College		299	71.2	40.1	61.7
=82 Cumbria		220	78.7	0.0	61.7
84 Glyndŵr		203	73.5	55.0	61.4
85 London South Bank	23.3	256	76.5	10.3	60.1
86 Greenwich	3.3	287	67.9	33.3	58.5
87 University for Creative Arts		274	58.9	58.3	58.2
88 Queen's, Belfast		351	67.8	17.0	57.3
89 Essex		252		16.1	52.1

» Broadcast Journalism Training Council: **www.bjtc.org.uk**
» Chartered Institute of Journalists: **www.cioj.co.uk**
» National Union of Journalists: **www.nuj.org.uk**
» Creative Skillset: **www.creativeskillset.org**

Computer Science

Computer science saw the biggest increase in applications of any major subject in 2013, the latest lurch in a rollercoaster pattern of applications over recent years. After several years of falling demand for places, computer science and the other specialist computing degrees began to turn the corner in 2010. But, while the decline was less than the national average, growth in demand did not survive the move to higher fees in 2012. The subject was one of the biggest recruiters in Clearing, but there was still a 5 per cent drop in the numbers beginning degrees. The 12 per cent increase in applications in 2013 suggests that computer science is once again seen as a natural route to employment by school leaver, although mature students are yet to return in the same numbers. Computer science is in the top 20 for starting salaries but, while it has shed the unwanted distinction of recording the highest level of unemployment of any subject, this year's 17 per cent jobless rate is still well above average. Almost 60 per cent go straight into professional jobs, however.

Cambridge remains at the top of the table, with the highest entry standards and the best grades in the 2008 Research Assessment Exercise, when 45 per cent of the university's research was considered world-leading. But Imperial College has narrowed the gap and St Andrews, which has overtaken Oxford to take third place, might have been higher still with a better research performance. St Andrews registered a rare 100 per cent score for

Computer Science cont

employment and one of the highest satisfaction ratings in any subject, with 98 per cent of final-year undergraduates giving their approval.

Cardiff has overtaken both Aberystwyth and Swansea to take the lead in Wales. Lincoln is the only one of almost 50 post-1992 universities in the table to reach the top 40. Entry standards are spread more widely than in any other subject, average scores on the UCAS tariff ranging from more than 600 points to only 182. Some of the leading universities demand maths at A level, or the equivalent. Three years after graduation, more than a quarter of computing students said they would be "very likely" to choose a different course if they had their time again – the second-highest total among 19 groups of subjects.

Universities we were unable to include this year because of insufficient data: Bolton, Chichester, Newman.

Employed in professional job:	57%	Employed in non-professional job and studying:	1%
Employed in professional job and studying:	2%	Employed in non-professional job:	15%
Studying:	8%	Unemployed:	17%
Average starting professional salary:	£23,103	Average starting non-professional salary:	£15,697

Computer Science	Research quality %	Entry standards	Student satisfaction %	Graduate prospects %	Overall rating
1 Cambridge	60.0	622	85.2	96.7	100.0
2 Imperial College	51.7	552	89.6	93.5	97.4
3 St Andrews	30.0	517	97.6	100.0	97.1
4 Oxford	50.0	576	83.0	85.3	92.7
5 Southampton	51.7	470	84.0	94.9	92.0
6 Birmingham	45.0	422	89.7	92.0	91.3
7 Bristol	43.3	506	81.6	96.6	90.4
8 Glasgow	46.7	477	87.2	81.0	89.9
9 Bath	41.7	467	82.1	96.7	89.0
10 Edinburgh	51.7	490	78.3	90.9	88.8
11 Durham	35.0	472	85.9	91.7	88.7
12 York	41.7	470	85.1	85.4	88.4
13 University College London	50.0	466	77.0	93.9	87.6
14 Manchester	48.3	425	83.4	85.9	87.5
15 Sheffield	31.7	403	88.3	92.5	87.1
16 Liverpool	45.0	388	83.5	85.3	85.4
17 Newcastle	36.7	377	85.5	88.1	84.9
18 Warwick	31.7	493	73.8	97.4	83.5
19 Exeter	31.7	435			83.3
20 Loughborough	28.3	376	84.9	89.6	83.0
21 Cardiff	36.7	404	81.2	84.3	82.7
22 Strathclyde	26.7	425	82.6	86.1	82.4
23 Nottingham	46.7	363	77.0	89.0	82.3
24 Kent	31.7	370	82.8	88.3	82.1
25 Leicester	35.0	362	80.7	87.4	81.3

26 Aberdeen	36.7	415	80.7	76.7	81.2
27 Leeds	43.3	382	79.3	78.0	81.1
28 Queen's, Belfast	30.0	358	82.3	87.7	81.0
29 Heriot-Watt	30.0	358	85.4	79.1	80.8
30 Surrey	23.3	387	84.0	84.7	80.7
31 Lancaster	43.3	355	80.4	75.5	80.2
32 Essex	31.7	297	88.4	76.2	80.1
33 Royal Holloway	38.3	365	81.0	76.1	79.9
34 Sussex	36.7	355	78.3	81.1	78.8
35 Queen Mary, London	41.7	340	78.2	73.8	77.8
36 King's College London	30.0	382	77.9	77.9	77.4
37 Swansea	40.0	359	68.4	94.3	77.3
38 Dundee	31.7	409	82.8	56.6	76.8
39 Goldsmiths College	33.3	307	79.4	77.8	76.3
40 Lincoln	26.7	322	81.7	74.0	75.8
41 East Anglia	35.0	366	75.3	74.1	75.7
42 Brunel	30.0	334	78.4	75.0	75.4
43 Hull	13.3	328	85.4	75.1	75.2
44 Reading	13.3	350	74.7	93.8	74.2
45 Plymouth	41.7	303	74.6	68.6	73.6
46 City	28.3	360	74.3	74.0	73.5
47 Bournemouth	15.0	337	76.7	84.6	73.3
48 Aston	18.3	352	79.8	69.2	73.0
49 West of England	21.7	295	76.8	80.8	72.6
=50 Robert Gordon	18.3	350	77.0	73.8	72.4
=50 Abertay		362	79.7	84.6	72.4
52 Aberystwyth	40.0	302	71.1	72.0	72.0
=53 Coventry	13.5	255	85.1	71.7	71.9
=53 Central Lancashire		312	87.1	71.6	71.9
55 De Montfort	22.5	309	79.3	65.2	71.3
56 Stirling	18.3	358	78.4	63.6	71.2
57 Brighton	28.3	265	75.7	74.1	71.0
58 Sunderland	11.7	275	84.9	64.6	70.6
59 Manchester Metropolitan	15.0	310	78.5	70.6	70.4
60 Middlesex	18.3	200	86.2	63.2	69.9
61 Edinburgh Napier	10.1	295	81.7	67.0	69.7
=62 Liverpool John Moores	20.0	300	80.4	57.3	69.4
=62 Edge Hill		273	86.7	67.2	69.4
64 Keele		336	83.6	61.8	68.8
65 Salford	31.7	268	74.0	63.1	68.7
66 Cardiff Metropolitan		293	83.0	68.8	68.5
67 Ulster	25.0	271	76.5	62.2	68.4
68 Teesside	25.0	335	75.6	52.5	68.1
=69 Nottingham Trent	10.0	301	73.2	79.2	68.0
=69 Bradford	18.3	270	78.2	63.1	68.0
=71 Glasgow Caledonian	5.0	331	78.4	65.7	67.8
=71 Hertfordshire	25.0	277	76.5	58.2	67.8

	Research quality %	Entry standards	Student satisfaction %	Graduate prospects %	Overall rating
73 Greenwich	6.7	274	86.3	51.3	67.3
74 Oxford Brookes	26.7	317	69.2	65.9	67.2
75 Staffordshire	10.0	260	78.9	67.6	67.1
76 Portsmouth	11.7	304	78.5	58.3	66.8
77 Northampton		273	83.5	60.3	66.3
78 Sheffield Hallam	11.7	274	75.6	66.8	66.1
79 Northumbria		287	79.8	66.0	66.0
80 Chester		275	79.2	67.8	65.6
81 Birmingham City		304	79.2	61.3	65.2
82 Kingston	15.0	296	72.9	60.0	64.7
=83 Derby		298	70.1	76.4	63.4
=83 Glyndŵr	16.7	209	76.5	57.1	63.4
85 Bangor	26.7	229	65.8	69.2	63.2
86 Worcester		259	77.0	62.8	62.9
87 Huddersfield	11.7	299	67.8	66.8	62.8
88 Anglia Ruskin		215	77.3	66.3	62.3
89 Westminster	11.7	257	74.3	54.2	62.1
90 Canterbury Christ Church		237	75.7	64.3	61.8
91 Roehampton		214	80.3	55.9	61.6
92 Leeds Metropolitan		240	76.0	61.1	61.3
93 West of Scotland	10.0	274	74.3	44.4	60.3
94 Gloucestershire		263	66.6	72.3	59.5
95 London South Bank	13.3	219	73.2	46.3	59.0
96 London Metropolitan	3.3	204	78.5	43.0	58.3
97 Bedfordshire	10.0	190	72.7	50.0	57.8
98 Southampton Solent		226	67.7	64.4	57.2
99 West London	5.0	182	69.6	58.3	56.5
100 East London		235	74.9	39.6	56.0
101 Buckinghamshire New		228	69.6	38.5	52.7

» BCS, The Chartered Institute for IT: **www.bcs.org**

Dentistry

Like last year, dentistry is the only subject in our *Guide* to command average starting salaries of more than £30,000. There is no figure for non-graduate jobs because virtually everyone who completes a degree goes on to become a dentist, so the subject is also in the top two for employment. Half of the 14 undergraduate dental schools registered full employment for their graduates and none dropped below 95 per cent. This measure is not used to determine positions so as not to exaggerate the impact of tiny numbers delaying their entry into the profession. Even so, there was an 8 per cent drop in applications in 2012 to follow a smaller decline in the previous year.

Most degrees last five years, although several universities offer a six-year option for those without the necessary scientific qualifications. The number of places has been increased in recent years to tackle shortages in the profession, but there are still ten applications to the place – more than in any subject except medicine. Entry standards are correspondingly high: none of the schools averages less than 480 points. Most demand chemistry and many give preference to candidates who also have biology; some also demand maths or physics.

Scores in the subject are so close that the ranking changes frequently, but Glasgow has opened up a considerable lead over King's College London at the top. Glasgow leads on entry standards and student satisfaction, where it boasts an unusually high score. Manchester recorded the best performance in the 2008 Research Assessment Exercise. Plymouth is the first post-1992 university to enter the ranking in its own right, having previously partnered Exeter in the Peninsula Medical and Dental School. The two universities went their own ways in 2013 and Plymouth alone will offer dentistry. It will be joined in future *Guide*s by Central Lancashire, which opened a purpose-built dental school in 2007, but does not yet have sufficient data to be ranked.

Dentistry	Research quality %	Entry standards	Student satisfaction %	Graduate prospects %	Overall rating
1 Glasgow	30.0	549	96.5	100.0	100.0
2 King's College London	43.3	506	88.2	99.2	95.6
3 Queen Mary, London	41.7	492	91.2		95.0
4 Sheffield	33.3	509	91.7	97.7	94.8
5 Newcastle	30.0	509	90.6	98.5	93.6
6 Dundee	23.3	527	89.8	95.8	93.5
7 Manchester	45.0	516	78.4	98.1	93.2
8 Leeds	33.3	488	90.9	100.0	92.4
9 Queen's, Belfast	25.0	475	95.2	100.0	90.9
10 Birmingham	26.7	486	89.6	100.0	90.1
11 Bristol	33.3	467	87.2	100.0	89.0
12 Liverpool	20.0	493	87.4	100.0	88.4
13 Cardiff	31.7	489	75.7	96.2	86.1
14 Plymouth	11.7		88.0	100.0	84.9

Employed in professional job:	94%	Employed in non-professional job and studying:	0%
Employed in professional job and studying:	3%	Employed in non-professional job:	0%
Studying:	1%	Unemployed:	1%
Average starting professional salary:	£30,681	Average starting non-professional salary:	n/a

» British Dental Association: **www.bda.org**

Drama, Dance and Cinematics

Drama has become one of the most popular subjects in UK higher education – consistently in the top 20 for degree applications. But it suffered a 15 per cent drop in degree applications when fees rose in 2012, with an even steeper decline in Foundation degrees and other courses. The smaller area of dance and the various degrees categorised as cinematics, which include photography as well as film studies, saw even greater falls in the demand for places. However, the numbers eventually enrolling, while down, were much closer to 2011 figures. Drama still had more than six applications to the place and dance almost six. The subjects' popularity has never been reflected in high entry grades, although 13 of the 91 universities and colleges in the table average more than 400 points at entry. Only five universities average less than 250 points.

Exeter tops the table for drama, dance and cinematics for the first time, bringing an end to Warwick's three-year tenure. Surrey has the best employment score and was one of only four universities where three-quarters of those finishing courses were in professional jobs or on postgraduate courses six months after graduation. Tenth-placed Glasgow has the highest entry grades, while Queen Mary, University of London, had much the best results in the 2008 Research Assessment Exercise, when half of its submission was rated world-leading. Roehampton's research in dance achieved an even higher score, but it was not sustained over the whole group of subjects in this category.

The majority of institutions offering drama, dance or cinematics are post-1992 universities, but only Cardiff Metropolitan makes the top 20. It nearly shared top position for student satisfaction with Essex. This is another table where the gulf in qualifications between entrants to new and old universities has a clear impact on positions, although for drama and dance in particular, this is unlikely to be the main criterion for selection. Some drama courses do demand English literature A level, however. The subjects are in the bottom four both for employment prospects and graduate salaries. Freelancing and periods of temporary employment are common throughout the performing arts, and less than half of all new graduates were in graduate-level jobs or still studying when the last employment survey was conducted. Even at some top-20 universities more than half of the leavers were unemployed or in low-level work six months after graduation.

Universities we were unable to include this year because of insufficient data: Oxford Brookes, St Mark and St John.

Employed in professional job:	36%	Employed in non-professional job and studying:	2%
Employed in professional job and studying:	2%	Employed in non-professional job:	38%
Studying:	7%	Unemployed:	15%
Average starting professional salary:	£17,384	Average starting non-professional salary:	£14,107

Drama, Dance and Cinematics	Research quality %	Entry standards	Student satisfaction %	Graduate prospects %	Overall rating
1 Exeter	48.3	441	89.8	77.0	100.0
2 Warwick	48.3	479	89.5	63.4	98.4
3 Queen Mary, London	63.3	416	88.2	59.4	96.1
4 Manchester	58.3	451	83.7	61.0	95.4

5 Bristol	55.0	451	78.6	66.0	93.7
6 Birmingham	31.7	412	87.9	75.9	93.6
7 Kent	46.7	396	86.5	61.8	91.3
8 Sheffield	38.3	382	83.0	76.0	90.9
9 Surrey	33.3	372	83.0	80.5	90.5
10 Glasgow	55.0	488	82.2	33.5	88.8
11 Royal Holloway	48.3	416	78.5	55.7	87.3
12 Lancaster	43.3	399	76.2	63.1	86.2
13 Loughborough	23.3	405	85.7	58.3	85.6
14 Edinburgh	50.0	456	73.7	47.4	85.5
15 Nottingham	31.7	391	84.0	56.9	85.3
16 Essex	25.0	364	95.8	46.2	85.1
17 Leeds	36.7	382	87.4	47.0	84.8
18 Cardiff Metropolitan		331	95.6	71.7	84.7
19 East Anglia		448	93.2	50.0	84.6
20 York	55.0	437	66.7	56.5	84.5
21 Central School of Speech and Drama	28.3	368	83.6	52.7	82.0
22 Coventry	23.3	320	84.0	65.3	81.7
23 Queen's, Belfast	28.3	353	90.9	41.5	81.5
24 Roehampton	46.0	299	83.3	46.7	79.8
25 Royal Conservatoire of Scotland		329	84.2	72.1	79.3
26 The Arts University at Bournemouth	3.3	322	84.2	70.0	79.0
27 Aberdeen	31.7		84.0	42.9	78.4
28 De Montfort	30.0	329	86.1	41.7	78.3
29 Middlesex	31.7	293	80.5	56.0	77.6
30 Goldsmiths College	35.0	370	73.3	46.6	76.9
31 Lincoln	10.0	327	80.5	62.1	76.8
32 Chichester	13.3	351	84.7	46.1	76.5
=33 West of England		336	85.3	58.2	76.4
=33 Northampton	8.3	317	89.2	48.8	76.4
35 Reading	38.3	327	74.9	47.2	76.0
36 Sussex		402	88.8	35.0	75.7
37 Huddersfield		324	83.4	58.2	74.8
38 Brunel	23.3	329	83.6	37.6	74.5
39 Hull	25.0	348	83.4	30.1	73.8
40 Nottingham Trent		332	85.1	49.1	73.6
=41 Aberystwyth	40.0	301	71.8	46.2	73.0
=41 Brighton	45.0	299	72.0	42.1	73.0
43 Greenwich		324	84.7	48.6	72.9
=44 Manchester Metropolitan	13.3	334	75.9	51.6	72.8
=44 Chester	13.3	295	77.9	56.4	72.8
=44 Birmingham City		340	78.8	55.4	72.8
47 Kingston	15.0	344	79.6	39.0	72.1
48 Norwich University of the Arts		289	83.2	54.8	71.7
49 Plymouth	20.5	306	86.4	28.4	71.4
50 Central Lancashire		298	80.5	55.2	71.1
=51 Edge Hill		338	84.1	39.8	71.0

Drama, Dance and Cinematics cont

		Research quality %	Entry standards	Student satisfaction %	Graduate prospects %	Overall rating
=51	Bath Spa		356	73.1	55.3	71.0
53	Winchester	15.0	287	79.2	47.0	70.7
54	Liverpool John Moores		336	84.7	36.9	70.4
55	Portsmouth	3.3	328	78.6	45.2	69.9
56	Leeds Metropolitan		270	82.1	52.5	69.5
57	Derby		304	81.1	45.3	69.0
58	Northumbria		298	83.5	42.0	68.9
59	Edinburgh Napier		334	70.1	55.6	68.3
60	Bolton		301	84.2	36.4	67.9
61	Queen Margaret Edinburgh	0.0	375	63.0	57.1	67.8
62	University of the Arts, London		325	71.9	51.4	67.5
63	Gloucestershire		308	75.5	46.8	67.0
64	Newman		295	88.3	26.2	66.8
65	St Mary's College		307	80.7	36.5	66.6
66	Westminster		363	65.7	50.0	66.4
=67	Worcester		276	79.9	42.4	66.1
=67	Cumbria		254	91.0	27.6	66.1
=69	York St John	15.0	297	70.7	40.7	65.6
=69	University for Creative Arts		295	71.1	52.4	65.6
71	Staffordshire	11.7	264	82.8	29.1	65.5
72	Canterbury Christ Church		275	79.1	41.0	65.2
73	West of Scotland		303	81.9	28.8	64.9
74	Sheffield Hallam		327	73.3	37.6	64.6
75	Hertfordshire	8.3	319	64.5	47.7	64.4
=76	London South Bank		270	76.5	42.4	64.1
=76	Falmouth		289	65.5	57.9	64.1
78	Salford	10.0	316	66.4	42.3	64.0
79	Sunderland	8.3	258	77.0	36.6	63.7
80	West London		274	67.6	53.2	63.0
=81	Bournemouth		327	69.6	36.8	62.6
=81	Teesside		314	74.4	31.0	62.6
83	Southampton Solent		311	72.9	33.7	62.3
=84	Ulster		264	85.5	19.9	61.9
=84	Anglia Ruskin		241	77.0	40.0	61.9
86	Bedfordshire	23.3	224	68.2	37.3	60.9
87	Buckinghamshire New		255	76.6	29.6	59.8
88	East London	15.0	253	69.3	31.0	59.7
89	Glyndŵr		211	76.6	38.5	59.5
90	London Metropolitan	8.3	240	71.1	31.8	58.6
91	Bishop Grosseteste		213	77.3	23.9	56.1

» The Stage: **www.thestage.co.uk**

» UKP-Arts: **www.ukperformingarts.co.uk**

East and South Asian Studies

Degrees in these subjects attracted fewer than 500 new students 2012, most taking either Japanese or Chinese. The subjects are officially classed as "vulnerable" because of their small size and their economic and cultural importance, although the number of universities in the East and South Asian studies ranking has doubled since the subjects were placed in this category. Universities have always come in and out of the table because small student numbers mean that reliable averages cannot always be compiled, even though courses are still running.

Numbers may well grow in future years, with the clamour for more interaction with China and India, but non-European languages have been among the hardest hit by increased fees. Although there were still eight applications for every place – one of the highest ratios for any subject – only 144 undergraduates started degrees in Japanese studies, down by a quarter on 2011. The decline in enrolments for Chinese was marginally less steep, but the 844 applications still lagged behind the total for Japanese. The well-publicised growth in the number of schools teaching Mandarin may have an effect on the demand for Chinese studies, but in 2012 there were fewer than five applications for every place.

Cambridge has lost the leadership in East and South Asian studies for the only time since the table was first compiled, having been overtaken by both Oxford and Cardiff, which tie for first place. Oxford has the highest entry standards, while Cardiff produced the best results in the 2008 Research Assessment Exercise. The most satisfied students are at Oxford Brookes, the only post-1992 university with enough students taking the subjects to qualify for the ranking. Edinburgh has much the best employment score, but more than 30 per cent of the graduates at seven of the ten universities, including Oxford and Cambridge, were in lower-level jobs or unemployed six months after graduating in 2012.

The small numbers make for exaggerated swings even in the national statistics. The latest unemployment rate of 18 per cent is among the three highest in the employment table, but East and South Asian studies are still not far below halfway for positive destinations or starting salaries in graduate-level jobs. Four out of five students enter with tariff scores that are above average for all subjects, so degree classifications are also high. Most learn their chosen language from scratch, although universities expect to see evidence of potential in other modern language qualifications.

Universities we were unable to include this year because of insufficient data: Liverpool John Moores, Westminster.

Employed in professional job:	40%	Employed in non-professional job and studying:	3%
Employed in professional job and studying:	3%	Employed in non-professional job:	19%
Studying:	17%	Unemployed:	18%
Average starting professional salary:	£19,799	Average starting non-professional salary:	£16,317

» Association of South-East Asian Studies in the UK: **http://aseasuk.org.uk**
» British Association for Chinese Studies: **www.bacsuk.org.uk**
» British Association for Japanese Studies: **www.bajs.org.uk**
» British Association for Korean Studies: **www.baks.org.uk**
» British Association for South Asian Studies: **www.basas.org.uk**
» Royal Asiatic Society: **www.royalasiaticsociety.org**
» Royal Society for Asian Affairs: **www.rsaa.org.uk**

East and South Asian Studies	Research quality %	Entry standards	Student satisfaction %	Graduate prospects %	Overall rating
=1 Oxford	35.0	603	75.4	68.8	100.0
=1 Cardiff	46.7	368	84.3		100.0
3 Cambridge	26.7	577	75.8	69.0	97.0
4 SOAS London	41.7	445	77.2	63.6	94.9
5 Edinburgh	18.3	487	71.7	85.8	93.3
6 Nottingham	16.7	383	79.6	76.6	90.8
7 Leeds	18.3	432	84.8	53.8	89.9
8 Sheffield	13.3	425	79.6	67.5	89.0
9 Manchester	18.3	448	70.8	60.0	83.8
10 Oxford Brookes		378	86.5	47.2	81.8

Economics

Economics is in the top six for graduate starting salaries, reflecting the value that employers place on a subject that they see combining the skills of the sciences and the arts. Although it is lower for overall employment rates, the subject is still comfortably in the top 25. Its reputation as a highly marketable degree helped economics to withstand the impact of higher fees better than most subjects. The numbers starting degrees in 2012 was 6 per cent down on the previous year, but applications recovered in 2013. Competition for places remains stiff, with around seven applications for every degree place.

Many prospective students underestimate the mathematical skills required for an economics degree. Most of the leading universities demand maths at A level or its equivalent as part of offers that are consistently high. Entry standards in this year's table reflect that, with the top five universities all averaging over 550 points – the equivalent of more than four As at A level and another at AS level. Another 16 have averages of at least 450 points, while only one of the 66 institutions in the ranking averages less than 250 points.

Cambridge has regained the lead it lost last year to Oxford, recording the best employment score as well as the highest entry standards. Not enough Cambridge economists responded to the 2013 National Student Survey for a score to be compiled on this measure, so one is generated from Cambridge's performance on the other indicators. The result leaves the university well ahead of Oxford, in second place. Both of the ancient universities were eclipsed by the third-placed London School of Economics and also by University College London, in fifth, in the 2008 Research Assessment Exercise (RAE). The most satisfied students are at Coventry, which would have been higher than 44th place if it had entered the RAE in this category. The University of the West of England is the leading post-1992 university, at =34th. Strathclyde has overtaken both Glasgow and Edinburgh to become the leading university in Scotland, although all three slipped back this year, while Cardiff remains top in Wales.

A quarter of all economists continue studying after their first degree, either full- or part-time. But some of those going straight into employment command high salaries: Cambridge economists' £40,000 average six months after graduation was the highest figure anywhere when the Unistats website published the first salary figures by subject in 2012.

Universities we were unable to include this year because of insufficient data: Oxford Brookes, Salford, Staffordshire.

Employed in professional job:	46%	Employed in non-professional job and studying:	2%
Employed in professional job and studying:	8%	Employed in non-professional job:	15%
Studying:	15%	Unemployed:	15%
Average starting professional salary:	£26,146	Average starting non-professional salary:	£17,343

Economics

	Research quality %	Entry standards	Student satisfaction %	Graduate prospects %	Overall rating
1 Cambridge	45.0	638		97.4	100.0
2 Oxford	58.3	608	86.8	79.5	95.3
3 London School of Economics	71.7	587	78.9	88.5	95.1
4 Warwick	58.3	573	83.8	86.2	94.1
5 University College London	68.3	553	79.3	82.5	92.2
6 Queen Mary, London	48.3	445	91.4	85.0	91.6
7 Bath	43.3	514	81.6	88.9	88.5
8 Nottingham	48.3	487	81.0	82.2	86.8
9 Exeter	38.3	498	82.9	84.7	86.7
10 Surrey	31.7	457	89.4	76.5	85.7
11 Bristol	48.3	502	78.6	80.1	85.6
12 East Anglia	31.7	425	92.2	72.1	85.2
13 Durham	28.3	555	79.7	85.4	85.0
14 York	37.1	473	82.0	83.4	84.9
15 Lancaster	41.7	457	82.6	77.9	84.4
16 Strathclyde	38.3	464	86.0	69.8	84.0
=17 Edinburgh	40.0	479	75.5	84.5	82.5
=17 St Andrews	28.3	510	81.7	75.8	82.5
19 Kent	35.0	410	86.6	69.5	81.8
20 Essex	58.3	385	82.9	59.4	81.6
21 Aberdeen	35.0	450	77.1	83.5	81.1
22 Cardiff	46.7	440	73.1	82.9	80.9
23 Leicester	36.7	402	83.6	71.6	80.8
24 Birmingham	31.7	464	77.0	79.6	80.0
=25 Leeds	36.7	451	76.8	77.0	79.9
=25 Sheffield	33.3	435	82.6	68.6	79.9
27 Manchester	43.3	450	76.9	69.7	79.7
28 Swansea	30.0	349	80.7	87.3	79.6
29 Newcastle	23.3	442	83.0	71.4	79.0
30 City	25.0	431	86.7	61.6	78.8
31 Glasgow	41.7	491	75.1	65.0	78.7
32 SOAS London	20.0	473	78.5	78.7	78.5
33 Heriot-Watt	21.7	364	89.1	66.7	78.3
=34 Loughborough	18.3	427	80.7	78.3	77.8
=34 Queen's, Belfast	28.3	380	86.8	61.0	77.8

	Research quality %	Entry standards	Student satisfaction %	Graduate prospects %	Overall rating
=34 West of England	10.0	330	91.3	75.0	77.8
37 Southampton	40.0	447	72.1	75.9	77.7
38 Royal Holloway	40.0	396	74.3	77.8	77.6
39 Liverpool	23.3	392	84.1	69.0	77.4
40 Reading	23.3	371	77.0	81.7	75.7
41 Keele	21.7	322	79.4	77.9	74.2
42 Birmingham City	11.7	300	89.0	57.9	72.2
43 Aberystwyth	13.3	330	80.6	72.0	72.1
44 Coventry		307	95.2	51.2	71.9
45 Sussex	26.7	394	78.6	53.5	71.8
46 Bradford	23.1	275	80.8	66.7	71.3
47 Dundee	18.3	336	79.5		70.4
48 Portsmouth	15.0	317	77.1	72.1	70.3
49 Plymouth	13.3	289	87.6	51.7	70.1
=50 Greenwich	10.0	279	89.1	51.0	69.7
=50 Central Lancashire	13.3	296	82.9		69.7
52 Stirling	30.0	400	78.3	36.5	68.8
53 Manchester Metropolitan	3.3	324	82.9	60.8	68.7
54 Brunel	26.7	345	74.6	54.1	68.2
55 De Montfort		300	86.5	54.5	67.8
56 Hull	18.3	332	77.2	51.7	67.0
57 Hertfordshire	15.0	296	73.8	60.0	65.2
58 Nottingham Trent	13.3	335	74.3	53.2	64.8
59 Brighton	28.3	301	69.3		64.3
60 Ulster		274	81.7	45.8	62.5
61 East London		231	83.4	44.3	61.6
62 Liverpool John Moores	1.7		75.5	53.6	61.3
63 Kingston	10.0	307	64.9	64.6	60.7
64 London Metropolitan	11.7	206	80.0	39.1	60.3
65 Middlesex		255	81.9	31.7	58.9
66 Leeds Metropolitan		278	66.9	59.1	57.7

» Economics, Business and Enterprise Association: **www.ebea.org.uk**
» Royal Economic Society: **www.res.org.uk**
» Why Study? Economics: **www.whystudyeconomics.ac.uk**

Education

The Government's rebalancing of teacher training in England is intended to steer more students towards schools, rather than universities, for their training. But so far, it has not affected the BEd courses, which provide most of the data for this table, as much as the postgraduate route. Continuing shortages of teachers in primary schools may mean that places continue to be available on a similar scale in 2014. Although the volume of applications dropped when higher fees were introduced in 2012, there were still more than seven to every place and more students actually began training than in the previous year. Other courses in education did see a decline in enrolments.

Education is the only ranking that still contains teaching scores – because teacher training assessments are carried out by Ofsted at English universities. Sixteen universities, including two from outside the top 30 – Chichester and Worcester – tie for the best scores from the inspections. Cambridge and Durham, the top two overall, are among the others. Cambridge maintains a clear lead in the table with entry standards that are over 100 points ahead of its nearest challenger and much the best research grades. Huddersfield, in =17th place, has the most satisfied students, but is not the top post-1992 university. That distinction goes to West of Scotland, which has slipped two places to equal fifth after a meteoric rise last year, but is still the only modern university in the top 10. Even that is not enough to make it the top university in Scotland: Stirling is the highest-placed of three Scottish universities in the top 10. Satisfaction levels are high generally, not only among the final-year undergraduates who complete the National Student Survey, but also in the early stage of careers. Three years after graduation, those with education degrees were among the most satisfied at work and least inclined to wish they had taken a different subject.

Employment scores at different universities reflect to some extent the variations in demand for new staff between primary and secondary schools as well as between different parts of the UK. Universities that specialise in primary training are at an advantage at the moment because vacancies are more plentiful in primary than secondary schools. Aberdeen, which focuses on primary training, has a rare 100 per cent score for employment, but there were 11 universities where under 60 per cent of leavers went straight into graduate-level jobs or continued their studies.

Some of the best-known education departments are absent from the table because they offer only the postgraduate courses that have become the normal route into secondary teaching and an increasingly popular choice for those wanting a career in primary schools. As such, they are not included in the National Student Survey for the subject and neither entry scores nor graduate destinations are comparable. The University of London's Institute of Education, which achieved the top grades in the 2008 research assessments, is one example; Oxford and King's College London, which ran it close, are others. Low entry scores have been a concern to successive governments, but for the first time no university averages less than 200 points in the latest table and only two are below 250 points.

University we were unable to include this year because of insufficient data: Bath.

Employed in professional job:	56%	Employed in non-professional job and studying:	2%
Employed in professional job and studying:	3%	Employed in non-professional job:	21%
Studying:	11%	Unemployed:	7%
Average starting professional salary:	£21,122	Average starting non-professional salary:	£14,053

» Graduate Teacher Training Registry (GTTR): **www.gttr.ac.uk**
» Get into Teaching: **www.education.gov.uk/get-into-teaching**

Education

		Research quality %	Teaching quality/5	Entry standards	Student satisfaction %	Graduate prospects %	Overall rating
1	Cambridge	41.7	4.0	563	82.6		100.0
2	Durham	31.7	4.0	437	87.4	86.0	92.1
3	York	30.0	4.0	402	85.7	76.1	88.1
4	Stirling	28.3		382	80.2	93.3	86.8
=5	West of Scotland	13.3		372	87.3	91.5	85.6
=5	Glasgow	16.7		401	80.0	98.0	85.6
7	Sheffield	23.3	3.0	400	89.4		84.2
8	Birmingham	21.7	4.0	360	85.4	73.5	84.1
9	East Anglia	26.7	4.0	358	81.7	75.0	83.8
10	Manchester	31.7	4.0	320	89.2	59.0	83.7
11	Brighton	18.3	4.0	314	86.5	82.8	83.4
12	Dundee	10.0		367	82.9	94.6	82.9
13	Canterbury Christ Church	18.3	4.0	325	82.0	87.9	82.8
14	Manchester Metropolitan	31.7	4.0	324	80.1	73.9	82.6
15	Birmingham City	11.7	4.0	317	87.5	83.0	82.5
16	Aberdeen	11.7		400	74.2	100.0	81.8
=17	Cardiff	35.0		384	79.6	58.3	81.5
=17	Huddersfield	8.3	3.5	323	93.4	79.2	81.5
=19	Northumbria		4.0	321	87.8	89.4	81.4
=19	Edinburgh	25.0		415	67.4	93.9	81.4
21	Reading	16.7	3.5	341	87.0	78.9	81.3
22	Leeds	33.3	3.0	337	85.6	72.7	80.7
=23	Brunel	8.3	3.5	356	84.0	88.5	80.5
=23	Strathclyde	13.3		401	76.0	86.8	80.5
25	Keele	31.7	3.5	300	88.3	60.3	80.4
26	Warwick	33.3	3.8	370	69.2	69.2	78.8
27	St Mary's College	3.3	4.0	314	78.6	92.5	78.7
28	Edge Hill	1.7	4.0	337	80.5	83.2	78.5
29	Bath Spa	5.0	4.0	326	82.3	75.1	78.2
30	Chichester		4.0	317	83.8	79.4	78.1
31	Oxford Brookes	13.3	3.5	334	82.0	72.6	77.4
32	West of England	8.3	3.8	311	83.2	70.5	77.0
33	Winchester	16.7	3.5	309	82.9	66.9	76.5
=34	Plymouth	16.7	3.5	302	83.9	65.8	76.4
=34	Sheffield Hallam	11.7	3.5	324	78.9	78.9	76.4
36	St Mark and St John	1.7	3.3	259	90.1	85.7	76.2
37	Gloucestershire	15.0	3.8	309	77.7	68.7	75.8
38	Chester	5.0	3.8	292	81.7	74.9	75.6
39	Northampton	8.3	3.5	308	83.6	68.3	75.2
40	Glyndŵr	1.7		271	89.8	72.5	74.9
41	Derby		3.0	309	93.0	66.9	74.7
42	York St John	0.0	3.0	311	85.1	85.5	74.5
43	Hull	11.7	3.3	325	82.7	62.3	74.3

44	Kingston	8.3	3.0	285	86.2	76.2	74.2
=45	Leeds Metropolitan	6.7	3.0	301	84.7	76.7	74.0
=45	Newman	8.3	3.0	300	87.6	67.4	74.0
=47	Leeds Trinity		3.5	298	82.5	76.1	73.8
=47	Sunderland	8.3	3.0	297	82.3	80.9	73.8
49	Roehampton	13.3	3.5	291	80.7	61.7	73.4
50	Bangor	16.7		291	79.0	65.0	73.0
51	Worcester		4.0	281	76.1	75.5	72.9
52	Goldsmiths College	16.7	3.0	271	84.4	62.5	72.5
53	Liverpool John Moores	6.7	3.0	342	83.2	58.4	72.2
54	Middlesex		3.0	273	81.6	86.7	71.8
55	Hertfordshire	6.7	3.0	314	75.0	82.4	71.5
56	Bishop Grosseteste	3.3	3.5	253	81.0	69.6	71.1
57	Southampton Solent			289	82.1	63.2	70.2
58	Nottingham Trent		3.0	294	84.2	63.1	69.9
59	Cumbria	1.7	3.0	272	78.8	78.8	69.7
60	Ulster	15.0		270	82.4	44.7	69.1
61	Portsmouth		3.5	305	79.2	51.7	69.0
62	Cardiff Metropolitan	0.0		305	83.2	51.6	68.7
63	Greenwich	6.7	3.3	283	72.9	67.9	68.6
=64	Central Lancashire	1.7		274	82.4	57.5	68.4
=64	Aberystwyth			278	78.7	65.8	68.4
66	London Metropolitan	23.3	3.0	219	73.3	51.6	65.5
67	Anglia Ruskin		2.0	250	83.4	75.2	64.9
68	East London	11.7	3.0	229	76.8	42.5	63.5
69	Bedfordshire		2.7	253	72.4	71.1	63.3
70	Teesside			298	80.7	28.0	62.6
71	De Montfort			301	62.4	48.1	57.2

Electrical and Electronic Engineering

While the demand for places in other branches of engineering began to recover in 2013, electrical and electronic courses continued to decline. The subjects had been recruiting more strongly after numbers had dropped for much of the last decade, but that did not survive the introduction of higher fees. The numbers starting courses in 2012 were 8 per cent down on the previous year and applications dropped again in 2013. Some natural applicants have been diverted into subjects such as computer games design, but the Royal Academy of Engineering has expressed concern about the more general courses. About half of the students – more in electrical engineering – come with qualifications other than A levels. Most of the top courses demand maths and physics at A level, or the equivalent.

Cambridge's lead in electrical and electronic engineering is one of the biggest in any subject. It has by far the best research grades and a lead of more than 80 points on entry standards. Having slipped from second to eighth place last year, Surrey has made the reverse journey in the new table with strong scores across the board. Manchester, in sixth place, is top for student satisfaction, just ahead of 48th-placed Greenwich, while Newcastle has the

Electrical and Electronic Engineering cont

best employment score with 98 per cent of graduates going straight into professional jobs or further study. Glasgow remains the top university in Scotland, while Bangor is the leader in Wales. Robert Gordon is the highest-placed post-1992 institution in 25th place, in a subject where old universities predominate.

Electrical and electronic engineering are back in the top 20 for employment prospects for the first time in five years, although still behind most other branches of the discipline. Only one university in the top 20 saw less than 80 per cent of leavers go straight into graduate jobs or further training, although the proportion still dropped below 50 per cent at four universities in the table. The subjects do better still in the earnings table, where they are in the top ten. The gap between those in professional jobs and lower-level employment is among the widest of any subject, at almost £10,000. More than 70 per cent of graduates go straight into professional jobs or continue their studies, but the 15 per cent unemployment rate is above the average for all subjects.

Universities we were unable to include this year because of insufficient data: Sussex, Ulster.

Employed in professional job:	56%	Employed in non-professional job and studying:	1%
Employed in professional job and studying:	3%	Employed in non-professional job:	14%
Studying:	11%	Unemployed:	15%
Average starting professional salary:	£24,506	Average starting non-professional salary:	£14,708

Electrical and Electronic Engineering	Research quality %	Entry standards	Student satisfaction %	Graduate prospects %	Overall rating
1 Cambridge	60.0	631	84.6	96.2	100.0
2 Surrey	43.3	473	88.5	85.9	89.2
3 Imperial College	38.3	550	83.7	85.3	88.2
4 Southampton	38.3	498	80.5	93.4	86.2
5 Bath	36.7	414	90.1	84.1	85.5
6 Manchester	40.0	378	91.2	82.8	85.3
=7 Leeds	46.7	402	80.6	90.6	84.6
=7 Glasgow	35.0	441	88.6	80.4	84.6
9 Bristol	28.3	446	86.5	94.4	84.5
10 Strathclyde	26.7	467	83.6	92.4	83.1
11 Sheffield	32.7	384	86.3	89.8	82.5
12 Birmingham	26.7	408	84.9	92.9	81.5
13 University College London	36.7	466	80.7	73.4	80.9
14 Edinburgh	28.3	468	79.4	88.0	80.7
15 Newcastle	30.0	387	80.8	97.6	80.6
16 Queen's, Belfast	33.3	374	81.2	83.0	78.5
=17 York	25.0	393	85.2	81.1	78.4
=17 Bangor	43.3	269	84.2		78.4
19 Lancaster	25.0	451	80.0		77.8
=20 Loughborough	30.0	363	80.6	87.5	77.7
=20 Liverpool	28.3	337	86.7		77.7

22	Essex	33.3	358	79.9		76.3
23	Aberdeen	31.7	415	75.6		75.7
24	Heriot-Watt	25.0	366	79.1	87.1	75.6
25	Robert Gordon	10.0	390	80.2	97.0	74.6
26	Cardiff	23.3	414	73.7	87.0	74.3
27	Brunel	20.0	351	83.1	78.3	73.8
28	City	21.7	366	85.6	65.5	73.6
29	Nottingham	28.3	381	74.7	78.2	73.3
30	Reading	16.7	348	80.6	86.1	73.1
31	Hull	13.3	310	89.7		72.5
32	Exeter	25.0	440	66.7	85.3	72.1
33	Kent	23.3	337	81.1	68.8	71.5
34	Coventry	20.0	250	83.0	78.8	70.1
35	Queen Mary, London	26.7	357	77.5	60.5	69.9
=36	Portsmouth	11.7	296	78.4	87.3	68.8
=36	Aston	18.3	320	80.1		68.8
38	Liverpool John Moores	33.3	305	74.8	59.4	68.3
39	Swansea	16.7	344	75.8	73.3	68.2
40	Derby		290	88.4	77.1	68.1
41	Huddersfield	15.0	335	79.1	68.1	67.9
42	Sheffield Hallam	15.0	264	77.8	84.1	67.7
43	West of England	25.0	298	69.0	82.3	67.2
44	Staffordshire	20.0	231	83.3		67.0
45	Central Lancashire	10.0	270	84.6	67.1	66.5
46	Hertfordshire	26.7	300	78.7	45.8	65.5
47	Manchester Metropolitan	11.7	287	86.0	50.0	65.0
48	Greenwich		274	90.8	57.1	64.9
49	Brighton	26.7	339	76.6	40.0	64.8
50	Northumbria	20.0	253	77.3	64.0	64.7
51	Salford	31.7	308	68.5	55.0	64.1
52	Teesside		321	83.6	53.1	62.4
53	Westminster	5.0	283	81.5	55.0	61.8
54	De Montfort	15.0	292	74.6	54.9	61.6
=55	Bradford	3.3	300	79.3		61.5
=55	London South Bank	23.3	263	78.2	38.5	61.5
57	Aberystwyth		286	71.4	84.0	61.1
58	Bolton		295	80.4	52.9	59.8
59	Birmingham City		318	74.5	56.7	58.6
60	Plymouth	10.0	305	67.7	58.8	58.1
61	London Metropolitan		204	88.1	40.0	57.6
62	Anglia Ruskin		179	74.1	60.0	53.8
63	Southampton Solent		223	54.2	65.7	47.0

» Institute of Electrical and Electronics Engineers, UK section: **http://ieee-ukri.org**
» Institution of Engineering and Technology: **www.theiet.org**

English

Degrees in English are a perennial favourite of university applicants, despite the fact that they never feature among the top 50 subjects for employment prospects or professional starting salaries. Applications dropped by about the average for all subjects when the fees went up in 2012, but English remained among the top ten choices for a degree. There were still almost six applications for every place and entry grades remained high. Seven of the top ten universities in the new table average more than 500 points and only six drop below 250.

Oxford's three-year run at the top of the table has come to a spectacular end, with the university dropping to sixth after a big decline in the proportion of graduates with positive destinations. Cambridge, which has the highest entry standards, takes over at the top, while University College London moves up to second. Durham, in third place, has the best employment score and York, in seventh, produced the best results in the 2008 Research Assessment Exercise, when three-quarters of its work was judged to be world-leading or internationally excellent. The most satisfied students are to be found much further down the table, however. Cumbria only just makes the top 50, but 97 per cent of its undergraduates in English gave their course the seal of approval.

St Andrews returns as the top university in Scotland, while Cardiff remains well clear in Wales. The table is dominated by older universities, but De Montfort, Edinburgh Napier, Coventry and Buckingham make the top 40. Only Durham saw eight out of ten graduates go straight into graduate-level work or further study, but eleven institutions did not manage even four out of ten.

Almost a third of English graduates continue their studies – almost as many as go into graduate-level jobs alone. Unemployment is no higher than average for all subjects, but more than a third of all graduates start out in lower-level jobs. However, English has produced consistently good scores in the National Student Survey. In the results published in 2013, only the bottom four out of 99 universities failed to satisfy at least three-quarters of the final-year undergraduates.

Universities we were unable to include this year because of insufficient data: Derby, Glyndŵr.

English	Research quality %	Entry standards	Student satisfaction %	Graduate prospects %	Overall rating
1 Cambridge	48.3	563	90.4	79.3	100.0
2 University College London	41.7	498	93.5	79.5	98.4
3 Durham	40.0	557	87.2	86.0	97.9
4 Exeter	51.7	502	88.4	70.2	95.3
5 St Andrews	46.7	519	84.7	78.9	94.8
6 Oxford	48.3	542	87.4	66.7	94.6
7 York	55.0	514	85.8	68.7	94.4
8 Newcastle	40.0	454	86.5	71.7	90.6
9 Warwick	45.0	518	81.9	67.6	90.1
10 Nottingham	46.7	473	82.3	71.4	90.0
11 Bristol	36.7	498	80.9	78.1	89.7
12 East Anglia	35.0	452	89.7	59.7	88.7

13	Edinburgh	50.0	494	78.9	67.7	88.5
=14	Lancaster	33.3	468	84.9	67.9	88.0
=14	Cardiff	43.3	449	82.1	69.5	88.0
=16	Leeds	45.0	451	83.0	65.1	87.9
=16	Sheffield	38.3	464	86.3	60.4	87.9
=18	Southampton	38.3	452	86.3	61.8	87.8
=18	Queen Mary, London	50.0	426	82.8	64.5	87.8
20	Royal Holloway	41.7	428	84.2	66.8	87.6
21	Glasgow	46.7	474	83.2	57.1	87.2
22	Leicester	30.0	419	85.1	70.0	86.3
23	Manchester	45.0	475	79.6	60.5	85.6
24	Kent	41.7	409	82.3	64.3	85.2
25	Aberdeen	41.7	447	82.0	58.9	85.1
=26	Liverpool	41.7	442	82.2	57.5	84.7
=26	Sussex	31.7	428	86.6	56.7	84.7
28	Birmingham	36.7	443	77.4	71.3	84.2
29	Loughborough	23.3	418	88.3	56.4	83.7
30	Queen's, Belfast	45.0	395	84.4	49.4	83.1
31	Brunel	25.0	360	91.9	48.7	82.3
=32	Reading	38.3	395	83.3	50.6	81.5
=32	Aston	10.0	374	89.7	60.7	81.5
34	De Montfort	46.7	318	87.8	43.4	81.4
35	Edinburgh Napier	10.0	371	87.9	62.5	80.7
36	Keele	23.3	363	85.9	57.3	80.6
37	Essex	25.0	400	89.6	40.6	80.5
38	Swansea	26.7	353	77.8	74.9	80.3
=39	Coventry	6.7	291	90.6	67.1	80.0
=39	Buckingham		310	92.3	65.6	80.0
=41	Goldsmiths College	31.7	394	81.8	47.1	78.5
=41	Chester	10.0	316	89.9	55.8	78.5
=43	Huddersfield	10.0	353	84.2	64.1	78.3
=43	Dundee	21.7	382	86.1	45.3	78.3
45	Strathclyde	25.0	463	82.8	38.0	78.0
46	Newman		306	85.4	74.3	77.9
47	Bath Spa	13.3	359	87.9	48.9	77.8
=48	Surrey		437	83.2	59.1	77.5
=48	West of England	13.3	339	86.2	54.8	77.5
50	Cumbria	3.3	226	96.7	52.8	77.4
51	Sunderland	20.0	283	92.5	41.0	77.3
=52	Hull	25.0	350	81.8	53.0	77.1
=52	Plymouth	16.7	328	86.4	51.7	77.1
54	Northampton	5.0	308	88.7	57.9	77.0
55	Winchester		327	87.7	61.0	76.8
56	Bishop Grosseteste	0.0	255	88.4	69.3	76.7
=57	Bangor	25.0	335	79.7	57.0	76.3
=57	Oxford Brookes	16.7	370	84.6	46.6	76.3
59	King's College London	33.3	472	69.4	55.6	76.2

English cont

		Research quality %	Entry standards	Student satisfaction %	Graduate prospects %	Overall rating
60	Gloucestershire	15.0	307	86.6	51.2	76.1
61	Lincoln		341	84.2	63.9	76.0
=62	Portsmouth	25.0	325	81.3	50.6	75.4
=62	Edge Hill	6.7	306	86.9	54.4	75.4
64	Manchester Metropolitan	21.7	336	82.2	49.2	75.3
65	St Mary's College	13.3	302	89.8	41.1	75.1
66	Anglia Ruskin	30.0	269	83.3	48.1	75.0
=67	Stirling	25.0	391	79.5	43.3	74.9
=67	Chichester	8.3	312	84.7	55.7	74.9
69	Roehampton	18.3	306	82.3	52.2	74.4
=70	Greenwich	8.3	284	85.6	54.1	74.1
=70	Northumbria	11.7	350	82.5	49.5	74.1
72	Hertfordshire	21.7	336	81.6	44.8	73.9
73	Bradford	11.7	283	85.7	50.0	73.8
74	Kingston	20.0	312	78.6	56.4	73.7
75	Aberystwyth	20.0	366	78.3	45.5	72.9
76	Nottingham Trent	25.0	321	78.8	46.3	72.8
77	Cardiff Metropolitan		294	87.3	48.9	72.7
78	Salford	18.3	308	77.4	56.3	72.6
79	Liverpool John Moores	13.3	332	86.0	34.9	72.4
=80	Birmingham City	10.0	305	79.0	56.0	71.7
=80	Worcester	11.7	290	84.5	43.0	71.7
82	Bedfordshire	23.3	218	85.8	40.0	71.6
83	Sheffield Hallam	13.3	340	82.4	38.7	71.5
84	Brighton	15.0	333	80.2	42.8	71.3
85	Teesside		345	84.5	38.6	70.4
86	Falmouth		281	83.3	50.0	70.2
=87	Westminster	6.7	316	77.7	53.3	70.1
=87	York St John	3.3	299	82.1	47.6	70.1
89	Ulster	15.0	281	84.2	33.0	69.5
90	Canterbury Christ Church	6.7	290	85.1	33.8	68.9
91	Central Lancashire	6.7	299	83.7	33.8	68.5
92	London Metropolitan		219	79.7	56.3	67.3
93	Leeds Metropolitan		284	80.2	43.1	66.8
94	St Mark and St John	0.0	247	88.2	22.2	65.4
95	Leeds Trinity	11.7	289	75.0	38.3	65.0
96	Middlesex	15.0	262	68.5	53.1	64.4
97	Staffordshire	11.7	239	74.3	38.3	63.0
98	East London		237	77.1	37.5	62.0
99	Bolton	3.3	254	69.4	45.2	60.6

» Poetry Society: **www.poetrysociety.org.uk**
» Royal Society of Literature: **www.rslit.org**

» Society of Authors: **www.societyofauthors.org**
» Society for Editors and Proofreaders: **www.sfep.org.uk**
» Teaching English as a Foreign Language: **www.tefl.com**

Employed in professional job:	29%	Employed in non-professional job and studying:	4%
Employed in professional job and studying:	3%	Employed in non-professional job:	31%
Studying:	21%	Unemployed:	13%
Average starting professional salary:	£18,071	Average starting non-professional salary:	£14,396

Food Science

The top two in food science are unchanged, with King's College London extending its lead over Leeds at the head of the table. King's has the highest entry grades and managed the best results in the 2008 Research Assessment Exercise, when two-thirds of its submission in nutritional sciences was considered world-leading or internationally excellent. But its greatest achievement in the new table is a 100 per cent employment rate, the first in the subject for eight years. Leeds has the most satisfied students, but most of the movement comes further down the table. Liverpool John Moores, for example, has jumped 15 places to 14th, just ahead of Newcastle, which has dropped nine places. Robert Gordon is the highest-placed modern university and the leader in Scotland, having moved up four places to sixth. Cardiff Metropolitan is the only university in Wales to qualify for the food science table.

The majority of the 33 institutions in the ranking are new universities, although higher entry standards and research grades ensure that their older counterparts fill eight of the top ten places. Entry standards have been rising – for the first time, none of the universities in this year's ranking averages less than 250 points – but there were little more than three applications per place in 2012. The volume of applications fell as higher fees were introduced, following three years of growth, but there was a surprise increase in the number of students actually starting courses in 2012. Almost a third of entrants to food science courses arrive with alternative qualifications to A levels.

Career prospects are good, with more than half of those completing courses going straight into graduate-level jobs and only 11 per cent without work six months after graduation. Food science is also in the top half of the graduate salaries league, with an average starting rate of more than £21,000 in professional jobs.

Universities we were unable to include this year because of insufficient data: Brighton, Central Lancashire, Huddersfield.

Employed in professional job:	50%	Employed in non-professional job and studying:	2%
Employed in professional job and studying:	3%	Employed in non-professional job:	22%
Studying:	12%	Unemployed:	11%
Average starting professional salary:	£21,009	Average starting non-professional salary:	£15,709

» Institute of Food Science and Technology: **www.ifst.org**
» Society of Food Hygiene and Technology: **www.sofht.co.uk**

Food Science

Food Science	Research quality %	Entry standards	Student satisfaction %	Graduate prospects %	Overall rating
1 King's College London	41.7	473	79.4	100.0	100.0
2 Leeds	31.7	411	94.6	81.8	96.6
3 Surrey	33.3	421	87.2	90.6	96.0
4 Nottingham	30.0	382	82.1	76.1	87.2
5 Reading	21.7	380	80.2	89.7	86.3
6 Robert Gordon		450	89.5	76.9	85.9
7 Queen's, Belfast	13.3	366	88.2	80.0	84.8
8 Heriot-Watt	16.7			81.8	84.5
9 Coventry		355	94.4	85.3	83.9
10 Ulster	11.7	317	93.3	71.2	81.8
11 Leeds Metropolitan		343	91.6	72.2	79.3
=12 Chester	5.0	322	84.7	85.7	78.8
=12 Glasgow Caledonian		358	88.3	72.7	78.8
14 Liverpool John Moores	11.7	320	84.6	73.3	78.3
15 Newcastle	18.3	398	66.8	80.0	78.1
16 Plymouth	3.3	283	89.2	75.7	76.1
=17 Sheffield Hallam		315	85.2	70.2	74.1
=17 Bournemouth		319	93.1	50.0	74.1
19 Northumbria	10.9	330	75.1	72.2	74.0
20 Oxford Brookes		368	80.9	62.5	73.8
21 Bath Spa		330	86.8	55.2	72.8
22 Queen Margaret Edinburgh		328	76.5	78.6	72.4
23 Harper Adams	8.3	283	83.8		72.3
24 Greenwich	13.3	310	74.0		70.5
25 London Metropolitan	1.7	269	72.6	93.8	70.3
26 Cardiff Metropolitan	8.3	282	83.0	53.5	70.2
=27 Manchester Metropolitan	10.0	320	79.0	44.7	69.5
=27 Westminster	15.0	284	77.0	53.2	69.5
29 Royal Agricultural University	5.0	310	77.1		69.0
30 St Mary's College		274	83.5	57.1	68.1
31 Lincoln	6.7	310	73.1	52.9	66.7
32 Roehampton		250	79.3	45.5	62.3
33 Kingston		289	76.7	26.1	59.7

French

Until the introduction of higher fees, French at degree level had avoided the decline in the take-up of modern languages seen in secondary schools. But there was a 15 per cent drop in both applications and enrolments in 2012, as all languages struggled to recruit undergraduates. French is still in a better position than other European (or world) languages but, with the decline continuing at A level, there is not a lot of leeway for many departments.

Only 586 students started degrees in French in 2012, with another 2,700 taking broader modern language courses.

Nevertheless, entry to the top courses in particular remains competitive and there were nearly six applications to the place in 2012. More than half of the 47 universities in the table averaged more than 400 points and only three had an average of less than 300. Perhaps not surprisingly, nine out of ten undergraduates enter with A levels or their equivalents, although some universities will teach the language from scratch, especially as part of joint degrees.

Oxford retains the slim lead over Cambridge that it established four years ago, thanks to the best performance in the 2008 Research Assessment Exercise, when 30 per cent of its submission was rated world-leading. Cambridge is ahead on all the other indicators and has the highest entry grades in the table. Leicester, in 18th place, has the best employment score, while Northumbria, in 27th place, has the most satisfied students. Northumbria is also the top post-1992 university and the only one in the top 30. Warwick has moved up to third, but Exeter has made the most progress in the upper reaches of the table, rising eight places to sixth.

French has dropped ten places in the employment table this year, but is still in the top half. The unemployment rate has doubled since the last edition of the *Guide*, when it was among the lowest in any subject, although it is still below the average. French has also dropped four places in the earnings league, with average starting salaries in professional jobs slightly lower than in the last edition, at a little below £20,000.

Universities we were unable to include this year because of insufficient data: Aberystwyth, York.

Employed in professional job:	41%	Employed in non-professional job and studying:	3%
Employed in professional job and studying:	3%	Employed in non-professional job:	22%
Studying:	18%	Unemployed:	12%
Average starting professional salary:	£19,921	Average starting non-professional salary:	£16,090

French	Research quality %	Entry standards	Student satisfaction %	Graduate prospects %	Overall rating
1 Oxford	41.7	557	88.5	78.2	100.0
2 Cambridge	31.7	577	91.2	80.0	99.5
3 Warwick	35.0	486	88.7	70.7	93.5
4 Southampton	38.3	454	89.7	66.7	92.9
5 Durham	26.7	529	82.9	83.2	92.4
6 Exeter	26.7	460	87.4	77.1	90.7
7 Bath	21.7	478	87.4	78.9	90.3
8 King's College London	38.3	469	78.9		89.6
9 St Andrews	26.7	503	88.3	63.0	89.5
10 Newcastle	26.7	430	87.5	75.5	89.2
11 Leeds	28.3	442	89.3	66.7	89.1
12 Glasgow	25.0	485	87.8	62.9	88.1
13 Sheffield	33.3	456	82.0	67.1	87.4
14 Nottingham	31.7	456	81.9	68.6	87.2
15 Birmingham	21.7	425	84.0	80.5	86.8

French cont

	Research quality %	Entry standards	Student satisfaction %	Graduate prospects %	Overall rating
16 University College London	25.0	496	77.2	76.2	86.0
17 Heriot-Watt	16.7	416	84.4	83.5	85.8
18 Leicester	8.3	430	85.4	88.5	85.4
19 Queen's, Belfast	20.0	392	86.7	71.6	84.3
20 Cardiff	25.0	441	82.1	66.1	84.1
21 Kent	26.7	371	89.5	58.1	83.9
22 Manchester	26.7	451	79.0	68.0	83.8
23 Reading	28.3	349	80.9	77.8	83.6
24 Aberdeen	31.7	456	76.2	65.5	83.5
25 Hull	25.0	346	86.7		83.1
26 Liverpool	23.3	406	83.0	67.5	83.0
27 Northumbria		359	96.7	73.2	82.5
28 Bristol	15.0	469	80.3	70.9	82.2
=29 Edinburgh	25.0	497	77.0	55.2	81.0
=29 Swansea	15.0	356	80.0	85.2	81.0
31 Royal Holloway	25.0	393	81.1	62.9	80.9
32 Lancaster	15.0	427	82.2	67.6	80.8
33 Stirling	13.3	372	81.9	70.4	78.6
34 Strathclyde		454	85.5	60.9	77.4
35 Aston	10.0	378	83.3	62.9	76.8
36 Queen Mary, London	25.0	395	78.4	51.0	76.7
37 Bangor		352	86.9	64.9	75.0
38 East Anglia		387	85.9	56.3	73.9
39 Portsmouth	25.0	314	75.5		73.6
=40 Chester		322	76.0	76.0	70.7
=40 Salford	12.5	329	77.5	55.0	70.7
42 Oxford Brookes	15.0	329	76.1		70.6
43 Sussex		431	85.6	27.9	68.9
44 Westminster	8.3	293	79.1		68.1
=45 Ulster	11.7	293	77.0		68.0
=45 Nottingham Trent	10.0	297	75.3	56.7	68.0
47 Manchester Metropolitan	6.7	321	71.8	42.3	62.7

» Alliance Française de Londres: **www.alliancefrancaise.org.uk**
» Chartered Institute of Linguists: **www.iol.org.uk**
» National Centre for Languages (CILT): **www.cilt.org.uk**
» Society for French Studies: **www.sfs.ac.uk**

General Engineering

Many aspiring engineers appear to have opted for the breadth of a general course, rather than specialising, when £9,000 fees arrived in 2012. The numbers starting courses in the General Engineering category rose by 15 per cent while other branches of engineering – and most other subjects – were in decline. They may have made the right decision if a high starting salary was their aim: general engineering is in the top four of this year's earnings table, with those in professional jobs averaging more than £27,000 a year. The subject is just outside the top ten for employment prospects six months after graduation.

Cambridge has extended its lead yet further at the top of the table, with the highest entry standards, the best employment record and the top grades in the 2008 Research Assessment Exercise, when 45 per cent of the university's work was classified as world-leading. Imperial, which remains in third place, had the best results in the National Student Survey. The University of the West of England is the leading post-1992 university and the only one in the top ten. Nottingham moved up three places to second, while Durham has moved up seven places to fourth. Cardiff remains the top university in Wales, while Aberdeen has that distinction in Scotland. Strathclyde, the previous leader north of the border, is one of six universities to have dropped out of the table because of low numbers.

As in the specialist branches of engineering, there is an enormous spread of entry grades, from more than 600 points at Cambridge to less than 200 at London South Bank. However, there were less than four applications per place in 2012, making admissions the least competitive in the engineering disciplines. Like other engineering degrees, most of the general courses will require both maths and physics at A level, with further maths and design technology welcome additions.

Universities we were unable to include this year because of insufficient data: Aston, Greenwich, Lancaster, Nottingham Trent, Strathclyde.

Employed in professional job:	63%	Employed in non-professional job and studying:	0%
Employed in professional job and studying:	2%	Employed in non-professional job:	10%
Studying:	13%	Unemployed:	12%
Average starting professional salary:	£27,221	Average starting non-professional salary:	£17,665

General Engineering	Research quality %	Entry standards	Student satisfaction %	Graduate prospects %	Overall rating
1 Cambridge	60.0	631	83.5	96.2	100.0
2 Nottingham	41.7	459	89.0		91.6
3 Imperial College	41.7	549	89.2	73.9	89.7
4 Durham	26.7	542	79.6	88.8	84.9
5 Warwick	36.7	494	77.7		83.9
6 Exeter	25.0	440	85.9	85.3	83.7
7 Oxford	45.0	591	73.9	70.8	83.4
8 Cardiff	35.5	377	84.1		83.2
9 West of England	25.0	351	86.2		79.9
10 Aberdeen	31.7	391	77.0		77.8
11 Edinburgh Napier	13.3	327	84.6	82.4	76.1

General Engineering cont	Research quality %	Entry standards	Student satisfaction %	Graduate prospects %	Overall rating
12 Swansea	36.7	338	64.5	90.9	75.0
13 Bournemouth	16.7	280	75.4	94.4	74.4
14 Queen Mary, London	21.7	373	81.5	66.7	73.8
15 Liverpool John Moores	33.3	279	74.2	67.6	70.9
16 Leicester	25.0	366	70.4	73.3	70.8
17 Ulster		273	86.3	77.0	70.4
18 De Montfort	13.3	242	80.1		67.8
19 London South Bank	23.3	175	72.0	78.9	67.3
20 Sheffield Hallam	15.0	273	72.5	69.9	65.7
21 Bradford	17.3	281	70.6		64.5
22 Glasgow Caledonian	6.7	303	66.7	80.0	64.3
23 Central Lancashire	10.0	264	82.8	46.2	62.7
24 Birmingham City		293	73.6	64.3	61.4

» Engineering Council: **www.engc.org.uk**
» EngineeringUK: **www.engineeringuk.com**
» Institution of Engineering and Technology: **www.theiet.org**

Geography and Environmental Sciences

Geography and environmental sciences continue to benefit from strong interest in "green" issues among prospective students. Environmental sciences and both human and social geography recruited almost the same numbers of students in 2012 as they had before the fees went up. And the trend has continued in 2013, with the subjects now well ahead of their recruitment in 2010. The subjects' attractions do not seem to be related to career prospects since geography and environmental science are only just in the top 50 in the employment table. They fare better in the comparison of earnings, although the £20,293 average starting salary in professional jobs is only a slight improvement on last year.

Cambridge remains top of the table, but Durham is close behind, having overtaken Oxford this year. Cambridge has the highest entry standards and one of the best research scores. The top four in the table all had 30 per cent of their research rated as world-leading in the 2008 assessments. Derby, although only just in the top 50, has the most satisfied students, while Durham has easily the best of generally mediocre set of employment scores. Only three of the 72 universities saw 80 per cent or more of leavers go straight into professional jobs or further study and the proportion dropped below 40 per cent at four of them.

St Andrews has enjoyed a meteoric rise up the table, jumping 20 places to fifth and becoming the leader in Scotland, while Cardiff has risen ten places to move clear of the competition in Wales. Coventry, at 33rd, is the highest-placed post-1992 university and, with Chester, the only two in the top 40. Entry scores have risen since last year. Six universities average more than 500 points and more than a third of the institutions in the table top 400 points. For environmental science, most of the leading universities will ask for two from biology, chemistry, maths, physics and geography at A level.

Employed in professional job:	33%	Employed in non-professional job and studying:	3%		
Employed in professional job and studying:	2%	Employed in non-professional job:	27%		
Studying:	20%	Unemployed:	14%		
Average starting professional salary:	£20,293	Average starting non-professional salary:	£14,449		

Geography and Environmental Sciences	Research quality %	Entry standards	Student satisfaction %	Graduate prospects %	Overall rating
1 Cambridge	43.3	566	87.8	81.7	100.0
2 Durham	43.3	512	87.1	88.8	99.2
3 Oxford	43.3	555	84.6	76.4	96.6
4 Bristol	43.3	490	83.5	77.4	93.8
5 St Andrews	33.3	526	84.8	70.4	91.9
6 Cardiff	37.8	371	88.7	79.3	91.5
7 East Anglia	39.0	432	88.2	67.5	91.1
8 Sheffield	36.7	440	89.3	64.9	90.9
9 London School of Economics	36.7	472	80.6	76.6	89.7
10 Exeter	33.3	441	86.7	68.5	89.5
=11 University College London	38.3	513	76.9	76.4	89.4
=11 Manchester	31.7	435	87.8	68.0	89.4
13 Lancaster	33.3	435	86.6	68.1	89.1
14 Nottingham	33.3	444	82.9	75.8	89.0
15 King's College London	36.7	428	83.0	71.7	88.3
=16 Southampton	35.0	435	82.2	70.0	87.4
=16 Glasgow	22.2	456	87.1	67.6	87.4
18 Queen Mary, London	41.7	389	87.1	54.9	86.8
19 Reading	37.6	386	82.9	69.9	86.6
20 Loughborough	23.3	409	87.0	69.9	86.4
=21 Leeds	40.0	426	81.1	63.6	86.2
=21 Dundee	30.0	403	89.8	55.6	86.2
23 Edinburgh	31.7	504	79.1	63.9	85.9
=24 Swansea	30.0	377	80.6	82.3	85.8
=24 Birmingham	28.3	424	82.1	72.4	85.8
=24 Royal Holloway	35.0	371	89.7	53.8	85.8
27 York	26.7	384	86.7	68.0	85.7
28 Newcastle	25.0	404	83.6	73.4	85.4
29 Aberdeen	23.3	418	85.3	68.1	85.3
30 Leicester	20.0	413	82.9	71.1	83.6
31 Liverpool	25.0	403	85.0	57.4	82.6
32 Aberystwyth	35.0	353	83.4	55.2	81.8
33 Coventry	6.7	315	93.5	59.6	80.4
34 Strathclyde	6.7	470	87.5	49.0	80.3
35 Hull	28.3	332	84.6	55.3	80.1
36 Queen's, Belfast	23.3	340	88.4	48.2	79.9
37 Stirling	16.7	375	81.8	64.7	79.4
38 Chester	3.3	304	90.1	68.0	79.1

Geography and Environmental Sciences cont

		Research quality %	Entry standards	Student satisfaction %	Graduate prospects %	Overall rating
39	Keele		359	85.6	72.0	78.6
40	Sussex	31.7	409	77.3	45.5	77.4
41	Gloucestershire	5.0	272	91.7	58.3	77.1
42	Plymouth	21.4	314	82.3	54.5	76.3
43	Portsmouth	13.3	316	88.3	46.9	76.2
44	Bradford	30.0	268	84.3	45.2	75.7
45	West of England	6.7	311	85.2	58.9	75.3
46	Northampton	7.7	285	87.1	53.6	74.5
47	Highlands and Islands	16.7	319			73.6
=48	Worcester	3.3	303	84.7	54.6	73.0
=48	Derby		267	94.5	38.8	73.0
50	Ulster	16.7	262	85.7	43.9	72.9
51	Bangor		328	83.7	54.7	72.5
52	Sheffield Hallam	30.0	336	76.0	40.5	72.4
53	Northumbria		328	88.2	40.7	72.1
54	Central Lancashire		277	88.9	46.9	72.0
=55	Oxford Brookes		324	86.1	45.4	71.7
=55	Manchester Metropolitan	16.5	304	78.8	50.0	71.7
57	Edge Hill	1.7	270	89.0	43.5	71.4
58	Liverpool John Moores		300	92.0	31.6	71.2
59	Brighton	13.3	306	80.5	45.1	70.9
60	Bath Spa	5.0	302	84.2	43.9	70.7
61	Canterbury Christ Church		291	86.5	41.1	69.8
=62	Greenwich		264	87.0	41.2	69.1
=62	Sunderland	3.3		74.4	66.7	69.1
64	Staffordshire		243	80.5	60.0	68.8
65	Nottingham Trent	1.7	293	85.3	36.8	68.6
66	Hertfordshire		306	82.6	40.5	68.0
67	Leeds Metropolitan		274	82.5	45.5	67.9
68	Salford	13.3	253	75.1	46.2	66.1
69	Kingston	13.3	297	68.9	52.1	65.5
70	Bournemouth	21.7	308	70.0	29.6	63.5
71	Southampton Solent		235	72.0	45.5	60.4
72	Cumbria		244	70.9	43.6	59.6

» British Cartographic Society: **www.cartography.org.uk**
» Royal Geographical Society (with the Institute of British Geographers): **www.rgs.org**
» Royal Scottish Geographical Society: **www.rsgs.org**

Geology

Starting salaries for graduate geologists shot up by more than £3,500 in last year's *Guide*, propelling the subject into the top ten from outside the top 20, where it has generally been in the past. The figure looked like an anomaly but even after a £1,000 drop this year, average starting salaries are in the top 15. The subject has also survived the switch to higher fees, with both applications and enrolment reaching record levels in 2012 after small increases at a time when demand was dropping in most subjects.

Cambridge remains well clear of the field in geology, with the best performance in the 2008 Research Assessment Exercise and has the highest entry standards in the table. Imperial College, which has overtaken Oxford to take second place, has the best of a stellar set of ratings in the 2013 National Student Survey. Its 99 per cent satisfaction rating was among the best in any subject and even Derby, one place off the bottom of the table, managed 92 per cent. Aberystwyth has the best employment record with 100 per cent of graduates gaining a professional job or going on to further study. All but four of the 27 institutions in this year's ranking are pre-1992 universities. Plymouth is again the highest-placed of the newer foundations, while Cardiff is the leading university in Wales, and St Andrews is the clear leader in Scotland after moving up four places to fourth.

Outside the top three, there is less contrast in entry standards in geology than in many other subjects. The average is above 300 points at all but two universities in the ranking and is above 400 at practically all of the top 20. Some of the leading universities expect candidates to have two, or even three, scientific or mathematical subjects at A level. Relatively few places are filled in Clearing. Geology's mid-table position for employment prospects does not match its performance on salaries. The unemployment level is above the average for all subjects, having jumped from 10 to 15 per cent this year, but nearly two-thirds of geologists go on to professional jobs or further study within six months of graduation.

University we were unable to include this year because of insufficient data: Kingston.

Employed in professional job:	36%	Employed in non-professional job and studying:	1%
Employed in professional job and studying:	1%	Employed in non-professional job:	19%
Studying:	27%	Unemployed:	15%
Average starting professional salary:	£23,766	Average starting non-professional salary:	£14,320

Geology	Research quality %	Entry standards	Student satisfaction %	Graduate prospects %	Overall rating
1 Cambridge	56.7	651	88.8	86.1	100.0
2 Imperial College	40.0	528	99.5	82.5	95.9
3 Oxford	51.7	626	78.3	82.8	91.8
4 St Andrews	33.3	478	87.6	96.8	89.6
5 Durham	33.3	482	83.9	95.0	87.5
6 Southampton	36.7	419	89.4	80.5	86.0
7 Royal Holloway	36.7	357	88.0	79.0	83.0
8 University College London	43.3	472	77.6		82.3
9 East Anglia	40.0	412	90.0	57.9	82.1
10 Liverpool	35.0	408	86.7	67.9	81.1

Geology cont	Research quality %	Entry standards	Student satisfaction %	Graduate prospects %	Overall rating
11 Bristol	41.7	467	79.1	63.8	80.2
12 Edinburgh	33.3	504	77.4	71.1	79.7
13 Leicester	28.3	414	87.5	65.8	79.4
14 Exeter	15.0	407	90.7	75.9	79.2
15 Leeds	33.3	411	82.7	67.2	78.6
16 Aberdeen	26.7	413	78.8	82.5	78.1
=17 Manchester	36.7	402	77.3	70.1	77.2
=17 Birmingham	31.7	404	78.8	73.0	77.2
19 Cardiff	33.3	397	79.7	67.4	76.7
20 Glasgow	21.7	449	86.1	53.7	75.3
21 Plymouth	21.4	308	93.8	55.1	74.8
22 Aberystwyth		327	82.0	100.0	73.3
23 Bangor	26.7	302	81.9		71.7
=24 Keele		347	89.6	56.0	68.1
=24 Brighton	13.3	313	81.8	61.5	68.1
26 Derby		285	91.8	55.1	67.1
27 Portsmouth	18.3	286	78.3	58.9	66.3

» Geological Society: **www.geolsoc.org.uk**

German

Fewer than 200 students began degrees in German in 2012, down by almost a third on the previous year, although many others are learning the language as part of a broader degree. There was little sign of a recovery in the 2013 applications. The introduction of £9,000 fees undoubtedly contributed to the fall, but there has been a worldwide decline in the language that has been worrying the German government, as well as academic linguists. Five more universities have dropped out of the table this year because their student numbers were too small to compile reliable averages on some measures, although only East Anglia has ceased to offer degrees in the subject.

Cambridge makes it eight years in a row as the leader in German, but Warwick has moved up four places to become the nearest challenger, registering the best score in the 2013 National Student Survey. Satisfaction levels remained high throughout the table. Only University College London failed to satisfy at least 75 per cent of final-year undergraduates, but it was also the only university to see 90 per cent of graduates go straight into professional employment or further study.

Southampton had the best results in the 2008 Research Assessment Exercise. Fifth-placed St Andrews remains the leading university in Scotland, while Swansea has overtaken Cardiff in Wales. Portsmouth is one of just three post-1992 universities left in the ranking and the only one in the top 25.

Despite the recruitment difficulties in German departments, there are still almost six applications for every place. Nine out of ten undergraduates enter with A levels or equivalent qualifications, and entry standards are relatively high, especially at the leading universities. At two-thirds of the universities in the table, entrants average at least 400 points.

As in other modern languages, career prospects are reasonable, although the unemployment rate has more than doubled since last year's *Guide*. Two-thirds of leavers go straight into graduate jobs or further study. German is a little below average for starting salaries, which have dropped by £750 since the last edition. Most universities in the table offer German from scratch as part of a languages package, as well as catering for those who took the subject at A level.

Universities we were unable to include this year because of insufficient data: Aberdeen, Bangor, East Anglia, Exeter, Hull.

German	Research quality %	Entry Standards	Student satisfaction %	Graduate prospects %	Overall rating
1 Cambridge	35.0	577	91.2	80.0	100.0
2 Warwick	25.0	468	93.4	87.6	96.0
3 Oxford	35.0	597	85.7	71.5	95.7
4 Durham	33.3	529	82.9	83.2	94.0
5 St Andrews	33.3	489	86.1		93.8
6 Southampton	38.3	472	89.6	65.5	92.8
7 Birmingham	30.0	436	84.3	84.0	90.5
8 Newcastle	28.3	427	88.5	77.1	90.3
9 University College London	35.0	488	73.3	90.3	89.6
10 Bath	21.7	454	87.6	79.3	89.3
11 Leeds	33.3	444	89.6	60.0	88.9
12 Royal Holloway	31.7	399	85.8		88.5
13 Edinburgh	33.3	494	81.7	66.7	88.1
14 King's College London	36.7	425	80.2		87.8
15 Glasgow	18.3	502	85.9	71.4	87.3
16 Bristol	26.7	444	81.6	76.6	86.6
17 Heriot-Watt	16.7	416	84.4	83.5	85.8
18 Manchester	31.7	426	85.0	60.5	85.4
19 Swansea	23.3	370	87.0	72.4	84.7
20 Nottingham	20.0	424	85.0	71.0	84.3
21 Liverpool	21.7		81.6	76.2	84.2
22 Sheffield	16.7	471	79.0	70.7	81.8
23 Cardiff	25.0	364	80.3		80.2
24 Reading	16.7	354	83.1		78.4
25 Portsmouth	25.0	309	75.5	75.4	77.6
26 Lancaster	15.0	407	79.2		77.5
27 Kent	10.0	355	83.2		75.8
28 Queen Mary, London	16.7	375	77.6		75.5
29 Aston	10.0	420	76.7		74.3
30 Manchester Metropolitan	6.7	321	76.5	43.5	65.3
31 Nottingham Trent		297	75.3	56.7	65.0

German cont

Employed in professional job:	45%	Employed in non-professional job and studying:	3%
Employed in professional job and studying:	3%	Employed in non-professional job:	20%
Studying:	17%	Unemployed:	13%
Average starting professional salary:	£20,263	Average starting non-professional salary:	£15,288

» Chartered Institute of Linguists: **www.iol.org.uk**
» Goethe-Institut: **www.goethe.de/enindex.htm**
» National Centre for Languages (CILT): **www.cilt.org.uk**

History

History remains close to the top ten subjects as a degree choice, despite being equally close to the bottom ten for employment. More historians are in non-professional jobs than those categorised as professional occupations six months after completing a degree. Yet history survived the introduction of higher fees with only a minuscule drop in the number of students taking up places and there was further improvement in 2013. The subject is among the most competitive at entry, with almost six applications to every place in 2012. Surveys have shown a strong representation of historians among business leaders, celebrities and senior politicians, but starting salaries in professional jobs are still slightly below average.

Durham and Cambridge have been taking it in turns to lead the history table for the last four years, and remain less than a point apart. Durham is top in the latest edition, thanks to the best employment record and a high score for student satisfaction. Cambridge has the highest entry standards and shares the best research score with University College London. In fact, Imperial College's work on the history of science won the top grade in the 2008 Research Assessment Exercise, but history is not an undergraduate subject at Imperial so it does not appear in this table.

For the third successive year, the most satisfied students are at Derby, which is not among the top 70 universities in the ranking. Satisfaction levels are high throughout the ranking: all but one university has at least a 70 per cent approval rating. The older institutions continue to dominate the table: only Oxford Brookes, of the modern universities, appears in the top 30, with Portsmouth, Huddersfield and Winchester joining it in the top 40. St Andrews remains the top university in Scotland, while Cardiff does the same in Wales.

Average entry scores at eight of the top ten universities are over 500 points, the equivalent of more than four As at A level, and only one institution averages less than 250 points. But employment scores are much more variable and at eight universities less than a third of those graduating in 2012 had found professional jobs or started postgraduate courses by the end of the year.

University we were unable to include this year because of insufficient data: Bishop Grosseteste.

» Historical Association: **www.history.org.uk**
» Royal Historical Society: **www.royalhistoricalsociety.org**

History

	Research quality %	Entry standards	Student satisfaction %	Graduate prospects %	Overall rating
1 Durham	33.3	561	92.1	84.3	100.0
2 Cambridge	48.3	581	87.6	74.8	99.2
3 Oxford	46.7	567	87.3	72.8	97.8
4 Warwick	45.0	499	85.3	81.2	95.6
5 London School of Economics	45.0	529	86.6	71.1	95.4
6 Exeter	33.3	505	91.2	73.2	95.3
7 University College London	48.3	502	84.3	70.0	93.6
8 St Andrews	33.3	528	85.7	77.1	93.5
9 York	35.0	510	83.9	72.0	91.1
10 Sheffield	45.0	478	85.2	62.2	91.0
11 King's College London	36.7	500	83.1	72.8	90.8
12 Southampton	43.3	444	86.1	64.3	90.5
13 Kent	46.7	407	87.0	63.7	90.4
14 Glasgow	36.7	477	88.7	55.2	89.9
15 Liverpool	46.7	416	88.2	55.4	89.8
16 Newcastle	23.3	439	89.0	72.7	89.4
17 East Anglia	33.3	440	88.6	58.3	88.5
18 Lancaster	28.3	459	86.0	67.5	88.3
19 Queen Mary, London	40.0	435	81.3	68.8	87.5
20 Leeds	31.7	477	85.0	58.7	87.2
21 Birmingham	33.3	436	82.4	70.5	87.1
22 Royal Holloway	33.3	423	85.3	62.6	86.8
23 Manchester	37.1	464	80.8	63.3	86.3
24 SOAS London	40.0	415	81.7	64.6	86.1
25 Aberdeen	40.0	430	85.7	49.4	86.0
26 Bristol	28.3	491	76.3	78.2	85.6
27 Leicester	30.0	416	86.3	58.1	85.5
28 Nottingham	26.7	467	81.5	66.9	85.3
29 Oxford Brookes	38.3	379	87.2	51.2	85.2
30 Keele	31.7	354	88.1	58.0	84.9
31 Queen's, Belfast	30.0	374	87.9	53.2	84.1
32 Portsmouth	25.0	319	89.9	59.8	83.7
33 Sussex	38.3	424	82.8	48.6	83.5
=34 Hull	31.7	368	88.3	47.4	83.3
=34 Huddersfield	18.3	349	89.0	62.5	83.3
=36 Cardiff	21.7	438	86.0	52.0	83.0
=36 Dundee	31.7	384	89.2	40.6	83.0
38 Winchester	28.3	324	92.8	42.4	82.9
39 Edinburgh	36.7	494	76.2	54.7	82.7
=40 Swansea	26.7	367	84.9	59.6	82.6
=40 Essex	46.7	379	84.8	36.4	82.6
42 Chester	25.0	321	85.8	65.9	82.5
43 Loughborough		419	87.4	66.7	81.5

History cont	Research quality %	Entry standards	Student satisfaction %	Graduate prospects %	Overall rating
44 Reading	23.3	395	83.2	54.2	80.6
45 Strathclyde	16.7	454	82.6	52.7	80.5
46 Teesside	23.3	328	86.7	50.7	79.9
47 Hertfordshire	40.0	321	80.8	51.4	79.7
=48 Brighton	45.0	300	80.1		79.4
=48 Stirling	26.7	402	83.3	43.2	79.4
50 Bangor	26.7	308	85.3	52.1	79.3
51 Sunderland	21.7	258	92.3	43.3	79.1
52 Anglia Ruskin	33.3	271	86.0	44.7	78.5
53 Lincoln	13.3	333	85.4	56.2	78.1
54 Northumbria	6.7	359	86.3	54.4	77.8
55 Brunel		348	93.3	41.8	77.7
56 Roehampton	18.3	315	85.8	46.0	76.8
=57 Greenwich	18.3	278	88.0	45.0	76.7
=57 Staffordshire		274	93.1	50.0	76.7
=57 Goldsmiths College	16.7	363	83.9	44.9	76.7
60 Nottingham Trent	13.3	337	84.5	47.5	75.9
61 Chichester	10.0	308	89.6	40.0	75.8
62 Aberystwyth	21.7	343	81.1	45.5	75.4
63 Northampton	16.7	276	85.7	47.0	75.3
64 Leeds Trinity	11.7	256	91.2	37.0	74.9
65 St Mary's College		321	86.8	50.5	74.5
=66 Manchester Metropolitan	6.7	325	83.0	52.0	74.1
=66 Ulster	28.3	275	82.8	37.6	74.1
68 Edge Hill	15.0	306	85.1	39.2	74.0
69 Plymouth	8.3	318	83.2	47.4	73.4
70 Gloucestershire	11.7	305	81.3	51.2	73.3
=71 Derby		268	93.7	31.5	73.2
=71 De Montfort	15.0	309	83.0	41.7	73.2
73 West of England	16.7	333	82.6	36.0	73.0
74 Coventry		291	90.4	35.4	72.7
75 Canterbury Christ Church	10.0	287	88.3	30.9	72.5
76 Newman	0.0	316	91.1	23.9	71.6
77 Bath Spa	18.3	324	78.7	39.0	71.3
=78 Central Lancashire	18.3	305	80.1	37.0	71.1
=78 Westminster	5.0	301	83.1	42.5	71.1
80 Glyndŵr		278	81.7	51.7	70.2
81 Sheffield Hallam	16.7	308	81.5	28.3	69.9
82 Worcester	0.0	289	83.1	41.9	69.4
83 Leeds Metropolitan		236	80.7	48.9	67.6
84 Liverpool John Moores	5.0	331	79.3	27.9	66.7
85 York St John		312	79.9	32.0	66.2
86 Kingston	13.3	284	74.0	38.7	66.0

87 Salford		11.7	311	68.8	46.0	64.8
88 Cumbria		6.7			28.6	63.1
89 Bradford		11.7	311	71.0	28.6	62.5

Employed in professional job:	26%	Employed in non-professional job and studying:	4%
Employed in professional job and studying:	3%	Employed in non-professional job:	30%
Studying:	23%	Unemployed:	14%
Average starting professional salary:	£20,759	Average starting non-professional salary:	£14,582

History of Art, Architecture and Design

Oxford has held on to top place in the history of art, architecture and design, even though it does not lead on any single measure. East Anglia has made the most progress, moving up seven places to second and sharing the best score in the 2013 National Student Survey with third-placed Glasgow, which also has the top research grades. In the 2008 Research Assessment Exercise, 85 per cent of its work was classified as world-leading or internationally excellent. But the year's outstanding performance was by Birmingham, where every graduate was in a professional job or on a postgraduate course within six months of graduating in a subject that is not normally considered a sure thing in the employment market. Overall, the subject is only just in the top 50 for positive destinations, with an above-average unemployment rate. The specialised nature of the jobs market has always made for uncertain prospects immediately after graduation, but history of art has moved out of the bottom 20 for starting salaries after a £1,000 increase since the last *Guide*.

There were good scores for most universities in the 2013 National Student Survey, although no university satisfied more nine out of ten final-year undergraduates. All 27 institutions in the ranking had satisfaction scores of more than 70 per cent. The majority of students are female and entry standards are high. Two-thirds of the universities in the table average more than 400 points – nearly twice as many as two years ago – and for the first time none has an average below 300. Neither history nor art is required at A level, although admissions officers might be sceptical if neither subject was among a candidate's qualifications.

Two universities have dropped out of the table this year because of low numbers in some categories, but 36 institutions expect to offer courses in the history of art in 2014. Only five post-1992 universities are left in the ranking, with Oxford Brookes the highest-placed, just inside the top 20. Glasgow is the top university in Scotland, while Aberystwyth is the only Welsh representative in the table.

Universities we were unable to include this year because of insufficient data: Aberdeen, Sheffield Hallam.

Employed in professional job:	32%	Employed in non-professional job and studying:	4%
Employed in professional job and studying:	2%	Employed in non-professional job:	27%
Studying:	19%	Unemployed:	15%
Average starting professional salary:	£19,446	Average starting non-professional salary:	£14,962

History of Art, Architecture and Design	Research quality %	Entry standards	Student satisfaction %	Graduate prospects %	Overall rating
1 Oxford	46.7	545	86.9		100.0
2 East Anglia	56.7	433	88.7	67.2	97.5
3 Glasgow	58.3	490	88.7	51.6	97.4
4 Cambridge	26.7	582	87.6	66.7	96.2
5 Birmingham	43.3	412	82.5	100.0	95.4
=6 University College London	46.7	489	84.1	71.9	95.3
=6 York	53.3	431	86.6	66.7	95.3
8 St Andrews	35.0	501	85.9	75.0	95.1
9 Courtauld	53.3	492	76.3	83.3	93.6
10 Sussex	53.3	454	82.8	46.9	90.4
11 Manchester	53.3	437	81.7	54.6	90.3
12 Essex	41.7	399	85.2		89.8
13 Warwick	33.3	476	85.5	47.5	88.9
=14 Leeds	31.7	402	85.0	60.6	87.7
=14 Reading	30.0	384	85.6	64.9	87.7
16 Nottingham	38.3	413	82.4	60.0	87.6
17 SOAS London	36.7	404	81.7	65.2	87.4
18 Goldsmiths College	30.0	414	83.9	52.2	85.7
19 Oxford Brookes	28.3	367	87.2	43.1	84.2
20 Edinburgh	30.0	459	75.8	59.7	83.3
21 Leicester	20.0	379	85.3	43.8	81.8
22 Bristol	25.0	469	75.1	56.1	81.6
23 Plymouth	21.7	305	83.2	51.7	79.4
24 Brighton	45.0	300	81.4	29.4	79.0
25 Manchester Metropolitan	21.7	342	83.0	30.8	77.1
26 Aberystwyth	11.7	333	81.1		74.7
27 Kingston	23.3	328	74.0	44.8	73.4

» Association of Art Historians: **www.aah.org.uk**
» Society of Architectural Historians of Great Britain: **www.sahgb.org.uk**

Hospitality, Leisure, Recreation and Tourism

This group of subjects covers a variety of courses directed towards management in the leisure and tourism industries, mainly delivered at modern universities. It remains in the top 20 for applications, but has slipped into the bottom two in the employment table with the largest proportion of graduates in any subject (41 per cent) beginning their careers in lower-level jobs. The numbers starting courses fell by 10 per cent when higher fees arrived in 2012. It is in the bottom 20 for graduate starting salaries.

Only eight institutions in the table are pre-1992 universities, but three of them fill the top three positions. Surrey remains clear at the top, with its 40-year reputation in hotel and tourism management. It is one of only six universities with average entry grades of more than 350 points and it had the best score in the 2008 Research Assessment Exercise (RAE). Stirling, in second place, has narrowed the gap on Surrey this year, while Exeter, in third, boasts the highest entry standards. Birmingham, which would have finished higher than tenth place if it had entered the RAE in this category, has the best employment score. Only 15 of the 49 universities and colleges in the table did. Even in the top 20, some universities saw fewer than 40 per cent of graduates going into graduate-level jobs or further study. However, starting salaries in professional jobs have improved by more than £1,000 since the last *Guide*, moving the subjects out of the bottom 15 in the earnings table.

Satisfaction rates are generally high, the most satisfied students being at Sunderland; only four universities failed to achieve at least 70 per cent approval in the 2013 National Student Survey. Sheffield Hallam has overtaken Central Lancashire to take fourth place and become the highest-placed post-1992 university. They are joined in the top ten by Manchester Metropolitan, Chester, Hertfordshire and Bournemouth. Cardiff Metropolitan is the only university in the table from Wales since the withdrawal of the new University of South Wales from this year's tables.

Universities we were unable to include this year because of insufficient data: Glasgow Caledonian, Strathclyde.

Employed in professional job:	38%	Employed in non-professional job and studying:	2%
Employed in professional job and studying:	1%	Employed in non-professional job:	41%
Studying:	4%	Unemployed:	14%
Average starting professional salary:	£19,021	Average starting non-professional salary:	£15,285

Hospitality, Leisure, Recreation and Tourism	Research quality %	Entry standards	Student satisfaction %	Graduate prospects %	Overall rating
1 Surrey	23.3	367	91.5	46.7	100.0
2 Stirling	20.9	395	81.1	53.4	96.4
3 Exeter		455	83.6	82.3	92.9
4 Sheffield Hallam	18.3	314	85.1	57.6	91.9
5 Central Lancashire	21.7	289	80.8	45.2	87.6
6 Manchester Metropolitan	15.0	307	75.8	58.2	84.4
=7 Chester	11.7	269	86.2	54.3	83.7
=7 Hertfordshire	15.0	317	81.0	40.8	83.7
9 Bournemouth	13.3	325	74.5	51.5	82.2
10 Birmingham		357	75.2	83.3	82.1
11 Brighton	18.3	264	83.8	31.6	81.8
12 Plymouth	14.1	284	80.4	39.2	80.0
13 Sunderland	13.3	251	92.2	24.7	79.9
14 Oxford Brookes		321	80.1	71.9	79.5
15 Cardiff Metropolitan	11.7	300	80.3	37.1	78.8
16 Robert Gordon		327	83.6	59.1	78.7
17 Manchester		360	81.8	52.9	78.6

Hospitality, Leisure, Recreation and Tourism cont

	Research quality %	Entry standards	Student satisfaction %	Graduate prospects %	Overall rating
18 Lincoln		295	80.4	67.7	76.9
19 University of the Arts, London		359	73.3	62.5	76.5
20 Salford	13.3	299	73.7	36.0	76.4
21 Coventry		276	86.6	52.9	75.3
22 Edinburgh Napier		339	79.6	45.9	74.5
=23 Northampton		281	85.5	48.9	74.2
=23 The Arts University at Bournemouth		300	71.1	75.0	74.2
25 Liverpool John Moores		318	85.5	31.4	72.7
=26 Chichester		249	84.9	52.2	72.4
=26 Leeds Metropolitan		280	77.5	58.8	72.4
=28 Derby		270	82.4	44.1	70.8
=28 West of England	6.7	301	72.9		70.8
30 Huddersfield		277	77.6	52.2	70.6
31 Westminster		283	82.4	35.9	69.8
32 Gloucestershire		293	74.2	50.0	69.5
33 Southampton Solent		270	73.7	52.1	68.2
34 Ulster		246	87.3	28.8	68.1
35 West London		219	84.4	42.2	67.9
=36 Greenwich		283	73.5	41.0	66.4
=36 Queen Margaret Edinburgh		270	77.0	36.9	66.4
38 Buckinghamshire New		235	76.8	42.9	65.2
39 London South Bank		221	79.7	40.0	65.0
40 Portsmouth		245	72.6	47.4	64.8
41 Winchester		297	75.9	23.9	64.7
=42 Canterbury Christ Church		241	77.0	38.2	64.6
=42 Bedfordshire	10.0	185	72.7	31.8	64.6
44 West of Scotland		258	77.3	31.0	64.3
45 Hull		278	82.0	8.3	62.9
46 Staffordshire		208	69.0	41.7	59.1
47 Middlesex		231	67.6	37.6	59.0
48 St Mary's College		261	64.1	33.7	58.4
49 London Metropolitan		231	56.5	40.3	54.0

» Association for Tourism in Higher Education: **www.athe.org.uk**
» Council for Hospitality Management Education: **www.chme.org.uk**
» Institute of Hospitality: **www.instituteofhospitality.org**
» Leisure Studies Association:
www.leisure-studies-association.info/LSAWEB/Index.html

Iberian Languages

Spanish has been gaining on French as the most popular language at degree level, following its rise at school level. But still fewer than 400 students started courses when the fees went up in 2012 – a 15 per cent decline on the previous year. The table also includes Portuguese, which saw its numbers quadruple in the same year. The statistic would be more impressive if there had been more than one student embarking on single honours in 2011. Nevertheless, more than 20 universities intend to offer courses in 2014, mainly in combination with other languages, including with Czech at Bristol.

Cambridge has extended its lead at the top of the table, with Durham moving ahead of Oxford into second place. Oxford has the highest entry standards but Aston, in 18th place, has a fractionally higher score than Cambridge in the 2013 National Student Survey. Stirling has easily the best employment record, while Nottingham and Manchester tied for the best performance in the 2008 Research Assessment Exercise. Only four of the 42 institutions in the ranking are post-1992 universities; four others have dropped out since last year. Northumbria is the highest-placed, while Portsmouth, one place lower, makes the top 30 for the sixth year in a row. St Andrews, in sixth place, is the top university in Scotland, while Swansea has that distinction in Wales.

There are high levels of student satisfaction in most universities. Only two failed to satisfy at least 70 per cent of final-year undergraduates. Entry standards have continued to rise: more than half of the universities in the table average over 400 points and five have averages of more than 500. However, Iberian languages have dropped into the bottom half of the employment table this year and they are in the bottom 20 for starting salaries in graduate jobs, after a second successive drop in average earnings six months after graduation.

Universities we were unable to include this year because of insufficient data: Chester, Liverpool John Moores, Roehampton, Westminster.

Employed in professional job:	40%	Employed in non-professional job and studying:	2%
Employed in professional job and studying:	4%	Employed in non-professional job:	24%
Studying:	18%	Unemployed:	13%
Average starting professional salary:	£19,405	Average starting non-professional salary:	£15,406

Iberian Languages	Research quality %	Entry standards	Student satisfaction %	Graduate prospects %	Overall rating
1 Cambridge	43.3	577	91.2	80.0	100.0
2 Durham	35.0	529	82.9	83.2	92.3
3 Oxford	30.0	588	87.7	66.7	92.1
4 Southampton	38.3	459	87.4	80.0	91.9
5 Newcastle	26.7	455	87.7	86.0	90.1
6 St Andrews	28.3	530	81.7	75.0	88.1
=7 Leeds	33.3	457	83.6	76.5	87.7
=7 Bath	21.7	473	88.2	76.8	87.7
9 Leicester	20.0	435	88.5	78.6	86.2

Iberian Languages cont

	Research quality %	Entry standards	Student satisfaction %	Graduate prospects %	Overall rating
10 Nottingham	45.0	446	82.1	58.9	85.6
11 Queen's, Belfast	28.3	385	87.5	75.8	85.3
12 Sheffield	35.0	438	84.5	64.8	85.2
13 Heriot-Watt	16.7	416	84.4	83.5	83.6
=14 Exeter	25.0	463	84.3	56.8	81.6
=14 Manchester	45.0	448	72.4	62.6	81.6
16 Glasgow	13.3	465	79.3	80.0	81.3
17 Aberdeen	21.7	446	81.3		81.1
18 Aston	10.0	387	91.6		80.8
19 Stirling	13.3	351	82.5	90.2	80.6
20 Birmingham	20.0	395	79.1	79.5	80.0
21 Bristol	16.7	466	77.0	75.0	79.9
=22 University College London	21.7	506	69.5	78.3	79.8
=22 Queen Mary, London	36.7	390	79.0	59.7	79.8
24 Royal Holloway	25.0	375	78.7	70.4	78.3
25 Strathclyde	6.7	446	83.7		77.4
26 Swansea	21.7	342	81.5	65.5	76.3
27 Northumbria		357	87.2	74.4	76.1
28 Portsmouth	25.0	326	75.5	75.4	75.8
=29 Edinburgh	26.7	496	68.5	58.0	75.6
=29 Kent	11.7	351	86.1		75.6
=29 Cardiff	25.0	395	78.6	55.3	75.6
32 Liverpool	26.7	384	82.7	44.4	75.2
33 Lancaster	15.0	397	79.4		74.8
34 Sussex		421	89.4	50.7	74.4
35 King's College London	37.5	448	71.7	40.9	74.3
36 East Anglia		419	86.2	48.5	72.2
37 Hull		371	85.7	51.4	70.6
38 Salford	12.5	332	76.7	55.2	68.7
39 Manchester Metropolitan	6.7	332	78.8	54.2	68.0
40 Bangor	11.7	284	74.9		64.4
41 Nottingham Trent		297	75.3	56.7	63.5
42 Ulster	3.3	274	75.0		60.9

» Association for Contemporary Iberian Studies: **www.iberianstudies.net**
» Association of Hispanists of Great Britain and Ireland: **www.dur.ac.uk/hispanists**
» Instituto Cervantes: **http://londres.cervantes.es/en/default.shtm**

Italian

Five more universities plan to offer Italian in 2014, giving students 36 to choose from. Only 47 undergraduates started degrees in Italian in 2012 – 18 down on the previous year – but many more will have included it in broader language degrees or in combination with subjects such as business studies. A relatively high proportion of the places are filled in Clearing. Most students have no previous knowledge of Italian, although they are likely to have taken another language at A level.

The low numbers can make for big swings in the annual statistics: in last year's *Guide*, for example, starting salaries had gone up by more than £1,000, but they are back to their previous level in the latest edition, leaving Italian just outside the bottom ten subjects. Cambridge, which has extended its already considerable lead over Oxford again this year, registered the top grades in the 2008 Research Assessment Exercise, when 80 per cent of its submission was judged to be world-leading or internationally excellent. But it has lost the lead on the other indicators. Oxford has fractionally higher entry standards, Leeds has the most satisfied students and University College London has the best employment record. Edinburgh has overtaken St Andrews to become the top university in Scotland, while Cardiff remains ahead of Swansea in Wales. There are only three post-1992 universities left in the table, with Portsmouth the clear leader.

Italian	Research quality %	Entry standards	Student satisfaction %	Graduate prospects %	Overall rating
1 Cambridge	56.7	577	91.2	80.0	100.0
2 Oxford	40.0	578	87.7	60.0	89.5
3 Warwick	40.0	477	81.9	76.6	86.8
4 Reading	38.3	364	90.9		86.7
5 Bristol	31.7	441	83.8	76.5	84.3
=6 Durham	11.7	529	82.9	83.2	84.0
=6 Birmingham	26.7		83.2	78.8	84.0
8 Bath	21.7	465	86.1	76.0	83.8
9 Leeds	41.7	427	92.2	47.6	83.3
10 Exeter	18.3	459	87.6	73.8	83.0
11 University College London	28.3	496	70.7	90.4	82.5
12 Edinburgh	8.3	492	83.3		78.6
=13 Manchester	31.7	386	75.4	69.0	76.2
=13 Cardiff	25.0	426	77.8	64.3	76.2
=15 St Andrews	13.3	479	74.0		73.4
=15 Swansea	13.3	346	84.3		73.4
17 Portsmouth	25.0	309	75.5	75.4	73.3
18 Royal Holloway	16.7	377	73.9		69.3
19 Salford	12.5	351	74.6		67.1
20 Nottingham Trent		297	75.3	56.7	62.2
21 Manchester Metropolitan	6.7	321	76.5	43.5	62.1

Italian cont

There were more than five applications to the place in 2012, and entry standards remained high. The top two average more than 570 points at entry and more than half of the 21 universities in the ranking top 400 points. There is a high response rate and scores have generally been good in the National Student Survey. No university failed to satisfy at least seven out of ten final-year undergraduates taking Italian.

Universities we were unable to include this year because of insufficient data: Glasgow, Lancaster, Strathclyde.

Employed in professional job:	43%	Employed in non-professional job and studying:	3%
Employed in professional job and studying:	2%	Employed in non-professional job:	22%
Studying:	19%	Unemployed:	11%
Average starting professional salary:	£18,732	Average starting non-professional salary:	£15,490

» Chartered Institute of Linguists: **www.iol.org.uk**
» National Centre for Languages (CILT): **www.cilt.org.uk**
» Society for Italian Studies: **http://italianstudies.org.uk**

Land and Property Management

Two more universities have joined the land and property management table this year, at a time when new employment categorisation has reduced the size of many rankings. Even so, the table is less than half the size of a decade ago. The economic downturn has taken its toll, although the subject is up 17 places in the employment table this year and well inside the top 20. Graduate starting salaries are still £1,000 lower than they were in the 2011 *Guide*, but a substantial increase since the last edition at least takes the subjects back into the top half of the earnings table.

Because land and property management tend to have small intakes, it is impossible to compile reliable scores for some universities, even though they are still offering one or more of the subjects. More than 20 universities and a number of colleges expect to offer degrees in this field starting in 2014.

Cambridge has a predictably huge lead, despite not achieving enough responses from its final-year undergraduates for a satisfaction score to be compiled. It has entry standards that are more than 140 points higher than at second-placed Reading and 250 points above most of the other universities in the table. Cambridge also registered the best performance in the 2008 Research Assessment Exercise. Reading tops the employment measure, with an impressive 98 per cent of graduates going straight into professional jobs or continuing their studies.

Greenwich, although next to bottom of the table, again has the most satisfied students. Only Queen's, Belfast failed to satisfy at least 70 per cent of final-year undergraduates in the 2013 National Student Survey. Sheffield Hallam remains the highest-placed of five post-1992 universities in the ranking. There are no representatives of Scotland or Wales in the table, although Aberystwyth, Aberdeen and Glasgow Caledonian all offer courses.

Employed in professional job:	57%	Employed in non-professional job and studying:	1%
Employed in professional job and studying:	9%	Employed in non-professional job:	14%
Studying:	8%	Unemployed:	11%
Average starting professional salary:	£20,804	Average starting non-professional salary:	£15,209

Land and Property Management	Research quality %	Entry standards	Student satisfaction %	Graduate prospects %	Overall rating
1 Cambridge	45.0	558		91.2	100.0
2 Reading	36.7	417	76.6	98.4	87.3
3 Ulster	31.7	276	83.6	67.3	78.8
4 Sheffield Hallam	30.0	324	79.1	71.4	78.4
5 Birmingham City	15.0	303	83.0		75.9
6 Nottingham Trent	10.0	298	75.5	86.8	72.4
7 Westminster	11.7	303	74.3	79.2	71.0
8 Greenwich	20.0	235	84.9	40.0	69.6
9 Queen's, Belfast	16.7	368	65.5		66.7

» Chartered Institute of Housing: **www.cih.org**
» Institute of Residential Property Management: **www.irpm.org.uk**
» Royal Institution of Chartered Surveyors: **www.rics.org/uk**

Law

Only nursing had attracted more applications than law in 2012. While other subjects suffered from the introduction of higher fees, law managed small increases in both applications and enrolments. Entry standards reflect law's popularity: only in medicine do so many universities make such testing demands. A dozen universities average more than 500 points and more than a third of the 95 universities have average entry scores of over 400 points. Only nine universities slip below 250 points, although the 5.5 applications to each place in 2012 were below average for all subjects.

Cambridge has taken back the top place it lost to Oxford three years ago, despite leading the table on only one of the measures: entry standards. Cambridge students did not respond to the 2013 National Student Survey in sufficient numbers for a satisfaction score to be compiled and its grades in the last Research Assessment Exercise were surprisingly moderate by its own standards. The London School of Economics has also overtaken Oxford and could hardly be closer to Cambridge's overall score. The LSE achieved the best grades in the 2008 Research Assessment Exercise, when three-quarters of its submission was rated world-leading or internationally excellent.

Buckingham, in 41st place, has the best record for graduate destinations, followed by Glasgow which has overtaken Edinburgh to become the top university in Scotland for law. Once again, the most satisfied students are not at one of the leading universities in the table, but at Cumbria, in =37th place. There were good performances throughout the table. Only the bottom two – compared with six last year – failed to satisfy at least 70 per cent of the undergraduates. Portsmouth is the leading post-1992 university, in a creditable 35th place.

Law cont

Aspiring solicitors go on to take the Legal Practice Course, while those aiming to be barristers take the Bar Vocational Course, so it is no surprise that over 40 per cent of all law graduates are engaged in postgraduate study six months after completing a degree. The unemployment rate for law is better than average, at 11 per cent, and the subject is just inside the top 30 for early career employment prospects, and there are some surprisingly low scores at the bottom of the ranking. Average starting salaries are not as high as many might believe, partly because of training salaries in law firms and also because only about half of all law graduates find their way into the profession. The latest figure is almost £1,500 down on the last edition of the *Guide*, leaving law in the bottom 20 of the earnings table.

Universities we were unable to include this year because of insufficient data: Bolton, St Mary's College.

Employed in professional job:	24%	Employed in non-professional job and studying:	7%
Employed in professional job and studying:	5%	Employed in non-professional job:	22%
Studying:	31%	Unemployed:	11%
Average starting professional salary:	£19,229	Average starting non-professional salary:	£15,381

Law	Research quality %	Entry standards	Student satisfaction %	Graduate prospects %	Overall rating
1 Cambridge	36.7	617		82.4	100.0
2 London School of Economics	55.0	562	86.0	81.5	99.8
3 Oxford	46.7	578	85.9	86.4	99.5
4 Nottingham	41.7	503	88.9	86.3	97.9
5 Durham	41.7	528	86.8	88.1	97.8
6 University College London	48.3	564	83.0	73.2	94.7
7 Glasgow	28.3	529	83.6	88.5	93.1
8 Queen Mary, London	33.3	489	85.5	80.7	92.3
9 Queen's, Belfast	36.7	444	88.5	75.6	92.2
10 Kent	41.7	387	86.5	78.9	91.1
11 Reading	33.3	423	86.9	75.9	90.0
12 Newcastle	13.3	476	89.3	80.8	89.7
13 Aberdeen	15.0	484	85.7	85.0	89.2
14 Bristol	28.3	521	80.2	80.7	89.0
15 Edinburgh	38.3	518	75.3	83.0	88.8
16 Lancaster	18.3	463	86.1	79.0	88.1
=17 Leeds	28.3	459	83.6	73.6	87.4
=17 East Anglia	16.7	439	88.1	75.4	87.4
19 King's College London	26.7	524	78.3	79.6	87.3
20 Exeter	21.7	486	82.5	77.2	87.1
=21 Birmingham	30.0	476	79.6	77.8	86.9
=21 Manchester	23.3	462	82.7	77.7	86.9
=21 Cardiff	36.7	432	79.7	76.9	86.9
=24 Strathclyde	33.3	515	76.5	76.7	86.8
=24 Surrey	13.3	418	87.8	79.6	86.8

26 York		485	88.2	82.0	86.7
27 Leicester	16.7	420	82.7	82.3	85.2
28 Liverpool	25.0	427	82.7	71.3	84.7
=29 SOAS London	18.3	427	82.3	76.3	84.1
=29 Dundee	20.0	445	80.7	76.0	84.1
=31 Warwick	21.7	506	77.8	72.1	83.7
=31 Southampton	20.0	463	79.7	74.4	83.7
33 Sussex	21.7	421	88.0	56.3	83.4
34 Swansea	18.3	345	83.2	80.6	83.1
35 Portsmouth	15.0	344	84.3	77.6	82.2
36 Sheffield	26.7	429	80.4	62.5	81.7
=37 Keele	23.3	374	81.4	69.4	81.4
=37 Cumbria		241	90.9	85.0	81.4
39 West of England	10.0	326	84.2	73.7	79.7
40 Brunel	20.0	374	81.7	63.4	79.5
41 Buckingham		332	79.6	93.2	79.4
42 Hull	18.3	384	81.2	62.7	79.0
43 Abertay	6.7	365	86.0	63.6	78.8
44 City	15.0	386	77.5	72.7	78.4
45 Westminster	11.7	344	81.3	70.8	78.2
46 Salford	6.7	339	83.9	68.0	77.8
47 Coventry	1.7	301	87.2	67.6	77.4
=48 Central Lancashire	5.0	307	81.6	77.5	77.3
=48 Lincoln	3.3	336	84.7	67.2	77.3
=48 Huddersfield		348	83.8	70.9	77.3
51 Ulster	31.7	313	84.8	42.9	77.2
52 Essex	20.0	373	79.0	60.3	77.1
53 Stirling	16.7	418	74.6	67.9	76.9
=54 Northumbria		366	82.3	70.4	76.8
=54 Derby		313	87.1	65.1	76.8
56 Oxford Brookes	21.7	376	78.7	57.5	76.7
57 Winchester		309	87.1	63.4	76.2
58 Edinburgh Napier	1.7	374	86.3	53.7	75.9
59 Nottingham Trent	3.3	347	80.3	69.6	75.6
60 Manchester Metropolitan	15.0	360	74.9	70.0	75.5
=61 Chester		318	78.9	78.7	75.2
=61 Aberystwyth	15.0	332	78.7	63.3	75.2
63 Brighton	28.3	299	74.9	63.3	74.9
=64 Plymouth	15.0	325	85.1	46.1	74.8
=64 Bradford	25.0	330	74.4	63.3	74.8
66 Hertfordshire	15.0	316	74.7	71.2	74.2
67 Teesside		318	83.9	60.9	74.1
68 Robert Gordon	1.7	386	73.6	76.4	74.0
69 Bournemouth	0.0	366	74.5	77.0	73.7
70 Bangor		309	81.6	63.8	73.1
71 Staffordshire		292	83.2	60.4	72.7
72 Liverpool John Moores		324	83.2	54.0	72.2

	Research quality %	Entry standards	Student satisfaction %	Graduate prospects %	Overall rating
73 Greenwich	1.7	328	82.1	53.3	71.9
=74 Sheffield Hallam	1.7	347	78.6	58.5	71.6
=74 Gloucestershire		301	84.4	51.4	71.6
=74 Middlesex	5.0	269	80.0	62.3	71.6
=74 Glasgow Caledonian	5.0	409	76.6	52.0	71.6
78 Northampton		280	82.9	56.8	71.3
79 Edge Hill		275	85.1	49.3	70.7
80 De Montfort	6.7	308	77.9	56.0	70.5
81 Anglia Ruskin		262	83.5	50.9	69.8
82 Buckinghamshire New		242	83.0	54.2	69.5
83 Birmingham City		304	75.2	65.2	69.4
84 Sunderland	0.0	275	84.3	43.3	68.8
85 East London	15.0	230	77.7	50.8	68.5
86 Roehampton		241	85.3	43.8	68.4
87 Kingston	3.3	302	76.8	53.7	68.3
88 London Metropolitan	3.3	235	78.4	57.1	68.0
89 London South Bank		239	80.3	53.9	67.8
90 Leeds Metropolitan		297	72.7	64.8	67.6
91 Canterbury Christ Church		252	80.9	44.8	66.5
92 Bedfordshire		204	84.8	38.5	65.8
93 West London		245	71.5	58.1	63.7
94 West of Scotland	0.0	283	68.4	37.5	58.3
95 Southampton Solent	0.0	247	61.6	57.8	57.8

» Law Society of England and Wales: **www.lawsociety.org.uk**
» Law Society of Northern Ireland: **www.lawsoc-ni.org**
» Law Society of Scotland: **www.lawscot.org.uk**

Librarianship and Information Management

Only one subject has seen a bigger increase in graduate starting salaries than librarianship and information management: the £24,038 average is some £3,500 up on last year's *Guide*. However, the small numbers graduating make for exaggerated swings. Last year's figure was £2,500 up on the previous edition. Little more than 100 undergraduates started degrees in information services in 2012, although even this was an improvement on the previous year. As a result, while 49 universities and colleges expect to offer courses in this area in 2014, only five universities – compared with nine last year – had enough entrants and graduates to qualify for the table.

Sheffield has ended Loughborough's four-year tenure at the top of the table for librarianship and information management. Loughborough still has the highest entry standards and employment record in the table, but Sheffield has more satisfied students and the best score for research of those universities remaining in the table. King's College

London actually produced the top results in the 2008 Research Assessment Exercise, but does not have undergraduate courses in this field so does not appear in the table. Northumbria, which has moved up three places to third and becomes the leading post-1992 university, has the most satisfied students of all.

Student satisfaction is high in all five universities: none of them had an approval rating of less than 75 per cent in the 2013 National Student Survey. The same cannot be said for employment prospects, which range from 81 per cent positive destinations at Loughborough to only 15 per cent at Aberystwyth. The subjects had the second-highest unemployment rate last year. While that figure has come down only slightly, at 13 per cent, it is now no higher than average for all subjects.

Universities we were unable to include this year because of insufficient data: Brighton, Leeds, Liverpool John Moores, London South Bank.

Employed in professional job:	51%	Employed in non-professional job and studying:	3%
Employed in professional job and studying:	1%	Employed in non-professional job:	24%
Studying:	8%	Unemployed:	13%
Average starting professional salary:	£24,038	Average starting non-professional salary:	£15,900

Librarianship and Information Management	Research quality %	Entry standards	Student satisfaction %	Graduate prospects %	Overall rating
1 Sheffield	41.7	346	84.2	69.6	100.0
2 Loughborough	28.3	361	81.5	81.5	97.7
3 Northumbria	6.7	284	90.0	73.7	91.4
4 Aberystwyth	23.3	274	79.6	14.8	81.2
5 Manchester Metropolitan	6.7		76.3	20.0	75.5

» Association for Information Management: **www.aslib.com**
» Chartered Institute of Library and Information Professionals: **www.cilip.org.uk**

Linguistics

Linguistics might have looked likely to be a prime victim of the switch to higher fees, but almost exactly the same number of undergraduates started courses in 2012 as in the previous year. With only 529 students enrolling and less than five applications to the place, the subject might become vulnerable in some institutions, but 53 universities plan to offer courses in 2014. Even Cambridge, at the top of the table, did not have enough graduates in linguistics to compile an employment score. The same applied to five others in the table and three more dropped out because this was not the only gap in their data.

Cambridge apart, there is much more movement in linguistics than in most other tables. Edinburgh has moved up seven places to second and Cardiff by the same amount to fourth. By contrast, Oxford, which topped the table two years ago, has slipped to fifth, despite having the highest entry standards. The University of the West of England, which also moved up seven places, has by far the most satisfied students and is now the highest-placed modern university. Lancaster, in third place, was the only university to see 80 per cent of graduates go

Linguistics cont

into professional jobs or further study in 2012, while Queen Mary, University of London, and Cardiff tie for the best grades in the 2008 Research Assessment Exercise.

Entry standards are comparatively high: only two of the 24 universities average less than 300 points and half have an average in excess of 400 points. Linguistics is in bottom ten subjects for starting salaries in graduate jobs, averaging only a little more than £18,000. Graduates' immediate employment prospects are slightly better, but more than a third start their careers in low-level jobs.

Universities we were unable to include this year because of insufficient data: Aberdeen, Portsmouth, Sussex.

Employed in professional job:	32%	Employed in non-professional job and studying:	4%
Employed in professional job and studying:	2%	Employed in non-professional job:	30%
Studying:	19%	Unemployed:	13%
Average starting professional salary:	£18,120	Average starting non-professional salary:	£14,339

Linguistics	Research quality %	Entry standards	Student satisfaction %	Graduate prospects %	Overall rating
1 Cambridge	30.0	564	90.4		100.0
2 Edinburgh	40.0	496	84.4	76.9	96.7
3 Lancaster	28.3	449	89.5	80.0	94.3
4 Cardiff	43.3	398	85.0	71.4	92.4
5 Oxford	20.0	572	82.0	74.0	91.7
6 York	35.0	437	87.1	57.7	89.0
7 Newcastle	23.3	385	84.6	77.6	86.9
8 Leeds	20.0	442	84.3	70.0	86.2
9 University College London	30.0	454	78.1	66.7	85.8
10 Essex	36.7	406	86.0	45.2	84.4
11 Sheffield	33.3	441	83.7	47.5	84.3
12 Queen Mary, London	43.3	380	76.3	54.9	83.0
13 West of England	21.7	320	97.0	45.5	81.6
14 Kent	26.7	368	77.7	64.5	80.3
15 Ulster	23.3	293	84.0		77.2
16 Manchester	25.0	421	72.6	52.6	76.4
17 Bangor	15.0	327	75.4	71.7	75.6
18 SOAS London	18.3	406	71.8		73.4
19 King's College London		408	72.5	70.6	72.6
20 Hertfordshire	21.7	326	82.5	37.8	72.5
21 York St John		290	86.8	50.0	69.4
22 Salford	15.0	317	70.9		66.3
23 Westminster	6.7	300	76.8		65.8
24 Brighton	3.3	332	75.8		65.5

» British Association for Applied Linguistics: **www.baal.org.uk**
» Linguistics Association of Great Britain: **www.lagb.org.uk**

Materials Technology

Courses in this category cover four distinct areas: materials science, mining engineering, textiles technology and printing, and marine technology. The various subjects are highly specialised and attract relatively few applicants, but have generally held their own with the onset of higher fees. There was only a small drop in the number of students starting courses in materials technology itself, for example, in 2012, but there were still fewer than four applications per place. The leading universities demand chemistry and sometimes also physics, maths or design technology at A level or its equivalent.

Cambridge has retained the leadership it won from Oxford four years ago, while Imperial College has moved up three places to second. Cambridge has the best grades from the 2008 Research Assessment Exercise, when only 5 per cent of the university's research was considered less than world-leading or internationally excellent. It also has much the highest entry standards, but it no longer leads on student satisfaction. That distinction goes to De Montfort, in 11th place and still the leading post-1992 university. Swansea, which now shares third place with Oxford, has a rare 100 per cent employment score and is the only university in the table from outside England.

Outside the top three, entry scores are tightly bunched throughout most of the table: no university has an average of more than 450 points or less than 230. Employment prospects are slightly below average for all subjects: the proportion going straight into graduate-level work has dropped by more than 10 percentage points since the last edition of the *Guide*, and the 15 per cent unemployment rate is above the norm. However, average starting salaries have shot up since the last edition. A rise of more than £4,000 has put the subject in the top ten for earnings, up 21 places, although the small numbers may mean that this turns out to be a blip.

Materials Technology	Research quality %	Entry standards	Student satisfaction %	Graduate prospects %	Overall rating
1 Cambridge	58.3	651	84.6	86.1	100.0
2 Imperial College	31.7	548	83.1	85.0	88.2
=3 Oxford	43.3	610	73.9	72.2	86.1
=3 Swansea	30.0	337	87.9	100.0	86.1
5 Loughborough	36.7	363	82.9	96.2	85.4
6 Sheffield	31.7	400	82.9	86.4	83.3
7 Birmingham	35.0	405	81.0	83.0	82.6
=8 Manchester	40.0	429	79.7	64.0	79.8
=8 Exeter	15.0	384	84.9	88.9	79.8
10 Queen Mary, London	28.3	359	87.6	66.7	78.7
11 De Montfort	13.3	323	90.8	70.7	76.0
12 Birmingham City		445	88.2	57.7	72.5
13 Manchester Metropolitan	10.0		75.5	83.3	71.6
14 Huddersfield		353	68.6	50.7	58.0
15 Buckinghamshire New		246	82.3	33.9	57.1
16 Bolton	15.0	237	66.6		56.8
17 London Metropolitan	0.0	325	61.0	55.0	54.2

Materials Technology cont

Universities we were unable to include this year because of insufficient data: Leeds, Sheffield Hallam.

Employed in professional job:	42%	Employed in non-professional job and studying:	1%
Employed in professional job and studying:	1%	Employed in non-professional job:	20%
Studying:	21%	Unemployed:	15%
Average starting professional salary:	£24,707	Average starting non-professional salary:	£17,776

» Institute of Materials, Minerals and Mining: **www.iom3.org**

Mathematics

Entry standards in maths are among the highest in any subject, boosted by the fact that most successful candidates for the leading universities have taken two A levels in the subject, as well as two or three others. The top eight in the table all average more than 540 points, headed by Cambridge, whose total of 669 points last year was the highest there has ever been for any subject in the *Guide*. Its new score is only six points lower and still equates to almost four A* grades and two As at AS level. Not all universities attract such high-fliers, however: six average less than 300 points. There was a small decline in both applications and enrolments when higher fees were introduced in 2012, but maths has held onto most of the gains it has made in recent years. The subject still attracted almost 13,000 more applications than it did in 2005.

Cambridge finishes ahead of Oxford in maths for the first time in five years. The light blues have the highest entry standards in the table, but Oxford is ahead in two of the three of the subjects grouped together as mathematics in the 2008 Research Assessment Exercise. The two universities tied for the best grades in applied maths, but 90 per cent of Oxford's work in statistics and operational research was considered world-leading or internationally excellent. Imperial was top for pure mathematics. St Andrews, in fourth place, has the best employment score, while Greenwich has the most satisfied students, despite only just securing a place in the top 40. Northumbria is the only post-1992 university in the top 20.

Generally, mathematicians seem well satisfied with their courses: for the second year in a row, only one university fell below a 70 per cent approval rating.

Maths is often cited as one of the subjects most likely to lead to a lucrative career, and the earnings table seems to bear this out. Although not quite in the top ten this year, starting salaries in graduate jobs averaged almost £24,500 at the time of the latest survey. The subject is also in the top 20 for the proportion of graduates going straight into professional jobs or becoming postgraduate students. Although there were surprisingly low figures at Central Lancashire and Essex, more than half of the 67 universities in the table saw 70 per cent of 2012 graduates achieve such positive destinations.

Universities we were unable to include this year because of insufficient data: Bolton, Cumbria, Glasgow Caledonian.

Employed in graduate job:	40%	Employed in non-graduate job and studying:	1%
Employed in graduate job and studying:	7%	Employed in non-graduate job:	15%
Studying:	23%	Unemployed:	13%
Average starting graduate salary:	£24,438	Average starting non-graduate salary:	£15,980

Mathematics

Mathematics	Research quality % Pure Mathematics	Research quality % Applied Mathematics	Research quality % Statistics	Entry standards	Student satisfaction %	Graduate prospects %	Overall rating
1 Cambridge	45.0	45.0	45.0	663	87.5	90.0	100.0
2 Oxford	48.3	45.0	56.7	618	86.2	86.3	98.1
3 Warwick	50.0	40.0	40.0	586	83.6	89.1	95.0
4 St Andrews	15.0	40.0	26.7	569	86.8	92.9	93.0
5 Imperial College	55.0	35.0	41.7	616	81.4	82.9	92.9
6 Bath	36.7	36.7	33.3	542	87.5	84.4	92.7
7 University College London	33.3	23.3	23.3	550	83.6	85.3	88.6
8 Durham	33.3	35.0	20.0	590	79.7	83.6	88.4
=9 Heriot-Watt	40.0	31.7	21.7	422	87.7	81.1	87.0
=9 Surrey		33.3		474	86.2	72.8	87.0
11 Bristol	43.3	40.0	40.0	548	75.7	79.6	86.7
12 Nottingham	26.7	35.0	36.7	499	81.8	76.7	86.0
13 Exeter	25.0	26.7		482	84.6	80.1	85.9
14 Newcastle	15.0	30.0	25.0	451	85.3	82.7	85.3
15 Birmingham	28.3	21.7		482	83.5	80.6	85.0
16 Lancaster	23.3		30.0	476	80.4	83.3	84.5
17 Swansea	16.7			375	90.3	80.7	83.6
=18 Keele		30.0		365	89.3	66.8	83.4
=18 London School of Economics	18.3		28.3	555	79.0	76.4	83.4
=20 Cardiff	16.7			473	81.4	87.4	82.8
=20 Northumbria		20.0		376	90.2	72.9	82.8
22 Manchester	33.3	36.7	31.7	516	78.4	65.7	82.6
23 Sheffield	28.3	21.7	26.7	463	82.6	72.0	82.4
=24 King's College London	36.7	31.7		497	79.0	65.2	82.2
=24 Dundee		21.7		444	78.3	90.6	82.2
26 Loughborough	25.0	23.3		445	82.4	75.3	82.0
27 East Anglia	30.0	18.3		425	87.5	63.6	81.9
=28 Glasgow	28.3	23.3	26.7	483	79.4	74.6	81.8
=28 Southampton	20.0	33.3	31.7	494	75.0	81.2	81.8
30 Queen's, Belfast	18.3			411	85.3	77.1	81.6
31 Portsmouth		35.0		312	85.4	68.7	81.3
=32 Leeds	25.0	28.3	38.3	464	80.2	67.9	81.1
=32 Edinburgh	40.0	31.7	21.7	511	73.3	73.4	81.1
34 York	21.7	23.3		507	76.5	76.0	80.3
35 Leicester	23.3	18.3		417	79.1	81.8	79.8
36 Aberdeen	35.0			442	78.3	60.0	79.3
37 Brunel		23.3	26.7	340	84.7	69.1	79.1
38 Greenwich			13.3	301	95.1	59.6	78.9
39 Sheffield Hallam	11.7	11.7	11.7	327	88.7	74.1	78.6
=40 Stirling		16.7		401	84.3		78.4
=40 Reading		16.7	15.0	377	86.5	66.3	78.4
42 Liverpool	21.7	30.0	11.7	427	79.3	64.1	77.7

		Research quality % Pure Mathematics	Research quality % Applied Mathematics	Research quality % Statistics	Entry standards	Student satisfaction %	Graduate prospects %	Overall rating
43	Aston	18.3	18.3	18.3	389	79.1	76.5	77.2
44	Plymouth		8.3	10.9	357	89.4	59.8	76.5
45	Nottingham Trent	13.3	13.3	13.3	329	89.3	59.0	76.3
46	Royal Holloway	8.3			405	86.7	61.0	76.1
47	Sussex		23.3		389	80.1	60.4	75.8
48	Oxford Brookes		3.3		363	89.9	62.1	75.6
49	Kent	11.7	21.7	35.0	361	74.0	74.1	75.0
50	Brighton		5.0		293	86.3	73.6	74.4
51	Queen Mary, London	26.7	23.3	20.0	397	75.2	64.3	74.3
52	Edge Hill				313		85.7	73.9
53	Hertfordshire	28.3			294	81.9	52.9	73.8
54	Strathclyde		23.3	20.0	438	68.9	75.5	73.7
55	Chester		5.0		319	83.8	73.3	73.6
56	Manchester Metropolitan	18.3			321	82.2	58.8	73.3
57	Coventry	6.7	6.7		292	82.4	76.9	73.2
58	Derby				281	81.4	78.6	70.9
59	Aberystwyth	16.7			380	81.9	41.1	70.8
60	City		10.0		389	77.3	58.0	70.2
61	Liverpool John Moores				326		68.6	69.1
62	West of England		3.3		339	79.8	60.3	68.8
63	London Metropolitan	18.3		11.7	216	84.9	46.6	68.4
64	Essex				360	83.4	31.6	64.6
65	Kingston				305	76.6	53.0	63.6
66	Staffordshire		0.0		247		40.0	56.6
67	Central Lancashire				357	71.6	23.3	56.1

» London Mathematical Society: **www.lms.ac.uk**
» Maths Careers: **www.mathscareers.org.uk**
» Royal Statistical Society: **www.rss.org.uk**

Mechanical Engineering

Mechanical engineering is just outside the top 10 most popular subjects at degree level and attracts more applicants than any other branch of the wider discipline. The arrival of higher fees cemented this position, as both applications and enrolments rose in 2012 – the latest in a series of substantial rises. The number of places has also grown in recent years, allowing almost 6,900 students to start degrees in 2012, but more than six applications for every place still made it the most competitive branch of engineering. It is not hard to see why. Despite the economic downturn, mechanical engineering is among the top ten subjects for early career prospects and in the top five for starting salaries in graduate jobs. Another substantial rise took the average in such jobs beyond £26,000 at the end of 2012. Most universities demand maths – preferably with a strong component of mechanics – and another science subject (usually physics) at A level or its equivalent.

Cambridge remains well ahead of Imperial College at the top of the mechanical engineering table, with Sheffield not far behind in third place. Cambridge, which was ranked third in the world in mechanical engineering earlier in 2013, has by far the highest entry standards, the best research grades and a very high employment score. Even so, it cannot match Sheffield or 14th-placed Lancaster's record of 97 per cent positive destinations for its 2012 graduates. Once again, the top score in the 2013 National Student Survey is to be found much further down the table. Central Lancashire is only just in the top 50, but 94 per cent of final year undergraduates were satisfied with their course. Liverpool John Moores is the highest-placed post-1992 university, just outside the top 20.

High satisfaction scores are spread through most of the table, with only four universities, compared with ten last year, failing to win the approval of at least 70 per cent of final-year undergraduates. Entry scores are also rising, with five universities averaging more than 500 points and only three, compared with six last year, averaging less than 250 points. The large numbers of mature students upgrading their qualifications in mechanical engineering mean that more than a third of the entrants at post-1992 universities are admitted without A levels or their equivalent. There are four additional universities in the table this year: King's

Mechanical Engineering	Research quality %	Entry standards	Student satisfaction %	Graduate prospects %	Overall rating
1 Cambridge	60.0	631	83.5	96.2	100.0
2 Imperial College	46.7	578	86.2	89.4	93.9
3 Sheffield	45.0	472	86.1	96.7	91.5
4 Leeds	38.3	418	92.4	89.4	88.8
5 Bristol	40.0	532	76.6	95.5	87.6
6 Bath	25.0	507	89.7	86.4	86.2
=7 Loughborough	36.7	445	84.4	86.2	84.9
=7 Surrey	35.0	414	88.7	84.4	84.9
9 Strathclyde	26.2	522	82.2	91.1	84.8
10 Cardiff	35.0	437	85.4	86.4	84.6
11 Nottingham	41.7	432	79.1	90.3	84.5
12 Southampton	30.0	499	79.4	92.0	84.0
13 Birmingham	36.7	464	74.9	93.5	83.1
14 Lancaster	23.3	424	83.8	96.6	82.7
15 Warwick	36.7	430	80.7	85.5	82.5
16 Exeter	25.0	440	85.9	85.3	81.9
17 Newcastle	31.7	446	79.9	87.1	81.7
18 Queen's, Belfast	31.7	399	85.3	83.1	81.5
19 Heriot-Watt	25.0	424	84.7	85.5	80.8
20 Manchester	36.7	442	78.5	79.0	80.4
21 Liverpool John Moores	33.3	314	85.7	85.7	79.9
22 Liverpool	35.4	415	79.9	76.9	79.2
23 Swansea	21.7	359	85.2	87.0	78.2
24 Edinburgh	28.3	499	67.4	89.6	77.6

Mechanical Engineering cont

	Research quality %	Entry standards	Student satisfaction %	Graduate prospects %	Overall rating
25 Brunel	23.3	378	87.1	74.0	77.0
26 King's College London	21.7		85.5	77.3	76.6
27 Glasgow	21.7	452	80.5	74.7	76.3
28 Aberdeen	31.7	418	70.8	84.0	75.9
29 Robert Gordon	10.0	371	79.3	96.2	74.9
=30 Coventry	7.4	298	88.6	85.5	73.2
=30 Harper Adams		315	90.2	88.6	73.2
32 Sussex	26.7	348	76.8	76.9	73.0
33 Staffordshire	20.0	244	91.2	72.1	72.8
34 Aston	18.3	364	77.8	80.0	72.4
35 Bradford	20.0	300	83.8		72.2
36 West of England	25.0	320	72.0	87.7	72.1
37 Plymouth	8.3	319	81.4	89.3	71.9
38 Queen Mary, London	21.7	377	81.9	64.3	71.8
39 Dundee		348	88.1	80.0	71.3
40 Greenwich	43.3	286	77.5	57.3	71.1
41 De Montfort	20.0	312	85.1	66.7	71.0
42 University College London	31.7	478	62.1	69.6	70.5
43 Huddersfield	15.0	300	77.5	83.7	70.0
44 Northumbria	20.0	316	77.1	75.0	69.7
45 Ulster		269	84.1	90.0	69.2
46 Manchester Metropolitan	11.7	312	80.4	75.0	68.6
47 Central Lancashire		270	93.6	66.7	67.8
=48 Salford	23.3	324	75.7	63.6	67.4
=48 Teesside		380	85.3	64.7	67.4
50 Brighton	26.7	287	71.4	71.4	67.1
51 Portsmouth	18.3	305	76.1	69.3	66.9
=52 Hertfordshire	26.7	300	75.0	60.7	66.5
=52 Sunderland	10.0	266	78.3	78.6	66.5
54 City	21.7	359	84.6	40.0	66.4
55 Hull	13.3	327	85.9	51.0	66.2
56 Oxford Brookes		366	75.3	68.8	63.4
57 West of Scotland		309	71.1	81.8	62.8
58 Birmingham City		306	70.5	80.6	62.1
59 Sheffield Hallam	15.0	265	68.0	68.5	60.8
60 Bolton	15.0	237	72.0		60.3
61 Kingston	11.7	275	67.8	65.8	59.4
62 London South Bank	23.3	240	71.2	50.0	59.2

Employed in professional job:	63%	Employed in non-professional job and studying:	1%
Employed in professional job and studying:	2%	Employed in non-professional job:	10%
Studying:	12%	Unemployed:	12%
Average starting professional salary:	£26,175	Average starting non-professional salary:	£17,542

College London, Salford, Teesside and West of Scotland. Overall, however, there are two more universities in the latest ranking than in last year's *Guide*.

University we were unable to include this year because of insufficient data: Glyndŵr.

» Engineering UK: **www.engineeringuk.com**
» Institution of Mechanical Engineers: **www.imeche.org**

Medicine

Medicine has become one of the most stable rankings in the *Guide*. The top four have been the same for the last four years and there is no change in the top six since the last *Guide* was published. Oxford has extended its lead over Cambridge and the top two continue to pull away from the rest. Oxford has the most satisfied students – challenged only by Keele, which is in the bottom five overall – while Cambridge has the best research score and the highest entry standards. At least 80 per cent of its research was considered world-leading or internationally excellent in all but one of the eight specialisms in which it submitted work. Universities were able to submit research in up to 12 areas (called units of assessment, UoA). Full details can be seen for UoA 1–9, 12, 14 and 15 at **www.rae.ac.uk/results**.

Medicine is the perennial leader of the employment table, but it has dropped to third in the earnings league, with slightly lower average starting salaries than last year. Employment scores for individual schools are no longer used as a measure (although they are still shown for guidance) to avoid small differences distorting positions in a subject where virtually all graduates become junior doctors or researchers. Fourteen schools, compared with four last year, registered less than full employment six months after graduation, but only six dropped below 99 per cent and one below 90 per cent. Undergraduates have to be prepared to work long hours, particularly towards the end of the course. But student satisfaction is generally high: in only two schools did the approval rating drop below 70 per cent.

The introduction of A* grades at A level produced another step change in the already fearsome entry grades at UK medical schools. Only four schools average less than 500 points in the latest table, and three of them have averages of more than 490 points. No other subject has such high standards. Yet only four subjects attract more applications, even though candidates are restricted to four medical schools. There was only a small decline when £9,000 fees arrived in 2012 and all the available places were filled. The opening of new medical schools a decade ago was expected to ease this pressure on places, but there were still more than ten applications to every place in 2012.

Nearly all schools demand chemistry and most biology. Physics or maths is required by some, either as an alternative or addition to biology Universities will want to see evidence of commitment to the subject through work experience or voluntary work. Almost all schools interview candidates, and several use one of the two specialist aptitude tests (*see* chapter 1). The figures for Exeter and Plymouth, in joint 15th place, relate to the Peninsula Medical School, which was run jointly by the two universities. From 2013, the school has separated and applications should be made to the University of Exeter Medical School or Plymouth University Peninsula Medical School.

Medicine	Research quality %	Entry standards	Student satisfaction %	Graduate prospects %	Overall rating
1 Oxford	47.6	620	96.8	90.7	100.0
2 Cambridge	51.9	640	75.5	89.3	94.9
3 Edinburgh	44.3	580	78.5	98.9	88.9
4 University College London	42.7	564	83.0	100.0	88.8
5 Aberdeen	36.2	538	86.6	100.0	86.1
6 Imperial College	40.5	567	75.7	99.3	85.7
7 Queen Mary, London	37.1	528	86.4	99.3	85.6
8 St Andrews	23.3	546	91.3	98.9	84.7
9 Newcastle	27.9	538	87.8	100.0	84.2
=10 Manchester	33.4	534	81.4	99.5	83.1
=10 Birmingham	29.3	547	82.1	99.7	83.1
12 Dundee	24.1	541	84.4	99.2	82.0
13 Leeds	27.5	508	88.1	100.0	81.8
14 Hull-York	32.3	537	76.4	97.8	81.1
=15 Exeter	22.8	524	86.3	100.0	81.0
=15 Plymouth	22.8	524	86.3	100.0	81.0
17 Queen's, Belfast	21.6	518	87.8	100.0	80.7
18 Southampton	28.9	504	82.6	100.0	79.8
=19 Glasgow	28.1	511	80.6	100.0	79.4
=19 Cardiff	22.7	543	78.1	99.6	79.4
=19 East Anglia	18.3	515	87.6	97.3	79.4
22 Nottingham	15.2	530	85.8	100.0	79.0
23 Sheffield	23.2	501	84.0	100.0	78.4
24 Warwick	21.9		81.3	100.0	78.3
25 Brighton & Sussex Medical School	15.0	498	90.8	100.0	78.2
26 Bristol	29.2	506	76.6	100.0	77.8
27 Keele	14.8	470	95.5	100.0	77.7
28 Leicester	20.1	520	80.5	99.5	77.6
=29 King's College London	29.6	530	61.0	99.4	74.0
=29 Liverpool	26.7	494	70.8	100.0	74.0
31 St George's	18.7	492	67.1	100.0	70.0

Employed in professional job:	92%	Employed in non-professional job and studying:	0%
Employed in professional job and studying:	1%	Employed in non-professional job:	0%
Studying:	6%	Unemployed:	1%
Average starting professional salary:	£28,862	Average starting non-professional salary:	n/a

» British Medical Association: **www.bma.org.uk**
» NHS Careers: **www.nhscareers.nhs.uk**
» Student BMJ: **http://student.bmj.com**

Middle Eastern and African Studies

Universities report increased interest in Middle Eastern courses, but still relatively few undergraduates take a whole degree, rather than individual modules. A few more students started Middle Eastern Studies in 2012 than in the previous year, despite much higher fees, but the total was only 114. There were further falls in both applications and enrolments for African Studies, but 13 universities expect to offer degrees in this area in 2014.

Cambridge has built a much larger lead in the table this year, and Durham has overtaken Oxford to take second place. Cambridge has the highest entry standards and is fractionally behind Oxford for research. Forty per cent of Oxford's submission to the 2008 Research Assessment Exercise was regarded as world-leading. Leeds has the most satisfied students, while Durham has this year's top employment record, 10 percentage points ahead of its nearest rival. Only six of the ten universities in the table had enough graduates for a reliable score on this measure. St Andrews remains in fourth place in the ranking, ahead of Edinburgh as the leading university north of the border. There are no representatives of Wales or Northern Ireland. Westminster is the only post-1992 university in the table.

The small numbers make for big swings even in the national statistics. The 24 per cent unemployment rate is the worst of any subject and almost twice last year's rate. But the subjects are not in the bottom 20 for the proportion of graduates in professional jobs or postgraduate study. They rank only slightly lower for average earnings, which have stabilised this year after big differences recently.

University we were unable to include this year because of insufficient data: Birmingham.

Employed in professional job:	35%	Employed in non-professional job and studying:	4%
Employed in professional job and studying:	5%	Employed in non-professional job:	16%
Studying:	17%	Unemployed:	24%
Average starting professional salary:	£19,363	Average starting non-professional salary:	£14,320

Middle Eastern and African Studies	Research quality %	Entry standards	Student satisfaction %	Graduate prospects %	Overall rating
1 Cambridge	48.3	612	80.7		100.0
2 Durham	35.0	522	80.5	89.0	92.6
3 Oxford	50.0	581	75.4	55.1	91.5
4 St Andrews	33.3	497	84.7		90.8
5 SOAS London	36.7	407	79.4	77.1	86.7
6 Edinburgh	40.0	457	70.4		80.8
7 Leeds		410	89.0	79.1	79.7
8 Exeter	23.3	448	77.6		78.1
9 Manchester	30.0	385	73.2	45.6	74.8
10 Westminster		300	79.8	40.6	64.3

» African Studies Association of the UK: **www.asauk.net**
» British Society for Middle Eastern Studies: **www.brismes.ac.uk**

Music

Music suffered a big drop in applications when the fees went up in 2012, but the numbers eventually starting courses were down by less than 200 across the whole of the UK. One effect was that the competition for entry dropped below five applications per place. Entry grades are relatively low at most universities – more than 20 average less than 300 UCAS points – although music grades and the quality of auditions are more significant. Nine out of ten degree applicants come with A levels and most university departments expect music to be among them, although they may accept a distinction or merit in Grade 8 music exams. The character of courses vary considerably, from the practical and vocational programmes in conservatoires to the more theoretical degrees in some of the older universities.

Music	Research quality %	Entry standards	Student satisfaction %	Graduate prospects %	Overall rating
1 Manchester	61.7	563	88.3	81.8	100.0
2 Oxford	58.3	535	87.3	79.2	96.9
3 Cambridge	58.3	550	76.3	81.8	93.2
4 Royal Holloway	70.0	439	86.5	70.5	92.3
5 Birmingham	61.7	490	72.3	88.8	90.8
=6 King's College London	58.3	518	74.1	81.3	90.5
=6 York	58.3	452	85.7	72.3	90.5
8 Newcastle	50.0	463	85.3	75.6	89.9
=9 Nottingham	45.0	411	89.2	79.0	88.9
=9 Queen's, Belfast	46.7	410	91.0	74.2	88.9
11 City	41.7	426	89.5	75.0	88.1
12 Sheffield	56.7	433	86.1	65.6	87.9
13 Glasgow	45.0	476	84.1	69.2	87.4
14 Edinburgh	35.0	472	89.4	68.3	87.3
15 Southampton	60.0	404	79.9	73.6	86.2
16 Bristol	35.0	461	85.8	71.3	85.8
17 Roehampton	65.0	301	85.3		84.2
18 Royal Academy of Music	40.0	338	79.3	96.2	83.9
19 Surrey	35.0	476	85.2	57.6	83.0
20 Cardiff	33.3	395	87.2	66.1	81.7
=21 Durham	40.0	497	67.8	70.8	80.3
=21 SOAS London	50.0	410	74.3		80.3
=21 Lancaster	43.3	395	79.4	66.4	80.3
24 Bangor	40.0	352	84.1	67.1	79.9
25 Leeds	35.0	403	84.6	57.9	79.3
26 Birmingham City	23.3	319	80.5	89.2	78.4
27 Royal College of Music	26.7	318	74.4	94.0	77.4
28 Huddersfield	38.3	333	81.7	65.0	77.0
=29 Keele	35.0	340	85.2	59.5	76.9
=29 Royal Northern College of Music	15.0	337	80.4	86.9	76.9
31 Goldsmiths College	43.3	364	76.8	61.0	76.4

32	Aberdeen	20.0	441	78.5	56.0	74.7
33	Bath Spa	16.7	395	78.3	65.8	74.0
34	Liverpool	26.7	398	83.5	45.3	73.8
35	Sussex	35.0	393	74.3	53.5	73.1
=36	Brighton	45.0	290	88.2	37.5	72.8
=36	Royal Conservatoire of Scotland	23.3	329	69.9	84.1	72.8
38	Essex		249	95.8	70.0	72.5
39	Plymouth	25.0	272	88.7	52.1	71.4
40	Oxford Brookes	21.7	308	89.9	44.9	71.2
41	Hull	16.7	378	84.9	44.6	71.1
42	Brunel	25.0	341	83.0	47.2	70.9
43	East Anglia	13.3	419	67.8	68.8	70.3
44	Gloucestershire		265	87.2	72.7	70.0
45	York St John	15.0	235	77.5	76.2	68.1
46	Coventry	23.3	337	70.9	60.7	68.0
47	Anglia Ruskin	8.3	254	76.9	71.4	66.2
48	Ulster	10.0	298	82.6	49.0	65.9
49	Edinburgh Napier	1.7	384	77.2	47.9	65.5
50	Chester	13.3	294	78.7		65.1
51	Derby		301	92.6	34.4	65.0
52	Hertfordshire	8.3	298	71.8	62.7	63.9
53	Northampton	8.3	298	77.1	49.2	63.1
54	Westminster	15.0	292	66.7	62.3	62.6
=55	Salford	8.3	341	68.2	54.7	62.4
=55	Canterbury Christ Church	16.7	278	76.7	43.8	62.4
=55	West London	3.3	259	73.5	65.3	62.4
=58	West of Scotland		346	82.0	33.6	62.1
=58	Cumbria		277	91.0	30.0	62.1
60	De Montfort	28.3	286	74.4	34.5	62.0
61	Middlesex		266	72.7	62.5	60.9
62	Chichester		306	71.2	55.5	60.5
63	Manchester Metropolitan		335	67.7	54.9	60.1
64	Southampton Solent		309	78.3	36.9	59.4
65	Central Lancashire		284	75.1	45.1	58.7
66	Falmouth		255	71.3	53.8	57.7
67	Kingston	3.3	322	64.7	47.8	57.1
68	Kent		348	60.3	53.3	57.0
69	Bournemouth		319	63.0	44.8	54.8
70	Liverpool John Moores		342	72.2	20.0	54.2
71	Sunderland	8.3	250	63.6	37.5	51.8
72	Buckinghamshire New		235	67.1	40.8	51.7
73	East London		266	53.7	59.1	51.4

Employed in professional job:	36%	Employed in non-professional job and studying:		3%
Employed in professional job and studying:	4%	Employed in non-professional job:		28%
Studying:	17%	Unemployed:		13%
Average starting professional salary:	£16,406	Average starting non-professional salary:		£13,914

Music cont

Manchester has leapt to the top of the music ranking this year, moving up five places with higher entry scores than Oxford or Cambridge, which fill the next two places. Essex has the most satisfied students, but is restricted to 38th place because it did not enter the 2008 Research Assessment Exercise in this subject. Royal Holloway, which has moved up to fourth place from outside the top ten, had the best grades in a high-scoring set of assessments, with no less than 90 per cent of its research considered world-leading or internationally excellent. Roehampton, which is new to the table this year, is the only post-1992 university in the top 20. Glasgow and Cardiff remain the top universities in Scotland and Wales respectively.

The Royal Academy of Music again has the best employment score, and it is noticeable that the specialist institutions do far better than even the leading university departments on this measure. While the specialists produced four of the five best employment scores, 20 universities saw fewer than half of their graduates go straight into professional jobs or further training. The 9 per cent unemployment rate in the last survey had risen to 13 per cent this year but was still no worse than the average for all subjects, despite the fact that career prospects for musicians are notoriously uncertain. The subject finishes in the bottom half of the employment table because more than 30 per cent of leavers were in non-graduate occupations six months after graduation. Salaries in those jobs were the lowest for any subject at the time of the latest survey, as were those for graduates who found employment classified as professional.

Universities we were unable to include this year because of insufficient data: Cardiff Metropolitan, Strathclyde.

» Incorporated Society of Musicians: **www.ism.org**
» Royal Musical Association: **www.rma.ac.uk**

Nursing

Nursing continues to attract by far the largest numbers of applications in higher education. There has been phenomenal growth since the move towards an all-graduate profession, with the number of applications passing 100,000 for the first time in 2008 and reaching 200,000 by 2011. Although there were small declines in both applications and enrolments when higher fees arrived in 2012, there were still almost nine applications per place and the upward trajectory has since resumed. With the diploma route into the profession withdrawn this year, it is safe to assume that there will continue to be strong competition for places in 2014. Entry requirements are low, however. Only the top two in the table average over 400 points on the UCAS tariff and eight have averages of less than 250 points.

Glasgow has taken over from Edinburgh at the top of the table without leading on any single indicator. Edinburgh has the highest entry standards, while Manchester, in tenth place, produced the best grades in the 2008 Research Assessment Exercise, with 85 per cent of its submission considered world-leading or internationally excellent. Huddersfield, which shares tenth place with Manchester, registered the best of many good scores in the 2013 National Student Survey. Manchester Metropolitan, in eighth, is the highest-placed post-1992 university. It is one of seven universities, compared with 11 last year, with 100 per cent employment records. The others are Liverpool, Birmingham, Queen Margaret, De Montfort,

Keele and Bangor. The employment figures are not quite as good as last year's, but still only seven institutions saw fewer than nine out of ten nurses go straight into the profession or on to further study. The subject remains in the top three for employment prospects, but is only just in the top 20 in the earnings league, with average starting salaries just above £22,500.

Less than a third of the institutions in the table are pre-1992 universities. Seven modern universities – two more than last year – make it to the top 20. Cardiff is the top university in Wales, while Ulster, which secured one of the best grades in the 2008 Research Assessment Exercise, outperforms Queen's, Belfast in Northern Ireland, taking fifth place. Almost two-thirds of the students arrive without A levels, many of them upgrading other health-related qualifications. A quarter of those who join pre-registration programmes drop out, but the rate is nearer 10 per cent thereafter.

University we were unable to include this year because of insufficient data: Lincoln.

Employed in professional job:	89%
Employed in professional job and studying:	3%
Studying:	1%
Average starting professional salary:	£22,514

Employed in non-professional job and studying:	0%
Employed in non-professional job:	3%
Unemployed:	4%
Average starting non-professional salary:	£15,417

Nursing

		Research quality %	Entry standards	Student satisfaction %	Graduate prospects %	Overall rating
1	Glasgow	30.0	451	88.5		100.0
2	Edinburgh	41.7	468	87.4	95.5	99.0
3	Liverpool	20.0	362	92.2	100.0	95.4
4	Southampton	58.3	328	79.0	99.2	94.4
5	Ulster	53.3	310	84.7	96.2	93.8
6	Nottingham	31.7	374	83.8	98.3	93.7
7	York	46.7	318	84.3	97.3	93.4
8	Manchester Metropolitan	10.0	339	90.9	100.0	92.5
9	Cardiff	25.0	347	84.3	98.6	91.9
=10	Manchester	61.7	369	74.0	91.9	91.5
=10	Huddersfield		378	92.3	96.2	91.5
=12	Surrey	1.7	397	85.1	98.9	90.9
=12	De Montfort	16.7	308	87.3	100.0	90.9
14	Queen Margaret Edinburgh		334	90.2	100.0	90.6
=15	Birmingham		366	86.0	100.0	90.3
=15	Northumbria	26.7	290	86.9	97.0	90.3
=17	Swansea	18.3	341	81.1	99.0	89.7
=17	Portsmouth		390	88.6	94.1	89.7
19	King's College London	23.3	359	77.0	98.7	89.5
20	East Anglia	20.0	365	76.8	98.9	89.2
21	Leeds	36.7	348	73.2	96.8	88.7
=22	Coventry		304	91.3	96.7	88.4
=22	Teesside		325	88.4	97.5	88.4
=22	Glyndŵr	8.3	289	89.3	97.0	88.4
25	Hertfordshire	35.0	290	78.1	97.5	88.3

Nursing cont

		Research quality %	Entry standards	Student satisfaction %	Graduate prospects %	Overall rating
26	Greenwich	13.3	358	85.2	92.1	88.2
27	Bournemouth	20.0	309	78.5	96.0	86.3
28	Queen's, Belfast	20.0	283	83.6	93.5	86.2
29	West of England	16.7	297	78.5	97.4	86.0
30	Edge Hill	13.3	308	85.8	90.8	85.9
31	West London	20.0	258	80.4	97.8	85.8
32	Glasgow Caledonian	30.0	272	86.8	86.6	85.6
=33	Birmingham City		306	81.6	98.2	85.4
=33	Keele		258	84.5	100.0	85.4
=33	Liverpool John Moores	16.7	321	80.1	92.3	85.4
36	Salford	20.0	290	77.4	96.3	85.3
37	Northampton		304	82.9	96.8	85.2
38	Plymouth	16.7	296	79.4	94.3	85.0
39	Oxford Brookes		310	83.8	94.3	84.7
40	Stirling	30.0	219	82.6	92.9	84.5
41	Kingston/St George's	25.0	287	76.2	93.6	84.3
42	Brighton	5.0	290	77.9	98.0	84.0
43	Dundee	23.3	231	79.4	95.6	83.9
44	Worcester		255	85.0	95.9	83.7
45	Leeds Metropolitan		251	85.1	95.7	83.5
46	Cumbria		292	79.0	97.1	83.4
=47	City	43.3	277	73.9	87.9	83.3
=47	Bangor		259	78.9	100.0	83.3
49	Chester	5.0	260	80.5	96.6	83.2
=50	Canterbury Christ Church		308	75.5	97.7	82.9
=50	Sheffield Hallam	18.3	299	81.0	87.1	82.9
52	London South Bank	15.0	254	76.2	95.8	82.5
=53	Central Lancashire	23.3	277	72.5	93.9	82.4
=53	Staffordshire		253	82.3	95.5	82.4
55	Edinburgh Napier	16.7	252	75.8	94.5	82.0
56	Hull		304	77.8	92.7	81.5
57	Bedfordshire		246	76.5	97.2	80.6
58	Anglia Ruskin		249	73.7	98.5	80.3
59	Bradford	18.3	283	73.4	86.2	79.0
60	Robert Gordon		203	78.3	93.2	77.9
61	West of Scotland		249	81.6	82.8	76.6
62	Middlesex	15.0	247	80.0	78.9	76.4
63	Buckinghamshire New	3.3	240	79.0	78.3	73.8
64	Abertay		261	68.3	86.7	73.6

» NHS Careers: **www.nhscareers.nhs.uk**
» The Royal British Nurses' Association: **www.rbna.org.uk**
» Royal College of Nursing: **www.rcn.org.uk**

Other Subjects Allied to Medicine

This table has been shorn of two of the most popular choices: by popular demand, physiotherapy and radiography now have rankings of their own. Seven universities have dropped out of the table, either because they specialised in those areas or because their remaining numbers were too low to compile a reliable score. The remaining subjects include audiology, complementary therapies, counselling, health services management, health sciences, nutrition, occupational therapy, optometry, ophthalmology, orthoptics, osteopathy, podiatry and speech therapy. Taken together, the subjects suffered only a marginal decline at the introduction of higher fees. Ophthalmics actually recruited more students in 2012 than in the previous year, although complementary medicine suffered a serious decline of more than 45 per cent after the closure of some courses.

Since the removal of physiotherapy and radiography, traditional universities no longer monopolise the upper reaches of the table, but they still occupy the top five places. Aston, second last year and famously strong in ophthalmics, is the new leader, although it does not lead on any single indicator. Glasgow, last year's top university in this category, is one of those to drop. Cambridge, which is restricted to fourth place because it did not enter the 2008 Research Assessment Exercise in this category, has average entry grades that are almost 200 points ahead of its nearest challenger. Cumbria, which is only just in the top 30, has the most satisfied students, while second-placed University College London and Leeds, three places lower, share the best of a mediocre set of research grades.

Leeds also shares the best employment score. Like Abertay, in 37th place, all its leavers went straight into graduate-level work or further study in 2012. The choice of specialism naturally affects graduate employment rates, which range from better than 90 per cent positive destinations at nine universities to less than 60 per cent at a handful of universities in the bottom half of the table. Entry grades are relatively low: even a number of older universities average less than 400 points. Hertfordshire is the only post-1992 university in the top 10, but it is joined in the top 20 by Oxford Brookes, Glasgow Caledonian, Portsmouth and Anglia Ruskin. Across the whole range of subjects, almost half of the students arrive without A levels.

The subjects are in the top 20 for early employment prospects, but slightly lower since the loss of physiotherapy and radiography, which both have strong employment records. Seventy per cent of those completing a degree go straight into professional jobs or continue their studies and the 11 per cent unemployment rate is below average for all subjects.

Universities we were unable to include this year because of insufficient data: Bangor, Bristol, Glasgow, Keele, Sunderland.

» Association of Health Professions in Ophthalmology: **www.ahpo.org**
» British Association and College of Occupational Therapists: **www.cot.org.uk**
» British Society of Audiology: **www.thebsa.org.uk**
» General Chiropractic Council: **www.gcc-uk.org**
» General Osteopathic Council: **www.osteopathy.org.uk**
» General Optical Council: **www.optical.org**
» Health and Care Professions Council: **www.hpc-uk.org**
» NHS Careers: **www.nhscareers.nhs.uk**
» Royal College of Speech and Language Therapists: **www.rcslt.org**
» Society of Chiropodists and Podiatrists: **www.scpod.org**

Other Subjects Allied to Medicine

		Research quality %	Entry standards	Student satisfaction %	Graduate prospects %	Overall rating
1	Aston	26.7	442	88.8	97.8	100.0
2	University College London	36.7	450	88.9	82.2	99.3
3	Cardiff	31.7	461	83.6	95.6	98.9
4	Cambridge		651	88.7	86.1	98.8
5	Leeds	36.7	339	86.3	100.0	97.4
6	Hertfordshire	26.0	346	92.6	95.5	96.9
7	Manchester	30.0	445	88.2	81.6	96.7
8	Newcastle	30.0	449	88.3	76.8	95.7
9	Strathclyde	30.0	457	84.5	78.8	94.5
10	Lancaster	33.3	417	84.3	76.7	93.1
11	Oxford Brookes	16.7	379	92.0	84.2	92.6
12	Glasgow Caledonian	30.0	421	79.0	89.1	92.5
13	Exeter	30.0	451	78.5		91.9
14	City	18.3	391	85.5	90.6	91.7
15	Sheffield	30.0	434	85.2	63.7	90.1
16	Warwick	28.3	458	77.6	70.4	88.2
=17	Portsmouth	28.3		75.7	87.5	87.9
=17	Bradford	16.2	381	83.0	84.9	87.9
19	Dundee	23.3	449	80.1	70.0	87.6
20	Anglia Ruskin	8.3	295	90.8	91.2	87.5
21	West of England	31.7	332	81.8	76.3	87.3
22	Liverpool	20.0	323	86.1	80.0	86.8
23	Ulster	31.0	330	87.7	60.9	86.3
24	Durham		453	87.6	72.4	85.9
25	Swansea	31.7	383	71.3	80.8	85.0
26	Teesside	6.7	316	91.7	76.2	84.7
27	King's College London	15.0		79.4	84.6	84.6
28	Birmingham		431	89.0	67.6	84.3
29	Cumbria	0.0	332	93.0	75.8	84.1
30	Nottingham	20.0	372	84.2	64.1	84.0
=31	Manchester Metropolitan	12.7	382	82.5	72.9	83.6
=31	Brighton	5.0	255	89.1	90.5	83.6
33	Southampton	8.3	332	81.9	83.6	82.4
34	East Anglia	5.0	403	83.1	71.4	82.3
35	Queen Margaret Edinburgh	1.7	356	79.3	90.7	82.1
36	York St John	1.7	320	86.2	81.8	81.9
=37	Chester	5.0	290	85.2	84.9	81.7
=37	Abertay	3.3	313	77.0	100.0	81.7
39	Sheffield Hallam	8.3	328	85.0	72.3	81.2
40	Nottingham Trent	30.0		75.7	64.3	80.8
41	Coventry	6.7	295	85.1	78.2	80.7
=42	Northampton	6.7	308	82.7	75.5	79.3
=42	St Mark and St John		370		73.1	79.3

44 Central Lancashire	13.3	283	85.2	64.9	78.8
45 Robert Gordon	10.0	363	76.7	72.2	78.7
46 Westminster	18.3	289	74.1	80.6	78.5
=47 West of Scotland	23.3	325	77.1	61.5	78.4
=47 Lincoln	3.3	313	83.4	73.3	78.4
49 Kent	16.7	380	76.0	61.5	78.3
50 Plymouth	3.3	318	81.6	75.4	78.2
51 Greenwich		315	84.5	72.7	78.0
52 Salford	15.0	295	78.6	71.4	77.9
53 Brunel	15.0	343	76.5	65.1	77.3
54 Huddersfield		284	83.6	76.7	77.1
55 Leeds Metropolitan	3.3	318	81.6	70.4	76.9
56 Cardiff Metropolitan	8.3	313	81.1	64.4	76.4
57 Essex		343	85.0	59.3	76.1
58 Bournemouth		318	83.5	64.7	75.6
59 St Mary's College		304	78.0	73.6	74.2
60 London Metropolitan	13.3	284	81.9	52.8	74.0
61 Bedfordshire		242	76.7	85.9	73.8
62 Liverpool John Moores	11.7	340	72.7	61.7	73.4
63 Middlesex	13.3	254	78.3	61.8	73.0
64 Edinburgh Napier	6.7		75.9	65.0	72.3
65 Derby		313	80.3	59.0	72.2
=66 Birmingham City		331	76.8	63.0	72.1
=66 St George's		397	72.5	60.0	72.1
68 Northumbria	13.3	310	68.0	68.6	71.7
69 De Montfort	11.7	303	74.8	55.9	71.4
=70 Canterbury Christ Church	1.7	237	79.6	66.7	70.8
=70 East London	16.7	252	73.4	60.0	70.8
72 Reading		422	72.9	47.6	70.3
73 Goldsmiths College	0.0	294			68.3
74 Hull	33.3	326	66.2	32.8	68.2

Employed in professional job:	55%	Employed in non-professional job and studying:	2%
Employed in professional job and studying:	4%	Employed in non-professional job:	17%
Studying:	11%	Unemployed:	11%
Average starting professional salary:	£20,007	Average starting non-professional salary:	£14,555

Pharmacology and Pharmacy

Pharmacology and pharmacy have been among the big successes of higher education, with substantial increases in applications and enrolments in recent years. Both held their own in 2012, in spite of the switch to higher fees, and have increased again in 2013. But this may come to an end, for pharmacy at least, in 2015 as the result of a Government-commissioned inquiry to examine whether there is now too much provision. It would not appear so from our employment table, which has pharmacology and pharmacy in third place, with an

Pharmacology and Pharmacy cont

unemployment rate of 4 per cent that is bettered only by medicine, dentistry and nursing. However, the number of English universities accredited for the MPharm course, which is the only direct route to professional registration as a pharmacist, has almost doubled in a decade. It is now offered at 21 institutions, compared with 12 in 2002, and two more universities are seeking full accreditation. Unlike medicine and dentistry, recruitment in the subjects has never been controlled centrally, but this is one of the options before the review. Any change of policy will not affect courses beginning in 2014, although it could have an impact on the demand for places. There were more than seven applications for every place in 2012.

Departments in England are evenly split between those specialising in pharmacy and pharmacology. Only four cover both. While the MPharm degree takes four years, pharmacology is available either as a three-year BSc or as an extended course. Most degrees require chemistry and another science or maths at A level or the equivalent. Surprisingly, given graduates' success in the labour market, the subjects are not high in the earnings league: average starting salaries have dropped since last year's *Guide* and average less than £20,000 in professional-level jobs.

Cambridge remains top of the table, where the university's normal high entry standards make the difference: they are 150 points ahead of the rest. Nottingham, which holds on to second place, has the best research score. Edinburgh actually achieved the best grades in the 2008 Research Assessment Exercise, but is one of six universities to have dropped out of the table this year. The most satisfied students are at Queen's, Belfast and, like last year,

Employed in professional job:	75%	Employed in non-professional job and studying:	0%
Employed in professional job and studying:	6%	Employed in non-professional job:	4%
Studying:	9%	Unemployed:	6%
Average starting professional salary:	£19,744	Average starting non-professional salary:	£14,243

Pharmacology and Pharmacy	Research quality %	Entry standards	Student satisfaction %	Graduate prospects %	Overall rating
1 Cambridge	33.3	651	88.7	86.1	100.0
2 Nottingham	50.0	470	83.4	96.7	96.4
3 Queen's, Belfast	28.3	433	95.6	99.2	94.4
4 Aston	26.7	459	91.8	100.0	93.3
5 Bath	33.3	450	88.1	100.0	93.2
6 Cardiff	28.3	454	90.2	97.9	92.4
7 Manchester	43.3	463	81.2	93.8	92.3
8 Dundee	38.3	403	86.9		91.8
9 East Anglia	28.3	442	88.6	100.0	91.5
10 Newcastle	33.3		90.3	76.5	89.2
11 Bristol	28.3	468	82.9	95.2	89.0
12 Leeds	30.0	409	91.6	77.8	87.9
13 King's College London	28.3	436	81.5	93.9	86.6
14 Glasgow	28.3	486	80.0	85.0	86.4
=15 Strathclyde	28.3	507	72.8	93.0	85.3
=15 Portsmouth	28.3	353	88.1	89.8	85.3

17 Reading	21.7	378	84.7	100.0	84.6
18 Bradford	28.3	376	82.2	95.8	84.5
19 University College London	36.1	450	69.9	93.5	83.8
20 Brighton	18.3	379	85.7	97.9	83.7
21 Liverpool	30.2	435	80.6	77.3	83.6
22 Huddersfield	8.3	376	89.9	97.7	82.5
=23 Hertfordshire	15.0	346	87.2	97.2	81.7
=23 Keele	5.0	388	89.4	97.9	81.7
=25 Central Lancashire		392	88.6	100.0	80.3
=25 Robert Gordon		450	83.9	98.2	80.3
27 Kent	15.5	364	76.0	100.0	77.7
28 De Montfort	18.3	345	80.6	87.3	77.6
29 Sunderland	6.7	376	74.6	100.0	74.8
30 Liverpool John Moores	11.7	397	70.8	96.4	74.7
31 Glasgow Caledonian	13.3	391	74.7		72.6
32 Greenwich	11.7	305	81.1	67.6	70.3
33 Kingston	11.7	302	66.3	78.6	64.9
34 East London		254	85.0	30.8	59.4
35 London Metropolitan		250	79.5	20.0	54.5

seven universities saw all their graduates go into professional jobs or further study. They were Aston, Bath, East Anglia, Reading, Central Lancashire, Kent and Sunderland. Entry standards are high: half of the universities in the table average more than 400 points and only two less than 300. Dundee is now the leading university in Scotland, while Cardiff remains the only representative of Wales. Portsmouth is the highest-placed post-1992 university and is joined by Brighton in the top 20.

Universities we were unable to include this year because of insufficient data: Aberdeen, Edinburgh, Hull, Nottingham Trent, Ulster.

» Association of Pharmacy Technicians, UK: **www.aptuk.org**
» British Pharmacological Society: **www.bps.ac.uk**
» General Pharmaceutical Council: **www.pharmacyregulation.org**
» Royal Pharmaceutical Society: **www.rpharms.com**

Philosophy

Philosophy confounded the sceptics who predicted a decline for subjects without a clear pathway to employment in the era of £3,000 fees. With almost six applications to the place in 2011, it was one of the most competitive subjects in the arts and social sciences. But there were ominous signs in 2012, as fees rose again, with applications and enrolments dropping by much more than the national average. Entry scores dropped at some of the leading universities, although more than half of the 44 universities in the table averaged more than 400 points.

Oxford is back on top of the table, a year after losing the leadership to Cambridge. It has the highest entry standards in the table, but University College London, in eighth place, produced the best results in the 2008 Research Assessment Exercise, when three-quarters

Philosophy cont

of its submission was rated world-leading or internationally excellent. The University of the West of England has the most satisfied students and is the top post-1992 university and it is joined by Brighton in the top 30. Philosophers are generally satisfied with their courses: only five universities had an approval rating below 80 per cent in the 2013 National Student Survey.

Employment is more of a problem, however. Exeter, which is up 12 places to sixth this year, was the only university to see 80 per cent of philosophers go straight into professional jobs or onto postgraduate courses. At 15 universities, fewer than half of the graduates were in this position and at Dundee the proportion dropped to a quarter. Philosophy remains just in the bottom 20 subjects in the employment table, but salaries for those who do find professional-level jobs are in the top 30, at close to £21,000.

Relatively few philosophy undergraduates studied the subject at A level – indeed, Bristol warns that even an A in the subject is "not necessarily evidence of aptitude for philosophy at university". Degrees can require more mathematical skills than many candidates expect, especially when there is an emphasis on logic in the syllabus. St Andrews remains the top university in Scotland, despite slipping three places to seventh, while Cardiff is now the only Welsh university in the table.

University we were unable to include this year because of insufficient data: Roehampton.

Employed in professional job:	28%	Employed in non-professional job and studying:	4%
Employed in professional job and studying:	3%	Employed in non-professional job:	26%
Studying:	24%	Unemployed:	16%
Average starting professional salary:	£20,807	Average starting non-professional salary:	£14,717

Philosophy	Research quality %	Entry standards	Student satisfaction %	Graduate prospects %	Overall rating
1 Oxford	45.0	594	86.6	75.3	100.0
2 Cambridge	42.7	581	84.7	77.8	98.3
3 Durham	28.3	550	89.6	74.6	97.2
4 London School of Economics	45.0	508	85.0	77.8	96.5
5 King's College London	48.3	490	84.3	76.7	95.9
6 Exeter	31.7	483	87.6	81.4	95.5
7 St Andrews	51.7	524	82.6	67.3	94.7
8 University College London	55.0	477	80.4	71.8	93.2
9 Newcastle	26.7	418	88.8	72.7	91.5
10 Bristol	41.7	483	80.2	74.7	91.2
11 Sheffield	46.7	455	84.4	56.9	90.7
12 East Anglia	15.0	406	93.9	64.0	90.6
13 Nottingham	36.7	417	83.5	71.6	89.7
14 Southampton	16.7	407	87.9	78.1	89.6
=15 Warwick	28.3	532	82.5	62.0	89.5
=15 York	28.3	470	83.3	70.4	89.5
17 Essex	38.3	370	90.2	45.0	87.9
=18 Birmingham	18.3	414	86.4	70.3	87.7

=18 Edinburgh	35.0	496	78.8	64.7	87.7
20 Reading	45.0	390	86.0	46.3	87.3
21 Sussex	26.7	425	90.7	40.6	86.9
22 Stirling	40.0	401	86.0	46.3	86.7
23 West of England	5.0	307	96.3	53.8	85.0
24 Manchester	21.7	477	78.7	64.5	84.3
25 Glasgow	21.7	466	85.1	39.1	83.4
26 Kent	18.3	375	83.7	63.4	83.3
27 Cardiff	13.3	419	81.3	67.2	83.0
28 Keele	16.7	351	87.0	54.1	82.6
29 Brighton	45.0	288	82.9	47.8	82.1
30 Lancaster	20.0	427	80.9	54.2	81.8
31 Leeds	35.0	413	78.9	45.6	81.3
32 Queen's, Belfast	25.0	379	83.3	42.1	80.5
33 Oxford Brookes	0.0	333	86.5	54.9	78.7
34 Dundee	21.7	375	86.2	25.0	78.4
35 Aberdeen	8.3	406	84.1	36.7	77.7
36 Heythrop College	1.7	360	82.8	54.5	77.4
37 Hertfordshire	11.7	335	82.3	41.4	75.6
38 Hull	15.0	342	76.8	50.1	74.5
39 Liverpool	8.3	425	74.1	49.0	74.0
40 Manchester Metropolitan	16.7	317	81.1	33.9	73.8
41 Central Lancashire		296	88.7	26.6	73.6
42 Greenwich		267	80.4	50.9	71.7
43 Anglia Ruskin		242	81.7	41.4	69.9
44 Staffordshire	6.7	252	80.2		69.5

» British Philosophical Association: **www.bpa.ac.uk**
» Philosophical Society of England:
   http://atschool.eduweb.co.uk/cite/staff/philosopher/philsocindex.htm
» Royal Institute of Philosophy: **www.royalinstitutephilosophy.org**

Physics and Astronomy

There has been concern about the state of physics for at least 20 years, with sixth-form numbers dropping and university departments closing. But the numbers starting physics degrees have gone up by 50 per cent in six years and even the prospect of £9,000 fees could not prevent further significant rises in both applications and enrolments in 2012. The 8 per cent growth in the demand for places even gave physics more applications than chemistry for the first time. The "Brian Cox effect" has been credited with the recent boom in popularity, in recognition of the engaging Manchester University professor's many television appearances.

There were almost six applications to the place in 2011 and physics is now one of the most competitive tables, with high scores among the leading universities. No fewer than 11 universities, led by top-placed Cambridge, average more than 500 points at entry and only one has an average of less than 300. Like last year, Cambridge has the slimmest possible

Physics and Astronomy

	Research quality %	Entry standards	Student satisfaction %	Graduate prospects %	Overall rating
1 Cambridge	38.3	651	88.8	86.1	100.0
2 St Andrews	38.3	530	94.4	88.4	99.9
3 Birmingham	33.3	538	92.3	85.0	96.4
4 Imperial College	35.0	609	84.6	88.6	95.9
5 Nottingham	38.3	473	88.3	83.2	93.8
6 Bath	36.7	488	83.8	93.8	93.7
7 Oxford	31.7	628	82.3	86.5	93.5
8 Durham	33.3	584	83.2	87.0	93.4
9 Manchester	31.7	566	86.3	75.9	91.4
=10 Sheffield	33.3	474	88.8	79.1	91.3
=10 Surrey	25.0	439	89.4	95.4	91.3
12 Warwick	26.7	540	81.4	94.6	90.5
13 Lancaster	40.0	498	84.9	70.0	90.3
14 Sussex	30.0	427	89.4	83.3	90.0
15 Exeter	30.0	476	82.5	91.9	89.7
16 Glasgow	33.3	481	84.0	79.2	89.0
17 Bristol	31.7	529	78.8	82.5	87.9
18 University College London	33.3	509	80.7	76.6	87.5
19 Edinburgh	35.0	520	78.4	75.5	87.0
20 Heriot-Watt	28.3	399	90.0	73.6	86.7
21 Queen's, Belfast	23.3	413	85.4	88.9	86.3
=22 Southampton	28.3	474	81.5	80.6	86.0
=22 Leicester	28.3	416	86.7	76.0	86.0
24 Leeds	26.7	428	89.7	69.4	85.8
25 Cardiff	20.0	445	84.3	86.6	85.0
26 York	28.3	444	82.3	75.5	84.3
27 Royal Holloway	25.0	407	89.8	67.5	84.2
28 Aberdeen	31.7	443	79.1		83.5
29 Liverpool	31.7	449	80.2	67.9	82.9
30 Strathclyde	16.7	422	87.7	76.4	82.5
31 Loughborough	26.7	402	87.5	60.3	81.7
32 Nottingham Trent	28.3	322	94.1	51.5	81.5
33 Hertfordshire	28.3	346	84.7	68.2	81.0
34 King's College London	23.3	453	79.0	69.0	79.6
=35 Keele	16.7	368	92.2	57.7	79.0
=35 Salford	23.3	312	85.8		79.0
37 Swansea	23.3	349	83.6	66.7	78.4
38 Central Lancashire	16.7	326	88.2		78.0
39 Hull	20.0	350	86.6	52.9	75.6
40 Kent	26.5	368	72.6	71.3	75.3
41 Queen Mary, London	27.4	372	72.5	64.7	74.3
42 Aberystwyth	10.0	310	78.2	55.9	67.0
43 West of Scotland	6.7	260	80.9		65.3

lead over St Andrews, which had the top score in the 2013 National Student Survey. Oxford has dropped four places to seventh, with Birmingham taking over in third. Cambridge has the highest entry standards, but Lancaster is top for research under the more detailed presentation of surprisingly modest scores from the 2008 assessments.

Surrey is the top performer in an improved set of employment scores, but physics has slipped out of the top ten subjects in the overall employment table. Unemployment is above average, at 15 per cent, and little more than a third of graduates went straight into professional jobs, although 45 per cent of physics graduates continued their studies, either full or part-time. The subject is also just outside the top 10 for starting salaries, averaging just over £24,500.

Physics has produced consistently high scores for student satisfaction, with almost every university satisfying at least three-quarters of their undergraduates in the last three years' results. Cardiff has retaken the lead from Swansea in Wales, while Nottingham Trent is just ahead of Hertfordshire as the highest-placed of the four post-1992 universities in the table.

Most universities demand physics and maths at A level for both physics and astronomy, as well as good grades overall. Only one undergraduate in five is female and a similarly small proportion arrives without A levels or their equivalent. About 5 per cent transfer to other courses or drop out, usually at the end of the first year, but well over half of those who remain get firsts or 2:1s.

Employed in professional job:	31%	Employed in non-professional job and studying:	1%
Employed in professional job and studying:	4%	Employed in non-professional job:	9%
Studying:	40%	Unemployed:	15%
Average starting professional salary:	£24,504	Average starting non-professional salary:	£14,990

» British Astronomical Association: **http://britastro/.org/baa/**
» Institute of Physics: **www.iop.org**

Physiotherapy

Physiotherapy is one of two new tables in the *Guide* this year. Courses in the subject were part of the ranking of "other subjects allied to medicine", but it has been sufficiently popular in recent years to warrant a separate table. Indeed, the subject became so popular in the latter half of the last decade that unemployment among physiotherapy graduates became a serious problem, but its first appearance in our employment table is in the top ten. Indeed, only seven subjects have lower unemployment rates and nearly 80 per cent of 2011 graduates went straight into professional jobs. Physiotherapy cannot match that performance in the earnings table, but average starting salaries of £21,500 in professional jobs still place it in the top half of all subjects.

The Chartered Society of Physiotherapy now accredits degrees at all 35 institutions offering the subject in the UK. Most of the leading courses demand Biology A level or equivalent, but some may also want another science or maths. Applications and enrolments fell when higher fees were introduced in 2012, but by much less than the national average, and demand recovered in 2013. Cardiff tops the first physiotherapy table, with Nottingham its nearest challenger. Entry grades are relatively low and closely bunched. Only Robert

Physiotherapy cont

Gordon, the leading modern university in the table, averages more than 450 points, but no university has average scores below 300 points.

Cardiff and the University of the West of England tied for the best grades in the 2008 Research Assessment Exercise, but the standard in physiotherapy was lower than in most other subjects. York St John has the most satisfied students and is one of ten post-1992 universities in the top 20. Keele registers a rare 100 per cent employment score and only four universities drop below 80 per cent for the proportion of graduates with positive destinations.

Physiotherapy	Research quality %	Entry standards	Student satisfaction %	Graduate prospects %	Overall rating
1 Cardiff	31.7	445	89.2	95.7	100.0
2 Nottingham	20.0	419	87.6	97.0	95.1
3 Keele	23.3	376	88.2	100.0	94.5
4 Liverpool	20.0	400	88.8	89.3	92.7
=5 Birmingham		449	89.3	95.2	92.2
=5 Robert Gordon	10.0	485	84.7	85.7	92.2
7 Oxford Brookes	16.7	398	86.6	94.4	92.0
8 Brunel	15.0	383	94.8	83.0	91.8
9 Glasgow Caledonian	30.0	443	74.4	89.6	90.8
10 King's College London	15.0	425	81.3	93.9	90.4
11 Teesside	6.7	408	90.0	88.9	90.3
12 Bradford	16.7	353	90.1	90.9	90.2
=13 York St John	1.7	368	95.6	89.3	89.6
=13 Northumbria	13.3	384	85.3	93.9	89.6
15 West of England	31.7	356	83.8	83.7	89.4
=16 Salford	15.0	383	90.5	80.0	89.0
=16 East Anglia	5.0	396	89.9	88.2	89.0
18 Brighton	5.0	354	91.8	93.8	88.9
=19 Sheffield Hallam	8.3	373	89.1	89.3	88.4
=19 Coventry	6.7	372	90.5	88.4	88.4
21 East London	16.7	307	86.1	97.4	87.3
22 Kingston/St George's	11.7	362	87.4	82.8	86.2
23 Bournemouth		367	89.4	88.9	86.0
24 Plymouth	3.3	369	83.9	91.3	84.9
25 Hertfordshire		385	82.7	89.2	83.8
26 Ulster	31.0	365	87.3	52.2	83.7
27 Southampton	8.3	437	74.9	82.8	83.6
28 Manchester Metropolitan	13.5	385	82.5	72.5	83.1
29 Queen Margaret Edinburgh	1.7		84.8	85.7	83.0
30 Leeds Metropolitan	3.3	332	90.4	72.0	81.2
31 Central Lancashire	13.3	332	78.7	82.1	80.5
32 Cumbria	0.0	307	86.5	71.4	76.9

» Chartered Society of Physiotherapy: **www.csp.org.uk**

Employed in graduate job:	78%	Employed in non-graduate job and studying:	0%
Employed in graduate job and studying:	1%	Employed in non-graduate job:	9%
Studying:	2%	Unemployed:	8%
Average starting graduate salary:	£21,502	Average starting non-graduate salary:	£13,953

Politics

Politics has been enjoying a boom as a degree subject, applications growing by almost a quarter in the first two years of the decade. The trend was reversed in 2012, with a big drop in the demand for places as £9,000 fees were introduced, but the numbers actually taking up places were down by less than the average for all subjects and there was a recovery in 2013.

With six applications for every place, entry scores have been rising. The table contains two more universities than last year. This year 26 of the top 30 – more than twice as many as in the 2009 *Guide* – average over 400 points and only two universities fall below 250 points.

The top three remain unchanged, with Oxford in first place. It has the highest entry grades, ahead of Cambridge in second place. Sheffield, in third, shares the best score from the 2008 Research Assessment Exercise with Essex, which would be higher than equal sixth but for a poor year for graduate employment. Both had three-quarters of their research rated world-leading or internationally excellent. Cardiff has overtaken Aberystwyth as the top university in Wales, while St Andrews remains the leader in Scotland. No post-1992 university makes the top 30, and Huddersfield, which has the most satisfied students, is again the only one in the top 40.

Satisfaction scores in politics were generally high in the 2013 National Student Survey: none of the 73 universities failed to satisfy at least 70 per cent of their final-year undergraduates. The best employment prospects are at University College London, in equal sixth place, the only institution to see 90 per cent of graduates go straight into professional jobs or further study. Scores elsewhere are variable, with 14 universities failing to register positive destinations for half of their politics graduates. The subject has dropped out of the top 20 in the earnings league, in spite of a small increase in average salaries. It is nearly 20 places lower for overall employment prospects. Unemployment is above average for all subjects, at 15 per cent, and more than a quarter of all graduates start off in lower-level jobs.

Universities we were unable to include this year because of insufficient data: Birmingham City, Cardiff Metropolitan.

Politics	Research quality %	Entry Standards	Student satisfaction %	Graduate prospects %	Overall rating
1 Oxford	43.3	596	85.3	80.2	100.0
2 Cambridge	30.0	558		79.7	97.3
3 Sheffield	55.0	486	82.7	68.1	94.7
=4 Exeter	31.7	483	85.0	79.9	93.1
=4 University College London	35.0	555	75.9	89.9	93.1
=6 Durham	26.7	511	81.6	89.0	92.9
=6 Essex	55.0	413	86.2	61.5	92.9
=8 Bath	21.7	472	88.0	82.4	92.8

Politics cont

	Research quality	Entry standards	Student satisfaction %	Graduate prospects %	Overall rating
=8 London School of Economics	40.0	550	78.9	75.5	92.8
10 York	25.0	471	87.5	78.5	92.4
11 Warwick	33.3	512	79.8	81.0	91.6
12 St Andrews	21.7	524	83.5	78.1	90.9
13 Cardiff	25.0	462	83.4	79.2	89.7
14 Newcastle	23.3	417	85.7	73.1	87.8
15 Bristol	20.0	476	81.7	77.9	87.7
16 Birmingham	18.3	416	82.2	83.9	86.8
17 Nottingham	26.7	438	83.8	66.1	86.7
18 Brunel	11.7	349	92.0	64.4	84.7
=19 Glasgow	25.0	465	81.7	59.4	84.5
=19 SOAS London	30.0	478	77.5	63.4	84.5
21 Manchester	30.0	470	77.9	63.7	84.4
=22 King's College London	25.0	480	79.8	61.6	84.3
=22 Loughborough	20.0	376	85.0	68.8	84.3
=24 East Anglia	15.0	409	88.1	60.1	84.2
=24 Kent	11.7	385	85.2	75.4	84.2
26 Lancaster	10.0	436	84.6	70.6	84.1
27 Surrey	13.3	406	88.7	56.9	83.4
28 Edinburgh	25.0	498	74.1	67.5	82.8
=29 Royal Holloway	13.3	412	80.8	73.2	82.3
=29 Aston	10.0	369	84.3	73.6	82.3
=31 Sussex	29.1	419	84.1	45.1	82.2
=31 Huddersfield	0.0	296	94.8	66.2	82.2
33 Leicester	8.3	407	85.8	64.2	82.1
34 Aberystwyth	48.3	334	76.0	56.1	81.3
=35 Queen Mary, London	18.3	439	75.9	71.0	81.0
=35 Reading	18.3	366	81.6	66.7	81.0
37 Hull	18.3	379	84.9	54.7	80.9
38 Aberdeen	11.7	443	77.1	73.1	80.8
39 Leeds	8.3	439	79.7	69.1	80.6
40 Southampton	13.3	418	77.8	71.4	80.4
41 Queen's, Belfast	23.3	390	80.1	57.2	80.0
42 Lincoln	10.0	304	90.9	54.5	79.9
43 Portsmouth	25.0	303	85.0	53.5	79.6
44 Dundee	16.7	384	83.3	52.8	79.3
45 City		396	84.3	65.6	79.2
46 Liverpool	5.0	418	81.2	63.9	78.8
47 Bradford	26.7	304	78.5	64.8	78.6
=48 Oxford Brookes	6.7	350	79.2	75.3	78.1
=48 Strathclyde	10.0	449	80.2	52.7	78.1
50 Keele	16.7	330	82.9	54.5	77.5
51 West of England	5.0	320	87.6	54.9	77.4

52	Plymouth	19.5	290	80.0	63.0	76.9
=53	Nottingham Trent		284	87.1	62.5	76.3
=53	Swansea	10.0	363	75.6	71.3	76.3
55	Stirling	8.3	412	80.8	49.2	76.0
56	Westminster	10.0	330	84.3	49.7	75.8
57	Leeds Metropolitan		246	86.2	68.2	75.7
58	Goldsmiths College	16.7	348	77.5	54.5	74.9
59	Sunderland	1.7	306	83.6		73.4
60	Coventry	6.7	284	79.5	61.7	73.1
61	Ulster	18.3	269	81.4	42.5	72.3
=62	Northumbria	15.0	355	70.0	59.6	71.3
=62	De Montfort	10.0	299	82.6	39.1	71.3
64	Canterbury Christ Church		277	84.0	48.0	71.0
65	Sheffield Hallam		279	84.4	44.1	70.5
66	London Metropolitan	10.0	227	78.9	54.2	69.9
=67	Brighton	45.0	298	70.4	23.8	68.8
=67	Central Lancashire	1.7	349	79.2	38.3	68.8
=67	Winchester		307	81.7	39.1	68.8
70	Manchester Metropolitan	6.7	309	75.1	45.8	67.8
71	Kingston	10.0	293	74.7	44.3	67.5
72	Greenwich	0.0	254	74.7	50.0	65.0
73	Salford	11.7	296	70.7	37.8	64.1

Employed in professional job:	36%	Employed in non-professional job and studying:		3%
Employed in professional job and studying:	4%	Employed in non-professional job:		23%
Studying:	20%	Unemployed:		15%
Average starting professional salary:	£21,655	Average starting non-professional salary:		£15,291

» Political Studies Association: **www.psa.ac.uk**
» Study Politics: **www.psa.ac.uk/psa-communities/specialist-groups/schools**

Psychology

Psychology is the biggest table in the *Guide*, despite two Welsh universities dropping out after declining to release data for league tables this year. Another four have joined, making 107 in all. Applications fell by 6 per cent in 2012, but only nursing and design attracted bigger totals. There was a smaller decline in the numbers actually starting degrees and the demand for places was back to previous levels in 2013. The popularity of the subject endures in spite of poor performances in the graduate employment market: it is in the bottom ten for the proportion of graduates with "positive destinations" and the bottom 15 for average starting salaries in professional-level jobs. Although unemployment is below average at 12 per cent, more than 40 per cent of graduates begin their careers in low-level jobs.

Most undergraduate programmes are accredited by the British Psychological Society, which ensures that key topics are covered, but the clinical and biological content of courses still varies considerably. Some universities require maths and/or biology A levels among

Psychology cont

three high-grade passes, but others are much less demanding. The contrast is obvious in the ranking, with 31 universities averaging more than 400 points at entry but six below 250 points.

Cambridge remains top of the table, with Bath replacing Oxford in second place. Cambridge has the highest entry scores by a margin of more than 100 points and the best grades in the 2008 Research Assessment Exercise, when 80 per cent of research considered world-leading or internationally excellent. The top two are the only universities to see three-quarters of their psychology graduates go straight into professional jobs or join postgraduate courses. The top scores for student satisfaction could hardly be closer, with four universities within a fraction of a point of each other. Lincoln, the only modern university in the top 20, pips Edge Hill, Chester and Bath, each with approval ratings of more than 90 per cent. Only three universities at the bottom of the table dropped below 70 per cent.

There have been some big moves in the overall table for psychology. Birmingham is up 15 places to fifth and Lincoln enjoyed an even bigger rise. However, Sheffield is down 16 places and Sussex 25. Glasgow remains the top university in Scotland and Cardiff the same in Wales.

Employed in professional job:	26%	Employed in non-professional job and studying:	5%
Employed in professional job and studying:	4%	Employed in non-professional job:	36%
Studying:	16%	Unemployed:	12%
Average starting professional salary:	£19,006	Average starting non-professional salary:	£14,287

Psychology	Research quality %	Entry standards	Student satisfaction %	Graduate prospects %	Overall rating
1 Cambridge	51.7	651	88.4	79.7	100.0
2 Bath	48.3	538	90.3	79.2	96.2
3 Oxford	50.0	544	89.0	67.2	93.0
4 Glasgow	33.3	477	87.9	74.3	88.4
5 Birmingham	43.3	461	84.3	64.9	85.7
6 Durham	30.0	484	83.4	71.6	84.8
7 York	35.0	487	87.2	57.6	84.4
8 University College London	45.0	522	82.1	54.4	84.3
9 St Andrews	35.0	528	80.4	64.5	84.1
10 Exeter	28.3	492	84.6	66.4	84.0
11 Bristol	26.7	481	87.1	62.5	83.6
12 Cardiff	40.0	459	85.3	55.6	83.0
13 Loughborough	36.7	418	82.8	65.1	82.0
14 Southampton	30.0	444	84.6	61.5	81.5
15 Nottingham	26.7	437	85.5	60.5	80.7
16 Bangor	35.0	346	85.8	63.5	80.3
17 Kent	20.0	413	83.9	70.1	80.1
18 Lincoln	11.7	362	90.9	69.5	80.0
19 Newcastle	20.0	455	85.0	59.4	79.3
=20 Surrey	20.0	440	85.8	59.3	79.2
=20 Royal Holloway	33.3	441	84.8	49.8	79.2

22 Lancaster	20.0	442	78.4	67.6	77.6
23 Warwick	25.0	470	77.4	61.2	77.5
24 Edinburgh	30.0	479	75.1	60.0	77.4
25 Leeds	23.3	447	79.0	61.5	77.2
26 Reading	26.7	395	82.0	58.6	77.0
=27 Sheffield	30.0	452	82.0	47.6	76.8
=27 Portsmouth	8.3	349	88.8	66.0	76.8
29 Strathclyde	10.0	473	86.1	51.9	76.4
30 Aberdeen	20.0	393	82.2	60.1	75.9
=31 Sussex	30.0	422	79.3	53.0	75.7
=31 City	20.0	392	89.3	45.0	75.7
33 Manchester	23.0	444	82.5	48.8	75.6
34 Goldsmiths College	23.3	346	83.8	57.3	75.2
35 Leicester	8.3	407	85.9	57.5	75.1
36 Queen Mary, London	20.0	407	74.2	70.0	74.9
37 Aston	26.7	394	83.3	47.9	74.8
38 Chester	5.0	310	90.7	61.3	74.6
39 Essex	25.0	368	83.8	48.2	73.9
40 East Anglia	5.0	424	84.7	53.6	73.4
41 Swansea	15.0	375	77.6	63.4	72.7
42 Coventry	6.2	316	82.9	66.7	72.4
43 Queen's, Belfast	13.3	383	81.0	55.2	72.3
44 Dundee	15.0	385	84.0	47.5	72.2
45 Stirling	8.3	398	82.3	53.9	72.1
46 Plymouth	13.3	341	81.8	56.4	71.5
47 Liverpool	13.3	414	79.4	50.8	71.4
48 Heriot-Watt	1.7	389	78.4	64.9	71.2
49 York St John	0.0	317	87.7	57.1	71.1
=50 Keele	8.3	352	83.6	53.5	71.0
=50 Nottingham Trent	5.0	350	86.1	51.4	71.0
52 Oxford Brookes	8.3	389	85.7	41.8	70.4
53 Glasgow Caledonian	3.3	392	82.5	51.1	70.1
=54 Manchester Metropolitan	17.4	350	78.1	53.2	70.0
=54 Queen Margaret Edinburgh		338	84.6	56.3	70.0
56 Huddersfield		310	85.5	56.2	69.4
=57 Hull	15.0	358	79.6	48.3	69.3
=57 Bradford	23.3	283	82.5	45.6	69.3
59 Salford	15.0	314	83.7	43.4	68.6
60 Hertfordshire	13.3	345	77.7	51.1	68.2
61 Edge Hill		308	90.8	40.7	68.1
62 Greenwich	5.0	304	84.8	48.5	68.0
=63 Abertay	5.0	293	79.5	60.5	67.9
=63 Chichester	10.0	282	84.8	47.1	67.9
65 Brunel	15.0	370	75.6	49.1	67.8
66 West of Scotland		308	88.0	43.9	67.5
67 De Montfort		317	87.1	44.0	67.4
68 Central Lancashire	10.0	322	78.6	51.1	67.1

Psychology cont

		Research quality %	Entry standards	Student satisfaction %	Graduate prospects %	Overall rating
69	Bournemouth	15.0	357	84.2	30.6	67.0
70	Liverpool John Moores	11.7	329	81.9	41.0	66.9
71	Bath Spa	1.7	350	81.9	45.5	66.6
72	Cumbria		223	87.0	52.2	66.2
73	West of England	16.7	329	72.6	52.2	66.0
74	Leeds Trinity	0.0	303	84.8	44.7	65.9
75	Cardiff Metropolitan	8.3	291	82.6	42.9	65.6
76	Teesside		315	84.3	40.4	64.9
77	Sunderland	1.7	274	86.0	40.3	64.7
=78	Anglia Ruskin	18.3	266	83.4	31.9	64.6
=78	Middlesex	3.3	281	73.5	62.6	64.6
=78	Gloucestershire	3.3	297	83.3	40.8	64.6
81	Westminster	5.0	311	77.7	48.2	64.5
=82	Northumbria	8.3	350	73.6	48.0	64.4
=82	Sheffield Hallam	3.3	338	78.4	44.3	64.4
84	London South Bank	6.7	292	80.3	43.7	64.3
85	Roehampton	6.7	263	77.5	52.7	64.2
86	Brighton	11.7	341	74.9	41.9	63.9
87	Derby	3.3	278	75.0	56.1	63.7
88	Aberystwyth	5.0	298	71.8	57.3	63.3
89	Worcester		298	78.4	48.1	63.2
90	Ulster	11.7	282	84.7	27.5	63.1
91	Winchester		319	75.8	48.4	62.7
92	East London	6.7	236	82.7	38.0	62.2
93	West London	0.0	227	76.1	57.1	62.0
=94	Canterbury Christ Church		286	77.1	45.6	61.6
=94	Staffordshire	10.0	298	75.2	39.9	61.6
96	Newman		308	80.0	36.5	61.4
=97	Northampton		307	79.1	37.9	61.3
=97	Birmingham City		317	74.9	44.8	61.3
99	Edinburgh Napier	1.7	337	80.4	27.9	60.8
100	Bolton	1.7	288	73.6	46.8	60.5
101	Southampton Solent		287	71.1	52.7	60.3
102	Leeds Metropolitan		311	70.6	43.7	58.5
103	Buckinghamshire New		244	75.9	39.7	58.0
104	St Mary's College		304	69.8	38.3	56.5
105	Kingston	6.7	317	61.6	46.3	56.2
106	Bedfordshire		225	76.1	34.2	56.0
107	London Metropolitan	3.3	237	68.9	39.1	54.7

» British Psychological Society: **www.bps.org.uk**

Radiography

Radiography is the second new subject to have its own table this year, having been listed among "other subjects allied to medicine" in previous *Guides*. Courses are divided into diagnostic and therapeutic specialisms. Diagnostic courses usually involve two years of studying anatomy, physiology and physics followed by further training in sociology, management and ethics, and the practice and science of imaging. The therapeutic branch covers much of the same scientific content in the first year, but follows this with training in oncology, psycho-social studies and other modules. Degrees require at least one science subject, usually biology, among three A levels or the equivalent.

A total of 24 universities expect to offer the subject in 2014, one more than the number in our first table, which is headed by Exeter. More than half of them are post-1992 universities, led by Robert Gordon in second place, which has one of the four 100 per cent employment records. The others are at Portsmouth, Queen Margaret and Bangor, which is only four places

Employed in graduate job:	85%
Employed in graduate job and studying:	1%
Studying:	2%
Average starting graduate salary:	£21,899

Employed in non-graduate job and studying:	0%
Employed in non-graduate job:	5%
Unemployed:	6%
Average starting non-graduate salary:	£14,615

Radiography	Research quality	Entry standards	Student satisfaction %	Graduate prospects %	Overall rating
1 Exeter	30.0	381	86.2	97.9	100.0
2 Robert Gordon	10.0	366	88.4	100.0	96.3
3 Cardiff	31.7	334	87.9	92.5	96.0
4 Portsmouth	28.3	346	81.6	100.0	95.9
5 Glasgow Caledonian	30.0	362	82.0	92.0	95.1
6 Leeds	36.7	359	74.6	96.6	94.6
7 West of England	31.7	311	80.6	96.4	92.5
8 Teesside	6.7	353	93.9	85.2	92.1
9 Queen Margaret Edinburgh	1.7	382	76.9	100.0	90.9
=10 Liverpool	20.0	348	73.3	97.7	90.2
=10 Bradford	16.7	342	81.5	90.9	90.2
12 Kingston/St George's	11.7	324	85.4	92.3	89.9
13 City	18.3	294	89.4	85.1	88.5
14 Ulster	27.2	331	89.2	68.4	87.7
15 Salford	15.0		84.6	82.9	86.8
16 Sheffield Hallam	8.3	316	75.3	96.4	85.8
17 Hertfordshire		305	83.1	90.5	84.6
18 Cumbria	0.0	310	81.9	88.6	83.8
19 London South Bank	15.0	280	71.2	93.8	82.1
20 Bangor		267	74.8	100.0	81.4
21 Derby		282	82.6	85.7	81.1
22 Birmingham City		316	73.7	87.8	80.7
23 Canterbury Christ Church	1.7	278	80.9	80.0	78.7

Radiography cont

off the bottom of the table. Radiography is in the top five subjects for employment, with 86 per cent going straight into professional jobs and only 6 per cent unemployed, a rate bettered only by medicine, dentistry and nursing. However, it is just outside the top 20 for starting salaries, averaging a little below £22,000.

Entry scores are low: no university comes close to an average of 400 points, although none drops below 260 points either. Queen Margaret, in ninth place, has the highest entry grades, just ahead of Exeter, while Teesside, in eighth place, is the only university to satisfy 90 per cent of final-year undergraduates. Leeds, in sixth place, managed the best of a low set of research assessments in 2008. Cardiff, in third place, is the leading university of two in Wales offering the subject, while Robert Gordon is top in Scotland.

» Society of Radiographers: **www.sor.org**
» Royal College of Radiologists: **www.rcr.ac.uk**

Russian and Eastern European Languages

Only 88 students began degrees in Russian and/or Eastern European studies in 2011; by the following year, with much higher fees, the total was down to 65 from a much-reduced pool of applicants. Only half of the 16 universities in this year's table had enough graduates at the time of the latest survey to compile a reliable employment score. Nevertheless, 19 universities, including the new, private Regent's University, intend to offer courses in 2014. The small numbers make for exaggerated swings in statistics. Average starting salaries in graduate-level jobs shot up by £4,600 in the last year's table, for example, propelling the subjects almost into the top ten. This year Russian is only just in the top 20 for earnings and only one subject has higher unemployment than its 22 per cent rate.

Oxford has taken first place back from Cambridge after only a year. Oxford tied with Manchester for the best performance in Russian and Eastern European languages in the 2008 Research Assessment Exercise. Cambridge has the highest entry standards and the most satisfied students. The two ancient universities are well clear of Bath, Sheffield and Manchester. Bristol, in eighth place, has much the best employment score. Portsmouth is the sole representative of the post-1992 universities and there are no institutions from Wales or Northern Ireland. St Andrews, in tenth place, remains the leader in Scotland.

Russian has been growing in popularity in schools, although most undergraduates learn the language from scratch. Nationally, there were little more than five applications for each place in 2011. But entry standards are high throughout the table: only Portsmouth averages less than 400 points on the UCAS tariff. Satisfaction levels are also high. Nearly every university in the table satisfied at least three-quarters of its final-year undergraduates.

Employed in professional job:	35%	Employed in non-professional job and studying:	2%
Employed in professional job and studying:	3%	Employed in non-professional job:	17%
Studying:	22%	Unemployed:	22%
Average starting professional salary:	£22,880	Average starting non-professional salary:	£17,340

» British Association for Slavonic and East European Studies: **www.basees.org.uk**
» National Centre for Languages (CILT): **www.cilt.org.uk**

Russian and East European Languages	Research quality %	Entry standards	Student satisfaction %	Graduate prospects %	Overall rating
1 Oxford	46.7	561	87.7		100.0
2 Cambridge	35.0	577	91.6	80.0	98.0
3 Bath	21.7	468	87.9		88.0
=4 Sheffield	40.0	442	84.5	72.0	87.8
=4 Manchester	46.7	407	83.3		87.8
6 Exeter	23.3	459	87.3	73.8	87.1
7 Durham	16.7	529	81.1	83.2	86.7
8 Bristol	30.0	431	78.8	90.5	85.1
9 Birmingham	28.3	422	84.6		84.8
10 St Andrews	6.7	516	82.7		82.7
11 University College London	21.7	478	76.7	71.4	81.0
12 Nottingham	33.3	423	77.0		80.3
13 Leeds	8.3	451	83.0		79.7
14 Glasgow	1.7	531	85.5	34.4	77.9
15 Edinburgh	16.7	445	77.2		77.1
16 Portsmouth		309	73.8	75.4	68.4

Social Policy

The London School of Economics (LSE) has been joined at the top of the Social Policy table by Leeds, the first time since the table was first published more than 15 years ago that it has not had a clear lead. The reasons are a dip in graduate prospects at the LSE and dramatic improvements across the board at Leeds, which has leapt seven places this year. The LSE still has by far the highest entry standards and the best grades performance in the 2008 Research Assessment Exercise, when 80 per cent of its submission in the wider category of social work and policy and administration was rated world-leading or internationally excellent. But it is 10 points behind Leeds for the percentage of graduates in professional jobs or postgraduate study six months after graduation. Bristol has the best score on this measure and was the only university to register positive destinations for three-quarters of its graduates. Social policy is in the bottom five subjects for employment prospects, with 40 per cent of graduates starting their careers in lower-level jobs.

Entrance grades are also low. There were barely three applications per place in 2012 and only two universities averaged more than 400 points at entry. Seven universities drop below 300 points and one below 200. Loughborough has the top score from the 2013 National Student Survey, with almost 90 per cent satisfaction among its final-year undergraduates. Scores were generally high, with only three universities failing to reach 75 per cent. Bolton is the only post-1992 university in the top ten. Swansea is top in Wales, while Stirling is the only Scottish university in the table.

More than 60 universities expect to offer courses in social policy starting in 2014, but many courses are small. A dozen universities have dropped out of the table this year because they have too few graduates to compile a reliable score for employment under the new categorisation of jobs by the Higher Education Statistics Agency. The subject enjoyed a 14 per cent increase in applications in 2011, but much of these gains were lost when higher

Social Policy cont

fees arrived in 2012. The numbers starting courses dropped by 12 per cent. Although two-thirds of entrants come with A levels or their equivalent, some courses cater very largely for mature students – the group most reluctant to pay fees of up to £9,000 a year.

Universities we were unable to include this year because of insufficient data: Bradford, City, Edinburgh, Glasgow, Glyndŵr, Leeds Metropolitan, London South Bank, Manchester, Manchester Metropolitan, Nottingham Trent, Queen's, Belfast, West of Scotland.

Employed in professional job:	28%	Employed in non-professional job and studying:	4%
Employed in professional job and studying:	3%	Employed in non-professional job:	36%
Studying:	13%	Unemployed:	15%
Average starting professional salary:	£18,764	Average starting non-professional salary:	£14,428

Social Policy	Research quality %	Entry standards	Student satisfaction %	Graduate prospects %	Overall rating
=1 Leeds	45.0	373	84.7	70.7	100.0
=1 London School of Economics	60.0	425	78.7	60.8	100.0
3 Bristol	33.3	376	85.2	78.1	99.2
4 Bath	48.3	401	80.8		98.5
5 York	38.3	348	78.9	60.5	91.3
6 Kent	43.3	325	79.4	56.3	90.8
7 Loughborough	31.7	355	89.5	25.8	90.6
8 Leicester	13.9	382	83.1	58.7	89.7
9 Keele	31.7	347	83.7	42.8	89.5
10 Bolton	18.3	242	87.5	70.7	89.3
11 Birmingham	30.0	334	77.4	64.4	88.4
12 Sheffield	35.0	337	80.5	44.8	88.0
13 Nottingham	23.3	319	79.2	66.7	87.8
14 Swansea	26.7	346	76.1	57.5	86.0
15 Lincoln	15.0	285	86.0		85.4
16 Cardiff	35.0	349	79.8	30.0	85.2
17 Aston	10.0	364	77.0	59.4	84.0
18 Sheffield Hallam	30.0	333	73.7	44.5	81.9
19 Brighton	11.7	307	80.1	47.3	81.4
20 Stirling	25.0		78.1	40.0	80.9
21 Ulster	26.7	264	80.8	34.6	80.7
22 Salford	20.0	223	83.9	32.4	78.9
23 Canterbury Christ Church		257	76.7	64.9	77.3
24 London Metropolitan	23.3	231	78.8	30.8	76.3
25 Plymouth	21.7		73.2	39.5	75.3
26 Birmingham City	10.0	309	71.6	45.5	74.9
27 Anglia Ruskin	13.3	175	79.1	32.0	71.6

» National Institute of Economic and Social Research: **www.niesr.ac.uk**
» UK Social Policy Association: **www.social-policy.org.uk**

Social Work

Despite the frequent pillorying of social workers in Parliament and the press, social work is among the most popular choices for higher education candidates. Until this year, it has also been in the top 20 for employment prospects and – more surprisingly – in the top ten for starting salaries. Perhaps as a result of early cuts in local authority budgets, the results from the end of 2012 sent the subject into the bottom half of the employment table and down seven places for starting salaries, which had dropped by £1,000 in a year. There was an 18 per cent drop in applications when higher fees arrived in 2012 but, with six applications for every place, social work courses still admitted as many students as in the previous year.

There are big changes in the latest table, not least because eight universities have dropped out with numbers too low to compile a score on more than one measure. The table had grown by 48 universities in five years, as thousands of places were added in the move to a graduate profession. Not a single one of the 75 universities that remain is in the same position as last year. Edinburgh has leapt 18 places to fifth, while Portsmouth and Anglia Ruskin are both up at least 30 places. Sussex is the new leader in social work, having climbed three places. It is the only university to average more than 400 points at entry in a table where 16 universities have averages of less than 250 points and two slip below 200.

Bath, last year's leader, has the best research score, but has slipped to second. Coventry, in 17th place, has the most satisfied students, while the West of England has a 100 per cent employment record and is the leading modern university, just outside the top ten. The employment scores vary widely, with three other universities reaching 90 per cent, but two falling below 40 per cent of graduates in professional jobs or further study six months after graduation. The majority of the institutions in the table are modern universities, but most are in the bottom half. Entry grades are largely responsible.

Universities we were unable to include this year because of insufficient data: Keele, Oxford Brookes, Queen Margaret, Reading, Roehampton, Teesside.

Employed in professional job:	56%	Employed in non-professional job and studying:	2%
Employed in professional job and studying:	3%	Employed in non-professional job:	22%
Studying:	5%	Unemployed:	13%
Average starting professional salary:	£23,294	Average starting non-professional salary:	£14,536

Social Work	Research quality %	Entry standards	Student satisfaction %	Graduate prospects %	Overall rating
1 Sussex	30.0	403	85.5	84.8	100.0
2 Bath	48.3	384	79.9	69.6	98.2
3 Sheffield	35.0		85.0	88.0	98.1
4 Leeds	45.0	363	80.3	76.7	97.6
5 Edinburgh	41.7	395	72.0	81.3	96.0
6 Lancaster	33.3	357	78.2	88.5	95.2
7 Swansea	26.7		79.5	96.8	93.9
8 Kent	43.3	310	79.6	77.8	93.1
9 Stirling	25.0		78.7	92.9	91.4
10 Birmingham	30.0	344	77.3	82.5	91.3

Social Work cont

	Research quality %	Entry standards	Student satisfaction %	Graduate prospects %	Overall rating
11 West of England	8.3	306	86.6	100.0	90.2
=12 Robert Gordon		322	91.2	89.8	88.2
=12 Dundee	15.0	381	75.0	83.3	88.2
=14 York	38.3	364	64.1	77.8	88.1
=14 Hull	20.0	313	83.2	80.8	88.1
16 Portsmouth		331	86.3	90.0	86.7
=17 Coventry	11.7	272	94.5	75.7	86.5
=17 Huddersfield	21.7	293	85.4	73.8	86.5
19 Glasgow Caledonian		357	82.5	88.9	86.4
20 Glasgow	16.7		80.6	84.6	86.2
21 Bristol	33.3	384	78.9	40.0	85.6
22 Strathclyde	16.7	346	70.1	87.5	84.9
23 Queen's, Belfast	31.7	313	63.6	86.9	84.3
=24 Manchester	25.0	246	86.4	71.4	84.1
=24 East Anglia	25.0	298	76.5	75.0	84.1
26 Sheffield Hallam	18.3	316	80.1	66.1	82.7
27 Hertfordshire	5.0	313	82.0	77.0	81.8
28 Lincoln	15.0	303	72.0	85.6	81.7
=29 Bolton	18.3	223	81.4	85.0	81.3
=29 Ulster	26.7	285	81.4	55.8	81.3
=31 Manchester Metropolitan	10.0	298	79.0	78.0	81.1
=31 Southampton Solent		314	79.8	84.8	81.1
33 Bedfordshire	20.0		86.5	52.9	81.0
34 Middlesex	20.0	297	72.1	77.3	80.9
35 Anglia Ruskin	13.3	289	74.3	83.6	80.8
36 Northumbria	15.0	284	85.1	60.0	80.2
37 Brunel	15.0	338	66.4	78.3	79.8
=38 London South Bank	30.0	269	70.7	70.0	79.7
=38 Cardiff Metropolitan		288	83.0	81.0	79.7
40 Nottingham Trent	30.0	258	80.5	52.6	79.2
41 Bradford	23.3	286	73.4	65.3	78.9
42 Bournemouth		299	84.0	70.9	78.5
=43 Goldsmiths College	18.3	195	83.0	76.0	77.8
=43 Chester	5.0	294	82.0	66.7	77.8
45 De Montfort	13.3	272	78.2	68.8	77.6
46 Birmingham City	10.0	277	72.6	79.4	76.9
47 Derby		266	84.3	70.3	76.1
48 Northampton		318	75.2	71.4	75.9
49 Plymouth	21.7	283	68.7	62.4	75.2
50 West of Scotland	20.0		79.8	47.4	75.0
51 Gloucestershire	3.3	264	72.9	80.6	74.3
52 West London		264	77.5	75.0	74.0
53 Central Lancashire	20.0	230	80.7	51.4	73.7

54 Winchester		322	75.7	59.3	73.4
55 Essex		239	84.1	65.4	72.8
56 Glyndŵr	6.7	194	83.7	69.9	72.7
57 Chichester		300	81.7	49.2	72.2
58 Brighton	11.7	235	76.7	59.3	71.4
59 St Mark and St John		237	77.5	72.4	71.3
=60 Edge Hill	5.0	270	81.9	42.8	70.2
=60 Sunderland		256	83.9	49.8	70.2
62 East London	11.7	225	71.9	65.0	69.9
=63 London Metropolitan	23.3	205	61.9	74.0	69.8
=63 Liverpool John Moores		317	73.1	51.3	69.8
65 Leeds Metropolitan		236	79.8	58.7	69.0
66 Salford	20.0	286	56.9	58.8	68.4
67 Staffordshire		236	75.3	60.0	67.2
68 Buckinghamshire New		241	73.5	60.0	66.7
=69 Bangor	13.3	228	77.0	39.1	66.6
=69 Greenwich		268	68.5	60.7	66.6
71 Canterbury Christ Church		270	70.5	51.1	65.2
72 Newman		307		39.4	65.0
73 Worcester		241	66.0	59.8	63.1
74 Cumbria		209	50.2	60.3	53.6

» British Association of Social Workers: **www.basw.co.uk**
» Health and Care Professions Council: **www.hpc-uk.org**
» Social Care Association: **http://socialcareassociation.co.uk**

Sociology

Sociology is bottom of the employment table this year for the first time, with almost 60 per cent of those graduating in 2012 working in low-level jobs or unemployed at the end of the year. The subject had been growing in popularity, with substantial increases in the demand for places in 2010 and 2011, but the prospect of higher fees saw both applications and enrolments drop by more than 10 per cent in 2012. Competition for places was already moderate for the social sciences, with fewer than five applications to the place and manageable entry grades.

Cambridge remains well clear in first place, despite uncharacteristically low grades for research. The sociology panel for the 2008 assessments was no respecter of reputations: neither Cambridge nor the London School of Economics is among the top 15 universities on this measure. But Cambridge has entry grades that are nearly 100 points ahead of the nearest challenger and one the best of an inevitably poor set of employment scores. Birmingham was the only university to see more than 80 per cent of sociologists go straight into professional jobs or start postgraduate courses in 2012, although it is only just in the top 30 overall.

Bath, which dropped back to fourth this year, has the best research score, with three-quarters of the university's work judged to be world-leading or internationally excellent. It has been overtaken by Manchester and Loughborough, both of which have jumped more than 20 places to tie for second place. Huddersfield has the most satisfied students and is

Sociology

		Research quality %	Entry standards	Student satisfaction %	Graduate prospects %	Overall rating
1	Cambridge	31.7	558		79.7	100.0
=2	Manchester	46.7	408	86.6	54.0	89.2
=2	Loughborough	31.7	383	88.9	68.4	89.2
4	Bath	48.3	380	81.7	67.5	88.2
5	Warwick	38.3	429	83.4	62.5	88.1
6	Southampton	46.7	375	78.1	77.8	87.6
7	Exeter	31.7	412	88.3	54.3	87.2
8	York	40.0	386	83.5	62.8	86.8
9	Durham	30.0	440	81.8	64.6	86.2
10	Kent	43.3	325	84.0	66.5	86.1
11	Surrey	38.3	385	83.2	61.3	85.9
12	Lancaster	43.3	420	80.1	56.9	85.7
13	Leeds	45.0	396	80.2	56.9	85.1
14	Sheffield	35.0	358	86.0	48.0	83.1
15	Newcastle	26.7	381	82.1	63.2	82.9
16	Edinburgh	38.3	461	78.6	43.8	82.8
17	Bristol	23.3	427	79.7	60.0	82.1
18	Huddersfield	8.3	236	94.6	70.2	82.0
19	Essex	43.3	364	83.2	39.9	81.8
20	Goldsmiths College	43.3	331	85.9	36.3	81.4
21	Sussex	35.0	392	85.4	33.8	81.3
22	Glasgow	20.0	387	82.5	57.7	80.9
23	Aston	10.0	350	86.3	62.0	80.4
24	Cardiff	35.0	398	78.6	47.4	80.2
25	Leicester	16.7	370	86.9	47.6	80.1
26	Aberdeen	28.3	392	76.6	59.4	79.8
27	Portsmouth	25.0	304	85.3	55.0	79.7
28	Stirling	25.0	396	83.9	37.9	79.2
29	Birmingham	13.3	379	71.5	88.2	78.7
=30	Strathclyde	6.7	441	79.2	59.1	78.5
=30	London School of Economics	28.3	430	78.8	38.9	78.5
32	Coventry		281	86.1	73.8	77.6
33	Brunel	23.3	327	83.5	43.5	76.9
34	Nottingham	23.7	351	76.4	54.9	76.0
35	Chester	5.0	271	87.5	57.0	75.8
36	Northumbria	15.0	336	84.9	39.7	75.5
37	Queen's, Belfast	31.7	343	76.8	42.7	75.2
38	Lincoln		303	85.8	55.3	74.7
39	Liverpool	13.3	376	82.4	34.7	74.3
40	Oxford Brookes		357	86.7	37.0	73.7
=41	Salford	22.3	280	82.4	40.6	73.5
=41	City	25.0	375	76.7	35.1	73.5
43	Keele	31.7	316	79.3	32.1	73.4

44	Bradford	23.3	247	82.2	45.5	73.3
45	Abertay		290	83.1	59.0	73.2
=46	Robert Gordon	5.0	298	79.3	61.1	72.8
=46	Royal Holloway	21.7	325	77.3	43.8	72.8
48	Hull	20.0	322	79.8	38.0	72.7
49	Teesside	11.7	287	83.8	38.1	71.9
50	Leeds Metropolitan		240	89.1	44.1	71.8
51	Nottingham Trent		306	82.4	46.8	71.0
52	Brighton	14.4	297	79.0	41.0	70.6
=53	West of England	5.0	313	77.7	51.4	70.5
=53	Bath Spa		313	85.6	33.3	70.5
55	Manchester Metropolitan	15.0	311	80.1	33.2	70.4
56	Westminster		283	83.8	43.3	70.2
57	Edinburgh Napier	3.3	337	74.6	55.4	70.1
58	St Mary's College		267	81.6	51.8	69.9
59	Staffordshire	11.7	249	79.5	47.8	69.7
60	Anglia Ruskin		242	84.3	46.2	69.4
61	Ulster		262	88.1	28.4	68.9
62	Canterbury Christ Church		262	88.0	28.2	68.8
63	Glasgow Caledonian	11.2	369	72.8	37.1	68.4
64	Gloucestershire		286	81.4	38.3	67.9
65	Sunderland		247	83.1	40.6	67.8
66	Roehampton	13.3	247	79.1	37.0	67.6
=67	Derby		276	80.9	38.7	67.3
=67	Worcester		304	79.0	39.1	67.3
69	Sheffield Hallam		298	80.3	35.0	67.1
70	Plymouth	15.0	288	73.2	40.9	66.9
71	Bedfordshire	20.0	203	82.6	24.2	66.7
72	Kingston	10.0	285	74.4	41.3	66.5
=73	Northampton		280	81.7	30.3	66.3
=73	Greenwich		278	79.8	37.0	66.3
75	Buckinghamshire New		242	80.9	39.5	66.1
76	East London	20.0	216	77.7	32.8	66.0
=77	Southampton Solent		280	76.8	41.7	65.6
=77	Central Lancashire		309	77.2	34.3	65.6
79	Liverpool John Moores		302	81.0	24.1	65.5
=80	Birmingham City	10.0	291	75.3	32.3	65.4
=80	Edge Hill		256	85.4	20.0	65.4
=80	Bangor		277	71.9	56.0	65.4
83	London South Bank		230	77.2	35.8	62.6
84	Middlesex		244	70.7	40.1	60.2
85	London Metropolitan		208	70.6	45.8	59.8

Employed in graduate job:	27%	Employed in non-graduate job and studying:	4%
Employed in graduate job and studying:	2%	Employed in non-graduate job:	40%
Studying:	12%	Unemployed:	15%
Average starting graduate salary:	£18,819	Average starting non-graduate salary:	£14,720

the only post-1992 university in the top 20. Edinburgh has retaken top place in Scotland, overtaking three of its rivals in the process, while Cardiff remains the leader in Wales.

Other subjects such as criminology, urban studies, women's studies and some communication studies are included in the category of sociology, and a large number of institutions teach the subject as part of a combined studies or modular programme. A total of 113 universities and colleges expect to offer courses starting in 2014. The subject's low standing in the employment ranking is not repeated in the comparison of graduate earnings, although it has slipped into the bottom 20 this year after another drop in average starting salaries in graduate-level jobs.

University we were unable to include this year because of insufficient data: West of Scotland.

» The British Sociological Association: **www.britsoc.co.uk**

Sports Science

Sports science has been one of the big growth areas of UK higher education over the past decade – so much so that it has had its own table for the last five years. Although there was a substantial drop in applications with the introduction of higher fees in 2012, the numbers joining courses fell by only 200 and the demand for places recovered in 2013. Sports science remains on the verge of the top ten subjects at degree level. The subject covers more than 40 specialisms, from sports therapy to equestrian sport studies and marine sport technology. Many contain more science and less physical activity than candidates may expect. Essex, for example, requires maths or one of the sciences at A level. Many universities now offer sports scholarships for elite performers, but most are not tied to a particular course and, officially at least, do not mean that the normal entry requirements are waived.

Loughborough, the most famous name in university sport, has lost the leadership of the table for the first time, after a dip in student satisfaction. All the four universities ahead of it this year have excellent sports facilities and highly successful teams. But it is their performance in research and degree courses in sports and exercise science that counts here. Durham has climbed from fifth place to top the table with the best employment score. It was the only university to see more than 80 per cent of leavers go straight into graduate-level employment or start postgraduate courses in 2012. Only 10 per cent of graduates nationally were unemployed at the end of that year, but the subject is still in the bottom 20 for positive destinations. It was lower still for graduate earnings.

Glasgow, which has dropped four places to sixth but is still the leading university in Scotland, has the highest entry standards, as the only university averaging more than 450 points. Eleven of the 73 universities average less than 250 points. The most satisfied students are at Exeter, in second place overall, while Loughborough ties with second-placed Birmingham for the best record in the 2008 Research Assessment Exercise (RAE). Both had 60 per cent of their research rated world-leading or internationally excellent. Portsmouth is the only post-1992 university in the top ten, but the year's most spectacular improvement was by Robert Gordon, three places lower in the table. It jumped 62 places to twelfth place, despite scoring no points for research because it did not enter the RAE in this subject.

Universities we were unable to include this year because of insufficient data: Bolton, Dundee, Strathclyde.

Employed in professional job:	36%	Employed in non-professional job and studying:	3%
Employed in professional job and studying:	4%	Employed in non-professional job:	33%
Studying:	14%	Unemployed:	10%
Average starting professional salary:	£18,539	Average starting non-professional salary:	£14,032

Sports Science

		Research quality %	Entry standards	Student satisfaction %	Graduate prospects %	Overall rating
1	Durham	30.0	397	88.1	87.8	100.0
2	Birmingham	36.7	405	84.6	77.9	97.9
3	Exeter	18.3	413	93.0	78.4	97.4
4	Bath	21.7	421	91.9	74.6	97.2
5	Loughborough	36.7	425	80.7	72.3	95.4
6	Glasgow	31.7	455	91.2	40.8	92.4
7	Edinburgh	25.0	400	77.3	78.0	90.4
8	Stirling	23.3	431	79.8		90.3
9	Portsmouth	28.3	335	89.5	59.8	89.3
10	Kent	25.0	333	81.2	71.0	86.9
11	Liverpool John Moores	33.3	339	85.3	52.7	86.8
12	Robert Gordon		364	88.3	76.5	86.5
=13	Chester	11.7	298	90.1	72.9	86.3
=13	Leeds Metropolitan	23.3	331	85.0	63.6	86.3
15	Bangor	18.3	283	90.0	68.2	86.2
16	Leeds	16.7	393	80.4	66.4	86.0
17	Brunel	21.7	356	82.9	55.9	84.0
18	Cardiff Metropolitan	11.7	363	85.1	61.1	83.9
=19	Swansea	0.0	354	81.8	75.0	82.1
=19	Hertfordshire	15.0	321	83.8	61.6	82.1
21	Lincoln		327	84.5	72.6	81.4
22	Nottingham Trent	0.0	341	89.3	59.8	81.2
23	Bournemouth		338	88.4	61.5	81.0
24	Coventry	5.0	289	83.1	75.2	80.9
25	Essex	16.7	327	79.5	61.8	80.8
26	Sheffield Hallam	18.3	340	79.7	55.8	80.5
27	Hull	3.3	332	89.3	54.0	80.1
28	Salford	15.0	307	83.5	56.7	80.0
29	Southampton Solent		306	91.5	56.3	79.6
30	Brighton	18.3	291	80.7	59.5	79.4
=31	Chichester	10.0	303	80.7	64.7	78.9
=31	Newman	0.0	312	83.3	68.4	78.9
33	Aberdeen	13.3		85.7	51.0	78.8
34	Oxford Brookes		338	87.6	53.9	78.5
35	East Anglia		388	74.9	66.7	78.1
36	Huddersfield		274	78.2	80.0	77.4
37	York St John	0.0	300	86.5	57.0	76.8
38	St Mary's College	3.3	293	80.8	65.1	76.6

Sports Science cont	Research quality %	Entry standards	Student satisfaction %	Graduate prospects %	Overall rating
39 Glyndŵr		266	88.5	57.9	76.3
40 Heriot-Watt	15.0		74.6	63.1	76.1
41 Derby		272	87.4	57.9	76.0
42 Northampton		296	85.6	54.6	75.5
43 Worcester		279	80.7	63.3	74.3
44 Teesside		315	84.1	48.5	74.0
=45 Abertay		278	76.7	68.4	73.6
=45 Manchester Metropolitan	12.7	300	79.6	44.7	73.6
47 Sunderland	13.3	254	84.5	43.1	73.4
48 Gloucestershire	3.3	308	74.0	62.2	73.1
=49 West of England		298	75.5	64.4	72.9
=49 Ulster	13.3	286	77.5	48.4	72.9
=51 Kingston		282	86.6	45.5	72.7
=51 Middlesex		215	82.9	65.4	72.7
53 Cumbria		223	87.2	54.9	72.5
54 East London		217	88.7	52.1	72.2
55 London South Bank	11.7	241	79.5		72.1
56 Edge Hill		330	84.8	36.1	71.8
57 Staffordshire	6.7	230	80.2	56.7	71.7
58 Leeds Trinity		301	81.1	47.9	71.5
=59 Anglia Ruskin		208	84.8	57.9	71.2
=59 Plymouth		269	89.9	36.1	71.2
=61 Canterbury Christ Church	6.7	258	83.8	42.3	71.1
=61 St Mark and St John	0.0	244	85.0	50.0	71.1
63 Roehampton	0.0	232	78.7	63.2	70.7
64 Winchester		266	81.9	49.0	70.4
=65 Edinburgh Napier		302	82.7	39.3	70.1
=65 Bedfordshire	10.0	220	77.4	55.0	70.1
67 Greenwich		286	76.9	53.5	70.0
68 Central Lancashire		297	79.0	46.6	69.9
69 Northumbria	10.0	279	75.1	44.9	69.3
70 Aberystwyth	5.0	278	68.9	54.3	67.1
71 Buckinghamshire New	1.7	211	73.4	54.8	65.1
72 West of Scotland		281	67.1	50.7	63.9
73 London Metropolitan		227	62.4	68.3	63.4

» British Association of Sport and Exercise Sciences: **www.bases.org.uk**
» English Institute of Sport: **www.eis2win.co.uk**
» Sports Scotland Institute of Sport: **www.sisport.com**
» Sport Wales: **www.sportwales.org.uk**

Theology and Religious Studies

The table for theology and religious studies shows its fourth change of leadership in as many years. Cambridge has regained the top position it last held three years ago, replacing Durham, which has slipped to equal third. Exeter has moved up to second, despite having the lowest research grade in the top ten. Cambridge has the highest entry standards and Exeter the most satisfied students. Durham produced the best results in the 2008 Research Assessment Exercise, when two-thirds of its work was considered world-leading or internationally excellent. St Andrews, in sixth place, produced the best employment score for 2012 graduates in a table where more than a third of the institutions dropped below 60 per cent on this measure.

More than 1,100 students began degrees in theology or religious studies when higher fees arrived in 2012, but this represented a 15 per cent drop on the previous year. It was already one of the least competitive subjects in the arts and social sciences, with little more than four applications to the place. This is not fully reflected in the entry grades, however. Although only a dozen institutions average more than 400 points, only one has an average of (just) less than 250.

There is particularly keen competition north of the border, where Aberdeen has overtaken Edinburgh and St Andrews. The three universities are all in the top ten for the subjects. Cardiff is the leader in Wales, while Chester, at 20th, is the highest-placed modern university. Thirteen of the 34 institutions in the table are post-1992 universities or colleges, but older institutions monopolise the top half of the table with superior research scores and entry qualifications. Theology and religious studies have dropped down the graduate destinations table, having been close to the top 20 last year. Although the unemployment rate is still below average, little more than a third of 2012 graduates went straight into professional jobs. By no means all graduates go into the church, but the vocation has helped to maintain healthy employment records up to now. Average starting salaries were still outside the bottom 20 for all subjects at the time of the latest survey.

Universities we were unable to include this year because of insufficient data: Hull, Oxford Brookes, Stirling.

Employed in professional job:	29%	Employed in non-professional job and studying:	5%
Employed in professional job and studying:	5%	Employed in non-professional job:	24%
Studying:	27%	Unemployed:	11%
Average starting professional salary:	£19,648	Average starting non-professional salary:	£14,662

» British Association for the Study of Religions: **www.basr.ac.uk**
» Society for the Study of Theology: **www.theologysociety.org.uk**

Theology and Religious Studies

	Research quality %	Entry standards	Student satisfaction %	Graduate prospects %	Overall rating
1 Cambridge	43.3	549	90.7	79.8	100.0
2 Exeter	23.3	478	96.7	78.0	97.2
=3 Durham	48.3	481	82.2	87.4	94.6
=3 Oxford	41.7	531	84.4	77.4	94.6
5 Aberdeen	36.7	426	89.8	75.0	93.0
6 St Andrews	30.0	484	82.5	88.0	91.3
7 Birmingham	30.0	389	89.0	79.9	90.8
8 Edinburgh	40.0	446	84.7	64.5	89.1
9 Sheffield	35.0	385	85.3		87.6
10 Lancaster	28.3	420	82.0	77.8	86.6
11 Nottingham	33.3	402	81.2	75.0	86.0
12 Manchester	38.3	419	83.6	53.5	85.2
13 Cardiff	15.0	381	87.1	70.4	84.6
14 Bristol	25.0	432	79.4	75.6	84.3
15 King's College London	28.3	427	84.3	53.4	83.9
16 Leeds	25.0	396	87.0	50.5	83.4
17 SOAS London	31.7	362	77.7	81.0	83.1
18 Glasgow	21.7	384	87.0	50.0	82.3
19 Queen's, Belfast		381	88.8	65.9	82.0
20 Chester	10.0	300	84.3	85.1	81.7
21 Kent	20.0	344	81.0	73.0	80.9
=22 Bangor	13.3		85.8	58.1	80.1
=22 Newman		295	92.9	57.5	80.1
24 St Mary's College	20.0	298	81.0	75.7	79.8
25 Bath Spa	3.3	334	86.5	64.4	79.2
26 Chichester	5.0	291	88.9		78.5
27 Heythrop College	3.3	320	85.4	63.0	77.8
28 York St John	1.7	285	90.4	47.0	76.6
29 Canterbury Christ Church	6.7	303	85.4	55.2	76.5
30 Roehampton	10.0	288	84.9	52.5	75.8
31 Gloucestershire	13.3	327	87.0	24.1	73.9
32 Winchester	3.3	332	83.5	44.8	73.7
33 Leeds Trinity	13.3	255	77.9	62.2	72.6
34 Cumbria	8.3	249		56.3	72.2

Town and Country Planning and Landscape

The number of students joining courses in town and country planning, or the smaller area of landscape design, dropped by more than 20 per cent in 2012. There had been a fall in the demand for places after the 2008 recession, but applications had begun to recover before the introduction of £9,000 fees. Overall, there were fewer than four applications for each of the 756 places. Low numbers have caused four universities to drop out of the planning table this year, but more than 30 universities and colleges in each of the main areas expect to offer courses in 2014. About a quarter of the courses in landscape design will be in further education colleges.

Cambridge continues to have a big lead in the table, with the best research grades, the top employment score and entry standards that are more than 100 points higher than the nearest challenger. Only two other universities average more than 400 points at entry, although just one, compared with three last year, now drops below 250. Competition was tight in the 2008 Research Assessment Exercise: Cambridge had the most work placed in the top two categories, but Sheffield – which remains in second place overall – had a higher proportion judged to be world-leading. Sheffield also has the most satisfied students in this year's table.

Employment scores are in the top 20 for all subjects, although they were in the top ten only four years ago. Starting salaries in professional-level jobs remain just in the bottom half of the table, although the average is back above £20,000. Reading, which registered 100 per cent employment scores for five years in a row, did not have enough graduates in

Town and Country Planning and Landscape	Research quality %	Entry standards	Student satisfaction %	Graduate prospects %	Overall rating
1 Cambridge	45.0	558		91.2	100.0
2 Sheffield	42.2	370	90.9	73.6	87.4
3 Aberdeen	33.3			87.1	85.6
4 Newcastle	38.3	353	84.6	86.7	85.5
5 University College London	33.3	440	79.8		85.1
6 Heriot-Watt	30.0	361	84.8	87.5	84.1
7 Reading	36.7	409	76.2		82.0
8 Cardiff	41.7	357	76.8	77.5	80.5
9 Edinburgh	40.0	391	72.4		79.5
10 Northumbria	20.0	336	84.1	83.1	79.3
11 Manchester	33.3	368	80.0	70.0	79.0
12 Oxford Brookes	16.7	345	82.2	87.5	78.9
13 Loughborough	41.7	343	81.6	61.1	78.8
14 West of England	19.5	311	85.4	79.4	78.0
15 Liverpool	23.3	355	83.0	68.4	77.2
16 Birmingham	23.3	390	75.9		76.5
17 Queen's, Belfast	16.7	345	80.0	72.1	74.5
=18 Gloucestershire	16.7	262		90.0	73.7
=18 Nottingham Trent	10.0	328	80.2	78.6	73.7
20 Birmingham City	15.0	258	79.8	86.7	73.4
21 Manchester Metropolitan	15.0	292	75.7	87.5	73.0
22 Glasgow Caledonian	30.0	359	66.9	64.3	70.0
=23 Leeds Metropolitan		272	88.2	60.0	68.9
=23 Sheffield Hallam	30.0	296	77.0	48.3	68.9
25 Westminster	11.7	320	75.4		68.4
26 Ulster		248	78.6	52.2	61.4
27 Kingston	3.3	280	69.4	61.5	61.0

Town and Country Planning and Landscape cont

2012 for a score to be included in the new table. Almost half of the institutions in the table are post-1992 universities, but only Northumbria makes the top ten. Aberdeen, which has moved up eight places to third, is the top university outside England, while Cardiff is the only institution from Wales.

Universities we were unable to include this year because of insufficient data: Dundee, Greenwich, Liverpool John Moores, London South Bank.

Employed in professional job:	51%	Employed in non-professional job and studying:	2%
Employed in professional job and studying:	5%	Employed in non-professional job:	17%
Studying:	13%	Unemployed:	12%
Average starting professional salary:	£20,267	Average starting non-professional salary:	£15,604

» Royal Town Planning Institute: **www.rtpi.org.uk**
» Planning Officers Society: **www.planningofficers.org.uk**
» Landscape Institute: **www.landscapeinstitute.org**

Veterinary Medicine

A new veterinary school has opened in 2013 at the University of Surrey, but it will be several years before there are enough data to include it in this table. But the performance of the last new arrival must offer hope for future success. Nottingham, which opened only in 2006, is enjoying its second year as the top school. This is the first year that it has had a full set of statistics and it has maintained its lead with by far the best rating for student satisfaction and good scores on the other indicators. Veterinary medicine is another of the rankings in which employment scores have been removed from the calculations that determine universities' positions. The scores are still shown in the table, but the review group of academic planners consulted on the *Guide* agreed that employment rates in the subject were so tightly bunched that small differences could distort the overall ranking.

Veterinary Medicine	Research quality %	Entry standards	Student satisfaction %	Graduate prospects %	Overall rating
1 Nottingham	30.0	467	91.9	95.1	100.0
2 Edinburgh	31.7	529	81.0	92.6	98.5
3 Cambridge	18.3	597	81.2	89.4	97.5
4 Royal Veterinary College	25.0	516	80.0	85.8	94.1
5 Liverpool	18.3	487	84.8	96.7	92.0
6 Glasgow	21.7	514	76.2	91.1	90.2
7 Bristol	13.3	485	84.3	79.0	89.4

Cambridge has much the highest entry standards in veterinary medicine, as in other subjects, but it has lost second place to Edinburgh, which produced the best performance in the 2008 Research Assessment Exercise. There are no degrees in veterinary medicine in Wales or Northern Ireland. Veterinary medicine has been a fixture in the top five for both graduate destinations and starting salaries in professional jobs, but no longer features in either. Indeed, the subject is down to seventh in the earnings table, despite average salaries of more than £26,000 in 2012. Although the small numbers taking lower-level employment earned more than the graduates of any other subject in non-graduate work, vets have fallen behind economists and engineers in graduate-level jobs.

Veterinary medicine was one of the select band of subjects to see more applicants and enrolments when £9,000 fees were introduced in 2012. There were almost nine applications per place and entry standards bettered only by medicine itself. Most courses demand high grades in chemistry and biology, with some accepting physics or maths as one alternative subject. Cambridge and the Royal Veterinary College also set applicants a specialist aptitude test that is used by a number of medical schools. Few candidates win places without evidence of practical commitment to the subject, through work experience, either in veterinary practices or laboratories. The norm for veterinary science degrees is five years, but the Cambridge course takes six years and both Bristol and Nottingham provide a "pre-veterinary" year. Both Edinburgh and the Royal Veterinary College run four-year courses for graduates.

Employed in professional job:	84%	Employed in non-professional job and studying:	0%
Employed in professional job and studying:	1%	Employed in non-professional job:	5%
Studying:	2%	Unemployed:	7%
Average starting professional salary:	£26,045	Average starting non-professional salary:	£18,467

» Royal College of Veterinary Surgeons: **www.rcvs.org.uk**

The top university for each of the subjects covered in this chapter

Cambridge
Aeronautical and Manufacturing Engineering
Anatomy and Physiology
Anthropology
Architecture
Biological Sciences
Celtic studies
Chemical Engineering
Chemistry
Civil Engineering
Classics and Ancient History
Computer Science
Economics
Education
Electrical and Electronic Engineering
English
General Engineering
Geography and Environmental Science
Geology
German
Iberian Languages
Italian
Land and Property Management
Law
Linguistics
Materials Technology
Mathematics
Mechanical Engineering
Middle Eastern and African Studies
Pharmacology and Pharmacy
Physics and Astronomy
Psychology
Sociology
Theology and Religious Studies
Town and Country Planning and Landscape

Oxford
Archaeology
Art and Design
Business Studies
East and South Asian Studies
French
History of Art, Architecture and Design
Medicine
Philosophy

Oxford cont
Politics
Russian and East European Languages

Cardiff
East and South Asian Studies
Physiotherapy

Durham
History
Sport Science

Exeter
Drama, Dance and Cinematics
Radiography

Glasgow
Dentistry
Nursing

Nottingham
Agriculture and Forestry
Veterinary Medicine

Warwick
American Studies
Communication and Media Studies

Aston
Other Subjects Allied to Medicine

Bath
Accounting and Finance

King's College London
Food Science

Leeds
Social Policy

Loughborough
Building

LSE
Social Policy

Manchester
Music

Sheffield
Librarianship and Information
  Management

Surrey
Hospitality, Leisure, Recreation and
  Tourism

Sussex
Social Work

6 Making Your Application

In an era when there are relatively few interviews and more candidates each year achieve high A-level grades, what goes on your UCAS form is becoming more and more important – too important, many would say. The art of conveying knowledge of, and enthusiasm for, your chosen subject – preferably with supporting evidence from your school or college – can make all the difference.

Too many people take their eye off the ball when actually applying for a higher education place. Surprising numbers of applicants each year spell their own name wrongly, or enter an inaccurate date of birth, or the wrong course code. And that is to say nothing of the damage that can be done in the personal statement and teachers' references. While UCAS will decode misspelt names, other errors in grammar or spelling present admissions officers with an easy starting point in cutting applications down to a more manageable number.

There was talk of a new application system, with only two choices and later deadlines. But, for the moment, applicants will continue to have five choices of course, and to make decisions well before they have their results. You do not have to take advantage of all five – some people make only a single application, perhaps because they do not want to leave home or they have very particular requirements – but you will give yourself the best chance of success if you go for the maximum.

A number of changes have been made to UCAS procedures for entry in 2014, but all are relatively minor. Perhaps the most important change allows candidates to submit a new personal statement if their initial applications are unsuccessful and they use the UCAS Extra process. This and other changes are outlined below.

The application process

Most applications for full-time higher education courses go through UCAS, although specialist admissions bodies still handle applications to the music conservatoires (Conservatoires UK Admissions Service: **www.cukas.ac.uk**) and some postgraduate courses, including teacher training (Graduate Teacher Training Registry: **www.gttr.ac.uk**). The trend is towards the UCAS model even among specialist providers, however: recruitment to nursing and midwifery diploma and degree courses in Scotland switched to the UCAS system in 2010 and the art and design courses that used to recruit using the separate "Route B" scheme have also moved to the main system.

Universities that have not filled all their places, even during Clearing, will accept direct applications up to and sometimes after the start of the academic year, but UCAS is both the official route and the only way into the most popular courses.

Since 2006, all UCAS applications have been made online. The Apply electronic system is accessed via the UCAS website and is straightforward to use. For those who do not have the internet at home and prefer not to use school or college computers, the UCAS website lists 900 libraries, all over the UK, where you can make your application. Apply is available 24 hours a day, and, when the time comes, information on the progress of your application may arrive at any time.

Registering with Apply

The first step in the process is to register. If you are at a school or college, you will need to obtain a "buzzword" from your tutor or careers adviser – it is used when you log on to register. It links your application to the school or college so that the application can be sent electronically to your referee (usually one of your teachers) for your reference to be attached. If you are no longer at a school or college, you do not need a "buzzword" but you will need details of your referee. More information is given on the UCAS website.

To register, go to the UCAS website and click on "Apply". The system will guide you through the business of providing your personal details and generating a username and password, as well as reminding you of basic points, such as amending your details in case of a change of address. You can register separate term-time and holiday addresses – a useful option for boarders, who could find offers and, particularly, the confirmation of a place, going to their school when they are miles away at home. Remember to keep a note of your username and password in a safe place.

Throughout the process, you will be in sole control of communications with UCAS and your chosen universities. Only if you nominate a representative and give them your unique nine-digit application number (sent automatically by UCAS when your application is submitted), can a parent or anyone else give or receive information on your behalf, perhaps because you are ill or out of the country.

Improved video guides on the application process have been posted by UCAS for the 2014 cycle. Once you are registered, you can start to complete the Apply screens. The sections that follow cover the main screens.

Personal details

This information is taken from your initial registration, and you will be asked for additional

---

The main screens to be completed in UCAS Apply

» Personal details and some additional non-educational details for UK applicants.
» Student finance, a section for UK-resident applicants used to speed up your loan application.
» Your course choices.
» Details of your education so far, including examination results and examinations still to be taken.
» Details of any paid jobs you have done.
» Your personal statement.
» A reference from one of your teachers.
» Payment details (in 2013 applications cost £23, or £12 to apply to just one course).
» A declaration that you confirm that the information is correct and that you will be bound by the UCAS rules.

information, for example, on ethnic origin and national identity, used to monitor equal opportunities in the application process. UK students will also be asked to complete a student finance section designed to speed up your loan application when you make it later in the process.

Choices

In most subjects, you will be able to apply to a maximum of five universities and/or colleges. The exceptions are medicine, dentistry and veterinary science, where the maximum is four, but you can use your fifth choice as a back-up to apply for a different subject.

The other important restriction concerns Oxford or Cambridge, because you can only apply to one or the other; you cannot apply to both Oxford and Cambridge in the same year, nor can you apply for more than one course. For both universities you may need to take a written test (see pages 20–21) and submit examples of your work, depending on the course selected. In addition, for Cambridge, you will be asked to complete a Supplementary Application Questionnaire once the university has received your application from UCAS. The deadline for Oxbridge applications – and for all medicine, dentistry and veterinary science courses – is 15 October. For all other applications the deadline is 15 January (or 24 March for some specified art and design courses).

Most applicants use all five choices. But if you do choose fewer than five courses, you can still add another to your form up to 30 June, as long as you have not accepted or declined any offers. Nor do you have to choose five different universities if more than one course at the same institution attracts you – perhaps because the institution itself is the real draw and one course has lower entrance requirements than the other. Universities are not allowed to see where else you have applied, or whether you have chosen the same subject elsewhere. But they will be aware of multiple applications within their own institution. It is, in any case, more difficult to write a convincing personal statement if it has to cover more than one subject.

For each course you select, you will need to put the UCAS code on the form – and you should check carefully that you have the correct code and understand any special requirements that may be detailed on the UCAS description of the course. You will also need to indicate whether you are applying for a deferred entry (for example, if you are taking a gap year – see page 203).

Education

In this section you will need to give details of the schools and colleges you have attended, and the qualifications you have obtained or are preparing for. The UCAS website gives plenty of advice on the ways in which you should enter this information, to ensure that all your relevant qualifications are included with their grades. While UCAS does not need to see qualification certificates, it can double-check results with the examination boards to ensure that no-one is tempted to modify their results. In the Employment section that follows add details of any paid jobs you have had (unpaid or voluntary work should be mentioned in your personal statement).

Personal statement

As the competition for places on popular courses has become more intense, so the value attached to the personal statement has increased. Admissions officers look for a sign of potential beyond the high grades that growing numbers of applicants offer. Many (but not all) academics responsible for admissions value success in extracurricular activities such as drama, sport or the Duke of Edinburgh's Award scheme. But your first priority should be to demonstrate an interest in and understanding of your chosen subject beyond the confines of the exam syllabus.

This is not easy in a relatively short statement that can readily sound trite or pretentious. You should resist any temptation to lie, particularly if there is any chance of an interview. A claim to have been inspired by a book that you have not read will backfire instantly under questioning and, even without an interview, experienced academics are likely to see through grandiose statements that appear at odds with a teacher's reference. Genuine experiences of after-hours clubs, lectures or visits – better still, work experience or actual reading around the syllabus – are much more likely to strike the right note. If you are applying for medicine, for example, any practical work experience or volunteering in medical or caring settings should be included. Take advice from teachers and, if there is still time before you make your application, look for some subject-related activities that will help fill out your statement.

UCAS top ten personal statement tips

1 Express interest in the subject and show real passion.
2 Go for a strong opening line to grab the reader's attention.
3 Relate outside interests to the course.
4 Think beyond university.
5 Get the basics right.
6 Don't try to sound too clever.
7 Take time and make it your best work.
8 Don't leave it until the last minute – remember the 15 January deadline!
9 Get a second opinion.
10 Honesty is the best policy.

Admissions officers are also looking for evidence of character that will make you a productive member of their university and, eventually, a successful graduate. Taking responsibility in any area of school or college life suggests this – leading activities outside your place of learning even more so. Evidence of initiative and self-discipline is also valuable, since higher education involves much more independent study than sixth-formers are used to.

Your overall aim in writing your personal statement is to persuade the admissions officer to pick yours out from the piles of applications. That means trying to stand out from an often rather dull and uniform set of statements based around the curriculum and the more predictable sixth-form activities. Everyone is going to say they love reading, for example; narrow your interest down to an area of (real) interest. Don't be afraid to include the unusual, but bear in mind that an academic's sense of humour may not be the same as yours.

Give particular thought to why you want to study your chosen subject – especially if it is not one you have taken at school or college. You need to show that your interests and skills are well-suited to the course and, if it is a vocational degree, that you know how you envisage using the qualification. Admissions officers want to feel that you will be committed to their subject for the length of the course, which could be three, four or even five years, and capable of achieving good results.

Your school or college should be the best source of advice, since they see personal statements every year, but there are others. The UCAS website has a useful checklist of themes that you may wish to address, while sites such as **www.studential.com** also provide tips. But do not fall into the trap of cutting and pasting from the model statements included on such sites – both UCAS and individual universities have software that will spot plagiarism immediately. In one year, no fewer than one in twenty applicants came to grief in this way. Plagiarists of this type are unlikely to be disqualified, but they destroy the credibility of their application.

Try not to cram in more than the limited space will allow – admissions officers will have many statements to go through, and judicious editing may be rewarded. As long as you write clearly – preferably in paragraphs and possibly with sub-headings – it will be up to you what to include. It is a *personal* statement. But consider the points listed below and make sure that you can answer all the questions raised. Once you have completed your statement show it to others you trust. It is really important to have others read your statement before submitting it – sometimes things that are clear to you may not be to fresh eyes.

The Apply system allows 4,000 characters (including spaces) or 47 lines for your statement. While there is no requirement to fill all the space, it should not look embarrassingly short. Indeed, from 2014, your statement will have to be at least 1,000 characters long. It is hard to believe that many candidates could not rustle up 200 words to support their application, but presumably a significant number have not been doing so. UCAS recommends using a word-processing package to compile the statement before pasting it into the application system. This is because Apply will time-out after 35 minutes of inactivity, so there is a danger of losing valuable material. Working offline also has the advantage of leaving you with a copy and making it easier to show it to others.

References

Hand in hand with your personal statement goes the reference from your school, college or, in the case of mature students, someone who knows you well but is not a friend or family member. From 2014, even referees who are not your teachers will be encouraged to predict your grades, although they will be allowed to opt out of this process. Whatever the source, the reference has to be independent – you are specifically forbidden to change any part of it if you send off your own application – but that does not mean you should not try to influence what it contains.

Most schools and colleges conduct informal interviews before compiling a reference, but it does no harm to draw up a list of the achievements that you would like to see included, and ensure your referee knows what subject you are applying for. Referees cannot know every detail of a candidate's interests and most welcome an aide-memoire.

The UCAS guidelines skirt around the candidate's right to see his or her reference, but it does exist. Schools' practices vary, but most now show the applicant the completed reference. Where this is not the case, the candidate can pay UCAS £10 for a copy, although at this stage it is obviously too late to influence the contents. Better, if you can, to see it before it goes off, in case there are factual inaccuracies that can be corrected.

Key points to consider in writing your personal statement

» What attracts you to this subject (or subjects, in the case of dual or combined honours)?

» Have you undertaken relevant work experience or voluntary activities, either through school or elsewhere?

» Have you taken part in other extra-curricular activities that demonstrate character – perhaps as a prefect, on the sports field or in the arts?

» Have you been involved in other academic pursuits, such as Gifted and Talented programmes, widening participation schemes, or courses in other subjects?

» Which aspects of your current courses have you found particularly stimulating?

» Are you planning a gap year? If so, explain what you intend to do and how it will affect your studies. Some subjects – notably maths – actively discourage a break in studies.

» What other outside interests might you include that show that you are well-rounded?

Timetable for applications (based on 2013-14 dates)

May onwards	Find out about courses and universities. Attend open days.
September	Registration starts for UCAS Apply.
mid-September	UCAS starts receiving applications.
15 October	Final day for applications to Oxford and Cambridge, and for all courses in medicine, dentistry and veterinary science.
15 January	Final day for all other applications from UK and EU students to ensure that your application is given equal consideration with all other applicants. Now also the deadline for all art and design courses except those which have a 24 March deadline (specified in UCAS Course Search).
16 January–30 June	New applications continue to be accepted by UCAS, but only considered by universities if the relevant courses have vacancies. All will be classed as "POST-15Jan".
25 February	Start of applications through UCAS Extra.
24 March	Final day for applications for those art and design courses that specify this date.
31 March	Universities should have sent decisions on all applications received by 15 January, but decisions may be later than this.
7 May	Final day by which applicants have to decide on their choices if application submitted by 15 January and all decisions received by 31 March (exact date for each applicant will be confirmed by UCAS). **If you do not reply to UCAS, they will decline your offers.**
8 May	UCAS must receive all decisions from universities if you applied by 15 January.
5 June	Final day by which applicants have to decide on their choices if all decisions received by 8 May (exact date for each applicant will be confirmed by UCAS).
26 June	Final day by which applicants have to decide on their choices if all decisions received by 5 June (exact date for each applicant will be confirmed by UCAS).
1 July	Any new application received from this date held until Clearing starts.
2 July	Final day for applications through UCAS Extra.
17 July	Universities must give decisions on all applications submitted by 30 June. You must make a decision on these offers by 24 July.
5 August	SQA results published. Scottish Clearing starts.
14 August	GCE results published. Full Clearing and Adjustment starts.
31 August	Adjustment closes.
20 September	Last day UCAS will accept applications for courses about to start.
30 September	Clearing vacancy service closes. Contact universities directly about vacancies.
22 October	Last date by which a university can accept you through Clearing. Last day to add a Clearing choice.

Timing

The general deadline for applications through UCAS is 15 January, but even those received up to 30 June will be considered if the relevant courses still have vacancies. After that, you will be limited to Clearing, or an application for the following year. In theory – and usually in practice – all applications submitted by the January deadline are given equal consideration. But the best advice is to get your application in early: before Christmas, or earlier if possible. Applications are accepted from mid-September onwards, so the autumn half-term is a sensible target date for completing the process. Although usually no offers are made before the deadline, many admissions officers look through applications as they come in and may make a mental note of promising candidates. If your form arrives with the deadline looming, you may appear less organised than those who submitted in good time; and your application may be one of a large batch that receives a more cursory first reading than the early arrivals. Under UCAS rules, last-minute applicants should not be at a disadvantage, but why take the risk?

Next steps

Once your application has been processed by UCAS, you will receive a welcome letter or email confirming your choices and summarising what will happen next. The letter will contain a reminder of your identification number and the username and password that you used to apply. These will also give you access to "Track", the online system that allows you to follow the progress of your application. Check all the details carefully: you have 14 days to contact UCAS to correct any errors. Since 2010, universities have been able to make direct contact with you through Track, including arranging interviews.

After that, it is just a matter of waiting for universities to make their decisions, which can take days, weeks or even months, depending on the university and the course. Some obviously see an advantage in being the first to make an offer – it is a memorable moment to be reassured that at least one of your chosen institutions wants you – and may send their response almost immediately. Others take much longer, perhaps because they have so many good applications to consider, or maybe because they are waiting to see which of their applicants withdraw when Oxford and Cambridge make their offers. Universities are asked to make all their decisions by the end of March, and most have done so long before that.

Interviews

Unless you are applying for a course in health or education that brings you into direct contact with the public, the chances are you will not have a selection interview. For prospective medics, vets, dentists or teachers, a face-to-face assessment of your suitability will be crucial to your chances of success. Likewise in the performing arts, the interview may be as important as your exam grades. Oxford and Cambridge still interview applicants in all subjects, and a few of the top universities see a significant proportion. But the expansion of higher education has made it impractical to interview everyone, and many admissions experts are sceptical about interviews.

What has become more common, however, is the "sales" interview, where the university is really selling itself to the candidate. There may still be testing questions, but the admissions staff have already made their minds up and are actually trying to persuade you to accept an offer. Indeed, you will probably be given a clear indication at the end of the interview that one is on its way. The technique seems to work, perhaps because you have invested time and nervous energy in a sometimes lengthy trip, as well as acquiring a more detailed impression of both the department and the university.

The difficulty can come in spotting which type of interview is which. The "real" ones require lengthy preparation, revisiting your personal statement and reading beyond the exam syllabus. Impressions count for a lot, so dress smartly and make sure that you are on time. Have a question of your own ready, as well as being prepared to give answers.

While you would not want to appear ignorant at a "sales" interview, lengthy preparation might be a waste of valuable time during a period of revision. Naturally, you should err on the side of caution, but if your predicted grades are well above the standard offer and the subject is not one that normally requires an interview, it is likely that the invitation is a sales pitch. It is still worth going, unless you have changed your mind about the application.

Offers

When your chosen universities respond to your application, there will be one of three answers:

» Unconditional Offer (U): This is a possibility only if you applied after satisfying the entrance requirements – usually if you are applying as a mature student, while on a gap year, after resitting exams or, in Scotland, after completing Highers.
» Conditional Offer (C): The university offers a place subject to you achieving set grades or points on the UCAS tariff.
» Rejection (R): You do not have the right qualifications, or have lost out to stronger competition.

If you have chosen wisely, you should have more than one offer to choose from, so you will be required to pick your favourite as your firm acceptance – known as UF if it was an unconditional offer and CF if it was conditional. Candidates with conditional offers can also accept a second offer, with lower grades, as an Insurance choice (CI). You must then decline any other offers that you have.

You do not have to make an Insurance choice – indeed, you may decline all your offers if you have changed your mind about your career path or regret your course decisions. But most people prefer the security of a back-up route into higher education if their grades fall short. You must be sure that your firm acceptance is definitely your first choice because you will be allocated a place automatically if you meet the university's conditions. It is no good at this stage deciding that you prefer your Insurance choice because UCAS rules will not allow a switch.

The only way round those rules, unless your results are better than your highest offer (see Adjustment below), is through direct contact with the universities concerned. Your firm acceptance institution has to be prepared to release you so that your new choice can award you a place in Clearing. Neither is under any obligation to do so but, in practice, it is rare for a university to insist that a student joins against his or her wishes. Admissions staff will do all they can to persuade you that your original choice was the right one – as it may well have been, if your research was thorough – but it will almost certainly be your decision in the end.

UCAS Extra

If things do go wrong and you receive five rejections, that need not be the end of your higher education ambitions. From the end of February until the end of June, you have another chance through UCAS Extra, a listing of courses that still have vacancies after the initial round of offers. Extra is sometimes dismissed (wrongly) as a repository of second-rate courses. In fact, even in the boom year for applications of 2010, most Russell Group universities still had hundreds of courses listed in a wide variety of subjects.

You will be notified if you are eligible for Extra and can then select courses marked as available on the UCAS website. In order to assist students who choose different subjects after a full set of rejections in their original application, from 2014 you will be able to submit a new personal statement for Extra. Applications are made, one at a time, through UCAS Track. If you do not receive an offer, or you choose to decline one, you can continue applying for other courses until you are successful. About half of those applying through Extra normally find a place. Nearly 8,000 were successful this way in 2012.

Results Day

Rule Number One on results day is to be at home, or at least in easy communication – you cannot afford to be on some remote beach if there are complications. The day is bound to be stressful, unless you are absolutely confident that you achieved the required grades – more of a possibility in an era of modular courses with marks along the way. But for thousands of students Track has removed the agony of opening the envelope or scanning a results noticeboard. On the morning of A-level results day, the system informs those who have already won a place on their chosen course. You will not learn your grades until later, but at least your immediate future is clear.

If you get the grades stipulated in your conditional offer, the process should work smoothly and you can begin celebrating. Track will let you know as soon as your place is confirmed and the paperwork will arrive in a day or two. You can phone the university to make quite sure, but it should not be necessary and you will be joining a long queue of people doing the same thing.

If the results are not what you hoped – and particularly if you just miss your grades – you need to be on the phone and taking advice from your school or college. In a year when results are better than expected, some universities will stick to the letter of their offers, perhaps refusing to accept your AAC grades when they had demanded ABB. Others will forgive a dropped grade to take a candidate who is regarded as promising, rather than go into Clearing to recruit an unknown quantity. Admissions staff may be persuadable – particularly if there are extenuating personal circumstances, or the dropped grade is in a subject that is not relevant to your chosen course. Try to get a teacher to support your case, and be persistent if there is any prospect of flexibility.

One option, if your results are lower than predicted, is to ask for papers to be re-marked, as growing numbers do each year. The school may ask for a whole batch to be re-marked, and you should ensure that your chosen universities know this if it may make the difference to whether or not you satisfy your offer. If your grades improve, the university will review its decision, but if by then it has filled all its places, you may have to wait until next year to start the course.

If you took Scottish Highers, you will have had your results for more than a week by the time the A-level grades are published. If you missed your grades, there is no need to wait for A levels before you begin approaching universities. Admissions staff at English universities may not wish to commit themselves before they see results from south of the border, but Scottish universities will be filling places immediately and all should be prepared to give you an idea of your prospects.

Adjustment

If your grades are better than those demanded by your first-choice university, there is now an opportunity to "trade up". Introduced in 2009, the Adjustment Period runs from when you receive your results until 31 August and you can only use it for five 24-hour periods during that period, so there is no time to waste. First, go into the Track system and click on "Register for Adjustment" and then contact your preferred institutions to find another place. If none is available, or you decide not to move, your initial offer will remain open. The number of students switching universities in this way more than doubled in 2012. Although the total was still only 1,350, the rise shows that the process is catching on and is certainly worth considering if you are eligible. UCAS does not publish a breakdown of which universities take part – some, such as Oxford and Cambridge simply do not have places available – but it is known that many students successfully go back to institutions that had rejected them at the initial application stage. Adjustment may well become more popular as it becomes better known, particularly if students become more cautious with their applications as the demand for places begins to rise again.

Clearing

If you do not have a place on Results Day, there will still be plenty of options through the UCAS Clearing scheme. More than 55,000 people – about one applicant in 12 – found a place through this route in 2012. There is no reason to think there will be fewer places filled through Clearing in 2014. Although the most popular courses fill up quickly, many remain open up to and beyond the start of the academic year. And, at least at the start of the process, the range of courses with vacancies is much wider than in Extra. Most universities will list some courses, and most subjects will be available somewhere.

Clearing runs from A-level Results Day until the end of September, matching students without places to full-time courses with vacancies. As long as you are not holding any offers and you have not withdrawn your application, you are eligible automatically. You will be sent a Clearing number via Track to quote to universities.

Now it is just a matter of trawling through the lists on the UCAS website, and elsewhere, before making a direct approach to the university offering the course that appeals most, and where you have a realistic chance of a place – do not waste time on courses where the standard offer is far above your grades. Universities run Clearing hotlines and have become adept at dealing with a large number of calls in a short period, but you can still spend a long time on the phone at a time when the most desirable places are beginning to disappear. If you can't get through send an email setting out your grades and the course that interests you.

The best advice is to plan ahead and not to wait for Results Day to draw up a list of possible Clearing targets. Many universities publish lists of courses that are likely to be in Clearing on their websites from the start of August. Think again about some of the courses that you considered when making your original application, or others at your chosen universities that had lower entrance requirements. But beware of switching to another subject simply because you have the right grades – you still have to sustain your interest and be capable of succeeding over three or more years. Many of the students who drop out of degrees are those who chose the wrong course in a rush during Clearing.

In short, you should start your search straight away if you do find yourself in Clearing, and act decisively, but do not panic. You can make as many approaches as you like, until you are accepted on the course of your choice. Remember that if you changed your personal statement for applications in Extra, this will be the one that goes to any universities that you approach in Clearing, so it may be difficult to return to the subjects in your original application.

Most of the available vacancies will appear in Clearing lists, but some of the universities towards the top of the league tables may have a limited number of openings that they choose not to advertise – either for reasons of status or because they do not want the administrative burden of fielding large numbers of calls to fill a handful of places. If there is a course that you find particularly attractive – especially if you have good grades and are applying late – it may be worth making a speculative call. Sometimes a number of candidates holding offers drop grades and you may be on the spot at the right moment.

What are the alternatives?

If your results are lower than expected and there is nothing you want in Clearing, there are several things you can do. The first is to resit one or more subjects. The modular nature of most courses means that you will have a clear idea of what you need to do to get better grades. You can go back to school or college, or try a "crammer". Although some colleges have a good success rate with re-takes, you have to be highly focused and realistic about the likely improvements. Some of the most competitive courses, such as medicine, may demand higher grades for a second application, so be sure you know the details before you commit yourself.

Other options are to get a job and study part-time, or to take a break from studying and return later in your career. The part-time route can be arduous – many young people find a job enough to handle without the extra burden of academic work. But others find it just the combination they need for a fulfilling life. It all depends on your job, your social life and your commitment to the subject you will study. It may be that a relatively short break is all that you need to rekindle your enthusiasm for studying. Many universities now have a majority of mature students, so you need not be out of place if this is your chosen route.

Taking a gap year

The other popular option is to take a gap year. In most years, about 7 per cent of applicants defer their entry until the following year while they travel, or do voluntary or paid work. A whole industry has grown up around tailor-made activities, many of them in Asia, Africa or Latin America. Some have been criticised for doing more for the organisers than the underprivileged communities that they purport to assist, but there are programmes that are useful and character-building, as well as safe. Most of the overseas programmes are not cheap, but raising the money can be part of the experience.

The alternative is to stay closer to home and make your contribution through organisations like Community Service Volunteers or to take a job that will make higher education more affordable when the time comes.

Many admissions staff are happy to facilitate gap years because they think it makes for more mature, rounded students than those who come straight from school, and graduate employers also value the initiative and skills gained. The right programme may even increase your chances of winning a place, if it is relevant to your course. But there are subjects – maths in particular – that discourage a break because it takes too long to pick up study skills where you left off. From the student's point of view, you should also bear in mind that a gap year postpones the moment at which you embark on a career. This may be important if your course is a long one, such as medicine or architecture.

If you are considering a gap year, it makes sense to apply for a deferred place, rather than waiting for your results before applying. The application form has a section for deferments. That allows you to sort out your immediate future before you start travelling or working, and leaves you the option of changing your mind if circumstances change.

Useful websites

The essential website for making an application is, of course, that of UCAS:
www.ucas.com/how-it-all-works/undergraduate/filling-your-application
For applications to music conservatoires: **www.cukas.ac.uk**
For applications for graduate teacher training: **www.gttr.ac.uk**
For advice on your personal statement:
www.ucas.com/students/how-it-all-works/undergraduate/filling-your-application/
  your-personal-statement
www.studential.com

Gap years

To help you consider options and start planning: **www.gapadvice.org**
For links to volunteering opportunities in the UK: **www.do-it.org.uk**
For links to many gap year organisations: **www.yearoutgroup.org**
For work placements relevant to university courses (the Year in Industry Scheme):
www.etrust.org.uk

Also consult:
Community Service Volunteers: **www.csv.org.uk**
vInspired (the national young volunteers service): **www.vinspired.com**

7 University Tuition Fees

Tuition fees at UK universities vary much more widely than it might appear from media reporting. Even just for undergraduates, it makes a big difference whether you are from inside or outside the European Union, studying full-time or part-time, and whether you are taking a Foundation degree or an honours programme. Non-European medical students may pay as much as £30,000 a year, Britons taking part-time Foundation degrees as little as £1,200. But all the attention has been focused on full-time honours degrees for British and other EU undergraduates because those are the courses for which the maximum fees shot up to £9,000 in 2012.

That maximum has now become the norm. Fewer than 20 universities will charge less than £9,000 in 2014, although many students will be eligible for scholarships or bursaries that will bring down the cost. Numbers dropped in the first year of higher fees, but prospective students now appear to have resigned themselves to the new charges. Both applications and enrolments recovered in 2013 and there was little sign that applicants were basing their choices on the marginal differences in fee levels at different universities. There was still concern, however, over the impact on part-time courses and, in years to come, on the numbers prepared to continue to postgraduate study.

Most readers of this guide will be choosing full-time undergraduate or Foundation degree courses. The fees for 2014–15 are listed alongside each university's profile in Chapter 14 and access agreements for universities in England, including full details of bursaries and scholarships, are on the website of the Office for Fair Access (OFFA). Institutions in Scotland, Wales and Northern Ireland will continue to have lower charges for their own residents, but charge varying amounts to students from other parts of the UK. Only those living in Scotland and studying at Scottish universities will escape all fees, although there will be discounts (described in more detail in the next chapter) available to those from Wales and Northern Ireland.

No one living in the UK will pay more than the £9,000 maximum introduced in 2012. Inflation is eating into tuition fee income – now a big part of universities' finances – and there is no longer any significant incentive to keep fees down. The number of bursaries and scholarships offered to reduce the burden on new students is also likely to fall since OFFA has suggested that such initiatives do little to attract students from low-income households. OFFA's evidence pre-dated £9,000 fees so may no longer be correct, but universities are already acting on its advice.

The Government and universities themselves distinguish between the "headline" fee and the average amount actually paid by undergraduates. The average fee is a slippery concept – the figure depends on whether you include only fee waivers or other forms of financial support as well – but there is no doubt that it went up marginally in 2013–14 and will almost certainly do so again in 2014–15. For most students, such movements will not matter because they would not have qualified for the various benefits in any case. But if your household income is below about £42,000, it may be worth checking the small print of your chosen university's access agreement on the OFFA website. For what it's worth, the average fee (however calculated) rose by about £90 in 2013–14, reaching almost £8,000 after all possible deductions were included.

The lowest full-time fee at an English university in 2014–15 will be £2,250 a year, charged for the small number of Foundation degrees at Leeds Trinity, one of the dozen new universities this year. But even there, honours degree students will pay £8,500. The lowest fee for an honours degree will be from London Metropolitan, where the average is expected to be £6,704.

More than 90 universities are charging the full £9,000 for at least some courses – all of them at 42 institutions – but the most expensive average fee after all possible deductions are taken into account will be £8,724 at City University London. Two universities (Chichester and University College Birmingham) will devote more than half of the income they receive above the basic £6,000 fee to access initiatives, including fee waivers and bursaries. At City, the proportion is only 20 per cent, and it falls lower still at a number of universities.

This may be regarded as good news by students who do not qualify for the benefits since a larger proportion of the fee will be spent on teaching them. But there is little evidence yet that fee levels have more than a marginal influence on choices of university or course. Many candidates appear to have decided that the possibility of repaying £27,000, rather than perhaps £24,000, over an extended period is not going to affect their preferences. So far, some of the most successful universities in terms of applications have charged the full £9,000 fees, while others have been equally successful at the opposite end of the scale. Predictions that old universities and/or vocational subjects would prosper at the expense of the rest have already been shown to be too simplistic.

For many young people, the options have not changed. If you want to be a doctor, a teacher or a social worker, there is no alternative to higher education. There is still no requirement to pay upfront, even if £9,000 fees do mean a greatly increased repayment period once your salary tops £21,000. It is in any case impossible to calculate exactly what a degree might cost, regardless of fee levels, because that will depend on your subsequent earnings, perhaps over 30 years, as that is the period after which any remaining loan is written off. The Government estimates that only a third of graduates will pay off all their loans, so marginal differences in fee levels may make no difference at all to the amount that is repaid in the end.

Some further education colleges will offer substantial savings on the cost of a degree, or Foundation degree, but they tend to have very local appeal, generally in a limited range of vocational subjects.

Similarly, the private sector may be expected to compete more vigorously in future, following the success of two-year degrees at Buckingham University and BPP University in particular. Most will continue to undercut the traditional universities, although Regent's University, one of the latest to be awarded that title, has been charging £14,200 and the New

College of the Humanities, also in London, £18,800. Like other private institutions, both are yet to set fees for 2014–15.

Elsewhere, even if it is closer to business as usual than many universities dared hope in the run-up to such a dramatic hike in fees, that does not mean that financial considerations will be completely irrelevant to the decision-making process. In the current economic circumstances, students will want to keep their debts to a minimum and are bound to take the cost of living into account. They will also want the best possible career prospects and may choose their subject accordingly.

Impact on subject and university choice

While there has been no stampede out of purely academic subjects, higher fees do appear to have accelerated the drift towards more vocational degrees and those that are perceived to be winners in the labour market. Every group of subjects, with the sole exception of those allied to medicine, saw a fall in applications at the start of 2012. A more detailed look shows surprising variations – who would have guessed that anthropology would have enjoyed the biggest increase after nursing, with a rise of nearly 24 per cent, and then register another big rise in 2013, for example?

In the first round of applications, vocational subjects such as mechanical engineering, medical technology and finance degrees were all up substantially, but others including architecture and degrees in hospitality, leisure, tourism and sport declined in popularity. Even teacher training, journalism, media studies and social work – all subjects that have grown consistently in recent years – struggled to attract applicants. Some of these recruitment patterns were repeated in 2013, but already there are signs of some subjects recapturing their allure. Media studies, for example, enjoyed a 14 per cent increase at the start of 2013.

In general, the new fees have been bearable for the sciences and very bad news for languages and the creative arts. In 2013, most subjects shared in the recovery, with science and engineering doing particularly well. Computer sciences, after a number of lean years, produced the biggest rise in applications, but law also did well. Languages, however, continued a worrying decline. But sixth formers studying English, history and French cannot suddenly switch to a chemistry degree. It will take time to detect whether the new fees regime brings about more fundamental changes in subject choice, starting at A level or the equivalent, if not before that. There were signs in schools, well before the fees went up, of a renaissance in the sciences.

In short, applicants are looking more carefully at future career prospects when choosing a degree, but they have decided (rightly or wrongly) that some careers are more secure, or more lucrative, than others. Applications for law remain buoyant and medicine is holding its own, despite a long and now much more expensive training. But civil engineering and building have dropped in both years of the new fees. Anthropology is not the only non-vocational subject to have held its own, however. There was a surge in demand for music degrees in 2013, with a 21 per cent increase in applications, more than compensating for an 8 per cent decline the previous year. But the same has been true for computer science, with an 8 per cent decline followed by a 15 per cent increase.

Clearly, no real pattern has been established since the fees went up, and those hoping to start courses in 2014 would be unwise to jump to conclusions about levels of competition in different subjects, or whole universities. A drop in applications may mean less competition for places, or it may lead universities to close courses and possibly even intensify the race for entry. The only reliable forecast is that competition for places on the most popular courses will remain stiff, just as it has been since before students paid any fees.

Getting the best deal

There is still considerable variation in fees and student support packages in 2014–15, so it will be possible to shop around, particularly if your family income is low. But remember that the best deal, even in purely financial terms, is one that leads to a rewarding career. By all means compare the full packages offered by individual universities, but consider whether marginal differences in headline fees really matter as much as the quality of the course and the likely advantages it will confer in the employment market. Higher career earnings will soon account for more than £3,000 or even £6,000 in extra fees to be repaid over 30 years. It is all a matter of judgement – Scottish students can save themselves £27,000 by opting to study north of the border. That is a very different matter to the much smaller saving that is available to students in England, particularly if the Scottish university is of comparable quality to the alternatives elsewhere.

Nor can those who may be eligible for means-tested bursaries afford to ignore the financial assistance they offer, even if the attractions of a course at another university prove too strong to resist in the end. No one has to pay tuition fees while they are a student, but you still have to find thousands of pounds in living costs to take a full-time degree. In some cases, bursaries may make the difference between being able to afford higher education and having to pass up a potentially life-changing opportunity. Some are worth up to £3,000 a year, although most are less generous than this, often because large numbers of students qualify for an award.

Some scholarships are even more valuable – at the University of Bedfordshire, for example, the Vice-Chancellor's Scholarship is worth the full £27,000 fees to one student in each faculty in 2013–14. Most scholarships, including the Bedfordshire example, are not means-tested, but a few are open only to students who are both high performers academically and from low-income families.

For those who are swayed by fee levels, it is important to compare charges within universities as well as between them. While the big names will continue to charge £9,000 a year for every subject, many universities have a range of fees for different subjects. Some, like Bournemouth and Derby are charging more for their most popular and prestigious courses. Others are adding a premium for courses that cost most to run – generally engineering or science courses.

How the new fees work

What follows is a summary of the position for British students in spring 2013. While there are substantial differences between the four countries of the UK, there is one important piece of common ground. Up-front payment of fees is not compulsory, as students can take out a fee loan from the Student Loan Company to cover them (see chapter 8). This is repayable in instalments after graduation, when earnings reach £21,000 for English students, a threshold set by the Government.

With undergraduate fees remaining at a maximum of £9,000, the most you can borrow to pay fees will also stay at £9,000, with lower sums set for private colleges and part-time study. There are different levels of fees and support for UK students who are not from England. Students from other EU countries will pay the same rate as home students in the UK nation in which they study. Those from outside the EU are not affected by the changes, and may well have to pay quite a lot more than home and European students. The latest information on individual universities' fees at the time of going to press is listed at the end of this chapter and alongside their profiles in chapter 14.

With changes, large or small, becoming almost an annual occurrence, it is essential to consult the latest information provided on the websites of the relevant Government agencies.

Fees in England

In England, the maximum tuition fee for full-time undergraduates from the UK or anywhere in the European Union will be £9,000 a year in 2014–15. Some private colleges and further education colleges are charging considerably less than this for 2013–14, particularly for Foundation degrees, but very few university degrees will be available for the £6,000 fee that ministers once hoped would be the norm. Indeed, even in 2012–13, every university set some or all of its fees above the basic level of £6,000.

Most universities have opted for fees of £9,000, or close to it, in order to recoup the money removed from Government grants and leave room for further investment and student support. But this is only the headline figure. Almost all universities offer bursaries and scholarships that make the actual cost lower for students from less affluent backgrounds. In many cases, these will reduce the cost by up to a third for those from homes where the combined salaries are less than £25,000.

In many public universities, the lowest fees will be for Foundation degrees and Higher National Diplomas. Although some universities have chosen to charge the same for all courses, in many universities and further education colleges, these two-year courses will remain a cost-effective stepping stone to a full degree or a qualification in their own right. Those universities that offer extended work placements as part of a degree course will charge much less than the normal fee for the "year out"; at Manchester Metropolitan University, for example, the "sandwich year" will cost £680 in 2014–15.

Fees in Scotland

At Scottish universities and colleges, students from Scotland and those from other EU countries outside the UK pay no fees directly. The universities' vice-chancellors and principals have appealed for charges to be introduced at some level to save their institutions from falling behind their English rivals in financial terms, but Alex Salmond, Scotland's First Minister, famously declared that the "rocks will melt with the sun" before this happens. This is regarded as an election promise which he would find it hard to draw back from.

Students whose home is in Scotland and are who studying at a Scottish university apply to the Student Awards Agency for Scotland (SAAS) to have their fees paid for them. Note, too, that three-year degrees are rare in Scotland, so most students can expect to pay four years of living costs.

Students from England, Wales and Northern Ireland studying in Scotland will pay fees at something like the level that applies in England and will have access to finance at similar levels to those available for study in England. Several Scottish universities are offering a "free" fourth year to bring their total fees into line with English universities, but Edinburgh and St Andrews are charging £9,000 in all four years of their degree courses.

Fees in Wales

Welsh universities have applied a range of fees up to £9,000, but a number have opted for fees below this level. Students who live in Wales will be able to apply for a Tuition Fee Loan as well as a Tuition Fee Grant, wherever they study. The grant is intended to pay fees beyond

£3,575 a year in 2013–14 (the 2014–15 arrangements have not been announced at the time of writing.

Fees in Northern Ireland

The two universities of Northern Ireland are charging local students £3,575 a year for 2013–14. Students can receive a fee loan to postpone paying this until their earnings are above £15,975 a year. For students from elsewhere in the UK, the fee is currently £6,000 a year at Ulster, still good value compared to much English provision, and £9,000 at Queen's, Belfast. The arrangements for 2014–15 have not been announced at the time of writing.

Useful websites

With changes, large or small, becoming almost an annual occurrence, it is essential to consult the latest information provided by Government agencies. It is worth checking the following websites for the latest information:

England: **www.gov.uk/student-finance** and **www.sfengland.slc.co.uk**

Wales: **www.studentfinancewales.co.uk**

Scotland: **www.saas.gov.uk**

Northern Ireland: **www.studentfinanceni.co.uk**

University tuition fees for UK/EU and international students

England

The fees given for UK/EU undergraduates are those for **2014–15**. The fees shown are for full degrees and do not include the sometimes lower fees charged for Foundation degrees or for Foundation years (Year 0). The International student fees are for **2013–14**. Please check university websites for the most recent information.

	Undergraduate fees UK / EU students 2014–15	Undergraduate fees International students 2013–14
Anglia Ruskin	£9,000	£9,800–£10,300
Arts University Bournemouth	£9,000	£11,600
Aston	£9,000	£12,500–£15,600
Bath	£9,000	£13,000–£16,500
Bath Spa	£9,000	£10,535–£13,690
Bedfordshire	£9,000	£9,600
Birkbeck	£6,750[1]	£11,334–£11,925 (full-time courses)
Birmingham	£9,000	£12,140–£16,000; £16,000–£28,100 (medicine)
Birmingham City	£7,500–£9,000	£10,100–£11,300; £14,600–£13,000 (Conservatoire and acting)
University College Birmingham	£8,282	£8,800
Bishop Grosseteste	£8,500	£8,800
Bolton	£9,000	£9,400
Bournemouth	£9,000	£9,500–£12,000
Bradford	£9,000	£11,000–£13,100
Brighton	£9,000	£10,900–£12,900; £24,860 (medicine)
Bristol	£9,000	£14,250–£17,250; £32,000 (dentistry, medicine, veterinary medicine)
Brunel	£9,000	£12,000–£15,000
Buckingham	£11,960[2]	£16,480[2]
Buckinghamshire New	£9,000	£9,200
Cambridge	£9,000	£13,662–£20,790: £33,069 (medicine)[3]
Canterbury Christ Church	£8,500	£9,425
Central Lancashire	£9,000	£10,450–£11,450
Chester	£9,000	£10,600
Chichester	£8,500	9,660–£11,025
City	£9,000	£12,000–£14,000
Coventry	£8,088–£9,000	£10,080–£12,000 (Coventry); £9,990–£10,375 (London)
Cumbria	£9,000	£9,960–£14,965
De Montfort	£9,000	£10,750–£11,250
Derby	£8,100–£9,000	£9,945–£10,510
Durham	£9,000	£13,300–£17,000
East Anglia	£9,000	£12,300–£14,900; £27,500 (medicine)
East London	£9,000	£9,900
Edge Hill	£9,000	£10,800
Essex	£9,000	£11,500–£13,500
Exeter	£9,000	£14,500–£17,000; £17,000–£29,000 (medicine)
Falmouth	£9,000	£10,900
Gloucestershire	£9,000	£10,200
Goldsmiths	£9,000	£11,700–£16,200

	Undergraduate fees UK / EU students 2014–15	Undergraduate fees International students 2013–14
Greenwich	£9,000	£10,100
Harper Adams	£9,000	£9,650
Hertfordshire	£9,000	£9,500–£10,000
Huddersfield	£8,250	£11,500–£12,500
Hull	£9,000	£11,760–£14,070; £24,680 (medicine)
Imperial	£9,000	£25,000; £27,500–£39,150 (medicine)
Keele	£9,000	£10,500–£12,500; £21,000 (medicine)
Kent	£9,000	£12,030–£14,360
King's College London	£9,000	£15,000–£19,000; £35,000 (medicine & dentistry)
Kingston	£9,000	£10,750–£12,350
Lancaster	£9,000	£12,640–£15,850
Leeds	£9,000	£12,900–£16,200; £18,000–£29,950 (medicine)
Leeds Metropolitan	£9,000	£9,500
Leeds Trinity	£8,500	£9,300–£11,000
Leicester	£9,000	£12,365–£15,815; £27,710 (medicine)
Lincoln	£9,000	£11,130–£12,755
Liverpool	£9,000	£11,862–£15,251; £23,108 (dentistry & medicine)
Liverpool Hope	£9,000	£9,000
Liverpool John Moores	£9,000	£11,055–£12,040
London Metropolitan	£4,500–£9,000	£9,000
London School of Economics	£9,000	£15,768
London South Bank	£9,000	£10,500
Loughborough	£9,000	£13,250–£16,750
Manchester	£9,000	£13,000–£17,000; £16,500–£30,000 (medicine)
Manchester Metropolitan	£9,000	£10,250–£16,500
Middlesex	£9,000	£10,400
Newcastle	£9,000	£11,500–£14,750; £14,750–£27,305 (medicine & dentistry)
Newman	£9,000	£8,900
Northampton	£9,000	£9,750–£10,750 (podiatry); £10,750 (2-year fast-track)
Northumbria	£9,000	£10,700–£11,500; £12,700 (nursing, physiotherapy)
Norwich University of the Arts	£9,000	£11,400
Nottingham	£9,000	£12,830–£16,510; £17,400–£30,240 (medicine) £16,510–£24,470 (veterinary medicine)
Nottingham Trent	£9,000	£11,100–£11,600
Oxford	£9,000	£13,860–£20,405; £28,100 (clinical medicine)[4]
Oxford Brookes	£9,000	£11,400–£12,200; £13,150 (physiotherapy)
Plymouth	£9,000	£10,750; £15,000–£22,500 (medicine)
Portsmouth	£9,000	£10,500–£11,900
Queen Mary	£9,000	£12,750–£15,500; £19,400–£29,600 (medicine)
Reading	£9,000	£12,000–£15,000
Roehampton	£8,750	£10,950
Royal Agricultural University	£9,000	£9,000
Royal Holloway	£9,000	£12,600–£14,250
St Mark and St John	£9,000	£9,400–£10,350
Salford	£9,000	£10,870–£12,200

	Undergraduate fees UK / EU students 2014–15	Undergraduate fees International students 2013–14
SOAS London	£9,000	£14,590
Sheffield	£9,000	£12,760–£16,640; £30,080 (medicine)
Sheffield Hallam	£9,000	£10,680–£11,880
Southampton	£9,000	£12,420–£15,250; £29,450 medicine
Southampton Solent	£9,000	£9,785–£10,815
Staffordshire	£7,610–£8,610 £9,000 (2-year fast track)	£9,875
Sunderland	£7,800–£8,500	£9,000
Surrey	£9,000	£12,130–£1,5160
Sussex	£9,000	£13,000–£16,200; £24,860 (medicine)
Teesside	£7,950–£8,450	£10,450
University of the Arts London	£9,000	£13,800
University College London	£9,000	£14,750–£19,500; £29,000 (medicine)
University for the Creative Arts	£9,000	£11,140
Warwick	£9,000	£14,420–18,390; £16,840–£29,340 (medicine)
West London	£8,500–£9,000	£9,350
West of England	£9,000	£10,750
Westminster	£9,000	£11,370
Winchester	£8,500	£10,500; £4,600 (Fast Track)
Wolverhampton	£8,900	£10,420
Worcester	£8,900	£10,600
York	£9,000	£13,580–£17,650; £24,680 (medicine)
York St John	£9,000	£9,000–£11,500

1 On the basis of students studying for four years at 75 per cent intensity, equivalent to £9,000 full-time fees.
2 Courses starting in July 2014. Note that courses only lasts two years (eight terms).
3 Plus Cambridge College fees (£5,000–£6,500). UK & EU students who are eligible for tuition fee support not liable for College fees.
4 Plus Oxford College fees (£6,465). UK & EU students who are eligible for tuition fee support not liable for College fees.

Wales

For **2014–15**, universities can to charge up to £9,000, with the Welsh Assembly paying fees above £3,575 (2013–14) for Welsh students.

Aberystwyth	£9,000	£9,750–£10,750

	Undergraduate fees UK / EU students 2014–15	Undergraduate fees International students 2013–14
Bangor	£9,000	£10,300–£12,500
Cardiff	£9,000	£12,700–£16,000; £29,000 (medicine & dentistry)
Cardiff Metropolitan	£9,000	£9,700; £11,400 (podiatry)
Glyndŵr	£7,400–£8,450	£8,950–£9,450
South Wales[1]	£8,250–£9,000	£9,950–£11,000[2]
Swansea	£9,000	£10,500–£13,500
Trinity St David (UWTSD)	£7,500[2]	£9,576–£10,000[2]

1 Glamorgan and Newport have amalgamated to become the University of South Wales.
2 Figures for 2013–14. UWTSD now includes Swansea Metropolitan.

Scotland

In **2013–14** there are no fees for Scottish and EU students, but there are fees for students from elsewhere in the UK. As Scottish Honours degrees are 4 years in length, the cost of some degrees in Scotland for students from the rest of the UK will be higher than in England, although some universities have put a maximum cap on charges to maintain equality with English fees. There is some financial support from the universities specifically for students from the rest of the UK. Please consult university websites for the fees to be charged in **2014–15**, as arrangements have not been announced at time of writing. The fees for International students are for **2013–14**.

	Fees for Scottish students and eligible non-UK EU students 2013–14[1]	Fees for students from elsewhere in the UK 2013–14	Undergraduate fees International students 2013–14
Aberdeen	No fee	£9,000[2]	£12,000–£15,000; £26,500 (medicine)
Abertay	No fee	£7,000[3]	£10,250
Dundee	No fee	£9,000[2]	£10,200–£14,850; £18,750–£28,750 (medicine & dentistry)
Edinburgh	No fee	£9,000	£13,300– £17,500 £21,650–£36,600 (medicine) £27,900 (veterinary studies)
Edinburgh Napier	No fee	£6,630 £19,890 for 3-year course	£10,080–£11,700
Glasgow	No fee	£6,750 £9,000[4]	£13,000–£16,500 £30,000
Glasgow Caledonian	No fee	£7,000[3]	£10,200–£14,500
Heriot Watt	No fee	£9,000[2]	£11,370–£14,340
Highlands and Islands	No fee	£7,740[5]	£8,244–£9,786
Queen Margaret	No fee	£6,750	£10,170–£12,090
Robert Gordon	No fee	£5,000–£6,750	£9,900–£12,000
St Andrews	No fee	£9,000	£15,460; £23,540 (medical science)
Stirling	No fee	£6,750	£10,750–£12,900
Strathclyde	No fee	£9,000[2]	£10,500–£15,600
West of Scotland	No fee	£7,250	£10,000–£10,500

1 For all eligible students, SAAS will pay fees of £1,820 direct to the universities.
2 Capped at £27,000 for 4-year courses
3 Capped at £21,000 for 4-year courses
4 Medicine , dentistry, veterinary science
5 Capped at £23,220 for 4-year courses

Northern Ireland

For **2013–14** there will be different fees for students resident in Northern Ireland and students coming from other parts of the UK. There is some financial support from the universities specifically for students from the rest of the UK. Please consult university websites for the fees to be charged in **2014–15**, as arrangements were announced at the time of writing.

	Fees for Northern Irish students and eligible non–UK EU students 2013–14	Fees for students from elsewhere in the UK 2013–14	Undergraduate fees International students 2013–14
Queen's Belfast	£3,575	£9,000	£11,500–£14,750 £15,225–£28,720 (medicine) £23,322 (dentistry)
Ulster	£3,575	£6,000	£9,805

8 The Cost of Studying

There is a little good news for those entering higher education in 2014: for the second year in a row, the maximum fee for British undergraduates will not be going up. The downside is that more universities in England and Wales are charging the full £9,000. And even Scottish universities will not provide a cheaper option unless you live in Scotland. Other Brits are likely to find it more expensive to study north of the border because most will take four years over a degree, with the associated extra living costs and loss of earnings.

Anyone reading this *Guide* already knows that they need to think hard about how they will pay for their higher education. Fees at English universities are now equal to the top of the range worldwide, and of course you have to live whilst studying. But funding is available, especially for those from less affluent backgrounds, to help make college affordable. These funds are growing in importance as economic hardship continues.

Despite the costs, most independent research continues to show that it is worth investing in a degree – as long as you pick the right course and work hard enough to pass. The extra amount you earn, over and above what you would have made without a degree, should far outstrip the cost of your higher education in most subjects at most universities. The latest study, by London Economics for the Million Plus group of post-1992 universities, puts the average graduate premium at £115,000 over working lifetime.

In addition, there are many satisfying careers that are open only to graduates – and others where the vast majority of new entrants have degrees. However, graduates are no longer a tiny social elite, so a degree has ceased to have rarity value as an entry point to working life. An increasing number of careers now expect a higher-level qualification such as a master's degree, not just a three-year BA or BSc.

Graduate salary expectations vary from subject to subject. You may love the movies, but you cannot expect your film studies course to do you as much good financially as a degree in engineering. Average starting salaries by subject groups were given in chapter 2.

Funding help

Even under the new fees regime, there are sources of funding to enable most students to meet the costs of higher education and live reasonably. The drawback is that you will build up debts in the process. The Government points out that long-term finance is available to ease the pain of servicing this debt.

Depending on your family income and where you live in the UK, you may be entitled to a range of grants, bursaries or scholarships. (Yes, you are legally an adult, but your student finance options depend heavily on your family income, which in practice means your mother's and father's earning power, or your partner's if you are married or in a civil partnership.) Unlike loans, these have the great virtue that you don't have to pay them back. The only problem is that this means complex calculations on sources of financial support, fee levels, the length of courses and the cost of living at different universities. With many families feeling the pinch, it has never been more important to get it right.

Getting into debt is now a fact of life for almost all students. In mid-2012, graduates and current students still on courses owed £40.3 billion between them in England alone, making them a major component of the public finances. Virtually all of this debt was in the form of income-contingent loans. The money was owed by 3.8 million borrowers, of whom 2.5 million were earning enough to make repayments, making the average debt just over £10,000 per person. However, most of this debt was run up by students in an era of much lower fees than we see today. Most research now puts average graduate debt at around £20,000. In England, interest rates on these sums are less than for most commercial finance. The rate is set at 3 per cent more than inflation as measured by the Retail Price Index, and at the time of writing was 6.6 per cent for courses that started in 2012. Repayments begin when you are earning £21,000 a year. By the time you graduate, the interest rate will probably have changed and the repayment threshold will have risen, if only by inflation.

Careful financial planning and research into help that is available can go a long way to helping you emerge from your university education with a level of debt that is not going to become a millstone for life.

Tuition

The first problem is paying for your course. The fees will be up to £9,000 a year, but up-front payment of fees is not compulsory, as students can take out a fee loan to cover them. This is repayable in instalments after graduation, when your earnings reach the threshold set by the Government. So although these sums are painfully large, it is not true to say that students pay to go to university. Graduates pay for having gone. It is a decision for you whether you

---

Tuition Fees 2014–15

The figures below show the maximum fees that can be charged.

Domicile of student	Location of institution			
	England	Scotland	Wales	Northern Ireland
England	£9,000	£9,000[1]	£9,000	£9,000
Scotland[1]	£9,000	No fee	£9,000	£9,000
Wales [2]	£3,575	£3,575	£3,575	£3,575
Northern Ireland	£9,000	£9,000[1]	£9,000	£3,575[3]
European Union	£9,000	No fee	£9,000	£3,575
Other international	Variable	Variable	Variable	Variable

1 Note that honours degrees in Scotland take four years and some universities charge £9,000 a year. Figures are for 2013–14.
2 Welsh-domiciled students are entitled to a tuition fee grant for any fees above £3,575 (2013–14; 2014–15 figure to be announced).
3 Figure for 2013–14.

wish to save money by going to a university which has come in at under £9,000 a year as its basic fee, but bear in mind that you will be no better off while you are a student.

If you are studying full-time at a public university, you can borrow up to £9,000 a year, which will cover your full tuition costs. If you are at a private institution the figure comes down to £6,000. This is a problem if you are at A.C. Grayling's much-discussed New College of the Humanities, with fees of £18,000 a year. If you are studying part-time you can borrow up to £6,750 a year at a public university and £4,500 at a private one to cover tuition. You will never see this cash. It is paid straight to the university.

As the table opposite shows fees can be different for UK students who are not from England. Students from other EU countries will pay the same rate as home students in the UK nation in which they study. Those from outside the EU are not affected by the changes, and may well have to pay quite a lot more than home and European students. International students, those from outside the EU, are a major source of cash flow for UK universities.

Living cost support

However much your university charges for your tuition, you will still need to survive the three or more years of your course. A range of grants and loans are available to help. If you are eligible, grants are better than loans for a simple reason. You don't have to pay them back.

As well as student loans, which are accessible at relatively generous interest rates and under very favourable terms, you can shop around for university bursaries, scholarships and other sponsorship packages, and seek out supplementary support to which you may be entitled. The University of Bristol, normally a £9,000-a-year institution, was offering a fee waiver for 2014 entrants from households with incomes below £25,000, ranging from a reduction in fees to £3,500 for those from homes with an income of less than £15,000 to a £6,000 fee for children of families with incomes between £20,000 and £25,000. You can also opt to take some of this waiver as non-repayable cash. This is only an example, and such waivers are widespread under the so-called National Scholarship Programme (NSP). There are also price cuts for a range of other groups, including local students, which vary widely from university to university and which are often detailed on university web sites.

You may be entitled to a maintenance grant: despite recent changes in eligibility, these are available to a much larger slice of the population than was the case in the early years of tuition fees. It can range from £3,387 a year for English students from homes with less than £25,000 income all the way to a rather more modest £50 for those from homes whose incomes approach £42,620. You apply for such a grant via the Student Loans Company alongside your application for a loan, and if you get one, your loan will be correspondingly reduced.

The amount you can borrow as a so-called maintenance loan depends on your need. For 2014 entry it will vary from a maximum of £4,418 for those living at home, to £5,555 for people living away from home outside London, and £7,751 for those living away from home in London. You can even get £6,600 for a year studying abroad as part of a UK course. This might be fine in Egypt, but will not get you far in Japan or Switzerland. At least, from 2014, tuition fees for a year abroad will be capped at 15 per cent of the university's headline rate.

How well you can live on these sums will vary from person to person. But most people will need to gather together all the resources they can just to survive. Analysis by the National Union of Students suggests that it is not possible to get by on student loans and grants alone. Savings, earnings, and help from family and friends have to be added to the pot.

The information provided here will help you understand how big your pot needs to be, and what you can expect to be added and taken away from it.

With changes, large or small, becoming almost an annual occurrence, it is essential to consult the latest information provided by Government agencies. It is worth checking the following websites for the latest information:

» England: **www.gov.uk/student-finance** and **www.sfengland.slc.co.uk**
» Wales: **www.studentfinancewales.co.uk**
» Scotland: **www.saas.gov.uk**
» Northern Ireland: **www.studentfinanceni.co.uk**

Student loans

Around 80 per cent of students take out a student loan, and it is not difficult to see why. First of all, as we saw earlier, it is very difficult to get by financially without one. The UK Border Agency, which had to decide whether incoming international students can support themselves, reckoned that a single student needs £1,000 a month to live in London, although prices are lower elsewhere in the UK. If you don't take out a loan to cover your fees and living costs, you will have to pay for them up front. Most students find it impossible to cover everything on savings and earnings alone. The only reasons to consider paying your fees up front might be if your parents are offering to meet the costs, or if a university is offering a discount if you do so.

There are two types of student loan – one to cover the cost of tuition fees and another to help you cover the cost of living.

Tuition fees loan

You can borrow up to the full amount needed to cover the cost of your tuition fees wherever you study in the UK and it is not dependent upon your household income. Scots studying

---

Maintenance grant and loan example for a first-year English student 2014

The mixture of grant and loan for a first-year English student in 2014–15 who is studying full-time and living away from home (but not in London). The maximum loan is £5,555, payable when the household income is £42,875. The loan thereafter declines to a minimum of £3,610 by £62,132.

Household income	Non-repayable grant	Maintenance loan	Total
£25,000 or less	£3,387	£3,862	£7,249
£30,000	£2,441	£4,335	£6,776
£35,000	£1,494	£4,808	£6,302
£40,000	£547	£5,282	£5,829
£42,620	£50	£5,530	£5,580
£42,875	£0	£5,555	£5,555
£45,000	£0	£5,341	£5,341
£50,000	£0	£4,836	£4,836
Over £62,131	£0	£3,610	£3,610

Department for Business, Innovation and Skills

in Scotland are even better off, as there are no tuition fees for them to pay, so no need for a loan or for repayments later.

Tuition fees loans for part-time students
The most that universities or colleges can charge for part-time courses is between £4,500 and £6,750 a year for 2014–15. They cannot charge more than 75 per cent of the full-time course fee. New part-time students will be able to apply for a tuition fee loan that is not dependent on household income or on age, which has led to some courses having a surprising number of pensioner students. Eligibility depends on the "intensity" of the course being at least 25 per cent of a full-time course. This measure works by comparing the course to a full-time equivalent. So if a course takes six years to complete and the full-time equivalent takes three, the intensity will be 50 per cent.

Maintenance loan
The second type of student loan, a maintenance loan, is means-tested. The amount you can borrow depends on a number of factors, including your family income, where you intend to study, and whether you expect to be living at home. Final-year students receive less than those in earlier years. As we saw above, the maximum maintenance loan for students starting in 2014 will be £5,555 outside London for those who leave home to study; £7,751 if you live away from home and study in London; £4,418 for those living at home; and £6,600 if you are spending a year of your course outside the UK.

Sixty-five per cent of the maintenance loan is available to you regardless of your family circumstances, while the remaining 35 per cent is means-tested. If your parents are separated, divorced or widowed, then only the parent with whom you normally live will be assessed. However, if that parent has married again, entered into a civil partnership, or has a partner of the opposite sex, both their incomes will be taken into account.

Note, too, that there is extra cash available for future teachers, social workers and healthcare workers, including doctors and dentists. The student finance web sites for the various UK nations have the details.

Maintenance loans in Scotland
In Scotland, the rules and regulations for maintenance loans are different and there was considerable change for students starting in 2013. Loans of £5,500 (£4,500 for students from households with incomes over £34,000) are available alongside bursaries ranging from £1,750 for people from families with under £17,000 annual income to zero for students from families with over £34,000 annual income. All the latest details can be found at **www.saas.gov.uk**. Higher loans but more limited bursaries are available for "independent" students, those without family support.

Maintenance loans for mature students
Mature students (those who are over the age of 25, married, or have supported themselves for at least three years before entering university) are assessed for loan and grant entitlements on their own income plus that of their spouse or partner. Grants are also available for those with children, for single parents, and for students with adult dependents. Further support is available for students with children through the Childcare Grant, the Parents' Learning Allowance, the Adult Dependants' Grant and Child Tax Credit system. You have to be under 60 to receive a living cost loan if you are studying full-time. But

remember that the student finance system is mainly open only to people taking a degree for the first time, and funding for graduates taking a similar level of qualification to one they have already completed is problematic.

Applying for loans

When you apply for tuition fee and maintenance loans, you will automatically be assessed for any maintenance grants (see below). English students should apply for grants and loans through Student Finance England, Welsh students through Student Finance Wales, Scottish students through the Student Awards Agency for Scotland, and those in Northern Ireland through Student Finance NI or their Education and Library Board. You should make your application as soon as you have received an offer of a place at university. Maintenance loans are usually paid in three instalments a year into your bank or building society account. European Union students from outside the UK will usually be sent an application form for tuition fee loans by the university that has offered them a place.

Repaying loans

Full-time students will begin accumulating interest during their course and will start repaying in the April after graduation, if they earn over £21,000. They will then pay 9 per cent of their income above £21,000, but repayments will stop during any period in which annual income falls below the threshold. Repayments are normally taken automatically through tax and National Insurance. If the loan has not been paid off after 30 years, no further repayments will be required.

Funding timetable

It is vital that you sort out your funding arrangements before you start university. Each funding agency has its own arrangements, and it is very important that you find out the exact details from them. The dates below give general indications of key dates.

March/April
» Online and paper application forms become available from funding agencies.
» You must contact the appropriate funding agency to make an application. For funding in England contact **www.sfengland.slc.co.uk** rather than your LEA.
» Complete application form as soon as possible. At this stage select the university offer that will be your first choice.
» Check details of bursaries and scholarships available from your selected universities.

May/June
» Funding agencies will give you details of the financial support they can offer.
» Last date for making an application to ensure funding is ready for you at the start of term (exact date varies significantly between agencies).

August
» Tell your funding agency if the university or course you have been accepted for is different from that originally given them.

September
» Take letter confirming funding to your university for registration.
» After registration, the first part of funds will be released to you.

During the repayment period, the amount of interest will vary according to how much you earn. If you earn less than £21,000, interest will be at the rate of inflation; between £21,000 and £41,000 you will be charged inflation plus up to 3 per cent; and if you earn over £41,000, interest will be at inflation plus the full 3 per cent. The Government website set up to guide prospective students through the changes includes a repayments calculator based on starting salaries for a range of careers, at **www.gov.uk/student-finance**. At the time of writing, anyone earning £25,000 a year would face monthly repayments of £23 a month. If you are on £60,000, the sum rises to £285 a month, a fair bite even from that healthy paycheque.

Maintenance grants

In the good old days, most students didn't have to pay fees and many received relatively generous maintenance grants to help them cover day-to-day costs. After a brief disappearance, these non-repayable grants have made a comeback, and are particularly significant if you come from a low-income family. The size and type of grants available, and the rules and regulations governing their distribution, are different for each country of the UK. Your eligibility for a grant is assessed when you apply for a tuition fee and maintenance loan (see above). In addition, there are various types of bursaries and scholarships you can apply for, and other types of grants or support in each country to help students in particular circumstances, such as those that have a disability. What follows is a description of the maintenance grant arrangements country by country.

England

Students from England can apply for a maintenance grant from the Government and a bursary from their university. Those on full-time courses are entitled to a full grant if their household income is £25,000 or less, or a partial grant if household income is between £25,000 and £42,611. Grants are paid into the student's bank account at the beginning of each term. One important rule to bear in mind is that for every £1 you receive in maintenance grant, the amount you can borrow in student loans falls by £1. Thus, it is not possible to have both a full grant and a maximum student loan.

In addition, the Government will fund the National Scholarship Programme to the tune of £150 million in 2014–15 to help students whose household income is £25,000 or less. Assistance may include reduced tuition fees ("fee waivers")or accommodation discounts. Each university will determine its own pattern of support and method of application. Some examples are given alongside the university profiles in chapter 13 and details are available on university and college websites.

Northern Ireland

Students from Northern Ireland can get grants and loans on a similar basis to English students. For 2013–14 the grants range from £3,475 for students with household incomes of less than £19,203, to zero if the figure is more than £41,065. Maintenance loans vary from £3,750 for students living at home, all the way to £6,780 in London. There are also extra sums for people doing courses longer than 30 weeks a year, worth up to £108 a week if you are in London. As in England, there are also special funds for people with disabilities and other special needs, and for those with children or adult dependants. There are modest special bursaries of up to £2,000 for students studying in the Republic of Ireland, who also have their fees paid by their local Education and Library Board.

Wales

In addition to the normal tuition and maintenance loans, students in Wales will also be able to apply for Assembly Learning Grants of up to £5,161. They will be scaled according to household income, which in 2013–14 ranged from £18,370 for a full grant to £50,020 for the smallest payment. The loan you can get is reduced by 50p for every £1 of grant you receive up to £2,575.

Scotland

The Scottish Government has a commitment to a minimum income of £7,000 a year for students from poorer backgrounds, not bad in a setting where tuition is also free. Students from a family with an income below £17,000 can get a £1,750 Young Students' Bursary (YSB) as well as a loan of £5,500. This bursary does not have to be repaid. It tapers off to zero for family incomes of £34,000, at which point the maximum loan also falls from £5,500 to £4,500.

Students with disabilities

Extra financial help will be available to disabled students studying on a part-time basis through Disabled Students' Allowances, which are paid in addition to the standard student finance package. They are available for help with education-related conditions such as dyslexia, and for other physical and mental disability. They do not depend on income and do not have to be repaid. The cash is available for extra travel costs, equipment and to pay helpers. The maximum for a non-medical helper is £20,725 a year, or £15,543 a year for a part-time student. Student Finance England has online videos on this support in British Sign Language.

University bursaries and scholarships

Bursaries and scholarships offered by universities and colleges are an important part of the student financial support system ushered in by the former Labour Government to try to ensure that no one was excluded from university because they could not afford it. Virtually all institutions have expanded their activities in this area as fees have risen. They are under pressure from Government and the Office of Fair Access to improve their performance in this area. Most support is targeted on students from poor backgrounds, but many scholarships are available (for academic achievement or sporting prowess) purely on merit. Some combine eligibility by family circumstances with academic excellence. Most schemes focus on entrants to degree courses, but some also reward performance at university.

Finding out about bursaries

There is now a bewildering variety of bursaries and scholarships on offer at UK universities. It is worth shopping around to see what you can get. The websites of individual institutions carry details of scholarships, bursaries and other financial support which they have available.

   The system of bursaries and scholarships is overseen for England by the Office for Fair Access. It requires all universities to submit what are called "Access Agreements" that contain details of what fees they intend to charge and what scholarships and bursaries they are offering. Access Agreements also describe other kinds of financial support such as "hardship funds". Some awards are guaranteed depending on your personal circumstances, while others are available through open competition. Copies of access agreements can be found at **www.offa.org.uk/access-agreements/**. For example, Anglia Ruskin has details of fee waivers via the NSP. It expects to award 704 of these in 2014–15.

Applying for bursaries and scholarships

Do take note of the application procedures for scholarships and bursaries, as these vary from institution to institution, and even from course to course within individual institutions. There may be a deadline you have to meet to apply for an award. In some cases the university will work out for you whether you are entitled to an award by referring to your funding agency's financial assessment. If your personal circumstances change part-way through a course, your entitlement to a scholarship or bursary may be reviewed.

If you feel you still need more help or advice on scholarships or bursaries, you can usually find it on a university's website or in its prospectus. Some institutions also maintain a helpline. Some questions you will need answered include whether the bursary or scholarship is automatic or conditional and, if the latter, when you will find out whether your application has been successful. For some awards, you won't know whether you have qualified until you get your exam results.

Another obvious question is how the scholarship or bursary on offer compares with awards made by another university you might consider applying to. Watch out for institutions that list entitlements that others don't mention, but which you would get anyway. Some institutions offer "fee remission" or "fee waiver" (a lower tuition fee) rather than scholarships or bursaries, which means you will have no more cash in hand during your course, but will owe less after you have graduated.

Living in one country, studying in another

As each of the countries of the UK develops its own distinctive system of student finance, the effects on students leaving home in one UK nation to go and study in another have become knottier. UK students who cross borders to study pay the tuition fees of their chosen university and are eligible for a fee loan, and maybe a partial grant, to cover them. They are also entitled to apply for the scholarships or bursaries on offer from that institution (apart from NSP awards at English universities which are only available to English students). Any maintenance loan or grant will still come from the awarding body of their home country. You must check with the authorities in your home country. The funds available there may differ from those for home students.

European Union laws stipulate that EU students from outside the UK must be charged the same tuition fees as those paid by nationals of the country where they are studying, rather than the higher fees paid by students from outside the EU. They can also apply for a fee loan and may be considered for some of the scholarships and bursaries offered by individual institutions. Only students who have been living and studying in the UK for at least three years can apply for a maintenance loan or grant. If you haven't, then you will need to apply for such assistance from the authorities in your own country. Tuition fee rules for non-UK European Union students are the same in Scotland as for Scottish students – that is, they do not have to pay tuition fees. There are also no fees to pay for exchange students coming to the UK, including those on the Socrates Programme.

Further sources of income

If you are feeling daunted by the potential costs, you can take some comfort from this section, which outlines just some of the ways you can raise additional funds.

Taking a gap year

Gap years have become increasingly popular both for travelling and to earn some money to help pay for higher education. Many students will simply want to travel, but others will be more focused on boosting the bank balance in preparation for life as a student. Of course, there is more to taking a gap year than short-term financial gain. The longer-term benefits of taking part in cultural exchanges and courses, expeditions, volunteering or structured work placements may be an advantage in the graduate employment market. Both university admissions officers and employers look for evidence that candidates have more about them than academic ability. The experience you gain on a gap year can help you develop many of the attributes they are looking for, such as interpersonal, organisational and teamwork skills, leadership, creativity, experience of new cultures or work environments, and enterprise. But the university may be less impressed if you spent the time partying in Thailand with your friends from school.

Various organisations can help you find voluntary work, if this is the way you prefer to spend at least some of your year out. Some examples include v (**www.vinspired.com**), Lattitude Global Volunteering (**www.lattitude.org.uk**) and Volunteer Africa (**www. volunteerafrica.org**). Voluntary Service Overseas (**www.vso.org.uk**) works mainly with older volunteers but has an offshoot, run with five other volunteering organisations, International Citizen Service (**www.volunteerics.org**), that places 18–25 year olds around the world.

Work placements can be structured or casual. An example of the structured variety is the Year in Industry Scheme (**www.etrust.org.uk**). Sponsorship is also available, mainly to those wishing to study science, engineering or business. There are also sites such as **www.gapyearjobs.co.uk**. Buyer beware: we cannot vouch for any of these and you need to be clear whether the aim is to make money or to plump up your CV. If it is the second, you may end up spending money, not saving it.

Further Government support

There are various types of support available from Government sources for students in particular circumstances, other than the main loans, grants and bursaries.

» Undergraduates in financial difficulties can apply for help from the Access to Learning Fund (Financial Contingency Fund in Wales, Hardship Fund in Scotland, Support Funds in Northern Ireland). These are allocated by universities to provide support for anything from day-to-day study and living costs to unexpected or exceptional expense. The university decides which students need help and how much money to award them. These funds are often targeted at older or disadvantaged students, and finalists who are in danger of dropping out. The sums range up to a few thousand pounds, are not repayable and do not count against other income.

» Students with children can apply for a Childcare Grant, worth £150.23 a week if you have one child and £257.55 a week if you have two or more children under 15, or under 17 with special needs; and a Parents' Learning Allowance, for help with course-related costs, of between £50 and £1,523 a year.

» Any students with a partner, or another adult family member who is financially dependent on them, can apply for an Adult Dependants' Grant of up to £2,668 a year.

If you do not qualify for any of this kind of financial support you may still be able to apply for a Professional and Career Development Loan available from certain banks, in partnership with the National Careers Service. Students on a wide range of vocational courses can borrow from £300 to £10,000 at a fixed rate of interest to fund up to two years of learning, but the loans cannot be used for first full-time degrees.

In addition, many universities and student unions have some money available for students who have hit the rocks financially. Institutions are very reluctant to see students drop out for financial reasons.

Part-time work

The need to hold down a part-time job during term time is now a fact of life for more than half of students. Students from a working-class background are more likely to need to earn while they learn.

If you need to earn during term time, it is important to try to ensure that you do not work so many hours that it starts to affect your studies. A survey by the NUS found that 59 per cent of students who worked felt it had an impact on their studies, with 38 per cent missing lectures and over a fifth failing to submit coursework because of their part-time jobs. You will find that new universities are better geared-up to cope with working students than more traditional institutions.

Student employment agencies, which can now be found on many university campuses, can help you get the balance right. These introduce employers with work to students seeking work, sometimes even offering jobs within the university itself. But they also abide by codes of practice that regulate both minimum wages and the maximum number of hours worked in term time (typically 15 hours a week). It is worth thinking how much paid work is enough. In a 2012 survey, Lloyds TSB found that 49 per cent of students said they had taken on paid work, and a quarter of those employed in term time say it had a negative effect on their studies.

Some firms, such as the big supermarkets, offer continuing part-time employment to their school part-time employees when they go to university. Some students make use of their expertise in areas like web design to earn some extra money, but most take on casual work in retail stores, restaurants, bars and call centres.

Most students, including those who don't work during term time, get a job during vacations. A Government survey found that 86 per cent of students in their second year of study or above worked during their summer vacation. Most of this kind of work is casual, but some is formalised in a scheme like STEP (**www.step.org.uk**) or may be part of a sponsorship programme. Many vacation jobs are fairly mundane, but it is possible to find more interesting work. Some students broaden their experience by working abroad, others work as film extras, do tutoring, or do a variety of jobs at big events such as festivals. It is also a good idea to try to use the summer holidays to get some work experience in a field that has some relevance to your career aspirations. Even if you don't get paid, this can significantly enhance your chances of finding employment after graduation.

What you will need to spend money on

Living costs

The NUS estimated that in 2012–13, a student living in London would have an average cost of living of £13,388, not including tuition fees, books or equipment. Although the sums are lower outside the capital (the NUS estimated £12,056 living costs outside London in 2012), even these can readily outstrip student grants, loans and bursaries. Little surprise, then, that a growing number of students are choosing to work while studying, or to live at home and study at a local university. However, even this option is not necessarily cheap, once travel to and from the university is taken into account.

Certain costs are unavoidable. You have to have a roof over your head, eat enough, clothe yourself, and probably do a certain amount of travelling. But the cost of even these essential items can be cut down significantly through a mixture of shopping around and careful budgeting. If you set aside a certain amount of money a week for food, you will find it goes much further if you keep takeaways and ready-meals to a minimum, and stick to a shopping list when you go to a supermarket. Some catering outlets at your university or in the students' union may well offer good value meals, but probably the most economical way to eat is to cook and share meals with fellow students with whom you may be living in a shared house. Make sure you make full use of student travel cards and other offers and facilities available locally to help you cut the cost of travel. In certain locations, a bicycle is a very worthwhile investment (as is buying a lock for it).

If you can keep your essential costs down, you will have more money for what you would probably prefer to spend your money on – going out, and personal items. Most students spend a proportion of their budget on socialising, and this is certainly an important part of the university experience. You can have plenty of fun and keep your leisure costs down by making the most of your student union's facilities and events.

The latest version of an annual survey of student life by the company Sodexo suggests that half of all students have altered their eating habits for lack of money. It found that students have been cutting back on fun, with their reported spend on leisure down from £24 a week in 2010 to £18.70 in 2012. A quarter of overseas students and 17 per cent of new university students claim to spend no money at all on leisure and, interestingly, 58 per cent of students claim to spend nothing on books.

The same survey suggested that while 30 per cent of students graduating in 2012 expected to have debts of over £20,000, up from virtually zero in 2002, a growing percentage of students (75 per cent in 2012) regard university as a worthwhile investment.

Studying costs

The latest NUS survey estimated that the average student spent about £1,000 a year on costs associated with course work and studying, mainly books and equipment. The amount you spend will be determined largely by the nature of your course and what you study. Additional financial support may be available for certain expenditure, but this is unlikely to cover you fully for spending on books, stationery, equipment, fieldwork or electives. A long reading list could prove very expensive if you tried to buy all of the required books brand new. Find out as soon as possible which books are available either in your university library or local libraries. Another approach is to buy books second-hand from students who no longer need them. Your students' union or your university may run second-hand book sales or offer a service helping students to buy and sell books.

Other costs

Keep any other costs you may incur as low as possible. This may sound trite, but it is easy to let "other costs" get out of hand to the extent that they start to eat into your budget for day-to-day living. Mobile phone bills are a case in point. Look at your previous bills, or think carefully about your usage, and then shop around for the best deal to cover what you need. Extras like downloading games or music, or sending pictures, can add significantly to your bill. Most of all, try to avoid getting tied up with an expensive and inflexible contract.

Overdrafts and credit cards

"Other costs" it is best to avoid are the more expensive forms of debt. Many banks offer free overdraft facilities for students, but if you go over that limit without prior arrangement, you can end up paying way over the odds for your borrowing. Credits cards can be useful if managed properly. The best way to manage a credit card is to set up a direct debit to pay off your balance in full every month, which means you will avoid paying any interest. One of the worst ways is just paying the minimum charge each month, which can cost you a small fortune over a long period. If you are the kind of person who spends impulsively and doesn't keep track of your spending, you are probably better off without a credit card. That way, you can't spend money you don't have.

Insurance

One kind of additional spending that can actually end up saving you money is getting insurance cover for your possessions. Most students arrive at university with laptops and other goodies such as digital cameras, mobile phones and iPods, not to mention bikes, that are tempting to petty thieves. It is estimated that around a third of students fall victim to crime at some point during their time at university. If you shop around, you should be able to get a reasonable amount of cover for these kinds of items without its costing you an arm and a leg. It may also be possible to add this cover cheaply to your parents' domestic contents policy.

Planning your budget

University websites, the National Union of Students and many other sites offer guidance on preparing a budget, usually with the basic headings provided for you to complete. First, list all your likely income (grants, bursaries, loans, part-time work, savings, parental support) and then see how this compares with what you will spend. Try to be realistic, and not too optimistic, about both sides of the equation. With care, you will end up either only slightly in the red, or preferably far enough in the black for you to be able to afford things you would really like to spend your money on.

Above all, keep track of your finances so that your university experience isn't ruined by money worries, or finding you can't go to the ball because the cash machine has eaten your card. Spreadsheets make doing this simpler, and it is one skill you can learn at college that you are definitely going to need for the rest of your life.

If all else fails, your campus almost certainly has a student money adviser who is a member of NASMA, the National Association of Student Money Advisers. You can find them via **www.nasma.org.uk**. NASMA reports that some students, especially those with children or whose family circumstances force them to drive to university, are noticing steep inflation right now. However, the bargains available in student shops can mean that you might not experience the painful price rises that newspaper headline suggest are affecting the bulk of consumers.

NASMA's Jo Gibson says that many student advisers spend time helping people with low levels of basic financial awareness and planning ability. In addition, they have noticed that students are increasingly likely to spend money they cannot afford on TV and online gambling, so make sure to avoid this temptation.

She adds that the overall pattern of student finance is a complex one. For example, university hardship funds have been cut, but the fact that child benefit is not taken into account for housing benefit has been good for students with children. The message is: stay informed and you might get through university in better financial shape than you had imagined.

Useful websites

For the basics of fees, loans, grants and other allowances:
www.gov.uk/student-finance
www.gov.uk/browse/education/student-finance

UCAS provides helpful advice: **www.ucas.com/how-it-works/studentfinance**
For England, visit Student Finance England : **www.sfengland.slc.co.uk**
Office for Fair Access: **www.offa.org.uk**
For Wales, visit Student Finance Wales: **www.studentfinancewales.co.uk**
For Scotland, visit the Student Awards Agency for Scotland: **www.saas.gov.uk**
For arrangements for Scottish students studying in the UK o EU, and for students
from the rest of the UK studying in Scotland: **www.scotland.gov.uk/Topics/Education/**
UniversitiesColleges/16640/financial-help.
For Northern Ireland, visit Student Finance Northern Ireland: **www.studentfinanceni.co.uk**
All UK student loans are administered by the Student Loan Company: **www.slc.co.uk**
HM Revenue and Customs: **www.hmrc.gov.uk/students**
NHS Student Bursaries for students on pre-registration health professional and social work
training courses: **www.nhsbsa.nhs.uk/students**
For finding out about availability of scholarships: **www.scholarship-search.org.uk**

9 Finding Somewhere to Live

The first decision of your university life – even before choosing which course options to take – is where to live. And, with some student rents now amounting to more than the entire maintenance loan, it is vitally important to get it right. Particularly in your first year – and even more so if it is your first time away from home – you are likely to be happier and more successful academically in accommodation of reasonable quality, preferably in a setting that helps you meet other students. But, equally obviously, whatever you choose has to be affordable.

As the number of students has risen in all parts of the UK, the search for reasonably priced and acceptable housing has become tougher. The property bubble may have burst, but rents have continued to rise, particularly in the student market. Where student numbers dropped in 2012–13, there was less pressure on university halls of residence and other student housing. But the latest accommodation survey by the National Union of Students (NUS) shows no sign of average rents dropping as a result. Unlike some private landlords, universities generally did not reduce charges, even where they had empty rooms, and the union reported a 25 per cent increase in rents in the three years ending in 2012–13, with the average student now paying more than £124 a week. In London, that figure rises to £157, according to the survey, with upmarket studio flats costing £10,900 a year. The average rents for university accommodation quoted in chapter 14 also show another increase this year.

Living at home

For a growing number of undergraduates, the solution to this problem is to live at home. With repayments starting only after graduation, the new fee regime leaves students no worse off during their time at university. But many undergraduates will be more careful about the debts they run up, and housing is the biggest single item in the student budget.

The pattern of recent applications shows that the trend towards studying at home is accelerating, and there is no reason to think that will change while the economic downturn continues. Indeed, it may be a permanent shift, given the rising costs and the willingness of many young people to live with their parents well into their twenties.

The proportion of students living at home grew from 13 per cent to 18 per cent in three years before undergraduate fees went up, according to the last *Sodexo University Lifestyle Survey*. This figure includes mature students, many of whom are restricted by family circumstances, but it would be surprising if it did not rise further in the immediate future. Women are more likely than men to stay at home: 20 per cent of them do, compared to 15 per cent of men. Asian women are particularly likely to take this option. Home study is also four times more common at post-1992 universities than older institutions, again reflecting the larger numbers of mature students at the newer universities and a generally more affluent student population at the older ones.

Living away from home

Most of those who can afford it still see moving away to study as integral to the rite of passage that student life represents. Some have little option because, in spite of the expansion of higher education, the course they want is not available locally. Others are happy to travel to secure their ideal place and widen their experience.

For the lucky majority, the search for accommodation will be over quickly because the university can offer a place in one of its halls of residence or self-catering flats. The choice may come down to the type of accommodation and whether or not to do your own cooking. For others, however, the offer of a degree place will be the start of an anxious search for a room in a strange city.

Going to university will oblige those who take the "away" route to think for the first time about practicalities of living independently. This can make the decision about where to live – both in terms of location and the type of accommodation – doubly difficult. It may even influence your choice of university, since there are big differences across the sector in the cost and standard of accommodation – as well as its availability.

Term-time type of accommodation of full-time and sandwich students

	2010/11	2011/12
University maintained property	18.5%	18.4%
Private-sector halls	5%	4.8%
Parental/guardian home	19%	18.9%
Own residence	16%	15.8%
Other rented accommodation	29%	29.3%
Other	4%	4.4%
Not known	8.5%	8.4%

HESA 2013 (adapted)

How much will it cost?

Students in the UK are estimated to spend almost twice as much on rent as their combined spending on food, going out, books and music. The NUS survey found enormous variations: while those living in London were paying more than £150 a week, average rents in Northern Ireland were still under £85 week and in Wales under £95. Such averages are becoming meaningless, however, because the range of rents is so wide, particularly in London.

There is undoubtedly a growing luxury end to the student market, even while others live in much cheaper, often sub-standard accommodation. Most universities with a range of accommodation find that their most expensive rooms fill up first and students appear to have higher expectations – almost half of all the rooms in the NUS survey had en-suite facilities. The downside of this trend is that there can be fewer university-owned places available at the lowest price band, which is also the one where rents have been the biggest percentage rises. The privately run blocks, which the union blames for pushing up prices, certainly tend to be well-appointed as well as popular. A survey by Deloitte Real Estate found that 2,660 purpose-built residential places had been added in London in 2010–11, with another 7,700 under construction – almost twice as many as in the previous year.

Generally speaking, the cost of student accommodation is highest in London and the southeast of England and lowest in the Midlands and North of England, Wales, Scotland and Northern Ireland. But even within those regions there is considerable variation. Renting in new blocks of flats – and especially those that are en suite – is often more expensive than sharing a house with friends, but the latter is a lot more common after the first year.

It is important to remember that both your living costs and your potential earnings should be factored into your calculations when deciding where to live. While living costs in London are, unsurprisingly, by far the highest, potential part-time earnings are nearly double those in other parts of the country.

The choices you have

No longer are you faced with a straightforward choice between a university hall of residence and a poor-quality rented house. The NUS puts accommodation into 16 categories, ranging from luxurious university halls to a bedsit in a shared house. The choices include:

» University hall of residence, with individual study bedrooms and a full catering service; many will have en-suite accommodation.
» University halls, flats or houses where you have to provide your own food.
» Private, purpose-built student accommodation.
» Rented houses or flats, shared with fellow students.
» Living at home.
» Living as a lodger in a private house.

This chapter will provide you with more information to help you decide where you would like to live and whether you can afford it.

Making your choice

Finance is not the only factor you should consider when deciding where to live. Feeling comfortable and happy in your student home is of crucial importance to your success at university and to the quality of your experience. It is therefore worth investing some time to find the right place, and to avoid the false economy of choosing somewhere cheap where you may end up feeling depressed and isolated. Most students who drop out of university do so in the first few months, when homesickness and loneliness can be felt most acutely.

Being warm and well fed is likely to have a positive effect on your studies. Perhaps for these reasons, most undergraduates in their first year plump for living in university halls, which offer a convenient, safe and reliable standard of accommodation, along with a supportive community environment. If meals are included, then this adds further peace of mind both for students and their parents: the difference in cost between full board and self-catering is £45–75 a week on average, according to the NUS survey – not unreasonable for two hot meals a day. But nowadays most are self-catering, with groups of students sharing a kitchen. The sheer number of students – especially first years – in halls also makes this form of accommodation an easy way of meeting people from a wide range of courses and making friends.

Wherever you chose to live, there are some general points you will need to consider, such as how safe the neighbourhood seems to be, and how long it might take you to travel to and from the university – especially during rush hour. A recent survey of travel time between term-time accommodation and the university found that most students in London can expect a commute of at least 30 minutes and often over an hour, while students living in Wales are usually much less than 30 minutes away from their university. Be sure to make use of any local or national Student Travel Card and any university or students' union transport system that may be provided to help you get back to your accommodation cheaply and safely.

In the university profiles (chapter 14), we provide details of what accommodation each university offers, covering the number of places, costs and policy towards first-year students.

Continuing to live at home

The first decision must be whether to move at all. The potential financial benefits of remaining at home are obvious, and there may also be advantages in terms of academic work if the alternative involves shopping, cooking and cleaning, as well as the other distractions of a student flat. The downside is that you may miss out on a lot of the student experience, especially the social scene and the opportunity to make new friends.

There is no evidence that students living at home do any worse academically. The quality of your home environment should influence your decision when weighing up whether or not to take this option. If it is stressful or not conducive to studying, then you are probably better off moving out, even if it means having to take a job to make ends meet. On the other hand, there is a lot to be said for making use of supportive and flexible home conditions where these exist. If you are studying at a post-1992 university, you are more likely to have fellow students who also live at home.

What universities offer

You might think that opting to live in university accommodation is the most straightforward choice, especially since first-year students are invariably given priority in the allocation of places in halls of residence. Certainly if you go for university residences you benefit from being able to make arrangements in advance and at a distance, rather than having to be in the right place at the right time, as is often the way when searching for private housing. However, you may still need to select from a range of options because some universities will have a variety of accommodation on offer. You will need to consider which best suits your pocket and your preferred lifestyle.

New university accommodation

At the top end of the market, partnerships between universities and private firms have begun

---

Money paid monthly for accommodation

Average monthly spend

	Catered halls	Self-catered halls/flats houses	Rented flats/ houses off campus	Own flats/ houses off campus	Home parents/family off campus
Overall					
£342.70	£542.80	£428.20	£375.30	£334.20	£96.10

Monthly level of payments made by students as a percentage of all students surveyed*

£0	£1–£200	£201–£300	£301–£400	£401–£500	£501–£1,000	Over £1,001
15%	6%	19%	26%	14%	9%	2%

* In addition to the figures shown, 8 per cent of respondents did not know their monthly accommodation costs.

Adapted from *Sodexo University Lifestyle Survey 2012*

to lead the way in recent years. Private organisations such as UPP, UNITE plc and Liberty Living have been paid by universities to build and manage some of the most luxurious student accommodation the UK sector has ever seen. Rooms in these complexes are nearly always en suite and include facilities such as your own phone line, satellite TV and internet access. Shared kitchens are also top quality and fitted out with all the latest equipment.

This kind of accommodation naturally comes at a higher price, but offers the advantages of flexibility both in living arrangements and through a range of payment options. Overall, according to the NUS survey, higher education institutions charged average rents of £118.49 for their own accommodation and £119.83 for rooms managed by private companies under contract, while private providers operating outside institutional links charged an average of £140.07. Private companies have invested more than £5 billion into new student flats in recent years, continuing to do so even while the recession brought the rest of the construction business to a halt.

Halls of residence

Many new or recently refurbished university-owned halls offer a standard of accommodation that is not far short of the privately built residences. One of the reasons for this is that rooms in these halls can be offered to conference delegates during vacations. Even though these halls are also at the pricier end of the spectrum, you will probably find that they are in great demand, and you may have to get your name down for one quickly to secure one of the fancier rooms. That said, you can often get a guarantee of some kind of university accommodation if you give a firm acceptance of an offered place by a certain date in the summer. This may not be the case if you have gained your place through Clearing – although rooms in private halls might still be on offer at this stage.

While a few halls are single-sex, most are mixed, and often house over 500 students. They are therefore great places for making friends and becoming part of the social scene. One possible downside is that they can also be noisy places where it can be difficult at times to get down to some work. The more successful students learn, before too many essay deadlines and exams start to loom, to get the balance right between all-night partying and escaping to the library for some undisturbed study time. Some libraries, especially new ones, are also now open 24 hours a day. If you feel in need of either personal or study support, this is often at hand either through a counselling service or from fellow students.

University self-catering accommodation

An alternative to the halls offered particularly by older universities, are smaller, self-catering properties fitted out with a shared kitchen and other living areas. Students looking for a more independent and flexible lifestyle often prefer this option. Remember that if you choose this kind of university housing, you will be responsible for feeding yourself, and you may also have heating and lighting bills to pay. University properties are often on campus or nearby, and so travel costs should not pose a problem.

Catering in university accommodation

Many universities have responded to a general increase in demand from students for a more independent lifestyle, by providing more flexible catering facilities. A range of eateries, from fast food outlets to more traditional refectories, can usually be found on campus or in student villages. Students in university accommodation may be offered pay-as-you-eat deals as an alternative to full-board packages.

What after the first year?

After your first year of living in university residences you may well wish, and will probably be expected, to move out to other accommodation. The main exceptions are the collegiate universities – particularly Oxford and Cambridge – which may allow you to stay on in college halls for another year or two, and particularly for your final year. Students from outside the EU are also sometimes guaranteed accommodation. At some universities, such as Loughborough, where there is a sufficiently large stock of residential accommodation, it is not uncommon for students to move back in to halls for their final year.

Practical details

Whether or not you have decided to start out in university accommodation, you will probably be expected to sign an agreement to cover rent. Contract lengths vary. They can be for around 40 weeks, which includes the Christmas and Easter holiday periods or for just the length of the three university terms. These term-time contracts are common when a university uses its rooms for conferences during vacations, and you will be required to leave your room empty during these weeks. It is therefore advisable to check whether the university has secure storage space for you to leave your belongings – otherwise you will have to make arrangements to take all your belongings home or to store them privately between terms. International students may be offered special arrangements, in which they can stay in halls during the short vacation periods. Organisations like **www.hostuk.org** can also arrange for international students to stay in a UK family home at holiday times such as the Christmas break.

Parental purchases

One option for affluent families is to buy a house or flat and take in student lodgers. This might not be the safe bet it once appeared, but it is still tempting for many parents. The *Sodexo University Lifestyle Survey* found a surprisingly large number of students living in houses owned by their own or fellow students' parents. Those who are considering this route tend to do so from the first year of study to maximise the return on the investment.

Being a lodger or staying in a hostel

A small number of students live as a lodger in a family home, an option most frequently taken up by international students. The usual arrangement is for a study bedroom and some meals to be provided, while other facilities such as a washing machine are shared. Students with particular religious affiliations or those from certain countries may wish to consider living in one of a number of hostels run by charities catering for certain groups. Most of these can be found in London.

Renting from the private sector

More than a third of students live in privately rented flats or houses, according to the Sodexo survey. Every university city or town is awash with such accommodation, available via agencies or direct from landlords. Indeed, there has been so much of it that so-called "student ghettoes", where local residents feel outnumbered, have become hot political issues. Into this traditional market in rented flats and houses have come the new private-sector complexes and residences, often created in partnership with universities, adding considerably to the private-sector options. Some are on university campuses. Others are in city centres and usually open to students of more than one university. Examples can be seen online; some sites are listed at the end of this chapter.

While there are always exceptions, a much more professional attitude and approach to managing rented accommodation has emerged among smaller providers, thanks to a combination of greater regulation and increasing competition. Nevertheless, it is wise to take certain precautions when seeking out private residences.

How to start looking for rented property

Contact your university's accommodation service and ask for their list of approved rented properties. Some have a Student Accommodation Accreditation Scheme, run in collaboration with the local council. To get onto an approved list under such schemes, landlords must show they are adhering to basic standards of safety and security, such as having an up-to-date gas and electric safety certificate. University accommodation officers should also be able to advise you on any hidden charges. For instance, you may be asked to pay a booking or reservation fee to secure a place in a particular property, and fees for references or drawing up a tenancy agreement are also sometimes charged. The practice of charging a "joining fee", however, has been outlawed. It would also be wise to speak to older students with first-hand experience of renting in the area. Certain companies in the area will often be notorious among second and third years and therefore you can seek to avoid them.

Making a choice

Once you have made an initial choice of the area you would like to live in and the size of property you are looking for, the next stage is to look at possible places. If you plan to share, it is important that you all have a look at the property. If you will be living by yourself, take a friend with you when you go to view a property, since he or she can help you assess what you see objectively, and avoid any irrational or rushed on-the-spot decisions. Don't let yourself be pushed into signing on the dotted line there and then. Take time to visit and consider a number of options. It is often helpful to spend some time in the area in which you may be living, to check out the local facilities, transport and the general environment at various times of the day and different days of the week.

If you are living in private rented accommodation, it is likely that at least some of your neighbours will not be students. Local people often welcome students, but resentment can build up, particularly in areas of towns and cities that are dominated by student housing. It is important to respect your neighbours' rights, and not to behave in an anti-social manner.

Preparing for sharing

The people you are planning to share a house with may have some habits that you find at least mildly irritating. How well you cope with some of the downsides of sharing will be partly down to the kind of person you are – where you are on the spectrum between laid back and highly strung – but it will help a lot if you are co-habiting with people whose outlook on day-to-day living is not too far out of line with your own. Some students sign for their second year houses as early as November and while it is good to be ahead of the rush, in such a short time at the university you may not have met your best friends yet. If you have not selected your own group of friends, universities and landlords can help by taking personal preferences and lifestyle into account when grouping tenants together. You can make this task easier if you give full details about yourself when filling in accommodation application forms.

Potential issues to consider when deciding whether to move into a shared house include whether any of the housemates smoke, own a loud musical instrument that they may decide to play at any time of the day or night, or have a habit of spending hours on the telephone. With most students owning a mobile phone, the latter should not be a problem unless someone decides to save on their mobile bills by using a landline in your shared house instead. If this is the case, then you should arrange for individual billing, provided by a number of phone companies. It will also be important to sort out broadband arrangements that will work for everyone in the house, and that you will be able to arrange access to the university system. It is also a good idea to agree from the outset a rota for everyone to share in the household cleaning chores. Otherwise it is almost certain that you will live in a state of unhygienic squalor or that one or two individuals will be left to clear up everyone else's mess.

The practical details about renting

It is a good idea to ask whether your house is covered by an accreditation scheme or code of standards. Such codes provide a clear outline of what constitutes good practice as well as the responsibilities of both landlords and tenants. Adhering to schemes like the National Code of Standards for Larger Student Developments compiled by Accreditation Network UK (**www. anuk.org.uk**) may well become a requirement for larger properties, including those managed by universities, now that the Housing Act is in force.

At the very least, make sure that if you are renting from a private landlord, you have his or her telephone number and home address. Some can be remarkably difficult to contact when repairs are needed or deposits returned.

Multiple occupation

If you are renting a private house it may be subject to the 2004 Housing Act in England and Wales (similar legislation applies in Scotland and Northern Ireland). Licenses are compulsory for all private Houses in Multiple Occupation (HMOs) with three or more stories that house five or more unrelated residents. The provisions of the Act also allow local authorities to designate whole areas in which HMOs of all sizes must be licensed. The good news is that these regulations can be applied in sections of university towns and cities where most students live. This means that a house must be licensed, well-managed and must meet various health and safety standards, and its owner subject to various financial regulations. The bad news is that this could lead to a reduction in the number and range of privately rented properties on the market, or an increase in rental prices. Oxford City Council was the first authority to require HMOs of all sizes within the city to be licensed by 2012.

Tenancy agreements

Whatever kind of accommodation you go for, you must be sure to have all the paperwork in order and be clear about what you are signing up to before you move in. If you are taking up residence in a shared house, flat or bedsit, the first document you will have to grapple with is a tenancy agreement or lease offering you an "assured shorthold tenancy". Since this is a binding legal document you should be prepared to go through every clause with a fine-tooth comb. Remember that it is much more difficult to make changes or overcome problems arising from unfair agreements once you are a tenant than before you become one.

You would be well advised to seek help, in the likely event of your not fully understanding some of the clauses. Your university accommodation office or students' union is a good place to start – they should know all the ins and outs, and have model tenancy agreements to refer to. A Citizens Advice Bureau or Law Advice Centre should also be able to offer you free advice. In particular, watch out for clauses that may make you jointly responsible for the actions of others with whom you are sharing the property. If you name a parent as a guarantor to cover any costs not covered by you, then they may also be liable for charges levied on all tenants for any damage that might not be your fault. A rent review clause could allow your landlord to increase the rent at will, whereas without such a clause, they are restricted to one rent rise a year. Make sure you keep a copy of all documents, and get a receipt (and keep it somewhere safe) for anything you have had to pay for that is the landlord's responsibility.

Contracts with private landlords tend to be longer than for university accommodation – they will frequently commit you to paying rent for 52 weeks of the year. There are probably more advantages than disadvantages to this kind of arrangement. It means you don't have to move out during vacation periods, which you might have to in university halls. You can store your belongings in your room when you go away (but don't leave anything really valuable behind if you can help it). You may be able to negotiate a rent discount for those periods when you are not staying in the property. The other advantage, particularly important for cash-strapped students, is that you have a base from which to find work and hold down a job during the vacations. Term dates are also not as dictatorial as they might be in halls; if you rent your own house then you can come back when you wish.

Deposits

On top of the agreed rent, you will need to provide a deposit or bond to cover any possible breakages or damage. This will probably set you back the equivalent of another month's rent. The deposit should be returned, less any deductions, at the end of the contract. However, be warned that disputes over the return of deposits are quite common, with the question of what constitutes reasonable wear and tear often the subject of disagreements between landlords and tenants. To protect students from unscrupulous landlords who withhold deposits without good reason, the 2004 Housing Act has introduced a National Tenancy Deposit Scheme under which deposits are held by an independent body rather than by the landlord. This is designed to ensure that deposits are fairly returned, and that any disputes are resolved swiftly and cheaply.

Inventories and other paperwork

You should get an inventory and schedule of condition of everything in the property. This

---

Security in rented accommodation

Students in private housing are twice as likely to be burgled as those in university halls. When looking at accommodation, use this NUS security checklist:

» Check that the front and back doors are fitted with five-lever mortise locks in addition to standard catch locks.
» Make sure the door to your room has a lock, and always lock up when you leave it, especially for long periods such as during vacations.
» Check the locks and catches on accessible windows, especially those at ground-floor level.
» Before you move in, try to talk to neighbours about how safe the area is and whether there have been many instances of burglary or car crime.
» Ask your landlord to ensure that all previous tenants and holders of keys no longer have copies.
» If you find a property that you like but have some security concerns, discuss these with the letting agency or landlord. They may be able to make the necessary changes to make the property more secure before you move in.

is another document that you should check very carefully – and make sure that everything listed is as described. Write on the document anything that is different. The NUS even suggests taking photographs of rooms and equipment when you first move in (putting the date on the pictures if you are using a digital camera), to provide you with additional proof should any dispute arise when your contract ends and you want to get your deposit back. If you are not offered an inventory, then make one of your own. You should have someone else witness and sign this, send it to your landlord, and keep your own copy. Keeping in contact with your landlord throughout the year and developing a good relationship with him or her will also do you no harm, and may be to your advantage in the long run.

You should ask your landlord for a recent gas safety certificate issued by a qualified CORGI engineer, a fire safety certificate covering the furnishings, and a record of current gas and electricity meter readings. Take your own readings of meters when you move in to make sure these match up with what you have been given, or make your own records if the landlord doesn't supply this information. This also applies to water meters if you are expected to pay water rates (although this isn't usually the case). If you are sharing a house only with other full-time students, then you will not have to pay Council Tax. However, you may be liable to pay a proportion of the Council Tax bill if you are sharing with anyone who is not a full-time student. You may need to get a Council Tax exemption certificate from your university as evidence that you do not need to pay Council Tax or should pay only a proportion, depending on the circumstances.

Safety and security

Once you have arrived and settled in, remember to take care of your own safety and the security of your possessions. You are particularly vulnerable as a fresher, when you are still getting used to your new-found independence. This may help explain why a fifth of students are burgled or robbed in the first six weeks of the academic year. Take care with valuable portable items such as mobile phones, iPods and laptops, all of which are tempting for criminals. Ensure you don't have them obviously on display when you are out and about and that you have insurance cover. If your mobile phone is stolen, call your network or 08701 123123 to immobilise it. Students' unions, universities and the police will provide plenty of practical guidance when you arrive. Following their advice will reduce the chance of you becoming a victim of crime, and so able to enjoy living in the new surroundings of your chosen university town.

Useful websites

For advice on a range of housing issues, visit: **www.nus.org.uk/en/student-life/housing-advice**
The Shelter website has separate sections covering different housing regulations in England, Wales, Scotland and Northern Ireland: **www.shelter.org.uk**

As examples of providers of private hall accommodation, visit:
www.unite-students.com or **www.libertyliving.co.uk**

There are a number of sites that will help you find accommodation and/or potential housemates. Among the best-known are:

www.accommodationforstudents.com	**www.let4students.com**
www.homesforstudents.co.uk	**www.studentbunk.com**
www.studentpad.co.uk	**http://student.spareroom.co.uk**

10 Sporting Opportunities

Sport now occupies an important place at the heart of university life. Both in elite sport and the everyday recreation and fitness activities that are the experience of most students, the opportunities are greater than ever before. Over the past decade in particular, there has been unprecedented expansion and upgrading of facilities all over the country. Such has been the scale of investment that some of the biggest multi-sports developments have been on university campuses, where facilities nationally are said to be worth an astonishing £20 billion. As a result, half of all universities were chosen as pre-Olympics training bases for Great Britain squads and 30 hosted other nations' teams in the run-up to the 2012 Games.

If the students and alumni of UK universities and colleges had been a team at the London Games, they would have finished fifth in the medals table. They claimed 20 of Team GB's 29 gold medals and more than 60 per cent of the overall medals haul, with more than 50 institutions contributing. The successes came in a wide range of sports – the medal-winning women's hockey team was composed entirely of students and graduates – and some of Great Britain's most celebrated stars, such as Jessica Ennis and Mo Farrah, acknowledged their debt to their alma mater.

Naturally, most students will never aspire to such heights, but may still welcome the chance to use top-grade facilities. Until recently, sport was a side issue at best for most students choosing universities. It still does not rate with the quality of course or the location of the university in the list of most applicants' priorities, but you only have to look at the investment in campus facilities to know that universities themselves think it is important.

Gone are the days when physical exercise was a minority pursuit on campus and regarded as not cool. Today it is said that at least 1.7 million students take part in regular physical activity, from gym sessions to competitive individual or team sports. Some specialist facilities may be reserved at times for elite (often international) performers, but all universities are conscious of the need for wider access. Surveys show that two-thirds of sessions at university sports facilities are taken by students, roughly a quarter by the local community and the rest by staff.

Sporting opportunities

Being a full-time student offers unrivalled opportunities to discover and play a vast range of sports. Many universities still encourage departments not to schedule lectures and seminars on Wednesday afternoons, to give students free time for sport. Even those who spend long hours in the laboratory have more time for leisure activities as a student than they will be able to spare later in life. There are student-run clubs for all the major sports and – particularly at the larger universities – a host of minor ones. Or you can content yourself with high-quality gyms, with staff on hand to devise personalised training regimes and run popular activities such as zumba and pilates. The cost varies widely between universities, and membership fees can represent a large amount to lay out at the start of the year, but most provide good value if you are going to be a regular user.

More and more students want to keep fit, even if they do not play competitive sport, and universities have joined a race of their own to provide the best facilities. Sport may still be a secondary consideration for most applicants, but particularly good (or particularly poor) facilities can sometimes tip the balance.

Sport for all

For most universities, it is in the area of "sport for all" that most attention has been focused. Beginners are welcomed and coaching provided in a range of sports, from ultimate Frisbee to tai-chi, that would be difficult to match outside the higher education system. Check on university websites to see whether your usual sport is available, but do not be surprised if you come across a new favourite when you have the opportunity to try out something different as a student. Many universities have programmes designed to encourage students to take up a new sport, with expert coaching provided.

All universities are conscious of the need to provide for a spread of ability. Sports scholarships for elite performers are now commonplace, but there will be plenty of opportunities, too, for beginners. University teams demand a hefty commitment in terms of training and practice sessions – often several times a week – and in many sports standards are high. University teams often compete in local and national leagues.

For those who do not aspire to such heights, or whose interests are primarily social, there are thriving internal, or intramural, leagues. These provide opportunities for groups from halls of residence or faculties, or even a group of friends, to form a team and participate on a regular basis. A recent survey conducted by British Universities and Colleges Sport (BUCS) found 41,000 participants in the intramural programmes of 41 institutions. The largest programme was at the University of Brighton, where more than 6,000 students were playing sports ranging from football, rugby and badminton to softball, orienteering and fencing. Nor is university sport a male preserve – student teams were among the pioneers in mixed sport and are still strong in areas such as women's cricket, football and rugby. More than a third of the teams entered in national leagues in 2010–11 – nearly 4,300 teams – were female.

First-year sport

Halls of residence and university-owned flats will often provide an array of sports teams. At some universities, these are part of the intramural network of leagues, while others have separate arrangements for first years. In such cases, a Sports Captain, elected the year previously as part of the Junior Common Room, takes responsibility for organising trials and picking the teams, as well as arranging fixtures for the year. Hall sport is a great way of meeting like-minded people from your accommodation and over the course of the years, friendly rivalries often develop with other halls or flats. Generally there will be teams for football (both five- and 11-a-side), hockey, netball, cricket, tennis, squash, badminton and even golf. If your lodgings are smaller then don't worry, they are often twinned with similar flats to enable as many first-year students as possible to get involved in freshers' sport.

Other opportunities

You may even end up wanting to coach, umpire or referee – and this is another area in which higher education has much to offer. Many university clubs and sports unions provide subsidised courses for students to gain qualifications that may be of use to the individual in later life, as well as benefiting university teams in the short term. Or you might want to try your hand at some sports administration, with an eye to your career. In most universities there is a sports (or athletic) union, with autonomy from the main students' union, which organises matches and looks after the wider interests of those who play. There are plenty of opportunities for those seeking an apprenticeship in the art of running a club, or larger organisation. Southampton Solent University, for example, deploy students on volunteer coaching placements in more than 70 local schools. These placements increase a university's community engagement as well as enhancing student employability with minimal investment.

Universities that excel

A few universities are known particularly for sport – Exeter and Loughborough men's teams play national Premier League hockey, for example, while Bath and Northumbria both have teams in the Netball Super League. The University of London women's volleyball team has won the English Volleyball Championships, and "Team Bath" have tasted success in the FA Cup as a university team. Several of this elite group had a head start as former physical education colleges. Loughborough is probably the best-known of them, but Leeds Metropolitan and Brunel are others with a similar pedigree. Other universities with different traditions, such as Bath and the University of East Anglia, also have a variety of outstanding facilities, while the likes of Stirling and Cardiff Metropolitan have the same in a narrower range of sports. As in so much else, Oxford and Cambridge are in a category of their own. The Boat Race and the Varsity Match (in rugby union) are the only UK university sporting events with a big popular following – although there are varsity matches in several university cities that have become big occasions for students – and there is a good standard of competition in other sports. But you should not assume that success in school sport will be a passport to an Oxbridge place, for the days of special consideration for sporty undergraduates appear to be over.

Representative sport

Competitive standards have been rising in university sport, as have the numbers taking part in it. More than 5,000 students participated in the last BUCS Gatorade Nationals in Sheffield. The British Universities and Colleges Sport (BUCS: **www.bucs.org.uk**) runs competitions in almost 50 sports, and ranks participating institutions based on the points earned in the competitive programme. Over 4,800 teams compete in BUCS leagues, making the organisation the largest provider of league sport across Europe. More than a third of those teams are female and many others mixed. There is also international competition in a number of sports, and the World Student Games have become one of the biggest occasions in the international sporting calendar.

BUCS is the national organisation for higher education sport in the UK, providing a comprehensive, multi-sport competition structure and managing the development of services and facilities for participative, grass-roots sport and healthy campuses, through to high-performance elite athletes. Its mission is to raise the profile of student sport and drive the university sport agenda by influencing government and key stakeholders in the sector.

University sports facilities

Even the smallest university should provide reasonable indoor and outdoor sports facilities – a sports hall, modern gym equipment and outdoor pitches (usually including an all-weather surface and floodlights). Many will also have a swimming pool and extras such as climbing walls, but some smaller universities make arrangements for students to use local sports centres and clubs when it is not feasible to provide for minority sports. The same goes for the really expensive sports, like golf, which is usually the subject of an arrangement with one or more local clubs that give students a discount. Specialist facilities, like boat houses and climbing huts, obviously depend on location, but the most landlocked university is likely to have a sailing club that organises regular activities away from campus, and a skiing club that runs at least annual trips to the mountains.

Many of the larger universities have spent millions of pounds improving their sports facilities, sometimes in partnership with local authorities or national sporting bodies. University campuses are ideal locations for national coaching centres, and many have been established in recent years. Although elite coaching generally takes place in closed sessions, students can occasionally find themselves rubbing shoulders with star players.

It is estimated that close to £500 million has been spent on new or upgraded sports facilities at UK universities over the past decade, and planned investment for the next three years will add at least £170 million to this figure. Universities now boast a significant proportion of the UK's 50-metre pools, for example, and more are planned to follow the recent opening at the University of Surrey. Other innovative schemes include Leeds Metropolitan's development of the Headingley cricket and rugby league grounds, providing teaching space for students during the week and improved facilities for players and spectators on match days.

Both the scale of investment and the emphasis on sport increased as the 2012 Olympics approached. The BUCS Visa Outdoor Athletics Championships was chosen as the test event for the Olympic Stadium and the Olympic Torch relay visited many university campuses before the Games took place. The legacy for students – not just in London – should be considerable, as it was following the Commonwealth Games in Manchester and the World Student Games in Sheffield.

Beyond scrutinising the prospectus for the extent of university facilities, there are two important questions to ask: how much do they cost and where are they? Neither is easy to track down on the average university website.

How much?

University prospectuses tend to major on the quality of the sports facilities without being as forthcoming about the prices. Students who are used to free (if inferior) facilities at school often get a nasty surprise when they find that they are expected to pay to join the Athletic Union and then pay again to use the gym or play football. Because most university sport is subsidised, the charges are reasonable compared to commercial facilities, but the best deal may require a considerable outlay at the start. Some campus gyms and swimming pools now charge more than £300 a year, for example, which is still considerably cheaper than paying per visit if you intend to use the facilities regularly (and provides an incentive to carry on doing so). Some universities are offering sports facility membership as part of the £9,000 fee, but most offer a variety of peak and off-peak membership packages – some for the entire length of your course.

Outdoor sports are usually charged by the hour, although clubs will also charge a membership fee. You may be required to pay up to £25 for membership of the Athletic Union (although not all universities require this). Fees for intramural sport are seldom substantial; teams will usually pay a fee for the season, while courts for racket sports tend to be marginally cheaper per session than in other clubs.

How far away?

The other common complaint by students is that the playing fields are too far from the campus – understandable in the case of city-centre universities, but still aggravating if you have to arrange your own transport. This is where campus universities have a clear advantage. For the rest, there has to be some trade-off between the quality of outdoor facilities and the distance you have to travel to use them. But universities are beginning to realise that long journeys depress usage of important (and expensive) facilities, and some have tried to find suitable land closer to lectures and halls of residence. Indoor sports centres should all be within easy reach.

Sport as a degree subject

Sports science and other courses associated with sport had seen consistent increases in applications until the imposition of higher fees. The subject is in the top dozen in terms of popularity, with more than 58,000 applications at degree level in 2013. The demand for places had recovered from a decline in 2012. A separate ranking for the subject is on page 186. If you are hoping to be rewarded with an academic qualification for three years on the sports field, you will be disappointed because there is serious science involved. However, sport is a growing employment field and one that demands qualifications like any other.

Other degrees in the sports area are more closely focused on management, with careers in the leisure industry in mind – golf course management, for example, has proved popular with students despite being a target of those who see anything beyond the traditional academic portfolio as "dumbing down". The question is not whether the courses are up to standard, but whether a less specialised one will offer more career flexibility if a decline in popularity for the particular sport limits future opportunities.

Sports scholarships

The number and range of sports scholarships have expanded just as rapidly as courses in the subject, but the two are usually not connected. Sports scholarships are for elite performers, regardless of what they are studying – indeed, they exist at universities with barely any degrees in the field. Imported from the USA, scholarships now exist in an array of sports. At Birmingham University, for example, there are specialist golf awards (as there are at ten other universities) and a scholarship for triathletes, as well as others open to any sport.

The value of scholarships varies considerably – sometimes according to individual prowess. The Royal and Ancient scholarships for golfers, for example, range from £500 for promising handicap golfers to £10,000 for full internationals. All of them demand that you meet the normal entrance requirements for your course and maintain the necessary academic standards, as well as progressing in your sport. In practice, most departments will be flexible about attendance and deadlines, as long as you make your requests well in advance.

Many sports scholarships offer benefits in kind, in the form of coaching, equipment or access to facilities. The Government-funded Talented Athlete Scholarship Scheme (TASS), which is restricted to students at English universities who have achieved national recognition at under-18 level and are eligible to represent England, is one such example. Winning Students is a similar scheme in Scotland. Some 200 current or former TASS athletes took part in the London Olympics, 44 of them winning a medal. The scholarships are worth £3,500 a year and can be put towards costs such as competition and training costs, equipment or mentoring. Further details are available at **www.tass.gov.uk.**

Part-time work

University sports centres are an excellent source of term-time (and out-of-term) employment. You may also be trained in first aid, fire safety, customer care and risk assessment – all useful skills for future employment. The experience will help you secure employment in commercial or local authority facilities – and even for jobs such as stewarding at football grounds and music venues. Most universities also have a sabbatical post in the Athletic Union or similar body, a paid position with responsibility for organising university sport and representing the sporting community within the university.

University sporting facilities

Different students look for different things from their sport while at university and the table overleaf gives an initial guide to what's on offer at different institutions and, where appropriate, their various campuses.

The table is based on a detailed survey of university sport undertaken by British University and Colleges Sport (BUCS) in early 2012 and updated in 2013. The information in the table relates only to the facilities and services that universities provide centrally for all their students and does not include any facilities there may be in halls of residence or colleges.

The table contains a mix of factual information and "1–5" rankings, with five dots the best and one dot the worst. If there is no dot there is no facility. All the ratings take account of the number of students at each university, or on each campus, so they provide comparative information. The information in the table includes:

» The university's overall BUCS ranking and number of teams in BUCS competitions. Teams get points each year for their success in inter-university competitions and BUCS uses them to compile an annual league table. Some multi-site universities (eg, Manchester Metropolitan) have a BUCS ranking for each of their campuses, others (eg, Cumbria) have only one.

» The type of pool, if any (25m, 50m or other) at each university and the extent of its availability to students. The availability rating takes account of the extent to which the pool may be reserved for outside users, for example by a local swimming club or squad.

» Ratings for the range and availability of indoor dry sports facilities, such as sports halls, dance studios, squash courts and fitness gyms, derived from the total at-one-time capacity of the facilities and number of students. The more dots in the "Range" column, the more extensive the facilities in relation to the student population. A significant difference in the rating for range and availability indicates that while facilities exist, students may have restricted access to them.

» The total number of fitness training machines, plus an asterisk if the university's fitness facilities are accredited under the Inclusive Fitness Initiative (IFI) by the English Federation of Disability Sport. However, note that the IFI scheme does not operate in

Northern Ireland, Scotland or Wales.
» Ratings for the range and availability of outdoor grass and artificial pitches and tennis or netball courts.
» The number of sports with intramural competitions.
» The availability of taught or instructor-led classes.
» The number of sports scholarships or bursaries available; they may be any mix of funding and free access to facilities or elite athlete support services.
» The number of different forms of support for achieving sporting excellence, such as coaching, sports psychology, nutritional advice, access to sports medicine or specialist strength and conditioning training.

University sports websites are given in the university profiles (chapter 14).

University sporting facilities

Name	BUCS Ranking 2012–13	Teams in BUCS Leagues	Swimming pool	Availability of pools	Range of indoor dry sports facilities	Availability of indoor dry sports facilities
Aberdeen	33	53	Other	•	•••••	••••
Abertay	82	15			••	•••
Aberystwyth	65	21	Other	••	••••	•••••
Anglia Ruskin	87	1			•••	•••
Arts University, Bournemouth	=148	No information available				
Aston	95	25	Other	•	••••	•••••
Bangor	68	35			•••	••••
Bath	4	71	50m	•••••	•••	••••
Bath Spa	118	No information available				
Bedfordshire	70	6			•••••	•••••
Birmingham	3	65	25m	•••	••	••
Birmingham City	120	No information available				
University College Birmingham	116	No information available				
Bishop Grosseteste	136	No information available				
Bolton	129	No information available				
Bournemouth	34	32			•	••
Bradford	96	29	25m	•	••••	••••
Brighton (Brighton)	37	40			•••	••
Brighton (Eastbourne)	37	40	25m	••	••••••	••••••
Bristol	13	48			••	•
Brunel West London	27	No information available				
Buckingham	141	0			•••••	•••••
Buckinghamshire New	86	No information available				
Cambridge	16	37			•••••	••••
Canterbury Christ Church	79	No information available				
Cardiff	19	57			•••••	•••••
Cardiff Metropolitan	12	37			•	•
Central Lancashire	44	31			••	•••
Chester (Chester)	88	No information available				
Chester (Warrington)	140	No information available				
Chichester	51	29			•••••	•••••
City	94	13			•	•
Coventry	54	31			••	•••
Creative Arts	=148	No information available				
Cumbria (Ambleside)	115	0			••••	•••••
Cumbria (Carlisle)	115	3			•	•
Cumbria (Lancaster)	115	13			•	••
Cumbria (Penrith)	115	2			•••••	•••••
Cumbria (Preston)	115	0			•	•••
De Montfort	93	30			•	•
Derby	66	27			••	••
Dundee	40	39	25m	•••	•••	••••
Durham	2	61			••••	•••
East Anglia	56	26	50m			
East London	63	0			•	•
Edge Hill	84	30			•••	•••

Fitness machines	Number of winter pitches	Availability of winter pitches	Outdoor courts	Availability of outdoor courts	Sports with intramural competitions	Availability of taught classes	Sports scholarships/ bursaries	Forms of elite athlete support
200	•••••	•••••	•	•	1	•••••	29	6
35					1	•	0	10
76	••••	••••	•••••	•••••	1	•••••	30	5
20					3	••••	25	0
103	••••	•••	•	••	0	••	6	2
93	•••	•••	••	••	6	•••	10	0
101*	••••	•••	••••	•••	2	•••	39	10
19	•••	•••	•••	•••	6	•	67	2
90*	••••	••••	•	•	6	•••••	67	10
55					10	•••	55	9
100*	••	•	•••	•••	17	•••	8	0
88	•••	•••	••••	••••	8	•	30	10
47	••••	••••	•••••	•••••	7	••••	30	10
100	••••	•••	••••	•	9	••	26	10
16	••	••			1	•••••	0	0
470					19	••	15	5
90	••	•••	•	••	3	••	60	9
55	•	•	•	•	2	•	28	6
108	••	•	••••	••••	1	••••	12	8
28	•••••	•••••	•••	•••	2	•	16	3
0					5	••	0	0
86	••	••			10	••	65	10
0	•	•			0	••	0	0
21					0	••	10	7
17	•••	•••			0	•	10	7
15	•••••	•••••			5		10	7
0	••	••	••••	•	0	•	0	8
90					6	•	0	0
37	•	•	••	••	0		6	10
125	••	••	•••	•••	8	•••••	12	10
242	•••••	•••••	••••	••••	20	•••	45	10
80							0	0
10					6	•	22	10
56	••••	•••			0	••••	18	10

Name	BUCS Ranking 2012–13	Teams in BUCS Leagues	Swimming pool	Availability of pools	Range of indoor dry sports facilities	Availability of indoor dry sports facilities
Edinburgh	6	71	25m	•••	•••••	••••
Edinburgh Napier	78	13			••	•••
Essex	42	64			••••	••••
Exeter	5	58	25m	•••	•••••	•••••
Falmouth	117	0			•••	••••
Glasgow	28	36	25m	•••••	••	•
Glasgow Caledonian	83	18			•	•
Gloucestershire	35	46			•••••	•••••
Glyndŵr	142	No information available				
Goldsmiths	130	8			•••••	•
Greenwich	119	13			•	••
Harper Adams	103	18			•••••	•••••
Heriot-Watt	55	28			•••	•••
Hertfordshire	46	33	25m	••••	•••	•••
Highlands and Islands	113	No information available				
Huddersfield	98	16			•	•
Hull	62	48			•	••
Imperial College	18	48	25m	•••••	•••••	•••••
Keele	=76	25			••••	•••••
Kent	30	41			•	•
King's College London	53	57			••	••
Kingston	72	26			•	•
Lancaster	45	41	25m	••••	••••	••••
Leeds	14	70	25m	••••	•••	••
Leeds Metropolitan	8	66	Other	••	•••	•••
Leeds Trinity	138	15			••••	•••••
Leicester	64	34			•••••	••
Lincoln	57	34			••	••
Liverpool	36	81	25m	••••	••	•••
Liverpool Hope	108	No information available				
Liverpool John Moores	58	No information available				
London Metropolitan	121	No information available				
LSE	71	No information available				
London South Bank	101	No information available				
Loughborough	1	66	50m	•••••	•••••	••••
Manchester	9	77	50 m	•••	••	••
Manchester Metropolitan (MMU)	60	29			••••	•••
MMU (Cheshire)	89	0			••••	••••
Middlesex	69	19			••	••
Newcastle	10	69			••	••••
Newman	=148	No information available				
Northampton	81	No information available				
Northumbria	15	68	25m	•	•••••	•••
Nottingham	7	72	25m	•••••	•••	••••
Nottingham Trent	17	44			•••	••
Oxford	11	No information available				
Oxford Brookes	52	35	25m	••	••••	••
Plymouth	32	23			•	•
Portsmouth	29	51			••	•••

Fitness machines	Number of winter pitches	Availability of winter pitches	Outdoor courts	Availability of outdoor courts	Sports with intramural competitions	Availability of taught classes	Sports scholarships/ bursaries	Forms of elite athlete support
266	••	••	•	••	11	••••	278	10
57					0	•	4	1
88	•••	••••	•••	•••	20	•••	7	10
125	•••••	•••••	•••••	•••••	16	•••••	60	10
40			•••	•••	2	••••	6	3
145	•••	•••	••••	••••	4	•••••	38	4
110					0	•••••	18	5
40*	•••••	•••••	•••••	•••••	4	•••••	18	10
113	•	•	••	••	3	••••	0	0
38*	•	•	•••	•••	0		0	3
22	•••••	•••••	•••••	•••••	0	••••	1	1
51	••••	••••	•••	•••	5	•••••	41	6
102*	•••••	•••••	•••	•••	2	•••	20	10
26					3	••	0	0
53*	•••	••	•••	•••	2	•	0	10
242	•••••	•••••	••	•••	7	••••	44	10
57	•••	•••	•	•	1	••••	0	2
110					9		51	9
32	••	•••	••	••	0	•	0	1
40	•	•	••	•	3	•	8	10
90	•••	••••	••	•••	16	•••••	0	0
221*	•	••	••	••	17	•••	35	10
169	•••	••••	•••	••••	4	•	52	10
16	•••••	•••••	•••	•••	8	••••	0	3
96	••	••	••••	••••	13	•••	5	4
44*	••••	••••	••	••	5	••	15	7
92	•••	••••	••	••	7	••••	40	10
233	•••••	•••••	•••••	•••••	45	••••	135	10
105	•	•	•	••	12	•••	40	8
178*			•	•	0		0	10
50	•••••	•••••	•••••	•••••	3		0	10
78			•	•	8	••	43	10
108	••	•••	••	••	7	••	32	9
240	•••	•••			0		100	10
184	•••	••••	•••••	•••••	8	•••	35	10
140	••••	••••	••	••	4	•••	50	10
107	•••	•••	•••••	•••••	5	••••	25	8
43					10	••	20	6
96	•	•	••	••	13	•••••	15	6

Name	BUCS Ranking 2012–13	Teams in BUCS Leagues	Swimming pool	Availability of pools	Range of indoor dry sports facilities	Availability of indoor dry sports facilities
Queen Margaret	109	7			•••••	•••••
Queen Mary	73	34			•••	••
Queen's, Belfast	114	No information available				
Reading	39	51			••••	••••
Robert Gordon	75	22	25m		•••••	•••
Roehampton	102	23			•••	•••••
Royal Holloway	61	46			•••	•••
St Andrews	26	51			•••	•••
St Mark and St John (Marjon)	=76	19	25m	••	•••••	•••••
Salford	112	22	25m	••	•	•
SOAS	134	No information available				
Sheffield	20	56	25m	••••	••	•
Sheffield Hallam	24	46			•	•
South Wales (Newport)	110	11			•••	••••
South Wales (Pontiprydd)	41	31			••••	••••
Southampton	23	57	25m			
Southampton Solent	74	17			•••••	•••••
Staffordshire	85	38			•••••	•••
Stirling	21	41	50m	•••••	••••	•••••
Strathclyde	49	0	Other	•	••	•
Sunderland	92	20			••	••
Surrey	48	40	50m	•••••	•••••	•••••
Sussex	47	30			•••	••
Swansea	25	No information available				
Swansea Metropolitan	132	No information available				
Teesside	90	26			••	••
Trinity St David	127	No information available				
Ulster	137	0			•	•
University College London	38	66			•	•
University of the Arts London	128	No information available				
UWE, Bristol	31	39			••	•
UWE, Hartpury	67	No information available				
Warwick	22	3	25 m	••••	••••	•••
West London	146	No information available				
West of Scotland	126	No information available				
Westminster	91	No information available				
Winchester	105	No information available				
Wolverhampton	106	18			•	•
Wolverhampton (Walsall)	106	18	25 m	•	•••••	•••••
Worcester	59	38			••••	••••
York	43	55	25 m	•••	•••	•••
York St John	100	26			•	••

Fitness machines	Number of winter pitches	Availability of winter pitches	Outdoor courts	Availability of outdoor courts	Sports with intramural competitions	Availability of taught classes	Sports scholarships/ bursaries	Forms of elite athlete support
50					0	•••••	0	0
70	•		•		4	•••	0	2
103	•••	•••	••••	••••	3	•••••	40	7
98*					0	••••	20	9
37*	•	•	••••	••••	0		23	10
48	••	••	•••••	•••••	0		28	4
45	•••••	•••••	•••••	•••••	14	••••	15	8
45	•••••	•••••	•••••	•••••	3	•••••	5	4
46	•	•			0	•	0	6
140	••	••			0		27	5
98	•	•	•	•	5	•••	36	10
35	•	•	•••	••••	3	••••	15	10
134	••••	••••			7	•••	24	9
140					11			
175	••••	••	•	•	20	•••	28	10
68	•••••	•••••	•••••	•••••	2	••	0	10
86	••••	••••	••••	••••	3	•••••	91	8
97	•	••			3	•••	44	5
60					0		10	10
110	•••••	•••••	•••••	••••	0		14	10
103	•••	••	•••	•••	5	•••	27	4
50*	••	••			3	••••	12	10
45	••	••			2	•	0	9
75*	•	•	•	•	3	••	26	7
100*	•	•			5	••	19	10
98*	••••	••••	••	•	7	••••	No	9
17					7	••	0	10
38	••••	••••	••••	••••	7	••••	30	10
60	•••••	••••			1	••	27	10
71*	•••	••	•••••	•••••	14	•	13	4
18	••	•••			0		1	9

11 What Parents Should Do

Even before tuition fees rocketed towards £9,000, parents had become more involved in their children's higher education – and especially in their choice of university. Open days are now organised with parents, as well as prospective students, in mind. Often it is the parents (usually mothers) who ask the most direct and practical questions, sometimes to the embarrassment of their children. But in general, today's sixth-formers and college students seem happy to have their parents' help and advice – even if they do not take it in the end. Research by the Knowledge Partnership consultancy found that more than half of the parents of first-year undergraduates felt they had exerted some influence on their children's choices of university and course, although only about 7 per cent characterised this as "a lot".

There is a certain irony in the fact that higher fees have been the catalyst for increased parental involvement since the new system places the responsibility for payment squarely on the student in later life. Parents will not even know when loan repayments begin since the trigger will be a graduate's salary reaching £21,000. In reality, however, it is not tuition but living costs that most parents are helping to meet. A survey conducted by *The Daily Telegraph* in 2011 suggested that up to half of the students at some leading universities did not take out maintenance loans (as opposed to those for tuition) at all. It is fair to assume that they were being supported by their families and that many other students were at least partly reliant on this source of income.

Spiralling student debt has left parents feeling more obliged than ever to help their children through university. Their involvement often continues beyond the decision-making process to the pursuance of value for money from the student experience. This chapter looks at where to draw the line between constructive involvement and unwelcome interference.

Nearly all students are adults, and university offers an environment where they can begin to make their own decisions and develop as individuals. A good starting point is to offer advice only when it is sought, and to leave direct contact with university administrators and academics to the student. Of course, throughout the *Guide*, all references to parents apply equally to guardians and step-parents.

Student finance and parental involvement

No matter how independent students are meant to be, most parents will still want to help out when they can. The new student finance system is designed to enable undergraduates to pay their own way through a degree course – albeit building up considerable debts. Even those who do take out maintenance loans will not find them sufficient to make ends meet, however moderate their standard of living. What is more, part of the maintenance loan is income-assessed and families may be expected to contribute towards living expenses, especially in Scotland, where loans are less generous.

Hundreds of thousands of students – particularly mature students – pay their own way through university. Many undergraduates of all ages supplement their income with term-time and vacation jobs. But every survey shows that families play an important (and growing) role where students move straight from school to higher education. The Knowledge Partnership research suggested that at least half of parents were meeting part or all of the costs of accommodation, food, clothing and books.

"Helicopter parents"

Universities have found that anxious mothers and fathers are more inclined than ever to question what their children are getting for their increasingly substantial fees. There have been stories of parents challenging not just the amount and quality of tuition, but even the marking of essays and exams. The phenomenon, first reported in the USA, has given rise to the phrase "helicopter parents" – so called because they hover over their children's education when they should be letting go. No one wants to think of themselves in that category, but it is not surprising – or reprehensible – that parents are taking more of an interest. Many more of today's parents have been to university themselves, so have the knowledge and confidence to offer advice, both in choosing where and what to study, and in the decisions facing students at university. One of the reasons that some then overstep the mark is that they are shocked that the amount of teaching and size of seminar groups are not what they recall from their own "free" higher education. The new fees are meant to herald improvements in the student experience, including more contact hours, but it remains to be seen if these materialise. Few universities now have more money to spend on teaching, and it may be that fewer and larger seminars are here to stay in the arts and social sciences, where almost all state support has been withdrawn.

An associated reason for greater parental involvement is that family relationships have changed. Many teenage applicants are glad to accept a lift to an open day to get a second opinion on a university and their prospective course. They are also more likely than previous generations of students to come home at the weekend – or to live there in the first place – and to air any grievances.

Laying the ground

The first thing any parent can do to smooth the path to university is to be encouraging about the value of higher education. Ideally, this should have started long before the application process, but it is especially important at this point. Now that student debt has become a frequent media topic and the economic downturn has hit graduate employment prospects, it is only natural for sixth-formers and others to have second thoughts about higher education. The lure of a regular wage packet will be tempting, should one be available, and there are plenty of young people who are not suited to full-time higher education. More big companies are choosing to employ promising 18-year-olds, rather than rely entirely on graduate recruitment, and there has been a rapid expansion of apprenticeships. Even after the years of enormous university expansion, most people still do not go to university. Nevertheless, those who are capable of going generally do not regret the decision. Many people look back on their student days as the best period of their life, as well as the one that shaped their personality and their career. Time as a student should still pay off for the individual in terms of lifetime earnings, as well as personal development. A little reassurance at this stage may make all the difference.

Making the choice

Any parent wants to help a son or daughter through the difficult business of choosing where and what to study. How big a role you play will depend on a number of factors, not the least of which is the extent to which your advice is wanted. In the end, it is the student's decision, and you can do no more than offer relevant information.

One important factor is the quality of advice available at school or college. If this is good, parental involvement should be marginal. But often that is not the case, and you may have to call on other resources, including your own research.

A second factor is your own level of expertise: you may have opinions about particular universities or subjects, but are they up-to-date and based on evidence? Try not to give advice that is coloured by memories of your own student days. That was probably a quarter of a century ago, and higher education has changed out of all recognition in the intervening years. Avoid second-hand opinions gleaned through the media or dinner party gossip. You may think that some subjects are a sure-fire route to lucrative employment, while others are shunned by employers, but are you right? And do you really know the strengths and weaknesses of more than 100 universities? The tables in chapters 2 and 4 offer a reality check, but even they cannot take account of the differences within institutions. The subject tables in chapter 5 show that the best graduate employment rates are often not at the obvious universities.

Above all, do not try to rewind your own career decisions through your children. The fact that you enjoyed – or hated – a subject or a university does not mean that they will. You may have always regretted missing out on the chance to go to Oxbridge or to become a brain surgeon, but they have their own lives to lead. Students who switch courses or drop out frequently complain that they were pressured into their original choice by their parents.

Check that choices are being made for sensible reasons, not on the basis of questionable gossip or trivial criteria. But beyond that, you should stay in the background unless there is a very good reason to play a more substantive role. Make a point of looking for important aspects of university life that the applicant might miss. Security, for example, usually does not feature near the top of a teenager's list of priorities; likewise other practical issues, such as the proximity of student accommodation to lectures, the library and the students' union.

Many universities now publish guides specifically for parents and put on programmes for them at Open Days. The latter may be a way of separating prospective applicants from their more demanding "minders", but the programmes themselves can be interesting and informative. Do not worry that you will be an embarrassment by attending Open Days – thousands of parents do so, and you may add a critical edge to the proceedings. Like prospectuses, Open Days are part of the sales process, and it is easy for a sixth-former to be carried away by the excitement surrounding a lively university. You are much more likely to spot the defects – even if they are ignored in the final decision.

Finding a place

Once the choices have been made, get to know the UCAS system and quietly ensure that deadlines are being met. The school should be doing this, but there is no harm in providing a little back-up, especially on parts of the process that take time and thought, such as writing the personal statement. There is little a parent can do as the offers and/or rejections come rolling in, other than to be supportive. If the worst happens and there are five rejections, you may have to start the advice process all over again for a new round of applications through UCAS Extra. If so, a cool head is even more necessary, but the same principles apply.

Results day

Then, before you know it, results day is upon you. Make sure you are at home, rather than in some isolated holiday retreat. Your son or daughter needs to have access to instant advice at school or college, and to be able to contact universities straight away if Clearing or Adjustment is required. And your moral support will be much more effective face to face, rather than down a telephone line. Whatever happens, try not to transmit the anxiety that you will inevitably be feeling to your son or daughter, especially if the results are not what was wanted. It is easy to make rash decisions about re-sitting exams or rejecting an insurance offer in the heat of the moment. Try to slow the process down and encourage clear and realistic thinking. Make sure you know in advance what might be required, such as where to access Clearing lists, and if Clearing or Adjustment is being used, you will need to be on hand to offer advice and help with visits to possible universities. Clearing or Adjustment is all but over in a week, so the agony should be short-lived.

Before they go

Little more than a month after the tension of results day, everything should be ready for the start of term. Unless your son or daughter is one of the growing band choosing to stay at home to study, there will be forms to fill in to secure university accommodation, as well as student loans to sort out and registration to complete. You can perform useful services, like supplying recipe books if the first year is to be spent in self-catering accommodation, but now is the time for independence to become reality. Make sure that important details like insurance are not forgotten, but otherwise stand clear.

Then it is just a matter of agreeing a budget, assuming you are in a position to make a financial contribution. How large that contribution is will depend on family circumstances and your attitude to independent living. Some parents want to ensure that their children leave university debt-free; others could never afford to do that, while yet others believe that paying your own way is part of the learning experience. The important thing is that students and parents know where they stand.

After they've left

Any new student is going to be nervous if he or she is leaving home for the first time and having to settle into a strange environment. But in most cases it is not going to last long because everyone is in the same boat and freshers' weeks hardly leave time for homesickness. In any case, they will not want to let their apprehension show. The people who are most likely to be emotional are the parents – especially if they are left with an empty nest for the first time. It can take a while to get used to an orderly, quiet house after all those years of mayhem.

Resist any temptation to decorate their bedroom and turn it into an office – it is more common than you might think, and psychologists say it can do lasting damage to family relationships. Keep in touch by phone, text or email, but try not to pry. You're not going to be told everything anyway – which is probably just as well. They will be back soon enough and, just as you were getting used to having the place to yourself, a weekend visit or the Christmas vacation will remind you of how things used to be. If things are not going smoothly at university, this may be the time for more reassurance – more students drop out at Christmas of their first year than at any other time.

Lastly, do not become a helicopter parent. Your son or daughter may well seek your advice if they are dissatisfied with the course, their accommodation or some other aspect of university life. By all means, give advice, but leave them to sort the problem out. Universities will cite the Data Protection Act, in any case, to say they can only deal with students, not parents. What they really mean is that students are adults and should look after themselves.

Useful websites

Many universities have sections on their websites for parents of prospective students. UCAS has a Parents section and a regular newsletter on its website: **www.ucas.com/how-it-all-works/parents-and-guardians**

To find out more about open days, visit: **www.opendays.com**

12 Coming to the UK to Study

All around the world, more and more young people are choosing to study outside their own country – 3.7 million did so in 2009. Sometimes this is because their home universities are poorly regarded, or just full. In other cases it is to master a different language, experience another culture or take the first step on an international career ladder.

The UK is one of the prime destinations of choice for those seeking to broaden their horizons. Only the USA, with its vast higher education system, attracts more international students. Global surveys have shown that UK universities are seen as offering high quality in a relatively safe environment. And, while their Achilles heel in such research is the perceived cost, there are compensations in the recent state of the pound and in the reduced living expenses offered by courses that are relatively short by international standards.

UK universities have been growing in popularity among international students for many years, although their "market share" has dropped as countries such as Australia and Germany have competed aggressively. Numbers have risen further as the value of the pound has made courses more affordable, while higher visa charges and changes in immigration regulations seem not to have dimmed global enthusiasm for UK higher education. The country's international student population rose by more than 5 per cent in 2010–11, and overseas applications for undergraduate places were up again at the start of 2012.

Both EU students (who pay the same fees as their British counterparts) and those from the rest of the world (who pay considerably more) have shared in the boom, but applications for 2012 courses saw a predictable parting of the ways. Those from EU countries for first degree courses were down by 12 per cent, as fees rose at English universities. Beyond the EU, where the new fees do not apply, applications were up by another 13 per cent. When postgraduates are included, the largest numbers continue to come from China and India.

There have been suggestions, even from the Prime Minister, that fees for non-EU students may fall (or at least rise more slowly) when British students are paying more. The logic behind the argument is that if the new rates for UK and other EU undergraduates reflect the full cost of teaching, international applicants and their sponsors will not expect to pay more. There is little sign as yet, however, of universities moving towards a single fee.

Why study in the UK?
Aside from the strong reputation of UK degree courses and the opportunity to be taught

and immerse yourself in English, new research shows that most graduates are handsomely rewarded when they return home. A report from the Department for Business, Innovation and Skills (BIS) shows that UK graduates earn much higher salaries than those who studied in their own country. The starting salaries of UK graduates in China and India were more than twice as high as those for graduates educated at home, while even those returning to the USA enjoyed a salary premium of more than 10 per cent.

Some premium is to be expected – you are likely to be bright and highly motivated if you are prepared to uproot yourself to take a degree. And most students have to be from a relatively wealthy background to afford the fees and other expenses of international study. A higher salary will probably be a necessity to compensate for the cost of the course. But the scale of increase demonstrated in the report suggests that a UK degree remains a good investment. Three years after graduation, 95 per cent of the international graduates surveyed were in work or further study. More than 90 per cent had been satisfied with their learning experience and almost as many would recommend their university to others.

A popular choice
Nearly all UK universities are cosmopolitan places that welcome international students in large numbers. Recent surveys by i-graduate, the student polling organisation which also produced the BIS report, put the country close behind the USA among the world's most

The top countries for sending international students to the UK

EU Countries (top 20)		%	Non-EU Countries (top 20)		%
Germany	7,288	9.8	China	32,112	26.1
Cyprus (EU)	7,154	9.7	Malaysia	10,810	8.8
France	7,115	9.6	Hong Kong	8,881	7.2
Ireland	6,209	8.4	India	6,455	5.2
Greece	4,775	6.5	Nigeria	5,800	4.7
Bulgaria	4,582	6.2	United States	4,197	3.4
Romania	4,519	6.1	Saudi Arabia	4,159	3.4
Lithuania	4,369	5.9	Singapore	3,856	3.1
Poland	3,998	5.4	Norway	3,193	2.6
Italy	3,185	4.3	Pakistan	2,996	2.4
Spain	3,004	4.1	Canada	2,662	2.2
Sweden	2,488	3.4	Korea (South)	2,164	1.8
Latvia	1,872	2.5	Sri Lanka	2,143	1.7
Belgium	1,860	2.5	Vietnam	1,798	1.5
Netherlands	1,400	1.9	Bangladesh	1,723	1.4
Finland	1,360	1.8	Russia	1,648	1.3
Portugal	1,139	1.5	Brunei	1,583	1.3
Slovakia	985	1.3	United Arab Emirates	1,516	1.2
Estonia	960	1.3	Switzerland	1,491	1.2
Austria	923	1.2	Kenya	1,341	1.1
All EU students	**74,004**		**All non-EU students**	**123,038**	

Note: First degree non-UK students .

attractive study destinations. More than 420,000 international students were taking higher education courses in the UK in 2010–11, around half of them at undergraduate level. They now make up over 17 per cent of all students at UK universities and colleges. More full-time postgraduates – the fastest-growing group – come from outside the UK than within it. In many UK universities you can expect to have fellow students from over 100 countries.

More than 90 per cent of international students declare themselves satisfied with their experience of UK universities in i-graduate surveys, although they are less sanguine in the National Student Survey and more likely than UK students to make official complaints. Nevertheless, satisfaction increased by 8 percentage points in four years, according to i-graduate, reflecting greater efforts to keep ahead of the global competition. International students are particularly complimentary about students' unions, multiculturalism, teaching standards and places of worship. Their main concerns tend to be financial, with the UK considered the second-most expensive study location in the world (after the USA), partly because of a lack of employment opportunities (in one survey, only 56 per cent were satisfied with the ability to earn money while studying).

One way round this in a growing number of countries is to take a UK degree through a local institution or a full branch campus of a UK university. Indeed, there are now almost as many international students taking UK degrees in their own country as there are in Britain, 320,000 of them outside the EU. The numbers grew by 70 per cent in a decade and are likely to rise further if the UK Government prevents universities increasing the number of students coming to Britain.

Where to study in the UK

The vast majority of the UK's universities and other higher education institutions are in England. Of the 120 universities covered in this *Guide*, 103 are in England, 15 in Scotland, 8 in Wales and 2 in Northern Ireland. Fee limits in higher education for UK and EU students are determined separately in each administrative area, which in some cases has brought benefits for EU students. All undergraduates from other EU countries are charged the same fees as those from the part of the UK where their chosen university is located, so EU students currently pay no tuition fees in Scotland, for example.

Within the UK, the cost of living varies by geographical area. Although London is the most expensive, accommodation costs in particular can also be high in many other major cities. You should certainly find out as much as you can about what living in Britain will be like. Further advice and information is available through the British Council at its offices worldwide, at more than 60 university exhibitions that it holds around the world every year, or at its Education UK website (**www.educationuk.org**). Another useful website for international students is provided by the UK Council for International Student Affairs (UKCISA) at **www.ukcisa.org.uk**.

Universities in all parts of the UK have a worldwide reputation for high quality teaching and research, as evidenced in global rankings such as those shown on pages 52–54. They maintain this standing by investing heavily in the best academic staff, buildings and equipment, and by taking part in rigorous quality assurance monitoring. The main regulatory bodies include the Quality Assurance Agency for Higher Education (QAA), higher education funding councils for each country of the UK, and the Office for Standards in Education, all of which publish reports on their websites. Professional bodies also play an important role, and there is an Independent Adjudicator for Higher Education who handles student complaints that have not been resolved by universities' own internal procedures.

Although many people from outside the UK associate British universities with Oxford and Cambridge, in reality most higher education institutions are nothing like this. Some universities do still maintain a traditional culture, but most are modern institutions that place at least as much emphasis on teaching as research and offer many vocational programmes, often with close links with business, industry and the professions. The table below shows the universities that are most popular with international students at undergraduate level. Although some of those at the top of the lists are among the most famous names in higher education, others achieved university status only in the last 20 years.

What subjects to study?

One of the reasons for such diversity is that strongly vocational courses are favoured by international students. Many of these in professional areas such as architecture, dentistry or medicine take one or two years longer to complete than most other degree courses. Traditional first degrees are mostly awarded at Bachelor level (BA, BEng, BSc, etc.) and last three to four years. There are also some "enhanced" first degrees (MEng, MChem, etc.) that take four years to complete. The relatively new Foundation degree programmes are almost all vocational and take two years to complete as a full-time course, with an option to study for a further year to gain a full degree. The tables at the end of this chapter select the 20 most popular subjects and show which universities for each subject have the greatest numbers of students. Remember, though, that you need also to consider the details of any course that you wish to study and to look at the ranking of that university in our main league table in

The universities most favoured by EU and non-EU students

Institution (top 20)	EU Students	Institution (top 20)	Non-EU Students
Aberdeen	1,863	Manchester	4,380
Coventry	1,690	University College London	3,257
London Metropolitan	1,656	Nottingham	3,031
Edinburgh	1,643	University of the Arts London	2,973
Middlesex	1,639	Edinburgh	2,678
Glasgow	1,553	Warwick	2,387
Manchester	1,517	Imperial College	2,384
Essex	1,469	Sheffield	2,264
University of the Arts London	1,441	Liverpool	2,241
Westminster	1,420	Coventry	2,183
Portsmouth	1,231	Hertfordshire	1,941
Edinburgh Napier	1,227	St Andrews	1,888
Kingston	1,196	Sheffield Hallam	1,822
University College London	1,167	Portsmouth	1,795
Kent	1,154	Exeter	1,793
King's College London	1,086	Middlesex	1,761
Salford	1,074	Northumbria	1,702
Imperial College	1,015	Leeds	1,621
Brighton	1,004	Leicester	1,610
Warwick	943	Southampton	1,606

chapter 4 and in the subject tables in chapter 5.

English language proficiency

The universities maintain high standards partly by setting high entry requirements, including proficiency in English. For international students, this usually includes a score of 6 or 7 in the International English Language Testing System (IELTS), which assesses English language ability through listening, speaking, reading and writing tests. Under new visa regulations introduced in 2011, universities are able to vouch for a student's ability in English. This proficiency will need to be equivalent to an "upper intermediate" level (level B2) of the CEFR (Common European Framework of Reference) for studying at an undergraduate level.

There are many private and publicly funded colleges throughout the UK that run courses designed to bring the English language skills of prospective higher education students up to the required standard. However, not all of these are Government approved. Some private organisations such as INTO (**www.into.uk.com**) have joined with universities to create centres running programmes preparing international students for degree-level study. The British Council also runs English language courses at its centres around the world.

Tougher student visa regulations were introduced in April 2012. Although universities' international students will not be denied entry to the UK, some lower-level preparatory

The most popular subjects for international students

Subject Group	EU Students	Non-EU Students	Total	%
Business and administrative studies	16,808	40,247	57,055	29%
Engineering and technology	6,966	18,585	25,551	13%
Social studies	7,720	10,820	18,539	9%
Creative arts and design	6,823	6,694	13,517	7%
Subjects allied to medicine	4,825	6,554	11,379	6%
Law	3,731	7,543	11,274	6%
Biological sciences	5,851	4,742	10,593	5%
Computer science	3,752	5,689	9,442	5%
Languages	4,506	2,839	7,345	4%
Architecture, building and planning	2,453	3,017	5,470	3%
Physical sciences	2,493	2,766	5,259	3%
Mass communications and documentation	2,710	2,400	5,109	3%
Mathematical sciences	1,270	3,786	5,055	3%
Medicine and dentistry	1,093	3,640	4,733	2%
Historical and philosophical studies	1,852	1,693	3,546	2%
Education	466	580	1,046	1%
Veterinary science	104	749	853	0%
Agriculture and related subjects	323	378	700	0%
Combined	260	316	576	0%
Total	**74,004**	**123,038**	**197,042**	**100%**

Note: First degree non-UK students
*Subjects allied to medicine include pharmacy and nursing

courses taken by international students will be affected. It is, therefore, doubly important to consult the official UK government list of approved institutions (web address given at the end of this chapter) before lodging an application.

How to apply

You should read the information below in conjunction with that provided in chapter 6, which deals with the application process in some detail.

Some international students apply directly to a UK university for a place on a course, and others make their applications via an agent in their home country. But most applying for a full-time first degree course do so through the Universities and Colleges Admissions Service (UCAS). If you take this route, you will need to fill in an online UCAS application form at home, at school or perhaps at your nearest British Council office. There is lots of advice on the UCAS website about the process of finding a course and the details of the application system (**www.ucas.com/how-it-all-works/international**).

Whichever way you apply, the deadlines for getting your application in are the same. For those applying from within an EU country, application forms for most courses starting in 2014 must be received at UCAS by 15 January 2014. Note that applications for Oxford and Cambridge and for all courses in medicine, dentistry and veterinary science have to be received at UCAS by 15 October 2013, while some art and design courses have a later deadline of 24 March 2014.

If you are applying from a non-EU country to study in 2014, you can submit your application to UCAS at any time between 1 September 2013 and 30 June 2014. Most people will apply well before the 30 June 2014 deadline to make sure that places are still available and to allow plenty of time for immigration regulations, and to make arrangements for travel and accommodation.

Entry and employment regulations

Visa regulations have been the subject of frequent controversy in the UK and many new rules and regulations have recently been introduced, often hotly contested by universities. The Government was criticised for increasing visa fees, doubling the cost of visa extensions, and ending the right to appeal against a refusal of a visa.

It also introduced a points system for entry – known as Tier 4 – which came into effect in March 2009. Under this scheme, prospective students can check whether they are eligible for entry against published criteria, and so assess their points score. Universities are also required to provide a Certificate of Acceptance for Study to their international student entrants and they must have "Highly Trusted" status on the Register of Sponsors. Prospective students have to demonstrate that, as well as the necessary qualifications, they have English language proficiency and enough money for the first year of their specified course. This includes the full fees for the first year and living costs of £9,000 if you are studying in inner London (£7,200 elsewhere). Under the new visa requirements, details of financial support will be checked in more detail.

Since September 2007, all students wishing to enter the UK to study have been required to obtain entry clearance before arrival. The only exceptions are British nationals living overseas, British overseas territories citizens, British Protected persons, British subjects, and non-visa national short-term students who may enter under a new Student Visitor route. Visa fees have been increased again and the details of the regulations have been reviewed by the UK Border Agency. You can find more about all the latest rules and regulations for entry and visa requirements at **www.ukba.homeoffice.gov.uk/visas-immigration/studying**.

The rules and regulations governing permission to work vary according to your country of origin and the level of course you undertake. If you are from a European Economic Area (EEA) country (the EU plus Iceland, Liechtenstein and Norway) or Switzerland, you do not need permission to work in the UK, although you will need to be ready to show an employer your passport or identity card to prove you are a national of an EEA country. Students from outside the EEA who are here as Tier 4 students are allowed to work part-time for up to 20 hours a week during term time and to work full-time during vacations. These arrangements apply to students on degree courses; stricter limits were introduced in 2010 for lower-level courses. If you wish to stay on after you have graduated, you can apply for permission under Tier 2 under the new points-based immigration system, but you will need a sponsor and the work must be considered "graduate level", commanding a salary of at least £20,000. The latest reforms abolished the Tier 1 two-year post-study period for graduates who do not have such a sponsor. They will be required to apply for a new visa from scratch. Full details are on the UK Border Agency website.

A new Graduate Entrepreneur Scheme will enable up to 1,000 graduates to remain in the UK longer than others if they have developed "world class innovative ideas or entrepreneurial skills". Successful applicants, who will be selected by their university, will be allowed to stay in the UK for 12 months, with the possibility of a further 12-month extension.

Bringing your family

Since 2010, international students on courses of six months or less have been forbidden to bring a partner or children into the UK, and the latest reforms extend this prohibition to all undergraduates except those who are government sponsored. Postgraduates will still be able to bring dependants to the UK and most universities can help to arrange facilities and accommodation for families as well as for single students. The family members you are allowed to bring with you are your husband or wife, civil partner (a same-sex relationship that has been formally registered in the UK or your home country) and dependent children.

If you are a national of any country from outside the EEA, your family will be subject to immigration policy. Those who are eligible to bring dependants will need to show that they can support them financially, arrange appropriate accommodation, and that they will leave the UK when the student has finished his or her studies. Such family members will usually be able to study (children under 16 are required to attend full-time education), and any over the age of 16 should be able to work as long as you have permission to stay for over 12 months and are following a degree or Foundation degree course. You can find out more about getting entry clearance for your family at **www.ukcisa.org.uk/**.

Support from British universities

Support for international students is more comprehensive than in many countries, and begins long before you arrive in the UK. Many universities have advisers in other countries. Some will arrange to put you in touch with current students or graduates who can give you a first-hand account of what life is like at a particular university. Pre-departure receptions for students and their families, as well as meet-and-greet arrangements for newly arrived students, are common. You can also expect an orientation and induction programme in your first week, and many universities now have "buddying" systems where current students are assigned to new arrivals to help them find their way around, adjust to their new surroundings and make new friends. Each university also has a students' union that organises social, cultural and sporting events and clubs, including many specifically for international students. Both the university and the students' union are likely to have full-time staff whose job it is to look after the welfare of students from overseas.

International students also benefit from free medical and subsidised dental and optical care and treatment under the UK National Health Service, plus access to a professional counselling service and a university careers service.

At university, you will naturally encounter people from a wide range of cultures and walks of life. Getting involved in student societies, sport, voluntary work, and any of the wide range of social activities on offer will help you gain first-hand experience of British culture, and, if you need it, will help improve your command of the English language.

The 20 most popular subjects and universities for international students

1 Business Studies

	EU	Non-EU
Coventry	398	699
Middlesex	297	686
Aston	329	652
Ulster	77	860
Manchester	216	650
Westminster	497	323
Hertfordshire	256	551
London Metropolitan	447	339
Glyndŵr	13	762
Sunderland	105	641
All overseas students	**11,935**	**24,506**

3 Law

	EU	Non-EU
King's College London	250	276
Leicester	168	331
Kent	133	331
Essex	296	97
Manchester	94	284
Warwick	50	272
Buckingham	26	257
Queen Mary, London	135	148
Bristol	22	246
University College London	90	177
All overseas students	**3,731**	**7,543**

2 Accounting & Finance

	EU	Non-EU
Manchester	81	570
Exeter	24	604
City	127	483
Lancaster	111	467
Sheffield Hallam	15	511
Essex	127	396
Bangor	4	498
Warwick	77	312
De Montfort	44	331
Liverpool	8	342
All overseas students	**2,351**	**13,135**

4 Computer Science

	EU	Non-EU
East London	28	499
Greenwich	41	328
Middlesex	51	301
Manchester	171	129
Coventry	162	134
Teesside	66	227
Imperial College	165	110
Edinburgh	189	61
Bedfordshire	25	201
Portsmouth	102	80
All overseas students	**3,752**	**5,689**

The 20 most popular subjects and universities for international students cont

5 Economics

	EU	Non-EU
University College London	100	552
Warwick	113	461
London School of Economics	50	489
Manchester	60	340
Leicester	38	287
Essex	163	155
Exeter	73	239
Royal Holloway	78	196
St Andrews	64	197
Edinburgh	48	208
All overseas students	2,455	6,474

8 Politics

	EU	Non-EU
St Andrews	91	439
Kent	234	47
Aberdeen	229	38
Edinburgh	46	183
Essex	150	68
London School of Economics	55	150
Warwick	61	129
Queen Mary, London	100	65
York	112	51
Royal Holloway	91	66
All overseas students	3,298	2,623

6 Art & Design

	EU	Non-EU
University of the Arts London	867	2,106
University for Creative Arts	229	85
Middlesex	194	69
Kingston	91	145
Coventry	102	125
Nottingham Trent	51	155
Northumbria	36	168
London Metropolitan	123	78
Birmingham City	77	123
Goldsmiths College	51	131
All overseas students	3,434	4,537

9 Mechanical Engineering

	EU	Non-EU
Imperial College	100	216
Coventry	57	250
Nottingham	35	208
Sheffield	19	219
Bath	78	98
Manchester	33	141
Southampton	67	101
University College London	22	143
Hertfordshire	25	126
Bristol	12	133
All overseas students	1,432	4,297

7 Electrical and Electronic Engineering

	EU	Non-EU
Imperial College	83	320
Manchester	43	281
Liverpool	10	271
Sheffield	33	230
Birmingham	16	224
Northumbria	26	212
Coventry	21	203
Birmingham City	47	140
Southampton	40	141
Strathclyde	25	151
All overseas students	1,281	5,668

10 Biological Sciences

	EU	Non-EU
Edinburgh	242	191
Imperial College	90	181
University College London	68	154
Manchester	89	114
Aberdeen	168	24
Glasgow	117	33
Liverpool	16	129
Cambridge	65	65
Oxford	50	60
Nottingham	38	72
All overseas students	2,611	2,657

The 20 most popular subjects and universities for international students cont

11 Mathematics

	EU	Non-EU
Imperial College	74	334
University College London	66	325
Warwick	74	282
Manchester	57	270
London School of Economics	23	244
Cambridge	112	140
Liverpool	9	221
Oxford	63	156
Southampton	25	129
Leicester	30	118
All overseas students	**1,270**	**3,786**

14 Psychology

	EU	Non-EU
Aberdeen	187	35
Glasgow	155	18
York	41	111
University College London	47	102
St Andrews	47	92
Essex	67	63
Middlesex	74	44
Edinburgh	57	54
Royal Holloway	62	30
Ulster	85	0
All overseas students	**2,701**	**1,882**

12 Hospitality, Leisure, Recreation & Tourism

	EU	Non-EU
West London	155	339
University College Birmingham	217	246
Surrey	73	245
University of the Arts, London	42	213
Bournemouth	101	92
London Metropolitan	129	64
Brighton	152	37
Sheffield Hallam	27	149
Edinburgh Napier	83	61
Leeds Metropolitan	96	47
All overseas students	**2,403**	**2,429**

15 Civil Engineering

	EU	Non-EU
Aberdeen	187	35
Glasgow	155	18
York	41	111
University College London	47	102
St Andrews	47	92
Essex	67	63
Middlesex	74	44
Edinburgh	57	54
Royal Holloway	62	30
Ulster	85	0
All overseas students	**2,701**	**1,882**

13 Communication and Media Studies

	EU	Non-EU
University of the Arts London	172	187
Middlesex	202	87
Goldsmiths College	65	149
London Metropolitan	139	48
Westminster	116	60
Liverpool John Moores	13	139
Leicester	23	113
Bournemouth	90	45
Southampton Solent	111	19
Coventry	83	44
All overseas students	**2,623**	**2,129**

16 Medicine

	EU	Non-EU
Imperial College	88	226
Manchester	40	256
Nottingham	40	196
King's College London	63	171
Edinburgh	20	168
University College London	48	133
Glasgow	61	117
Leicester	27	150
Cambridge	57	108
Birmingham	21	141
All overseas students	**1,027**	**3,360**

The 20 most popular subjects and universities for international students cont

17 Architecture

	EU	Non-EU
Nottingham	62	272
London Metropolitan	118	53
Manchester Metropolitan	83	80
Westminster	115	47
Portsmouth	97	55
Brighton	96	38
Edinburgh	43	90
Plymouth	115	14
Liverpool	36	81
Bath	33	82
All overseas students	**1,934**	**1,786**

19 Pharmacology & Pharmacy

	EU	Non-EU
Sunderland	105	302
Nottingham	18	263
Strathclyde	10	224
Liverpool John Moores	17	198
Brighton	97	116
University College London	27	159
Bath	26	145
Manchester	20	147
Robert Gordon	146	12
King's College London	30	80
All overseas students	**876**	**2,329**

18 Drama, Dance and Cinematics

	EU	Non-EU
University of the Arts London	196	275
The Arts University College at Bournemouth	70	83
Middlesex	105	28
University for Creative Arts	108	23
Kingston	76	53
Central School of Speech and Drama	38	53
Royal Holloway	47	37
Hertfordshire	38	45
Surrey	33	36
Aberystwyth	52	16
All overseas students	**2,011**	**1,220**

20 Other Subjects Allied to Medicine

	EU	Non-EU
Bournemouth	189	165
Queen Margaret Edinburgh	59	100
Imperial College	54	105
Greenwich	88	64
London Metropolitan	25	119
Cambridge	66	67
Middlesex	69	53
Sheffield	18	97
Bedfordshire	65	47
Newcastle	20	77
All overseas students	**1,489**	**1,684**

Useful websites

The British Council, with its dedicated Education UK site designed for those wishing to find out more about studying in the UK:

www.educationuk.org

The UK Council for International Student Affairs (UKCISA) provides a wide range of information on all aspects of studying in the UK:

www.ukcisa.org.uk

UCAS, for full details of courses available and an explanation of the application process:

www.ucas.com/how-it-all-works/international

For the latest information on entry and visa requirements, visit the UK Border Agency:

www.ukba.homeoffice.gov.uk/visas-immigration/studying

Register of Sponsors for Tier 4 educational establishments:

www.ukba.homeoffice.gov.uk/sitecontent/documents/employersandsponsors/
pointsbasedsystem/registerofsponsorseducation

For a general guide to Britain, available in many languages:

www.visitbr itain.com

13 Applying to Oxbridge

Oxbridge (as Oxford and Cambridge are called collectively) not only dominates UK higher education; the two universities are recognised as among the best in the world, regularly featuring among the top five in global rankings. But that is not why they merit a separate chapter in this *Guide*.

The two ancient universities have different admissions arrangements to the rest of the higher education system. Although part of the UCAS network, they have different deadlines from other universities, you can only apply to one or the other, and selection is in the hands of the colleges rather than the university centrally. Most candidates apply to a specific college, although you can make an open application if you are happy to go anywhere.

There have been reforms to the admissions system at both universities in recent years, in order to make the process more user-friendly to those who do not have school or family experience to draw upon. In particular, the business of choosing a college has been intimidating for many prospective applicants. Candidates are now distributed around colleges more efficiently, regardless of the choices they make initially.

There is little to choose between the two universities in terms of entrance requirements, and a formidable number of successful applicants have the maximum possible grades. However, that does not mean that the talented student should be shy about applying: both have fewer applicants per place than many less prestigious universities, and admissions tutors are always looking to extend the range of schools and colleges from which they recruit. For those with a realistic chance of success, there is little to lose except the possibility of one wasted space out of five on the UCAS application.

Overall, there are about five applicants to every place at Oxford and Cambridge, but there are big differences between subjects and colleges. As the tables in this chapter show, competition is particularly fierce in subjects such as medicine and English, but those qualified to read geology or classics have a much better chance of success. The pattern is similar to that in other universities, although the high degree of selection (and self-selection) that precedes an Oxbridge application means that even in the less popular subjects the field of candidates is certain to be strong.

The two universities' power to intimidate prospective applicants is based partly on myth. Both have done their best to live down the *Brideshead Revisited* image, but many sixth-formers still fear that they would be out of their depth there, academically and socially. In fact, the state sector produces nearly 58 per cent of entrants to Oxford and Cambridge, and the dropout rate is lower than at almost any other university. The "champagne set" is still present and its activities are well publicised, but most students are hard-working high achievers with the same concerns as their counterparts on other campuses. A joint poll by the two universities' student newspapers showed that undergraduates were spending much of their time in the library or worrying about their employment prospects, and relatively little time on the river or even in the college bar.

State school applicants

Both universities and their student organisations have put a great deal of effort into trying to encourage applications from state schools, and many colleges have launched their own campaigns. Such has been the determination to convince state school pupils that they will get a fair crack of the whip that a new concern has grown up of possible bias against independent school pupils. In reality, however, the dispersed nature of Oxbridge admissions rules out any conspiracy. Some colleges set relatively low standard offers to encourage applicants from the state sector, who may reveal their potential at interview. Some admissions tutors may give the edge to well-qualified candidates from comprehensive schools over those from highly academic independent schools because they consider theirs the greater achievement in the circumstances. Others stick with tried and trusted sources of good students. The independent sector still enjoys a degree of success out of proportion to its share of the school population.

Choosing the right college

Simply in terms of winning a place at Oxford or Cambridge, choosing the right college is not quite as important as it used to be. Both universities have got better at assessing candidates' strengths and finding a suitable college for those who either make an open application or are not taken by their first-choice college.

Cambridge: The Tompkins Table 2013

College	2013	2012	College	2013	2012
Trinity	1	1	Corpus Christi	16	3
Pembroke	2	4	Gonville and Caius	17	16
Trinity Hall	3	8	Selwyn	18	6
Emmanuel	4	2	Sidney Sussex	19	17
Churchill	5	5	Fitzwilliam	20	19
Jesus	6	7	Girton	21	22
Queens'	7	12	Robinson	22	21
Christ's	8	9	Newnham	23	23
St Catharine's	9	10	Murray Edwards	24	24
Peterhouse	10	18	Wolfson	25	25
Clare	11	11	Homerton	26	27
Downing	12	20	Hughes Hall	27	26
St John's	13	14	Lucy Cavendish	28	29
King's	14	13	St Edmund's	29	28
Magdalene	15	15			

At Oxford, subject tutors from around the university put candidates into bands at the start of the selection process, using the results of admissions tests as well as exam results and references. Applicants are spread around the colleges for interview and may not be seen by their preferred college if the tutors think their chances of a place are better elsewhere. Almost a quarter of last year's successful candidates were offered places by a college other than the one they applied to.

Cambridge relies on the "pool", which gives the most promising candidates a second chance if they were not offered a place at the college to which they applied. Those placed in the pool are invited back for a second round of interviews early in the new year. The system lowers the stakes for those who apply to the most selective colleges – in 2010 over 18 per cent of offers came via the pool. Cambridge still interviews about 90 per cent of applicants, whereas the new system at Oxford has resulted in more immediate rejections in some subjects. In medicine, fewer than a third of Oxford's applicants were interviewed in 2010, while in biochemistry almost all were.

However, most Oxbridge applicants still apply direct to a particular college, not only to maximise their chances of getting in, but because that is where they will be living and socialising, as well as learning. Most colleges may look the same to the uninitiated, but there are important differences. Famously sporty colleges, for example, can be trying for those in search of peace and quiet.

Thorough research is needed to find the right place. Even within colleges, different admissions tutors may have different approaches, so personal contact is essential. The tables in this chapter give an idea of the relative academic strengths of the colleges, as well as the varying levels of competition for a place in different subjects. But only individual research will suggest where you will feel most at home. For example, women may favour one of the few remaining single-sex colleges (Murray Edwards, Newnham and Lucy Cavendish at Cambridge). Men have no such option.

Oxford: The Norrington Table 2013

College	2013	2012	College	2013	2012
New	1	3	St Edmund Hall	16	28
St John's	2	=4	Christ Church	17	7
Merton	3	14	Wadham	18	=4
Trinity	4	18	Hertford	19	23
Harris Manchester	5	25	St Peter's	20	26
Magdalen	6	1	St Hilda's	21	22
Lincoln	7	6	St Catherine's	22	10
Brasenose	8	2	University	23	17
Oriel	9	13	St Hugh's	24	19
Balliol	10	9	Corpus Christi	25	20
Worcester	11	12	Queen's	26	21
St Anne's	12	24	Keble	27	8
Jesus	13	15	Exeter	28	11
Mansfield	14	16	Somerville	29	27
Pembroke	15	30	Lady Margaret Hall	30	29

Cambridge applications and acceptances by course

	Applications		Acceptances		Acceptances to Applications %	
Arts, Humanities and Social Sciences	**2012**	**2011**	**2012**	**2011**	**2012**	**2011**
Anglo-Saxon, Norse and Celtic	57	58	25	24	43.9	41.4
Archaeology and Anthropology	140	162	56	73	40.9	45.1
Architecture	456	458	45	41	9.9	9.0
Asian and Middle Eastern Studies	135	143	41	46	30.4	32.2
Classics	153	153	71	77	46.4	50.3
Classics (4 years)	40	35	14	12	35.0	34.3
Economics	1,328	1,255	171	163	12.9	13.0
Education	75	97	29	37	38.7	38.1
English	743	811	210	187	28.3	23.1
Geography	262	320	101	99	38.5	30.9
History	591	672	199	191	33.7	28.4
History of Art	104	110	26	22	25.0	20.0
Land Economy	228	234	48	57	21.1	24.4
Law	1,021	1,011	215	193	21.1	19.1
Linguistics	91	91	34	33	37.4	36.3
Modern and Medieval Languages	476	502	178	160	37.4	31.9
Music	142	151	53	73	37.3	48.3
Philosophy	245	266	48	48	19.6	18.0
Politics, Psychology and Sociology	669	796	104	120	15.5	15.1
Theology and Religious Studies	105	108	43	48	41.0	44.4
Total Arts, Humanities and Social Sciences	**7,061**	**7,433**	**1,725**	**1,704**	**24.4**	**22.9**
Science and Technology	**2012**	**2011**	**2012**	**2011**	**2012**	**2011**
Computer Science	394	352	84	70	21.3	19.9
Engineering	1,862	1,652	331	307	17.8	18.6
Mathematics	1,382	1,127	253	238	18.3	21.1
Medical Sciences	1,897	1,916	302	279	12.8	14.6
Natural Sciences	2,670	2,490	675	607	25.3	24.4
Veterinary Medicine	435	419	66	69	15.2	16.5
Total Science and Technology	**8,640**	**7,956**	**1,712**	**1,570**	**19.8**	**19.7**
Total	**15,701**	**15,389**	**3,437**	**3,274**	**21.9**	**21.3**

Note: the dates refer to the year in which the acceptances were made.

Mathematics includes mathematics and mathematics with physics. Medical sciences includes medicine and the graduate course in medicine.

The Tripos courses in chemical engineering, management studies and manufacturing engineering can be taken only after Part 1 in another subject. Applications and acceptances for these courses are recorded under the first year subjects taken by the applicants involved.

Archaeology and anthropology, and Politics, psychology and sociology were discontinued in 2012. Two new courses have been introduced for 2013: Human, social and political sciences and Psychological and behavioural sciences.

Oxford applications and acceptances by course

Arts	Applications		Acceptances		Acceptances to Applications %	
	2012	2011	2012	2011	2012	2011
Ancient and Modern History	74	74	13	16	17.6	21.6
Archaeology and Anthropology	106	87	23	25	21.7	28.7
Classical Archaeology and Ancient History	85	107	17	22	20	20.6
Classics	330	292	127	117	38.5	40.1
Classics and English	29	36	5	7	17.2	19.4
Classics and Modern Languages	33	38	7	12	21.2	31.6
Computer Science and Philosophy	26	-	8	-	30.8	-
Economics and Management	1,107	1,086	94	89	8.5	8.2
English	1,268	1,152	245	220	19.3	19.1
English and Modern Languages	149	166	17	20	11.4	12
European and Middle Eastern Languages	36	54	6	15	16.7	27.8
Fine Art	174	193	21	23	12.1	11.9
Geography	416	344	85	81	20.4	23.5
History	1,012	960	227	225	22.4	23.4
History and Economics	87	85	13	14	14.9	16.5
History and English	86	86	10	13	11.6	15.1
History and Modern Languages	81	94	17	16	21	17
History and Politics	303	316	46	48	15.2	15.2
History of Art	130	105	14	14	10.8	13.3
Law	1,226	1,223	187	202	15.3	16.5
Law with Law Studies in Europe	301	341	29	28	9.6	8.2
Mathematics and Philosophy	92	95	19	16	20.7	16.8
Modern Languages	567	582	179	185	31.6	31.8
Modern Languages and Linguistics	77	68	25	15	32.5	22.1
Music	218	232	76	65	34.9	28
Oriental Studies	159	150	41	41	25.8	27.3
Philosophy and Modern Languages	64	79	18	16	28.1	20.3
Philosophy and Theology	92	96	24	25	26.1	26
Physics and Philosophy	123	116	18	25	14.6	21.6
Philosophy, Politics and Economics (PPE)	1,726	1,676	260	248	15.1	14.8
Theology	105	107	40	31	38.1	29
Theology and Oriental Studies	8	6	1	2	12.5	33.3
Total Arts	**10,290**	**10,046**	**1,912**	**1,876**	**18.6**	**18.7**

The findings in the Tompkins Table (see page 277) are not officially endorsed by Cambridge University itself. However, since 2007 we have been able to publish the "official" Norrington Table from Oxford. Sanctioned or not, both tables give an indication of where the academic powerhouses lie – information which can be as useful to those trying to avoid them as to those seeking the ultimate challenge. Although there can be a great deal of movement year by year, both tables tend to be dominated by the rich, old foundations. Both tables are

Oxford applications and acceptances by course cont

Sciences	Applications		Acceptances		Acceptances to Applications %	
	2012	2011	2012	2011	2012	2011
Biochemistry	386	391	101	90	26.2	23
Biological Sciences	390	399	108	102	27.7	25.6
Biomedical Sciences	213	204	33	31	15.5	15.2
Chemistry	546	560	181	188	33.2	33.6
Computer Science	139	151	25	25	18	16.6
Earth Sciences (Geology)	154	146	34	35	22.1	24
Engineering Science	666	820	156	156	23.4	19
Engineering, Economics and Management	106	131	9	11	8.5	8.4
Experimental Psychology	327	262	64	47	19.6	17.9
Human Sciences	135	167	28	28	20.7	16.8
Materials Science (including MEM)	133	106	36	28	27.1	26.4
Mathematics	950	1133	172	173	18.1	15.3
Mathematics and Computer Science	117	99	24	26	20.5	26.3
Mathematics and Statistics	160	209	13	26	8.1	12.4
Medicine	1,511	1487	155	151	10.3	10.2
Physics	916	893	167	166	18.2	18.6
Psychology and Philosophy	102	139	15	27	14.7	19.4
Total Sciences	**6,951**	**7,297**	**1,321**	**1,310**	**19**	**18**
Total Arts and Sciences	**17,241**	**17,343**	**3,233**	**3,186**	**18.8**	**18.4**

Note: the dates refer to the year in which the acceptances were made

compiled from the degree results of final-year undergraduates. A first is worth five points; a 2:1, four; a 2:2, three; a third, one point. The total is divided by the number of candidates to produce each college's average.

In both universities, teaching for most students is based in the colleges. In practice, however, in the sciences this arrangement holds good only for the first year. One-to-one tutorials, which are Oxbridge's traditional strength for undergraduates, are by no means universal. Teaching groups remain much smaller than in most universities, and the tutor remains an inspiration for many students.

The applications procedure

Both universities have set a UCAS deadline of 15 October 2013 for entry in 2014. You may also need to take a written test and submit examples of your work – the exact requirements vary depending on the course you select, so check this carefully. See pages 20–21 for details of application tests. In addition, once Cambridge receives your UCAS form, you will be asked to complete an online Supplementary Application Questionnaire (SAQ). The deadline for this will be 22 October 2013 in most cases. For international applications to Cambridge you must also submit a Cambridge Online Preliminary Application (COPA), in some cases by 9 September 2013; check the Cambridge website for full details.

You may apply to either Oxford or Cambridge (but not both) in the same admissions year, unless you are seeking an Organ award at both universities. Interviews take place in December for those short-listed (for international applicants, Cambridge hold some interviews overseas while Oxford holds some interviews over the internet, though medicine interviewees must come to Oxford). Applicants to Oxford will receive either a conditional offer or a rejection by Christmas, while in Cambridge the news arrives early in the new year. For more information about the application process and preparation for interviews, visit **www.cam.ac.uk/study-at-cambridge** and **www.ox.ac.uk/admissions.**

Oxford College Profiles

Balliol

Oxford OX1 3BJ   01865 277777   www.balliol.ox.ac.uk

Undergraduates: 387   Postgraduates: 325   undergrad.admissions@balliol.ox.ac.uk

Famous as the *alma mater* of many prominent post-war politicians, Balliol has maintained a strong presence in university life and is usually well represented in the Union and most other societies. Academic standards are formidably high, as might be expected in the college of Wyclif and Adam Smith, notably in the classics and social sciences, and it was tenth in the 2013 Norrington Table. PPE is notoriously popular, while library facilities are good and include the Taylor law library. Balliol began admitting overseas students in the 19th century and has cultivated an attractively cosmopolitan atmosphere. It is now the only college to have an entirely student-run bar, the focal point for evening socialising. Most undergraduates are offered guaranteed accommodation in college for their first and final years, with second-year accommodation mostly off-site. Graduate students are usually lodged in the Graduate Centre at Holywell Manor.

Brasenose

Oxford OX1 4AJ   01865 277510 (admissions)   www.bnc.ox.ac.uk

Undergraduates: 364   Postgraduates: 205   admissions@bnc.ox.ac.uk

Brasenose may not be the most famous Oxford college, but it makes up for its discreet image with an advantageous city-centre position, nestled beside the stunning Radcliffe Camera, and was eighth in the 2013 college league table (second in 2012). The *alma mater* of David Cameron, Brasenose was one of the first colleges to admit women in the 1970s, and now usually has a near-even split within each year. BNC, as the college is often known, has a strong rugby reputation, having won the rugby cuppers 14 times over the years, and also has among the lowest proportion of students from state schools in the university. Named after the door knocker on the 13th-century Brasenose Hall, the college has a pleasant, intimate ambience which most find conducive to study. Law, PPE, medicine and modern history are traditional strengths, and competition for places in these subjects is intense. The library is open 24 hours a day and there is a separate law library. Sporting standards are as high as at many much larger colleges and BNC's rowing club is one of the oldest in the university. The annexe at Frewin Court means nearly all undergraduates can live in, and many postgraduates can also live in the St Cross Building.

Christic Church

Oxford OX1 1DP   01865 276181 (admissions)   www.chch.ox.ac.uk

Undergraduates: 434   Postgraduates: 188   admissions@chch.ox.ac.uk

The college founded by Cardinal Wolsey in 1525 and affectionately known as "The House" has come a long way since Evelyn Waugh mythologised its aristocratic excesses in *Brideshead Revisited*. Around half of offers tend to be made to state school pupils, which still leaves Christ Church with among the highest proportion of private school students. Academic pressure is reasonably relaxed, although natural high achievers prosper, and the college's history and law teaching is highly regarded. The college was 17th in the most recent Norrington Table, falling from seventh the year before. The magnificent 18th-century library is one of the best in Oxford and is supplemented by a separate law library. Christ Church has its own art gallery, which holds over 2,000 works of mainly Italian Renaissance art. Sport, especially rugby and football, is an important part of college life. The college has good squash courts and the river is close by for the aspiring oarsman, though the men's crew recently surrendered its position as Head of the River to Oriel College. Accommodation for all three years is rated by college undergraduates as excellent and includes flats off Iffley Road as well as a number of beautifully panelled shared sets (double rooms) in college. Its chapel is also the cathedral of the Diocese of Oxford – England's smallest medieval cathedral.

Corpus Christi

Oxford OX1 4JF   01865 276693 (admissions)   www.ccc.ox.ac.uk

Undergraduates: 252   Postgraduates: 98   admissions.office@ccc.ox.ac.uk

Corpus, one of Oxford's smallest colleges, is naturally overshadowed by its Goliath-like neighbour, Christ Church, but makes the most of its intimate, friendly atmosphere and exquisite beauty. Although the college has only around 350 students including postgraduates, it has an admirable library open 24 hours a day. Academic expectations are high and English, Classics, PPE and medicine are especially well-established. The college came 25th in the 2013 Norrington Table, a significant fall from second in 2010 and 20th last year. Corpus has stormed to victory in University Challenge twice in recent years, although after their 2008 win the team were subsequently disqualified and stripped of their title. Corpus is able to offer accommodation to all its undergraduates, one of its many attractions to those seeking a smaller community in Oxford. The college is also one of the most generous with bursaries, giving travel, book and vacation grants at an almost unparalleled level across the university. Scholars are particularly well rewarded.

Exeter

Oxford OX1 3DP   01865 279648 (academic secretary)   www.exeter.ox.ac.uk

Undergraduates: 337   Postgraduates: 216   admissions@exeter.ox.ac.uk

Exeter is the fourth oldest college in the university and was founded in 1314 by Walter de Stapeldon, Bishop of Exeter. Nestling between the High Street and Broad Street, site of most of the city's bookshops, it could hardly be more central. The college boasts handsome buildings, the exceptional Fellows' garden and attractive accommodation for most undergraduates for all three years of their university careers, although many second year students currently live out. The college has recently refurbished its graduate accommodation in the east of the city to a high standard. Having climbed to 11th in the 2012 Norrington table, it fell back down to 28th in 2013. It is, however, often accused of being rather dull. Given its glittering roll-call of alumni, which includes Martin Amis, J.R.R. Tolkien, Alan

Bennett, Richard Burton, Imogen Stubbs and Tariq Ali, this seems an accusation that, on the face of it at least, is hard to sustain. The arrival of Frances Cairncross, the former managing editor of *The Economist*, in 2004 created a new dynamic at the college, with regular, high-profile speaker events, and the incorporation of a college careers service. The college has taken over the buildings of Ruskin College in Walton Street, which will provide further accommodation.

Harris Manchester

Oxford OX1 3TD 01865 271009 (admissions tutor) www.hmc.ox.ac.uk
Undergraduates: 98 Postgraduates: 116 enquiries@hmc.ox.ac.uk
Founded in Manchester in 1786 to provide education for non-Anglican students, Harris Manchester finally settled in Oxford in 1889 after spells in both York and London. A full university college since 1996, its central location with fine buildings and grounds in Holywell Street is very convenient for the Bodleian, although the college itself does have an excellent library. Harris Manchester admits only mature students to read for both undergraduate and graduate degrees, predominantly in the arts. All students must be 21 or older, though the average age has come down slightly in recent years. There are also groups of visiting students from American universities and students training for the ministry. Most members live in and all meals are provided – indeed the college encourages its members to dine regularly in hall. The college has few sporting facilities (a croquet lawn and a college punt), but members can use two central Oxford gyms without charge and can play football, cricket, chess and swim, as well as playing on other college or university teams. Other outlets include the college Drama Society and the chapel, a focal point for many there.

Hertford

Oxford OX1 3BW 01865 279404 (admissions) www.hertford.ox.ac.uk
Undergraduates: 409 Postgraduates: 187 admissions@hertford.ox.ac.uk
Though tracing its roots to the 13th century, Hertford is determinedly modern. It was one of the first colleges to admit women (in 1975). Hertford also helped set the trend towards offers of places conditional on A levels, which paved the way for the abolition of the entrance examination. It is popular with state school applicants, and is one of the least stuffy colleges, with a reputation for attracting students from a broad range of backgrounds. The college lacks the grandeur of Magdalen, of which it was once an annex, but has its own architectural trademark in the Bridge of Sighs. It is also close to the History Faculty library (Hertford's neighbour), the Bodleian and the King's Arms, perhaps Oxford's most popular pub. Academic pressure at Hertford is relaxed and, though the college occupies the lower half of the Norrington Table, the quality of teaching, especially in English, is generally thought admirable. Accommodation has improved, thanks in part to the Abingdon House and Warnock House complex close to the Thames near Folly Bridge, and the college can now lodge all of its undergraduates at any one time, often at subsidised rates, albeit in disparate parts of the city.

Jesus

Oxford OX1 3DW 01865 279721 (admissions) www.jesus.ox.ac.uk
Undergraduates: 347 Postgraduates: 168 admissions.officer@jesus.ox.ac.uk
Jesus, the only Oxford college to be founded in the reign of Elizabeth I, suffers from something of an unfair reputation for insularity. Its students, whose predecessors include T.E.

Lawrence and Harold Wilson, describe it as "friendly but gossipy" and shrug off the legend that all its undergraduates are Welsh. Close to most of Oxford's main facilities, Jesus has three compact quads, the second of which is especially enticing in the summer. The college's JCR is well-equipped, with a pool table, large projector screen television, and a hatch serving tea and toast throughout the day. Academic standards are high and most subjects are taught in college. Physics, chemistry and engineering are especially strong. Rugby and rowing also tend to be taken seriously. Accommodation is almost universally excellent and relatively inexpensive. Self-catering flats in north and east Oxford have enabled every graduate to live in throughout his or her Oxford career. The range of accommodation available to undergraduates is similarly good and is available for the full length of any course. The new Ship Street Centre contains 33 en-suite rooms for first-year students and a lecture theatre. The college's Cowley Road development, next to the college's sports ground, was described by the students' union as "some of the plushest student housing in Oxford".

Keble

Oxford OX1 3PG   01865 272711 (admissions)   www.keble.ox.ac.uk
Undergraduates: 443   Postgraduates: 224   college.office@keble.ox.ac.uk

Keble is one of Oxford's most distinct colleges, with its unmistakable Victorian Gothic architecture and brickwork walls gleaming around the grand quads. Named after John Keble, the leader of the Oxford Movement, Keble was founded in 1870 with the intention of making Oxford education more accessible, and the college remains proud of "the legacy of a social conscience". With around 400 undergraduates, Keble is one of the biggest colleges in Oxford and its academic performance varies, finishing 27th in the Norrington Table in 2013 (and 8th in 2012). It is strong in the sciences, where it benefits from easy access to the Science Area, the Radcliffe Science Library and the Mathematical Institute. The college's sporting record remains exemplary, with the rugby team regularly dominating university competitions. Though the overflow of the sporting ethos into the college's social life can be a little overbearing, it by no means dominates the life of a college, which has numerous music and drama societies as well as a highly successful annual Arts Week. Undergraduates are guaranteed accommodation in their first two years and the college can also accommodate most undergraduates in their final year. The cosy, wood-panelled library is open 24 hours a day. The college hall, where students wishing to dine must wear gowns six nights a week, has recently been intensively cleaned to restore it to its former glory and is one of the most impressive in the university. The college also has a well-equipped gym and the modern O'Reilly theatre, the acoustics of which are rated the best in the university.

Lady Margaret Hall

Oxford OX2 6QA   01865 274310 (admissions)   www.lmh.ox.ac.uk
Undergraduates: 401   Postgraduates: 203   admissions@lmh.ox.ac.uk

Lady Margaret Hall, Oxford's first college for women, has been co-educational since 1978 and now enjoys an equal gender balance. For many students, LMH's comparative isolation – the college is three-quarters of a mile north of the city centre – is a real advantage, ensuring a clear distinction between college life and university activities, and a refuge from tourists. For others it means a long journey to central library facilities. Although the neo-Georgian architecture is not to everyone's taste, the college's beautiful gardens back onto the Cherwell River, allowing LMH to have its own punt house and 12 acres of land. The students' union describes life at the college as "relaxed". It generally hovers around the lower reaches of the Norrington Table (30th in 2013), although English is strong, producing a high proportion of firsts each year, as do maths, physics and history. Accommodation is guaranteed for first, second and third years since the opening of the Pipe Partridge building, which has considerably enlarged undergraduate accommodation and houses a new JCR, dining hall and lecture theatre. Ongoing building works aim to provide further graduate rooms as well as a new gym, due for completion by autumn 2014. LMH shares most of its sports facilities with Trinity College, though it has tennis courts on site and has become a leading rowing college. The library is open 24 hours and is well-stocked for English and Classics, with a separate law library. It has long been one of Oxford's dramatic centres, with at least five student productions a year, put on at the Simpkins Lee lecture theatre.

Lincoln

Oxford OX1 3DR 01865 279836 (admissions) www.lincoln.ox.ac.uk

Undergraduates: 306 Postgraduates: 291 admissions@lincoln.ox.ac.uk

Small, central Lincoln cultivates a lower profile than many other colleges with comparable assets. The college's 15th-century buildings and beautiful library – a converted Queen Anne church – combine to produce a delightful environment in which to spend three years. Academic standards are high, particularly in arts and social science subjects, and the college finished sixth in the Norrington Table in 2013. The college's relaxed atmosphere is justly celebrated and city-centre accommodation is provided by the college for all undergraduates throughout their careers and includes rooms above the Mitre, a medieval inn. The college has a healthy rivalry with neighbouring Brasenose. Historically, Lincoln students must invite their Brasenose counterparts into the bar for free drinks every Ascension Day, in recognition of a time when a Lincoln and Brasenose student were both being chased by a town mob and the Brasenose student was denied access to Lincoln, leaving him to be killed by the mob. Graduate students have their own centre a few minutes' walk away in Bear Lane and at the EPA Science Centre close to the university science area. Finalists live in a recently refurbished complex on Museum Road, by Keble and the University Parks. Lincoln's small size and self-sufficiency have led to the college being accused of insularity. Lincoln's food is outstanding, among the best in the university. Sporting achievement is impressive for a college of this size, in part a reflection of its good facilities, with a successful cup-winning football team in recent years.

Magdalen

Oxford OX1 4AU 01865 276063 (admissions) www.magd.ox.ac.uk

Undergraduates: 411 Postgraduates: 184 admissions@magd.ox.ac.uk

Perhaps the most beautiful Oxbridge college of all, Magdalen is known around the world for its tower, its deer park and its May morning celebrations – when students threw themselves off Magdalen Bridge into the River Cherwell (this practice has now been banned after shallow water resulted in a large number of injuries). The college has shaken off its public school image to become a truly cosmopolitan place, with a large intake from overseas and one of the highest proportion of state school pupils. Magdalen's record in English, history and law is second to none, while its science park at Sandford bolsters its reputation in these subjects. The college is academically very strong and topped the Norrington Table in 2012 having come top in 2010 and fourth in 2011, with almost half of finalists last year achieving firsts. Library facilities are excellent, especially in history and law. First-year students are accommodated in the Waynflete Building and are allocated rooms in subsequent years by ballot. Undergraduates can be housed in college for the full length of their course. Rents are not cheap compared to other colleges, but there is always financial help on offer. Magdalen is also conveniently placed between the city centre and east Oxford, where there is a plethora of pubs and restaurants and a lively music scene. The college bar is one of the best in Oxford and the college is a pluralistic place, proud of its drama society and choir. In recent years the college has become particularly strong at rowing. Elsewhere, enthusiasm on the sports field makes up for a traditional lack of athletic prowess.

Mansfield

Oxford OX1 3TF   01865 270920 (admissions)   www.mansfield.ox.ac.uk
Undergraduates: 214   Postgraduates: 102   admissions@mansfield.ox.ac.uk

Mansfield's graduation to full Oxford college status in 1995 marked the culmination of a long history of development since 1886. Its spacious, attractive site is fairly central, close to the libraries, the shops, the University Parks and the river Cherwell. With just over 200 undergraduates, the community is close-knit, although this can verge on the claustrophobic. Recent moves to increase intake numbers may change that. The less intimidating atmosphere of Mansfield is, perhaps, helped by its strong representation of state-school students; among the highest ratio in the university with 78 per cent of places going to state-school applicants in the past three years. First and third years live in college accommodation while second-years live in private houses nearby. The library is open 24 hours and the JCR is among the largest of any college, while Mansfield students share Merton's excellent sports ground and have numerous college teams. In recent years the college has produced many student journalists and contributes many performers to theatre and music productions. Despite its former theological background, students are not admitted on the basis of religion and can read a wide variety of subjects. Mansfield is home to the Oxford Centre for the Environment, Ethics and Society (OCEES) and the American Studies Institute backs onto its gardens, evidence of the strong links between Mansfield and the USA, which is reflected by some 35 visiting students annually. It also spearheads the Oxford FE Initiative, which encourages applications to the university from further education colleges.

Merton

Oxford OX1 4JD   01865 276299 (admissions)   www.merton.ox.ac.uk
Undergraduates: 300   Postgraduates: 291   admissions@admin.merton.ox.ac.uk

Founded in 1264 by Walter de Merton, Bishop of Rochester and Chancellor of England, Merton is one of Oxford's oldest and most prestigious colleges. Quiet and beautiful, with the oldest quad in the university, Merton has high academic expectations of its undergraduates, normally reflected in its position at or near the top of the Norrington Table (it was third in 2013). History, English, physics, PPE and chemistry all enjoy a formidable track record. The medieval library is the envy of many other colleges. Accommodation is some of the cheapest in the university, of a good standard and offered to students for all three years. Merton's food is well-priced and among the best in the university; formal Hall is served six times a week. Kitchens are provided for second years who live in off-site accommodation while Merton's many diversions include the Merton Floats, its dramatic society, the Neave Society (politics), an excellent Christmas Ball and the peculiar Time Ceremony, which celebrates the return of GMT. Sports facilities are excellent, although participation tends to be more important than the final score.

New College

Oxford OX1 3BN	01865 279512 (admissions)	www.new.ox.ac.uk
Undergraduates: 441	Postgraduates: 285	admissions@new.ox.ac.uk

New College is actually rather old (founded in 1379 by William of Wykeham), large and much more relaxed than most expect when first confronting its daunting facade. It is a bustling place, as proud of its excellent music and its bar as of its strength in classics, chemistry, music and maths. The college topped in the Norrington Table in 2013, having been third in 2011 and 2012. Traditionally in the bottom third of colleges for attracting state-school students, the college has been making particular efforts to increase this proportion, inviting applications from schools that have never sent candidates to Oxford. The Target Schools Scheme, designed to increase applications from state schools, is well established, but the proportion of places going to state-school students remains under half. All first, second and fourth-year students can live in college and almost all of the third-years who want to live in usually can. The college's library facilities are impressive, especially in law, classics and PPE. The sports ground is nearby and includes good tennis courts. Women's sport is particularly strong, especially on the river. A sports complex, named after Brian Johnston, opened in 1997, at St Cross Road. The sheer beauty of New College remains one of its principal assets and the college gardens are a memorable sight in the summer, especially the other-worldly Mound in the heart of the college. Music is a feature of college life, and the college has some of the best practice facilities in the university. The Commemoration Ball, held every three years, is a highlight of Oxford's social calendar.

Oriel

Oxford OX1 4EW	01865 276522 (admissions)	www.oriel.ox.ac.uk
Undergraduates: 306	Postgraduates: 180	admissions@oriel.ox.ac.uk

In spite of its reputation as a rower's paradise, Oriel is a friendly, centrally located college with a strong sense of identity. The college is traditionally described as having "a strong crew spirit" reflecting its traditions on the river, and the Oriel crew have regained their position as Head of the River in the last few years after a dip in fortunes. Academic pressure is relaxed by Oxford standards and it tends to inhabit the middle reaches of the Norrington Table, though climbing to ninth in 2013. The well-stocked library is open 24 hours a day. Oriel's sporting reputation is certainly deserved and sports other than rowing are well catered for, even if their facilities are considerably farther away than the boathouse, which is only a short jog away. Accommodation is of variable quality, but Oriel can provide rooms for the duration of the course – be it three years or four – for those students who require them. Extensive accommodation is provided one mile away off the Cowley Road and at the Island Site on Oriel Street. Oriel also offers a lively drama society, a Shakespearian production taking place each summer in the front quad. College meals are generally considered cheap, too.

Pembroke

Oxford OX1 1DW	01865 276412 (admissions)	www.pmb.ox.ac.uk
Undergraduates: 354	Postgraduates: 190	admissions@pmb.ox.ac.uk

Although its alumni include such extrovert characters as Dr Johnson and Michael Heseltine, Pembroke is stereotypically one of Oxford's least dynamic colleges. The college is historically poor financially, though its modern art collection draws in visitors and revenue. Normally mid-table in terms of exam results (15th in 2013), the college had slipped to bottom place in the Norrington Table in 2012. It has Fellows and lecturers in almost all the major university subjects. Pembroke is now able to accommodate all undergraduates after a new extension opened in October 2012, and the Sir Geoffrey Arthur building on the river, ten minutes' walk from the college, offers excellent facilities; in addition to 100 student rooms there is a concert room, computer room and a multi-gym. College food is reasonable, with formal hall three times a week. Rugby and rowing are strong, with Pembroke usually behind only Oriel and Magdalen on the river, and squash and tennis courts are available at the nearby sports ground. The college's netball, football and hockey teams have all reached the finals of college cup competitions in recent years. Over the past few years Pembroke's intake has had the lowest proportion of state-school students in the university, though it is running access schemes to improve this ratio.

Queen's

Oxford OX1 4AW   01865 279161   www.queens.ox.ac.uk

Undergraduates: 348   Postgraduates: 113   admissions@queens.ox.ac.uk

One of the most striking sights of the High Street, Queen's is one of Oxford's liveliest and most attractive colleges. The college's academic record is average, occupying the lower end of the Norrington Table (26th in 2013). Modern languages, chemistry and mathematics are reckoned among the strongest subjects. Queen's does not normally admit undergraduates for the single honour schools of theology, computer science or geography, but is seen as strong in history and politics. The library is as beautiful as it is well stocked. All students are offered accommodation, first years being housed in modernist annexes in east Oxford, and the college has converted a large number of rooms into en-suite facilities. Queen's can be insular and is largely apolitical, but has a strong college enthusiasm for sport, particularly rugby and netball. The college's beer cellar is one of the most popular in the university and the JCR facilities are also better than average. An annual dinner commemorates a student who is said to have fended off a bear by thrusting a volume of Aristotle into its mouth. Postgraduates are accommodated in St Aldate's House, a modern building close to the centre of town.

St Anne's

Oxford OX2 6HS   01865 274840 (admissions)   www.st-annes.ox.ac.uk

Undergraduates: 428   Postgraduates: 281   enquiries@st-annes.ox.ac.uk

Architecturally uninspiring (a Victorian row with concrete "stack-a-studies" dropped into their back gardens), St Anne's makes up in community spirit what it lacks in awesome grandeur. One of the largest colleges, it has an above average proportion of state-school students. A women's college until 1979, its academic standing has fluctuated, having been in last place in the Norrington Table in the middle of the last decade, but now scoring around mid-table – 12th in 2013, rising from 24th the previous year. PPE is particularly strong. The library, which is now open 24 hours, is very well-stocked and is rich in law, Chinese and medieval history texts. The college has recently a strong presence in the university journalism scene, and its football teams usually do very well. Accommodation is guaranteed to all undergraduates, and the college also operates an equalisation scheme which gives grants to students wishing to live out. The college is situated to the north of the city centre. Three new accommodation blocks contain 150 student rooms, including four for disabled students, while the older rooms have been refurbished. Half of all rooms are en suite.

St Catherine's

Oxford OX1 3UJ   01865 271703 (admissions)   www.stcatz.ox.ac.uk

Undergraduates: 487   Postgraduates: 268   admissions@stcatz.ox.ac.uk

Arne Jacobsen's modernist design for "Catz", one of Oxford's youngest and largest under-graduate colleges, has attracted much attention as the most striking contrast in the university to the lofty spires of Magdalen and New College. Close to the law, English and social science faculties, the university science area and the pleasantly rural Holywell Great Meadow, St Catherine's is nevertheless only a few minutes' walk from the city centre. Academic standards are especially high in mathematics and physics but the college fell down to 22nd in the Norrington Table in 2013 (from 10th in 2012). The well-liked Wolfson library is open till midnight on most days. Rooms are small but tend to be warmer than in other, more venerable, colleges, and are now available on site for first, second and third years. There is an excellent theatre, as well as an on-site punt house, gym and squash courts. The college is host to the Cameron Mackintosh Chair of Contemporary Theatre, whose incumbents have included Meera Syal, Kevin Spacey, Arthur Miller and Sir Ian McKellen. St Catherine's has one of the best JCR facilities in Oxford.

St Edmund Hall

Oxford OX1 4AR   01865 279011 (admissions)   www.seh.ox.ac.uk

Undergraduates: 427   Postgraduates: 230   admissions@seh.ox.ac.uk

St Edmund Hall – "Teddy Hall" – has one of Oxford's smallest college sites but also one of its most populous. The college offers students the chance to live in its medieval quads right in the heart of the city. With the male/female ratio nearly equal, the college is shedding its image as a home for "hearties", and the authorities have gone out of their way to tone down younger members' rowdier excesses. Nonetheless, the sporting culture is still vigorous and the college usually does well in rugby, football and hockey. Academically, Teddy Hall tends to yo-yo between the middle and the bottom of the Norrington Table; it was 16th in 2013. But the college has some impressive names among its fellowship as well as a marvellous library, originally a Norman church. It hosts three annual prizes for journalism, including a £500 award for a student from St Edmund Hall. College accommodation is reasonable and can be offered for three years, either on the main site or in three annexes, one near the University Parks, and two on Iffley Road, where many of the rooms have private bathrooms.

St Hilda's

Oxford OX4 1DY   01865 286620 (admissions)   www.st-hildas.ox.ac.uk

Undergraduates: 395   Postgraduates: 189   college.office@st-hildas.ox.ac.uk

October 2008 marked a milestone for St Hilda's and the university as a whole, as the college welcomed its first mixed sex intake. Although the college, founded in 1893, lasted more than 100 years as an all-female institution, the governing body voted in 2006 to admit men. Male students now make up nearly half of first years. The college has long languished at the bottom end of the Norrington Table, though is slowly rising towards mid-table, being 21st in 2013. However, it is a distinctive part of the Oxford landscape and is usually well represented in university life. The library is growing fast and accommodation for readers was extended in 2005. Around 55 per cent of successful applicants to St Hilda's in the past three years have been from state-sector students, just below the average for all Oxford colleges. Accommodation is guaranteed to first years and finalists and the bar and common room have been renovated and enlarged with improved disabled access. The JCR has its own punts, which are available free for college members and their guests. Many of the rooms offer some of the best river views in Oxford. The standard of food is high, and the college has recently stopped fining students for serious misbehaviour, but rather is asking them to do community service.

St Hugh's

Oxford OX2 6LE   01865 274910 (admissions)   www.st-hughs.ox.ac.uk

Undergraduates: 430   Postgraduates: 255   admissions@st-hughs.ox.ac.uk

One of the lesser-known colleges, St Hugh's was criticised by students in 1986 when it began admitting men. There is now an equal male/female ratio, a better balance than at most Oxford colleges. Like Lady Margaret Hall, St Hugh's picturesque setting is a bicycle ride from the city centre. It is an ideal college for those seeking a place to live and study away from the madding crowd, and is well liked for its pleasantly bohemian atmosphere and beautiful gardens. Academic pressure remains comparatively low. After a brief jump up the Norrington Table the college is now back down the table, coming 24th in 2013. St Hugh's guarantees accommodation to undergraduates for all three years, although the standard of rooms is variable. Sport, particularly football, is taken quite seriously. As the college enjoys extensive grounds compared to most colleges, there is space for a croquet lawn and tennis courts. Following a £10-million donation from a Hong Kong businessman, the Dickson Poon building for the university's China Centre is due to open in Easter 2014.

St John's

Oxford OX1 3JP   01865 277317 (admissions)   www.sjc.ox.ac.uk

Undergraduates: 392   Postgraduates: 194   admissions@sjc.ox.ac.uk

St John's is one of Oxford's powerhouses, excelling in almost every field and boasting arguably the most beautiful gardens in the university. Founded in 1555 by a London merchant, it is richly endowed and makes the most of its resources to provide under-graduates with an agreeable and challenging three years. The work ethic is very much part of the St John's ethos, and academic standards are high, with English, chemistry and history among the traditional strengths, though all students benefit from the impressive library. The college is usually challenging for the top spot in the Norrington Table, and climbed back to second in 2013 after falling to 11th in 2011. As might be expected of a wealthy college, the accommodation is excellent and guaranteed for three or four years, boosted by the completion of a new quad with en-suite rooms and a new gym, café and law library. The college's riches allow it to subsidise accommodation costs, as well as providing generous book grants and prizes. St John's has a strong sporting tradition and offers good facilities, but the social scene is relatively limited. As befits such an all-round strong college, entry is fiercely competitive. The college is very close to two of Oxford's landmark pubs: the Eagle and Child and the Lamb and Flag.

St Peter's

Oxford OX1 2DL   01865 278863 (admissions)   www.spc.ox.ac.uk

Undergraduates: 336   Postgraduates: 115   admissions@spc.ox.ac.uk

Opened as St Peter's Hall in 1929, St Peter's has been an Oxford college since 1961. Its medieval, Georgian and 19th-century buildings are in the city centre and close to most of Oxford's main facilities. Though still young, St Peter's is well-represented in university life and has pockets of academic excellence, rising to tenth in the Norrington Table in 2004, although it has since fallen far back into the bottom half, making 20th in 2013. History tutoring is particularly good and accommodation is offered to students in their first and third years. Student rooms vary from traditional rooms in college to new purpose-built rooms a few minutes' walk away. The college's facilities are impressive, including one of the university's best JCRs. The college has a proud sporting heritage, being particularly strong at rugby and rowing. St Peter's is known as one of Oxford's most vibrant colleges socially. It is strong in acting and journalism, and has a recently refurbished bar, although the college has recently suffered from a severe shortage in funding.

Somerville

Oxford OX2 6HD   01865 270619 (admissions)   www.some.ox.ac.uk

Undergraduates: 394   Postgraduates: 131   secretariat@some.ox.ac.uk

The announcement, early in 1992, that Somerville was to go co-educational sparked an unusually acrimonious and persistent dispute within this most tranquil of colleges. Protests were doomed to failure, however; the first male undergraduates arrived in 1994 and men now account for half the students. The college's atmosphere appears to have survived the momentous change. The college, *alma mater* to chemistry graduate Margaret Thatcher has an average state-school representation. Accommodation, including 30 small flats, is of a reasonable standard, and was supplemented recently by a 68-room building, so that all first, third and fourth-year students can live in, as well as around three-quarters of second-years. There are kitchens in all college buildings, but hall food is towards the cheaper end of the university. Sport is strong at Somerville and the women's rowing eight usually finishes near the head of the river. The college's hockey pitches and tennis courts are nearby. The library is open 24 hours a day and is the second largest college library as well as one of the most beautiful in Oxford. The college also has an active music society and strong drama presence.

Trinity

Oxford OX1 3BH   01865 279860 (admissions)   www.trinity.ox.ac.uk

Undergraduates: 305   Postgraduates: 105   admissions@trinity.ox.ac.uk

Architecturally impressive and boasting beautiful lawns (which you can actually walk on), Trinity is one of Oxford's least populous colleges, admitting some 80 undergraduates each year. It is ideally located, beside the Bodleian, Blackwell's bookshop and the White Horse pub, a short stroll from the University Parks and the town centre. Cardinal Newman, an alumnus of Trinity, is said to have regarded Trinity's motto as "Drink, drink, drink". Academic pressure varies, but the college had recently made impressive steps up the ranks of the Norrington Table and climbing from 18th in 2012 to 4th in 2013. Trinity has shaken off its reputation for apathy, and whilst members are active in all walks of university life, the college has its own debating and drama societies, as well as sharing a fierce rivalry with neighbouring Balliol. Usually, all undergraduates are given a room on the main site in their first and second years, with the majority of third and fourth years living in a purpose-built block a mile and a half north of the main site. Students rate the food highly and the atmosphere is close-knit

University

Oxford OX1 4BH   01865 276959 (admissions)   www.univ.ox.ac.uk

Undergraduates: 372   Postgraduates: 221   admissions@univ.ox.ac.uk

University is the first Oxford college to be able to boast a former student in the Oval Office as the former President Clinton was a Rhodes Scholar at University in the late 1960s. The college is probably Oxford's oldest – a claim fought over with Merton – though highly unlikely to have been founded by King Alfred, as legend claims. Academic expectations are high and the college prospers in most subjects, though it has slid from 6th in Norrington Table in 2011 to 23rd in 2013. Physics, PPE and maths are particularly strong. Students who are accepted to read courses with a mathematical element are invited to a free week-long maths course just before the beginning of their first term, providing a head start in their studies. Accommodation is guaranteed to undergraduates for all three years, with third years lodged in an annexe in north Oxford about a mile and a half from the college site on the High Street, although the vast majority of third years choose to live out in rented accommodation. Sport is strong and University has been successful on the rugby field in the last few years, but the college has a reputation for being quiet socially. Students from the state sector can benefit from a generous bursary scheme, and its proactive access schemes in recent years have resulted in an increase to about 55 per cent of places going to state-sector students in the past three years.

Wadham

Oxford OX1 3PN   01865 277545 (admissions)   www.wadh.ox.ac.uk
Undergraduates: 448   Postgraduates: 128   admissions@wadh.ox.ac.uk

Founded by Dorothy Wadham in 1609, Wadham is known in about equal measure for its academic track record – the college generally ranks around mid-table (18th in 2013), though it was joint fourth in 2012 – and its leftist politics. The JCR – or student union as it has rebranded itself – is famously dynamic and politically active, although the breadth of political opinion is greater than its left-wing stereotype suggests. Wadham students are notoriously trendy, although some in the university find the atmosphere at the college slightly forced. That said, the college is very strong on admitting students from state schools. And for somewhere supposedly unconcerned with such fripperies, its gardens are surprisingly beautiful. The somewhat rough-hewn chapel is similarly memorable. The college has a good 24-hour library. Accommodation is guaranteed for at least two years and there are many large, shared rooms on offer. Journalism, music and drama play an important part. Highlights in the social calendar are Queer Festival, a riotous celebration of all things gay, and Wadstock, the college's open-air summer music festival. Tickets to both are always sold out.

Worcester

Oxford OX1 2HB   01865 278391 (admissions)   www.worc.ox.ac.uk
Undergraduates: 412   Postgraduates: 180   admissions@worc.ox.ac.uk

Worcester is to the west of Oxford what Magdalen is to the east: an open, rural contrast to the urban rush of the city centre. The college's rather mediocre exterior conceals a delightful environment, including some characteristically muscular Baroque Hawksmoor architecture, a garden and a lake. The college had been rising up the Norrington Table, being ranked sixth in 2011, but it fell back to 11th in 2013. The 24-hour library is strongest in the arts. Accommodation, guaranteed for two years and provided for the majority of third years, varies in quality from ordinary to conference standard in the Canal Building. More en-suite accommodation, next to the new gym, is also available. Sport plays an important part in college life, as befits the only college with playing fields on site. Worcester's hockey team is not quite what it once was, but the college has had five successful rowing teams since the first term of 2010/11 and is a noted powerhouse in men's football. Reasonably priced formal halls are available four nights a week. Like Magdalen and New, it is home to the Commemoration

Ball once every three years, a highlight of the Oxford social calendar. Of the 2012 intake, 67 per cent was from the state system, well above the average of 57.5 per cent across Oxford colleges.

Cambridge College Profiles

Christ's

Cambridge CB2 3BU   01223 334983 (admissions)   www.christs.cam.ac.uk
Undergraduates: 434   Postgraduates: 150   admissions@christs.cam.ac.uk

Christ's is the proud *alma mater* of some of Cambridge's most famous alumni including John Milton and Charles Darwin. It is one of the colleges with the widest breadth of subject strength and a reputation for natural science and maths being balanced by a thriving art scene. Christ's is well known for its Visual Arts Centre where each year they welcome a recent graduate to work as artist-in-residence (the only college to do this in the university), while the Yusuf Hamied Centre, a gallery and performance space renovated in 2008, hosts everything from Shakespeare to film screenings. Accommodation is spread between the old-world splendour of First and Second Court and modern rooms in New Court, an award-winning piece of architecture fondly dubbed "the Typewriter". Just over 40 per cent of the rooms are en suite and the newer ones have private balconies. Not many Christ's students spend a lot of time in college though, as Cambridge city centre is less than ten steps from the front gate. It's a little further to the college playing fields – about a ten-minute cycle ride – which they share with St. Catharine's. Sport flourishes and the Christ's football team has won Cuppers more times than any other college. They also have a recently renovated swimming pool in the seventeenth-century Fellows Garden, a popular place to cool off in summer.

Churchill

Cambridge CB3 0DS   01223 336202 (admissions)   www.chu.cam.ac.uk
Undergraduates: 492   Postgraduates: 238   admissions@chu.cam.ac.uk

Forty-two acres of grounds make Churchill the most spacious of the colleges, although not the most beautiful. Founded in 1958, its modern buildings allow for some of the best facilities of any Cambridge college including a new gym, a theatre-cum-cinema and a brand new music room with recording equipment. It also has squash and tennis courts and grass pitches on site. One of the major benefits of the space is the college's ability to house all students for the first three years of their undergraduate degree (which for most covers their entire time at Cambridge). Plans are well underway for a new court of 70 undergraduate rooms which will all be en suite. Some students do move out to be nearer to the centre, as Churchill is about a 15-minute cycle to town and to most lecture halls. It was the first of the all-male colleges to welcome female students in 1972, and students are allowed to walk on the grass (a rarity on Cambridge's hallowed lawns) and don't wear academic gowns when dining formally in hall. Relaxed attitudes do not mean that Churchill students slack off, however, and it has been in the Tompkins Table top ten for the past six years. With a founding remit to address the "national need for scientists and engineers and to forge links with industry", it is more science-focused and largely male-dominated, although this is beginning to change. It is proud of having one of the highest proportions of state-educated students in the university, currently 68 per cent.

Clare

Cambridge CB2 1TL   01223 333246 (admissions)   www.clare.cam.ac.uk
Undergraduates: 497   Postgraduates: 193   admissions@clare.cam.ac.uk

The second oldest college in Cambridge doesn't look it with bright, clean architecture making Clare one of the most picturesque. It is a quiet haven despite its central location on "the Backs" and its gardens are much loved by students. Music of all genres is one of Clare's strongest assets. It has a renowned college choir, a strong Music Society and live music and dance sessions. It has squash courts on site, but an oft-heard complaint is that the rest of the college's sports facilities are 15 minutes away by bike and are shared with both Peterhouse and the graduate college, Clare Hall. What it lacks in sports facilities, it makes up for in accommodation. Lerner Court, opened in 2009, sits conveniently opposite the University Library and provides en-suite undergraduate accommodation. Next door to this, Memorial Court provides more first-year accommodation and boasts its own computer facilities, common room and music room as well as the relatively new college library. While some love living close by the library, others prefer living a little further from college in "Clare Colony", about ten minutes from the main site near Magdalene. Overall, Clare is one of the most popular colleges with competition for places standing on average at eight to one.

Corpus Christi

Cambridge CB2 1RH   01223 338056 (admissions)   www.corpus.cam.ac.uk
Undergraduates: 280   Postgraduates: 161   admissions@corpus.cam.ac.uk

The only Oxbridge college to have been founded by townspeople, Corpus is one of the smallest colleges in Cambridge, giving it an intimate atmosphere. While some students find this claustrophobic, its situation on Trumpington Street makes it very easy to get out of college to the Sidgwick Site for arts students, to the Downing Site for sciences, or into the town centre. None of these is more than five minutes on a bike. Despite its size, Corpus is home to not one, but two libraries. The Taylor Library, the main one for undergraduates, was opened in 2008, while the older Parker Library holds the college's collection rare books and manuscripts. Corpus usually performs well in the Tompkins Table (but 16th in 2013), which may be to do with the college policy of partly allocating rooms based on exam results – a rule not much loved by students. All undergraduates do have the option of living in college accommodation for all three years of their degree either in the historic courts or in nearby hostels. Accommodation in hostels is very comfortable with particularly good kitchens, but sets in Old Court, whilst beautiful, lack en-suite bathrooms. State-of-the-art sports facilities are just over a mile away on the Leckhampton site, but the provision does not always translate into success on the games field. A popular bar (recently visited by alumnus Hugh Bonneville, to the student's delight) is a cosy hub of activity, as is the tiny but well provided Corpus Playroom that underwent a £100,000 refurbishment in 2011.

Downing

Cambridge CB2 1DQ   01223 334826 (admissions)   www.dow.cam.ac.uk
Undergraduates: 436   Postgraduates: 169   admissions@dow.cam.ac.uk

In some ways Downing feels like a stately home with its neo-Classical buildings set round a large quadrangle. Near to the centre of Cambridge, but not in the thick of it, the college was founded in 1800 for the study of law. Now its location – next door to the Downing Site containing many of the university's science facilities – means that it attracts many medics and engineers as well as lawyers. It's not all work though: Downing has a fearsome reputation on the river where it often wins inter-college competitions known as "Bumps", and with an on-site gym as well as tennis, netball and squash courts, it also excels off the water. In November 2012, its refurbished bar was opened, and a new accommodation block done up in Art Deco style was unveiled in July. Generally, student accommodation is known to be very high standard with first and third years housed on site, and second year accommodation a short walk away along Lensfield Road. For the less sporty, Downing has an active cultural scene with recently knighted alumnus Quentin Blake putting his name to the Blake Society for arts and, thanks to a generous grant from the Howard Foundation, the college now has a much used 120-seater theatre with its own exhibition space.

Emmanuel

Cambridge CB2 3AP   01223 334290 (admissions)   www.emma.cam.ac.uk

Undergraduates: 505   Postgraduates: 163   admissions@emma.cam.ac.uk

Founded in the 1584 with a Puritan ethic (one of the earliest alumni was John Harvard of Harvard University fame), it is one of the most openly friendly colleges. It has a strong academic reputation and regularly competes with Trinity for the Tompkins Table top spot. Thanks to being one of the wealthier colleges, "Emma" provides cheaper accommodation than most colleges and offers many generous grants for travel, books and welfare. It is also the only college to provide an in-college laundry service as part of the rent, allowing all students to take in one (large) load a week. First and third years live either in college or along its edge overlooking one of Cambridge's biggest green spaces, Parker's Piece. Second years live in rooms a maximum ten-minute cycle ride from college. With self-catering limited, many students appreciate not being far from hall where the award-winning Emmanuel chefs serve up heavily subsidised food which is reliably good, if not always exciting. The gender balance in Emmanuel is nearly 50:50, and the college fields a number of inclusive sports teams.

Fitzwilliam

Cambridge CB3 0DG   01223 332030 (admissions)   www.fitz.cam.ac.uk

Undergraduates: 461   Postgraduates: 252   admissions@fitz.cam.ac.uk

Set up on the hill next door to Murray Edwards, "Fitz" can proudly lay claim to having the highest point in Cambridge: the top of their recently built library which opened in 2010 after £5-million investment. Designed by award-winning architect Edward Cullinan, it is probably one of the most beautiful of the college buildings which are renowned more for good facilities than for looks. With just over 400 rooms in college and a further 167 in houses nearby, all undergraduates are comfortably accommodated. Fitzwilliam was originally established in 1869 in order to widen access to the university and it is known for a multicultural and mixed social environment. As home to the most drinking societies of any college and an impressive array of sports teams, Fitz enjoys something of a party reputation. The sports teams also achieve highly on the pitch and there are well-kept sports facilities close by for football, rugby, cricket, hockey and tennis, as well as a gym. All the extracurricular activity does not stop the college producing results on the academic front. While less pressurised than some of its older counterparts, a quarter of all students graduated last year with a first.

Girton

Cambridge CB3 0JG   01223 338972 (admissions)   www.girton.cam.ac.uk
Undergraduates: 499   Postgraduates: 157   admissions@girton.cam.ac.uk

Not many know that Girton is one of Cambridge's most beautiful colleges as it is a 15-minute cycle away up the Huntingdon Road. For some this is a disadvantage, but many enjoy the peace and quiet this allows. It also means that Girton's 50 acres of grounds can provide some of the best facilities of all colleges including, uniquely, an indoor swimming pool (currently being refurbished), a gym, tennis, squash and basketball courts, and an orchard that is much loved in summer. A new sports pavilion opened in 2013. The college library, extended in 2005, holds 95,000 books, making it one of the largest of all the college libraries and the college also has a strong artistic bent, housing its own museum, which dates from the involvement of the Pre-Raphaelites at its foundation. Second years have the opportunity to live closer to town in Wolfson Court, where any student can go for lunch if they don't have time to get back to the college dining hall between lectures. All other students have space to live in very reasonably priced rooms on campus and the community atmosphere this promotes is strong. Although it was originally an all-female college, since opening its doors to men in 1977, Girton's student body has become just over half male. However, the college does still boast the highest number of female Fellows of any co-ed college.

Gonville and Caius

Cambridge CB2 1TA   01223 332440 (admissions)   www.cai.cam.ac.uk
Undergraduates: 575   Postgraduates: 182   admissions@cai.cam.ac.uk

Gonville and Caius (pronounced "keys") is a tucked away just off Cambridge's market square. It was founded in 1348 as Gonville Hall which makes it one of the oldest colleges, although it was re-founded in its current state in 1557. It is usually in the middle of the Tompkins Table, coming 17th in the most recent rankings, which may in part be thanks to its stunning student library in the Cockerell Building, previously the University Library. As one of the oldest colleges, it has also held on to a somewhat old-fashioned reputation. Gowns are required in hall every night of the week whether students are attending the "informal" early hall or the later "formal" hall. Accommodation is of a high standard in parts: Harvey Court, renovated in 2011, provides 100 en-suite rooms to undergraduates while next door, the £13 million Stephen Hawking building offers another 75 en suite rooms. Both are a five minute walk from the college across the Backs. The rest of the accommodation is tucked into the college's small but stunning historic courts or a 10 minute cycle ride away near the station. The Harvey Court complex is also home to a well-equipped gym and the college has won the "Bumps" rowing competition in recent years. Every two years, Caius also holds one of Cambridge's most popular May Balls for which tickets are keenly sought.

Homerton

Cambridge CB2 8PH   01223 747252 (admissions)   www.homerton.cam.ac.uk
Undergraduates: 582   Postgraduates: 699   admissions@homerton.cam.ac.uk

Despite being situated in Cambridge since the 1890s (the college was founded in London), Homerton has only been part of the university for 37 years and officially a college since 2010. It is the largest of all the Cambridge colleges with over 1,000 students, which makes it a diverse place to be a part of. Originally it was a teacher training college and, although still home to those taking the PGCE course, Homerton does offer the full range of subjects. Like

Girton, many students comment on the college's location near the station, a relatively short cycle ride from the town centre. Its relative newness and the space it occupies mean that students enjoy an experience more akin to a campus university. Its grounds host two large halls of residence where students are accommodated for three years of undergraduate study as well as squash courts, football pitches, a rugby-training strip and a croquet lawn in summer. Sporting success has been most notable on the river in recent years where Homerton won the Pegasus Cup for the most successful college boat club in the annual "Bumps". It also boasts some eclectic musical provision with college instruments ranging from harpsichords to marimbas. Academically Homerton hovers towards the lower end of the scale but what it lacks in brains it makes up for in extra-curricular excellence.

Hughes Hall

Cambridge CB1 2EW   01223 334897 (admissions)k   www.hughes.cam.ac.uk
Undergraduates: 87   Postgraduates: 483   admissions@hughes.cam.ac.u

Starting as a small institution for women training to be teachers with just 14 students in its first intake, Hughes Hall is the oldest of the five graduate colleges in Cambridge. Named after its first principal, Elizabeth Hughes, who travelled widely abroad, it follows her precedent by welcoming one of the most internationally diverse communities of any college. Most students range between the ages of 21 and 35. Hughes is one of the sportiest colleges with two members of its prestigious boat club rowing for the university in the 2013 Boat Race. Accommodation is provided within college for all single undergraduates and affiliated students throughout their course, but family accommodation is harder to secure as the college is low on funds. A new library was built in 2008 in order to expand the existing small one, although most postgraduate students tend to gravitate toward their faculties. A big draw of the location is its proximity to a more diverse side of Cambridge on the much-loved and cosmopolitan Mill Road. Food in college is well regarded, and formal hall is a regular in the social calendar.

Jesus

Cambridge CB5 8BL   01223 339455 (admissions)   www.jesus.cam.ac.uk
Undergraduates: 518   Postgraduates: 231   undergraduate-admissions@jesus.cam.ac.uk

Jesus' extensive grounds backed by Jesus Green on one side and the town centre on the other make it quite the envy of other colleges. Although regularly in the top ten colleges academically, it is known for sporting prowess. With football, rugby and cricket pitches in college as well as ten tennis courts and three squash courts, this reputation is no surprise. It has an extensive collection of sculpture spread throughout the grounds, and is home to the university's Visual Arts Society. Also popular are the Jesus College "Chapel Sessions" – concerts of music from all eras and genres held in the college chapel, whose choir recently went on tour to India and whose services are occasionally broadcast by the BBC. Jesus is near the famous ADC theatre, home of the Cambridge Footlights with its much-loved bar, and prides itself on an extensive annual May Ball. Despite being one of the bigger colleges, teaching provision is excellent, with a high ratio of Fellows to students. Accommodation is available within the grounds for all first years and half of the third-year students, while all other students live in well-appointed college houses across the road. Many appreciate this as it fosters a more "authentic" university experience. In September 2012 the college opened the newly refurbished Chapel Court with en-suite rooms for undergraduates.

King's

Cambridge CB2 1ST   01223 331255 (admissions)   www.kings.cam.ac.uk

Undergraduates: 402 Postgraduates: 200 undergraduate.admissions@kings.cam.ac.uk

Thousands tune in to listen to the carols from King's College Chapel every Christmas Eve but King's has much more going on beside its world famous chapel. Originally founded in 1441 for boys from Eton College, it has completely thrown off the traditionalist image and is known in the town for its leftist leanings. A favourite debate among students is whether or not the hammer and sickle flag should remain hanging above the bar. It has also done away with many of the traditions associated with Cambridge life including gowns, the Fellow's "High Table" in hall and rooms allocation based on academic achievement. Formal Halls happen once a term to much acclaim and the students have pushed for much of the food to be ethically sourced. King's students are also proud of their anti-May Ball, the "King's Affair", which has been known to attract queues two hours long for tickets. The college was among the first of the all-male colleges to admit women, and it is active in trying to attract students from economically and socially disadvantaged backgrounds. The proportion of students from state schools is habitually over 70 per cent. King's also boasts an extensive library of 130,000, the highest ratio of Fellows to students and came 14th in the most recent Tompkins rankings.

Lucy Cavendish

Cambridge CB3 0BU   01223 330280 (admissions)   www.lucy-cav.cam.ac.uk

Undergraduates: 120 (women only) Postgraduates: 168 lcc-admissions@lists.cam.ac.uk

Lucy Cavendish is not just the only college for mature female students in Cambridge, it is unique for this in the UK as a whole. It works on the remit that it provides a hard-working atmosphere for high-achieving women. Although all students are over 21, the age mix is diverse with some 20 per cent over the age of 40 and some in their 60s. Although it is one of the "hill colleges", a ten-minute cycle from town up the Huntingdon Road, it is a short walk from the Maths and Veterinary faculties and the Sidgwick Site which is home to most of the arts faculties. "Lucy", as it is fondly known, is not a big college and has a close knit community. It is not a social hub – the bar is only open three nights a week – but many appreciate this as it fosters a supportive working environment. Accommodation is provided for all students either in college or in houses nearby. For sportier women, they share a boathouse with Hughes Hall, which tends to draw out a competitive streak, and have a well-equipped gym. The college is particularly strong on the medical side and also has a good reputation for social sciences and English.

Magdalene

Cambridge CB3 0AG   01223 332135 (admissions)   www.magd.cam.ac.uk

Undergraduates: 360   Postgraduates: 140   admissions@magd.cam.ac.uk

Magdalene, founded in the 1420s, is one of Cambridge's oldest colleges and one of its most traditional. Students outside the college know it for its white-tie ball, only held every three years, and its candlelit formal dinner which, priced at just £4.95 last year, is one of the cheapest in Cambridge. Living up to Cambridge clichés, its image is enhanced by becoming the last college to admit women in 1988 and in the most recent intake women outnumbered men. Rowing and rugby are strong, and the college shares sports grounds with the equally sporty St John's. It also has its own Eton fives court. On the musical side, Magdalene choir sing twice weekly in the stunning chapel, and the college offers a number of choral, music and organ scholarships. Cripps Court, which was completed in 2005, also has a 140-seat auditorium where concerts are regularly held. About 60 undergraduate rooms are in Cripps while the rest of the accommodation is either in other areas of college or in its 21 houses and hostels, none more than a two-minute walk away. Magdalene has the longest river frontage of any Cambridge college and the college punts are often booked out on a sunny afternoon. While it slipped down the most recent Tompkins Table rankings from ninth to fifteenth, Magdalene students are high achievers and in 2013, Rowan Williams, the former Archbishop of Canterbury, became Master of the college.

Murray Edwards

Cambridge CB3 0DF   01223 762229 (admissions)   www.murrayedwards.cam.ac.uk
Undergraduates: 386 (women) Postgraduates: 93 admissions@murrayedwards.cam.ac.uk

Things are not always quick to change in Cambridge and although Murray Edwards benefitted from a £30 million endowment and a new name in 2008, it is still often called by its unofficial previous name "New Hall". One of three female-only colleges in Cambridge, Murray Edwards enjoys a less stridently feminist reputation than the other two. It has been 24th for the last two years in the Tompkins Table. Students at Murray Edwards enjoy its atmosphere and it is known for being a friendly, relaxed place with airy modern buildings and informal gardens. The distinctive dome sits above the light dining hall where food is good. Strong on the sporting front, the college won the Pegasus cup for most successful college boat crew in 2011 and many of the students fill teams on a university level. Unlike many colleges, Murray Edwards does not have a chapel or any religious stance adding to the egalitarian ambiance. It is the proud owner of the second largest collection of contemporary women's art in the world and also has an onsite art studio with dark room facilities. The bar is unusually split over two levels and while many students like to get out of college to socialise, they do put on popular events such as "Band in the Bar". Accommodation is comfortable and, with 40 per cent of new rooms being en suite, not many have to share with anyone.

Newnham

Cambridge CB3 9DF   01223 335783 (admissions)   www.newn.cam.ac.uk
Undergraduates: 400 (women)   Postgraduates: 222   admissions@newn.cam.ac.uk

The first college to be set up for women to allow them to attend lectures at Cambridge, Newnham boasts a stellar line up of alumni including Sylvia Plath, Germaine Greer and Mary Beard. It remains a women-only college and with an all female fellowship. In fact, Newnhamites are a diverse bunch and take a lively role in university life. Sports teams are enthusiastic, if not always high achieving. The 18-acre grounds mean that all sports pitches and tennis courts are on site alongside the much loved gardens whose stunning lawns are a favourite fixture for students in summer. Also in the gardens is "The Old Labs" performing arts centre which is home to Newnham's drama and music groups, as well as the college's two grand pianos. Weekly lunchtime recitals are held in term time. All students who want to live in college can and take full advantage of the three common rooms and the 50-inch plasma TV in the Buttery. The college is best known for its strength in arts subjects – not a surprise as the lecture halls of Sidgwick are a minute from the college doors.

Pembroke

Cambridge CB2 1RF   01223 338154 (admissions)   www.pem.cam.ac.uk

Undergraduates: 428   Postgraduates: 186   adm@pem.cam.ac.uk

Tucked into the corner of Pembroke and Trumpington Streets, the grounds of Pembroke are an oasis in the midst of the city bustle. With a stunning chapel – Christopher Wren's first commission – and a 17th-century library, Pembroke is one of Cambridge's most beautiful colleges off the tourist trail. It is gradually shaking off a more traditionalist image. Men and women have nearly reached parity (54 per cent male last year) and the state to public school ratio sticks at around 60:40. The conventional Cambridge sports of rowing and rugby are strong, but the arts are increasingly becoming a regular feature of college life. The Old Library holds regular concerts as well as comedy "smokers" and the Pembroke Players is a well-known drama society which has counted Eric Idle, Peter Cooke, Bill Oddie and Tim Brooke-Taylor among its numbers. It has ranked in the top five of the Tompkins Table for the past three years and is traditionally known for its strength in sciences. It helps that it is a two-minute walk from the main science faculties. Pembroke is known for great food in a canteen, but accommodation is of variable quality. Kitchen facilities are basic and while many undergraduates can live in college, second years and some third years live out in pokey college hostels. Freshers live in the recently done up Foundress Court where rooms are spacious and modern. Pembroke also has a lively media with a student poetry journal *The Pem* as well as a bi-termly magazine.

Peterhouse

Cambridge CB2 1RD   01223 338223 (admissions)   www.pet.cam.ac.uk

Undergraduates: 260   Postgraduates: 108   admissions@pet.cam.ac.uk

Peterhouse is both the smallest and the oldest undergraduate college and is often perceived as traditionalist and fairly elite. However, this image belies a college which accepted 70 per cent of its state-school applicants in the last cycle (unusual among Cambridge colleges) and has male to female ratio of 60:40. Some find the small bounds of the college suffocating but the size of the student body means that rooms are generally large and at most ten minutes' walk from the college. It is particularly strong in the arts and performs very highly in Arts Tripos, but it does not have very good provision for scientists and this can pull it down the Tompkins Table, though in 2013 it rose to tenth. Beyond lectures, it has a rich array of societies to join: the Peterhouse Politics Society, the Heywood Society (resident dramatic society), the intellectual Perne Club, the scientific Kelvin Club, and the Music Society. However, with not many undergraduates to chose from and sports pitches shared with two other colleges, it is not known for its sport. Peterhouse students tend to be an eclectic lot and the cosy bar is much enjoyed by all. The 13th-century candle-lit formal is also a very Cantabrigian treat.

Queens'

Cambridge CB3 9ET   01223 335540 (admissions)   www.queens.cam.ac.uk

Undergraduates: 522   Postgraduates: 372   admissions@queens.cam.ac.uk

Although Queens' has one of the largest undergraduate bodies, its provision of on-site accommodation for all three years of a student's degree means that Queens' students all know each other well. Walnut Tree Court and Old Court are as idyllic as their names sound and have rooms highly sought after by third years. Most first years are housed across the Mathematical Bridge, designed by Sir Isaac Newton, in the noisier Cripps, also home to the large and popular bar. A large student body means many student societies. Sport ranges from a strong rowing team to a tiddlywinks club, and a multi-gym, squash and badminton courts in college complement the spacious sports ground they share with Robinson just under a mile away. The library is housed in the Old Chapel and apart from the occasional bell tolling is a peaceful place to work. Over half of the undergraduate intake comes from the state sector and generally around 45 per cent of the intake is female. In summer, Queens' students enjoy full use of the college punts, often with a stop at The Anchor pub just across the river. They also have an active drama society known as "BATS".

Robinson

Cambridge CB3 9AN   01223 339143 (admissions)   www.robinson.cam.ac.uk
Undergraduates: 401   Postgraduates: 108   apply@robinson.cam.ac.uk

Robinson is probably best known for its austere red brick architecture, which has led some to dub it "the car park". What the bricks hide are excellent facilities – a large auditorium, well-loved gardens and lake, the popular "Red Brick Café" and for those in the musical know, an outstanding chapel organ. Founded just over 40 years ago, Robinson's youthful atmosphere is also an unpretentious one. It typically accepts around 60 per cent of its intake from state schools and a quarter of the fellows are women. While rooms are comfortable and spacious with two recently built graduate buildings and 170 en-suite rooms, Robinson also commands the highest rents of all colleges and some students bemoan the lack of travel grants to explore studies abroad. On the plus side, the food is inexpensive and has been named amongst the best in Cambridge by *Varsity*, the student newspaper. The sport's grounds (shared with Queens') are less than a mile from the main site and the proximity to the University Real Tennis courts and the Blues rugby ground attracts a sporty student body. Academically it sits comfortably around the middle of the Tompkins Table most years, though towards the lower end most recently.

St Catharine's

Cambridge CB2 1RL   01223 338319 (admissions)   www.caths.cam.ac.uk
Undergraduates: 479   Postgraduates: 157   undergraduate.admissions@caths.cam.ac.uk

Not among the best known of Cambridge college, "Catz" as it is known, occupies a prominent position on King's Parade and dates from the 15th century. It has not one but two libraries on the belief of its original benefactor, Robert Woodlark, that books were central to learning. First-year rooms are all provided on site with a few en suite, while in second year, students move out to the popular flats in the St Chad's complex. Third years move back into college with a pick of the best rooms, some of which are extensive, and a preference is given to those who performed well in exams. It is known for its football squad and is the only college in the university to own an Astroturf pitch. It has also provided Blues rowers and, although not one of the biggest colleges, manages to field a surprising number of sports teams that vary in talent. It is an ethically minded place, too, proudly laying claim to being the first college in the town to be awarded Fair Trade status in 2006.

St Edmund's

Cambridge CB3 0BN   01223 336086 (admissions)   www.st-edmunds.cam.ac.uk
Undergraduates: 118   Postgraduates: 282   admissions@st-edmunds.cam.ac.uk

With a student body coming from over 50 different countries, St Edmund's can rightly lay claim to being the most international of the Cambridge colleges. Not far from the city centre to the northwest, it is the most central of the graduate colleges and also the sportiest. "Eddies" boys often make up a substantial number of the Blues rugby and rowing teams and the college rugby squad recently triumphed over Jesus in the 2012 "Cuppers" competition. The gym, which was refurbished and reopened in summer 2011, is well equipped. This was part of a development plan that reached its final stages in 2007 and saw the opening of three new accommodation blocks including the Brian Heap Building whose dining room-kitchens and en-suite facilities put rooms there in high demand. St Edmund's is one of the most flexible of colleges for accommodation with a number of small maisonettes for couples and students with children, and a good number of rooms for students with physical disabilities. Social life is vibrant for a primarily graduate college with a couple of "bops" each term, a good bar, free cake and tea at four o'clock on Sundays and regular international movie nights.

St John's

Cambridge CB2 1TP   01223 338703 (admissions)   www.joh.cam.ac.uk
Undergraduates: 586   Postgraduates: 234   admissions@joh.cam.ac.uk

St John's has quite a reputation in many fields. While not always academically brilliant – it has maintained a middling position in recent years' Tompkins Table – it is known for stunning grounds, excellent facilities, a vibrant if laddish social life and for being fierce on the sports field. The "Red Boys" rugby team consistently win various inter-college competitions and fill up many of the spaces on the Varsity rugby team (the team fielded by the university against Oxford). The college grounds straddle the River Cam which becomes blocked by punts on the night of the famous St John's May Ball as those not lucky enough to get tickets crowd into boats to watch the fireworks display. The chapel is home to a strong musical tradition and singers from all over the university audition for places in the John's choir. It is one of the biggest colleges, but this has not helped it to throw off its largely "posh boy" public school reputation. It has a state school intake of just over half, and it is a male dominated institution with the proportion of females reaching just over a third. Accommodation is of a high standard and under a new system, Johnians are allowed to keep their rooms year round (as opposed to moving out during the holidays). Food is also well renowned. The Buttery sells a range of takeaway food as well as steak dinners for the princely sum of £3 and invitations to John's formal are coveted university-wide.

Selwyn

Cambridge CB3 9DQ   01223 335896 (admissions)   www.sel.cam.ac.uk
Undergraduates: 389   Postgraduates: 143   admissions@sel.cam.ac.uk

Although some students complain that Selwyn is "miles" from a supermarket and other town facilities, it is only tucked just behind the university's Sidgwick Site. The slight distance from the centre gives it a quiet vibe that is enhanced by the lovely gardens. The location is also ideal for arts and humanities students who can roll out of bed into their faculty lecture halls next door. As one of the first colleges to admit women, it has maintained a nearly gender equal balance and is proud to have been the first college to appoint a female head porter in 2009. Accommodation for all students is either in the imposing red brick buildings in college or in Cripps Court over the road. A couple of hostels (essentially large houses) are also available for second and third years and are a popular choice. Food in hall rates quite low on the gourmet scale and the college has a popular, and fairly cheap, bar which was redecorated last year. Selwyn isn't always scrapping for the top places in inter-college sports competitions (though they don't do badly), but sports are strongly promoted through the Hermes and Sirens Club, longstanding male and female sports clubs, which fund bursaries and various teams. The college share sports fields with King's towards Grantchester. Selwyn is also well known for its Winter Ball – a high point on the Cambridge social calendar.

Sidney Sussex

Cambridge CB2 3HU   01223 338872 (admissions)   www.sid.cam.ac.uk
Undergraduates: 368   Postgraduate: 168   admissions@sid.cam.ac.uk

As one of the smaller colleges, Sidney students all tend to know each other and the college has an almost familial atmosphere. Some like this while others find it a bit much and Sidney students are certainly an active bunch outside of college. Sidney's location in the centre of town is a draw. Accommodation is split between hostels around town and rooms in college. The latter tend to be smaller unless you get a much-coveted room in Garden Court, which have enormous bay windows. Although Sidney faces onto Sidney Street, it is only a short walk down to Jesus Green and the boathouse on the other side of the Cam. Sidney boats are known to be keen and often come not far from the top in "Bumps". For all other sports, the college shares a sports ground with Christ's, a ten-minute cycle away. It is also a very short distance from Cambridge's main theatre and home to the Footlights, the ADC, and plays are also put on in the quiet gardens behind Front Court in summer. When not acting or rowing, students are often in the college bar which, along with Emmanuel, is one of the last student run college bars in the university. As a result, prices are cheap and "bops" are rowdy. Academically, it tends toward the middle of the Tompkins Table and took 19th place in the most recent results.

Trinity

Cambridge CB2 1TQ   01223 338422 (admissions)   www.trin.cam.ac.uk
Undergraduates: 676   Postgraduates: 263   admissions@trin.cam.ac.uk

Trinity is big in all ways. It is the richest Cambridge college and it also has the largest number of undergraduates about two thirds of whom are men. With an endowment almost as big as all the other colleges put together, it can afford to fund generous travel grants and maintains its facilities well. Scholars have first choice of rooms, but most are large and nearly half are en suite so there isn't much concern about this prioritising. Accommodation is also among the cheapest in Cambridge as it is heavily subsidised. In the last results, Trinity came top of the Tompkins Table for the third year in a row and nearly 42 per cent of students graduated with a first in 2013. Food is very good and one kind benefactor gave Trinity its own ice cream chef. Sports are strong, and the college provides a gym on site as well as hockey, tennis, netball, rugby, football, basketball and cricket pitches a short walk away. The grounds stretching down to the backs and famous Christopher Wren library make Trinity a tourist hotspot, but it is well policed by their bowler-hatted porters who keep the college quiet in exam term. With all the grandeur, it may not be a surprise that the number of students from the state sector has been historically low, hovering at around 40 per cent. Trinitarians tend to be regarded as falling into two categories: hard workers (it is strong on maths) and more fun-loving types. The tickets to the college's May Ball are one of the hottest sells in town.

Trinity Hall

Cambridge CB2 1TJ   01223 332535 (admissions)   www.trinhall.cam.ac.uk

Undergraduates: 387   Postgraduates: 183   admissions@trinhall.cam.ac.uk

Glorying in the nickname "Tit Hall", this small college is one of Cambridge's oldest. Thanks to its size, students enjoy living in a close community right on the river with a two-minute walk to town in one direction and a short cycle ride to the University Library in the other. It is back in third place in the Tompkins Table, having fallen to eighth in 2012, and it regularly achieves highly on the academic front. Although it was founded for the study of law, it is more or less 50:50 ratio of science to arts students and just over half the undergraduate body is female. For such a small college (and particularly small bar), it is a hive of activity socially. On the extra-curricular front it is one of the few colleges to field its own newspaper, *Hallmark*, and is home to one of the better college drama groups, the Preston Society. All undergraduates are provided with accommodation for all years of their course, including fourth years, and rents are very reasonable. The Wychfield Site, with its 90 en-suite rooms and pretty gardens, was opened in 2007, and is an especially popular choice. Most students continue to be housed in older accommodation in college. In the summer, the students not involved in the competitive and well-organised boat club, enjoy taking out the college punts for some more relaxed boating right from the college gate.

Wolfson

Cambridge CB3 9BB   01223 335918   www.wolfson.cam.ac.uk

Undergraduates: 172   Postgraduates: 575   ugadministrator@wolfson.cam.ac.uk

Originally founded as University College in 1965, Wolfson became known by its current name following a generous grant from the Wolfson Foundation. It is primarily for graduate students and has a significant number of post-doctoral research fellowships. However, it also welcomes around 170 mature or affiliated undergraduates and is one of the few colleges to offer part-time study. Like Hughes Hall, it basks in an internationally diverse community. The atmosphere is different to many Cambridge colleges as it does not uphold many of the university's better known customs like having a Fellow's table in hall. Also, rather than a Master, it is headed by a President. The position is currently held by the eminent historian Richard Evans. Not known to be one of the most beautiful colleges architecturally, it does boast tranquil and well-tended gardens. Its location out of town adds to the peaceful atmosphere, although some gripe that it is nearer to the M11 than to Cambridge. In reality, it is a 20-minute walk from the centre of town. Because of its diverse community, it also offers a packed cultural calendar including jam sessions, art film society screenings, lunchtime talks and many language classes. Accommodation is in either the "old" (1970s) blocks or "new" (1990s) buildings, both of which are seen as functional rather than glamorous. Most students can be accommodated, though, and there is even space for some couples.

14 University Profiles

This chapter provides profiles of every university that appears in *The Times and Sunday Times* league table. In addition there are profiles for Norwich University of the Arts and the Royal Agricultural University, both newly created as universities but which could not fairly be compared with generalist universities included in the league table, and the two major suppliers of part-time degrees, the Open University and Birkbeck College. There are also profiles for those institutions which did not release data for use in the table. However, we do not have separate profiles for specialist colleges and medical schools, such as the Royal College of Music (**www.rcm.ac.uk**) and St George's, University of London medical school (**sgul.ac.uk**), or institutions that only offer postgraduate degrees, such as Cranfield University (**www.cranfield.ac.uk**) and London Business School (**www.lbs.ac.uk**). Their omission is no reflection on their quality, simply a function of their particular roles. A number of additional institutions with degree-awarding powers are listed at the end of the book with their contact details.

Comments on campus facilities apply to the universities' own sites only. Newer universities, in particular, operate "franchised" courses at further education colleges, which are likely to have lower levels of provision. Prospective applicants should check out the library and social facilities before accepting a place away from the parent institution.

The profiles contain valuable information about each university. You can find contact details, including the postal address, the telephone number for admission enquiries, email or web addresses for admissions and prospectus enquiries, web addresses for the university, the students' union and for sports facilities, and any university grouping that the institution is affiliated to (Russell Group, etc.). In addition, each profile provides information under the following headings:

» **The Times and Sunday Times rankings** For the overall ranking, the figure in bold refers to the university's position in 2014 and the figure in brackets to 2013. All the information listed is taken from the main league table. See chapter 4 for explanations and the sources of the data.
» **Undergraduates** The first figure is for full-time undergraduates. The second figure (in brackets) gives the number of part-time undergraduates. The figures are for 2011–12, and are the most recent provided by Higher Education Statistics Agency (HESA).

- » **Postgraduates** The first figure is for full-time postgraduates. The second figure (in brackets) gives the number of part-time postgraduates. The figures are for 2011–12, and are the most recent provided by HESA.
- » **Mature students** The percentage of undergraduate entrants who were 21 or over at the start of their studies in 2012. The figures are from UCAS (except for Buckingham and Birkbeck, which are for 2011–12, as calculated by HESA).
- » **Overseas students** The number of undergraduate overseas students (both EU and non-EU) as a percentage of full-time undergraduates. The figures relate to 2011–12, and are based on HESA data.
- » **Applications per place** The number of applicants per place for 2012 as calculated by UCAS.
- » **From state-school sector** The number of young full-time undergraduate entrants from state schools or colleges in 2011–12 as a percentage of total young entrants. The figures are published by HESA.
- » **From working-class homes** The number of young full-time undergraduate entrants in 2011–12 whose parental occupations are skilled, manual, semi-skilled or unskilled (NS-SEC classes 4–7) as a percentage of total young entrants. The figures are published by HESA.
- » **Accommodation** The information was obtained through a survey made of all university accommodation services, and their help in compiling this information is gratefully acknowledged.

Undergraduate fees and bursaries

Details of tuition fees and financial support for students starting in 2014–15 are given wherever possible. Tuition fees for international students refer to 2013–14. For Scotland and Northern Ireland the figures refer to 2013–14, while for Wales details of government support for students are for 2013–14, as figures for 2014–15 were not available at the time this book went to press. It is of the utmost importance that you check university websites for the latest information. In England the Office for Fair Access (**www.offa.org.uk**) publishes "Access Agreements" for every English university. Each agreement outlines the university's plans for fees, financial support and measures being taken to widen access to that university and to encourage students to complete their courses. The agreements are available on the OFFA website. In the summary given on the profile pages:

- » NSP stands for National Scholarship Programme, a scheme of awards at English universities part-funded by the Government. They are only available to English students from households with a family income of below £25,000. English universities offer a limited number of NSP awards according to additional criteria that they select.
- » RUK describes students from the Rest of the UK at Scottish and Northern Irish universities. Fees and financial support given by universities differs from those available to students resident in Scotland or Northern Ireland.

Universities also offer a variety of scholarships and bursaries, for example, in particular subjects or to help people from particular places. There is not space in this book to give full details of such awards, and, again, you are advised to check university websites for details.

University of Aberdeen

Aberdeen took 500 additional students in 2012 – an increase of more than 20 per cent – despite receiving fewer applications. The university had been enjoying record demand for places and, with eight applicants to the place in 2011, calculated that there was room to expand without affecting standards. The extra students were attracted partly by a new range of "Sixth Century Courses", which include cross-disciplinary degrees such as risk in society, sustainability and the digital society. They provide the option of "sustained study programmes" in a language, computing or a business-related subject. The aim is to give graduates broader knowledge and more intellectual flexibility. The university has added 100 academic posts to deliver the new courses, as well as strengthening its research.

The early years of the university's sixth century have also seen a series of big capital projects. Aided by one the most successful fundraising schemes at any UK university, Aberdeen spent £28 million on a sports centre that opened in 2009 and £57 million on a futuristic new library that followed in 2011. The Sir Duncan Rice Library (named after the Principal who commissioned it) has since been named one of the 12 best new buildings in Scotland, and collecting an award from the Royal Institute of British Architects. Student services had already been transformed and the redeveloped Butchart Centre has given the Student's Association a new social focus on campus. In all, the university invested £229 million on capital projects in ten years up to 2009 and expects to spend another £148 million by 2019.

Aberdeen registered some good results in the 2008 Research Assessment Exercise, when more than half of the work submitted was judged to be world-leading or internationally excellent. Health services research and theology, divinity and religious studies produced the best results in the UK, while computer science and informatics, anthropology, English and history also did particularly well. Research income grew by more than a third over five years, cementing Aberdeen's ambitions to be recognised among the top 100 universities in the world.

Female students now outnumber the men, but Aberdeen still considers itself a "balanced" university because roughly half of its students study medicine, science or engineering, half the arts or social sciences. Even on traditional degree programmes, students can try out three or four subjects before committing themselves at the end of their first or even second year. The modular system is so flexible that the majority of students change their intended degree before graduation.

Aberdeen established the English-

King's College
Aberdeen AB24 3FX

01224 272090/91 (admissions)
sras@abdn.ac.uk
www.abdn.ac.uk
www.ausa.org.uk
Affiliation: none

The Times and Sunday Times **Rankings**
Overall Ranking: **40** (39)

Student satisfaction:	=57	(81.7%)
Research quality:	34	(20.7%)
Entry standards:	19	(443)
Student–staff ratio:	=36	(16.4)
Services & facilities/student:	47	(£1,599)
Expected completion rate:	88	(81.6%)
Good honours:	=37	(72%)
Graduate prospects:	21	(75.8%)

speaking world's first chair in medicine and has produced its share of advances since. The Institute of Medical Sciences, which has brought together all Aberdeen's work in this area, boasts high quality laboratory facilities. Another £20 million was invested in the Suttie Centre, a teaching and learning centre for medical education and clinical skills. Education is now also considered among Aberdeen's strengths, while biological sciences have developed considerably in recent years, becoming second only to the social sciences in terms of size. Biomedicine is particularly strong, and the university's links with the oil industry show in geology's high reputation.

Today's university is a fusion of two ancient institutions which came together in 1860. With King's College dating back to 1495 and Marischal College following almost a century later, Aberdeen likes to boast that for 250 years it had as many universities as the whole of England. The original King's College buildings are the focal point of an appealing campus, complete with cobbled main street and some sturdily handsome Georgian buildings, about a mile from the city centre.

Medicine is at Foresterhill, a 20-minute walk away, adjoining the Aberdeen Royal Infirmary. Buses link the two sites with the Hillhead residential complex. Almost a third of all students come from the north of Scotland, but taking one in six from

outside Britain ensures a cosmopolitan atmosphere. Students from England and the 120 nationalities from further afield are generally prepared for Aberdeen's remote location and, although the winters are long, the climate is warmer than the uninitiated might expect. Transport links are good. Students find the city lively and welcoming, but expensive: the JobLink service provides a good selection of part-time employment.

The students' centre in The Hub brings together dining and retail outlets with support services, including the accommodation office and the careers service. There is also first-class sports facilities, which have improved further with the opening of the Aberdeen Sports Village, part-funded by the City Council and Sports Scotland. The university ICT network has over 1,500 computers for student use. All new undergraduates are guaranteed housing.

Undergraduate Fees and Bursaries
» Fees for Scottish and EU students 2014–15   No fee
» Fees for Non-Scottish UK (RUK) students for 2014–15: £9,000 capped at a maximum of £27,000 regardless of course length, with the exception of enhanced degrees and medicine.
» Fees for international students 2014–15   £12,600–£15,700
    Medicine   £27,800
» For RUK students (2013–14): £2,000 accommodation bursary in Year 1. Access scholarships: household income below £20K, £3,000 for three years; household income £20K–£30K, £2,000 for three years. Merit scholarships (AAB at A level or equivalent) excluding medicine, £3,000 for four years.
» Range of other scholarships and bursaries available.

Students		
Undergraduates:	**10,620**	**(1,335)**
Postgraduates:	**2,185**	**(1,375)**
Mature students:	13.6%	
Overseas students:	21.5%	
Applications per place:	6.7	
From state-sector schools:	81.7%	
From working-class homes:	24.4%	
Satisfaction with students' union	64%	

For detailed information about sports facilities:
www.abdn.ac.uk/sportandexercise

Accommodation
Number of places and costs refer to 2013–14
University-provided places: about 2,717
Percentage catered: 14%
Catered costs: £149–£164 a week (39 weeks).
Self-catered costs: £89–£142 a week (39–48 weeks).
First-year students are guaranteed accommodation.
International students: as above.
Contact: studentaccomm@abdn.ac.uk

University of Abertay Dundee

Abertay has built an international reputation in computer arts and games design – so much so that it has a partnership with Peking University (one of China's top two) for computer games. It is the only UK university with official accreditation for both computer games technology and computer arts: the university hosts the first Interactive Media Academy in the UK and also the first national Centre for Excellence in Computer Games Education. Its courses hold five of only twelve degree accreditations in these areas awarded by Skillset, the Government-sponsored training council for the creative industries. Staff and students in the Institute for Art, Media and Computer Games work with industrial partners from across the broadcast, interactive and wider digital media sectors.

But Abertay resists any suggestion that it is a one-trick academic pony. It launched Scotland's first degrees in bioinformatics and biotechnology, and now claims to be a leader for teaching and research in environmental science. Nevertheless, it occupies a surprisingly low position in *The Times and Sunday Times* league table.

The university doubled in size during the 1990s and has grown further since tuition fees were abolished for Scottish students, but there are still only 5,500 students in total. Most are in Dundee, but Abertay's degrees are also taught as far away as Malaysia and China. The university attracted two huge increases in applications in the early years of this decade and enjoyed a more modest rise in 2012, when the numbers enrolling dropped slightly. There have been occasional suggestions that Abertay might merge with neighbouring Dundee University – most recently in 2011 – but it is now firmly on an independent path.

The former Dundee Institute of Technology had already established its academic credentials when its university title arrived in 1994, with teaching in economics rated more highly than in some of Scotland's elite universities. Subsequent assessments were solid, without living up to that early promise in most subjects. Abertay plays to its strengths with a limited range of courses, and is not shy about its achievements. Among them is a high-tech approach that permeates all five of the university's schools, while spending on libraries and IT has created one of the highest ratios of PC per student in Britain, providing almost one computer for every four students.

A series of specialist research centres has been established in areas as diverse as wood technology, urban water systems, bioinformatics and environmental sciences.

Bell Street

Dundee DD1 1HG

01382 308080
sro@abertay.ac.uk
www.abertay.ac.uk
www.uadsa.com
Affiliation: million+

The Times and Sunday Times Rankings

Overall Ranking: **105** (112)

Student satisfaction:	=103	(78.1)
Research quality:	=83	(3.0%)
Entry standards:	=73	(315)
Student–staff ratio:	117	(24)
Services & facilities/student:	=85	(£1,249)
Expected completion rate:	118	(71.6%)
Good honours:	=85	(59.9%)
Graduate prospects:	53	(67%)

The university opened Europe's first dedicated computer games and digital entertainment research centre, and more recently established a centre for research into systems pathology. Environmental sciences, urban water engineering and intelligent systems engineering produced the best scores in the 2008 research assessments. Those for law and psychology were the best at any post-1992 Scottish university.

All the university's teaching and learning buildings are within five minutes' walk of each other, mainly in the centre of Dundee. They are modern and functional, with new facilities being added gradually, such as the innovative White Space facility, the university's flagship creative learning and working environment, where students study alongside industry professionals who are working on real commercial or broadcast projects. A 500-bed student village opened in 2010 and new premises for a £5-million Business Prototyping Project to support the UK's creative industries followed in 2011.

Entrance requirements have been rising, although for most courses other than high-demand areas such as computer games, they are still modest. Well-qualified A-level students are eligible for direct entry into second year. Degrees are predominantly vocational, with more subjects being added every year. Food and consumer sciences, creative sound production, and ethical hacking and digital forensics are recent examples. All courses can be taken on a part-time basis, and new programmes aim to offer students the chance to spend at least 30 per cent of their time in industry.

Undergraduates take a maximum of eight modules a year, completing a Certificate of Higher Education after one year, a diploma after two, an ordinary degree after three, or honours in four years. The dropout rate has been improving and is now one in ten – considerably better than average for its courses and entry qualifications. Abertay is piloting problem- and work-based approaches to learning across a wide range of courses, focusing on real-world issues and teamwork.

Dundee has a large student population and the cost of living is modest. Around 27 per cent of the undergraduates are over 21 on entry, many living locally. All first years are given priority for accommodation.

Undergraduate Fees and Bursaries

» Fees for Scottish and EU students 2013–14   No fee
» Fees for Non-Scottish UK (RUK) students for 2013–14   £7,000 capped at £21,000 for all courses.
» Fees for international students 2013–14   £10,250
» For RUK students (2013–14): household income below £25K, annual bursary £1,500.
» Academic merit or personal achievement in music or sport scholarships, £1,500 a year.
» Check the university's website for the latest information.

Students

Undergraduates:	4,245	(220)
Postgraduates:	325	(140)
Mature students:	26.7%	
Overseas students:	12.2%	
Applications per place:	5.2	
From state-sector schools:	95.9%	
From working-class homes:	32.6%	
Satisfaction with students' union	72%	

For detailed information about sports facilities:
www.sport.abertay.ac.uk/

Accommodation

Number of places and costs refer to 2013–14
University-provided places: 668
Percentage catered: 0%
Self-catered costs: £59–£111 a week (38, 42 or 51 weeks).
New first years are given priority provided conditions are met.
Some residential restrictions.
International students: prioritised by distance from Dundee.
Contact: residences@abertay.ac.uk

Aberystwyth University

Aberystwyth has set itself the goals of becoming one of the top 30 universities in the UK and the top 250 in the world by 2017. But it has dropped 35 places and out of the top 80 in *The Times and Sunday Times* league table, mainly because of unusually low student satisfaction scores. The university has performed well in the National Student Survey in previous years, and it will be hoping that an emphasis on the student experience in a new strategic plan will pay dividends. However, both the number of applications and eventual enrolments dropped significantly in 2012, in spite of the fee concessions offered to Welsh students, who make up about a third of Aber's intake. Welsh-medium teaching is thriving, with more courses available in the language.

The university is investing over £48 million in its residences and teaching facilities to ensure it maintains its popularity. The prospectus includes QR (quick response) codes giving people with smart phones direct links to a website or video presentation. The attractive seaside location remains a draw for applicants and there had been strong growth in the demand for places over several years before the fees went up. Although the oldest of the Welsh universities, Aberystwyth has long prided

itself on a modern outlook: it was among the pioneers of the modular degree system and allowed students flexibility between subjects even before that. Uniquely in the UK, every student is offered the opportunity of a year's work experience in commerce, industry or the public sector, either at home or abroad. Those who have taken advantage of the scheme have achieved better than average degrees and enhanced their employment prospects.

Over 90 per cent of the undergraduates come from state schools or colleges – a higher proportion than the mix of subjects would imply – but the proportion of entrants from working-class homes had dropped below 30 per cent in the latest survey. The projected dropout rate of 10 per cent is one of the lowest in Wales.

Recent developments include a building on the main Penglais campus for the Institute of Biological, Environmental and Rural Sciences, which serves more than 1,000 undergraduate and research students and has a remit to look for creative solutions to some of the major challenges facing the world in sustainable land use, climate change, renewable energy and the security of food and water supplies. The institute, which has a link with Bangor University, has over 300 staff and an annual budget in excess of £25 million, making it one of the largest groups of scientists and support staff working in this field in Europe.

Old College
King Street
Aberystwyth
Ceredigion SY23 2AX

01970 622021 (admissions)
ug-admissions@aber.ac.uk
www.aber.ac.uk
www.abersu.co.uk
Affiliation: none

The Times and Sunday Times **Rankings**
Overall Ranking: **82** (47)

Student satisfaction:	109	(76.9%)
Research quality:	=35	(20.3%)
Entry standards:	=59	(327)
Student–staff ratio:	=72	(19.4)
Services & facilities/student:	96	(£1,186)
Expected completion rate:	=56	(86.5%)
Good honours:	92	(58.5%)
Graduate prospects:	101	(53.9%)

Aber has the widest range of land-related courses in the UK.

Other additions to the university estate include a new student health centre and crèche, new psychology and education buildings, as well as a new phenomics research facility on the Gogerddan campus. A £1.5-million Student Welcome Centre, opened in 2009, bringing together services such as the fees office and student support services that were previously distributed around the campus or in town.

Entrance scholarships and bursaries are available in a range of subjects, even though Welsh students have been spared the full impact of top-up fees. Aber boasts one of higher education's most informative websites and also publishes a special guide for parents. There is 24-hour access to the computer network, and the four university libraries are complemented by the National Library of Wales. International politics produced the best results in the 2008 research assessments, when computer science was the leader in Wales, while geography and earth sciences, Welsh, and theatre, film and television also did well.

The town of Aberystwyth is compact and travel to other parts of the UK slow, so applicants should be sure that they will be happy to spend three years or more in a tight-knit community. The students' guild is the largest entertainment venue in the region, and the prize-winning arts centre has been extended at a cost of £3.5 million. The seaside town of 25,000 people was voted the best university location in Wales and eighth in the UK in one survey. There is plenty of out-of-season accommodation to supplement the university's 3,700 places, all of which are now online. Another 1,000 residential places should become available in 2014 on land immediately adjacent to the award-winning Pentre Jane Morgan Student Village and within easy walking distance of its all facilities on the Penglais campus. Sports facilities are good for the size of institution and well used – participation in exercise classes increased by 90 per cent last year. A 400-metre running track has just been added to 50 acres of playing fields, a new 3G pitch, refurbished swimming pool, a climbing wall and specialist outdoor facilities for water sports.

Undergraduate Fees and Bursaries

» Fees for UK/EU students for 2014–15: £9,000, with Welsh Assembly non-means-tested grant to pay fees above £3,575 (2013–14) for Welsh students.
» International student fees 2013–14   £9,750–£10,750
» For all UK students (2013–14): household income less than £18,371, a bursary of £1,100 a year; sliding scale to £34,090, £950–£700; £400 bursary in Year 1 for those in university accommodation.
» Scholarships and subject-linked bursaries available, from £666 to £1,200.

Students

Undergraduates:	**8,050**	**(1,860)**
Postgraduates:	**1,080**	**(720)**
Mature students:	**10.1%**	
Overseas students:	**12.9%**	
Applications per place:	**4.1**	
From state-sector schools:	**94.0%**	
From working-class homes:	**27.4%**	
Satisfaction with students' union	**61%**	

For detailed information about sports facilities:
www.aber.ac.uk/sportscentre/

Accommodation

Number of places and costs refer to 2013–14
University-provided places: 3,750
Percentage catered: 12%
Catered costs: £70.00–£114.10 a week (31 or 37 weeks).
Self-catered costs: £57.75–£107.80 a week (37 weeks).
First years are guaranteed accommodation if conditions are met.
International students: accommodation guaranteed for students classed as overseas for fees.
Contact: www.aber.ac.uk/residential
accommodation@aber.ac.uk

Anglia Ruskin University

Anglia Ruskin is one of the largest universities in Eastern England, with some 30,000 full- and part-time students. And it is still growing, having bucked the national trend in 2012 with big increases in both applications and enrolments. The university was awarded 550 additional places as one of the institutions with relatively low fees and filled most of them. Although fees for degree courses were set at £8,300 (and held at that level for 2013–14), extra fee waivers for students from poor backgrounds brought the average cost down sufficiently to qualify for the extra places. The 8 per cent growth in applications followed a much bigger increase in the previous year. In 2014–15, however, fees will rise to £9,000.

The two main campuses are at Essex and Chelmsford, more than 40 miles apart, and there are smaller sites in Harlow, King's Lynn and Peterborough. The university has invested over £81 million in the last five years in the latest learning environments, including the £35-million redevelopment of the Cambridge campus and two buildings dedicated to Health and Social Care in Chelmsford. It has committed to investing a further £124 million over the next five years. Among the specialist study facilities are four university libraries and a mock courtroom. The two very different primary locations are far enough apart to limit contact, although electronic networking and a central administration mean that key academic facilities are available throughout the university. Three-quarters of the full-time undergraduate leavers who find jobs in the UK are working in East Anglia. The average salary of £21,000 for new graduates in 2011 was well above the national average.

Anglia was the last university to retain a polytechnic title, discarding it in 2005. The former APU took the name of John Ruskin, who founded the Cambridge School of Art, which evolved into the university. It has since acquired the former Homerton College School of Health Studies in Cambridge, after a long period of partnership, and opened the £9.3-million University Centre Harlow with Harlow College, Britain's oldest journalism school. In Chelmsford, the 22-acre Rivermead campus boasts an impressive business school and a sports hall, as well as the £15-million Marconi Building for law students. Recent additions include a new health and social care building with counselling rooms, simulated hospital wards, operating theatres and a complementary medicine suite.

Anglia Ruskin stresses its green credentials and was the first UK university to sign the Rio+20 Declaration of Higher Education Institutions. Its Global Sustainability Institute, established in 2011, is building an international reputation for

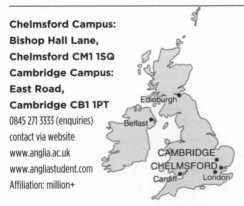

Chelmsford Campus:
Bishop Hall Lane,
Chelmsford CM1 1SQ
Cambridge Campus:
East Road,
Cambridge CB1 1PT
0845 271 3333 (enquiries)
contact via website
www.anglia.ac.uk
www.angliastudent.com
Affiliation: million+

The Times and Sunday Times **Rankings**
Overall Ranking: **110** (107)

Student satisfaction:	**=101**	(78.2%)
Research quality:	**=100**	(1.7%)
Entry standards:	**113**	(248)
Student–staff ratio:	**=84**	(20.2)
Services & facilities/student:	**98**	(£1,160)
Expected completion rate:	**87**	(81.7%)
Good honours:	**100**	(56.6%)
Graduate prospects:	**72**	(61.6%)

its research on behaviour change, resource scarcity and climate finance, and the university is aiming to make sustainability an important part of every student's experience. Only 71 academics were entered for the Research Assessment Exercise in 2008, but almost a third of their work was considered world-leading or internationally excellent. All but one of the nine subject areas had some top-rated research, with history, English and psychology producing the best grades. Psychology produced the best results among the post-1992 universities.

Nearly all the students attended state schools or colleges and more than a third are from working-class homes. The projected dropout rate had improved in the latest survey, and is significantly better than the national average for the university's subjects and entry grades. Each undergraduate has an adviser to help compile a degree package which looks at the chosen subject from different points of view to maximise future job prospects. There is also an employer mentoring scheme for second-year undergraduates planning for the transition from study to work. Each student is carefully matched with a mentor from their chosen career field who volunteers time to provide skills-building, support and encouragement.

Employers play a part in planning courses which are integrated into a modular system extending from degree level to professional programmes, including a modest selection of vocational two-year Foundation degrees. The Business School, for example, has developed a work-based course with Barclays Bank, where the students are sponsored and salaried for all three years of their course. The university has a history of providing innovative courses: the BOptom (Hons) is the only qualification of its kind in the UK and the Hearing Aid Audiology course was among the first to lead directly to registration.

Famous alumni include Pink Floyd members Dave Gilmour and the late Syd Barrett. The social scene varies between the two campuses, but the university has two art galleries and a theatre. There is limited collaboration with Cambridge University on the Cambridge Centre for Cricketing Excellence, and a base for Anglia Ruskin's Rowing Club. In the past, some students have found Chelmsford dull, but the social life is said to be improving, and neither main base is far from London by train.

Undergraduate Fees and Bursaries

» Fees for UK/EU students 2014–15 £9,000
Foundation degree £7,500
» International student fees 2013–14 £9,800–£10,300
» Over 700 NSP awards: £1,200 fee waiver, £1,000 cash and £800 university services, year 1, £1,200 fee waiver and £400 university services, years 2 and 3.
» Eligible but not receiving NSP: £750 fee waiver and £400 university services a year.
» Scholarship of £1,100 a year for those with ABB or above at A Level or equivalent and household income below£25K.

Students

Undergraduates:	**12,580**	**(5,660)**
Postgraduates:	**1,640**	**(1,720)**
Mature students:	**29.6%**	
Overseas students:	**11.9%**	
Applications per place:	**4.2**	
From state-sector schools:	**96.3%**	
From working-class homes:	**37.1%**	
Satisfaction with students' union	**64%**	

For detailed information about sports facilities: www.anglia.ac.uk/sport

Accommodation

Number of places and costs refer to 2013–14
University-provided places: Cambridge, 720 plus 800 referral rooms; Chelmsford, 511
Percentage catered: 0%
Self-catered costs: Cambridge: £79–£159 a week; Chelmsford: £101–£109 a week.
Most first years are accommodated. Distance restrictions apply.
International students: conditions and deadline apply.
Contact: cambaccom@anglia.ac.uk (Cambridge and Peterborough)
essexaccom@anglia.ac.uk (Chelmsford)

Arts University Bournemouth

Applications were up by 13 per cent even before the former Arts University College Bournemouth relaunched itself with its new title. It was decided not to confuse potential applicants with a new identity before the UCAS deadline passed, but word had obviously filtered through to sixth forms and colleges. The new Arts University Bournemouth (AUB) starts life with some 3,000 students based on a single campus, but it has operated as a specialist institution since 1885. It is now one of only 15 higher education institutions in the UK devoted solely to the study of art, design and media. Its strong reputation is reflected in a place in the top half of *The Times and Sunday Times* league table, higher than any of the other universities established in 2012. It is particularly strong in student satisfaction and employment prospects, both areas in which arts institutions tend to struggle. The university describes its courses as having a "highly practical streak" designed to give students an edge in a competitive creative world. AUB joins three other arts universities in the table by offering a sufficiently wide portfolio of courses to qualify for inclusion. There are degrees in acting, architecture, dance, event management and film production, as well as art and design subjects.

The campus in Wallisdown, which straddles Bournemouth and Poole, was opened in the 1980s by the Princess Royal, who returned in 2007 to open University House, the current flagship building. The Gallery showcases work by students and other contemporary artists, hosting talks, events and film nights to support the exhibition programme. There is also an Enterprise Pavilion (eP) on campus to develop, attract and retain new creative businesses in the South West. The purpose-built library has over 50,000 books covering a wide range of art, design, media and performance subjects, with a further collection of more than 45,000 e-books and over 300 specialist journal titles, many of which are available online. The Museum of Design in Plastics is located in the library and holds over 12,000 artefacts of predominantly 20th- and 21st-century mass-produced design and popular culture. The items are selected specifically to support the academic courses taught at the university.

Applications dropped steeply when higher fees were introduced in 2012, but the first-year intake was within 50 of the previous year. Almost a third of the students are from working-class homes and 95 per cent attended state schools or colleges – both figures close to the national average for AUB's subjects and entry qualifications.

**Wallisdown, Poole,
Dorset BH12 5HH**

01202 533011
general@aub.ac.uk
www.aub.ac.uk
http://aucbsu.co.uk
Affiliation: GuildHE

The Times and Sunday Times **Rankings**
Overall Ranking: **=52** (n/a)

Student satisfaction:	=29	(83.6%)
Research quality:	=115	(0.3%)
Entry standards:	=69	(316)
Student–staff ratio:	71	(19.3)
Services & facilities/student:	118	(£653)
Expected completion rate:	=27	(92.4%)
Good honours:	94	(57.8%)
Graduate prospects:	=46	(68.7%)

The low dropout rate is a point of particular pride – at less than 6 per cent, it is half the university's benchmark figure.

AUB was a university college for only three years, having been given degree awarding powers in 2008. It now boasts a Skillset Media Academy in partnership with Bournemouth University, offering eight accredited courses in animation, film and digital media production, photography, make-up for media and performance, graphic design and model-making. The two universities also bid successfully to become a Screen Academy, through which Skillset recognises excellence in film and the broader screen-based media, providing some students with access bursaries. The most recent audit of the university by the Quality Assurance Agency resulted in the highest possible grade, commending the academic standards and highlighting a number of features of good practice.

Students and staff work in partnership on an innovative programme of professional practice and research, with different disciplines encouraged to work together. The academics include many with experience in, and continuing engagement with, the creative industries, while the careers service provides students with subject-specific and generic advice on future employment. Industry liaison groups and visiting tutors keep the university abreast of developments in the creative industries,

while alumni return regularly as lecturers. Students are encouraged to join the university's European Exchange programme to study abroad.

The university has fewer than 200 places in its halls of residence and gives priority in their allocation to overseas students and those with disabilities or other medical conditions. There is plenty of privately rented accommodation in the area, for which the average rent in 2012–13 was £82 a week in a shared house. The university keeps a register of approved housing at the **www.aubstudentpad.com** website and runs accommodation days in July and August for current and prospective students to find potential housemates. Bournemouth has a large and cosmopolitan student population and one of the most vibrant club scenes outside London. The capital is less than two hours away and is easily reached by regular train and coach services or via good motorway links. Bournemouth and Southampton both have international airports providing good value flights to more than 50 destinations.

Undergraduate Fees and Bursaries

» Fees for UK/EU students 2014–15 £9,000
» Fees for International students 2013–14 £11,510
» 116 NSP awards: household income below £25K, benefits (four options) of £3,000, year 1; benefits (three options) of £1,500, years 2 and 3.
» Check the university's website for the latest information.

Students

Undergraduates:	**2,750**	**(60)**
Postgraduates:	**30**	**(25)**
Mature students:	**10.4%**	
Overseas students:	**11.0%**	
Applications per place:	**5.5**	
From state-sector schools:	**95.3%**	
From working-class homes:	**30.1%**	
Satisfaction with students' union	**68%**	

For detailed information about sports facilities:
http://aucbsu.co.uk/?page_id=22

Accommodation

Number of places and costs refer to 2013–14
University-provided places: 165
Percentage catered: 0%
Self-catered costs: £105 (single en suite); £110 (double, en suite); £115 (single studio); £125 (double studio) a week.
Priority is given to students with medical conditions/disabilities. International students have priority.
Contact: studentadvice@aub.ac.uk;
http://aub.ac.uk/accommodation/

University of the Arts London

The University of the Arts London is a federation of world-famous art, design, fashion and media colleges that markets itself as Europe's leading art and design university. But an inability, shared by most arts-based institutions, to match the high levels of student satisfaction seen at generalist universities holds it back in our league table. Overall satisfaction levels rose significantly in the 2013 National Student Survey, but still left the university in the bottom three on this measure. The demand for places had been growing by leaps and bounds before the introduction of £9,000 fees. Although applications fell sharply in 2012, there was a more manageable decline in the numbers eventually enrolling.

Five of the six component colleges originally came together as the London Institute in 1989 and became a university 15 years later. With almost 20,000 students spread through 14 sites around central London, it is Europe's largest arts university. A global reputation attracts more than 6,000 international students and 2,700 from other EU countries,. The five colleges became six when Wimbledon College of Art joined in 2006, bringing an international reputation in theatre design and the UK's largest school of theatre. The founding members, which continue to use their own names and enjoy considerable autonomy, were Camberwell College of Arts, Central Saint Martins College of Arts and Design, Chelsea College of Art and Design, London College of Fashion and London College of Communication (formerly the London College of Printing). The university offers one Foundation course across Camberwell, Chelsea and Wimbledon.

Big changes were already under way before the change of title was agreed: a £70-million development next door to the Tate Gallery produced prestigious new premises for Chelsea College, with extensive workshop facilities, studios and a new library. Another £32 million was spent on new headquarters for the College of Communication at the Elephant and Castle, south of the Thames, where a Special Archives and Collections Centre includes the archives of the filmmaker Stanley Kubrick. The college has Film Academy status. London's largest open-air art gallery was launched in 2008 on the Parade Ground at the heart of the Chelsea College, and final-year students' work is also showcased online at a virtual degree show. The university hopes to consolidate the London College of Fashion's three East London sites, but there are no detailed plans yet.

The biggest project of all has brought Central Saint Martins together on one site

272 High Holborn
London WC1V 7EY

0207 514 6197 (enquiries)
admissions@arts.ac.uk
www.arts.ac.uk
www.suarts.org
Affiliation: none

Edinburgh
Belfast
Cardiff
LONDON

The Times and Sunday Times **Rankings**

Overall Ranking: **=77** (60)

Student satisfaction:	=119	(74.3%)
Research quality:	=35	(20.3%)
Entry standards:	=69	(316)
Student–staff ratio:	108	(22.4)
Services & facilities/student:	66	(£1,372)
Expected completion rate:	34	(90.9%)
Good honours:	58	(65%)
Graduate prospects:	=102	(53.7%)

for the first time, moving to the new King's Cross development. The £200-million campus is based on a Grade II listed former granary, which accommodates a new School of Performing Arts as well as the college's existing art, fashion and design courses. There is a 350-seat public theatre, studios and rehearsal spaces, as well as four levels of workshops, studios and exhibition space, with facilities for students from across the university. The new building was voted the world's best higher education building in 2012.

Published assessments have barely done justice to the eminence of the colleges, although the 2008 Research Assessment Exercise saw half of the university's submission rated as world-leading or internationally excellent. All the colleges make good use of visiting lecturers, who keep students abreast of developments in their field. The university has also been running weekend classes and summer schools in an attempt to broaden the intake. The proportion of undergraduates from working-class homes is now more than 30 per cent. There have been big improvements in the dropout rate and the latest projection of less than 9 per cent is significantly better than the national average for the university's courses and entry grades.

Students have access to the largest art and design specialist careers centre in the country, in the Student Enterprise and Employability Service, while the pioneering Emerging Artists Programme continues to support graduates in the early years of their careers. The university holds the only recruitment festival tailored to the needs of creative graduates, providing access to hundreds of industry professionals for networking opportunities and advice.

The colleges vary considerably in character and facilities, although a single students' union serves them all. The university's new student hub provides a central place for students to work, socialise and share ideas, as well as being the location for student services such as housing and careers. The university is not overprovided with residential accommodation, although there are 13 residences spread around the colleges, providing more than 2,400 beds. House-hunting workshops help those who have to rely on an expensive private housing market. The university owns no sports facilities, although it has arranged student discounts with a number of providers.

Undergraduate Fees and Bursaries

» Fees for UK/EU students 2014–15 £9,000
» International student fees 2013–14 £13,800
» 1,055 NSP awards, with priority to those with household income below £16K, £3,000 fee waiver or combination totalling £3,000 of fee waiver, university services and cash, year 1; £1,000 cash for other years.
» £1,000 cash each year for students with household income below £25K who do not receive an NSP award.

Students

Undergraduates:	**13,245**	**(680)**
Postgraduates:	**2,470**	**(905)**
Mature students:	**26.6%**	
Overseas students:	**37.8%**	
Applications per place:	**6.4**	
From state-sector schools:	**95.9%**	
From working-class homes:	**28.9%**	
Satisfaction with students' union	**58%**	

For detailed information about sports facilities:
www.suarts.org/groups#club-society#sport

Accommodation

Number of places and costs refer to 2013–14
University-provided places: 2,507
Percentage catered: 0%
Self-catered costs: £130–£215 a week.
First-year students are offered accommodation if conditions are met. Priority for disabled students and those from outside London. International students: guaranteed if conditions met.
Contact: www.arts.ac.uk/housing/
accommodation@arts.ac.uk

Aston University

Aston was one of the few universities to make public its applications for 2013–14, largely because the demand for degree places was up by 10 per cent at the start of the year. This followed an increase in enrolments in spite of the introduction of £9,000 fees in 2012. Dame Professor Julia King, the Vice-Chancellor, was a member of the Browne Review, which recommended higher fees, and she argued that Aston's strong record for graduate employment justified the charges. Small and lively, set in the heart of Birmingham, the university has remained resolutely specialist in science and technology, business, languages and social science, concentrating on the sandwich degrees which have served its graduates so well in the employment market. But it is now aiming for "sustainable growth in key areas" to provide an improving student experience and the size necessary to boost research performance and become a top ten university.

Aston was named by QS among the top 50 universities in the world that are under 50 years old. Previously a college of advanced technology, it remains strong in engineering and the sciences, although the highly rated business school accounts for almost half of the students. Despite some modest growth, the university still has fewer than 8,000 undergraduates. But, with healthy funding from industry and commerce, Aston has been investing in its future, boosting staffing in business, engineering and languages, and developing the campus with a £215-million programme of improvements. An impressive new library, with glazed façade, opened in 2010. The Woodcock Sport Centre, which includes a Grade II listed swimming pool, followed in 2011 and has since acquired a new sports hall with indoor courts and team sports facilities. More chemistry and chemical engineering laboratories have been provided and £16.5 million spent on the European Bio Energy Research Centre.

Business and management led the way in the 2008 Research Assessment Exercise, with health subjects also producing good grades. While 45 per cent of the work in the four subject areas was judged to be world-leading or internationally excellent, the high proportion of academics entered for assessment helped to place Aston near the bottom of the tables of pre-1992 universities. New research centres have since been established in enterprise, healthy ageing, Europe and neuroscience and child development. The £6-million Aston Brain Centre opened in 2011, combining research and teaching in a single unique facility.

A £20-million extension to the business school has seen an increase in staff from 80 to over 120. New undergraduates are offered 12 online study skills modules in areas such

---

Aston Triangle
Birmingham B4 7ET

0121 204 4444 (course enquiries)
ugenquiries@aston.ac.uk
www.aston.ac.uk
www.astonunion.com
Affiliation: none

The Times and Sunday Times **Rankings**

Overall Ranking: **=29** (=36)

Student satisfaction:	=15	(84.6%)
Research quality:	50	(13.3%)
Entry standards:	36	(398)
Student–staff ratio:	=33	(16.2)
Services & facilities/student:	45	(£1,632)
Expected completion rate:	33	(91.1%)
Good honours:	=30	(73.5%)
Graduate prospects:	30	(73.6%)

as essay writing before the formal start of their course. Aston has also introduced a free programme of language tuition for all students, covering six languages from Arabic to Portuguese, as part of its efforts to help boost employability further. More than a quarter of first-year students have signed up for the programme.

There is a wide range of joint honours programmes for those who prefer not to specialise. Almost nine out of ten Aston graduates – far more than the national average – go straight into jobs, often returning to the scene of work placements, which have become the norm for seven out of ten of them. The tuition fee for the placement year is set at £1,000, and most students are paid by their host company. At the forefront of employer-led degrees, the university was awarded £1.6 million to set up a Foundation Degree Centre to establish new courses and explore other ways of delivering qualifications. Aston consistently features among the top 20 in the "High Fliers" survey of employers' favoured universities for graduate recruitment.

The projected dropout rate improved considerably in the latest statistics and, at less than 7 per cent, was well ahead of the national average for Aston's subjects. The intake is diverse, with just over a third of the undergraduates coming from working-class homes. Six out of ten undergraduates come from outside the West Midlands, around a fifth of them from outside the UK.

The 40-acre campus is a ten-minute walk from the centre of Birmingham. Recent building programmes have brought all residential and academic accommodation onto one carefully landscaped site. Almost half of the undergraduates live on campus, with places guaranteed for first years and overseas students. A new phase of construction for residential accommodation has been accelerated in order to provide another 2,400 en-suite rooms by the end of 2013. More than half of these are now available. Recent developments have helped to place Aston among the top dozen universities in the People and Planet Green League of sustainability for the past three years. It has been given "Platinum Eco Campus" status for demonstrating a lasting commitment to sustainability. The renamed Aston Students' Union remains active, both socially and in student welfare matters.

Undergraduate Fees and Bursaries

» Fees for UK/EU students 2014–15   £9,000
    Foundation degree   £6,000
» International student fees 2013–14   £12,500–£15,600
» 293 NSP awards, £1,000 fee waiver, £2,000 university accommodation discount, year 1; £500 fee waiver or cash, other years (£1,000 for sandwich year).
» Household income below £42K and no NSP award, £500 a year fee waiver, accommodation discount or cash.
» Excellence scholarships (AAB at A level or equivalent), £1,000 a year (including sandwich year).

Students

Undergraduates:	**7,270**	**(660)**
Postgraduates:	**1,530**	**(740)**
Mature students:	**12.3%**	
Overseas students:	**22.8%**	
Applications per place:	**4.9**	
From state-sector schools:	**91.2%**	
From working-class homes:	**34.8%**	
Satisfaction with students' union	**67%**	

For detailed information about sports facilities: www.aston.ac.uk/sport

Accommodation

Number of places and costs refer to 2013–14
University-provided places: 3,017
Percentage catered: 0%
Self-catered accommodation: £121–£131 a week.
First years are guaranteed accommodation if they fulfil requirements and apply by the deadline.
International fee-paying students: as above.
Contact: accom@aston.ac.uk; www.aston.ac.uk/accommodation

Bangor University

Bangor has the "fairest" workload of any UK university, according to polls of students in three of the last five years. The university also scored well in the 2013 *Times Higher Education* Student Experience Survey for the quality of residential accommodation, security and the overall campus environment. The "small and friendly" nature of the university and the city no doubt helped, although there are now more than 10,000 students based on the North Wales coast. Numbers dipped only slightly with the advent of higher fees in 2012, despite a 14 per cent drop in applications.

Bangor's community focus dates back to a 19th-century campaign which saw local quarrymen putting part of their weekly wages towards the establishment of a college. The School of Lifelong Learning continues the tradition with courses across North Wales, but the university has also built a worldwide reputation in areas such as environmental studies and ocean sciences. Like Swansea and Aberystwyth, it left the University of Wales to assert its independence, taking the title of Bangor University and awarding its own degrees.

The 2008 research assessments identified some world-leading work in all Bangor's 19 subject areas. The university claimed the grades for accounting and finance to be the best in the UK, with electronic engineering second and both sports science and Welsh in the top ten in their respective subjects. There is a high proportion of small-group teaching and tutorials, as well as one of Britain's largest peer guiding schemes, in which senior students mentor new arrivals. In addition, the Bangor Employability Award (BEA) has been introduced to enhance students' career prospects by accrediting co-curricular and extra-curricular activities such as volunteering and part-time work that are valued by employers.

Bangor merged with a nearby teacher training college, Coleg Normal, in 1996, and that site is now part of the university. The 24 academic schools are grouped into six colleges. A new School of Philosophy and Religion, developed out of a longstanding tradition in these areas, was established in 2012. All schools are within walking distance of each other, apart from the School of Ocean Sciences, which is two miles away in Menai Bridge.

The university estate has been re-developed, with the addition of a £5-million environmental sciences building, while a £3.5-million Cancer Research Institute is attracting specialists of international repute. A combination of private funds and a £5-million European grant was used to establish a new Business Management Centre on a waterfront site. A £40-million Arts and Innovation Centre is due to open

Bangor

Gwynedd LL57 2DG

01248 382017 (admissions)
ask-admissions@bangor.ac.uk
www.bangor.ac.uk
www.undeb.bangor.ac.uk
Affiliation: none

The Times and Sunday Times **Rankings**

Overall Ranking: **56** (56)

Student satisfaction:	=64	(81.3%)
Research quality:	=45	(16.0%)
Entry standards:	=75	(313)
Student–staff ratio:	55	(17.9)
Services & facilities/student:	102	(£1,113)
Expected completion rate:	=68	(84.7%)
Good honours:	=83	(60.1%)
Graduate prospects:	57	(64.4%)

in 2014, forming a bridge between the university's upper campus and the nearby science site. The centre will focus on science, technology and the creative arts and will include a theatre, studio, cinema, lecture theatres, exhibition spaces, bar and café.

Little more than a stone's throw from Snowdonia with its attractions for sports enthusiasts, Bangor is an expanding centre for Welsh-medium teaching. Although a majority of students come from outside Wales – there is a strong link with Ireland, for example – around 20 per cent of the students speak the language and one of the halls of residence is Welsh-speaking. The university also has a flourishing international exchange programme. Summer courses in South Korea, a year in Australia or a semester in Finland are some of the opportunities available to undergraduates. Under the new International Experience Programme, students will extend their degree by a year. No tuition fees will be charged for the year abroad and, "with International Experience" will be added to the degree title.

Around 94 per cent of the students come from state schools or colleges, and three in ten come from working-class homes. The university spends £2.5 million annually on bursaries and scholarships, which range from merit awards based on pre-entry examinations, to sports scholarships and excellence awards in several subject areas.

The university's Talent Opportunities Programme, which operates in schools across North Wales, targets potential applicants from lower socio-economic families, who have little or no history of going on to university.

There is a strong focus on student support including the Peer Guide Scheme for new students and the pioneering dyslexia unit offers individual and group support throughout students' courses. A new Study Skills Centre, which opened in 2013, will help with the transition to university and provide continuing academic support.

Eleven new halls of residence are part of a £35-million upgrade at the main university accommodation site. Bangor is one of the most cost-effective places in which to study – one survey made it the second-cheapest university in the UK. The university is also rated the "greenest" in Wales and twentieth in the UK in the People and Planet Green League.

Undergraduate Fees and Bursaries

» Fees for UK/EU students for 2014–15: £9,000, with Welsh Assembly non-means-tested grant to pay fees above £3,575 (2013–14) for Welsh students.
» International student fees 2013–14   £10,300–£12,500
» Bangor Bursary: household income below £25K, £1,500 a year; £25K–£40K, £750 a year. Welsh-medium study bursaries.
» Scholarships include Excellence Scholarships (up to £5,000) and Merit Scholarships (up to £3,000), awarded on Entrance Scholarship examinations.

Students

Undergraduates:	**7,365**	**(1,070)**
Postgraduates:	**1,830**	**(985)**
Mature students:	**17.5%**	
Overseas students:	**11.2%**	
Applications per place:	**4.4**	
From state-sector schools:	**94.1%**	
From working-class homes:	**30.6%**	
Satisfaction with students' union	**66%**	

For detailed information about sports facilities: www.maesglas.co.uk

Accommodation

Number of places and costs refer to 2013–14
University-provided places: around 2,450
Percentage catered: 0%
Self-catered costs: £71–£94 (standard); £105–£122 (en-suite or larger rooms) a week (40-week UG contract).
All first-year students are guaranteed places.
International UG students: as above.
Contact: halls@bangor.ac.uk; www.bangor.ac.uk/accommodation

University of Bath

Bath has been one of the few universities to see the demand for places continue to rise both when fees were increased to £9,000 and in the following year. Applications were up by more than 7 per cent at the start of 2013, with UK enquiries showing an even higher rate of growth. Improved performance in league tables may have been one factor, as the university reaped the benefit of consistently good student satisfaction scores. Students like the community feel of campus life, and one of the lowest dropout rates in Britain suggests that they are well supported. Bath attracted a much higher than average response to an optional question in the National Student Survey on whether it acted on students' comments.

With its origins as a technological university established in the 1960s, Bath is still a relatively small institution with a high proportion of postgraduates. The university enjoys both an attractive location and a high academic reputation – it has never been out of the top 20 in *The Times* league table. The modern campus on the edge of Bath cannot live up to the magnificence of the city's architecture, but the 200-acre site has pleasant grounds and is functional, with academic, recreational and residential facilities in close proximity. The university has twice been rated among

the top ten in the world in the GreenMetric environmental ranking. The sports facilities are outstanding and were used as a training base in sports as diverse as athletics, judo, swimming and beach volleyball in the run up to London 2012. The university's Sports Training Village was chosen to host the Paralympics GB team ahead of the Games. Some 25 athletes who train at the university were selected to compete across seven sports at the Games.

The university is in the midst of a three-year £100-million capital programme to provide new teaching space, student accommodation and a new arts centre. Additional teaching accommodation for 2,000 students will be connected to the main campus parade by a "skywalk" bridge due to open in time for the start of the new academic year. A £43-million student accommodation complex providing 708 additional en-suite bedrooms in 75 flats is due to open in summer 2014, shortly before the new Centre for the Arts, which will contain a theatre, performance and rehearsal studios, a gallery and teaching facilities. The programme will also see the refurbishment of existing teaching and research space over the next two years.

A new student centre and a dedicated centre for postgraduates opened in 2010, while additional lecture theatres and computer laboratories have eased the pressure on teaching space. Almost 500

Claverton Down
Bath BA2 7AY

01225 383019 (admissions)
admissions@bath.ac.uk
www.bath.ac.uk
www.bathstudent.com
Affiliation: none

The Times and Sunday Times Rankings
Overall Ranking: **7** (9)

Student satisfaction:	1	(87.9%)
Research quality:	=23	(23.3%)
Entry standards:	11	(480)
Student–staff ratio:	=42	(16.8)
Services & facilities/student:	34	(£1,734)
Expected completion rate:	=7	(96.8%)
Good honours:	9	(82.8%)
Graduate prospects:	3	(83.6%)

study bedrooms have also been added recently. The sports facilities were already among the best in Britain before the addition of a £35-million training village, funded with Lottery money. The campus acquired a 50-metre swimming pool by this route, to which it added an indoor running track, a multipurpose sports hall, eight indoor tennis courts, an indoor jumps and throws hall, air pistol and fencing sale, a judo dojo and a simulated bobsleigh. There is even a skeleton start area, as used by Amy Williams, 2010 Olympic gold medallist. There is a strong tradition in competitive sports: the university pioneered sports scholarships more than 20 years ago and there are courses to do the facilities justice.

Research is Bath's greatest strength: 60 per cent of the work submitted for the 2008 Research Assessment Exercise was judged to be world-leading or internationally excellent. Social work and social policy, business and management, physics, maths and pharmacy did particularly well, but there were good results in a number of areas. The university's research grants and contracts portfolio is worth more than £90 million. Most degree courses have a practical element, and assessors have praised the university for the work placements it offers. Most undergraduates take courses with placements or a period of study abroad, which helps to produce consistently outstanding graduate employment figures. Student entrepreneurship is actively encouraged through a number of initiatives and projects.

Students – nearly a quarter of whom were educated at independent schools – may find the campus quiet at weekends and struggle to afford some of Bath's attractions, but they value its location. The nightlife of Bristol is only a few minutes away by public transport, and the two cities have a combined student population of more than 50,000. The popular students' union – one of only four in the country to hold a SUEI Gold Award – is very active, and the university has been upgrading its student support services. Improvements include the introduction of a new virtual learning environment and establishment of a central base for the full range of student services. More than nine out of ten students surveyed say they would recommend the university to family and friends.

Undergraduate Fees and Bursaries

» Fees for UK/EU students 2014–15 £9,000
  Franchised Foundation degree £7,500
» International student fees 2013–14 £13,000–£16,500
» Household income £20K or below and other criteria, fee waiver of £3,000, years 1 and 2; full fee waiver in sandwich year.
» Household income £20K or below, bursary of £3,000, years 1 and 2; £1,500 for unpaid sandwich year; £1,000 in subsequent years.
» Check the university's website for the latest information.

Students

Undergraduates:	**9,995**	**(570)**
Postgraduates:	**1,955**	**(2,620)**
Mature students:	**3.7%**	
Overseas students:	**21.2%**	
Applications per place:	**6.8**	
From state-sector schools:	**75.3%**	
From working-class homes:	**16.1%**	
Satisfaction with students' union	**86%**	

For detailed information about sports facilities:
www.bathstudent.com/sport

Accommodation

Number of places and costs refer to 2013–14
University-provided places: 3,392
Percentage catered: 7%
Catered cost: £160–£190 a week.
Self-catered cost: £60 (shared) – £145 (en-suite single) a week.
First years guaranteed accommodation if conditions are met, and applications received by 1 July.
International students: as above. Exchange students are housed on a reciprocal basis.
Contact: www.bath.ac.uk/study/ug/accommodation/index.html

Bath Spa University

Bath Spa maintained its position in *The Times and Sunday Times* league table, ahead of many of the universities created in this millennium after moving up 14 places last year. It is far from new as an institution: the history of the predecessor colleges goes back 160 years, and it boasts some famous alumni, including Body Shop founder Anita Roddick and Turner Prize winner Sir Howard Hodgkin. The university's Newton Park headquarters, four miles outside the World Heritage city of Bath, is in grounds landscaped by Capability Brown in the 18th century, with a handsome Georgian manor house owned by the Duchy of Cornwall as its centrepiece.

The university is focusing on creativity, culture and enterprise under the direction of its new Vice-Chancellor, Professor Christina Slade, who is also expanding its international dimension. Students can collect a Global Citizenship award by completing a module that covers a range of cross-cutting issues with relevance to all subjects in the arts, humanities and sciences. There are about 200 overseas students from a variety of countries, and the university is actively seeking additional partnerships with institutions abroad.

Newton Park is the base for all students except those taking art and design subjects, and provides a study environment where historic buildings blend sympathetically with modern facilities such as the 200-seat University Theatre. The Creative Writing Centre is housed in the 14th-century gatehouse, a scheduled ancient monument. Significant further development is taking place at Newton Park and should be completed during 2014. The £70-million development will provide new teaching, social and residential facilities that will enable another 550 students to be housed on campus.

A second campus at Sion Hill, in Bath itself, houses the Bath School of Art and Design. It has recently undergone a £6-million redevelopment and boasts facilities that are among the most modern in the country. Meanwhile, the university has established a postgraduate centre at Corsham Court, a 16th-century manor house near Chippenham, and there is currently a teacher training centre on the site of Bath Community Academy. About a third of the students are postgraduates, including a large cohort training to be teachers.

Bath Spa has been awarding its own taught degrees since 1992 – much longer than some of the other new arrivals on the university scene – and research degrees since 2007. Results in the National Student Survey have been good, especially for teaching quality. Students like the "small and friendly" atmosphere. The university

---

Newton Park
Newton St Loe
Bath BA2 9BN

01225 875609 (admissions)
admissions@bathspa.ac.uk
www.bathspa.ac.uk
www.bathspasu.co.uk
Affiliation: million+

The Times and Sunday Times Rankings

Overall Ranking: **70** (70)

Student satisfaction:	=48	(82%)
Research quality:	=83	(3.0%)
Entry standards:	54	(339)
Student–staff ratio:	105	(21.8)
Services & facilities/student:	117	(£865)
Expected completion rate:	=53	(87.1%)
Good honours:	48	(68.6%)
Graduate prospects:	=89	(57.3%)

was designated a national centre for excellence in teaching and learning in the creative industries, bringing significant investment in the Schools of Music and Performing Arts, Humanities and Cultural Industries, and Bath School of Art and Design. Half of the subjects in which the university entered the 2008 Research Assessment Exercise (art and design, communication, cultural and media studies, English, history and music) were judged to have some world-leading work. The recent appointment of some high profile professors (such as Fay Weldon and Gavin Turk) has strengthened the university's profile for both research and teaching in key areas.

Despite a setting that would seem to be a magnet for applicants from independent schools, almost 94 per cent of the home intake is state-educated and more than 38 per cent are from working-class homes. Two-thirds of the students are female, reflecting the arts and social science bias in the curriculum, and a quarter are over 25. The latest projected dropout rate of less than 9 per cent is better than the national benchmark for the university's courses and entry grades. Bath Spa was one of many universities to experience a significant drop in applications when higher fees arrived in 2012, but it still managed to recruit almost as many degree students as in the previous year.

The university has a number of partner colleges in the region, both in the further education and private sectors, where a range of vocational two-year Foundation degrees are delivered. Many students then progress to the university campuses to complete an honours degree. Employment opportunities and skills are emphasised throughout all degree courses. Good links with employers and a significant student presence in the creative and cultural life of Bath and the region help with graduate employment.

Currently about 90 per cent of first years attending Bath Spa itself are offered university managed residential accommodation, and more is being built. The university is proud of its environmental successes and has a good record in the People and Planet Green League. Sports facilities are not extensive, but a new gym in the students' union has improved them, and some of the university's sports teams fare well in local competitions.

Undergraduate Fees and Bursaries

» Fees for UK/EU students 2014–15 — £9,000
Franchised Foundation degree — £7,500–£9,000
» International student fees 2013–14 — £10,535–£13,690
» 357 NSP awards with priority criteria: £3,000 fee waiver or £2,000 fee waiver or university services and £1,000 bursary, year 1; £500 fee waiver or university services, years 2 and 3, plus Bursary scheme awards as below.
» Bursary scheme: household income up to £17K, £500 a year; £17K–£22K, £400 a year; £22K–£25K, £350 a year.
» Check the university's website for the latest information.

Students

Undergraduates:	5,375	(340)
Postgraduates:	670	(2,170)
Mature students:	10.1%	
Overseas students:	2.8%	
Applications per place:	6.5	
From state-sector schools:	93.6%	
From working-class homes:	38.3%	
Satisfaction with students' union	56%	

For detailed information about sports facilities:
www.bathspasu.co.uk

Accommodation

Number of places and costs refer to 2013–14
University provided places: 959 in halls; 141 in Accredited Independent Housing
Percentage catered: 0%
Self catered: £110.00– £145.67 a week (40–48 weeks).
First years are housed provided requirements are met. Residential restrictions apply. Students with a disability or medical condition have priority.
International students: as above; Homestay option available.
Contact: http://housing.bathspa.ac.uk

University of Bedfordshire

Bedfordshire swapped one high-profile vice-chancellor for another when Professor Les Ebdon left to become the Director of the Government's Office for Fair Access and was replaced by Bill Rammell, a former Labour Higher Education Minister. Mr Rammell will oversee a campus development programme costing £120 million to follow the £180 million of improvements carried out since the university established a new identity in 2006. The move allowed the former Luton University to shed a name that – however unfairly – had become a liability. It has seesawed in our table and dropped out of the top 100 this year, but the demand for places nearly doubled in its first four years before declining when higher fees were introduced in 2012. Even then, Bedfordshire met its target for recruitment.

The new university has been expanding and developing its five campuses, adding a well-equipped media arts centre in Luton, where a new library is under construction. Further redevelopment is also planned in Bedford, the other main site, which already boasts a new campus centre comprising a 280-seat auditorium and a students' union, as well as an accommodation block for 500 students. A new campus centre opened in Luton in 2010, with teaching and exhibition space as well as the students' union, information desks and the careers and employment centre. New £40-million student halls are now open, with en-suite facilities, phone and high-speed internet access, as is the £20-million Postgraduate and Continuing Professional Development Centre.

The university is opening a new campus in Milton Keynes in 2013, in partnership with the local authority, with a strong focus on engineering and technology, while also providing popular courses in business and health subjects. University Campus Milton Keynes will cater initially for 120 students, mainly but not exclusively from the UK's fastest-growing city. There are also partner colleges in Bedford and Dunstable, but the bulk of the students remain in Luton. The Bedford campus is a 20-minute walk from the town centre in a "self-contained leafy setting". It houses the Faculty of Education, Sport and Tourism, with 3,000 students, making it the UK's largest provider of physical education teacher training, as well as a national centre for other subjects at primary and secondary level. There is also an attractive management centre and conference venue at Putteridge Bury, a neo-Elizabethan mansion. Nursing and midwifery students in the growing Faculty of Health and Social Sciences are based at the Butterfield Park campus, near Luton, or at the Oxford House development, in

University Square
Luton
Bedfordshire LU1 3JU

0844 848 2234
admissions@beds.ac.uk
www.beds.ac.uk
www.ubsu.co.uk
Affiliation: million+

The Times and Sunday Times Rankings
Overall Ranking: **115** (88)

Student satisfaction:	=111	(76.6%)
Research quality:	=100	(1.7%)
Entry standards:	121	(214)
Student–staff ratio:	109	(22.5)
Services & facilities/student:	43	(£1,644)
Expected completion rate:	=102	(79.1%)
Good honours:	117	(50.2%)
Graduate prospects:	104	(53.5%)

Aylesbury, Buckinghamshire. There are additional teaching facilities at Stoke Mandeville and Wycombe General hospitals. A postgraduate medical school is run in partnership with Hertfordshire and Cranfield universities.

Bedfordshire's courses are largely vocational. The portfolio of two-year Foundation degrees taught by the university has been scaled back, but subjects from animal management to sustainable construction are available through partner colleges. The university pioneered electronic assessment, with more than 10,000 students in disciplines from accountancy to biology tested by computer. Bedfordshire was also awarded a national centre of excellence in personal development planning and employability, aiming to link student learning with life after university. The university celebrated much-improved results in the 2008 Research Assessment Exercise, registering at least some world-leading work in earth systems and environmental science, social work, social policy and administration, sport, tourism and leisure, English language and literature, and communications, cultural and media studies.

Almost all of Bedfordshire's entrants are from state schools and 42 per cent come from working-class backgrounds. Around a quarter of the undergraduates are 21 or over on entry and about a third take part-time courses. Clearing numbers have dropped from nearly one in three to only one in ten, and the projected dropout rate has improved considerably. Although it was over 16 per cent in the last survey, that was better than the national average for the university's courses and entry qualifications. Surprisingly high numbers – nearly a third – are from outside the EU, many of them taking postgraduate courses.

Both Luton and Bedford have their share of pubs, clubs and restaurants, and London is only half an hour away by train. Bedford's impressive sports facilities were used to host athletes for the 2012 Olympics and are expected to have a role in the 2015 Rugby World Cup. The university broke into the top 20 in the People and Planet Green League in 2013, scoring highly for its reduction in carbon emissions.

Undergraduate Fees and Bursaries

- » Fees for UK/EU students 2014–15 £9,000
  Foundation degree £6,000
- » International student fees 2013–14 £9,600
- » NSP awards with priority criteria: £1,000 cash and £2,000 flexible support payments, year 1; £350, years 2 and 3..
- » Welcome package of £350 (£500 if from partner colleges) for university services.
- » Household income below £25K not receiving NSP, Welcome package plus flexible payment £150, year 1; £300, years 2 and 3.
- » Range of other scholarships and bursaries available.
- » Check the university's website for the latest information.

Students

Undergraduates:	**11,910**	**(3,495)**
Postgraduates:	**4,585**	**(2,280)**
Mature students:	**24.3%**	
Overseas students:	**14.5%**	
Applications per place:	**4.7**	
From state-sector schools:	**98.7%**	
From working-class homes:	**42.0%**	
Satisfaction with students' union	**64%**	

For detailed information about sports facilities:
www.beds.ac.uk/sportbeds

Accommodation

Number of places and costs refer to 2013–14
University-provided places: about 2,440
Percentage catered: 0%
Self-catered costs: £96–£140 a week.
First years cannot be guaranteed a place, but help is available to find alternative housing in the private sector.
International students: as above.
Contact: www.beds.ac.uk/studentlife/accommodation
Bedford campus: accommodationqueries@beds.ac.uk
Luton campus: info@studentvillagebeds.com

Birkbeck, University of London

Birkbeck, London's leading provider of part-time higher education, is expanding beyond its Bloomsbury base for the first time for the start of the 2013–14 academic year. It has been offering courses in Stratford, East London, since 2005, but will now share a new five-storey building with the University of East London to offer courses in law, business and subjects tailored for the creative industries. University Square Stratford is the first shared project of its kind in the capital. Facilities will include a 300-seat lecture theatre, learning centre, student support centre and seminar rooms for 3,400 students. As in Birkbeck's central London base, courses will be available either part-time or full-time.

Birkbeck now has its own degree-awarding powers, but is remaining part of the University of London. Although most of its courses are part-time, the college has doubled the number of three-year full-time degrees taught in the evening for 2013–14. It attracted the biggest increase in full-time applications of any university after another big expansion in the previous year. Recruitment to part-time courses was hit hard by the Labour government's removal of funding for graduates returning to take a different qualification. The introduction of the first Government loans for part-time undergraduates has enabled Birkbeck students to afford fees of between £6,000 and £6,750 a year for standard part-time degree courses, which is pro-rata the £8,000 a year cost for the three-year evening programme. Further cash bursaries and fee waivers are on offer for students with household incomes below £25,000. But, as in other institutions, numbers have yet to recover fully, in spite of a successful publicity campaign.

Birkbeck does not appear in the overall ranking of universities published in this *Guide* because, as a specialist provider of mainly part-time, evening higher education it cannot be compared fairly with other institutions on some of the measures. But the college has become an increasingly popular and prestigious choice for Londoners of all ages. There were over 70 part-time undergraduate degree courses to choose from in 2013. Courses are tailored to the employment market. For example, a new BSc in applied accounting and business is run in collaboration with the Institute of Chartered Accountants in England and Wales, allowing trainee accountants to combine work and study to gain their qualifications at a substantially lower cost and much sooner than if they took a degree before completing their professional qualification.

Malet Street
Bloomsbury
London WC1E 7HX

020 7631 6000 (general enquiries)
contact via website
www.bbk.ac.uk
www.birkbeckunion.org
Affiliation: 1994 Group

The Times and Sunday Times Rankings
The available data do not match the data used to rank the other full-time universities, so Birkbeck could not be included in the league table this year.

The college encourages applications from people without traditional qualifications and there is a flexible policy for entry at undergraduate level. In 2012, it received a national award for promoting and supporting women in the fields of science, technology, engineering, mathematics and medicine. Students aged over 21 are not asked for formal qualifications, but the college makes its own assessment of skills and knowledge, on the basis of interviews and/or short tests.

Founded in 1823, Birkbeck offers a wide range of subjects. Most are in the arts and social sciences, but the full-time evening degrees include biomedicine, law, and film and media. Students apply for full-time courses through UCAS, rather than direct to the college, as is the case for the part-time portfolio. The college has reorganised into a smaller number of "super-schools", increased its recruitment activity and set about improving the student experience. The strategy appears to be succeeding and brought the college a leadership award.

There are now over 18,000 students at the college. The My Birkbeck Student Centre acts as a front door to all the college's student support services, from help in choosing courses and submitting applications to information about financial support and study skills. Nine out of ten academics at the college are researchers as well as teachers. More than half of the work submitted to the 2008 Research Assessment Exercise was considered world-leading or internationally excellent. Earth Sciences, psychology, history, classics and archaeology, and history of art, film and visual media were rated in the top five nationally. Its research strength has helped Birkbeck to a place among the top 200 universities in the world, according to the 2012 *Times Higher Education* rankings.

Birkbeck is located close to the University of London's headquarters and main facilities, including university's excellent and underused students' union. Almost £20 million has been spent consolidating the college's buildings and bringing them under one roof. Bloomsbury is easily accessible by public transport and cycle routes. Most Birkbeck students live in the capital, but full-time students looking for housing can apply to the University of London Accommodation Office.

Undergraduate Fees and Bursaries
» Fees for UK/EU students 2014–15   £6,750
  (on the basis of students studying for four years at 75 per cent intensity, equivalent to £9,000 full-time fees).
» International student fees 2013–14   £11,334–£11,925
  (full-time courses)
» NSP awards: household income below £20K, £3,000 fee waiver for first 120 credits of study.
» Household income below £25K, up to £1,000 cash a year; for household income £25K–£35K, up to £800 a year, both awards depending on intensity of study.

Students
Undergraduates:	**320**	**(13,120)**
Postgraduates:	**1,360**	**(4,780)**
Mature students:	**60.1%**	
Overseas students:	**6.4%**	
Applications per place:	**2.7**	
From state-sector schools:	**77.4%**	
From working-class homes:	**25.0%**	
Satisfaction with students' union	**61%**	

For detailed information about sports facilities:
www.ulu.co.uk/content/621793/energybase/

Accommodation
Number of places and costs refer to 2013–14
The university has a limited number of places in the intercollegiate halls of residence, and these are normally reserved for full-time international students.
Catered costs: £130.90 (mini single) – £185.50 (standard single); £153.90 (twin); £206.50–£230.30 (en-suite single); £173.25 (en-suite twin) a week.
For further accommodation information see:
www.bbk.ac.uk/mybirkbeck/services/facilities/accommodation
www.bbk.ac.uk/prospective/international/accommodation

University of Birmingham

Birmingham responded to a drop in both applications and enrolments in the first year of higher fees with a bold initiative for courses beginning in 2013. The university promised unconditional offers for applicants in a dozen subjects who were predicted better than three As at A level. About 1,200 applicants were expected to receive the offer in subjects from maths to metallurgy and modern languages by committing to making Birmingham one of their two choices. Other subjects included accounting and finance, business management, classics, economics, international relations, philosophy, politics and sociology.

Birmingham was the original "redbrick" university. Vice-Chancellor Sir David Eastwood said on his appointment that he wanted the university to be the "best of the rest" outside Oxbridge and the top London colleges, and a series of initiatives in teaching and research are taking the university in the right direction. One of them has seen Birmingham partner with the University of Nottingham on a series of projects, mainly in research. It is our 2014 University of the Year.

The university is part way through a long-term programme of investment. Recent developments costing £700 million include a student facilities building at the medical school, a new home for sport and exercise sciences and a well-equipped learning centre, as well as refurbished student accommodation. The programme has also included a new music building with 450-seat auditorium, improved library and IT services, and enhanced student support. The university has also invested £3.5 million on an employability initiative which will include internships and mentoring by some of the university's most successful alumni.

Birmingham's 25,000 full-time students include 4,000 from 150 different countries. Three-quarters of them undertake work experience as part of their course. The university encourages interdisciplinary study, for example allowing undergraduates to combine technology with subjects ranging from Latin or modern Greek to the management of floods and other natural disasters.

The university has stepped up its efforts to widen participation to coincide with the introduction of £9,000 fees. Over 4,000 students are expected to benefit from its package of enhanced financial support for those from lower income backgrounds. The Access to Birmingham (A2B) scheme, which encourages students from the West Midlands whose families have little or no experience of higher education to apply to university, will be extended to students outside the Midlands.

The university's enduring reputation is

Edgbaston
Birmingham B15 2TT

0121 415 8900 (admissions)
admissions@bham.ac.uk
www.bham.ac.uk
www.guildofstudents.com
Affiliation: Russell Group

The Times and Sunday Times **Rankings**
Overall Ranking: **16** (=24)

Student satisfaction:	=54	(81.8%)
Research quality:	=21	(24.0%)
Entry standards:	18	(444)
Student–staff ratio:	=23	(14.8)
Services & facilities/student:	10	(£2,219)
Expected completion rate:	=13	(95.1%)
Good honours:	17	(78.8%)
Graduate prospects:	8	(80.8%)

based on its research, with 16 per cent of the work submitted for the Research Assessment Exercise regarded as world-leading. Birmingham took satisfaction from the broad range of subjects in which it produced good results, with music, physics, computer science, mechanical engineering, European studies, primary care, cancer sciences, psychology and law all doing well. Birmingham is the hub for a national STEM programme to promote interest in science, technology, engineering and maths among young people and enhance higher level skills in the workplace. It has also become the first link in a chain of Cancer Research UK Centres, while a £60-million fundraising campaign launched in 2009 will support projects ranging from research into brain injury, ageing and clean energy to scholarships and a centre for heritage and cultural learning.

The 230-acre campus in leafy Edgbaston is dominated by a 300-foot clock tower, one of the city's best-known landmarks, and boasts its own station. Dentistry is located in the city centre, while part of the School of Education is in Selly Oak, a mile from the Edgbaston campus. Drama is also located there, along with the BBC Drama Village, which is part of a strategic alliance between the university and the corporation.

The University of Birmingham's Teacher Education Partnership has been graded "outstanding" in all categories in its latest Ofsted report.

Most of the halls and university flats are conveniently located in an attractive parkland setting near the main campus. There are more than 4,200 university-owned beds, and accommodation in the private sector is also plentiful. The campus is less than three miles from the city centre, but the area has plenty of shops, pubs and restaurants. With its own nightclub among the facilities on campus, some students do not even stray that far, but the city is acquiring a growing reputation among the young. Some 40 per cent of Birmingham graduates make the city their home.

Student facilities on campus are on a par with the best in the country, and include a medical practice. An outdoor pursuits centre is by Coniston Water in the Lake District. The voluntary Active Lifestyles Programme attracts 4,000 students to 150 different courses.

Undergraduate Fees and Bursaries

- » Fees for UK/EU students 2014–15 £9,000
- » International student fees 2013–14 £12,140–£16,000
  Clinical medicine £28,100
- » For UK/EU students with household income below £16,190, either £3,000 university accommodation discount, £3,000 fee waiver, or £2,000 fee waiver and £1,000 cash, year 1; eligibility re-assessed each year, with £2,000 package.
- » With household income up to £36K, Chamberlain Awards of £1,000–£2,000 a year.
- » Check the university's website for the latest information.

Students

Undergraduates:	**17,855**	**(1,335)**
Postgraduates:	**7,095**	**(4,780)**
Mature students:	**7.6%**	
Overseas students:	**10.6%**	
Applications per place:	**7.6**	
From state-sector schools:	**76.1%**	
From working-class homes:	**21.2%**	
Satisfaction with students' union	**69%**	

For detailed information about sports facilities:
www.sport.bham.ac.uk

Accommodation

Number of places and costs refer to 2013–14
University-provided places: 4,279
Percentage catered: 28%
Catered costs: £116–£176 a week.
Self-catered costs: £81–£141 a week.
All first years are guaranteed housing (subject to conditions).
International students: as above.
Contact: living@contacts.bham.ac.uk
www.birmingham.ac.uk/students/accommodation

Birmingham City University

Birmingham City University (BCU) is opening the first phase of a new campus in the heart of the city in time for the 2013–14 academic year. Situated next to Millennium Point and opposite the newly opened Eastside City Park, the £125-million development should be complete by 2015 and become the university's main base. The project is intended to create a Learning Quarter in Eastside and provide a home for the Birmingham Institute of Art and Design (BIAD), one of the six faculties of the university. The BIAD is the largest institute of its kind outside London, and includes the world-famous School of Jewellery. The development will also feature a "media hub" with industry-standard TV, radio and photographic studios that will underpin the university's media production courses.

BCU has been remodelling its estate for some time, although it still has six sites in and around the city centre and a main base (scheduled for closure when the new campus is complete) three miles to the north. Millennium Point already houses computing and engineering, as well as the Birmingham School of Acting, while the Conservatoire – one of BCU's best-known features – is located in the city's convention centre. Courses from opera to world music have given it a reputation for innovation.

The Edgbaston campus has been refurbished for the Faculty of Health, with a prize-winning library, IT suites, teaching facilities and recreational space. Meanwhile, the Bournville campus, which occupies part of the Cadbury Village, will host a new college for overseas students to support BCU's international ambitions. Birmingham City University International College is due to open in September 2013, following the transfer of art and design courses to the new city campus, and will provide bespoke pathways leading to undergraduate and postgraduate courses at the university. The college is a joint venture with global education provider Navitas Ltd.

The university has thrived since adopting its new name in 2007, with record demand for places. Applications stalled with the move to higher fees in 2012, but the university still managed to fill more places than in the previous year. The switch from the previous identity as UCE Birmingham was designed to emphasise the university's location, reinforce its close relationship with the city and give the university a stronger identity. The university enjoys strong links with business and the professions.

As a pioneer in green technology, BCU is attracting support from national and regional partners to help support a green economy with the potential to create thousands of jobs. There is a strong emphasis on making graduates "job-ready",

---

City North Campus
Birmingham B42 2SU

0121 331 5595 (enquiries)
access via website
www.bcu.ac.uk
www.bcusu.com
Affiliation: million+

The Times and Sunday Times **Rankings**
Overall Ranking: **=91** (=75)

Student satisfaction:	=96	(78.7%)
Research quality:	=90	(2.3%)
Entry standards:	64	(323)
Student–staff ratio:	95	(21)
Services & facilities/student:	54	(£1,483)
Expected completion rate:	=84	(81.9%)
Good honours:	=88	(59.1%)
Graduate prospects:	=66	(62.4%)

with support schemes and work placements among a raft of initiatives designed to help develop skills and knowledge for the workplace. High-powered visiting lecturers and an innovative i-learning strategy contribute to this agenda, with students having access to learning tools and facilities, such as Shareville – a virtual town where students can engage with real-life scenarios.

The prize-winning Student Academic Partners scheme has spawned a formal agreement between the university and the students' union to improve the student experience. Internal student surveys have led to the introduction of internet tutorials in engineering and new help with research for law and social science undergraduates. Teacher education courses consistently produce among the best scores in Ofsted inspections. The university was also awarded a national teaching centre in health and social care.

More than 42 per cent of the students come from working-class homes and 97 per cent were state educated. About half come from the West Midlands, many from ethnic minorities. The dropout rate has been improving and now matches the national average for BCU's courses and entry grades. The university also has one of the largest programmes of part-time courses in Britain, making it the biggest provider of higher education in the region. With the city's other universities, BCU is working with schools in the region to maintain its record of inspiring more young people to go on to higher education. Many students enter through the network of associated further education colleges, which run foundation and access programmes.

The university has been increasing its portfolio of high-tech degree courses such as electronic commerce, communications and network engineering, and electronic systems. The 2008 Research Assessment Exercise recorded some world-leading work in all seven areas covered by the university's submission. In art and design, 30 per cent were given the top grade, placing Birmingham City in the top ten for the subject. Most research is applied, with an accent on employment in the region.

University-owned accommodation is guaranteed for first years. The city's student scene is highly rated and has been charted in a Lonely Planet guide.

Undergraduate Fees and Bursaries

» Fees for UK/EU students 2014–15   £7,500–£8,200
    Conservatoire, acting, jewellery and education   £9,000
    Foundation degree   £6,000
» International student fees 2013–14   £10,100–£11,300
    Conservatoire and acting   £13,000–£14,600
» Over 660 NSP awards with conditions (priority given to students from partner schools or colleges): £3,000 fee waiver, year 1; £1,250 fee waiver, year 2; £1,000 cash ,year 3.
» Check the university's website for the latest information.

Students

Undergraduates:	**15,470**	**(4,055)**
Postgraduates:	**1,895**	**(1,750)**
Mature students:	**30.9%**	
Overseas students:	**8.1%**	
Applications per place:	**5.4**	
From state-sector schools:	**97.0%**	
From working-class homes:	**42.2%**	
Satisfaction with students' union	**63%**	

For detailed information about sports facilities:
www.bcusu.com/sports

Accommodation

Number of places and costs refer to 2013–14
University-provided places: 2,485
Percentage catered: 0%
Self-catered costs: £83.50–£132.00 a week (40–42 weeks).
Accommodation guaranteed for first years if conditions are met.
International students are guaranteed accommodation.
Contact: http://www.bcu.ac.uk/student-info/accommodation
accommodation@bcu.ac.uk

University College Birmingham (UCB)

UCB is a unique among the universities in England in having more than a third of its students taking further education programmes. For that reason, the new university was concerned that it would be at a disadvantage in league tables and has instructed the Higher Education Statistics Agency not to release data this year. Consequently, it does not appear in our main league table or any of the subject tables. UCB is the largest of the dozen universities established when the criteria for university status changed – and the only one not to change its name. The others were quick to drop the word "college" from their titles to emphasise their new status, but a formulation that is good enough for University College London should also work in Birmingham. Against the national trend, applications went up when fees of £7,800 arrived in 2012. Students beginning degrees or Foundation degrees in 2014 will pay £8,282 – among the lowest charges at any university in England.

The new university traces its history back more than 100 years, to the foundation of a Municipal Technical School offering cookery and household science courses. Several different titles followed until it became a university college in 2007 and received degree awarding powers, although some degrees are still accredited by the University of Birmingham. UCB now has more than 5,500 higher education students and nearly 2,500 taking further education courses. The core subjects are hospitality, tourism, business, sport and education. The most recent Ofsted inspection rated the further education provision as outstanding, while 100 per cent of students in the most recent exit survey rated their postgraduate teacher training as good or better. Overall satisfaction among all final-year undergraduates slipped slightly in the 2013 National Student Survey, but the college was still close to the national average. UCB has an international reputation in hospitality and tourism, with about a third of the students coming from outside the UK.

UCB is based in Birmingham city centre, close to the International Convention Centre, Symphony Hall and Birmingham Central Library, as well as the main shopping areas. The main campus is at Summer Row, with New Street train station a five-minute walk away. As well as lecture theatres and computer suites, it has a student resource centre, language centre, careers and employability centre, library and Student Guild office. Specialist teaching facilities include high-quality training kitchens, commercial training restaurants, full bakery and a product development

Summer Row
Birmingham B3 1JB

0121 232 4300 (course enquiries)
admissions@ucb.ac.uk
www.ucb.ac.uk
www.ucbsu.com
Affiliation: GuildHE

***The Times and Sunday Times* Rankings**
University College Birmingham blocked the release of data from the Higher Education Statistics Agency and so we cannot give any ranking information.

kitchen. UCB is spending more than £50 million on new facilities for both further and higher education students. The £25-million first phase of development of a four-acre site in the city's Jewellery Quarter will open in 2014, increasing the university's teaching and learning facilities by 25 per cent. Built to the highest energy-efficient standards, the campus will include a dedicated Postgraduate Centre, a 24-hour flexible learning centre, lecture theatres, café and additional social breakout spaces. Work on Phase Two will begin at the end of 2013 and see the development of a new campus for further education students, which may allow new subjects to be added.

UCB focuses on giving students an advantage in the highly competitive graduate job market. As well as arranging placements in industry during courses, the Careers and Employability Centre team provides students with support to develop skills such as communication, teamwork, problem solving and time management through work experience, workshops, volunteering, part time and seasonal work. There are strong relationships with employers, including a job-shop service which is accessible 24 hours a day. Student ambassadors promote further and higher education to young people from a diverse range of backgrounds. Over 96 per cent of the undergraduates are state educated and almost half come from the four poorest socio-economic groups. However, the projected dropout rate of almost 18 per cent is significantly worse than the national average for UCB's courses and entry qualifications.

More than 1,000 students can be accommodated in UCB's halls of residence, and accommodation can be offered to all years and programmes of study. The Maltings halls are ten minutes' walk from UCB and Cambrian Hall is only 150 yards from the main campus. Both offer among the best value in the Midlands. The Spa, at Richmond House on Newhall Street, offers hairdressing salons, beauty therapy suites, sports therapy clinic, a multi-gym, and fitness assessment suite. There is also a gym and sports hall at the Maltings site, which are open on weekday evenings and at weekends. Two restaurants staffed by the university's students are open to the public, as well as to students and staff.

Undergraduate Fees and Bursaries

» Fees for UK/EU students 2014–15: £8,282
» International student fees 2013–14: £8,800
» Around 350 NSP awards: household income £16K or below, £3,000 fee waiver, year 1; £1,030 fee waiver, years 2 and 3. For other English students with household income below £16K, £1,030 fee waiver, years 1–3.
» £1,030 fee waiver in all years for students progressing from an FE course at UCB.
» Check the university's website for the latest information.

Students

Undergraduates:	**3,215**	**(1,255)**
Postgraduates:	**430**	**(90)**
From state-sector schools:	**96.9%**	
From working-class homes:	**48.6%**	
Satisfaction with students' union	**63%**	

For detailed information about sports facilities:
www.ucb.ac.uk/facilities/gym-and-sports.aspx

Accommodation

Places and costs refer to 2013–14
University-provided places: 1,074
Percentage catered: 0%
Self-catered costs: £76; £88 (standard) – £151 (twin) for 42 weeks.
Priority is given to disabled students (new and returning) and new full-time students by application date.
International students: guaranteed housing if application received by mid June
Contact: accommodation@ucb.ac.uk;
www.ucb.ac.uk/facilities/student-accommodation.aspx

Bishop Grosseteste University

Bishop Grosseteste celebrated 150 years of teacher training in 2012 with the award of university status. With only 2,000 students on its campus in Lincoln, the former university college used to be too small to become a university, but a change of rules allowed it to take the title at last. Although still best known for the training of teachers, which is highly rated by Ofsted, Bishop Grosseteste long since expanded into other academic areas, mainly in the arts and social sciences. It has awarded its own degrees since 2006. The university makes its debut in *The Times and Sunday Times* league table as the lowest of the new arrivals.

Named after a theologian and scholar who was bishop of Lincoln in the 13th century, BGU was originally known as the Diocesan Training School for Mistresses. It is still proudly associated with the Church of England, although it welcomes students of all faiths and none. Indeed, the new prospectus proclaims: "We've had a change of name (but not a change of heart)." It describes itself as a Church university within the Anglican tradition.

BGU occupies an attractive, leafy and secluded campus in uphill Lincoln, not far from the gothic cathedral and castle, built by the occupying Normans in 1086. The campus has a friendly, welcoming feel. The campus entrance and reception area has been remodelled at a cost of £250,000. Other recent developments have seen the campus theatre equipped with a new digital projection system, surround sound and fully refurbished seating to double as a cinema which can also stage theatrical productions. The Venue is now home to the Lincoln Film Society and is open to staff, students and the public. Also in 2012, the library was extended and given a new name: the Cornerstone Building is now home to Library Services and the Student Support and Learning Advice teams. The students' union building has had a major refit and new teaching and learning spaces added. The next phase of the university's campus investment will see the refurbishment and extension of its student accommodation.

Fees for degree courses were set at £7,500 for the first two years of higher charges, but will go up to £8,500 for 2014–15. Foundation degrees will cost £6,375 a year. Against the national trend, both applications and enrolments went up when the new fee regime arrived in 2012 – ahead of the announcement that university status would be awarded. Over 28 per cent of the undergraduates are from working-class families and 20 per cent come from areas of low participation in higher education – one of the largest proportions at any university.

Lincoln LN1 3DY

01522 527347
admissions@bishopg.ac.uk
www.bishopg.ac.uk
www.bgstudentsunion.org
Affiliation: GuildHE,
Cathedrals Group

The Times and Sunday Times **Rankings**
Overall Ranking: **=106** (n/a)

Student satisfaction:	**=54**	(81.8%)
Research quality:	**=115**	(0.3%)
Entry standards:	**114**	(247)
Student–staff ratio:	**120**	(32.9)
Services & facilities/student:	**120**	(£452)
Expected completion rate:	**31**	(91.6%)
Good honours:	**90**	(58.9%)
Graduate prospects:	**55**	(66.4%)

The new university is divided into two schools. The School of Teacher Development offers undergraduate and postgraduate training courses, as well as conducting research. The School of Culture, Education and Innovation covers a dozen disciplines and in subjects as diverse as mathematics and art. History, music, drama, sport, archaeology and theology are also offered in a portfolio of degree courses that includes a range of combined degrees. From 2013, students will be able to study tourism, psychology or enterprise and entrepreneurship in combination with another degree subject. Tourism will also be offered as a single honours degree. After its most recent Ofsted inspection in 2010, Initial Teacher Training at BGU was graded "Excellent" for primary teaching and "Good" for secondary teaching.

Business development is among the priorities identified in the new university's strategic plan. A business start-up centre has opened on campus and is proving popular with new businesses and entrepreneurs. BG Futures differs from other incubation centres by emphasising the university's values of equality and diversity.

New student accommodation costing £4.3 million is being built on campus to replace an older hall which has been demolished. It will have 126 en-suite bedrooms in groups of six with a shared common room and kitchen. The new development will increase the number of student rooms on campus from just over 200 to 280, and should be completed in time for the start of the academic year in 2013. The university also took on a purpose-built student accommodation with 79 additional rooms close to the campus in 2013. The Sport and Fitness Centre has a sports hall which can cater for a variety of different sporting activities and fitness classes and a well-appointed fitness suite. Ten acres of sports fields are close by. The city of Lincoln is one of the fastest-growing in the UK, with relatively low living costs. It may not compete with the big conurbations for youth culture, but it has a growing student population and a range of bars and nightclubs to serve it.

Undergraduate Fees and Bursaries

» Fees for UK/EU students 2014–15: £8,500
   Foundation degree £6,375
» International student fees 22013–14: £8,800
» 97 NSP awards, with conditions, of £1,000 cash bursary and £2,000 contribution to accommodation costs on or off campus, year 1; £1,021 package, years 2 and 3.
» Range of other scholarships and bursaries available.
» Check the university's website for the latest information.

Students

Undergraduates:	**1,845**	**(50)**
Postgraduates:	**110**	**(245)**
Mature students:	**10.7%**	
Overseas students:	**0%**	
Applications per place:	**3.4**	
From state-sector schools:	**97.4%**	
From working-class homes:	**46.4%**	
Satisfaction with students' union	**60%**	

For detailed information about sports facilities: www.bishopg.ac.uk/?_id=10236

Accommodation

Number of places and costs refer to 2013–14
University-provided places: 218 on campus; 79 off campus.
Percentage catered: 0%
Self-catered costs: £89 (shared) – £118 (en suite) for 33 weeks.
Priority is given to disabled and new full-time students on a first come, first served basis.
International students: limited accommodation is available.
Contact: www.bishopg.ac.uk/?_id=10432

University of Bolton

Bolton offered some of the lowest fees at any university in 2013, averaging less than £6,500 after all forms of financial support were taken into consideration. That figure will still be lower than most of its rivals' in 2014, but the headline fee is rising to £9,000. New enrolments dropped by a quarter with the initial rise in fees in 2012, as two years of healthy increases in the volume of applications came to an abrupt halt. With around 11,000 students – mainly in the town centre, but also in partner colleges in several Asian countries – the university was not planning further expansion, however. There is now a single campus in the centre of the town, as well as a branch campus in the United Arab Emirates. The Ras as Khaimah campus opened in 2008, offering a range of undergraduate and postgraduate courses identical to those taught at Bolton. The £1-million development near Dubai has 270 students and is intended to take 700 within five years. Students at Bolton also have the opportunity to study in the UAE for part of their degree course.

The university has spent £41 million on its Bolton campus. The rationalisation of sites in the town has provided additional · and enhanced teaching space, facilities to interact with industry and a new students' union. In 2013, the university has launched the Bolton Business School, which hosts business, law and accountancy courses, along with the Centre of Islamic Finance. The school includes a £100,000 law court for students to develop their advocacy skills. Bolton is also planning a purpose-built Centre for Advanced Performance Engineering, to be run in conjunction with a motorsports company.

The university traces its roots back as far as 1824 to one of the country's first three mechanics institutes. In spite of an international dimension that stretches to Malaysia, China, Zambia, Malawi and Vietnam, it sees itself as primarily a regional institution. A concrete example of this approach came with the opening of Bolton One, a £31-million health, leisure and research centre for students and the local community, built in partnership between Bolton Council, NHS Bolton and the university. The student population is one of the most ethnically diverse in the UK, with around a quarter of UK students coming from ethnic minority communities.

Bolton is not a research-driven university, but it has been accredited for research degrees for more than a decade. About 1,400 of the students are postgraduates, taking qualifications up to and including PhDs. Engineering, architecture and the built environment, social work and social policy all contained some world-leading research in the 2008

Deane Road
Bolton BL3 5AB

01204 903903 (course enquiries)
enquiries@bolton.ac.uk
www.bolton.ac.uk
www.ubsu.org.uk
Affiliation: million+

The Times and Sunday Times Rankings

Overall Ranking: **119** (115)

Student satisfaction:	=107	(77%)
Research quality:	=92	(2.0%)
Entry standards:	108	(270)
Student–staff ratio:	91	(20.6)
Services & facilities/student:	115	(£899)
Expected completion rate:	119	(68.6%)
Good honours:	118	(49.2%)
Graduate prospects:	=109	(52.8%)

assessments. An institute for research and innovation in materials was the first of a series of "knowledge exchange zones". Institutes for educational cybernetics and renewable energy and environmental technologies have followed, as well as a research centre for health and wellbeing.

The building programme at the Deane campus has included a design studio and three floors of teaching and learning space where students work on actual briefs for companies seeking design solutions, an Innovation Factory housing, among others, special effects laboratories and a product design studio. Within this development is a new social learning zone which includes students' union offices, advice centre, bar and social facilities, plus a computer access room. Bespoke facilities for arts students have been developed across the top floor of Eagle Tower.

Bolton One, which opened in 2012, boasts a 25-metre swimming pool and sports complex that includes a gym, dance studio, sports courts and climbing wall, as well as health service facilities. The building also contains teaching and research space. Some 700 residential places are reasonably priced and go a long way towards meeting the demand for accommodation in an institution with a high proportion of local students. Well over a third of the undergraduates are 21 or over at entry.

The university exceeds all the access measures designed to widen participation in higher education: more than 47 per cent are from working-class homes and the proportion from areas without a tradition of higher education is among the highest in the UK. The downside – and an important one – is that, despite a big improvement since the previous survey, the projected dropout rate remains by far the highest of any university in England. More than a quarter of the first years who entered in 2010 are expected to leave without a qualification – a rate that is considerably worse than the national average for Bolton's degree subjects and entry grades. However, the university says it has improved on some of the measures used in such exercises in the period since the statistics were collected.

Undergraduate Fees and Bursaries

» Fees for UK/EU students 2014–15: £9,000
   Courses at partner colleges: £5,400–£6,600
» International student fees 2013–14 £9,400
» 315 NSP awards: £3,000 fee waiver, year 1; £1,000 fee waiver, years 2 and 3.
» Grant of £400 each year for students from partner colleges with household income below £25K and not receiving NSP.
» Vice Chancellor's Award, up to £15,000, for most outstanding and academically gifted, students (max. three awards a year).
» Range of other scholarships and bursaries available.
» Check the university's website for the latest information.

Students

Undergraduates:	**4,330**	**(2,710)**
Postgraduates:	**615**	**(830)**
Mature students:	**36.5%**	
Overseas students:	**7.8%**	
Applications per place:	**4.5**	
From state-sector schools:	**98.6%**	
From working-class homes:	**47.7%**	
Satisfaction with students' union	**56%**	

For detailed information about sports facilities:
http://bolton.ac.uk/Sport/Home.aspx

Accommodation

Number of places and costs refer to 2013–14
University-provided places: 700
Percentage catered: 0%
Self-catered costs: £2,902 (38 weeks); £76.37 a week.
All first years are generally accommodated.
International students: accommodation is secured for these students.
Contact: accomm@bolton.ac.uk

Bournemouth University

Bournemouth has led a yo-yo existence in our league table, rising 27 places in four years and then slipping back 19 after scores in the National Student Survey collapsed last year. This year sees another big rise after student satisfaction recovered. The university did its best to compensate for the 2012 fees increase by promising every undergraduate a work placement, typically 40 weeks in length. An independent survey published in 2013 showed that Bournemouth had the highest proportion of graduates (almost 90 per cent) with some form of work experience on their CV – a feature that invariably translates into good graduate employment prospects. The retail management degree, for example, notched up eight successive years of full employment. However, Bournemouth still suffered big falls in applications and enrolments in 2012, when most degrees cost £8,250 a year. The norm has since gone up to £9,000, although Foundation degrees were still available at £6,000 a year for 2013–14.

The university has been changing its approach from one that once gloried in the absence of traditional academic disciplines. It appointed 150 academics in three years to "foster the development of an academically-led culture". Research moved up the agenda with a £1-million investment in 80

PhD studentships – only three universities showed more improvement in the last set of research assessments – and undergraduates' entry qualifications have been rising. Bournemouth has particular strengths in media subjects and boasts the National Centre of Computer Animation, a field in which the university was awarded a Queen's Anniversary Prize in 2012. State-of-the-art equipment includes a motion capture facility for real-time animation, which is used in teaching and available for use by outside companies. The university was designated as England's only centre for excellence in media practice.

Bournemouth claims a number of firsts in its portfolio of courses, notably in the area of tourism, media-related programmes and conservation. Degrees in public relations, retail management, script-writing and tax law were all ahead of their time. Foundation degrees are delivered in five further education colleges in Dorset and Somerset, as well as on the main campus. They support the needs of business in the creative arts, media and tourism. One even serves soldiers based in Afghanistan, who are studying business and management via the internet. Top-up courses are available for those who wish to turn their qualification into an honours degree.

Virtually all students take up the offer of personal development planning, both online and with trained staff, while 1,400 first

---

Fern Barrow
Talbot Campus
Poole
Dorset BH12 5BB

01202 961916 (enquiries)
askBUenquiries@
    bournemouth.ac.uk
www.bournemouth.ac.uk
www.subu.org.uk
Affiliation: University Alliance

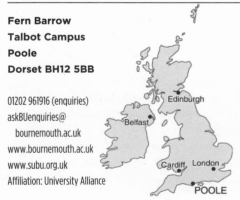

POOLE

The Times and Sunday Times Rankings
Overall Ranking: **67** (=81)

Student satisfaction:	100	(78.3%)
Research quality:	=70	(4.3%)
Entry standards:	51	(345)
Student–staff ratio:	99	(21.5)
Services & facilities/student:	63	(£1,377)
Expected completion rate:	=48	(87.2%)
Good honours:	49	(68.4%)
Graduate prospects:	=58	(63.9%)

years also take advantage of peer-assisted learning, receiving advice and mentoring from more experienced undergraduates. Bournemouth has also been increasing its use of education technology, for example to enable its part-time students to study from home or the workplace and reduce the amount of time they need spend on campus. The library's use of new technology helped it to the title of "best large library" in the UK, awarded by the Society of College, National and University Libraries. In the 2008 Research Assessment Exercise, eight of the ten subject areas contained at least some world-leading research, with art and design and communication, cultural and media studies producing the best grades.

New teaching and residential accommodation has been added in recent years, with more to come. There is a wide range of accommodation and students based in halls of residence in Poole enjoy a millionaire's view of the Harbour. Recent developments include a new Executive Business Centre, which is a focus for services to local companies, and £1.5 million has been spent on improvements to information technology. There are now two campuses – the original Talbot site in Poole and a dedicated campus in Bournemouth – with partner colleges in Bridgwater, Yeovil, Bournemouth and Poole, Dorchester and Weymouth. The university finished on the verge of the top ten in the 2013 People and Planet Green League of environmental performance.

The southern seaside location and the subject mix attract more middle-class students than most new universities, although 92 per cent attended state schools. The campuses are served by a subsidised bus service and students are discouraged from bringing cars. The students' union's Old Fire Station bar is among many nightlife options. The surf reef, off Boscombe seafront, is helping to transform the area into the UK's latest surfing hotspot and other water sports are catered for in Poole Harbour. Sports facilities have been improving and in 2012 there was a complete refurbishment of the gym suite, with the addition of a new multipurpose large studio.

Undergraduate Fees and Bursaries

» Fees for UK/EU students 2014–15 £9,000
   Foundation degree £6,000
   Foundation degree, long course £8,450
» International student fees 2013–14 £9,500–£12,000
» 596 NSP awards: £400 cash, £2,000 fee or accommodation waiver, £600 living expenses vouchers, year 1; £300 cash, £200 living expenses vouchers, £1,000 fee waiver or additional vouchers, years 2 and 3.
» Check the university's website for the latest information.

Students		
Undergraduates:	**13,160**	**(3,815)**
Postgraduates:	**1,510**	**(1,265)**
Mature students:	**19%**	
Overseas students:	**6.8%**	
Applications per place:	**5.5**	
From state-sector schools:	**92.4%**	
From working-class homes:	**28.2%**	
Satisfaction with students' union	**78%**	

For detailed information about sports facilities:
http://studentportal.bournemouth.ac.uk/things/sportbu/

Accommodation
Number of places and costs refer to 2013–14
University-provided places: about 3,246 (2,846 in halls; 400 head tenancy)
Percentage catered: 0%
Self-catered costs: £100–£112 (single); £131–£145 (studio) a week.
The university expects to offer all first years a place to live.
Residential restrictions apply.
International students: guaranteed if conditions are met.
Contact: accommodation@bournemouth.ac.uk

University of Bradford

Bradford pulled off something of a coup with the appointment as vice-chancellor of Professor Brian Cantor, the former Vice-Chancellor of York University. At York, Professor Cantor oversaw major expansion with the establishment of a new campus and took the university into the Russell Group, but he will face different challenges at Bradford. The university is at the heart of the city's plans for regeneration, but first-year enrolments were down by more than 18 per cent in 2012, as fees for degree courses hit £9,000.

The university has been a leading light in the green movement in higher education, with its "ecoversity" programme addressing issues of sustainable development in all the university's practices, including the curriculum. The most visible sign was the opening in 2011 of The Green, a sustainable student village catering mainly for 1,000 first-year and international students. The development, which won a Green Gown award for sustainability in 2012, is part of a £70-million modernisation plan that includes a £7-million investment in new and upgraded teaching facilities. Bradford was in the top ten in the People and Planet Green League of universities' environmental performance for 2013. A major refurbishment of the library made carbon savings by maximising insulation and natural ventilation, while the "edible campus" project allows gardeners to improve the inner-city site and to monitor biodiversity.

Still relatively small, Bradford has carved out a niche for itself with mature students, who now make up around a quarter of all undergraduates. They relish the vocational slant and the accent on work experience and placement courses which regularly place Bradford towards the top of the graduate employment tables. However, the university has slipped below a number of newer institutions in *The Times and Sunday Times* league table and is now one of the lowest-ranked pre-1992 institutions.

Nearly half of the undergraduates are from working-class homes – the biggest proportion at any of the older universities. Just over 16 per cent of the university's students are from overseas, many of them taught in partner institutions in locations as diverse as Poland, India, Iceland and Hong Kong. Nearer home, there are alliances with a number of further education colleges to help boost participation in a region where it is well below the national average. The colleges offer Foundation degrees in areas such as public sector administration, community justice, engineering technology and enterprise in IT. Perhaps the best known is in health and social care, where the university was already expanding opportunities locally, bringing about a

Richmond Road
Bradford
West Yorkshire BD7 1DP

0800 073 1225 (freephone)
course-enquiries@bradford.ac.uk
www.bradford.ac.uk
http://www.brad.ac.uk/
    students-union/
Affiliation: University
    Alliance

The Times and Sunday Times Rankings
Overall Ranking: =84 (67)

Student satisfaction:	(79.7%)Research quality:
	(10.0%)Entry standards:
	(311)
Student–staff ratio:	(19.4)Services & facilities/student:
	(£1,393)Expected completion rate:
	(82.8%)Good honours:
(52.8%)Graduate prospects:	
(69.8%)	

fourfold increase in enrolments by young women from South Asian families.

The relatively small, lively campus is close to the city centre. Health students have moved into a new state-of-the-art facility on campus; the highly rated management school is two miles away in a 14-acre parkland setting. Improvements in recent years have included upgraded laboratories for chemical and forensic science, and new sports facilities including a gym and climbing wall and an improved sports hall. There is also a distinctive four-storey Atrium, which has brought together all student support services in a single, open-plan social space, while "Student Central", which houses the students' union, opened in 2010.

Bradford is harnessing the power of technology for new and prospective students. A so-called "e-induction" offers online preparation for university life, while those who do win a place are offered a "self-audit" that gauges new students' levels of confidence in different academic areas and allows them to develop an action plan with their personal tutor. Computer-assisted learning is increasing in many subjects, making use of unusually extensive IT provision and a new wireless network. Some courses feature online assessment and the use of laptops in lectures.

Some 80 per cent of the work submitted for the 2008 Research Assessment Exercise was placed in the top two categories, although more than a third of the academics were not entered. Social work and social policy, politics, civil engineering and pharmacy produced the best results. Politics includes peace studies, which has acquired an international reputation, while the human studies programme, which combines psychology, literature and sociology with philosophy, is another imaginative construct.

Places in halls are reasonably priced and all have internet connections. The university has particularly good provision for disabled students, who account for 6 per cent of the university population. Bradford's senior management group includes a Dean of Students to ensure that the student voice is heard in future developments.

Undergraduate Fees and Bursaries

» Fees for UK/EU students 2014–15 £9,000
  Foundation degree £7,500
» International student fees 2013–14 £11,000–£13,100
» 644 NSP awards with priority criteria: £1,500 fee waiver, £1,000 university accommodation discount or further fee waiver, £500 for university services, year 1; fees waived, sandwich year.
» UK/EU students with at least ABB at A level or equivalent, £1,500 cash, year 1; £1,000 cash, years 2 and 3.
» Check the university's website for the latest information.

Students

Undergraduates:	**9,580**	**(2,030)**
Postgraduates:	**1,135**	**(1,465)**
Mature students:	**26.4%**	
Overseas students:	**16.1%**	
Applications per place:	**5.7**	
From state-sector schools:	**94.9%**	
From working-class homes:	**48.4%**	
Satisfaction with students' union	**75%**	

For detailed information about sports facilities:
www.bradford.ac.uk/unique/

Accommodation

Number of places and costs refer to 2013–14
University-provided places: 1,051
Percentage catered: 0%
Self-catered costs: £97.34 (town house) – £105.28 (en suite) a week (42-week contracts).
All first-year undergraduate students are guaranteed accommodation (terms and conditions apply).
Contact: halls-of-residence@bradford.ac.uk
www.brad.ac.uk/accommodation

University of Brighton

Brighton has seen its applications grow in 2013, with strong demand for courses in engineering, computer science, illustration and medicine. The university's newest campus in Hastings, which focuses on digital and broadcast media, has seen a 25 per cent increase. But Brighton is yet to recover the ground lost on the introduction of £9,000 fees. The university tried to compensate for higher charges with an increased focus on employability. Career planning and development, as well as employability skills, are now built into every course, while leadership skills, management training and enterprise are available as modules or in workshops. More than nine out of ten courses include a work placement or a sandwich year. Degrees are designed in collaboration with employers in the public and private sectors, three-quarters of them endorsed by professional associations. Applications still dropped by 15 per cent in 2012, although there was a much smaller decline in enrolments.

There are 22,000 students on five campuses, and the university has spent more than £100 million on new buildings and equipment in the last decade. The School of Education, as well as languages and literature students, moved into a new building on the Falmer campus, which now also boasts a £7.3-million sports centre. Meanwhile, at the Moulsecoomb site, the £23-million Huxley Building has provided a new home for pharmacy and biosciences. The developments have helped the university to fifth place in the People and Planet Green League, with the judges also praising its approach to sustainability in the curriculum. Brighton has set itself a target of reducing carbon emissions by 50 per cent in five years.

Brighton came of age as one of the first new universities to be awarded a medical school, but is equally well known for imaginative initiatives in its region. Its campus in Hastings runs a number of schemes to draw people from the region into higher education and to help them with practical problems. The £28.5-million medical school, run jointly with Sussex University, is training 128 doctors a year. Brighton was already heavily engaged in other health subjects, such as nursing and midwifery. The medical school's headquarters, on Brighton's Falmer campus, has also provided a new base for applied social sciences, such as criminology and applied psychology, which are among the university's most sought-after degrees.

The two universities have been collaborating since Brighton was a polytechnic. There is a joint research building for science policy and management studies, and a joint accord guarantees the offer of a place to

---

Mithras House
Lewes Road
Brighton BN2 4AT

01273 600900 (switchboard)
enquiries@brighton.ac.uk
www.brighton.ac.uk
www.bsms.ac.uk
www.brightonsu.com
Affiliation: none

The Times and Sunday Times **Rankings**
Overall Ranking: **76** (69)

Student satisfaction:	=73	(81%)
Research quality:	55	(9.7%)
Entry standards:	87	(304)
Student–staff ratio:	=66	(19)
Services & facilities/student:	114	(£929)
Expected completion rate:	64	(85.4%)
Good honours:	57	(65.3%)
Graduate prospects:	83	(58.6%)

all suitably qualified applicants from the Channel Island of Jersey. Brighton does the same for applicants from all of Sussex and leads a Learning Network for the county. Almost a third of undergraduates now come through these accords.

Brighton was again one of the top new universities in the last Research Assessment Exercise. Art and design produced the best results, with two-thirds of the work submitted considered world-leading or internationally excellent. Business management, sports studies and mechanical and aeronautical engineering also did well. Brighton's strengths in art and design – recognised in the award of national teaching centres in design and creativity – have been at the forefront of the university's popularity. But the university also has a growing reputation in areas such as sport and hospitality, as well as scoring well in teacher education rankings.

The Design Council's national archive is lodged on campus, and the four-year fashion textiles degree offers work placements in the USA, France and Italy, as well as Britain. Teaching facilities include a flight simulator, a fully functional newsroom for the university's sports journalists, modern clinical skills laboratories for pharmacy, and a custom-designed culinary arts studio. At Eastbourne there is a new library and extensive leisure and sports facilities, which attracted the Swedish tennis team for its

pre-Olympic preparations. Sport science laboratories and 354 en-suite residential places have been added, and improvements made to the learning resources centre, lecture theatres and refectory.

The university has a cosmopolitan air, with more overseas students and a more middle-class UK intake than most former polytechnics. Over a quarter of the full-time undergraduates are 21 or over on entry, often attracted by strongly vocational courses. Students have a personal tutor to advise on combinations within the modular degree scheme and there is an award-winning student services department.

Most like Brighton's lively social scene, despite the high cost of living for those not in hall. Eastbourne is also popular, and both towns offer plentiful accommodation to supplement the university's stock.

Undergraduate Fees and Bursaries

» Fees for UK/EU students 2014–15   £9,000
   Foundation degrees at partner colleges   £7,000–£7,500
» International student fees 2013–14   £10,900–£12,900
   Medicine   £24,860
» NSP awards with priority criteria: £1,000 cash, £1,000 fee waiver and £1,000 university services in year 1.
» Bursary for participants in Compact Plus outreach programme and eligible for NSP: £1,000 cash or university services, years 2 and 3; also £1,000 cash or university services in final year for those studying architecture, pharmacy and teaching and eligible for NSP.
» Check the university's website for the latest information.

Students

Undergraduates:	14,530	(3,130)
Postgraduates:	1,880	(2,530)
Mature students:	26.8%	
Overseas students:	10.7%	
Applications per place:	5.9	
From state-sector schools:	92.8%	
From working-class homes:	28.3%	
Satisfaction with students' union	56%	

For detailed information about sports facilities:
www.brighton.ac.uk/sportbrighton

Accommodation

Number of places and costs refer to 2013–14
University-provided places: 2,104; 300 in private sector university-managed houses or flats.
Percentage catered: 47%
Catered costs: £138–£159 a week.
Self-catered costs: £100–£150 a week.
First years have priority for housing if conditions are met.
International students: guaranteed accommodation if conditions are met.
Contact: accommodation@brighton.ac.uk

University of Bristol

Having resisted the temptation to expand over many years despite attracting more applications per place than any multi-faculty university in Britain, Bristol announced plans to take 600 more students when the fees went up and recruitment restrictions were lifted for the best-qualified applicants. In the event, it took 1,000 more, stretching its facilities to the limit. The university has long been a natural alternative to Oxbridge, favoured particularly by independent schools. In order to broaden the intake, departments may make slightly lower offers to the most promising applicants from the bottom 40 per cent of schools and colleges at A level.

The university's academic credentials are not in doubt – the QS rankings for 2012 placed it in the top 30 in the world. Entry standards are among the highest at any UK university and Bristol continued to live up to expectations in the last Research Assessment Exercise, when almost two-thirds of the work submitted was rated in the top two categories. Epidemiology and public health, health services research, chemistry, mathematics, drama, mechanical engineering and economics produced the best results. There are 33 Fellows of the Royal Society and similar numbers in other learned societies. The latest research development saw the opening in 2013 of an £18-million Centre for Power Electronics that will focus on delivering the underpinning science and engineering behind many low-carbon technologies.

There are now more than 13,000 full-time undergraduates, but Bristol remains among the smallest institutions in the Russell Group of elite research universities. The university's official strategy is to "stay relatively compact and nurture the collegial atmosphere that makes it a true community as well as an ambitious and challenging place to be." Bristol has tried hard to broaden its intake, spending more than £15 million since 2006 on recruiting and supporting students from disadvantaged backgrounds. However, in 2011–12 only 13 per cent came from a working-class home – the lowest proportion outside Oxbridge. Generous bursaries and fee waivers represent the latest attempt to broaden the intake. Local students who take the Access to Bristol course while at school or college will receive free education if their family income is less than £25,000.

The university celebrated its centenary in 2009 and launched a new fundraising campaign with a target of £100 million by 2014. The previous campaign helped the university to create new chairs and embark on a number of building projects, including a well-appointed centre for the highly rated chemistry department. Both chemistry and

Senate House
Tyndall Avenue
Bristol BS8 1TH

0117 928 9000 (switchboard)
ug-admissions@bristol.ac.uk
www.bristol.ac.uk
www.ubu.org.uk
Affiliation: Russell Group

The Times and Sunday Times **Rankings**
Overall Ranking: **15** (11)

Student satisfaction:	84	(80%)
Research quality:	=7	(29.7%)
Entry standards:	10	(487)
Student–staff ratio:	=17	(14.2)
Services & facilities/student:	19	(£2,034)
Expected completion rate:	3	(97.4%)
Good honours:	6	(84%)
Graduate prospects:	11	(79.1%)

medical sciences were chosen to house national teaching and learning centres, and the university was also awarded four centres to train doctoral scientists and engineers. The largest estate investment programme in the university's history is currently underway, with £200 million of projects due to be completed by 2016. A £54-million development of the Life Sciences Building, which will provide new teaching facilities and research laboratories for Biological Sciences and a range of related disciplines, is due to open early in 2014. A new hall of residence at the Stoke Bishop site will be ready for the 2014 intake, ensuring that the university continues to guarantee accommodation for all first years. A rolling programme of refurbishment is under way to modernise the existing halls.

An impressive sports complex with a well-equipped gym has been developed at the heart of the university precinct, where the careers centre has also been refurbished. The students' union houses one of the city's biggest live music venues as well as a café, bars, theatre and swimming pool. A £28-million refurbishment and redesign will be complete in 2014, providing more space for community activities and the 180 student societies and 50 sports clubs, as well as an extended café bar.

Bristol, as well as possessing a vibrant youth culture, is also relatively prosperous, offering job opportunities to students and graduates alike. The university merges into the centre, its famous gothic tower dominating the skyline from the junction of two of the main shopping streets. Despite its hills, Bristol is England's first Cycling City and was named Europe's best small city of the future for 2012/13 by FDI magazine.

The current students' union is less of a social centre than in some universities, partly because of the intense competition from nightclubs. Most students enjoy life in Bristol, although the high cost of living can be a drawback. The dropout rate is among the lowest in Britain, and one student in five stays in the city after graduation. Parts of the city suffer from the same security concerns as any big conurbation, but the university won a police-approved Secured Environments award for its crime protection work.

Undergraduate Fees and Bursaries

» Fees for UK/EU students 2014–15 £9,000
» International student fees 2013–14 £14,250–£16,250
    Dentistry, medicine, veterinary medicine £32,000
» For UK (excluding Welsh) students with household income £15K or below, £5,500 fee waiver; £15K–£20K, £4,500 fee waiver; £20K–£25K, £3,000 fee waiver; £2,000 of these fee waivers can be converted into a cash bursaries.
» For students in the Access to Bristol scheme with household income of £25K or below, a full fee waiver and annual maintenance bursary of £3,750.
» Range of other scholarships and bursaries available.
» Check the university's website for the latest information.

Students

Undergraduates:	**12,920**	**(515)**
Postgraduates:	**4,055**	**(1,660)**
Mature students:	**5.3%**	
Overseas students:	**14.3%**	
Applications per place:	**7.7**	
From state-sector schools:	**59.9%**	
From working-class homes:	**13.0%**	
Satisfaction with students' union	**48%**	

For detailed information about sports facilities:
www.bris.ac.uk/sport

Accommodation

Number of places and costs refer to 2013–14
University-provided places: about 4,304
Percentage catered: 42%
Catered costs: £115.95 (shared room) – £168.75 a week.
Self-catered costs: £62.50 (shared room) – £132.00 a week.
First years are guaranteed one offer of accommodation provided conditions are met.
International students: accommodation is guaranteed provided conditions are met.
Contact: www.bristol.ac.uk/accommodation/

Brunel University

Brunel's investment in buildings and infrastructure over the past decade is now in excess £400 million, with many new and refurbished social, teaching and recreational facilities, halls of residence, and more green spaces for students to enjoy. The programme has transformed the campus, which retains its original 1960s architecture but with the addition of striking new buildings and landscaping. Brunel's latest acquisition is the £30-million flagship Eastern Gateway Building that opened in July 2012, providing new teaching and research facilities, a large auditorium, a café and an art gallery. Previous developments have included a hugely extended library and sports facilities.

In recent years, Brunel has introduced more variety into a portfolio of degrees that was once given over almost entirely to sandwich courses. Many undergraduates take four-year degrees with extended work placements, but new developments have tended to focus on more conventional three-year arts, humanities or sports programmes. There has also been significant growth in courses specialising in new technologies, such as multimedia design and broadcast media, as well as health and social care. Other innovations include creative writing, professionally accredited journalism, sonic arts, aviation engineering and pilot studies, motorsport engineering and games design.

The university has tried to enhance graduates' prospects in the employment market through work placements and the inclusion in degree courses of skills modules, such as oral and written communication, business and computer literacy. Many courses are validated by professional institutions and a recent survey placed Brunel graduates 13th in the UK for average starting salaries. At more than £22,000, the figure was almost £3,000 above the national average. The latest strategic plan sets the goal of confirming the university's standing in the top third of UK higher education, working across academic boundaries and making stronger connections between teaching and research, as well as improving the quality of students' experience.

Professor Julia Buckingham, Brunel's Vice-Chancellor, has identified research as the university's top priority. Substantial investment in research centres and academic recruitment produced significant improvements in the last Research Assessment Exercise, when Brunel registered one of the biggest increases in the numbers of staff entered. Almost nine out of ten academics were assessed, compared with barely more than six out of ten in 2001. With 43 per cent of the work submitted judged to be world-leading or internationally excellent, the outcome

---

Kingston Lane
Uxbridge
Middlesex UB8 3PH

01895 265265 (admissions)
admissions@brunel.ac.uk
www.brunel.ac.uk
http://brunelstudents.com
Affiliation: none

The Times and Sunday Times **Rankings**
Overall Ranking: **46** (43)

Student satisfaction:	32	(83.3%)
Research quality:	=42	(17.0)
Entry standards:	46	(357)
Student–staff ratio:	51	(17.5)
Services & facilities/student:	33	(£1,757)
Expected completion rate:	=53	(87.1%)
Good honours:	=67	(62.5%)
Graduate prospects:	76	(60.5%)

was a 54 per cent increase in Brunel's research allocation from the Higher Education Funding Council for England. The extra money was invested in 40 senior academic posts. Benjamin Zephaniah took up his first academic position as Chair of Creative Writing, and Will Self has joined as Professor of Contemporary Thought. Brunel's Institute for the Environment won a Queen's Anniversary Prize for pioneering research revealing the link between chemicals in rivers and reproductive health.

Recent reviews of NHS-funded health programmes, including physiotherapy and occupational therapy, have been satisfactory and Brunel also scored well in its last institutional audit. Sporting excellence is also being maintained, and several students competed in the London 2012 Olympic and Paralympic Games. The level of facilities is such that Brunel hosted the South Korean Olympic and Canadian Paralympic teams.

The volume of applications held up well when £9,000 fees were introduced in 2012, although there was still a 14 per cent drop in first-year enrolments. Almost a third of the undergraduates are from working-class homes and more than half come from ethnic minorities. There is also a large contingent of international students. The International Pathways and Language Centre has been named as the top-performing British university language centre under the new British Council accreditation framework.

The projected dropout rates of less than 9 per cent is an improvement on the previous figure and much lower than the national average for Brunel's subjects and entry qualifications.

Brunel featured in the top 40 in the *Times Higher Education*'s latest ranking of the world's leading universities under 50 years old, scoring particularly highly for its international outlook. The university will reach its half-century in 2016, although it dates back to the 19th century in other guises. Student union facilities are good and the residential stock has been increased so that all new first years continue to be guaranteed accommodation on campus. Brunel has won awards for its provision for disabled students, and for its placement and careers service. Central London is within easy reach by public transport.

Undergraduate Fees and Bursaries

- » Fees for UK/EU students 2014–15 £9,000
- » International student fees 2013–14 £12,000–£15,000
- » 360 NSP awards with priority criteria, £2,000 fee waiver and £1,000 cash for each year.
- » Up to 150 Academic Excellence scholarship for those with at least AAA at A level or equivalent, £3,000 fee waiver or £2,000 fee waiver and £1,000 cash for three years.
- » 10 Local Borough scholarships, £5,000 fee waiver and £1,000 cash, accommodation discount or fee waiver each year.
- » 6 Alumni scholarships of £6,000 cash each year.
- » Other scholarships for care leavers, local students and some subjects.

Students

Undergraduates:	**10,135**	**(410)**
Postgraduates:	**3,890**	**(1,445)**
Mature students:	**13.6%**	
Overseas students:	**14.5%**	
Applications per place:	**7.7**	
From state-sector schools:	**94.1%**	
From working-class homes:	**31.9%**	
Satisfaction with students' union	**80%**	

For detailed information about sports facilities:
www.brunel.ac.uk/services/sport

Accommodation

Number of places and costs refer to 2013–14
University-provided places: 4,531
Percentage catered: 0%
Self-catered costs: £98.00 (standard) – £125.02 (en suite); £186.97 (studio flat) a week.
All new full-time first-year students are eligible for on-campus accommodation.
International students: as above.
Contact: www.brunel.ac.uk/services/accommodation
accom-uxb@brunel.ac.uk

University of Buckingham

Britain's first private, not-for-profit university of the modern era re-entered our league table two years ago after an absence of more than a decade and is now just outside the top 40. Buckingham had too few students to be classified in some measures in the intervening period, but has seen dramatic growth in the last few years. The total number of students increased from 1,300 in 2010 to 2,000 in 2012, when applications grew by an unprecedented 200 per cent. Staffing levels have not kept pace, although during 2012 the university tried to redress this by making new academic appointments and boosting spending on student facilities. This included refurbishment of the refectory, introducing Wi-Fi across the whole campus and expanding the library and teaching space. Buckingham's students have emerged as among the most satisfied in every year of the National Student Survey and the graduate employment rate is also among the best in the country.

Even before the latest rise in fees at universities around the UK, Buckingham claimed to be no more expensive than other universities because its intensive two-year degrees cut maintenance costs and accelerate entry into employment. Total fees for UK undergraduates taking the two-year degree from January 2014 will be just under £24,000, and there are further discounts for payment in advance. Overseas students pay just under £33,000 and there is a range of scholarships for both home and overseas candidates.

The university, which will celebrate its 40th anniversary in 2016, still has only around 2,000 full-time students. Small group tutorials, which have all but disappeared outside Oxbridge, are common at Buckingham. The average tutorial group contains about six students. Only its absence from the Research Assessment Exercise, which was open only to state-funded institutions, prevented the university from finishing higher in our table. However, the university has a number of research groups and over 170 research students. Research income in 2011 was around £847,000.

A Conservative-backed experiment of the 1970s, Buckingham is now an accepted part of the university system. Its degrees carry full currency in the academic world and teaching standards are high. The university's culture of responsiveness to students was praised by the Quality Assurance Agency in its report on the university this year. The university has no party political ties. Its own statement on its independence declares that Buckingham was founded on the principles of classical liberalism, and teaches the ideals of free-thinking and liberal political thought.

Hunter Street

Buckingham MK18 1EG

01280 814080

info@buckingham.ac.uk

www.buckingham.ac.uk

www.buckingham.ac.uk/
life/social/su

Affiliation: none

*The Times and Sunday Times **Rankings***

Overall Ranking: **41** (41)

Student satisfaction:	=4	(86.3%)
Research quality:	n/a	
Entry standards:	81	(310)
Student–staff ratio:	4	(11.4)
Services & facilities/student:	38	(£1,720)
Expected completion rate:	101	(79.5%)
Good honours:	121	(43.9%)
Graduate prospects:	4	(83.1%)

Professor Terence Kealey, a biochemist and libertarian commentator, has been Vice-Chancellor since April 2001, declaring an ambition for Buckingham to "one day" challenge the cream of American higher education.

The university runs on calendar years, rather than the traditional academic variety, although some courses give the option of entering in July or September. Most degree courses run for two 40-week years, minimising disruptive career breaks for the many mature students. Around half of the students are from overseas, but the proportion from Britain is growing. Students have the option of a three-year degree in the humanities and other schools are now following suit. Recent additions to the subjects on offer in Buckingham include a five-year dentistry degree, which is based at Leicester, a BSc in business enterprise and Masters programmes in finance and investment, security and intelligence studies, and diplomacy. Masters programmes in biography, military history, modern war studies and decorative arts are now taught in London, where a new MA in diplomacy and an MA in garden history, are also based. A new BA in art history and heritage management offers the opportunity of a term at the British Institute in Florence.

Education courses now have accreditation from the Training and Development Agency for Schools. The most striking development, however, has been the postgraduate medical school launched in 2008 with a two-year MD in clinical medicine. The course attracts overseas medical graduates who find it difficult to secure junior doctor posts as a result of Government restrictions. A four-and-a-half year undergraduate medical course starts in January 2015.

Buckingham operates on two sites within walking distance of each other, an academic centre containing computer suites, lecture theatres and student facilities providing a focal point. Two historic buildings have recently been refurbished at a cost of almost £2 million, and a new six-acre site has been acquired to make room for future expansion. Not surprisingly the social scene is quiet. A great benefit of being in leafy middle England is that Buckingham's campus has been judged to be the safest in the country. There is a university cinema, and the town of Buckingham is pretty, with a good selection of pubs and restaurants. Milton Keynes and Oxford are nearby.

Undergraduate Fees and Bursaries

» Fees for UK/EU students for degree course starting in July 2014, £11,960 a year. Note that the course only lasts two years (eight terms).

» Fees for International students for degree course starting in July 2014, £16,480 a year. Note that the course only lasts two years (eight terms).

» Scholarships of £1,000 a year for students from surrounding counties..

» Range of other scholarships and bursaries available.

Students

Undergraduates:	**1,225**	**(35)**
Postgraduates:	**595**	**(30)**
Mature students:	**28.0%**	
Overseas students:	**56.1%**	
Applications per place:	**12.4**	
From state-sector schools:	**79.8%**	
From working-class homes:	**20.2%**	
Satisfaction with students' union	**60%**	

For detailed information about sports facilities:
www.buckingham.ac.uk/life/thingstodo/sport

Accommodation

Number of places and costs refer to 2013–14
University-provided places: 643
Percentage catered: 0%
Self-catered accommodation: £85–£174 a week (47–50 weeks).
All first-year students are guaranteed accommodation if they follow the application process.
International students: same as above.
Contact: accommodation@buckingham.ac.uk

Buckinghamshire New University

Buckinghamshire New University took more new students in 2012 despite suffering a big drop in applications. It had set maximum fees of £8,000, increased to £8,200 in 2013 and £9,000 in 2014. The university had been enjoying demand for its places that far outstripped its days as a college of higher education. Based in High Wycombe, Bucks now has some 9,000 students, three-quarters of them taking degree courses. The first phase of a £200-million campus redevelopment was completed in 2009 and students have been responding enthusiastically to a portfolio of innovative courses and an attractive package of financial support and extracurricular benefits for students.

The redevelopment allows most students to be based at the main campus – the exception being those taking nursing, who have moved into a new building in nearby Uxbridge. The prize-winning Gateway Building at High Wycombe has transformed the town-centre campus with improved teaching, social and administrative space. The complex includes a new sports hall, gym, treatment rooms and sports laboratory, which are available to the public as well as to students. At the same time, collaboration with two of the world's biggest IT companies is resulting in one of the most advanced student networks in UK higher education.

The next phase of campus improvements should be complete by September 2014. It will include new student accommodation, changes to the external appearance of its main building and additional space for the students' union. Two new accommodation blocks at the student village in High Wycombe will add 108 bedrooms. There will also be new laboratories and teaching rooms on the Uxbridge campus. In addition to the building projects, the university is planning further improvements to its online learning and IT capabilities.

Sport is an important part of life at the new university, which partners the London Wasps rugby union team in a relationship which trades coaching for Bucks students for courses for Wasps players. But the university's main aim is to contribute to the social and economic life of the region, embracing workplace learning and close ties with local businesses. Employees of the bed company Dreams, which is based in High Wycombe, take a Foundation degree in retail management while at work, for example.

A further innovation in 2010 was the establishment of the National School of Furniture with local employers and further education colleges, offering qualifications

Queen Alexandra Road
High Wycombe
Buckinghamshire
HP11 2JZ

0800 0565 660 (enquiries)
advice@bucks.ac.uk
www.bucks.ac.uk
www.bucksstudent.com
Affiliations: GuildHE

The Times and Sunday Times Rankings
Overall Ranking: **113** (106)

Student satisfaction:	**=115**	(76.2%)
Research quality:	**=112**	(0.7)
Entry standards:	**117**	(237)
Student–staff ratio:	**118**	(24.1)
Services & facilities/student:	**13**	(£2,159)
Expected completion rate:	**=77**	(83.1%)
Good honours:	**120**	(46.4%)
Graduate prospects:	**121**	(43.7%)

from certificate level to PhD. Bucks has also won awards for its training of commercial pilots and courses for music industry management. Other Foundation degrees include animation and visual effects, protective security management, and sports coaching and performance, all run at partner colleges.

More than a quarter of the undergraduates are over 25 years old and nearly 60 per cent are female. Academic departments are divided into two faculties: Design, Media and Management, and Society and Health. The nursing provision is the largest in the London area and has growing links with the Imperial College London Healthcare Trust, including a joint appointment designed to promote innovation. The child nursing courses attract particularly good ratings. Only 26 staff were entered for the 2008 Research Assessment Exercise – half of them in art and design, which registered the only world-leading research. However, an institutional audit expressed "broad confidence" in academic standards.

The projected dropout rate for first years entering in 2010 improved again and, at just over 10 per cent, was considerably lower than at most comparable institutions and 6 percentage points better than the national average for its subjects and entry qualifications. This was not achieved by neglecting the Government's widening

participation agenda: almost all the entrants are from state schools or colleges, and almost 40 per cent are from working-class homes. The university has a particular focus on student support: the university's Big Deal, which was in place before the fees went up, provides free entertainment, recreational activities, events and sports.

However, scores in the National Student Survey have been consistently low. The university's own annual survey, carried out by independent academics, has been more complimentary. And the courses and lecturers attracted some of the most positive verdicts of any university on a national student reviews website. More residential accommodation was provided in the town centre in September 2012, and High Wycombe has the usual range of pubs and clubs for a medium-sized town.

Undergraduate Fees and Bursaries

» Fees for UK/EU students 2014–15 £9,000
   Franchised courses at partner colleges £6,000–£7,245
» International student fees 2013–14 £9,200
» 281 NSP awards with priority criteria: £3,000 (year 1) and £1,500 (years 2 and 3) as fee waiver, accommodation voucher, for course costs, discounted public transport, or to include a cash bursary of up to £1,000 a year.
» "Big Deal" package which encourages participation in a range of sporting, recreational and social activities.
» Check the university's website for the latest information.

Students

Undergraduates:	**5,610**	**(3,365)**
Postgraduates:	**240**	**(560)**
Mature students:	**34.6%**	
Overseas students:	**7.9%**	
Applications per place:	**4.2**	
From state-sector schools:	**96.9%**	
From working-class homes:	**39.1%**	
Satisfaction with students' union	**78%**	

For detailed information about sports facilities:
www.bucks.ac.uk/student_experience/sport

Accommodation

Number of places and costs refer to 2013–14
University-provided places: 944
Percentage catered: 0%
Self-catered costs: £96.79 (standard)–£161.19 (studio) a week (42 weeks).
First-year students cannot be guaranteed accommodation.
Residential restrictions apply.
International students: priority allocation for first years.
Contact: accom@bucks.ac.uk

University of Cambridge

Cambridge has returned to the top of our league table for the first time in 12 years, although it remains effectively in a dead heat with Oxford, so slim is the points margin. It already topped more than half of the subject tables and appeared as the top UK university in two of the three main world rankings. Now it has overtaken Oxford in *The Times and Sunday Times* table mainly because of a much better graduate employment rate and slightly higher levels of student satisfaction. Until 2001, Cambridge had enjoyed an unbroken run at the top of the table, and it has never been far from first place in the intervening years. The university produced the best results in the 2008 Research Assessment Exercise, when nearly a third of its research was considered world-leading and over 70 per cent was rated in the top two categories. It was also one of the minority of universities where applications rose when the fees went up to £9,000 in 2012.

Cambridge has the highest entry standards of any UK university. It demands AAA* at A level, although candidates may be made a lower offer if their school or personal circumstances are thought to disadvantage them. The only good news for applicants is that, for most degrees, the top grade can come in any subject. The bad news is that there will still be additional tests, such as Cambridge's own STEP papers, in a number of subjects. The university has been characteristically independent-minded on admissions, using the A* for selection before the Labour government wanted and publicly opposing the reform of AS levels proposed by the Coalition.

Close to 60 per cent of undergraduates now come from the state system, but the proportion of working-class undergraduates remains low, at little more than 10 per cent. Summer schools, student visits and, in some colleges, sympathetic selection procedures are helping to attract more applications from comprehensive schools and further education colleges. Although Cambridge is charging the full £9,000 undergraduate fee, there are £6,000 fee waivers for the poorest students and additional bursaries according to parental income. The application system has been simplified slightly, with candidates no longer required to complete an initial Cambridge form, as well as their UCAS form. However, they are still sent the Supplementary Application Questionnaire, after they have submitted their UCAS form, covering the applicant's academic experience in more detail. The tripos system was a forerunner of the currently fashionable modular degree, allowing students to change subjects (within limits) midway through their courses. Students receive a classification for each of the two parts of their degree.

The Old Schools
Trinity Lane
Cambridge CB2 1TN

01223 333308 (admissions)
admissions@cam.ac.uk
www.cam.ac.uk
www.cusu.cam.ac.uk
Affiliation: Russell Group

The Times and Sunday Times **Rankings**
Overall Ranking: **1** (2)

Student satisfaction:	=6	(86.2%)
Research quality:	1	(45.0)
Entry standards:	1	(610)
Student–staff ratio:	5	(11.6)
Services & facilities/student:	2	(£3,054)
Expected completion rate:	1	(98.8%)
Good honours:	2	(89.4%)
Graduate prospects:	2	(85.1%)

A lively alternative prospectus, available on the students' union website, used to say there was no such thing as Cambridge University, just a collection of colleges. Where applications are concerned, this is still true. Making the right choice of college is crucial, both to maximise the chances of winning a place and to ensure an enjoyable three years if you are successful. Applicants can take pot luck with an open application if they prefer not to opt for a particular college. But, though the statistics show that this route is equally successful, only a minority takes it. Most teaching is now university-based, especially in the sciences, and a shift of emphasis towards the centre has been taking place more generally.

Cambridge is involved in numerous national and international research networks. For example, it was chosen to host one of five Academic Health Science Centres to lead biomedical innovation. A £1-billion funding appeal to mark the university's 800th anniversary, in 2009, reached its target two years early, making Cambridge the first university outside the USA to raise such a sum. The money has gone into bursaries and scholarships, professorships and teaching posts, and new buildings for research, teaching and student accommodation. A new building for molecular biology costing more than £200 million, housing 600 scientists, PhD students and research staff, was opened by the Queen in 2013. A £16-million sports centre

opened in 2013, featuring a large sports hall and a strength and conditioning wing. In the longer term, the university now has planning permission for its first out-of-town site, which will cost £1 billion to develop and will include housing for staff, students and local people in its first phase.

With fewer than five applicants for each place – fewer still if you choose your subject carefully – the competition for places appears less intense than at the popular civic universities, but the real difference is that nine out of ten entrants have at least three A grades at A level. The amount of high-quality work to be crammed into eight-week terms can prove a strain, although the projected dropout rate of 1.1 per cent is the lowest at any university.

Undergraduate Fees and Bursaries

- » Fees for UK/EU students 2014–15 £9,000
- » International student fees 2013–14 £13,662–£20,790
  Medicine £33,069
  College fees £5,000–£6,500
- » Bursary of £3,500 a year for students (£5,650 for some mature students) with household income below £25K; in addition 339 NSP awards of £6,000 fee waiver in year 1, prioritised for students with lowest household income.
- » Household income £25K–£42.6K, a bursary of up to £3,500 a year.
- » Many college scholarships and bursaries.

Students

Undergraduates:	12,020	(200)
Postgraduates:	6,355	(1,370)
Mature students:	4.5%	
Overseas students:	17.7%	
Applications per place:	4.7	
From state-sector schools:	57.9%	
From working-class homes:	10.3%	
Satisfaction with students' union	42%	

For detailed information about sports facilities:
www.sport.cam.ac.uk

Accommodation

See chapter 13 for information about individual colleges.

Canterbury Christ Church University

Canterbury Christ Church marked its 50th anniversary in 2012, but the celebrations were punctuated by difficult decisions. The vice-chancellor left abruptly and without explanation, applications and enrolments dropped, and it was decided to close one of the five campuses. Rama Thirunamachandran, Deputy Vice-Chancellor and Provost of Keele University, takes over amid press leaks of a further decline in the demand for places. In other respects, however, he will find a university that has thrived since its change of status from a Church of England college in 2005. There are now 20,000 students on campuses in four locations and the university has become the region's largest provider of courses for the public services. The teacher training courses are rated "outstanding" by Ofsted and there are strong programmes in health and social care, nursing and policing. Primary education has a unique record of successive outstanding ratings since 1996.

The Folkestone campus has now closed to all but trainee teachers, but the university has bases in Broadstairs, Tunbridge Wells and Chatham, as well as its headquarters in Canterbury. The purpose-built campus at Broadstairs offers a range of subjects from commercial music to digital media, photography, and child and youth studies. The Tunbridge Wells campus, based in a country house just outside the town, caters exclusively for postgraduate courses, while the newly expanded Medway site at Chatham is shared with Greenwich and Kent universities, offering education and health programmes at a variety of levels, from Foundation degree to postgraduate.

The majority of the students, however, are at the university's main campus at Canterbury, a World Heritage Site and one of the safest UK university cities. The Canterbury campus, which dates from 1962, is a few minutes' walk from the city centre, but the university has several buildings in other parts of the city. Augustine House, a £35-million library and student services centre, with specialist teaching and IT facilities, opened in 2009. The Sidney Cooper Gallery, in the heart of the city, hosts exhibitions and workshops from visiting artists as well as work by students before the best goes on to be exhibited in London galleries. St George's Centre opened in 2012, housing the students' union, residential accommodation, bar and coffee lounge within easy reach of the high street. The university has also opened the newly renovated St Gregory's Centre for Music, an historic concert venue, and separate rehearsal, practice and performance space named after Sir Peter Maxwell Davies,

---

North Holmes Road
Canterbury CT1 1QU

01227 782900 (enquiries)
admissions@canterbury.ac.uk
www.canterbury.ac.uk
www.ccsu.co.uk
Affiliation: Cathedrals
Group; million+

The Times and Sunday Times **Rankings**
Overall Ranking: **90** (85)

Student satisfaction:	80	(80.5%)
Research quality:	=100	(1.7%)
Entry standards:	106	(273)
Student–staff ratio:	=75	(19.5)
Services & facilities/student:	104	(£1,100)
Expected completion rate:	=65	(85.2%)
Good honours:	65	(62.7%)
Graduate prospects:	=84	(57.9%)

who is a visiting professor. Christ Church broke into the top 20 in the People and Planet Green League of universities' environmental performance this year, drawing praise for its work on sustainability and rigorous environmental auditing.

The Church of England link was underlined with the installation of the Archbishop of Canterbury as the university's first Chancellor. The subject mix, with an emphasis on health subjects and education, means that seven out of ten students are female. Some 96 per cent of the undergraduates are state-educated and just over a third come from working-class homes. The dropout rate has improved consistently and, at less than 10 per cent, is significantly better than average for the university's courses and entry qualifications. Canterbury Christ Church was one of the new "teaching-led" universities, but was given the power to award research degrees in 2009. The university entered staff in seven areas in the 2008 Research Assessment Exercise. The best grades came in education and music, both of which had 10 per cent of their work assessed as world-leading.

All campuses are interconnected by a high speed data network, providing access to online teaching and learning materials, the student web portal and email. A new student support service – i-zone – was introduced in 2009, which can be accessed online or via staff at the i-zone desks. The Drill Hall

Library at Medway provides 110,000 items, 400 computers and 280 study spaces, while the Augustine House Library has over 300,000 books, 250 computers, plus extensive wireless coverage throughout the building. The award-winning i-Borrow scheme has 200 laptops available for self-service loan within the building.

Social and sports facilities naturally vary between the campuses, although the students' union is present on all of them. A new sports centre in Canterbury includes a fitness suite and a hall big enough for eight badminton courts. There is also a tennis court and netball court on campus and the university also has facilities at Polo Farm Sports Club close to the city. There are 12 acres of playing fields about a mile from the main campus. Residential accommodation is available to all first years. The pressure is eased to some extent because more than 60 per cent of the students come from Kent, many of them among the 7,600 taking part-time courses.

Undergraduate Fees and Bursaries

- » Fees for UK/EU students 2014–15   £9,000
  Foundation degree at partner colleges   £8,000
  Degree courses at partner colleges   £7,500–£8,000
- » International student fees 2013–14   £9,425
- » 976 NSP awards with priority criteria: £2,000 support package and £1,000 cash, year 1; £1,000 cash , years 2 and 3.
- » Household income below £25K and not in receipt of NSP award, £1,000 cash a year.
- » Sports and music scholarships available.

Students

Undergraduates:	**10,295**	**(4,730)**
Postgraduates:	**1,195**	**(2,890)**
Mature students:	**23.9%**	
Overseas students:	**8.1%**	
Applications per place:	**4.5**	
From state-sector schools:	**95.9%**	
From working-class homes:	**34.9%**	
Satisfaction with students' union	**62%**	

For detailed information about sports facilities:
www.canterbury.ac.uk/support/sport-recreation/

Accommodation

Number of places and costs refer to 2013–14
University-provided places: 1,616
Percentage catered: 0%
Self-catered costs: £87–£182 a week.
Accommodation guaranteed for first years if conditions are met.
International students: as above.
Contact: accommodation@canterbury.ac.uk
www.canterbury.ac.uk/support/accommodation

Cardiff University

Cardiff was one of the big winners when undergraduate fees went up to £9,000 in 2012, filling an extra 669 places – an increase of 13 per cent on the previous year. The university is the acknowledged leader of higher education in Wales and the only one in the top 200 of the world rankings. It is the Principality's only member of the Russell Group of research-led universities and has two Nobel Laureates on its staff. Entry requirements have been rising and more than half of all applicants achieve at least AAB grades at A Level. It is our 2014 Best Welsh University.

The university now has around 28,000 students and nearly 6,000 staff. The student population is diverse with international students accounting for around 12 per cent, while a third of the intake comes from Wales. The 2008 Research Assessment Exercise rated almost 60 per cent of the submitted work in the top two categories, with 33 of the 34 subject areas containing some world-leading research. Journalism, media and cultural studies, English, city and regional planning, and business produced the best results. Cardiff takes more than half of the research funding awarded in Wales and, with the additional fee income at its disposal, is expected to have considerable extra funds available for future developments. The university is already home to three major new research institutes, offering radical new approaches to neurosciences and mental health, cancer stem cells and sustainable places.

Courses are accredited by more than 50 different professional bodies. An audit by the Quality Assurance Agency complimented the university on its "powerful academic vision and well-developed and effectively articulated mission to achieve excellence in teaching and research". Student support services, including counselling facilities and the help offered to dyslexics, were among the features singled out for praise. Cardiff was the first Welsh university to be awarded the Frank Buttle Trust Quality Mark which recognises support for students who have been in care.

Many full-time degrees share a common first year, and the modular system makes undergraduate study flexible thereafter. Recent additions at degree level include marine geoscience, an MMath degree and a new portfolio of computing courses. Cardiff was ahead of the national trend with increases in applications in the physical sciences. One undergraduate in six comes from an independent school, but nearly one in five have a working-class background. The projected dropout rate is comfortably the lowest in Wales, at less than 6 per cent.

The university occupies a significant part of the civic complex around Cathays Park

---

Cardiff
Wales CF10 3XQ

029 2087 4455 (enquiries)
contact via website
www.cardiff.ac.uk
www.cardiffstudents.com
Affiliation: Russell Group

The Times and Sunday Times **Rankings**
Overall Ranking: **=33** (32)

Student satisfaction:	**=41**	(82.3%)
Research quality:	**=32**	(21.0%)
Entry standards:	**26**	(433)
Student–staff ratio:	**=17**	(14.2)
Services & facilities/student:	**78**	(£1,289)
Expected completion rate:	**24**	(93.1%)
Good honours:	**=27**	(74.5%)
Graduate prospects:	**16**	(77.6%)

in Cardiff. The five healthcare schools at the Heath Park campus share a 53-acre site with the University Hospital of Wales. The university's new health education centre opened in 2011, offering students the latest teaching, library and simulation facilities. The £18-million Cochrane Building provides teaching and learning facilities for all healthcare schools based on the Heath Park Campus.

In recent years, there has been major investment in new buildings and equipment, and extensive refurbishment including a £4-million extension to the School of Biosciences and a £21-million building to house the School of Optometry and Vision Sciences. Current projects include a £30-million building which will house highly advanced facilities for some of the university's world-leading scientific teams.

Library services continue to improve access to resources, increase the range of electronic resources, extend self-service provision and improve the environment for the study of rare collections. A new IT working environment gives students online access to information about their studies and social life, from reading lists and timetables to social events and networking groups. The campus is also wireless enabled.

Other recent developments include the Cardiff Award, providing students with an opportunity to gain official recognition for learning acquired via extracurricular activities to support their employment prospects, and the students union's state-of-the-art "Lounge" aimed at international students. The School of Dentistry recently launched a new Dental Education Clinic offering students some of the UK's most modern training facilities.

The university guarantees a residential place for those applying through the normal admissions cycle. The main residential site at Talybont boasts a "sports training village", and there is also a newly refurbished city-centre fitness suite and a sports ground. The university hosted competitors before and during the London 2012 Olympics and Paralympics for boxing, football and wheelchair basketball. Cardiff is a popular student city, relatively inexpensive and with a good range of nightlife and cultural venues.

Undergraduate Fees and Bursaries

» Fees for UK/EU students for 2014–15: £9,000, with Welsh Assembly non-means-tested grant to pay fees above £3,575 (2013–14) for Welsh students.

» International student fees 2013–14   £12,700–£16,000
  Medicine, dentistry   £29,000

» For 2013–14, Cardiff University Bursaries: for students with household income below £30K, government-funded support topped up to £7,500; £30–£42.6K, government-funded support topped up to £6,750.

» Around 100 scholarships of £1,500 (year 1) and £750 (years 2 and 3) to students achieving grades AAA at A-level or equivalent in selected subjects.

» Welsh medium and other subject scholarships available.

Students

Undergraduates:	**16,245**	**(4,365)**
Postgraduates:	**3,820**	**(3,315)**
Mature students:	**12.5%**	
Overseas students:	**12.3%**	
Applications per place:	**5.2**	
From state-sector schools:	**83.0%**	
From working-class homes:	**19.7%**	
Satisfaction with students' union	**82%**	

For detailed information about sports facilities:
 www.cardiff.ac.uk/sport

Accommodation

Number of places and costs refer to 2013–14
University-provided places: 5,172
Percentage catered: 5.4%
Catered costs: £94–£114 a week.
Self-catered costs: £78–£109 a week.
All first years (except Clearing students) are guaranteed accommodation if conditions are met.
Policy for international students: as above
Contact: residences@cardiff.ac.uk

Cardiff Metropolitan University

Cardiff Metropolitan successfully fought off the Welsh government's attempts to make it join the new University of South Wales with Newport and Glamorgan. The pressure came soon after it had changed its name from the University of Wales Institute to stress its location in the Principality's capital, but it threatened legal action to maintain its independence. Students starting courses in 2014 will pay fees of £9,000. Those from Wales, who account for two-thirds of the 13,500 students, will continue to pay only £3,575. Half of them are from Cardiff or the Vale of Glamorgan.

The university's three campuses have benefited from a £50-million programme of improvements. The £20-million Cardiff School of Management opened on the Llandaff campus in 2010, offering improved facilities for business, hospitality and tourism. A new campus centre, with a shop and catering facilities, was also added in 2010, along with an Information Zone for student services. The Cyncoed campus already had a new student centre with a nightclub and all the normal catering and leisure facilities. When the academic year starts in 2014, a £10-million building on the Llandaff campus will bring Cardiff School of Art and Design together on one site.

The university has a good record in the National Student Survey and does even better in the International Student Barometer. Ratings by overseas students from more than 140 countries placed Cardiff Met top in the UK for the learning experience, living experience, and for satisfaction with student support for a fourth year running. Cardiff Met has been awarded the Government's Charter Mark four times, the judges commenting particularly on the level of satisfaction among students. Overseas partnerships also offer the university's programmes in Egypt, Korea, Morocco, Sri Lanka and Singapore.

Some 93 per cent of the UK undergraduates attended state schools and nearly a third come from working-class homes. The dropout rate improved in the latest survey and, at nearly 14 per cent, is only marginally higher than the UK average for the university's subjects and entry grades. Entrance requirements are generally modest, but the menu of largely vocational courses means that many students come with qualifications other than A levels. Over a quarter are mature students and more than 1,000 are international students. Many are postgraduates, who make up nearly a quarter of the student population.

Cardiff Met is one of Britain's leading centres for university sport, with team performances to match some excellent

Llandaff Campus
Western Avenue
Cardiff CF5 2YB

029 2041 6070 (enquiries)
askadmissions@cardiffmet.ac.uk
www.cardiffmet.ac.uk
www.cardiffmetsu.co.uk
Affiliation: University
  Alliance

The Times and Sunday Times Rankings

Overall Ranking: **87** (=78)

Student satisfaction:	=48	(82%)
Research quality:	=78	(3.3)
Entry standards:	=78	(312)
Student–staff ratio:	112	(23.4)
Services & facilities/student:	=87	(£1,243)
Expected completion rate:	=71	(84.4%)
Good honours:	=88	(59.1%)
Graduate prospects:	112	(52%)

facilities. In recent years, the university has had British university champions in sports ranging from archery and gymnastics to squash, weightlifting and judo. More than 300 past or present students are internationals in 30 sports. Fifteen of them, including two gold medallists, took part in the London 2012 Olympic and Paralympic Games, where the university also provided three coaches and a physiologist. The £7-million National Indoor Athletics Centre is Cardiff Met's pride and joy, but other facilities are also of high quality. As well as participating in a thriving sports club scene, around 1,500 students pursue sport and dance related courses.

Academically, the large Cardiff School of Art and Design is the star performer, with 70 per cent of the work submitted to the 2008 Research Assessment Exercise rated either world-leading or internationally excellent. Sport also registered some world-leading research, and all six teacher training courses are rated as excellent by Estyn, the school inspectorate.

The three sites in Cardiff are all within three miles of the city centre. The Cyncoed campus, housing education and sport, is the main centre of activity, particularly for first years. As well as the new student centre, the athletics centre is there, together with a multitude of outdoor facilities and also the Welsh Sports Centre for the Disabled. Student facilities have been upgraded recently. The IT suite has 250 computers available 24 hours a day. For the moment, Howard Gardens is the home of fine art, while the Llandaff campus hosts design, engineering, food science and health courses. The student centre at Llandaff includes a dyslexia support unit among a number of advice and representation services, and a learning centre with more than 300 computers.

The enterprising students' union owns a nightclub and bar in the city centre to add to the campus choices. During term-time, the Rider bus service links all the campuses with other parts of Cardiff. The halls of residence are a mile from the main campus on the Plas Gwyn Residential Campus, where there are enough hall places to accommodate most first years.

Undergraduate Fees and Bursaries

» Fees for UK/EU students for 2014–15: £9,000, with Welsh Assembly non-means-tested grant to pay fees above £3,575 (2013–14) for Welsh students.

» International student fees 2013–14 £9,700
  Podiatry £11,400

» For 2013–14, scholarship of £3,000 for highest academic achievers on entry, based on UCAS score.

» For Welsh students from Community First areas, £1,000 package a year.

» Sports scholarships available.

Students

Undergraduates:	**7,675**	**(730)**
Postgraduates:	**2,175**	**(2,425)**
Mature students:	**27.3%**	
Overseas students:	**12.6%**	
Applications per place:	**3.3**	
From state-sector schools:	**93.0%**	
From working-class homes:	**32.5%**	
Satisfaction with students' union	**68%**	

For detailed information about sports facilities: www3.uwic.ac.uk/English/sport

Accommodation

Number of places and costs refer to 2013–14
University-provided places: 937
Percentage catered: 34%
Catered cost: £131–£139 a week (£87–£95 outwith term).
Self-catered costs: £86–£104 a week.
First-year students have no guarantee; terms and conditions apply.
International students: accommodation is reserved, subject to availability and if conditions are met.
Contact: accomm@cardiffmet.ac.uk

University of Central Lancashire (UCLan)

Already one of the largest universities in the UK, Central Lancashire added an international dimension in 2012, opening a branch campus in Cyprus. One of the few post-1992 universities to appear in the QS World University Rankings, now students at the university's Preston base will be able to take part of their course at UCLan Cyprus or at one of the other partner colleges overseas. Travel bursaries are available for study or work experience abroad, and there is free tuition is a variety of languages, including Arabic, Chinese, Japanese and Russian. The Confucius Institute, on the Preston campus, supports the development of Chinese culture throughout the North West and more than 500 students have been helped to visit China.

The university has invested over £100 million in new buildings and facilities, including the £13-million Sir Tom Finney Sports Centre and a £12.5-million building housing the university's forensic science, chemistry and fire courses. The campus also boasts Europe's largest 3-D lecture theatre and a 24-hour-access library. The dental school was one of the first to open in over a century, while the architecture degree was the first new such course for a decade. New courses include the BSc in airport security management – the first of its kind in the UK – and an MSc in counter terrorism.

With the introduction of £9,000 fees, the university launched UCLan Advantage: a package of benefits that aims to help students before and after graduation. The scheme includes the provision of guaranteed structured work experience for every student who requests it, as well as covering language and travel benefits. However, both applications and enrolments declined significantly in 2012, when the number of first-year undergraduates recruited through UCAS dropped by more than 1,000.

The university has a strong focus on entrepreneurship and has established a range of business incubation facilities for its students and graduates. The Futures Centre brings together advice on careers and work placements, employability and enterprise course electives, business start-up and self-employment services. UCLan ranks in the top three nationally for the number of graduate start-ups, about 70 per cent of which are still trading after three years. The university works with a wide variety of industrial partners and many undergraduate programmes are directly linked to them.

UCLan's roots stretch back to 1828 and the university has a high reputation in some unusual fields. Astrophysics benefits from two observatories in Britain and a share in the Southern African Large Telescope, its

---

Preston

Lancashire PR1 2HE

01772 892400 (enquiries)
cenquiries@uclan.ac.uk
www.uclan.ac.uk
www.yourunion.co.uk
Affiliation: million+

The Times and Sunday Times **Rankings**

Overall Ranking: **88** (71)

Student satisfaction:	=68	(81.2%)
Research quality:	=76	(3.7%)
Entry standards:	91	(298)
Student–staff ratio:	=66	(19)
Services & facilities/student:	35	(£1,730)
Expected completion rate:	=102	(79.1%)
Good honours:	107	(54.6%)
Graduate prospects:	97	(54.6%)

academics working closely with NASA. The university is a partner in a nanotechnology research team in China. Linguistics and journalism were classed as world-leading in the last Research Assessment Exercise and in total, 17 areas contained work considered world-leading or internationally excellent. The Undergraduate Research Internship Scheme enables students from all disciplines to work on research projects for up to ten weeks. Since its launch in 2008, over 200 interns have been sponsored to work in fields as diverse as digital publishing, wind power, and materials to clean up radioactive waste. UCLan students formed the UK's first Undergraduate Research Society, which funds conference visits and organises events. An overall rating of the teaching, research and facilities by QS gave the university four out of five stars.

Electives are used to broaden the curriculum; up to 11 per cent of students' time is spent on subjects outside their normal range. Four out of ten students come from working-class homes, and a high proportion are local people in their 20s or 30s. Almost a fifth of the UCLan's students are taught in colleges and UCLan has won official praise for the quality of its external programmes.

UCLan's Burnley campus gives local students the opportunity to take degree or Foundation degree courses without leaving home. In collaboration with Cisco Systems, the campus is the location for an advanced manufacturing facility incorporating robotics, computer vision, non-destructive testing and component assembly. A Centre for Outdoor Education is at Llangollen, North Wales, while the university's West Cumbrian Campus, in Westlakes, focuses primarily on nuclear skills training. UCLan is ranked among the top ten universities in the People and Planet Green League of environmental performance. It was the first university in the UK to install solar trackers.

UCLan's sports facilities were used as official training venues for the Olympic Games and the 2013 Rugby League World Cup. Compared with Manchester or Liverpool, the security risks and cost of living are both low. The students' union won the Best Campus Venue 2011 award from Live UK Music, and in 2012 was ranked in the top 25 per cent for its support, activities and academic representation.

Undergraduate Fees and Bursaries

» Fees for UK/EU students 2014–15	£9,000
Foundation year	£6,000
Burnley campus (Foundation year)	£7,000 (£6,000)
» Degree courses at partner colleges	£6,000–£9,000
» International student fees 2013–14	£9,450–£10,450

» In year 1 for all students with household income below £20K, £1,000 cash and £2,000 for university accommodation and other university services; household income £20K–£25K, £1,500 for university services.

» Check the university's website for the latest information.

Students

Undergraduates:	**19,225**	**(7,785)**
Postgraduates:	**1,540**	**(2,980)**
Mature students:	**25.7%**	
Overseas students:	**7.9%**	
Applications per place:	**5.0**	
From state-sector schools:	**98.3%**	
From working-class homes:	**40.0%**	
Satisfaction with students' union	**75%**	

For detailed information about sports facilities: www.uclansu.co.uk/uclansport.

Accommodation

Number of places and costs refer to 2013–14
University-provided places: around 2,200
Percentage catered: 0%
Self-catered costs: £79.03–£83.02 (standard) – £95.76–£99.47 (en suite) a week (42 weeks); £86.87–£107.80 (self-contained flats).
The Student Accommodation Service will assist all first years find suitable accommodation either in university owned/leased halls of residence, private sector registered halls or shared houses.
International students: as above.
Contact: www.uclan.ac.uk/study/accommodation/index.php

University of Chester

Chester began a concerted effort to improve the student experience four years ago, after criticism from its students and disappointing scores in the National Student Survey. The university spent £600,000 refurbishing the refectory, around £3 million overhauling the university's learning resources centre and another £1 million on sports facilities. The initiatives have produced big increases in student satisfaction, culminating in the university being named as the most improved institution in *Times Higher Education* magazine's student experience survey, winning it a place in the top 30.

In 2012, the university cut its intended fee of £9,000 for degree courses by £1,000 to gain access to the pool of places reserved for universities with low charges. It managed a small increase in first-year enrolments as a result; although there was a substantial decline in applications, there were still seven to every place. The following year the charges reverted to £9,000.

The picturesque Roman city of Chester is one of those places that outsiders probably always expected to have its own university. Indeed, William Gladstone was among the founders of the first Church of England teacher training college there in 1839. Although it took until 2005 for that college to achieve university status, it had been building up a solid reputation in a number of subjects beyond education. The main campus is only a short walk from the centre of Chester, a 32-acre site boasting manicured gardens and a number of new developments. A new students' union is just one of a stream of improvements, including the opening of a second campus in the city in 2007 as a base for the Faculty of Arts and Media. A third site was added in 2010, following the purchase of the city's historic County Hall, which now houses the faculties of Health and Social Care and Education and Children's Services.

The Warrington campus, which has eight halls of residence, focuses on the creative industries and public services. It has seen the addition of high-quality production facilities and the university has also signed a partnership agreement with the BBC, which is intended to open up new employment opportunities and develop new talent following the transfer of parts of the corporation to Salford. The library has been tripled in size, and a business centre opened for students and local firms.

Chester was the first of the universities created in 2005 to be granted the power to award research degrees. Four of the ten subject areas entered for the last Research Assessment Exercise contained at least some world-leading work. History was the most successful, with nearly half of its submission placed in the top two categories.

Parkgate Road
Chester CH1 4BJ

01244 512528 (admissions)
admissions@chester.ac.uk
www.chester.ac.uk
www.chestersu.com
Affiliation: Cathedrals Group

The Times and Sunday Times **Rankings**

Overall Ranking: **=52** (59)

Student satisfaction:	39	(82.8%)
Research quality:	=108	(1.0%)
Entry standards:	92	(296)
Student–staff ratio:	35	(16.3)
Services & facilities/student:	52	(£1,494)
Expected completion rate:	90	(81.2%)
Good honours:	69	(62.4%)
Graduate prospects:	43	(69.4%)

With almost 18,000 students, including part-timers, Chester is among the biggest of the new universities. More than a fifth of the undergraduates are over 20 on entry and two-thirds are female. Nearly all are state-educated, and 36 per cent have working-class roots. Progression agreements guarantee interviews to students at a number of local colleges, subject to certain conditions, but there is no reduction in entry requirements. The projected dropout rate has been improving and, at almost 14 per cent, now matches the national average for the university's courses and entry standards. There is also a limited range of Foundation degrees, mainly in health subjects. The Foundation degree in mortuary science was the first of its kind, as was one for guide dog trainers. Even the more traditional degrees have been designed to support the practical and vocational demands of the professions. Many include an extended period of work experience. Initial teacher training courses have been rated "outstanding" by Ofsted.

A student contract of the type that is becoming universal in higher education sets out clear conditions on the offer of a place, as well as detailing the university's responsibilities. Students promise to "study diligently, and to attend promptly and participate appropriately at lectures, courses, classes, seminars, tutorials, work placements and other activities which form part of the programme". The university undertakes to deliver the student's programme, but leaves itself considerable leeway beyond that.

There are extensive sports facilities at Warrington and especially on the main campus in Chester, where around £1 million has been spent on new tennis courts, a 100-metre sprint track and a floodlit 3G multi-use sports pitch. Another 200 residential places are being added for 2013–14, allowing most first years to be offered university accommodation. Student union facilities form the basis of the social scene on both campuses, but the city of Chester also has a great deal to offer.

Undergraduate Fees and Bursaries

» Fees for UK/EU students 2014–15 £9,000
   Foundation degrees at partner colleges £5,000–£7,650
» International student fees 2013–14 £10,450–11,450
» Over 380 NSP awards for students with lowest household income below £25K, £1,000 cash and £2,000 package of fee waiver and university services, year 1; £1,500 fee waiver, years 2 and 3; eligible for Chester Plus bursary of £500 in years 2 and 3.
» Chester Plus bursary: household income below £25K, £1,000 cash, year 1; £500, years 2 and 3.
» Students from targeted partner schools and colleges with household income below £42.6K, cash award of £1,000, year 1; £500, years 2 and 3.
» Students with at least ABB or equivalent with household income below £42.6K, cash award of £1,000, year 1; £500, years 2 and 3.

Students

Undergraduates:	8,050	(3,855)
Postgraduates:	900	(2,410)
Mature students:	19.3%	
Overseas students:	1.5%	
Applications per place:	7.0	
From state-sector schools:	97.4%	
From working-class homes:	36.0%	
Satisfaction with students' union	76%	

For detailed information about sports facilities:
www.chestersu.com/sports-societies

Accommodation

Number of places and costs refer to 2013–14
University-provided places: approx 1,169
Percentage catered: 36% (including semi-catered)
Catered costs: £82.25–£137.90 a week.
Self-catered costs: £73.15–£130.20 a week.
First years cannot be guaranteed accommodation.
International students: guaranteed accommodation if they apply by the advertised date.
Contact: www.chester.ac.uk/campus-life/accommodation

University of Chichester

Chichester is reinvesting a £2.9-million surplus generated mainly by strong student recruitment since it became a university in 2005. The money is being spent on improvements to the two campuses – carried out in the summer to minimise student inconvenience – in order to maintain its attractiveness in an increasingly competitive market. Just how competitive was obvious in 2012, when applications dropped by 20 per cent but the university was still able to fill more places than in the year before the fees went up. It has left the fees for degree courses at £8,500 in 2014, although bursaries and waivers should bring the average charge down to little more than £7,180.

The smallest of the nine universities created in 2005, Chichester features regularly among the leading modern universities in league tables, thanks mainly to consistently high levels of student satisfaction.

It traces its history back to 1839, when the college that subsequently bore his name was founded in memory of William Otter, the education-minded Bishop of Chichester. It became a teacher training college for women, who still account for two-thirds of the places, and eventually merged with the nearby Bognor Regis College of Education. The Chichester campus – now the larger of two – continues to carry the Bishop Otter name, signifying a continuing link with the Church of England.

The two faculties each operate on both sites, one covering business, teacher training and IT; the other the arts, history, media, sport and social sciences. The portfolio of some 300 courses ranges from adventure education to humanistic counselling, fine art and the psychology of sport and exercise. The PE teacher training course is one of the largest in the country – recently training one in five PE teachers in England – and is highly rated by Ofsted. Sport was the only area in which the university registered any world-leading work in the 2008 Research Assessment Exercise, but history and drama, dance and performing arts also produced good results.

The university is near to completing developments in Bognor Regis that cost £13 million, the majority of which has be spent transforming the Dome into a business and research centre and creating a new learning resources centre. Since May 2012, Chichester has been implementing the second phase of its investment plan, which aims to bring facilities on the Bishop Otter campus up to the same standard as those in Bognor Regis. The learning resources centre has been overhauled to provide easier access to books, online resources, media and computer facilities, as well as adding a coffee shop. The old library on the

---

Bishop Otter Campus
College Lane
Chichester
W. Sussex PO19 6PE

01243 816002 (admissions)
help@chi.ac.uk
www.chi.ac.uk
www.ucsu.org
Affiliation: Cathedrals
  Group; GuildHE

The Times and Sunday Times **Rankings**
Overall Ranking: **68** (61)

Student satisfaction:	**47**	(82.1%)
Research quality:	**=100**	(1.7%)
Entry standards:	**=82**	(307)
Student–staff ratio:	**=64**	(18.8)
Services & facilities/student:	**105**	(£1,098)
Expected completion rate:	**=35**	(90.7%)
Good honours:	**=83**	(60.1%)
Graduate prospects:	**81**	(59.4%)

Bognor Regis campus has been converted into a 150-seater lecture theatre and other teaching space. The former student support services building is being used as business incubator units for local firms. The Alexandra Theatre, in Bognor, is used as a base for the musical theatre programme and there are links, too, with the Chichester Festival Theatre. The Mathematics Centre, at Bognor, has an international reputation, working with over 30 countries as well as teaching the university's own students. It has become a focal point for curriculum development in Britain and elsewhere.

About one in seven of the 5,000 students are 21 or over on entry, but fewer than three in ten come from working-class homes, which is well below average for the university's courses and entry grades. An already low projected dropout rate improved still further in the latest survey. At little more than 5 per cent, it was less than half the benchmark figure. The university runs summer taster sessions and has a series of partnerships with schools in the Channel Islands and Sussex to encourage a broader intake. Courses are also run in collaboration with Isle of Wight College.

Both of the university's campuses are within ten minutes' walk of the sea and the residential places are roughly equally divided between them, enabling Chichester to guarantee accommodation to anyone making the university a firm choice before the January UCAS deadline. There is a university bus service linking the two and students' union bars at each. Sports facilities are good and the university was chosen to provide training facilities for competitors in athletics, boxing, road cycling and table tennis before the 2012 Olympic Games. Since then, a sports dome has been added to the existing tennis courts to provide an all-weather, multi-sport facility, and a new running track has been installed.

The small cathedral city of Chichester is best known as a yachting venue and Bognor is said to have the longest stretch of coastline in the south where all types of water sports are available. Both offer a good supply of private housing and some student-oriented bars. Much of the surrounding countryside has been designated an area of outstanding natural beauty.

Undergraduate Fees and Bursaries

» Fees for UK/EU students 2014–15 £8,500
» International student fees 2013–14 £9,660–£11,025
» Over 200 NSP awards, £3,000 fee waiver, year 1; £2,000 fee waiver and £1,000 cash or fee waiver, years 2 and 3.
» Students with household income below £25K, £2,000 fee waiver, £1,000 cash or fee waiver each year; household income £25K–£42K, £1,000 cash bursary.
» Range of other scholarships and bursaries available.
» Check the university's website for the latest information.

Students

Undergraduates:	4,025	(705)
Postgraduates:	305	(605)
Mature students:	13.5%	
Overseas students:	2.5%	
Applications per place:	4.3	
From state-sector schools:	96.5%	
From working-class homes:	28.9%	
Satisfaction with students' union	76%	

For detailed information about sports facilities:
www.chi.ac.uk/student-life/life-campus/sport

Accommodation

Number of places and costs refer to 2013–14
University-provided places: 647
Percentage catered: 66.5%
Catered costs: £119.98 (twin) – £158.27 (en-suite single) a week (37 or 40 weeks).
Self-catered costs: £109.97 (shared) – £144.20 (en suite) a week (37 or 40 weeks).
First-year accommodation is allocated using a randomised system.
International students: as above.
Contact: www.chi.ac.uk/student-life/accommodation

City University London

For two successive years, City set the highest undergraduate fee in England after fee waivers and other financial support were taken into account, according to OFFA figures, but for 2014–15, it fell to ninth highest. The university has a better record than most of its peers for widening participation in higher education, with over 40 per cent of its undergraduates coming from working-class homes. The university is offering over 230 National Student Scholarships and investing more than £1 million a year in outreach and retention activities such as summer schools. In addition, it has promised to invest heavily in new academic staff and student related facilities, focusing particularly on the recruitment of more research-oriented academics. City is aiming to be ranked among the world's top 200 universities and in the top 35 in the UK by 2016. It expects to be London's only university to be committed to business and the professions, as well as academic excellence. The university's strategy includes raising entry qualifications and focusing on the university's strongest subjects at the expense of weakest. Applications dropped by almost 18 per cent in 2012, but there was only a marginal drop in enrolments.

Marketing itself as the "international university in the heart of London", City added the name of the capital to its title to make the most of its greatest asset. Students come from more than 160 countries to study on the borders of the financial district. Once a college of advanced technology, City now has roughly a quarter of its students taking business courses, another quarter health and community subjects, and the remaining half law, computing, mathematics, engineering, journalism and the arts.

The university reaps the benefits of its strong links with business and the professions with consistently good graduate employment figures. City's graduates play their part, with nearly 2,000 of them offering practical help to current students through an online careers network. Courses have a practical edge, and many of the staff hold professional, as well as academic, qualifications. Some interdisciplinary centres have been launched to increase collaborative teaching and research, as well as to build stronger links between industry and academia. There are about 17,000 students, and because around a fifth of them are from outside the EU and more than a third are postgraduates, City is less dependent on Government funding than many other universities. It also remains among the most popular, with 7.5 applications for each undergraduate place.

Development is continuing at the university's Islington campus. Some £20

Northampton Square
London EC1V 0HB

020 7040 5060
contact via website
www.city.ac.uk
www.culsu.co.uk
Affiliation: none

The Times and Sunday Times **Rankings**
Overall Ranking: **43** (46)

Student satisfaction:	=70	(81.1%)
Research quality:	48	(14.3%)
Entry standards:	39	(390)
Student–staff ratio:	=61	(18.6)
Services & facilities/student:	22	(£1,952)
Expected completion rate:	=48	(87.2%)
Good honours:	43	(69.9%)
Graduate prospects:	=37	(71%)

million went into an impressive new building for the School of Social Sciences, interactive classrooms and a modern electronics laboratory in 2009 for the School of Engineering and Mathematical Sciences. The library has been renovated at a cost of £2.3 million, giving students more space, upgraded technology and better support. The Student Centre and Careers Centre have been refurbished and a new common room for students was put in over the summer of 2011. The School of Law was also upgraded over the summer of 2012. The School of Health Sciences has now moved to the main campus with new facilities including a new biomedical and clinical skills centre, as part of a £80-million building plan for the university.

The Cass Business School is one of City's great strengths, ranking among the top 50 business schools in the world. Based in the heart of the financial district, it has built up an impressive cadre of visiting practitioner lecturers who find it easy and convenient to visit. City has links with 50 European universities and many more further afield, and many students spend a year of their course abroad. The City Law School, which incorporated the Inns of Court School of Law in 2001, was the first in London to offer a "one-stop shop" for legal training, from undergraduate to professional courses. The School of Journalism, within the School of Arts is highly regarded and the university

has launched the UK's first graduate school of journalism in £12-million premises. There is a flourishing short course programme which ranges from sitcom writing to e-business.

City has a very high reputation in music, where it is associated with the Guildhall School of Music and Drama. Together with nursing and midwifery, music achieved the university's best results in the 2008 Research Assessment Exercise. Social work and social policy also produced good results.

The Students' Union is popular and the Student Centre, which provides advice on a range of topics, is the only one in the UK to be recognised by The Institute of Customer Service. The Sports Centre's redevelopment should be complete in 2014. Much-needed improvements will include a six-court sports hall, a 100-station fitness area, improved and expanded changing facilities and four multipurpose studios.

Undergraduate Fees and Bursaries

» Fees for UK/EU students 2014–15   £9,000
» International student fees 2013–14   £10,000–£12,000
» 233 NSP awards, with household income below £16K, £3,000 fee waiver and £1,000 cash or fee waiver, year 1; £1,000 fee waiver and £1,000 cash or fee waiver, year 2; £1,000 cash or fee waiver, year 3.
» Bursary of £1,000 a year for students with household income £16K–£42.6K.
» Lord Mayor of London Scholarship, from £1,000 a year for ABB at A Level or equivalent to £3,000 a year for at least A*AA.

Students

Undergraduates:	**8,140**	**(1,985)**
Postgraduates:	**6,220**	**(2,990)**
Mature students:	**22.0%**	
Overseas students:	**28.1%**	
Applications per place:	**7.5**	
From state-sector schools:	**89.3%**	
From working-class homes:	**40.3%**	
Satisfaction with students' union	**58%**	

For detailed information about sports facilities:
www.city.ac.uk/sport-and-leisure.

Accommodation

Number of places and costs refer to 2013–14
University-provided places: 1,250 through private providers
Percentage catered: 0%
Self-catered costs: £147–£299 a week.
Accommodation is guaranteed for first years if conditions are met.
Residential restrictions apply.
International students: guaranteed if conditions are met.
Contact: accomm@city.ac.uk
www.city.ac.uk/study/why-study-at-city/accommodation

Coventry University

Coventry has been more innovative than many other universities since it became clear that higher fees would usher in much greater competition between universities. It was among the first provincial universities to offer courses in London and then took its rivals by surprise by opening its own university college in 2012. Its courses will lead to Coventry degrees or diplomas, but fees in 2014 will be £5,500–£6,500 a year because most campus facilities will not be available. The initiative appears not to have affected the demand for places at the main university campus, where fees for 2014–15 will range from £8,088 to £9,000 for specialist subjects such as automotive engineering. Both applications and enrolments rose in 2012.

Coventry registered the biggest improvement in last year's table, going up more than 20 places, which it has built upon this year with another 10-place rise, making it the highest placed post-1992 university in our table. It is our Best Modern University this year. The university is in the throes of a £150-million investment scheme to rejuvenate its 33-acre campus close to the city centre. Much of the ten-year programme involves student facilities such as the showcase turreted library, which cost £20 million. The latest developments are the new building for engineering and computing, and The Hub, which contains the students' union, a music venue, plenty of informal study space, shops and restaurants. Other facilities have already been added, including more residential accommodation, an arts centre and a sports centre.

Coventry traces its origins back to 1843 and its links with the motor industry of the Midlands were reflected in its earlier title of Lanchester Polytechnic, named after a leading engineering figure. It has adopted an innovative approach to computer-assisted learning, supported by an expanded computer network. The university was chosen to house national centres of excellence in teaching for e-learning in health and social care, as well as in maths, and transport and product design. The university has a focus on employment, which is reflected in a predominantly vocational curriculum. The Start-Up Café encourages business networking and local employers are engaging with the programme of work-based learning. The Add+vantage scheme is designed to help full-time undergraduate students improve their employability while studying. Its modules cover a wide range of skills and help students gain work-related knowledge and prepare for a career.

Among the initiatives to improve the student experience has been the introduction of tangible rewards for excellent teaching and further development of electronic learning.

Priory Street
Coventry CV1 5FB

024 7615 2222 (admissions)
studentenquiries@coventry.ac.uk
www.coventry.ac.uk
www.cusu.org
Affiliation: University
   Alliance

The Times and Sunday Times **Rankings**

Overall Ranking: **45** (55)

Student satisfaction:	3	(86.9%)
Research quality:	=90	(2.3%)
Entry standards:	=94	(294)
Student–staff ratio:	=21	(14.6)
Services & facilities/student:	81	(£1,279)
Expected completion rate:	=74	(83.6%)
Good honours:	54	(66.1%)
Graduate prospects:	=37	(71%)

The Centre for Academic Writing offers advice on essays and theses, with group sessions and one-to-one appointments, while the Maths Support Centre includes a statistics advisory service and specialist support service for students with dyslexia. The majority of students exercise their right to take "free-choice modules" that cover the full range of university provision, with IT skills and languages particularly popular. Coventry has been building up its portfolio of courses, introducing eye-catching degrees in subjects such as ethical hacking and network security, disaster management, forensic chemistry, criminology and boat design.

Research grades improved in the 2008 assessments, when small amounts of world-leading work were recognised in seven of the sixteen areas the university submitted. Art and design and electrical and electronic engineering produced the best results. Design benefits from a £1.6-million digital modelling workshop, sponsored by the Bugatti Trust, which provides full-scale vehicle modelling facilities. The university also has a Technology Park, housing start-ups and small knowledge-based businesses.

The civic-minded approach of the university has created many town–gown links. The university's main buildings open out from the ruins of the bombed cathedral, as university and public facilities mingle in the city. Student residences are within easy walking distance of the campus and city centre. The London campus, which opened in 2013, is business-oriented and mainly for international students. A degree in global business management will include a workplace project and a period of study abroad, while one-year top-up programmes give international students entry into the final year of a BA degree. The campus includes a simulated financial trading floor to enhance business teaching and learning.

Nearly 40 per cent of the undergraduates have working-class backgrounds, and almost all attended state schools. For the second year in a row, the projected dropout rate had improved significantly in the latest survey. At less than 10 per cent, it is much better than the national average for the university's courses and entry qualifications. Students in Coventry welcome the relatively low cost of living there, and the city is not short of student-oriented nightlife.

Undergraduate Fees and Bursaries

» Fees for UK/EU students 2014–15   £8,088–£9,000
    Foundation degree   up to £6,000
» International student fees 2013–14:
    £10,080–£12,000 (Coventry); £9,990–£10,375 (London)
» 646 NSP awards (40 per cent targeted at students from institutions in the university's Phoenix Partnership scheme), £2,500 fee waiver and £500 cash, or £2,500 university accommodation credit and £500 cash in year 1, continued into year 2, based on performance.
» Scholarships for sporting excellence and exceptional academic achievement.

Students

Undergraduates:	**15,760**	**(10,335)**
Postgraduates:	**2,780**	**(2,170)**
Mature students:	**21.7%**	
Overseas students:	**14.7%**	
Applications per place:	**5.2**	
From state-sector schools:	**96.3%**	
From working-class homes:	**37.4%**	
Satisfaction with students' union	**81%**	

For detailed information about sports facilities:
www.coventry.ac.uk/life-on-campus/student-life/sport-coventry/

Accommodation

Number of places and costs refer to 2013–14
University-provided places: 2,431 (includes 235 beds on Nomination Agreements)
Percentage catered: 25%
Catered costs: £4,680 (38 weeks).
Self-catered costs: £3,980–£5,375 (40–44 weeks).
First years are guaranteed housing provided conditions are met.
International students: as above.
Contact: www.coventry.ac.uk/study-at-coventry/student-support/accommodation/

University for the Creative Arts (UCA)

The University for the Creative Arts (UCA) suffered the biggest drop in applications of any in the UK – almost 30 per cent – when its fees went up to £8,500 in 2012. But the fall in enrolments to 1,700 was less steep and broadly matched the national decline in the creative arts at degree level. The university has reduced its recruitment target to that level and joined others in raising fees for UK degree students to the maximum £9,000. Dr Simon Ofield-Kerr, the Vice-Chancellor, is planning to increase the number of international students, while also maintaining the university's local roots.

With around 6,000 students in total, UCA is sizeable by the standards of specialist institutions and applications had risen significantly before the switch to higher fees. The university is the product of a merger between two well-established arts institutes straddling Kent and Surrey. Indeed, the first version of its title was the unwieldy University for the Creative Arts at Canterbury, Epsom, Farnham, Maidstone and Rochester, although the multiple locations have since been dropped. The constituent colleges all date back to Victorian times, but university status arrived only in 2008. The location of each college is given in the map below: Canterbury (1), Epsom (2), Farnham (3), Maidstone (4) and Rochester (5).

By September 2014, the university will have moved out of the Maidstone campus that it shares with a further education college to focus activity on the four sites that it owns. Students taking the popular media courses will continue to use studios in the town at the largest independent studio complex in the UK. They are only 20 minutes by car from Rochester, the largest of the three existing campuses in Kent, which offers a full range of art and design, including fashion, photography and specialist design courses. The purpose-built campus is set on a hillside overlooking the city centre and River Medway. Halls of residence with 214 places are close to the campus, which has studio space, library and learning resource centre, and a gallery. At Canterbury, the accent is on architecture, but there are also degrees in fine art, interior design and more general art and design. The modern site is close to the city centre and contains purpose-built studios, workshops and lecture theatres. The Canterbury School of Architecture is the only such school to remain within a specialist art and design institution, encouraging collaboration between student architects, designers and fine artists.

By far the largest enrolment is at Farnham, in Surrey, where more than

---

UCA Canterbury
New Dover Road
Canterbury
Kent CT1 3AN

01252 892960 (enquiries)
admissions@ucreative.ac.uk
www.ucreative.ac.uk
www.ucasu.com
Affiliation: GuildHE

The Times and Sunday Times **Rankings**
Overall Ranking: **99** (103)

Student satisfaction:	=119	(74.3%)
Research quality:	=63	(5.0%)
Entry standards:	=82	(307)
Student–staff ratio:	=46	(17.1)
Services & facilities/student:	28	(£1,860)
Expected completion rate:	83	(82.1%)
Good honours:	=101	(56.3%)
Graduate prospects:	114	(51.2%)

2,000 students take courses in art, design, cinematics and communications. There is a purpose-built student village with 350 rooms in the centre of town and two galleries, as well as teaching space and a library and learning centre. The campus includes research centres in animation, crafts and sustainable design. Courses range from pre-degree Foundation courses in art and design to degrees in film production, motoring journalism and three-dimensional design. The second base in Surrey, at Epsom, specialises in fashion, graphics and new media, although it offers general art and design courses at further education level. Degrees include music journalism and fashion promotion and imaging. There is a modern library and learning resource centre for more than 1,200 students, a bar and café on campus and three halls of residence, the latest of which opened in 2010. A new £5.9-million teaching block includes learning and resource facilities, a 200-seat auditorium and a digital media centre. Photovoltaic cells on the roof and solar water heating will ensure that at least 20 per cent of the energy it uses is generated on site.

The university offers four-year degrees, incorporating a Foundation year, as well as the three-year format, and two-year Foundation degrees, which can be topped up to produce honours. Its courses are also taught in five partner colleges, including India's National Institute of Design, in Ahmedabad. However, results in the National Student Survey have been poor in all six years of polling, as they have been for art and design in most universities. The 2013 scores saw the university slip back into the bottom two for overall satisfaction among final-year undergraduates.

Many staff are practitioners as well as academics and the colleges have produced a string of famous graduates, such as Tracey Emin, Karen Millen and Zandra Rhodes, who has now become the university's Chancellor. There is also a strong research culture, although UCA had only limited success in the 2008 Research Assessment Exercise. Thirty per cent of the university's submission was considered world-leading or internationally excellent, but this left it well down the ranking for art and design.

Undergraduate Fees and Bursaries

» Fees for UK/EU students 2014–15 £9,000
» International student fees 2013–14 £11,140
» NSP awards to priority students, £3,000 package, year 1 only. All other students with household income below £25K, £900 bursary in year 1.
» 15 creative scholarships of £3,000 in year 1.
» Range of other scholarships and bursaries available.
» Check the university's website for the latest information.

Students

Undergraduates:	5,340	(120)
Postgraduates:	165	(130)
Mature students:	14.2%	
Overseas students:	9.6%	
Applications per place:	4.0	
From state-sector schools:	96.9%	
From working-class homes:	34.4%	
Satisfaction with students' union	56%	

For detailed information about sports facilities:
http://ucasu.com/clubs

Accommodation

Places and costs refer to 2013–14
University-provided places: 969
Percentage catered: 0%
Self catered costs: £65.85 (shared); £96.84–£140.65 (single); £121.92–£142.47 (en suite) a week.
Priority is given to disabled students (new and returning) and new full-time students by distance.
International students: guaranteed housing if application received by mid June
Contact: accommodation@ucreative.ac.uk; www.ucreative.ac.uk

University of Cumbria

Cumbria trades on its "small and friendly" image, with only about 10,500 students. But the university operates in no fewer than six different locations in or close to the county, as well as maintaining a base for teacher training in the East End of London, which is rated outstanding by Ofsted. More than a quarter of first years are 21 or over, and only a quarter come from Cumbria itself. The university is the largest provider of outdoor education degrees in the UK and is reopening its most attractive campus, at Ambleside, to capitalise on this position. It had been mothballed as a result of serious financial difficulties that have since been overcome, and is part of a ten-year estates plan. By 2015, the last students will have moved out of the Newton Rigg campus, outside Penrith, which presently houses some of the outdoor education and forestry courses. It is to become a field centre for research and development.

The university was finally established in 2007, after a series of false starts. It was formed by the amalgamation of a former teacher training college and an arts institute, with the addition of the two Cumbrian campuses of the University of Central Lancashire. It has been through a turbulent period, but the finances are now on an even keel after three successive surpluses.

The demand for places was strong as well before an 18 per cent drop in enrolments when the new fees regime arrived and some courses were closed. The university is by far the largest provider of higher education in the historically underprovided county of Cumbria. Its main campuses are in Carlisle, Penrith, Ambleside and Lancaster, but there is a new base at Furness College in Barrow in Furness, and another teaching centre in Workington. There are also partnerships with the four further education colleges in the county to provide higher education locally.

Although the headquarters remain in Carlisle, the biggest of the component parts is the former St Martin's College, which was founded in Lancaster by the Church of England in 1964 to train teachers and expanded during the 1990s with the addition of a nursing college. It forms the new university's main base, a ten-minute walk from Lancaster town centre. The Gateway, a £9.2-million development, opened in 2009, provides a range of student services and there is a modern library and excellent sports facilities, including a £2.5-million sports complex, gymnastics centre and fitness centre.

There are two main sites in Carlisle, the larger of which is in a parkland setting close to the River Eden. The second campus, closer to the city centre, boasts a new Learning Gateway, an innovative

---

Fusehill Street
Carlisle, Cumbria CA1 2HH

0845 606 1144 (enquiries)
contact via website
www.cumbria.ac.uk
www.ucsu.me
Affiliations: Cathedrals
  Group, million+

The Times and Sunday Times Rankings
Overall Ranking: **95** (=97)

Student satisfaction:	=73	(81%)
Research quality:	=115	(0.3%)
Entry standards:	=110	(253)
Student–staff ratio:	=61	(18.6)
Services & facilities/student:	116	(£871)
Expected completion rate:	81	(82.6%)
Good honours:	56	(65.7%)
Graduate prospects:	82	(59.2%)

multimedia learning resource centre, and a sports centre with a four-court sports hall and well-equipped fitness room.

The former Cumbria Institute of the Arts can trace its history in Carlisle back to 1822, eventually becoming the only specialist institute of the arts in the North West, and one of only a small number of such institutions in the country. The creative arts are one of the main areas for development in the university's initial planning. Policing will also move to Carlisle as part of the reorganisation.

Further education courses taught at Newton Rigg, a former agricultural college with two farms, are being taken over by Askham Bryan College. All other courses there will be transferred to Ambleside and some of the land sold off to help finance the reorganisation of the university's estate. The Ambleside campus will be refurbished and new amenities provided in conjunction with the Lake District National Park Authority. Research has already restarted there and the campus is intended to host more business and enterprise activity, as well as some new courses. The new University of Cumbria in Ambleside, the Lake District, looks like being popular with students: the courses that are moving from Newton Rigg to Ambleside have seen a 20 per cent increase in the numbers making it their first choice. The first phase of the redevelopment will establish an Institute of Leadership and Sustainability, which will be part of the business school and develop a portfolio of activities that make the best use of its unique setting.

The university was bottom of the initial rankings from the 2008 Research Assessment Exercise, recording only a small amount of world-leading research in theology, divinity and religious studies. But the focus of the university has been on attracting more students from a region of low participation in higher education, as well as on serving the social and economic needs of the county. Almost all the students are from state schools and colleges and more than a third are from working-class homes. The proportion from areas without a tradition of higher education is also well above the national average for the university's subjects and entry grades.

Undergraduate Fees and Bursaries

» Fees for UK/EU students 2014–15 £9,000
  Foundation degree £7,000
» International student fees 2013–14 £9,960–£14,965
» 200 NSP awards with priority criteria, £2,000 fee waiver or university services, £1,000 cash, year 1; £1,500 university services, years 2 and 3. Also 52 part-time NSP awards of £3,000 fee waiver over three years.
» Household income below £25K, up to 85 Cumbria bursaries of £1,000 university services a year.
» Check the university's website for the latest information.

Students

Undergraduates:	**6,285**	**(2,650)**
Postgraduates:	**810**	**(960)**
Mature students:	**25.4%**	
Overseas students:	**2.0%**	
Applications per place:	**4.0**	
From state-sector schools:	**96.2%**	
From working-class homes:	**35.6%**	
Satisfaction with students' union	**57%**	

For detailed information about sports facilities:
www.cumbria.ac.uk/StudentLife/Sport

Accommodation

Number of places and costs refer to 2013–14
University-provided places: 1,000
Percentage catered: 65%
Catered costs: £75.60–£81.90 a week (plus catering plan).
Self-catered costs: £60.40–£99.80 a week.
First years are guaranteed halls accommodation if Cumbria is first choice.
International students: guaranteed halls accommodation if conditions are met.
Contact: www.cumbria.ac.uk/FutureStudents/Accommodation

De Montfort University

De Montfort issued a £90-million bond to finance more campus improvements, having spent more than £140 million on the first round of developments to concentrate all its activities on its Leicester headquarters. The entire institution is now once again on one campus. The last piece in the jigsaw saw nursing and midwifery move into new premises for the health and life sciences. Now it plans to add to recent improvements such as the £8-million leisure centre with new facilities for the Faculty of Art, Design and Humanities, better catering facilities and the creation of a "green lung" in the heart of the campus, replacing redundant buildings with outdoor social space for students, staff and members of the public. The new leisure centre includes a 25-metre swimming pool, eight-court sports hall and a large fitness suite. The old centre will be used mainly for conferences and exhibitions.

De Montfort achieved one of the best performances any post-1992 university in the last Research Assessment Exercise, when 43 per cent of its work was rated world-leading or internationally excellent. Almost all the subject areas contained some world-leading research, and in the case of English language and literature the proportion reached an outstanding 40 per cent. Drama, dance and performing arts

and communication and media studies also produced excellent results. Successes in the previous assessments laid the foundation, helping to bring in an income of about £10 million a year in external research grants and contracts. The university has 500 staff engaged in research and 600 research degree students. Much of the successful work took place in the Institute of Creative Technologies, which acts as a catalyst for research that defies the traditional boundaries of computer science, the digital arts and humanities, and excites the interest of the business world. Some £3.7 million was spent on creative technology studios, which feature video, audio and radio production suites, recording studios and laboratories with the latest broadcast and audio analysis technology. A Performance Arts Centre for Excellence allows the university to deliver innovative teaching for students of dance, drama and music technology.

Other campus developments have included the diversion of part of the ring road to allow the university to open up the 15th-century Magazine Gateway building, which has become the focal point of a university quarter with public open spaces and new links to the city centre. A prize-winning building for business and law, which opened in 2010, is at its heart. The Hugh Aston Building cost £35 million and caters for around 6,000 students, and includes a court room, law library, dedicated

The Gateway
Leicester LE1 9BH

08459 454647 (enquiries)
enquiry@dmu.ac.uk
www.dmu.ac.uk
www.demontfortstudents.
  com
Affiliation: University
  Alliance

The Times and Sunday Times **Rankings**
Overall Ranking: **86** (72)

Student satisfaction:	79	(80.6%)
Research quality:	59	(6.0%)
Entry standards:	=75	(313)
Student–staff ratio:	=84	(20.2)
Services & facilities/student:	93	(£1,214)
Expected completion rate:	=65	(85.2%)
Good honours:	=74	(61.4%)
Graduate prospects:	=107	(53%)

law clinic and bookshop, as well as more conventional teaching facilities. Elsewhere, the 24-hour library was remodelled with wireless networks and rooms equipped with audio visual and IT facilities, and new game development studios have been installed to enable students to see their work in 3-D.

The professional accounting courses achieved "premier" status in a global accreditation scheme, and the university was awarded a national teaching centre for drama, dance and theatre studies. However, both applications and enrolments still dropped by more than 10 per cent in 2012. Among the recent additions to the portfolio of courses is a degree in digital marketing and social media. Others include a BSc in green energy technology and another in public and community health, tackling issues such as increases in sexually transmitted infections and obesity. Strong links with local business and industry manifest themselves in courses such as the BSc in media production, run in conjunction with the BBC. There is also an agreement to work with Hewlett-Packard on innovative educational programmes to better connect academia and business, as well as to collaborate on research.

Four further education colleges across the East Midlands are associates, linked into De Montfort's network and offering its courses. The dropout rate has improved consistently: at less than 10 per cent, it is now significantly lower than the national average for the university's courses and entry grades. De Montfort went back to a three-term year, rather than semesters, partly because it believed the prospect of imminent assessment encouraged some students to give up at Christmas in their first year. The university has a proud record for widening access to higher education with 40 per cent of students coming from working-class homes. It was one of the first to set up an employment agency to help students find part-time work as well as find careers upon graduation.

Accommodation difficulties have been addressed, with the addition of new halls within walking distance of lectures, although all first years cannot be guaranteed housing. Rents in the private sector are low.

Undergraduate Fees and Bursaries

» Fees for UK/EU students 2014–15   £9,000
  Foundation degree   £6.000
  Degree courses at partner colleges   £6,000–£7,800
» International student fees 2013–14   £10,750–£11,250
» 648 NSP awards for those with lowest household income, £2,000 fee waiver and £1,000 cash, year 1 only.
» Vice-Chancellor's Fund: academic scholarships of £1,000 a year and bursaries of £200 a year; bursaries of £1,000 a year for students on access courses.
» Range of other scholarships and bursaries available.
» Check the university's website for the latest information.

Students

Undergraduates:	**15,330**	**(2,620)**
Postgraduates:	**1,175**	**(2,665)**
Mature students:	**20.5%**	
Overseas students:	**7.9%**	
Applications per place:	**5.0**	
From state-sector schools:	**96.2%**	
From working-class homes:	**39.8%**	
Satisfaction with students' union	**74%**	

For information about sports facilities:
www.demontfortstudents.com/getinvolved/sports/

Accommodation

Number of places and costs refer to 2013–14
University-provided places: around 2,356
Percentage catered: 0%
Self-catered costs: £80–£148 a week.
First years cannot be guaranteed accommodation.
International students: new students are guaranteed accommodation.
Contact: accommodation@dmu.ac.uk

University of Derby

Professor John Coyne, Derby's Vice-Chancellor, has hinted at some rationalisation of courses after a 25 per cent drop in applications when higher fees were introduced in 2012. The decline followed two years of record demand for places, but enrolments still dropped by more than 500 at a time when the university had been allocated extra places for keeping its average fee below £7,500 a year. Professor Coyne said the university had "some big judgement calls to make about the precise Higher Education space we shall occupy, but we have the enormous benefit of a strong financial and physical environment in which to make real choices." Derby's target is to become the pre-eminent university of its type by 2020. Its yardsticks are student satisfaction, employability, service to business and flexibility, delivered cost effectively.

Higher entry grades have coincided with the recruitment of more students from affluent families, but still more than four in ten undergraduates are from working-class homes and two in ten are from areas of low participation in higher education – well above the national average for the courses and entry qualifications. The latest projected dropout rate saw another big improvement, but was still almost 18 per cent, a little above the benchmark figure for the university.

Campus developments are continuing, all part of a £75-million estates strategy that has created a University Quarter for the city of Derby. The second campus in Buxton is based in the former Devonshire Royal Hospital and offers courses in spa, outdoor recreation and hospitality management, as well as further education programmes. The landmark building houses a training restaurant, a beauty salon and a health spa, as well as more conventional teaching facilities. The UK's only degree in ecotourism will be launched there in September, while the Foundation degree in spa management will also be taught in London, at the London School of Beauty and Make-up. A new Sports Centre opened in Buxton in 2011.

There are two main sites in Derby. The extended academic campus at Kedleston Road, two miles from the city centre, caters for most of the main subjects including all business, computing, science, humanities and law courses. The residential campus close to the city's entertainment district is at Kedleston Road. The Markeaton cluster hosts arts, technology and some social science and health. The students' union, multi-faith centre and main sports facilities are here. The £1.5-million clinical skills suite features hospital wards, counselling rooms and diagnostic radiography facilities. The site's three tower blocks have been

---

Kedleston Road
Derby DE22 1GB

01332 592012 (enquiries)
askadmissions@derby.ac.uk
www.derby.ac.uk
www.udsu.co.uk
Affiliation: none

The Times and Sunday Times **Rankings**

Overall Ranking: **=84** (89)

Student satisfaction:	**=24**	(83.8%)
Research quality:	**=108**	(1.0%)
Entry standards:	**=97**	(288)
Student–staff ratio:	**=64**	(18.8)
Services & facilities/student:	**74**	(£1,312)
Expected completion rate:	**=96**	(80.3%)
Good honours:	**106**	(54.7%)
Graduate prospects:	**94**	(55.6%)

refurbished in a £13.5-million project, which will make them more energy efficient with the installation of photovoltaic panels and wind turbines. A new all-weather sports pitch was added in 2009. The university has acquired the 550-seat Derby Theatre to house theatre arts programmes as well as continuing as a producing theatre. Students have access to the main auditorium as well as their own 112-seat studio theatre.

The sites are within ten minutes walk of each other as well as being linked by free shuttle buses and the UniBus service, which also connects with the train station and city centre. Derby also has a centre in Chesterfield to teach nursing.

A Foundation programme allows students to begin work at a partner college before transferring to the university. Derby claims to award more work-based qualifications than any other UK university. Business and management is by far the university's biggest academic area, but work placements are encouraged in all relevant subjects. The accent on employability continues through the "Skillbuilder" career development programme, which covers a range of transferable skills to give graduates an edge in the employment market. Derby is at the forefront of development of a Higher Education Achievement Record that students can make available electronically to prospective employers. The university was quick to adopt new teaching methods,

pioneering the use of interactive video for a national scheme. Distance learning is a growth area, either online or through Derby's nine regional centres. Prospective students can even sample a virtual open evening. The university won an award for the imaginative use of distance learning.

The university spent £30 million in five years to maintain its guarantee of accommodation for all first years and has improved student facilities. The Institute for Learning Enhancement and Innovation is acting to enhance learning spaces across the university. At the Markeaton Street site, for example, flexible spaces have been created for work or social activities. "Learning pods" fitted with the latest audio-visual technologies contain 100 seats where students can work in groups or simply listen to music. Derby comes out well in its own satisfaction surveys, although this has not been reflected in the national equivalent.

Undergraduate Fees and Bursaries

» Fees for UK/EU students 2014–15   £8,100–£9,000
    Two-year accelerated degree   £9,000
» International student fees 2013–14   £9,945–£10,510
» 1,123 NSP awards with priority criteria, £2,000 university services and £1,000 cash in year 1 only.
» Bursary for students from Buxton and Leek Colleges. Undergraduate progression bursaries for those with household income below £25K also available.
» Range of other scholarships and bursaries available.
» Check the university's website for the latest information.

Students

Undergraduates:	**10,550**	**(4,990)**
Postgraduates:	**730**	**(2,225)**
Mature students:	**24.6%**	
Overseas students:	**6.9%**	
Applications per place:	**5.4**	
From state-sector schools:	**97.8%**	
From working-class homes:	**40.7%**	
Satisfaction with students' union	**63%**	

For detailed information about sports facilities:
 www.teamderby.com

Accommodation

Number of places and costs refer to 2013–14

University-provided places: 2,500

Percentage catered: 0%

Self-catered costs: £92.89–£115.00.

First-year students are guaranteed accommodation if they apply before 31 July.

Policy for international students: as above.

Contact: studentliving-housingteam@derby.ac.uk; www.derby.ac.uk/halls

University of Dundee

Dundee has completed a £200-million campus redevelopment designed by the leading architect, Sir Terry Farrell, and has been reaping the rewards in terms of popularity. The university was top in Scotland in *Times Higher Education* (THE) magazine's 2013 student experience survey. Its students voted it first for good, conveniently located facilities and in the top three north of the border for accommodation, students' union and social activities. Dundee is ranked in the top 200 in the world by both THE and QS, and its overseas students voted it into in the top five in the UK for overall satisfaction in the International Student Barometer. Applications rose again in 2012, although the number of undergraduate places filled was the lowest for seven years. The university doubled in size over two decades and there are now nearly 17,000 students, including a healthy number from overseas. Dundee has been looking outwards to achieve the "critical mass" which experts regard as essential to break into the higher education elite, with the acquisition of education, nursing and art colleges, which greatly increased its scope. But it resisted ministerial encouragement to amalgamate with Abertay University in 2012, while agreeing instead to collaborate more closely with its neighbour.

The university is best known for its work in the life sciences and medicine, where research into cancer and diabetes is recognised as world-class. Among the buildings added in recent years are those for clinical research, interdisciplinary research and applied computing. Biochemistry is the flagship department, housed in a complex that includes the £13-million Wellcome Trust Building and the Sir James Black Centre, which cost £21 million. Its academics were the first in Britain to be invited to take part in Japan's Human Frontier science programme and are now the most-quoted researchers in their field. Set in 20 acres of parkland, the medical school is the one of the few components of the university outside the compact city-centre campus – some of the nursing and midwifery students are 35 miles away in Kirkcaldy.

More than half the work submitted for the 2008 Research Assessment Exercise was rated world-leading or internationally excellent. Dundee recorded the best results in Scotland for art and design, civil engineering, biological and laboratory-based clinical sciences. The university is to lead one of four "knowledge exchange hubs for the creative economy", tasked with bringing academics together with business and charities, and raising public awareness of the creative industries. The highly rated design courses are taught at the former Duncan of Jordanstone College of Art.

Nethergate
Dundee DD1 4HN

01382 383838 (enquiries)
contactus@dundee.ac.uk
www.dundee.ac.uk
www.dusa.co.uk
Affiliation: none

The Times and Sunday Times **Rankings**
Overall Ranking: **49** (44)

Student satisfaction:	=57	(81.7%)
Research quality:	47	(15.7%)
Entry standards:	37	(396)
Student–staff ratio:	20	(14.4)
Services & facilities/student:	76	(£1,295)
Expected completion rate:	105	(78.9%)
Good honours:	=45	(69.3%)
Graduate prospects:	33	(71.8%)

Almost £40 million was spent on wireless-networked student residences. The IT facilities include a superfast broadband network and are among the best in the UK, allowing the latest technologies to be used to enhance teaching. Education and social work moved onto the main campus in 2008, and there have been extensions to the library and the sports centre. Vocational degrees predominate, helping to produce the university's consistently good graduate employment record. The university claims to send more graduates into the professions than any other institution in Scotland, and only Oxbridge graduates came out ahead of Dundee's in a national survey of starting salaries. Most degrees include a career planning module and an internship option, and students are now provided with their own personal development website. The Enterprise Gym gives students the chance to improve their self-reliance and employability and exercise their business creativity through business enterprise skills development training. Students can take the Scottish Internship Graduate Certificate, an eight-month programme combining a six-month internship with career management learning. There is a global equivalent, lasting seven months and with an internship in India or China.

Two-thirds of Dundee's students are from Scotland and nearly one in ten from Northern Ireland. About one in five come from areas with little tradition of higher education and almost a quarter are from working-class homes. Private accommodation is plentiful for those not housed by the university. Applicants have access to MyDundee, an online portal giving further information about the university during the application process and to prepare them for the academic year. The city is profiting from recent regeneration programmes and enjoys a cost of living that is among the lowest at any university city in the UK – 14 per cent lower than the UK average according to a NatWest survey in 2010. The university is experimenting with a range of three-year degree programmes for qualified candidates, rather than the regular four-year Scottish degree, bringing costs down further. Spectacular mountain and coastal scenery are close at hand, but social life tends to be concentrated on one of the most active students' unions in Scotland.

Undergraduate Fees and Bursaries

» Fees for Scottish and EU students for 2013–14   No fee
» Fees for Non-Scottish UK (RUK) students for 2013–14: £9,000 a year, capped at a maximum of £27,000 for all courses.
» Fees for international students for 2013–14   £10,200–£14,850
    Medicine and dentistry   £18,750–£28,750
» RUK students (2013–14), bursary of £3,000 a year if household income below £20K, and £1,000 a year if income £20K–£42K.
» Widening Access bursaries for Scottish students.
» A range of academic scholarships by subject of £1,000–£3,000 available (some restricted to RUK students).

Students		
Undergraduates:	**9,410**	**(1,530)**
Postgraduates:	**1,700**	**(3,855)**
Mature students:	**20.7%**	
Overseas students:	**12.0%**	
Applications per place:	**9.4**	
From state-sector schools:	**86.2%**	
From working-class homes:	**24.5%**	
Satisfaction with students' union	**82%**	

For detailed information about sports facilities:
www.dundee.ac.uk/ise

Accommodation

Number of places and costs refer to 2013–14
University-provided places: 1,587
Percentage catered: 0%
Self-catered costs: £110.32–£128.38 a week.
First-year students are guaranteed accommodation if conditions are met. No residential restrictions.
International students are guaranteed accommodation if conditions are met.
Contact: residences@dundee.ac.uk
www.dundee.ac.uk/studentservices/residences

Durham University

While most universities saw applications and enrolments drop with the introduction of higher fees, Durham saw substantial increases in both. As one of four universities to join the Russell Group of leading research universities in 2012, it was well placed to attract more highly qualified applicants when restrictions on their recruitment were lifted. Entrance requirements were already among the highest in Britain – and the projected dropout rate of little more than 2 per cent among the lowest. Durham slipped one place to sixth in our league table this year but has been moving up the world rankings, finishing in the top 100 in both the *Times Higher Education* and QS world rankings in 2012.

Long established as a leading alternative to Oxford and Cambridge, Durham has a collegiate structure and picturesque setting that attracts a largely middle-class student body. The university has been attracting more applicants from non-traditional backgrounds, partly through a scheme that targets able pupils from schools in County Durham and Teesside where progression to higher education is low. But still more than 40 per cent of undergraduates come from independent schools. In addition to the normal open days, all those who receive an

offer are invited to a special open day to see if Durham is the university for them. Since around 80 per cent come from outside the northeast of England, most are seeing the small cathedral city for the first time.

Undergraduates apply to one of 14 colleges, all of which have been mixed since 2004. Colleges range in size from 300 to 1,100 students and are the focal point of social life, although all teaching is done in central academic departments. There are significant differences in atmosphere and student profile, ranging from the historic University College, in Durham Castle, to modern buildings on the city's outskirts and on Queen's Campus, 23 miles away at Stockton-on-Tees. Investment continues on the Science Site with improved student facilities and an extension of the Bill Bryson Library (now named after Durham's former Chancellor). The new law school has been completed and the £16.6 million extension of the Business School is under way. But the main development has been the opening of the Palatine Centre, the culmination of a £50-million programme to create a student services hub at the heart of the university. The centre houses the full range of student services, which were previously spread around Durham city.

As the third-oldest university in England, Durham is generally quite traditional. Wherever possible, teaching takes place in small groups and most assessment is

---

University Office
The Palatine Centre
Stockton Road
Durham DH1 3LE

0191 334 6128 (admissions)
admissions@dur.ac.uk
www.dur.ac.uk
www.dsu.org.uk
Affiliation: Russell Group

***The Times and Sunday Times* Rankings**
Overall Ranking: **6** (5)

Student satisfaction:	23	(83.9%)
Research quality:	=7	(29.7%)
Entry standards:	7	(510)
Student–staff ratio:	25	(15.1)
Services & facilities/student:	5	(£2,365)
Expected completion rate:	10	(96.1%)
Good honours:	7	(83.9%)
Graduate prospects:	5	(82.6%)

by written examination. However, the establishment of Queen's Campus in Stockton-on-Tees broke the mould. Initially a joint venture with Teesside University, Stockton is now home to a wide range of courses including applied psychology, business and business finance, anthropology and primary education. The campus has also seen the fulfilment of Durham's long-held ambition to restore the medical education it lost when Newcastle University went its own way in 1963. An innovative joint project allows students to do the first two years of their training at Stockton, concentrating on community medicine, before transferring to Newcastle to complete their degree. The first cohort of pharmacy students will be welcomed to Queen's Campus in October.

Significant investment has been made to improve social facilities for the 2,000 students in Stockton, including the opening of a £5.5-million sports centre, relocating some of the university's elite sports activities from Durham as part of a strategy to increase integration between the two sites. The university's aim is for the campus to be equal in academic status to Durham City, focusing on interdisciplinary research and covering the full range of research, taught postgraduate and undergraduate study.

More than 60 per cent of the work submitted for the 2008 Research Assessment Exercise was rated world-leading or internationally excellent. Applied maths, archaeology and theology achieved among the best results in the UK. Music, English and geography and environmental science also did well.

The university dominates the city of Durham to an extent which sometimes causes resentment, but adds considerably to the local economy. For those looking for nightlife, or just a change of scene, Newcastle is a short train journey away. Sports facilities are excellent – with strong investment in facilities at both Durham and Stockton – and Durham is among the premier universities in national competitions. The university hosts centres of excellence in cricket, rowing and fencing, and offers a range of sports scholarships. Nine out of ten students take part in sport on a regular basis, and Durham's College Sport programme is the largest intramural competition in the UK. Some 380 teams compete in 15 sports every week.

Undergraduate Fees and Bursaries

» Fees for UK/EU students 2014–15 £9,000
» International student fees 2013–14 £13,300–£17,000
» Household income below £25K, £3,000 a year for college living expenses or as cash if living out; £25K–£42.6K, £1,000.
» Students from the Supported Progression Compact Scheme, £5,500 a year (in year 1, as an accommodation subsidy).
» Academic, music, art and sports scholarships based on circumstances or by competition, up to £2,000. Scholarships for local students up to £10,000 a year.

Students

Undergraduates:	**11,620**	**(190)**
Postgraduates:	**3,170**	**(1,590)**
Mature students:	**5.0%**	
Overseas students:	**12.8%**	
Applications per place:	**6.5**	
From state-sector schools:	**59.2%**	
From working-class homes:	**13.5%**	
Satisfaction with students' union	**50%**	

For detailed information about sports facilities: www.teamdurham.com

Accommodation

Number of places and costs refer to 2013–14
University-provided places: 5,398
Percentage catered: 70.6%
Catered costs: £153.72–£169.15; 29 weeks catered.
Self-catered costs: £119.97 (Durham); £119.97 (Queen's campus).
All full-time students become members of one of the university's colleges or societies and are allocated housing if they want it.
International students: first years are guaranteed housing.
Contact: admissions@durham.ac.uk; www.dur.ac.uk/colleges/

University of East Anglia

UEA has reached its highest-ever position in 20 years of our league table, thanks mainly to consistently high levels of student satisfaction and good staffing levels. It is seldom outside the top ten in the National Student Survey and was voted the top university in the UK for student satisfaction in the 2013 *Times Higher Education* Student Experience Survey. UEA was one of the few universities to meet its recruitment targets when the fees went up in 2012, filling marginally more places despite a drop in applications of more than 13 per cent. The 15,000 students appear to like the scale of this relatively small campus university, as well as the quality of its courses. They can bring any inquiries to four learning and teaching "hubs", one for postgraduates, another for nursing and two for undergraduates in the other 25 schools.

The university has been engaged in an ambitious building and refurbishment programme on the 320-acre site on the outskirts of Norwich. Recent projects include the refurbishment of the Law School's Earlham Hall complex, the addition of more student accommodation and common space facilities, and a Gymnastics Centre in UEA's community Sportspark. In recent years, it has also provided a new health centre, and extended and refurbished the central library, catering facilities and students' union. An Enterprise Centre to develop students' entrepreneurial skills is due to open in 2015, along with a new Medical Research Building for the Medical School. The new developments continue UEA's longstanding commitment to sustainability, which is reflected in a top-30 position in the People and Planet Green League of environmental performance.

As UEA celebrates its 50th anniversary, some of the broad subject combinations pioneered in its early days are still highly regarded in the academic world. The university is ranked among the top 200 in the world by *Times Higher Education* magazine. Environmental sciences is the flagship school, with UEA contributing more than any other university in the world to the 2007 Nobel Prize-winning Intergovernmental Panel on Climate Change. The Climatic Research Unit and the Government-funded Tyndall Centre for Climate Change Research, which has a hub in Shanghai, are among the leaders in the investigation of climate change.

History of art and culture and media did even better in the 2008 Research Assessment Exercise, when half of their research was considered world-leading. Art history has the benefit of the Sainsbury Centre for the Visual Arts, perhaps the greatest resource of its type on any British campus. The refurbished and extended

---

Norwich Research Park
Norwich NR4 7TJ

01603 591515 (admissions office)
admissions@uea.ac.uk
www.uea.ac.uk
www.ueastudent.com
Affiliation: 1994 Group

The Times and Sunday Times **Rankings**
Overall Ranking: **17** (28)

Student satisfaction:	2	(87.1%)
Research quality:	=32	(21.0%)
Entry standards:	=29	(418)
Student–staff ratio:	13	(13.5)
Services & facilities/student:	31	(£1,813)
Expected completion rate:	32	(91.3%)
Good honours:	40	(71.6%)
Graduate prospects:	=46	(68.7%)

centre houses a priceless collection of modern and tribal art in a building designed by Norman Foster. Creative writing is another of UEA's best-known features and the recipient of a Diamond Jubilee Queen's Anniversary Prize. Health studies have been among UEA's fastest-developing areas. The university was awarded one of the first new medical schools for 20 years, and has since added pharmacy and speech and language therapy degree courses.

Nearly nine out of ten undergraduates come from state schools or colleges, and almost a quarter have a working-class background. Most have the opportunity of work experience as part of their course. An academic adviser guides all students on their options under the modular course system and monitors their progress through to graduation. The university is focusing even more on employability since the introduction of £9,000 fees. UEA's strategy addresses the development of academic and wider skills through the curriculum while a Graduate Intern Programme enables recent graduates to work full- or part-time for between four and twelve weeks at a business in the eastern region.

UEA opened University Campus Suffolk in 2007, in partnership with Essex University, with a main site in Ipswich and smaller bases in Bury St Edmunds, Great Yarmouth, Lowestoft and Otley. It now also has a London campus for the growing numbers of international students. The site in the City of London offers preparatory courses run by INTO, the university's partner, as well as a range of business-related programmes. Dropout rates have improved enormously in recent years. The latest projected figure of 6 per cent was better than the national average for the university's subjects and entry standards.

The university is situated in parkland, with easy access to Norwich, voted one of the best small cities in the world and also England's first UNESCO City of Literature in 2012. The impressive Sportspark boasts an Olympic-sized swimming pool, fitness and aerobics centres, athletics track, gymnastics facilities, climbing wall, courts and pitches. The university was chosen as the base for the English Institute of Sport in the East.

Undergraduate Fees and Bursaries

» Fees for UK/EU students 2014–15   £9,000
   Courses at partner colleges   £5,900–£7,500
» International student fees 2013–14   £12,300–£14,900
   Medicine   £27,500
» For each year of study, students with household income below £16K, £3,000 as fee waiver or accommodation discount, or £1,000 cash and £2,000 accommodation discount or fee waiver (£4,500 for Foundation-year students in Science and Arts); £16K–£20K, £1,500 as cash, fee waiver or accommodation discount.
» Entry Scholarships, £1,500 cash for students with at least AAA or equivalent; subject scholarships.
» Annual progression Excellence Awards (£1,000) available.

Students

Undergraduates:	11,315	(1,590)
Postgraduates:	3,020	(1,680)
Mature students:	15.4%	
Overseas students:	16.8%	
Applications per place:	6.0	
From state-sector schools:	89.7%	
From working-class homes:	23.6%	
Satisfaction with students' union	84%	

For detailed information about sports facilities:
http://sportspark.co.uk

Accommodation

Number of places and costs refer to 2013–14
University-provided places: 3,457
Percentage catered: 0%
Self-catered costs: £2,630.74 – £8,259.30 (38 weeks).
First years are guaranteed accommodation if conditions are met.
Distance restrictions.
International students (non EU) are guaranteed accommodation if conditions are met.
Contact: accom@uea.ac.uk
www.uea.ac.uk/accommodation

University of East London

East London (UEL) has just climbed off the bottom of our league table after a year in which it was effectively level with two other universities. Its scores for graduate prospects, entry standards and completion are among the lowest in the UK. But the university is buoyant in many respects, after capitalising on the legacy of the London 2012 Olympics nearby and opening a new site, University Square, in partnership with Birkbeck, University of London. UEL was the closest university to the Olympic Park and hosted the United States team at its new £21-million sports and academic centre at the Docklands Campus, called the Sports Dock. The campus, which opened in 2000, was the first such venture in London for 50 years and gave the university a new focal point, with its modern version of traditional university features like cloisters and squares. The university spent more than £190 million on the campus in the shadow of Canary Wharf, where student residences and recreational facilities sit side by side with academic buildings in a prize-winning waterside development. The final pieces in the jigsaw were the business school and Knowledge Dock, a support centre for local companies, and a £40-million student village by the Royal Albert Dock, which added 800 more beds.

The university has spent more than £170 million in three years on new developments, with the focus shifting to nearby Stratford, the original headquarters in UEL's days as a pioneering polytechnic. The Great Hall in University House boasts a high-tech, 230-seat fully retractable lecture theatre, while the health and bioscience laboratories have been refurbished. The Cass School of Education has now opened and law is next on the development agenda. A new £14.7-million library opened in Stratford in 2013, and student residences and facilities for part-time and evening courses had already been added. The University Square development takes its first students in September 2013. It will house a selection of departments from UEL and Birkbeck and incorporates a range of flexible teaching and administrative spaces, alongside dedicated spaces for subjects including law, performing arts, dance, music and information technology that will be offered as daytime or evening courses.

UEL had been attracting big increases in applications before the introduction of the maximum £9,000 fee for degrees in every subject. Despite a "generous package" of scholarships and bursaries to ensure that potential students were not deterred from accessing higher education, the demand for places saw a 17 per cent decline and the first-year intake dropped by more than 1,000 students. Extending access to higher

---

Stratford Campus,
Water Lane
London E15 4LZ
Docklands Campus
University Way
London E16 2RD
020 8223 3333 (admissions)
study@uel.ac.uk
www.uel.ac.uk
www.uelunion.org
Affiliation: million+

The Times and Sunday Times **Rankings**
Overall Ranking: **120** (=116)

Student satisfaction:	**106**	(77.5%)
Research quality:	**=73**	(4.0%)
Entry standards:	**116**	(238)
Student–staff ratio:	**119**	(24.8)
Services & facilities/student:	**101**	(£1,118)
Expected completion rate:	**121**	(62.9%)
Good honours:	**119**	(49%)
Graduate prospects:	**120**	(43.8%)

education is UEL's top priority. Barely more than half of first years arrive with A levels and very nearly half are 21 or older on entry – many choosing to start courses in February. Almost half of the undergraduates come from working-class homes, many from the area's large ethnic minority populations. A successful mentoring scheme for black and Asian students has become a model for other institutions, while a guidance unit advises local people considering returning to education. The Noon Centre for Equality and Diversity in Business, which opened in 2013 at UEL's Royal Docks Business School, gives extra help to its Black Ethnic Minority (BME) students to prepare for a successful career in business. UEL is also strong on provision for disabled students and houses the Rix Centre for Innovation and Learning Disability.

The projected dropout rate has been improving – the latest figure of less than 14 per cent is considerably better than average for UEL's courses and entry qualifications.

Many degrees are vocational and almost 1,000 businesses are involved in mentoring programmes and/or a work-based learning initiative which offers accredited placements. All but one of the nine subject areas in which UEL entered the 2008 Research Assessment Exercise contained at least some world-leading research. Communication, culture and media studies,

produced particularly good results, while art and design and sociology also did well. Centres of excellence include an Islamic Banking and Finance Centre, launched in 2011 and partly funded by one of Saudi Arabia's biggest banks, which has become a hub for international scholars who are looking to conduct research in this field.

University housing is not plentiful, although there are now 1,200 bedspaces and the rents are good value for London. The social mix means that UEL has not been the place to look for the archetypal partying student lifestyle, although the Docklands campus has changed this to some extent and Stratford has been transformed since the Olympics. Sports facilities and new students' union premises have been added at both Stratford and Docklands.

Undergraduate Fees and Bursaries

» Fees for UK/EU students 2014–15 £9,000
» International student fees 2013–14 £9,900
» 628 NSP awards prioritised for students from local schools or colleges, £1,000 cash, £2,000 for accommodation and other study-related costs, year 1; £1,500 university services, years 2 and 3.
» UEL Progress Bursary for all who complete first semester: £500, year 1; £300, years 2 and 3
» Care leaver bursary £1,000 a year; sports scholarships, free textbook offer and enhanced study skills support.
» Range of other scholarships and bursaries available.
» Check the university's website for the latest information.

Students

Undergraduates:	**13,475**	**(3,595)**
Postgraduates:	**2,705**	**(3,445)**
Mature students:	**48.1%**	
Overseas students:	**12.8%**	
Applications per place:	**4.3**	
From state-sector schools:	**97.1%**	
From working-class homes:	**48.7%**	
Satisfaction with students' union	**61%**	

For detailed information about sports facilities: www.uel.ac.uk/sport

Accommodation

Number of places and costs refer to 2013–14

University-provided places: 1,200

Percentage catered: 0%

Self-catered costs: £120.45 (en-suite single) – £150.00 (studio flat) a week (39 weeks).

First years are guaranteed accommodation if conditions are met; priority given to disabled students and to those living furthest away.

International students: same as above.

Docklands Campus 020 8223 5409; dlres@uel.ac.uk

Edge Hill University

Edge Hill surprised many observers with its decision to charge £9,000 undergraduate fees in all subjects in 2012, but the outcome was an increase in applications across all programmes. In the end, the university filled 350 fewer places through UCAS than in 2011, but the decision paid off handsomely in financial terms. The university had promised to use most of the income to continue enhancing its students' learning experience after losing 95 per cent of its teaching grant in the switch to the new fees regime. Based at Ormskirk, Edge Hill has been one of the fastest growing universities in the UK, as well as one of the newest. It has more than doubled its complement of students since the millennium to reach over 22,000, although just over 9,000 of them are on full-time undergraduate courses. The largest numbers are on part-time postgraduate courses for the professions.

Edge Hill moved up nearly 30 places since 2009 in our league table. More than £180 million has been spent on the 160-acre campus over the past decade, and there are plans for significant expansion following the purchase of land adjoining the existing site. A new sports complex with indoor and outdoor facilities, including 3G pitches and tennis courts, was the first development on this site, ready for the 2013 intake. A £13.5-million spacious modern Student Hub building opened on the original campus in 2011. It houses the students' union and also contains open access computers, dining and shopping facilities, and social space. The latest major development is the £16-million Creative Edge building, opening this autumn, which will provide industry-standard facilities for students studying courses in media, film, animation, advertising and computing. It will also provide space for businesses to recruit students for internships and forge links with academic staff through research and consultancy projects.

Although university status arrived only in 2005, Edge Hill moved to its landscaped campus in the 1930s and has been training teachers since the 19th century. It has long since expanded into other subjects, but remains the largest provider of secondary teacher training and courses for classroom assistants. It has also won the lion's share of funding to deliver further training for qualified secondary school teachers. In 2011, the Faculty of Education achieved an unprecedented "outstanding" grade in all 33 possible graded areas of its Ofsted inspection across all three phases of its teacher-training provision.

A newly developed Arts Centre houses the university's Performing Arts Department and the Rose and Studio Theatres. The £2-million overhaul includes

St Helens Road
Ormskirk
Lancashire L39 4QP

01695 575171 (enquiries)
contact via website
www.edgehill.ac.uk
www.edgehillsu.org.uk
Affiliation: none

The Times and Sunday Times **Rankings**
Overall Ranking: **69** (=73)

Student satisfaction:	=24	(83.8%)
Research quality:	=112	(0.7%)
Entry standards:	=82	(307)
Student–staff ratio:	49	(17.2)
Services & facilities/student:	67	(£1,360)
Expected completion rate:	73	(83.7%)
Good honours:	98	(56.9%)
Graduate prospects:	75	(60.7%)

a seating, a bistro and an adjoining amphi-theatre. Resources for the performing arts were expanded in 2005, providing new facilities for animation, TV and other media areas. The SOLSTICE (Supported Online Learning for Students using Technology for Information and Communication in their Education) e-learning centre is recognised officially as a national centre of excellence in teaching and learning. It has a particular focus on learning in the workplace, but is involved with curriculum development and delivery in all three of the university's faculties. Nursing, midwifery and other health care programmes have been commended by inspectors. Three-quarters of all graduates leave with professional accreditation. Recent additions to the portfolio of degrees are digital marketing and music, sound and enterprise. All students have a personal tutor, as well as access to counsellors and financial advice.

Beyond Ormskirk, there are seven satellite campuses in Liverpool, Manchester and other parts of the North West to facilitate local learning. In addition, a range of further education colleges in the region teach the university's Foundation degrees. Edge Hill has one of the highest proportions of state-educated students in England – almost 99 per cent. Over 40 per cent of undergraduates have a working-class background and one in five come from areas without a tradition of higher education

– far above the national average for the university's courses and entry qualifications. The projected dropout rate of 11 per cent is also better than the university's benchmark.

Before the fees went up, Edge Hill won an award for a student finance support package that rewarded achievement, as well as encouraging students to complete their studies, rather than simply offering incentives for enrolling. Bursaries and scholarships have been extended since, and there are separate awards in sport, the performing arts, volunteering and the creative arts. The £3.9-million Sporting Edge complex, which was part funded by a Lottery grant, is open to staff, students and the local community. There are over 1,500 residential places on campus.

Undergraduate Fees and Bursaries

- » Fees for UK/EU students 2014–15 £9,000
  Foundation degree £6,000
- » International student fees 2013–14 £10,800
- » 809 NSP awards for those with household income below £25K who accept an offer by 14 May 2014, £1,000 cash and £2,000 university accommodation discount or fee waiver in year 1 only.
- » Scholarship of £1,000 for those with at least 320 UCAS points and not receiving an NSP award.
- » Access Scholarships of £1,000, year 1; £500, years 2 and 3, particularly for mature students.
- » Scholarship of £1,000, year 1, £500, years 2 and 3, based on personal achievements, in sport, performing arts, creative arts and volunteering.

Students

Undergraduates:	**9,425**	**(5,180)**
Postgraduates:	**685**	**(7,060)**
Mature students:	**18.6%**	
Overseas students:	**0.9%**	
Applications per place:	**5.3**	
From state-sector schools:	**98.5%**	
From working-class homes:	**40.5%**	
Satisfaction with students' union	**70%**	

For detailed information about sports facilities:
www.edgehill.ac.uk/EdgeHillSport

Accommodation

Number of places and costs refer to 2013–14
University provided places: 1,574
Percentage catered: 19.5%
Catered costs: £96 a week (40 weeks)
Self-catered costs: £59–£104 a week (40 weeks)
First years cannot be guaranteed housing. Residential restrictions apply.
Students designated overseas for fees are guaranteed accommodation if conditions are met.
Contact: www.edgehill.ac.uk/study/accommodation

University of Edinburgh

Becoming one of the two most expensive universities in the UK for undergraduates from England, Wales and Northern Ireland in 2012 did not stop Edinburgh attracting more applications and filling 10 per cent more places than in the previous year. Unlike most others in Scotland, the university charges students from other parts of the UK £9,000 for the full four years of a degree course. The university retains a special status north of the border, where it is regarded as the nearest thing to Oxbridge. Edinburgh's research strength won it a place in the top 20 in the 2013 QS World University Rankings, but unusually poor student satisfaction ratings have seen it drop eight places and out of our top 20 this year. The fact that almost a quarter of the 27,600 students come from outside the UK testifies to its worldwide reputation. Among the recent achievements celebrated by the university were the multiple Olympic gold medals won by Edinburgh alumnus Sir Chris Hoy and the confirmation of the discovery of the "God particle" by a team led by Professor Peter Higgs, which was marked by the establishment of the Higgs Centre for Theoretical Physics. The Centre will offer masters programmes and enable students to take up PhDs in relevant areas.

Edinburgh is the largest university in Scotland. Its buildings are spread around the city, but most border the historic Old Town. These include the university's main library, which has been redeveloped at a cost of £60 million. The science and engineering campus is two miles to the south.

Competition for places remains intense: more than eight applications for each place in 2012. Edinburgh has been trying to widen its intake, spending more than £1 million on undergraduate bursaries of at least £1,000 a year. Other measures include an eight-week summer school for local teenagers and support for students in the transition to higher education. The university has always attracted a high proportion of middle-class candidates – many from England – and is a favourite in independent schools, whose students take about three places in ten. Selection guidelines aim to look beyond grades to consider candidates' potential, giving particular weight to references and personal statements. The university gives extra credit in some oversubscribed programmes to applicants from Scotland and parts of the north of England.

Edinburgh, a member of the Russell Group of leading UK research universities, has stepped up its fundraising activities. The campaign has contributed to a new informatics building, as well as to the development of a "BioQuarter", a ground-breaking collaboration between the university and a number of public bodies

---

Old College
South Bridge
Edinburgh EH8 9YL

0131 650 4360 (admissions)
contact via website
www.ed.ac.uk
www.eusa.ed.ac.uk
Affiliation: Russell Group

The Times and Sunday Times **Rankings**
Overall Ranking: **22** (14)

Student satisfaction:	114	(76.4%)
Research quality:	6	(32.7%)
Entry standards:	9	(489)
Student–staff ratio:	15	(13.9)
Services & facilities/student:	12	(£2,185)
Expected completion rate:	=35	(90.7%)
Good honours:	10	(82.6%)
Graduate prospects:	24	(75.3%)

that is intended to consolidate Scotland's reputation as a world leader in biomedical science. In 2010, the author J.K. Rowling gave £10 million to the university to set up a new research clinic for multiple sclerosis. The Business School has relocated to the heart of the main campus and a new research centre has been established for the study of Islamic civilisation and issues relating to Islam in Britain. Elsewhere, £90 million has been spent on the redevelopment of the Easter Bush site. A veterinary school building, a research building for the recently incorporated Roslin Institute and a cancer centre opened in 2011, followed by a new building to house the MRC Centre for Regenerative Medicine at Little France.

Almost two-thirds of the work submitted for the last Research Assessment Exercise was rated as world-leading or internationally excellent, the highest proportion in Scotland. The university's entry was among the largest in the UK and produced strong results across the board. The College of Medicine and Veterinary Medicine was the star performer, with all of the work in hospital-based clinical subjects rated at the international level and 40 per cent at the highest grade. Informatics, linguistics and English literature also produced outstanding results. Departments organise visiting days in October for those thinking of applying and in the spring for

those holding offers, as well as the annual open day in June. New undergraduates generally take three subjects in both their first and second years. Every student has a director of studies to help them narrow down the selection of a final degree and give personal advice when necessary.

A new £4.5-million extension to the university's Centre for Sport and Exercise was unveiled in 2010, adding to the already impressive sports facilities. Considerable sums have also been spent making the university more accessible to disabled students. The students' union operates on several sites and there is a regular bus link between the science areas and the main university around George Square. The city is a treasure-trove of cultural and recreational opportunities, and most students thrive on Edinburgh life. Most first years are guaranteed an offer of accommodation.

Undergraduate Fees and Bursaries
» Fees for Scottish and EU students for 2013–14   No fee
» Fees for Non-Scottish UK (RUK) students for 2013–14: £9,000 a year, for up to 4 years (total £36,000).
» Fees for international students 2013–14   £13,300–£17,500 Medicine: £21,650–£36,600;   Veterinary studies: £27,900
» Accommodation bursaries of £500–£2,000 a year for Scottish students.
» Edinburgh RUK Bursary (2013–14) taken as fee waiver or cash: household income below £16K, £7,000 a year (£3,575 for Welsh students), and then a sliding scale to £42.6K, £5,700–£500 (£3,575–£500 for Welsh students).

Students

Undergraduates:	**18,175**	**(795)**
Postgraduates:	**6,745**	**(1,960)**
Mature students:	**10.2%**	
Overseas students:	**23.1%**	
Applications per place:	**8.6**	
From state-sector schools:	**70.3%**	
From working-class homes:	**16.5%**	
Satisfaction with students' union	**58%**	

For detailed information about sports facilities:
www.sport.ed.ac.uk

Accommodation
Number of places and costs refer to 2013–14
University-provided places: about 6,300
Percentage catered: about 30%
Catered costs: £115–£236 a week
Self-catered costs: £56–£137 a week.
First years are guaranteed an offer of accommodation providing they fulfil requirements. Residential restrictions apply.
International students: accommodation guaranteed if conditions are met.
Contact: www.accom.ed.ac.uk

Edinburgh Napier University

Edinburgh Napier set itself the target of becoming "one of the leading modern universities in the United Kingdom" by 2015. For two successive years, the university has enjoyed among the biggest increases in applications in the UK, defying the national trend in 2012 by registering another significant rise. Although partly fuelled by changes in art and design and nursing qualifications, the demand for places has been a clear reflection of the university's growing popularity. But it has dropped sharply in our league table this year, losing ground to its rivals on student satisfaction, completion and spending on facilities.

Edinburgh Napier is one of the largest universities in Scotland with 17,500 students, including more than 5,000 international students from over 100 different countries. It has been investing £100 million in its campuses. At Sighthill, the Faculty of Health, Life and Social Sciences has been brought together on one site for the first time. The student-focused campus includes a 5-storey learning resource centre, 25 specialised teaching rooms including clinical skills laboratories, an environmental chamber and biomechanics laboratory, a crime scene scenario room, 3 IT-enabled lecture theatres and seminar rooms as well as integrated sports facilities. Over the past year, further work has taken place on the Merchiston campus, bringing together the Faculty of Engineering, Computing and Creative Industries. The refurbishment includes a new student hub and reception area, as well as fully soundproofed music studios. The Napier Students' Association will also be based on the campus for the first time, and the library has been refurbished and is now open 24 hours a day.

Once Scotland's first and largest polytechnic, the university is named after John Napier, the inventor of logarithms. The 500-seat computing centre is open all hours and students have access to online lecture notes and study aids via Moodle, the university's Virtual Learning Environment. The web-based system supports learning, teaching and assessment via the student portal and is accessible from smart phones and tablet computers. The university has plans for continued development of study spaces to access technology-based learning. There are fully networked libraries on each campus and a multimedia language laboratory and adaptive learning centre for students with special needs.

The Craiglockhart campus houses the business school. It features a glass atrium housing a cyber café and two spherical lecture theatres. The Craiglockhart studio has been refurbished and is the venue for an assortment of fitness classes. The Screen Academy Scotland, run in partnership

---

Craiglockhart Campus
Edinburgh EH14 1DJ

08455 203050 (admissions)
ugadmissions@napier.ac.uk
www.napier.ac.uk
http://napierstudents.com
Affiliation: million+

The Times and Sunday Times Rankings		
Overall Ranking: **100** (84)		
Student satisfaction:	81	(80.4%)
Research quality:	=83	(3.0%)
Entry standards:	62	(325)
Student–staff ratio:	115	(23.8)
Services & facilities/student:	110	(£1,009)
Expected completion rate:	113	(75.2%)
Good honours:	53	(66.5%)
Graduate prospects:	65	(62.8%)

with Edinburgh College of Art, reflects the university's strong reputation in film education. The university is also opening a new student residence in the city centre for the start of the 2013–14 academic year. There are several smaller sites, mainly in the leafy south of Edinburgh, ranging from a converted church to a former school, as well as outposts in Melrose and Livingston.

Edinburgh Napier has over 3,000 students taking its degrees in Hong Kong, Singapore and India. Agreements with a number of partner universities and colleges enable students to complete their qualifications as undergraduates or postgraduates. A new dual degree with the State University of New York (SUNY) allows students to complete a degree from Edinburgh Napier and SUNY in four years. Closer to home, some 2,000 "college articulation routes" enable students to use their college qualifications to gain direct entry into year two or three of a university degree. Widening participation is high on the university's list of priorities. The 35 per cent share of undergraduate places going to students from working-class homes is greater than the UK average for the university's subjects and entry grades.

Many courses include a work placement, and a close relationship with industry has traditionally produced good employment prospects. The university's students and graduates are set to benefit from a new

£1.8-million initiative designed to ensure that this continues. The Stand Out project aims to improve graduate employment levels, partly by increasing the uptake of opportunities to study abroad as well as by improving links with small- and medium-sized enterprises.

The modular system allows movement between courses at all levels, and the option of starting courses in February, rather than September. A model to other universities trying to reduce non-completion rates, Edinburgh Napier uses its students to mentor newcomers, runs bridging programmes and offers pre-term introductions to staff and information on facilities, as well as running summer top-up courses in a variety of subjects and teaching employability skills and personal development. The latest projected dropout rate of 13.4 per cent matches the UK average for the subjects on offer, and represents continued improvement on previous years.

Undergraduate Fees and Bursaries

» Fees for Scottish and EU students for 2013–14   No fee
» Fees for Non-Scottish UK (RUK) students for 2013–14: £6,630 a year, for up to 4 years (total £26,520).
» Fees for international students 2013–14   £10,080–£11,700
» For RUK students (2013–14), household income below £25K, £2,000 bursary a year; household income £25K–£42.6K, £1,000 bursary a year.
» Range of other scholarships and bursaries available.
» Check the university's website for the latest information.

Students

Undergraduates:	**9,555**	**(1,820)**
Postgraduates:	**1,350**	**(1,340)**
Mature students:	**41.9%**	
Overseas students:	**18.9%**	
Applications per place:	**6.3**	
From state-sector schools:	**94.3%**	
From working-class homes:	**35.0%**	
Satisfaction with students' union	**57%**	

For detailed information about sports facilities:
www.napier.ac.uk/engage/

Accommodation

Number of places and costs refer to 2013–14
University-provided places: 1,404
Percentage catered: 0%
Self-catered costs: £102–£103 average cost a week; £120 (en suite) for 38 weeks.
First years and direct entrant undergraduates are guaranteed a place provided requirements are met. Residential restrictions apply.
International students: as above.
Contact: accommodation@napier.ac.uk

University of Essex

Essex is best known for the social sciences. The university received the only Regius Professorship in Political Science in the awards to mark the Queen's Diamond Jubilee and achieved the best results in the last Research Assessment Exercise for both politics and sociology. It was also in the top three for accounting and finance, history and economics. Essex featured in the top ten in more than half of the 14 areas in which it was assessed, demonstrating quality well beyond the old favourites. Essex has been building up its science departments, and is strong in biological sciences and computing. The university was one of the few to enjoy an increase in applications despite the introduction of £9,000 fees, although the first-year intake dropped slightly.

The main campus, two miles from Colchester, is set in 200 acres of parkland. The university has been carrying out major refurbishments to its 1960s buildings, at the same time as expanding student facilities. It has announced new developments costing more than £200 million in the run-up to the university's 50th anniversary in 2014. Recent projects have included a £1.4-million gym, renovation of the students' union bar, a café with adjoining learning space and an innovative shared IT workspace. Another £5 million has been spent on new teaching facilities and work has started on a £26-million Student Centre and library extension, which will provide a "one-stop-shop" for a range of student services, plus an integrated learning centre for group working, new IT facilities, and a 24-hour reading room. The current Large Reading Room is open 24 hours a day during the week with long weekend hours that are extended during revision and exam periods.

Wivenhoe House, the original centrepiece of the campus, has been converted into a thriving four-star hotel run by and home to the Edge Hotel School. Future developments include the Knowledge Gateway development, which will provide space for social sciences, research and development, and business. Essex Business School's new £21-million building, which will open in 2014, will feature low and zero carbon technology. The university is ranked third in the national Carbon Reduction Commitment rankings, a reward for green policies across its campuses.

The incorporation of the East 15 Acting School, in Loughton, as a department of the university was the university's first venture beyond Colchester. There has since been heavy investment in a third site in Southend – a modern multi-faculty campus offering courses in business, health and the arts. Situated in the town centre, the Southend Campus has been based

---

Wivenhoe Park
Colchester
Essex CO4 3SQ

01206 873666 (enquiries)
admit@essex.ac.uk
www.essex.ac.uk
www.essexstudent.com
Affiliation: 1994 Group

The Times and Sunday Times **Rankings**
Overall Ranking: **39** (40)

Student satisfaction:	=12	(85.4%)
Research quality:	=27	(22.7%)
Entry standards:	53	(342)
Student–staff ratio:	=36	(16.4)
Services & facilities/student:	23	(£1,946)
Expected completion rate:	63	(85.6%)
Good honours:	=79	(60.7%)
Graduate prospects:	113	(51.8%)

around the Gateway Building and Clifftown Studios, a former church that is now the university's theatre. University Square is an accommodation complex which also houses a gym and fitness studio. The Forum was added in 2013, a £27-million project comprising a public and academic library, learning facilities, café and gallery. Another regional project has seen Essex collaborate with the University of East Anglia on University Campus Suffolk, which offers courses in Ipswich and at smaller centres across the county. Essex degrees are also taught at Writtle College, near Chelmsford, the Colchester Institute and South East Essex College, in Southend.

The university now has almost 12,000 undergraduates. The student population is unusually diverse for a pre-1992 university, with high proportions of mature and overseas students. More than a third of undergraduates are from working-class homes and 95 per cent went to state schools or colleges – both higher figures than the subject mix would suggest. The Employability and Careers Centre has seen major investment over recent years. The university and students' union have established a Frontrunners placement scheme offering students paid work opportunities on its campuses, with placements of between one and three terms. Many courses offer work placement opportunities. Essex Abroad supports students studying, working or volunteering abroad, while the new Languages for All scheme offers all students language tuition at no extra cost. The university does not charge a fee for a full year abroad, and many courses also include work placement opportunities.

Social and sporting facilities are good, with an active students' union and some 40 acres of land on the Colchester campus devoted to sports facilities. All new first years are guaranteed a residential place in university accommodation, which has been voted some of the best in the UK. Some ground-floor flats have been adapted for disabled students. A £23-million new development will open on the main campus in October 2013 with 648 student bedrooms in flats and town houses. All the campuses are within easy access of London.

Undergraduate Fees and Bursaries

» Fees for UK/EU students for 2014–15   £9,000
» International student fees 2013–14   £11,500–£13,500
» NSP awards, £3,000 university services, or £1,000 cash and £2,000 university services, year 1, £1,000 cash, year 2; £500 cash, year 3.
» Academic Excellence scholarship of £2,000 a year for those with specified entry qualifications.
» Care leaver and refugee bursaries of up to £1,000.
» Range of other scholarships and bursaries available.
» Check the university's website for the latest information.

Students

Undergraduates:	**10,040**	**(1,970)**
Postgraduates:	**2,310**	**(900)**
Mature students:	**14.2%**	
Overseas students:	**25.3%**	
Applications per place:	**6.2**	
From state-sector schools:	**95.7%**	
From working-class homes:	**34.0%**	
Satisfaction with students' union	**74%**	

For detailed information about sports facilities:
www.essex.ac.uk/sport

Accommodation

Number of places and costs refer to 2013–14
University-provided places: 4,266
Percentage catered: 0%
Self-catered costs: Colchester: £70.00 (South Towers) – £126.84 (Meadows en suite) a week; Southend: £124.74 (en suite) – £154.00 (studio flat)
New first years are guaranteed accommodation if conditions met.
International students: new students are guaranteed accommodation if conditions are met.
Contact: admit@essex.ac.uk

University of Exeter

The Sunday Times University of the Year for 2012, Exeter attracted more students when the fees went up and outperformed its rivals again in 2013. Applications were up by 19 per cent at the start of the year, with highly competitive selection in most subjects. The university was one of the first to announce £9,000 fees, arguing that the maximum was needed to direct resources at widening participation, fair access and improving the student experience. One of four institutions to join the Russell Group of leading research universities in 2012, Exeter is becoming established in the top 10 in our league table, thanks particularly to consistently high levels of student satisfaction and a good performance in the Research Assessment Exercise (RAE).

The 2008 RAE saw Exeter move up the pecking order of research universities, with most of its work judged to be world-leading or internationally excellent despite a much larger submission (involving 95 per cent of academics) than most of its peers. English, classics, archaeology, and accounting and finance did particularly well. The successes produced one of the biggest increases in research funding at any university, and the research environment is being further improved with an investment of more than £230 million in infrastructure and staff.

Exeter's main Streatham Campus is one of the most attractive settings of any university, and has benefited from £380 million of investment. This ambitious programme includes £130 million for student residences, substantial investment in the Business School, a new Mood Disorders Centre and new facilities for biosciences and the Law School. The jewel in the crown of the new developments is the Forum, a £50-million development which creates a central hub and features an extended library, new student services centre, technology-rich learning spaces, a new auditorium and additional social and retail facilities.

The start of the academic year will see the first students admitted to the new University of Exeter Medical School, which has grown out of the former Peninsular College of Medicine and Dentistry, opened in association with Plymouth University in 2006. The partners have gone their separate ways, with Plymouth taking dentistry and Exeter offering a BSc in medical sciences in addition to the established Bachelor of Medicine, Bachelor of Surgery (BMBS). New degrees for 2014 on the main campus will include a BA in philosophy, politics and economics, a BSc in biological sciences with professional placement, a BA in human sciences and four-year integrated Masters programmes in several subjects.

Almost a third of Exeter's undergraduates come from independent schools – a

---

Northcote House
The Queen's Drive
Exeter, Devon EX4 4QJ

0844 620 0012 (admissions)
ug-ad@exeter.ac.uk
www.exeter.ac.uk
www.exeterguild.org
www.fxu.org.uk
Affiliation: Russell Group

The Times and Sunday Times **Rankings**
Overall Ranking: **8** (10)

Student satisfaction:	8	(86%)
Research quality:	=13	(28.0%)
Entry standards:	13	(470)
Student–staff ratio:	54	(17.8)
Services & facilities/student:	16	(£2,120)
Expected completion rate:	4	(97.1%)
Good honours:	8	(83.8%)
Graduate prospects:	=18	(77.1%)

much higher proportion than the national average for the university's subjects and entry qualifications, although this figure has been coming down gradually. The university used to focus its attempts to broaden the intake mainly on the rural South West, but is now targeting schools and colleges further afield. The share of places taken by students from working-class homes is among the lowest in the UK, at little more than 15 per cent. However, the dropout rate of less than 3 per cent is also among the lowest.

A £100-million campus near Falmouth has helped boost applications. Shared with Falmouth University, the Cornwall campus offers Exeter degrees in biosciences, geography, geology, renewable energy, English, history, politics and mining engineering. The latest development is a £30-million Environment and Sustainability Institute that will help put the university at the forefront of environmental and climate change research.

Exeter's longstanding international focus is exemplified by a large range of four-year programmes "with international study" and by its partner universities in over 40 countries. All students are offered tuition in foreign languages and even some three-year degrees include the option of a year abroad. Career management skills are built in and students have a wide range of work experience opportunities. The Career Zone has been expanded to increase career support and internships and graduate employment rates have been improving. The university's Exeter Award provides official recognition of all the extracurricular activities that students undertake.

The main campus is located near the city centre, while the highly rated department of sport and health sciences, the graduate school of education and the medical school are a mile away at the St Luke's Campus. Over £20 million has been invested in sports facilities in the last few years, and Exeter is one of only nine UK universities to have indoor tennis facilities to national competition standards.

There is no shortage of student-oriented bars and clubs, as well as more sophisticated cultural events. New first years are guaranteed accommodation.

Undergraduate Fees and Bursaries

» Fees for UK/EU students for 2014–15 £9,000
» International student fees 2013–14 £14,500–£17,000
  Medicine £17,000–£29,000
» For all eligible UK students: household income below £16K, £2,000 fee waiver and £1,400 cash, years 1 and 2; £1,400 bursary, year 3; household income 16K–£25K, £1,000 bursary each year; £25K–£35K, £750; £35K–£42.6K, £500.
» Sports and music scholarships available.
» Range of other scholarships and bursaries available.
» Check the university's website for the latest information.

Students

Undergraduates:	**14,080**	**(125)**
Postgraduates:	**3,535**	**(980)**
Mature students:	**9.2%**	
Overseas students:	**17.7%**	
Applications per place:	**6.0**	
From state-sector schools:	**67.4%**	
From working-class homes:	**15.2%**	
Satisfaction with students' union	**78%**	

For detailed information about sports facilities:
http://sport.exeter.ac.uk

Accommodation

Number of places and costs refer to 2013–14
University-provided places: 4,870
Percentage catered: 24%
Catered costs: £143.92–£212.03 a week (32 weeks).
Self-catered costs: £79.80–£142.94 a week (40, 42, 44 or 51 weeks).
Unaccompanied first years are guaranteed accommodation provided conditions are met.
International students: as above.
Contact: sid@exeter.ac.uk

University of Falmouth

Falmouth set itself three targets while still a university college: to achieve a university title by 2014, the power to award research degrees by 2016 and to be among the top five specialist arts universities by 2017. It is on target and will enrol its first students as a university this autumn. With fewer than 3,000 students, Falmouth had been too small to become a university until the rules changed. But while still an arts specialist, the new university offers degrees in advertising, animation, architecture, marketing, dance, digital media, fashion, creative writing and English, as well as conventional art and craft courses.

Founded in 1902 as Falmouth School of Art, the institution was granted the power to award taught degrees in 2005 and three years later merged with Dartington College of Arts, in south Devon, to add a range of performance-related courses to its portfolio. The former Dartington courses relocated to a purpose-built Performance Centre on the Tremough campus, at Penryn, in 2010. Falmouth has also collaborated with the University of Exeter since 2002 and students benefit from a £10-million joint venture between the two. The Exchange, which contains teaching and library space as well as study areas, opened in 2012 on the Tremough campus, where there has been a major extension to the library and the establishment of an Academy for Innovation and Research, which has a particular focus on the digital economy and sustainable design. More than 70 per cent of the staff submitted work to the 2008 Research Assessment Exercise in music, theatre, choreography, visual performance and performance writing. The research programme covers areas such as future transport solutions, eco-town developments and Britain's ageing population, as well as art.

The new university had grown rapidly over the last five years before receiving its new title, almost doubling in size. The original Falmouth campus, near the town centre, boasts subtropical gardens and an outdoor sculpture canopy, as well as studios, library and catering facilities. Applications dropped sharply when £9,000 fees were introduced in 2012, but Falmouth still managed a small increase in the size of its intake. Because portfolios or auditions are as important as A levels on many courses, more than half of the offers made to applicants are unconditional and others average only about 220 UCAS tariff points. About 60 per cent of the undergraduates are female, and 95 per cent were state educated, with almost 30 per cent coming from working-class homes. The university has an internal teaching qualification for staff to ensure high standards in teaching, learning

Woodlane
Falmouth, Cornwall TR11 4RH

01326 211 077 (admissions)
admissions@falmouth.ac.uk
www.falmouth.ac.uk
www.fxu.org.uk
Affiliation: GuildHE

The Times and Sunday Times **Rankings**
Overall Ranking: **=77** (n/a)

Student satisfaction:	105	(77.8%)
Research quality:	=92	(2.0%)
Entry standards:	96	(289)
Student–staff ratio:	116	(23.9)
Services & facilities/student:	25	(£1,916
Expected completion rate:	46	(88%)
Good honours:	59	(64.4%)
Graduate prospects:	78	(60.2%)

and assessment.

Most of the degrees are single honours, but those in the performing arts allow students to combine theatre, fine art, music, writing and choreography. The university intends to introduce new "externally facing" courses, including programmes that enable students to set up a business while studying. There will be new provision in growing creative industries sectors, with plans for courses in creative computing, gaming, social media, creative leadership, business and management, as well as a graduate entrepreneurship programme. There will also be a focus on the "learning and leisure" market, making use of Cornwall's tourist attractions, businesses and landmarks. Falmouth is involved in setting up a college based at the Eden Project for young people who have dropped out of education and training.

A new Photographic Centre opened on the Tremough Campus in 2007, with an extension to the Media Centre. Falmouth has been awarded Skillset Academy status for its media courses. The animation and visual effects department has become part of the Cross Channel Film Lab, a project that aims to develop an innovative visual effects for use in low-budget feature film production, working on films alongside experts from the within the industry. Partners include BBC Films, Film 4 and Arte France, and the university benefits from new computers, a 3D printer and stereoscopic projector, all of which will be available for student use.

Student residences are shared with the University of Exeter and there is a single students' union, FXU, to represent Falmouth students and those attending Exeter's Cornwall campus. Glasney Student Village, on the Tremough Campus, opened in 2004 and expanded in 2012 and there are also residential places in Falmouth, so the university can guarantee all full-time first years accommodation. The Sports Centre has a gymnasium, exercise studio and multi-use games area. As befits the seaside location, there are many water sports activities. Students make full use of Cornwall's coastline and rugged moors, but there are good transport links to London and Europe. Plenty of tourist-related work is available and the university also pays students to be mentors to newer arrivals.

Undergraduate Fees and Bursaries

- » Fees for UK/EU students 2014–15: £9,000
- » International student fees 2013–14: £10,900
- » 205 NSP awards to Cornish residents of £3,000, year 1; £1,500, years 2 and 3; of £6,000 total, £1,000 as cash, £5,000 as mix of fee waiver, accommodation discount and course expenses.
- » Bursaries for all students with household income below £25K, £750; £25K–£35K, £250.
- » Range of scholarships and bursaries by subject, for travel and for care leavers and disabled students.
- » Check the university's website for the latest information.

Students

Undergraduates:	**3,450**	**(55)**
Postgraduates:	**190**	**(165)**
Mature students:	**15.5%**	
Overseas students:	**4.0%**	
Applications per place:	**3.7**	
From state-sector schools:	**95.1%**	
From working-class homes:	**29.3%**	
Satisfaction with students' union	**73%**	

For detailed information about sports facilities: www.fxplus.ac.uk/enjoy/sports-recreation

Accommodation

Places and costs refer to 2013–14

University-provided places: approx. 1,400

Percentage catered: 0%

Self-catered costs: £73.92 (shared) – £123.20 (single en suite) for 40 weeks.

First year full time students are guaranteed housing if conditions are met.

International students: as above.

Contact: accommodation@fxplus.ac.uk; www.falmouth.ac.uk/140/student-life-6/accommodation-32.html

University of Glasgow

Glasgow almost caught its old rival, Edinburgh, in last year's league table, but both slipped back outside the top 20 in the latest edition. Student satisfaction and reduced staffing levels were mainly responsible. Glasgow is just outside the top 50 in the QS World University Rankings, however, and is enjoying sharply increased demand for places. Applications and enrolments both rose in 2012. With two-thirds of the students coming from Scotland – almost half of them from within 30 miles of Glasgow – the university benefits more than some of its rivals from the policy of free tuition for Scottish students. There has always been a high proportion of home-based students, but over 12 per cent are from outside the UK. They seem to enjoy the experience, having voted Glasgow third in the UK in i–graduate's independent International Student Barometer.

The university opened its first overseas branch in 2011, as part of an agreement with the Singapore Institute of Technology (SIT) to deliver joint engineering and mechatronics degree programmes. Students will complete three years at one of SIT's partner polytechnics before finishing their studies at the University of Glasgow Singapore. The university's Commonwealth Scholarship scheme celebrates the city's success as host of the 2014 Commonwealth Games by offering 53 awards for students from developing countries. The Centre for International Development, which was the first of its kind in Scotland and the largest in the UK, has helped to secure more than £20 million of research income. The university also has a campus at Dumfries, which is taking liberal arts and teacher education degrees to southwest Scotland.

Glasgow enjoys the rare distinction of having been established by Papal Bull, and began its existence in the chapterhouse of Glasgow Cathedral in 1451. Since 1871 it has been based on the Gilmorehill campus in the city's fashionable West End, with its 104 listed buildings – more than any other British university. Education occupies a separate campus nearby, while the Veterinary School and outdoor sports facilities are located at Garscube, four miles away. A new student centre opened in 2008, winning two architecture awards, while the environmental research building has also won awards as one of the "greenest" in Scotland. The university is about to embark on a major campus development, having bought 15 acres of land around Glasgow's Western Infirmary. Outline plans to reshape the university's estate should be ready in Spring 2014.

Glasgow is no stranger to innovation: it was the first university in Britain to have a school of engineering, for example, and

---

University Avenue
Glasgow G12 8QQ

0141 330 2000 (switchboard)
student.recruitment@
    glasgow.ac.uk
www.gla.ac.uk
www.guu.co.uk
www.qmu.org.uk
Affiliation: Russell Group

GLASGOW
Edinburgh
Belfast
London
Cardiff

The Times and Sunday Times **Rankings**
Overall Ranking: **25** (15)

Student satisfaction:	=36	(83.1%)
Research quality:	20	(24.3%)
Entry standards:	12	(477)
Student–staff ratio:	=36	(16.4)
Services & facilities/student:	11	(£2,206)
Expected completion rate:	43	(88.8%)
Good honours:	=27	(74.5%)
Graduate prospects:	27	(74.6%)

the first in Scotland to have a computer. It has now appointed Scotland's first Gaelic language officer and the country's first chair of Gaelic to promote both learning opportunities and cultural events. Glasgow is a member of the Russell Group of leading research universities. More than half of the work submitted for the last Research Assessment Exercise was considered world-leading or internationally excellent. Art history was the most highly rated in the UK and the Vet School joint top in its field, while the university finished in the top ten in 18 subject areas. The latest development is the £20-million Stratified Medicine Scotland Innovation Centre (SMS-IC) at the new South Glasgow Hospitals Campus, which involves a consortium of universities, NHS Scotland and industry partners, and opens in 2015.

Almost half of the university's applications are for arts or sciences degrees, rather than specific subjects, reflecting the popularity of a flexible system that allows students to delay choosing a specialism until the end of their second year. The university operates a number of access initiatives, including the Top Up programme, which has been working with schools in the West of Scotland since 1999, and the Talent Awards, which are worth £1,000 a year to 50 academically able entrants who could face financial difficulties in taking up a place at Glasgow. But little more than 20 per cent

of the undergraduates are from working-class homes. The projected dropout rate had improved slightly in the latest statistics but, at almost 11 per cent, is above average for Glasgow's subjects and entry qualifications. The Club 21 programme provides students with paid work experience placements in the UK and overseas. It involves more than 100 employers from Santander to T-Mobile, some of whom sponsor undergraduates at £1,000 a year.

Most students like the combination of campus and city life, with the added bonus that Glasgow has been rated among the most cost-effective cities in which to study. Undergraduates have the choice of two students' unions, plus a sports union supporting more than 40 clubs and activities.

Undergraduate Fees and Bursaries

» Fees for Scottish and EU students for 2013–14   No fee
» Fees for Non-Scottish UK (RUK) students for 2013–14, £6,750 a year (total £27,000); medicine , dentistry, veterinary science £9,000 (total £36,000).
» Fees for international students 2013–14   £13,000–£16,500 Medicine, dentistry and veterinary medicine   £28,500
» Talent Scholarships of £1,000 a year for those facing financial difficulties in taking up a place.
» For all RUK students (2013–14), £1,000 in year 1, as fee waiver or cash.
» Tuition fee waiver of £2,000 a year when household income below £20K, £1,000 (£20K–£30K), £500 (£30K–42.6K).
» Scholarship of £1,000 a year for students with at least AAB at A Level or equivalent and household income below £42.6K.

Students

Undergraduates:	**16,190**	**(3,725)**
Postgraduates:	**4,555**	**(1,825)**
Mature students:	**17.9%**	
Overseas students:	**12.2%**	
Applications per place:	**6.9**	
From state-sector schools:	**87.8%**	
From working-class homes:	**20.5%**	
Satisfaction with students' union	**76%**	

For detailed information about sports facilities:
www.gla.ac.uk/services/sport

Accommodation

Number of places and costs refer to 2013–14
University-provided places: 3,521
Percentage catered: 6.7%
Catered costs: £150.78–£166.81 a week.
Self-catered costs: £85.40 (twin) –£137.90 (large en suite) a week.
First years are guaranteed accommodation if conditions are met.
Deadline applies.
International students: first years are guaranteed accommodation if conditions are met. 10% of returners are also housed.
Contact: www.accom.gla.ac.uk; accom@gla.ac.uk

Glasgow Caledonian University

Glasgow Caledonian is arguably the most outgoing in Scotland. Not only was it the first Scottish university to open a campus for postgraduates in London, but there are also bases in Oman and Bangladesh. It even numbers the new President of Iran among its alumni: Dr Hassan Rouhani was awarded an MPhil and a PhD in the 1990s for theses on Islamic legislative power and Sharia law. However, the university's top priority remains the modern city-centre campus that continues to draw home and international students to Glasgow. There are plans for a £30-million redevelopment, with a striking new glass reception and atrium, a 500-seat teaching and conference facility, and a new eating mall. Two of the main buildings will be renovated and better connected to the campus centrepiece, the award-winning Saltire Centre.

The university has already spent more than £70 million transforming its facilities into a single campus that does justice to a thriving institution of almost 17,000 students. The campus includes the only INTO centre in Scotland, running preparatory courses for international students. The health building brings together teaching and research facilities that include a virtual hospital. Other learning resources include multimedia studios, a Fashion Factory and an eye clinic equipped with latest technologies for teaching and research. Student facilities include the Arc sports centre, 24-hour computer labs, an employability centre and a dedicated Students' Association building.

Many GCU courses benefit from accreditation from professional bodies and more than half include work placement opportunities. The university is one of the largest providers of health-related graduates to the NHS in Scotland, covering a wide range of professions, and as the only Scottish university delivering optometry degrees, for example, it trains 90 per cent of the country's eye care specialists. GCU has also launched its new Scottish Ambulance Academy, the only education establishment in the UK to be formally endorsed by the College of Paramedics and certified by the Health Professions Council. The School of Engineering and Built Environment teaches more than 75 per cent of Scotland's part-time construction students.

The Caledonian Business School boasts more undergraduates than any other such institution in Scotland, with almost 1,000 in each year group. The university pioneered subjects such as entrepreneurial studies and risk management and offers highly specialist degrees, such as tourism management, fashion marketing, leisure management

Cowcaddens Road
Glasgow G4 0BA

0141 331 8681 (enquiries)
studentenquiries@gcu.ac.uk
www.gcu.ac.uk
www.caledonianstudent.com
Affiliation: University Alliance

GLASGOW
Edinburgh
Belfast
London
Cardiff

The Times and Sunday Times **Rankings**
Overall Ranking: **81** (=81)

Student satisfaction:	**95**	(78.9%)
Research quality:	**=83**	(3.0%)
Entry standards:	**=47**	(356)
Student–staff ratio:	**98**	(21.4)
Services & facilities/student:	**49**	(£1,556)
Expected completion rate:	**91**	(81.1%)
Good honours:	**55**	(65.9%)
Graduate prospects:	**56**	(65.3%)

and consumer protection. A more recent innovation was the first full-time university MA course in fiction writing for television.

Widening participation in higher education has always been one of the university's main aims. Nearly a third of the undergraduates are from working-class homes and about three-quarters are the first in their family to attend university. GCU's Caledonian Club for children and families from disadvantaged communities was recognised by *Times Higher Education* as a national example of best practice in raising aspirations, building life skills and opening the university to the local community. The university has introduced a series of measures – such as better academic, social and financial support – for those at risk of dropping out. The projected dropout rate of just over 12 per cent in the most recent survey is better than the UK average for GCU's courses and entry qualifications.

The GCU Students' Association was named Scottish University Students' Association of the Year in 2011, when the university continued a run of good results in the International Barometer survey for overseas students. GCU has 1,500 international students and offers engineering in Oman and nursing in Bangladesh, as well as joint degrees in a variety of subjects at the Caledonian College at the University of Jinan, in China. Undergraduates are encouraged to participate in international exchanges and study abroad. Overall enrolments increased slightly in 2012, despite a marginal drop in applications.

Half of the 14 subject areas in which the university entered the 2008 Research Assessment Exercise contained at least some world-leading work, with 30 per cent of all researchers judged to have produced world-leading or internationally excellent work. Health subjects registered the best results and entered the largest numbers for assessment. There were particularly good results in rehabilitative health sciences, which covers long-term health conditions such as arthritis and strokes.

GCU is committed to environmental sustainability and has had success in the EcoCampus Environmental Management and Awards Scheme. Glasgow itself is a lively city with a large student population, where the cost of living is reasonable.

Undergraduate Fees and Bursaries

» Fees for Scottish and EU students for 2013–14   No fee
» Fees for Non-Scottish UK (RUK) students for 2013–14, £7,000 a year, capped at a maximum of £21,000 for all courses.
» Fees for international students 2013–14   £10,200–£14,500
» For Applied Health Professions and nursing, RUK fees paid by Scottish government.
» For RUK students (2013–14), household income below £25K, £2,000 a year fee waiver to total of £6,000. £1,000 a year fee waiver to total of £3,000 for students with at least ABB at A Level or equivalent.

Students

Undergraduates:	**10,550**	**(2,520)**
Postgraduates:	**1,830**	**(1,215)**
Mature students:	**31.8%**	
Overseas students:	**6.0%**	
Applications per place:	**6.1**	
From state-sector schools:	**96.2%**	
From working-class homes:	**32.2%**	
Satisfaction with students' union	**63%**	

For detailed information about sports facilities:
www.gcal.ac.uk/arc/

Accommodation

Number of places and costs refer to 2013–14
University-provided places: 660
Percentage catered: 0%
Self-catered costs: £89–£102 a week (39 weeks).
Students under 19 living outside the Glasgow area have priority for accommodation.
International students: new non-EU students guaranteed housing.
Contact: www.gcu.ac.uk/study/undergraduate/accommodation

University of Gloucestershire

Gloucestershire has dropped sharply in our new league table, mainly because of student satisfaction, entry standards and degree classifications. Its decline illustrates the highly competitive nature of the ranking: even though its student satisfaction score had stayed the same, other universities around them had improved. Gloucestershire is one of a number of universities to raise their fees to £9,000 for 2014, although the average after all forms of student support remains below £8,000. The university has promised to spend £4.4 million on bursaries, fee waivers, scholarships and other forms of support for new students, an increase of nearly £1 million on the current academic year. A new Care Leavers' Scholarship will be worth up to £13,500 a year in fees plus living costs to those who win places after being in local authority care, while students from one of the university's 50 "compact" partnership schools or colleges are also eligible for a £1,500 fee waiver for each year of study.

Gloucestershire was the first university for more than a century to have formal links with the Church of England when it achieved full university status in 2001. Applications were down by less than the national average in 2012 and there was also only a small decline in its intake of first-year students. The university's intake is diverse, with over 96 per cent of undergraduates from state schools and almost a third from working-class homes. About a third are recruited from Gloucestershire, and another third from elsewhere in the South West of England. The projected dropout rate has improved dramatically over recent years, and the latest projection of 8 per cent is well below the national average for the university's subjects and entry qualifications. In addition to its conventional degrees, the university is offering two-year "fast track" degrees in 18 subjects, from biology to events management and law. There is also a new joint venture with INTO providing preparatory programmes for international students.

Gloucestershire has a longstanding focus on green issues, and finished in the top three in the People and Planet Green League of universities' environmental performance. There are allotments for students, diplomas in environmentalism and an International Research Institute in Sustainability that brings together researchers from around the world, undertaking work for agencies such as UNESCO. Students are discouraged from bringing cars to university and bus fares between campuses are subsidised. The main campus, Park Campus, is on the attractive site of the former College of St Mary, a

---

The Park Campus
The Park
Cheltenham GL50 2RH

0844 8011100 (enquiries)
enquiries@glos.ac.uk
www.glos.ac.uk
www.yourstudentsunion
.com
Affiliations: Cathedrals
Group

The Times and Sunday Times **Rankings**
Overall Ranking: **=91** (=65)

Student satisfaction:	99	(78.4%)
Research quality:	=92	(2.0%)
Entry standards:	93	(295)
Student–staff ratio:	107	(22.3)
Services & facilities/student:	75	(£1,299)
Expected completion rate:	=71	(84.4%)
Good honours:	66	(62.6%)
Graduate prospects:	74	(61.1%)

mile outside Cheltenham. There has been considerable development of the Gloucester campus (Oxstalls), on the site of a former domestic science college which became part of the university in 2002. The two centres are only seven miles apart and students are not as isolated as they are in some split-site institutions.

Gloucestershire is investing £5 million in new teaching accommodation and social space after closing two campuses and dividing its courses between the three remaining sites. Student accommodation remains on the former Pittville campus in Cheltenham. The reorganisation has maintained the full range of subjects and added a media hub with new studio areas for fine art, photography and specialist design. Art and design students have transferred to Francis Close Hall, which they share with the Institute of Education and Public Services. The Park Campus is the main base for the Faculty of Business, Education and Professional Studies, which includes accounting and law. Sport and exercise sciences, playwork, leisure, tourism, hospitality and event management are based at the Oxstalls campus in Gloucester, which also houses the Countryside and Community Research Institute, the largest rural research centre in the UK.

The university prides itself on a good range of work placements for students, and the Degreeplus initiative combines internships with additional training to improve students' chances of getting a good job after graduating. Gloucestershire did not quite repeat in 2008 the success it enjoyed in the previous research assessments. Some world-leading research was found in five of the twelve areas in which the university submitted work, with the small education entry producing the best results. But less than 20 per cent of all work reached the top two categories. However, fourteen Gloucestershire academics have been awarded National Teaching Fellowships.

The sports facilities include a sports hall, gym and tennis courts. First years are given preference for hall places, and the university has access to private sector places. At both main sites facilities overall are improving.

Undergraduate Fees and Bursaries

» Fees for UK/EU students 2014–15   £9,000
    Foundation degrees and courses at partner college   £6,000
    Fast-track courses at partner colleges   £8,250
» International student fees 2013–14   £10,200
» 296 NSP awards with priority criteria, £2,000 fee waiver and £1,000 cash, year 1; £1,500 fee waiver, years 2 and 3.
» Students from Compact schools and Strategic Alliance partners not receiving NSP award: £1,500 a year fee waiver.
» Students with household income below £25K and not receiving NSP award, £1,000 a year fee waiver.
» For those with at least ABB at A Level or equivalent, £1,500 fee waiver and £1,000 cash, year 1; in years 2 and 3, if household income below £25K, £1,500 fee waiver.
» Check the university's website for the latest information.

Students		
Undergraduates:	**6,445**	**(750)**
Postgraduates:	**675**	**(1,210)**
Mature students:	**20.2%**	
Overseas students:	**5.2%**	
Applications per place:	**4.1**	
From state-sector schools:	**96.3%**	
From working-class homes:	**32.6%**	
Satisfaction with students' union	**60%**	

For detailed information about sports facilities:
www.glos.ac.uk/living/sport

Accommodation

Number of places and costs refer to 2013–14
University-provided places: about 1,349
Percentage catered: 0%
Self-catered costs: £95–£140 a week (40 weeks).
First-year undergraduates have priority for halls.
International students: first-year undergraduates are guaranteed accommodation if conditions are met.
Contact: accommodation@glos.ac.uk

Glyndŵr University

Glyndŵr is charging some of the lowest fees at any university in 2014, at a maximum of £8,450 for science, engineering and computing degrees for UK students from outside Wales. Those in business and the humanities will be the cheapest, at £7,400, while the remainder, in subjects such as journalism, the built environment and health, psychology and social care, will cost £7,800. Fees were lower than elsewhere in Wales in 2012, but the number of first-year students dropped by more than 20 per cent and there were barely more than three applicants for each place. The result is some of the lowest entry standards in our table contributing to a drop of 12 places overall.

The former North East Wales Institute of Higher Education took the name of the 15th-century Welsh prince Owain Glyndŵr (who championed the establishment of universities throughout Wales) when it was awarded university status in 2008. The new university is based on two campuses in Wrexham and one at Northop, in Flintshire, on the site of the former Welsh College of Horticulture. The Flintshire campus is the first university presence in the county, and £1.7 million has been invested to make it a centre of excellence for land- and animal-based studies.

In 2011, Glyndŵr became the only university to own an international football stadium – the oldest in the world – when it bought the Racecourse Ground to safeguard the future of Wrexham FC and provide more facilities for its students. The purchase included the club's well-equipped training ground. Glyndŵr already had a partnership with the club, whose land, next door to the university's Plas Coch site, hosts the 200-bed student village. Part of the Plas Coch Hostel was transformed in 2013 into a library featuring more than 13,000 books collected by a New York scholar. The campus also contains a modern sports centre with two floodlit artificial pitches, including an international standard hockey pitch, a human performance laboratory and indoor facilities that include a sports hall with a 1,000 square-metre sprung floor.

Glyndŵr has 8,800 students, but fewer than half are full-time undergraduates. Over half are 21 or over on entry and one in five comes from outside the European Union. The two campuses in Wrexham are within five minutes' walk of each other. The university's art school is based at the Regent Street campus, nearer the town centre. The university has also opened a new campus in London offering mainly business courses. Based at Elephant and Castle in South London, the new development is the result of a partnership with the London School of Management and Science.

The university has embarked on a series

Mold Road
Wrexham
N. Wales LL11 2AW

01978 293439 (enquiries)
contact via website
www.glyndwr.ac.uk
http://studentsguild.
glyndwr.ac.uk
Affiliation: none

of academic developments, including the opening of a £2-million Centre for the Child, Family and Society, based on a Scandinavian concept, to allow those working in the field of child development to hone their skills in both an academic and practical manner. The Advanced Composite Training and Development Centre, at Broughton, opened in 2010. It is a partnership with Airbus, which has a large plant nearby. Research carried out at the centre will help to improve the efficiency of aircraft and will feed into the university's undergraduate engineering courses, which are also developed in association with Airbus. The Centre for the Creative Industries opened in 2011 with new TV, radio and online production studios for students from disciplines such as art and design, media and computing. It plays a key role in the university's television degree, and is also the new regional home of BBC Cymru Wales. At St Asaph the university has a centre for the research and development of cutting-edge opto-electronics technology.

Nearly all the undergraduates are state-educated, 42 per cent of them coming from working-class homes – far more than average for the university's subjects and entry grades. Only one university in the UK takes a higher proportion of students from areas of low participation in higher education. Glyndŵr also has the largest proportion of disabled students in Wales

and was nominated for an award for its provision for them. There is a dedicated centre for students with disabilities that assesses students' needs before they embark on a course.

The university entered only 27 academics for the last Research Assessment Exercise, but almost a quarter of their work was judged to be world-leading or internationally excellent. Computer science and materials both reached the top grade for a small proportion of their work, and the university's research funding more than doubled as a result.

Two-thirds of the students are local, many living at home, which inevitably affects the social scene but eases the pressure on residential accommodation. The university added 320 places in its Wrexham Village, close to the main campus, in 2010. Wrexham is not without nightlife, and both Manchester and Liverpool are within easy reach.

Undergraduate Fees and Bursaries

» Fees for UK/EU students for 2014–15: £7,400–8,450, with Welsh Assembly non-means-tested grant to pay fees above £3,575 (2013–14) for Welsh students.
    Foundation degrees £5,400
» International student fees 2013–14 £8,950–£9,450
» Care Leaver's scholarship of £1,000 a year and other scholarships available.
» Check the university's website for the latest information.

Students

Undergraduates:	**4,395**	**(3,725)**
Postgraduates:	**850**	**(570)**
Mature students:	**12.4%**	
Overseas students:	**39.8%**	
Applications per place:	**3.1**	
From state-sector schools:	**98.8%**	
From working-class homes:	**42.1%**	
Satisfaction with students' union	**61%**	

For detailed information about sports facilities:
www.sport.glyndwr.ac.uk

Accommodation

Number of places and costs refer to 2013–14
University-provided places: 615
Percentage catered: 0%
Self-catered costs: £78 (single) – £105 (en suite) for 37–40 weeks.
First-year full-time undergraduates are given priority in accordance with the university's allocation policy.
International students: guaranteed housing if conditions are met.
Contact: www.glyndwr.ac.uk/en/Ourstudentsupport/Accommodation/
accommodation@glyndwr.ac.uk

Goldsmiths, University of London

Applications to Goldsmiths dropped by more than 20 per cent when the fees went up to £9,000 in 2012, but there was a small increase in the numbers taking up places because so many more candidates accepted offers. Goldsmiths has a stellar reputation in the arts, with alumni such as Damien Hirst and Antony Gormley as well as 2011 Mercury Prize nominees Katie B and James Blake. Graduates of the college have won the Turner Prize no fewer than six times. But Goldsmiths stresses that it brings the same creative approach to a wider range of subjects that span humanities, social sciences, computing and teacher training. More than half of the work submitted for the last Research Assessment Exercise was considered world-leading or internationally excellent. Indeed, it was among the top ten universities for the proportion of work (22 per cent) placed in the highest category. Recent world university rankings have placed Goldsmiths in the world's top 100 and the UK's top 20 for art and design, but the portfolio of courses includes computing, management and psychology.

Goldsmiths has a long tradition of community-based courses,. Evening and other part-time classes are almost as popular as conventional degree courses, and many subjects can be studied from basic to postgraduate levels. A history of providing educational opportunities for women is continuing – two-thirds of the students are female. A number of new degrees were introduced in 2013, including journalism, international studies with Chinese and BSc psychology pathways in clinical psychology and cognitive neuroscience.

Determinedly integrated into its southeast London locality, the campus has a cosmopolitan atmosphere. Around a third of new undergraduates are 21 or over on entry with a strong representation from the area's ethnic minorities, and there is a growing cohort of international students. Over a third of students are from working class backgrounds but only 5 per cent, half their target, are students from areas of low participation in higher education.

The campus is a mixture of old and new. The latest addition, a purpose-built, eco-friendly building for media and communications facilities and the Institute for Creative and Cultural Entrepreneurship, opened in September 2010. The Rutherford Building, containing library and IT services and a Grade II listed former baths building has been converted to provide more space for research and art studios. The Ben Pimlott Building, featuring a dramatic sculptural "scribble" by the acclaimed architect Will Alsop, contains state-of-the-art studio facilities and two multidisciplinary centres for interaction between the arts and social

Lewisham Way
New Cross
London SE14 6NW

020 7919 7766 (enquiries)
course-info@gold.ac.uk
www.gold.ac.uk
www.goldsmithssu.org
Affiliation: 1994 Group

The Times and Sunday Times Rankings

Overall Ranking: **48** (48)

Student satisfaction:	=48	(82%)
Research quality:	=18	(24.7%)
Entry standards:	44	(370)
Student–staff ratio:	=68	(19.2)
Services & facilities/student:	=112	(£954)
Expected completion rate:	70	(84.6%)
Good honours:	=30	(73.5%)
Graduate prospects:	111	(52.6%)

sciences. The main building on Lewisham Way is being refurbished at the start of the college's biggest programme of renewal for 50 years. The forecourt is being landscaped and turned into a social area with outdoor seating, improved access and a space that can be used for outdoor performances and events to make the area more inviting for the public, as well as students. Work has also started on the construction of a professional recording studio on campus.

There are nearly 7,000 full-time students and around 1,600 part-timers at Goldsmiths. With integrated work placements on many of their degrees, employment prospects are good, especially for an institution with such a high proportion of students taking performing arts subjects. Goldsmiths places great emphasis on equipping students with creative thinking skills and has introduced workshops to help students develop entrepreneurial skills. Personal development opportunities include the Gold Award, encouraging students to develop the skills and experience that employers are looking for. The projected dropout rate of a little more than 15 per cent is just above average for the courses and entry qualifications.

Student politics is alive and well at Goldsmiths, and a college in which Alex James and Graham Coxon, from Blur, are just two of a number of successful alumni cannot fail to have a thriving music scene. The union has a strong tradition in volunteering and an award-winning newspaper/magazine, and in recent years have been winners of several Sound Impact Awards, in recognition of work on ethical and environmental issues.

There are nearly 1,000 halls of residence places, most within a five-minute walking distance of the campus, but not enough to guarantee all first years accommodation. There are plenty of reasonably priced options in the vicinity. International students are given priority throughout their degree if they meet the application deadlines. There is a well-equipped and affordable gym on campus plus a swimming pool and indoor complex in Deptford and College Green on campus for training purposes but the main pitches are eight miles away.

Undergraduate Fees and Bursaries

» Fees for UK/EU students 2014–15 £9,000
» International student fees 2013–14 £11,700–£16,200
» 206 NSP awards of £3,000 package, year 1; £1,500, years 2 and 3.
» Ten £9,000 a year fee waivers for best students from Lewisham and 10 £4,500 a year fee waivers for students from local boroughs.
» Range of scholarships and bursaries for local students, mature students, care leavers, disabled students, computer, music and education students.
» Range of other scholarships and bursaries available.
» Check the university's website for the latest information.

Students

Undergraduates:	**4,695**	**(515)**
Postgraduates:	**2,195**	**(1,055)**
Mature students:	**29.4%**	
Overseas students:	**17.4%**	
Applications per place:	**5.1**	
From state-sector schools:	**88.6%**	
From working-class homes:	**34.1%**	
Satisfaction with students' union	**65%**	

For detailed information about sports facilities:
www.gold.ac.uk/sports/

Accommodation

Number of places and costs refer to 2013–14
University-provided places: 972 (College halls)
Percentage catered: 0%
Self-catered costs: £100 – £133.50 a week (includes heating and lighting costs).
Priority is given to new full-time students if conditions are met; distance restrictions apply.
International students will be given priority throughout their programme.
Contact: www.goldsmiths.ac.uk/accommodation

University of Greenwich

Greenwich claims to have "one of the grandest university settings in the world", and it is hard to argue. Its move into the former Royal Naval College buildings designed by Sir Christopher Wren provided a campus worthy of a name which conjured up images of history and science in equal measure. The main campus is now part of a World Heritage Site. Wren's baroque masterpiece is being used, with the former Dreadnought Hospital, to teach over half the university's students in humanities, law, business, maths, computing and maritime studies. The university has set itself some challenging targets to do justice to its palatial surroundings. Among them are the goals of reaching the top 50 in the UK and the top ten in London within five years. The strategic plan covers teaching and research, as well as aiming to foster a strong sense of community within the university.

Following two years of strong growth in the demand for places, applications declined when £9,000 fees were introduced in 2012 and the first-year intake was down by more than 20 per cent. However, the average entry tariff was the best ever, up by 24 UCAS points compared to 2011. Greenwich draws primarily from southeast London and Kent. The university has invested £76 million in a new building, due to open in 2014, to house the campus library, TV studios and academic facilities for disciplines including architecture, design and construction and will increase student numbers in Greenwich by about 20 per cent.

The prize-winning Medway campus, centred on the former Chatham naval base, has been developed in partnership with Kent and Canterbury Christ Church universities. Student accommodation opened there in 2008, together with an improved café. Greenwich put £20 million into the campus, which houses the schools of pharmacy, science and engineering, the Natural Resources Institute, nursing and some business courses. A joint learning resources centre serves the Chatham Maritime campus and the University of Kent's neighbouring premises. The campus has exceeded its original target of 6,000 students and now has improved teaching facilities and expanded student services. A BSc in paramedic science combines academic study with learning in the workplace as part of an ambulance crew.

Other schools are situated at Avery Hill, a Victorian mansion on the outskirts of southeast London, which boasts a £14-million sports and teaching centre with a café, sports hall and 220-seat lecture theatre. There are also laboratories for health courses that replicate NHS wards. The campus contains a student village of 1,300 rooms, alongside teaching

---

Old Royal Naval College
Park Row
Greenwich
London SE10 9LS

020 8331 9000 (course enquiries)
courseinfo@greenwich.ac.uk
www.gre.ac.uk
www.suug.co.uk
Affiliation: University
  Alliance

accommodation for the social sciences. The large education faculty is one of the few to offer both primary and secondary teacher training courses.

Greenwich achieved good results in the last Research Assessment Exercise, which showed a quarter of the work reaching world-leading or internationally excellent levels. The small mechanical, aeronautical and manufacturing engineering group produced by far the best results, but architecture and history also did well. A fifth of the university's income is from research and consultancy – the largest proportion at any former polytechnic – and it is planned that the total should reach £21 million. Greenwich is undertaking an ambitious programme of investment in research by increasing the proportion of research-active staff to 75 per cent. One in five of the 26,000 students is a postgraduate. Thirteen associated colleges in Kent and London teach the university's courses, while strong links with institutions in Europe and further afield provide a steady flow of overseas students, as well as exchange opportunities for those at Greenwich. The 5,000 students from outside the European Union put the university among the top six international recruiters. The university attracts more students than any other UK institution from India and large numbers from Bangladesh, Ghana, Sri Lanka, Mauritius and Nigeria.

A commitment to extending access is reflected in a high proportion of mature students. More than 97 per cent of undergraduates are state-educated, and more than half come from working-class homes – the biggest proportion in the UK. Both figures are significantly higher than the national average for Greenwich's courses and entrance qualifications. The downside has been the dropout rate. The latest projection of just under 20 per cent is still higher than the university's benchmark.

Greenwich is in the top six in the People and Planet Green League of universities' environmental performance. A new hall of residence for 358 students will open on the main campus in 2014 and will be powered by biomass and has green roofs on each of its three blocks, along with other sustainable features. First years are already guaranteed university housing.

Undergraduate Fees and Bursaries

» Fees for UK/EU students 2014–15   £9,000
    Foundation degree   £6,000–£8,400
» International student fees 2013–14   £10,100
» NSP awards of £1,000 university services and £2,000 fee waiver in year 1; £1,000 fee waiver in years 2 and 3. Conditions apply, with priority given to local students.
» Access Scholarship for students with household income below £25K and not receiving an NSP award, £500 for university services in year 1.
» Supporting Success bursary of £200 of university services for those not receiving other awards.

Students

Undergraduates:	**15,820**	**(5,220)**
Postgraduates:	**2,835**	**(2,565)**
Mature students:	**33.1%**	
Overseas students:	**11.8%**	
Applications per place:	**7.8**	
From state-sector schools:	**97.2%**	
From working-class homes:	**53.3%**	
Satisfaction with students' union	**61%**	

For detailed information about sports facilities: www.gre.ac.uk/about/sports

Accommodation

Number of places and costs refer to 2013–14
University-provided places: 2,300
Percentage catered: 0%
Self-catered costs: £103.46–£180.53 a week.
First years are guaranteed a place. Conditions apply.
International students: new students get priority.
Contact: www2.gre.ac.uk/study/accommodation
ah.accommodation@gre.ac.uk (Avery Hill Campus)
gr.accommodation@gre.ac.uk (Greenwich Campus)
me.accommodation@gre.ac.uk (Medway Campus)

Harper Adams University

Founded in 1901, Harper Adams was *The Sunday Times* University College of the Year for six years in a row before being awarded full university status in 2012. The former agricultural college has finished just outside the top half of the table in its debut in the new guide, benefiting from its customary high scores for student satisfaction and graduate prospects. Dr David Llewellyn, the founding Vice-Chancellor, said the new title would make Harper Adams "the leading university in the country for rural and land-based higher education, enhanced by our strong international links across several continents." Based in a single campus in the Shropshire countryside, the new university offers degrees in business, veterinary nursing and physiotherapy, land and property management, engineering and food studies, as well as agriculture. There is also a range of foundation degrees that can be converted into honours. New degrees in wildlife, conservation and resource management, and veterinary physiotherapy, are being offered in 2013.

Harper Adams has more than 4,000 students, little more than half of whom are taking undergraduate or postgraduate courses. The university has been making significant investments to upgrade the teaching and research facilities, as well as making new academic appointments. A new teaching block, due to open in time for the start of the new academic year, will add a 250-seat lecture theatre, IT classrooms, accessible computers and seminar rooms. The £2.9-million Engineering Building, incorporating the National Centre for Precision Farming, will also be open then. The Faccenda Centre, opened in 2011, is located at the heart of the campus and acts as a hub for students with the Students' Union, Careers Service and Graze Café under one roof. The building also contains social space with open access computers to allow students to work and socialise in the same space. Previous developments included the opening of the Countryside and Environment Resource Centre in 2009.

The Main Building, which dates from the opening of the college, was once the centre of all campus activities with bedrooms, teaching rooms and even a shooting gallery. The Bamford Library is one of the largest specialist land-based collections in the UK, 41,000 books and 3,000 journals. Open access computing areas are open 24 hours. But the new university's most prized feature is its 550-hectare commercial farm, which has been undergoing a multimillion pound development, including expanded dairy, pig and poultry units and a new food research centre. At the heart of the University Farm, Ancellor Yard is a redevelopment of the

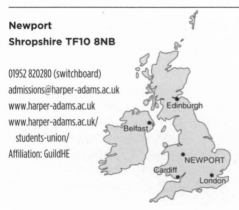

Newport

Shropshire TF10 8NB

01952 820280 (switchboard)
admissions@harper-adams.ac.uk
www.harper-adams.ac.uk
www.harper-adams.ac.uk/
students-union/
Affiliation: GuildHE

The Times and Sunday Times Rankings

Overall Ranking: =**64** (n/a)

Student satisfaction:	**18**	(84.5%)
Research quality:	**=92**	(2.0%)
Entry standards:	**=56**	(332)
Student–staff ratio:	**106**	(22.2)
Services & facilities/student:	**99**	(£1,158)
Expected completion rate:	**=58**	(86.2%)
Good honours:	**112**	(52.3%)
Graduate prospects:	**52**	(67.2%)

original farm courtyard, the former home of Thomas Harper Adams after whom the university is named. It houses the Frank Parkinson Farm Education Centre and the Frontier Crops Centre. The latest addition was the £2-million dairy unit, which serves 400 cows, and there is a £3-million anaerobic digestion plant that provides organic fertiliser across the estate.

Harper Adams has been close to the top in the National Student Survey in every year that it has been published, its students praising the personal attention they receive. Not surprisingly, given its agricultural specialisms, the university is one of a shrinking band where male students outnumber female. Approaching one in five of the undergraduates comes from independent schools, but still 44 per cent have a working-class background. The university enjoyed a significant increase in its first-year intake when £9,000 fees were introduced and its new status had been announced in 2012. Work placements are part of most courses, provided by a network of 500 regular placement employers, some of whom — including JCB and Claas — also endow student scholarships. They help Harper Adams to a consistently good graduate employment rate, while the projected dropout rate of less than 7 per cent is much better than the national average for the university's courses and entry qualifications.

Only 19 staff members were entered for the 2008 Research Assessment Exercise, when 25 per cent of the work was judged to be internationally excellent. The research/reach-out strategy is based on the theme of sustainable agri-food and land systems with strands in livestock and crop production, and their impact on, and relationship with, the food supply chain, food security, land use and natural resource management.

Nearly half of the students live on campus, where priority for residential places goes to first years. There are eight halls of residence, all within a short distance of each other, offering a range of accommodation options. The latest of them opened in 2012, with 55 en-suite bedrooms. A shuttle bus runs three times a day for students living in nearby Newport to get to campus and there is free parking for students. Sports facilities include a gymnasium, heated outdoor swimming pool, rugby, cricket, football and hockey pitches, tennis courts and an all-weather sports pitch. There is a dance/fitness studio and even a 4x4 club.

Undergraduate Fees and Bursaries

» Fees for UK/EU students 2014–15:   £9,000
» International student fees 2013–14:   £9,650
» 133 NSP awards, based on academic performance, of £3,000 fee waiver, year 1; £1,000 fee waiver, year 2; £600 fee waiver, sandwich year; £500 fee waiver, final year.
» Range of other scholarships and bursaries available.
» Check the university's website for the latest information.

Students

Undergraduates:	**2,170**	**(3,820)**
Postgraduates:	**60**	**(350)**
Mature students:	**7.5%**	
Overseas students:	**4.0%**	
Applications per place:	**3.4**	
From state-sector schools:	**80.5%**	
From working-class homes:	**44.6%**	
Satisfaction with students' union	**79%**	

For detailed information about sports facilities: www.harper-adams.ac.uk/facilities/sports.cfm

Accommodation

Places and costs refer to 2013–14
University-provided places: 700
Percentage catered: 60%
Catered costs: £3,399 (shared) – £5,643 (single, en suite).
Self-catered costs: £2,628 (shared) – £4,752 (single, en suite).
Priority is given to new full-time students on a first come first served basis. Provision for students with disabilities.
International students: entitled to housing for first year of study.
Contact: www.harper-adams.ac.uk/accommodation/on-campus.cfm

Heriot-Watt University

Heriot-Watt was *The Sunday Times* Scottish University of the Year in 2011 and 2012, recognised for its stellar record in the National Student Survey and consistently good graduate employment. The university enjoyed the biggest percentage increase in applications north of the border in 2012, but they did not turn into extra enrolments. The university is investing £5 million a year to boost its teaching and research in business and technology as part of a commitment to become a world-leading university within ten years. The university is already Scotland's most international institution, with a new, purpose-built campus in Dubai and another under construction in Malaysia. There are nearly 12,000 students in approved learning centres overseas or taking distance learning courses in 150 different countries. Overseas students also fill around a third of the places on the university's Edinburgh campus – one of the biggest proportions in the UK. Heriot-Watt won an award from the Scottish Council of Development and Industry, partly for its support for international students.

Heriot-Watt's strengths lie in the physical sciences, mathematics, business and management, engineering and the built environment. Concentration on these areas is fitting for a university which commemorates James Watt, the pioneer of steam power, and George Heriot, financier to King James VI. The university has fostered interdisciplinary teaching and research, with a battery of employment-related degrees.

Recent graduate employment figures showed further significant improvement at a time when many other universities experienced a decline. The projected dropout rate of under 10 per cent is better than the UK average for the university's subjects and entrance qualifications. More than half of the undergraduates are from Scotland, and just under 20 per cent from other parts of Britain. Over 90 per cent of them are from state schools and colleges, with 27 per cent from working-class homes.

Heriot-Watt is one of the most commercially diversified universities in Britain, deriving over 60 per cent of its income from non-government sources, particularly research income generated from business and industry. Its Research Park was the first of its kind in Europe, providing direct access to university expertise for a range of companies. Over the last three years the university has run a £6.5-million project to transfer knowledge and expertise to Scottish businesses, creating 300 private sector jobs and supporting the development of 17 new companies. More than half of the work submitted for the last Research Assessment Exercise was rated

---

Edinburgh Campus
Edinburgh EH14 4AS

0131 449 5111
enquiries@hw.ac.uk
www.hw.ac.uk
www.hwunion.com
Affiliation: none

EDINBURGH
Belfast
London
Cardiff

***The Times and Sunday Times* Rankings**
Overall Ranking: **38** (42)

Student satisfaction:	**20**	(84.2%)
Research quality:	**41**	(18.0%)
Entry standards:	**38**	(391)
Student–staff ratio:	**=56**	(18.3)
Services & facilities/student:	**71**	(£1,342)
Expected completion rate:	**67**	(84.8%)
Good honours:	**=45**	(69.3%)
Graduate prospects:	**15**	(77.7%)

world-leading or internationally excellent. Mathematics produced the best results, but there were good grades, too, in petroleum engineering, physics, general engineering, the built environment, and art and design.

The main campus, in an attractive parkland setting at Riccarton, on the outskirts of Edinburgh, still has a modern feel more than 40 years after it opened, and a £34-million project has seen the opening of new residences at both Heriot-Watt's Edinburgh and Scottish Borders campuses. The university remains small in terms of full-time students – there are about 7,500 on the Edinburgh campus. Students in Dubai take business, engineering, science, technology or textiles and design courses. Numbers in the Gulf state have risen to about 3,000 and continue to grow towards 6,000, as the university invests £35 million in the campus. The new Heriot-Watt University Malaysia is now accepting students, with a purpose-built campus scheduled to open in 2014.

Science, engineering, management and languages are located on the Edinburgh campus. The Scottish Borders Campus in Galashiels, 35 miles south of Edinburgh, specialises in textiles, fashion and design. Heriot-Watt and Borders College have signed a partnership agreement for a long-term collaboration to deliver higher and further education in the historically under-provided region, both institutions now sharing new campus facilities costing £12 million. In addition, there is a postgraduate campus at Stromness in Orkney, specialising in renewable energy.

The Edinburgh campus has the students' union, named Scottish Student Union of the Year by NUS Scotland. The 12 halls of residence are conveniently placed and house some 1,600 students. Built on the grounds of a country house, the landscaped campus boasts a loch and a sunken garden. Regular bus services link to the city centre and its wide range of nightlife and cultural events. The university has a programme of sports scholarships, and representative teams do well. Music also thrives: there is a professional Director of Music and a number of music scholarships, as well as a varied programme of musical events.

Undergraduate Fees and Bursaries

» Fees for Scottish and EU students for 2013–14   No fee
» Fees for Non-Scottish UK (RUK) students for 2013–14, £9,000 a year, capped at £27,000 for 3- or 4-year courses; and £36,000 for enhanced 5-year courses.
» Fees for international students 2013–14   £11,370–£14,340
» Range of scholarships and bursaries for Scottish students.
» For RUK students (2013–14) entering at year 1, £2,250 fee waiver a year plus £1,500 cash bursary in year 1. From year 2, and for students entering at year 2, with household income below £25K, £3,000 cash bursary a year; household income £25K–£42.6K, £2,000 cash bursary a year.
» RUK academic scholarship of £1,000 a year for students who achieve specified grades at A Level, or equivalent.

Students

Undergraduates:	**6,010**	**(605)**
Postgraduates:	**1,980**	**(2,270)**
Mature students:	**16.0%**	
Overseas students:	**31.4%**	
Applications per place:	**6.6**	
From state-sector schools:	**90.9%**	
From working-class homes:	**27.1%**	
Satisfaction with students' union	**67%**	

For detailed information about sports facilities:
www.hw.ac.uk/sports/sports-union.htm

Accommodation

Number of places and costs refer to 2013–14
University places provided: 1,683
Percentage catered: 0%
Self-catered costs: £95.13 (standard) – £138.00 (en suite) a week.
All new first years are guaranteed accommodation provided conditions are met and applications in place by 22 August.
International students: as above.
Contact : halls@hw.ac.uk;
www.hw.ac.uk/student-life/campus-life.htm

University of Hertfordshire

Hertfordshire describes itself as "the UK's leading business-facing university" and it certainly was ahead of a growing pack now using that description. It plays an important role in the regional economy and even runs the local bus service, as well as offering work placements on many courses. However, it has dropped almost 30 places in our league table this year, mainly due to declining student satisfaction. Until now, most undergraduates have paid £8,500 or less, but the full-time rate for all Honours degrees will go up to £9,000 in 2014. An extensive package of support for students from poor backgrounds is expected to keep the average fee below £8,200. The lower fees helped Hertfordshire to keep the number of applications in 2012 close to the previous year's total, but the eventual intake was still down by 900 students. Despite this, both applications and enrolments were in line with the healthy figures achieved after a succession of increases up to 2010.

A purpose-built £120-million campus, close to the existing Hatfield headquarters, opened in 2003, bringing the university together for the first time and providing outstanding facilities. The de Havilland campus, named after the aircraft manufacturer which once occupied the site, houses business, education and the humanities. It has a 24-hour learning resources centre, £15-million sports complex and 1,600 networked, en-suite residential places. The two sites are linked by cycleways, footpaths and university-owned shuttle buses. One of the biggest developments is a £38-million entertainment venue on the College Lane campus. The Forum has three entertainment spaces, a restaurant, a café and multiple bars, attracting young people from all over the county, as well as the university's students. A new learning and student zone, housing all student services, is due to open alongside it in 2014.

Health subjects account for the largest share of places. An innovative degree in paramedic science was Britain's first, its students using the UK's largest medical simulation centre to train how to treat patients in emergency situations. The opening of a School of Pharmacy and a postgraduate medical school strengthened its position in the health sector. The university is also working with the NHS Trusts in the East of England as a preferred provider for a BSc healthcare science degree. Increased research activity resulted in the establishment of the Health and Human Sciences Institute.

The creative arts have also been growing, particularly the multimedia courses. The School of the Creative Arts occupies a £10-million media centre on the College Lane campus, with the latest technology for

College Lane
Hatfield
Herts AL10 9AB

01707 284800 (admissions)
contact via website
www.herts.ac.uk
www.hertfordshire.su
Affiliation: University
   Alliance

The Times and Sunday Times Rankings
Overall Ranking: **=96** (68)

Student satisfaction:	**=107**	(77%)
Research quality:	**=78**	(3.3%)
Entry standards:	**=78**	(312)
Student–staff ratio:	**=75**	(19.5)
Services & facilities/student:	**46**	(£1,628)
Expected completion rate:	**=99**	(80.1%)
Good honours:	**72**	(61.6%)
Graduate prospects:	**=66**	(62.4%)

the teaching of music, animation, film, television and multimedia. It includes one of the largest art galleries in the eastern region. A 460-seat auditorium on the de Havilland campus enhances the cultural programme. An Automotive Centre has upgraded the teaching facilities for that branch of engineering, as well as boosting interaction with industry – every British Formula One team has at least one Hertfordshire graduate.

The student intake is more diverse than might be expected, given the location and subject mix: four in ten come from working-class homes and 97 per cent are state-educated. The projected dropout rate has improved but was still almost 17 per cent in the latest survey, marginally more than the national average for the university's subject mix and entry grades. The university's Careers and Placements Service offers graduates lifelong support on employment and career development issues, including help to set up their own business or social enterprise, to operate as a freelance or to take a new company to the next level.

Hertfordshire produced some of the best results of any post-1992 university in the 2008 Research Assessment Exercise, when nearly half of its submission was judged to be world-leading or internationally excellent. History, nursing and midwifery, engineering and computing collected the highest grades, but the Centre for Astrophysics Research also did well.

The university claims that 10 per cent of all known planets were discovered by Hertfordshire's astronomers.

The award-winning library and resource centre on the main campus is among Britain's biggest, offering 24-hour access to hundreds of computer workstations. A second centre on the de Havilland campus provides another 1,100 workstations. The StudyNet information system has been a leader in its field, giving all staff and students their own storage space. Students can use it for study, revision or communication, as well as to access university information.

About 3,400 students live on one of the two campuses and the university also owns or manages property nearby. A £15-million sports complex, the Hertfordshire Sports Village, includes a 110-station health and fitness centre, a 25-metre pool and a large, multipurpose sports hall. Principally for student use, it is also open to local residents.

Undergraduate Fees and Bursaries

» Fees for UK/EU students 2014–15 £9,000
Foundation degrees at partner colleges £5,500
» International student fees 2013–14 £9,500–£10,000
» Around 650 NSP awards with priority criteria, £1,000 fee waiver, £2,000 support package, year 1; £500 fee waiver, £400 cash and £600 support package, year 2; £550 fee waiver, £600 cash, £350 support package, year 3.
» Range of other scholarships and bursaries available.
» Check the university's website for the latest information.

Students

Undergraduates:	**17,535**	**(4,100)**
Postgraduates:	**2,625**	**(2,965)**
Mature students:	**23.8%**	
Overseas students:	**14.6%**	
Applications per place:	**6.5**	
From state-sector schools:	**96.9%**	
From working-class homes:	**38.7%**	
Satisfaction with students' union	**65%**	

For detailed information about sports facilities:
www.uhsport.co.uk

Accommodation

Number of places and costs refer to 2013–14
University-provided places: 3,400
Percentage catered: 0%
Self-catered costs: £70.63 (twin) – £117.67 (single en suite) a week.
First years are guaranteed accommodation if conditions are met.
International students: as above.
Contact: Accommodation@herts.ac.uk

University of the Highlands and Islands

A federation of 13 colleges and research institutions spread across hundreds of miles in the Highlands and Islands of Scotland, the University of the Highlands and Islands (UHI) is unlike any other in the UK. As such, it fits uneasily into our league table – it has proved impossible to calculate a meaningful staff/student ratio, for example, from the unique mix of part-time and full-time staff and students. UHI's colleges spread from Dunoon in the southwest to the village of Scalloway, the ancient capital of the Shetland Islands, in the north. But that does not begin to do justice to the university's network of campuses. Argyll College, for example, has 13 sites on the mainland and on islands such as Arran, Islay and Mull. UHI courses are also taught at more than 50 learning centres located throughout the Highlands and Islands, Moray and Perthshire. Some colleges are relatively large and located in the urban centres of the region such as Perth, Elgin and Inverness. Others are smaller institutions, including some whose primary focus is research. The university insists, however, that all have a student-centred culture and an individual approach.

Several of the colleges are in spectacular locations. Lews Castle College UHI, in Stornoway, in the Outer Hebrides, for example, is set in 600 acres of parkland. It claims "possibly the UK's most attractive location to study art" for its harbourside Lochmaddy campus in North Uist. Sabhal Mòr Ostaig UHI is the only Gaelic-medium college in the world, set in breathtaking scenery on the Isle of Skye, while the Highland Theological College UHI is in Dingwall. West Highland College UHI does not even have a central campus, although the single degree, in adventure tourism management, is taught in Fort William, close to Ben Nevis. North Highland College UHI has opened a new equestrian centre in Caithness, six miles from the main campus in Thurso. The site boasts international-sized outdoor and indoor arenas among the facilities for 45 full-time students enrolled on equestrian programmes ranging from National Certificate to BA degree.

UHI waited almost 20 years for university status – indeed, its establishment was recommended in 1990 in a report to the Highland Regional Council which envisaged that the process might take four years. The region had to wait a lot longer than that for a university: Perth was first identified as a suitable location for a university in 1425. The university's development has come in stages since its establishment was formally recommended in 1992. As the UHI Millennium Institute, it became a higher

---

Executive Office
Ness Walk
Inverness IV3 5QS

01463 279 000 (general enquiries)
contact via website
www.uhi.ac.uk
www.uhisa.org.uk
Affiliation: none

***The Times and Sunday Times* Rankings**

Overall Ranking: **116** (114)

Student satisfaction:	78	(80.7)
Research quality:	=92	(2.0%)
Entry standards:	=94	(294)
Student–staff ratio:	n/a	
Services & facilities/student:	119	(£592)
Expected completion rate:	116	(73.1%)
Good honours:	41	(70.8%)
Graduate prospects:	119	(43.9%)

education institute in 2001 and received degree-awarding powers in 2008. University status finally came in February 2011, by which time it had 8,000 students spread around its many campuses.

The university's priority is to give people living in the region local access to learning and research relevant to their needs and to those of local employers. The students are predominantly mature and part-time, drawn largely from the Highlands and Islands, but UHI is aiming to recruit more young entrants, as well as attracting greater numbers from the rest of Scotland, other parts of the UK and overseas. Students take a broad range of qualifications, from higher national certificates and diplomas and degrees to professional development awards. Teaching is increasingly through "blended" learning, combining online and face-to-face teaching, with small class sizes and extensive use of video conferencing. The university is widely acknowledged as a major asset to the regional economy, helping to create and sustain businesses, as well as championing local culture and the environment.

The university offers more than 100 undergraduate courses. Many courses are available entirely online, including a new international degree in sustainable development. Degree courses intended to lead to careers in renewable engineering, tourism and hospitality, health care, and

children's services were among the options for 2013. UHI became the first higher education institution to publish a Gaelic language plan in 2010, setting out ways to provide students with unique opportunities to learn Gaelic, improve existing skills, or study for qualifications entirely through the language. There is now a growing community of students with Gaelic skills throughout the UHI network and there are plans to extend the course portfolio before 2017. The university's mission statement is published in five languages, of which Gaelic is the first and staff are offered a one-day Gaelic Awareness course.

Environmental science produced the best results and made by far the largest submission in the 2008 Research Assessment Exercise, but there was some world-leading research in Celtic studies and archaeology. There are a dozen research centres specialising in everything from agronomy and marine science to Nordic studies, diabetes and rural childhood.

Undergraduate Fees and Bursaries

» Fees for Scottish and EU students for 2013–14   No fee
» Fees for Non-Scottish UK (RUK) students for 2013–14, £7,740, capped at a maximum of £23,200 for 3- or 4-year courses.
» Fees for international students 2013–14   £8,244–£9,786
» For RUK students (2013–14), household income below £20K, £1,500 fee waiver; £20K–£22.5K, £1,000 fee waiver; £22.5–£25K, £500 fee waiver, all for three years.
» Check the university's website for the latest information.

Students

Undergraduates:	**3,810**	**(2,970)**
Postgraduates:	**95**	**(350)**
Mature students:	**57.1%**	
Overseas students:	**3.8%**	
Applications per place:	**n/a**	
From state-sector schools:	**96.9%**	
From working-class homes:	**30.6%**	
Satisfaction with students' union	**55%**	

For detailed information about sports facilities: Sports provision for each campus is through local community facilities.

Accommodation

On-site halls of residence are available at four of the partner colleges. The other colleges provide lists of local lodgings or private rented accommodation. Some international students prefer to stay with host families.

Contact: Perth College UHI: pc.enquiries@perth.uhi.ac.uk
Sabhal Mòr Ostaig UHI: trusadh@smo.uhi.ac.uk
Lews Castle College UHI: enquiries@lews.uhi.ac.uk
NAFC Marine Centre UHI: www.nafc.ac.uk/Accommodation.aspx

University of Huddersfield

Huddersfield is one of the dwindling band of universities that will persevere with fees of less than £9,000 in 2014. The maximum fee for UK undergraduates will be £8,250 and the average, after taking account of all forms of student support, £7,839. The university managed a small increase in first-year enrolments with fees of less than £8,000 in 2012. Huddersfield is just outside the top half of our league table this year. It continues to score highly for student satisfaction and also for graduate employment, which benefits from the fact that a third of the students take sandwich courses – one of the highest proportions in the UK – while all of them do work some experience during their studies. Its links with employers helped Huddersfield to become Entrepreneurial University of the Year for 2012, an award which also recognised the way in which degree courses embed entrepreneurship into the curriculum and in particular the university's BA in enterprise development.

Huddersfield lives up to its mission to widen participation in higher education. Over 41 per cent of full-time undergraduates are from working-class homes – far more than the national average for the university's courses and entry qualifications – and the numbers coming from areas without a tradition of higher education are among the highest in the country. The university has opened satellite centres in Barnsley and Oldham to widen participation further. The dropout rate has improved, and the latest projection of almost 16 per cent is close to the national benchmark.

Imaginative conversions and new buildings have brought the university together on one town-centre campus. The university capitalised on Huddersfield's industrial past to ease the strain on facilities that were struggling to cope with student numbers that have now passed 23,000. Canalside, a refurbished mill complex, provided extra space for mathematics and computing, and education occupies another mill site. The university has created "pocket parks" and a landscaped area along the reopened Narrow Canal to provide additional green space. It spent £4 million on a new students' union, allowing drama courses to take over the existing union complex. The union building includes alcohol-free social areas to encourage participation by those overseas students and ethnic minorities who would otherwise avoid the facilities. Recent developments include a striking creative arts building, which cost around £16 million, and a similar sum was spent on a new business school, which opened in 2010. A £22.5-million Learning and Leisure Centre

---

Queensgate
Huddersfield
West Yorkshire HD1 3DH

0870 901 5555 (prospectus)
prospectus@hud.ac.uk
www.hud.ac.uk
www.huddersfield.su
Affiliation: University
Alliance

Edinburgh
Belfast
HUDDERSFIELD •
London
Cardiff

The Times and Sunday Times **Rankings**
Overall Ranking: **66** (57)

Student satisfaction:	=36	(83.1%)
Research quality:	=92	(2.0%)
Entry standards:	68	(317)
Student–staff ratio:	=59	(18.4)
Services & facilities/student:	79	(£1,287)
Expected completion rate:	=96	(80.3%)
Good honours:	77	(60.9%)
Graduate prospects:	51	(67.6%)

will open in 2014, bringing together library, computing, sport, leisure, eating, social and meeting facilities. The centre is part of a £58-million investment in teaching and research facilities.

The 19th-century Ramsden Building, the historical heart of the university, has been refurbished and there are ultra-modern facilities behind its carefully preserved exterior. A tradition of vocational education dates back to 1841, and the university has a long-established reputation in areas such as textile design and engineering. The university was awarded an £8-million Centre for Innovative Manufacturing in Advanced Metrology by the Engineering and Physical Sciences Research Council. Other strengths include music and social work, as well as teacher training, for which Huddersfield was awarded a national centre of excellence. Ten academics in the last six years have been selected as National Teaching Fellows, the largest total in the UK.

Most of the areas in which Huddersfield entered the 2008 Research Assessment Exercise contained at least some world-leading work. A third of the university's submission was placed in the top two categories, with music producing by far the best results and social work also doing well. The results brought a 45 per cent increase in research funding, which is supplemented by healthy private contracts. The university has sealed partnerships recently with the National Physical Laboratory, the Food and Environment Research Agency and the Royal Armouries in developments that it expects to benefit undergraduates as well as researchers.

The most popular courses are in human and health sciences. Many arts and social science courses have a vocational slant, for example, politics features a six-week placement, which often takes students to the House of Commons. The university's Chancellor, the actor Sir Patrick Stewart, teaches drama students in his capacity as professor of performing arts, as well as undertaking other duties.

Most residential accommodation is now concentrated in the Storthes Hall Park student village, but additional housing is available at Ashenhurst, just over a mile from the campus. Town–gown relations are good, although students tend to base their social life around the students' union. There is easy public transport access to Leeds and Manchester.

Undergraduate Fees and Bursaries

» Fees for UK/EU students 2014–15 £8,250
» International student fees 2013–14 £11,500–£12,500
» 1,200 NSP awards of £3,000 fee waiver in year 1 to students with household income below £25K and either a minimum of 280 UCAS points or joining Foundation programme in Science and Engineering.
» Additional support for care leavers.

Students

Undergraduates:	**13,800**	**(4,225)**
Postgraduates:	**1,590**	**(2,720)**
Mature students:	**26.9%**	
Overseas students:	**9.4%**	
Applications per place:	**4.7**	
From state-sector schools:	**98.0%**	
From working-class homes:	**41.4%**	
Satisfaction with students' union	**73%**	

For detailed information about sports facilities:
www.hud.ac.uk/sportandfitness/

Accommodation

Number of places and costs refer to 2013–14
University-provided places: 1,665 in privately-owned halls
Percentage catered: 0%
Self-catered costs: £74.50–£108 a week.
First years are housed on a first come, first served basis provided conditions are met.
International students: as above.
Contact: www.digstortheshall.co.uk; www.digashenhurst.co.uk

University of Hull

Students arriving at Hull in 2014 will have access to the redeveloped Brynmor Jones Library with a striking new atrium and revamped exterior that will become the centrepiece of the campus. The £27.4-million project is the latest example of an emphasis on the student experience that has helped to produce consistently high satisfaction ratings and eased the transition to £9,000 fees. The students' union has been refurbished and more than £2 million spent remodelling University House, which accommodates student services as well as the union. There has also been a focus on employability, which includes the option of a 20-credit module on career management skills. The careers service approaches undergraduates early in their time at Hull and sets up meetings with potential employers on campus. However, none of this could prevent applications dropping by 18 per cent in 2012, with 500 empty places as a result. The university has slipped out of the top 50 in our league table, hit by falls in student satisfaction and graduate employment.

The university and the city have always commanded loyalty among students, who appreciate the modest cost of living and ready availability of accommodation, as well as the quality of courses. There are now around 20,000 students on the main campus and at the former site of University College Scarborough. The medical school, which is run jointly with the University of York, occupies a landmark building on the former Humberside (now Lincoln) University campus. The West Campus also contains a Business Quarter, incorporating the Business School and a new Enterprise Centre to support local firms.

The original 94-acre main campus, less than three miles from the centre of Hull, has seen considerable development, with new buildings for languages and chemistry, a Graduate Research Institute and a state-of-the-art sport, health and exercise science laboratory. In 2010, the university opened a history centre in partnership with the city council, telling the story of the city over the centuries. It attracted 10,000 visitors in its first six weeks. The university spent more than £13 million in 2010 upgrading the teaching facilities and student accommodation.

The Scarborough campus has also seen investment, with new laboratories for music technology and digital arts, and a renovated café bar. A new enterprise lab opened in 2010, helping start-up firms and existing businesses to harness their innovations. Students' union facilities and teaching rooms have also been refurbished. Hull has always maintained a roughly equal balance between science and technology and the

---

Cottingham Road
Hull HU6 7RX

01482 466100 (admissions)
admissions@hull.ac.uk
www.hull.ac.uk
www.hyms.ac.uk
www.hullstudent.com
Affiliation: none

The Times and Sunday Times **Rankings**

Overall Ranking: **63** (49)

Student satisfaction:	=33	(83.2%)
Research quality:	=52	(11.0%)
Entry standards:	52	(344)
Student–staff ratio:	78	(19.8)
Services & facilities/student:	68	(£1,358)
Expected completion rate:	61	(86%)
Good honours:	93	(58.3%)
Graduate prospects:	96	(54.8%)

arts and social sciences, but the Scarborough campus tips the scales towards the arts.

A longstanding focus on Europe shows in the wide range of languages available at degree level, with the purpose-built Language Institute heavily used by all the students. Strength in politics – confirmed by one of three top research grades – is reflected in a steady flow of graduates into the House of Commons. The Westminster Hull Internship Programme (WHIP) offers a year-long placement and month-long internships for British politics and legislative studies students. The Legal Advice Centre, staffed by law students, provides guidance and advice to the public. The university offers 400 adult education modules, as well as 2,000 courses for its full-time students.

Research plaudits have been relatively thin on the ground, however. Hull had the lowest proportion of world-leading research among England's older universities in the 2008 Research Assessment Exercise. Health subjects, geography and environmental science, and drama, dance and performance achieved the best grades. A new biomedical research building, funded partly through a gift from a local businessman, will focus on cancer and cardiovascular and metabolic diseases – both areas in which the university has an international reputation. By bringing together both academics and health professionals, it aims to quickly translate research into tangible benefits for patients.

An Institute for Learning encourages academics to put research findings into practice, developing training courses and developing the university's interest in lifelong learning.

More than 90 per cent of Hull's undergraduates are state-educated, while almost three in ten are from working-class homes. The projected dropout rate of less than 10 per cent is better than the national average for the university's courses and entry qualifications. Student leisure facilities have been upgraded, and the students' union is one of only six in 2013 to achieve the top grade at the Best Bar None Awards. New football pitches have been added recently on campus and the Sports and Fitness Centre has been attracting praise. There is a rolling programme of refurbishment of the halls of residence in both Hull and Scarborough.

Undergraduate Fees and Bursaries

» Fees for UK/EU students 2014–15 £9,000
» International student fees 2013–14 £11,760–£14,070
  Medicine £24,680
» 642 NSP awards: £1,000 fee waiver, £2,000 credit package including up to £1,000 cash in year 1.
» University of Hull Scholarship of £1,000 fee waiver and £2,000 credit package each year, for English students with household income below £42.6K who achieved at least AAB at A Level or equivalent.
» HYMS has its own bursary scheme (in 2013, £3,000 package a year when household income below £25K).

Students

Undergraduates:	**12,975**	**(6,695)**
Postgraduates:	**2,320**	**(1,325)**
Mature students:	**29.9%**	
Overseas students:	**11.1%**	
Applications per place:	**3.8**	
From state-sector schools:	**91.0%**	
From working-class homes:	**29.2%**	
Satisfaction with students' union	**80%**	

For detailed information about sports facilities: www.hullstudent.com/activities/list

Accommodation

Number of places and costs refer to 2013–14
University-provided places: 2,601 (owned stock); 150 (leased/associated stock)
Percentage catered: 49%
Catered costs: £123.76–£144.13 (31 weeks).
Self-catered costs: £56.00–£127.40 (31–34 weeks).
Unaccompanied first years are guaranteed accommodation if conditions are met.
International students: as above.
Contact: www2.hull.ac.uk/student/accommodation.aspx

Imperial College of Science, Technology and Medicine

Imperial is branching out from the South Kensington campus where it has made its name as one of the world's leading universities of science, engineering and medicine. It opened a new medical school jointly with Nanyang University of Technology, in Singapore, in 2013, and is developing the £1-billion Imperial West campus near the former BBC Television Centre, at White City. There have been talks with China's Zhejiang University about occupying part of the site and an agreement with the Chinese communications company Huawei to collaborate on a research and innovation centre. At the heart of the new campus will be a £150-million Research and Translation Hub, which will bring together the academic and business communities.

Never out of the top five in our league table, Imperial also features in the top ten of both the QS and *Times Higher Education* world rankings. The 2,200 academics and researchers include 73 Fellows of the Royal Society, 77 Fellows of the Royal Academy of Engineering and 81 Fellows of the Academy of Medical Sciences. Imperial's submission for the 2008 Research Assessment Exercise contained a higher proportion of world-leading or internationally excellent work

(73 per cent) than any other university's submission. The results in pure mathematics, chemical engineering, civil engineering, mechanical, aeronautical and manufacturing engineering, and history of science were the best in the UK.

Entrance requirements are high. Even in subjects that struggle for candidates elsewhere, entrants average better than A*AA at A level. Applications and enrolments dropped only slightly when £9,000 fees were introduced in 2012. More than a third of the undergraduates are from independent schools – one of the highest proportions at any university and considerably more than the national average for Imperial's courses. Approaching 30 per cent of the 15,600 students are from outside the EU. The projected dropout rate of only 3 per cent is among the lowest in the UK.

The Faculty of Medicine is one of Europe's largest in terms of its staff and student numbers, as well as its research income. There are teaching bases attached to a number of hospitals in central and west London, while the UK's first Academic Health Science Centre (AHSC), run in partnership with Imperial College Health-care NHS Trust, aims to translate research advances into patient care. The centre is one of only five in the country, denoting international excellence in biomedical research, education and patient care.

Engineering degrees last four years and

South Kensington Campus
London SW7 2AZ

020 7589 5111 (switchboard)
contact via website
www.imperial.ac.uk
www.imperialcollege
union.org
Affiliation: Russell Group

The Times and Sunday Times **Rankings**

Overall Ranking: **5** (4)

Student satisfaction:	=33	(83.2%)
Research quality:	=4	(33.0%)
Entry standards:	3	(567)
Student–staff ratio:	=6	(11.7)
Services & facilities/student:	3	(£3,041)
Expected completion rate:	=5	(97%)
Good honours:	4	(84.6%)
Graduate prospects:	1	(89.2%)

lead to an MEng. Imperial is unique in the UK for providing teaching and research in the full range of engineering disciplines. The growing business school is Imperial's main venture beyond the world of science and technology. It is highly rated and is accredited by the three largest and most influential business school accreditation associations worldwide. There is also an environmental research campus at Silwood Park, 25 miles west of London.

The new Imperial Horizons programme, designed to give students an edge in their future career, includes opportunities to debate global challenges such as climate change, drawing on expertise from across the university. Many degrees offer a work placement or year abroad, and students are actively encouraged to seek summer internships. The Undergraduate Research Opportunities Programme offers "hands-on" research experience. It is especially popular in the summer vacation, when students can be paid bursaries and international undergraduates can participate without needing a work permit. The Careers Advisory Service's award-winning website has a section dedicated to international students. Imperial's graduates have the highest average starting salaries in the UK.

Imperial celebrated its centenary in 2007 having left the University of London to trade on its global reputation. It has been redeveloping and expanding facilities on its main campus, in South Kensington. A new sports centre, a second residential complex and refurbishments to the central library were followed by improvements to the students' union bar and nightclub. Most recently, the £73-million Imperial Centre for Translational and Experimental Medicine, was opened as a flagship biomedical research facility for the AHSC on the Hammersmith Hospital Campus, only 500 metres from the new Imperial West. Next will be a £24-million centre to speed up the development of new technologies in synthetic biology.

The students' union claims to have the largest selection of clubs and societies in the country. Outdoor sports facilities are remote, but the new and well-equipped sports centre at the South Kensington campus offers students free gym and swimming facilities.

Undergraduate Fees and Bursaries

- » Fees for UK/EU students 2013–14 — £9,000
- » International student fees 2013–14 — £25,000
  Medicine — £27,500–£39,150
- » Sliding scale of annual support: household income under £25K, support package of £6,000; £25K–£32K, support package of £4,600; £33K–42K, support package of £3,100.
- » Range of subject scholarships and Rector's Scholarships.
- » Check the university's website for the latest information.

Students		
Undergraduates:	9,050	(–)
Postgraduates:	5,445	(1,505)
Mature students:	4.3%	
Overseas students:	37.6%	
Applications per place:	6.6	
From state-sector schools:	62.7%	
From working-class homes:	15.5%	
Satisfaction with students' union	77%	

For detailed information about sports facilities: www3.imperial.ac.uk/sports

Accommodation

Number of places and costs refer to 2013–14
University-provided places: 2,363
Percentage catered: 0%
Self-catered costs: £60–£250 a week.
First-year undergraduates are guaranteed accommodation if application received by 26 July.
International students: as above.
Contact: accommodation@imperial.ac.uk

Keele University

Keele celebrated its 50th anniversary in 2012 and managed the transition to £9,000 fees better than many of its counterparts. Although numbers dropped, it was by less than the national average, as prospective students responded positively to a broad portfolio of courses and a string of good scores for student satisfaction and graduate employment. The broad Foundation course and four-year degree that made the university unique in its early years is now a fading memory, but half of the undergraduates still take more than one subject. The distinctive Keele Curriculum is the only one in the UK that can lead to accreditation by the Institute of Leadership and Management. A new student charter introduced in September 2012 focuses on ten "graduate attributes" that include independent thinking, synthesising information, creative problem solving, communicating clearly, and appreciating the social, environmental and global implications of all studies and activities. The university is one of the pilot institutions for a Higher Education Annual Report, which sets out in detail what undergraduates have achieved.

More than £115 million has been spent on the Keele's 600-acre campus – the largest in the country – since the turn of the century.

The latest phase aims to transform the heart of the campus, reconfiguring the Union Square plaza and providing a social hub for both informal and formal events. Two-thirds of all undergraduates, as well as many postgraduates and even some staff, live on a campus which includes an arboretum and has won a clutch of environmental awards. The university's commitment to green issues was underlined with the installation of environmental campaigner Jonathan Porritt as Chancellor in 2012. Keele topped the Environment Agency's inaugural energy efficiency ranking in 2011 and its new Sustainability Hub brings together a wide range of organisations and experts in the field. There is a degree in environment and sustainability and all undergraduates can take a module in sustainability or environmental studies.

The academic year divided into two 15-week semesters, with breaks at Christmas and Easter. Nearly all undergraduates have the option of spending a semester abroad at one of the university's 50 partner universities. Keele remains small by modern standards, with just over 10,000 students at all levels. There are plans for limited growth, especially at the postgraduate level. The proportion of postgraduates has already been growing, and almost a quarter of the students now take higher degrees. The university has been trying to broaden its intake by targeting 12- and

---

Keele

Staffordshire ST5 5BG

01782 734005 (admissions)
admissions.ukeu@keele.ac.uk
www.keele.ac.uk
www.keelesu.com
Affiliation: none

The Times and Sunday Times **Rankings**

Overall Ranking: **44** (45)

Student satisfaction:	11	(85.6%)
Research quality:	51	(12.7%)
Entry standards:	=47	(356)
Student–staff ratio:	39	(16.5)
Services & facilities/student:	95	(£1,195)
Expected completion rate:	39	(89.8%)
Good honours:	42	(70%)
Graduate prospects:	49	(68.1%)

13-year-olds with a special website, as well as running masterclasses in local schools and hosting a summer school. Nine out of ten undergraduates are state educated and approaching 30 per cent come from working-class homes. The projected dropout rate of less than 8 per cent is below the national average for the university's subjects and entry qualifications.

Health subjects have been the main focus of development in recent years. First degrees in physiotherapy and nursing and midwifery were added to the well-established postgraduate medical school. Keele also offers a five-year undergraduate medical course. Some 130 students each year are taught in new facilities on the Keele campus, at the University Hospital of North Staffordshire NHS Trust, three miles away, and at the Associate Teaching Hospital at the Shrewsbury and Telford Hospitals NHS Trust in Shropshire. Students take the new Keele undergraduate degree programme, which was approved by the GMC in 2011. New improved facilities for pharmacy and the natural sciences opened in 2010.

An increased emphasis on research brought limited success in the last Research Assessment Exercise. Almost half of the work submitted was judged to be world-leading or internationally excellent, but Keele was still towards the bottom of the traditional universities on this measure.

The most successful subjects were history and music, with some world-class work in primary care, physics, applied mathematics, business and management, law, social policy and administration, politics, Russian and English language and literature.

Located outside Stoke, the university is within an hour's drive of Manchester and Birmingham. Crime statistics suggest that Keele is the safest university campus in the West Midlands. More than 3,000 students live on campus and the cost of living in the Potteries and the surrounding area is relatively low. The highly rated students' union, which has undergone a £2.7-million renovation, offers entertainment on campus every night of the week. The sports facilities have benefited from a new all-weather pitch, and the leisure centre has a refurbished fitness suite. A new £2.9-million nursery caters for more than 100 children from three months to school age.

Undergraduate Fees and Bursaries

» Fees for UK/EU students 2014–15 £9,000
» International student fees 2013–14 £10,500–£12,500
  Medicine £21,000
» 330 NSP awards with priority criteria: £2,000 fee waiver and £1,000 cash bursary in year 1. £1,000 cash bursary for those with household income below £25K not receiving NSP award.
» In years 2 and 3, £1,000 cash for all students with household income below £25K.
» Scholarships for those with excellent pre-entry qualifications of up to £2,000 a year.

Students

Undergraduates:	7,565	(675)
Postgraduates:	815	(1,600)
Mature students:	15.1%	
Overseas students:	14.2%	
Applications per place:	8.9	
From state-sector schools:	90.9%	
From working-class homes:	28.7%	
Satisfaction with students' union	84%	

For detailed information about sports facilities:
www.keele.ac.uk/sport

Accommodation

Number of places and costs refer to 2013–14
University-provided places: 3,200
Percentage catered: 5%
Catered costs: £131–£150 a week.
Self-catered costs: £75–£128 a week.
First years are guaranteed accommodation on campus if Keele is first or firm choice university.
International students: guaranteed accommodation for the duration of their course. Deadlines apply.
Contact: accommodation@keele.ac.uk

University of Kent

Kent is offering scholarships of £2,000 a year (renewable annually) to candidates who achieve at least three As at A level, or the equivalent, and meet certain other criteria. The incentive, introduced in 2013, underlines the university's determination to attract high-fliers in today's more competitive higher education market. Applications and enrolments dropped by less than the national average when fees for UK students went up to £9,000 in 2012. Kent has a good record in the National Student Survey and has tried to safeguard teaching standards by encouraging all academics to take a Postgraduate Certificate in Higher Education. Kent academics have been awarded National Teaching Fellowships in four of the last five years.

The university has capitalised sensibly on its position near the Channel ports, specialising in international programmes, as well as in the flexible degree structures that have been the hallmark of most 1960s universities. Styling itself "the UK's European university", Kent now has postgraduate sites in Brussels, Paris, Athens and Rome, as well as giving many undergraduates the option of a year abroad. There are partnerships with over 100 European universities and Kent is one of the UK's most enthusiastic participants in the EU's Erasmus exchange programme, providing its undergraduates with study or work opportunities in countries from Spain to the Czech Republic.

The university has been broadening its horizons at home as well, assuming a regional role. Access courses throughout the county allow students to upgrade their qualifications to university standard, but the main focus is on the Medway towns, where Kent is involved in ambitious projects with Greenwich and Canterbury Christ Church universities and Mid-Kent College. The Medway campus, based in the old Chatham naval base, has already exceeded its target of 6,000 students, a third of whom are from Kent. The School of Pharmacy, which now has more than 550 undergraduates and nearly 300 postgraduates, is the main feature of a £50-million development. A new School of Arts opened in 2012, with flexible work spaces for painting, sculpture, printmaking, film, photography, music and performance projects. Additionally, the Dockyard's old Boiler Shop now features a £1-million sculpture workshop, while the old Foundry now houses recording studios. Further development has brought the number of residential places on the campus to 1,100.

The original low-rise campus is set in 300 acres of tidy parkland overlooking Canterbury. The student centre has a nightclub large enough to attract big-name bands, as well as a theatre, cinema and bars.

The Registry
Canterbury
Kent CT2 7NZ

01227 827272 (admissions)
information@kent.ac.uk
www.kent.ac.uk
www.kentunion.co.uk
Affiliation: none

The Times and Sunday Times **Rankings**
Overall Ranking: **=33** (34)

Student satisfaction:	40	(82.4%)
Research quality:	=42	(17.0%)
Entry standards:	41	(380)
Student–staff ratio:	=21	(14.6)
Services & facilities/student:	70	(£1,347)
Expected completion rate:	37	(90.5%)
Good honours:	=30	(73.5%)
Graduate prospects:	39	(70.7%)

A new concert hall and music building is now open, while other recent developments on the main campus have included the Canterbury Innovation Centre and a new sports pavilion. The university has another base in Tonbridge serving 3,000 part-time students across Kent, mainly taught in associate colleges. Entry grades for full-time degrees have been rising in most subjects. Offers are pitched according to the UCAS points tariff, although those taking A levels are expected to pass at least three subjects (one of which may be general studies).

The university has a more mixed intake than many in the south of England: over nine out of ten undergraduates are from state schools and more than a quarter come from working-class homes. The projected dropout rate of 8 per cent is lower than its benchmark for the university's subjects and entrance requirements. Graduates of all disciplines fare well in the employment market – the university regularly features among the top 20 for graduate starting salaries.

Kent was much more successful in the 2008 research assessments than in previous exercises, with more than half of its submission placed in the top two categories. Thirty per cent of research in social policy was considered world-leading. The university has been building up its science departments, among which computing is particularly well regarded, but still a majority of the students take arts or social science subjects. Kent has an £8-million postgraduate scholarship fund, including ten Erasmus Mundus fellowships in the humanities, research student scholarships, location-specific funding, sport and music scholarships and funding for overseas students.

Kent's students come from 120 countries, and campus security is good, although some complain that Canterbury itself is expensive and limited socially. Undergraduates on the main campus are attached to one of four colleges, although they do not select it themselves. The colleges act as the focus of social life, and include academic as well as residential facilities. The £25-million redevelopment of Keynes College in 2011 and further development of the Park Wood student village has brought the number of places available in Canterbury close to 5,000.

Undergraduate Fees and Bursaries
» Fees for UK/EU students 2014–15 £9,000
Partner colleges £6,000
» International student fees 2013–14 £12,030–£14,360
» For English students with household income below £42.6K and meeting various conditions, £1,000 cash and £2,000 package, year 1; £2,000 package, years 2 and 3.
» Subject scholarships and partner school and college scholarships.
» Scholarships of £2,000 a year for those with AAA at A level or equivalent. Check website for the latest information.

Students
Undergraduates:	**14,705**	**(1,800)**
Postgraduates:	**2,285**	**(1,520)**
Mature students:	**12.4%**	
Overseas students:	**17.3%**	
Applications per place:	**5.2**	
From state-sector schools:	**90.7%**	
From working-class homes:	**25.3%**	
Satisfaction with students' union	**69%**	

For detailed information about sports facilities: www.kent.ac.uk/sports

Accommodation
Number of places and costs refer to 2013–14
University-provided places: 4,756
Percentage catered: 16%
Catered costs: £119–£135 a week.
Self-catered costs: £101–£141 a week.
First years are guaranteed accommodation provided applications received before 31 July.
International students: as above
Contact: hospitality-enquiry@kent.ac.uk

King's College London

King's has taken to describing itself as "the most central university in London" because four of its five campuses are all within a single square mile around the banks of the Thames. The fifth is not far away at Denmark Hill in south London. The college's research strength won it a place in the top 20 of the QS World University Rankings this year, but declining student satisfaction ratings have seen it drop five places in our league table. The college more than justified those positions by attracting an additional 450 students when £9,000 fees came in and restrictions were lifted on the recruitment of those with the best A-level grades. Like other universities, King's saw its applications drop, but the first-year intake grew by more than 10 per cent while most suffered a decline. Once known primarily for science, King's now excels in a wide range of subjects in nine schools of study, including such unusual features as War Studies. In the 2008 Research Assessment Exercise, 60 per cent of the college's submission was judged to be world-leading or internationally excellent. Cardiovascular medicine, dentistry, nutritional sciences, philosophy, languages and the digital humanities were among the leaders in their fields.

King's is one of the oldest and largest of the University of London's colleges. It is Europe's largest centre for the education of doctors, dentists and other healthcare professionals, and home to six Medical Research Council Centres. King's Health Partners Academic Health Sciences Centre represents a pioneering collaboration between the college and three NHS foundation trusts. The original Strand site and the Waterloo campus, which includes the largest university building in London, house most of the non-medical departments. Nursing and midwifery and some biomedical subjects are also based at Waterloo, while medicine and dentistry are mainly at Guy's Hospital, near London Bridge, and in the St Thomas' Hospital campus, across the river from the Houses of Parliament. The Denmark Hill campus houses the Institute of Psychiatry, as well as more medicine and dentistry. Libraries are located on all the main campuses, specialising in the subjects taught locally.

The college has spent £60 million improving student facilities and further investment of £140 million is planned over the next few years. The expansion of the Strand Campus into the East Wing of Somerset House in 2012 has provided impressive new premises for the 175-year-old School of Law. The college has invested in new student centres on each campus and upgraded the library and student space on the Waterloo Campus, as well as

---

Strand

London WC2R 2LS

020 7836 5454 (enquiries)
contact via website
www.kcl.ac.uk
www.kclsu.org
Affiliation: Russell Group

The Times and Sunday Times **Rankings**

Overall Ranking: **27** (22)

Student satisfaction:	110	(76.8%)
Research quality:	=23	(23.3%)
Entry standards:	14	(467)
Student–staff ratio:	=6	(11.7)
Services & facilities/student:	21	(£1,975)
Expected completion rate:	25	(92.8%)
Good honours:	=12	(80.6%)
Graduate prospects:	6	(82%)

refurbishing teaching and social spaces at the Strand and Guy's. A £12-million science gallery will open on the Guy's campus in 2015. The conversion of the former Public Record Office in Chancery Lane created the largest new university library in Britain since World War II. A donation of £4 million by a graduate allowed the spectacular Maughan Library to be equipped with 1,600 networked reader places. King's is engaged in a £500-million fundraising campaign, with priority areas in neuroscience and mental health, leadership and society, cancer, global power and children's health.

About one student in five is from outside the European Union, many of them among the 8,600 postgraduates. An institutional audit by the Quality Assurance Agency gave King's the highest mark, stressing the excellence of the student support services. Graduates enjoy among the best employment rates in the UK and typically also earn some of the highest starting salaries. The college's location means King's students are in an enviable position for accessing opportunities for work experience. A new Internships Office is working with King's Careers Service to support development in this area.

Almost three undergraduates in ten come from independent schools, despite the college's efforts to widen its intake. King's launched a new Enhanced Support Dentistry Programme to attract talented school-leavers from lower performing schools, along the lines of its celebrated Access to Medicine course. Student facilities on the Strand, Waterloo and Guy's campuses have been upgraded, and the active students' union, which runs bars, cafes and a nightclub, puts on an extensive programme of events.

The college is well provided with accommodation in a variety of residences, in busy central locations as well as quieter, residential areas. Students have access to privately run residences and others run by the University of London, as well as more than 2,500 places in university-owned provision. Some of the outdoor sports facilities are a long train ride from the college. There are facilities for all the main sports, as well as rifle ranges, two gyms and a swimming pool.

Undergraduate Fees and Bursaries

» Fees for UK/EU students 2014–15   £9,000
    Foundation degree in education studies   £4,500
» International student fees 2013–14   £15,000–£19,000
    Medicine and dentistry   £35,000
» 661 NSP awards of £1,000 cash and £2,400 fee waiver or accommodation discount in year 1.
» King's Living Bursary fee waiver or accommodation discount of £1,500 (household income below £25K) or £1,000 (£25K–£42.6K).
» Bursaries and merit scholarships, including 40 Access to Professions scholarships of £9,000 in year 1; STEM awards of £5,000 a year; full fee waiver law scholarships.

Students

Undergraduates:	**12,790**	**(2,965)**
Postgraduates:	**6,425**	**(4,280)**
Mature students:	**17.7%**	
Overseas students:	**18.5%**	
Applications per place:	**7.8**	
From state-sector schools:	**70.6%**	
From working-class homes:	**22.6%**	
Satisfaction with students' union	**68%**	

For detailed information about sports facilities:
www.kcl.ac.uk/campuslife/sport

Accommodation

Number of places and costs refer to 2013–14
University-provided places: 2,166; 654 nominated; 752 intercollegiate.
Percentage catered: 21% overall; 100% intercollegiate
Catered costs: £130.90 (mini single) – £230.30 (en suite) a week.
Self-catered costs: £79.94–£195.00 (40 weeks); £230 (studio).
New full-time undergraduate students are guaranteed the offer of one year in accommodation if specific conditions are met.
International students: priority for new students.
Contact: 020 7848 2759; www.kcl.ac.uk/accomm

Kingston University

Kingston is one of a number of universities moving to a flat fee of £9,000 for all degree courses starting in 2014, having charged less than that for most subjects until now. The university had been growing rapidly, but applications dropped by more than 7,000 when the fees regime changed in 2012. Kingston has one of the most ethnically mixed student populations of any UK university, and many undergraduates are also the first in their family to experience higher education. At least 1,750 students are expected to receive some financial support in 2013–14. More than a quarter of Kingston's places go to mature students and 40 per cent to those from working-class families – both groups with low completion rates nationally. The latest projected dropout rate is just over 15 per cent, lower than the national average for the subjects on offer.

The university markets itself as in "lively, leafy London", making a virtue of its suburban location southwest of central London as well as its proximity to the bright lights. Two of its four campuses are close to Kingston town centre; another, two miles away, is at Kingston Hill; the fourth is in Roehampton Vale, where a site once used as an aerospace factory now contains a new technology block. A flight simulator and the university's own Learjet as well as a Foundation degree in aeronautical engineering continue the tradition as part of the third-largest engineering faculty in London.

Kingston is revitalising its four campuses, opening three impressive new buildings as part of a £123-million programme which will run to 2018. The new facilities include multiple projection systems, video conferencing, interactive displays and built-in voting systems. The centrepiece is the £20-million John Galsworthy Building at the heart of the Penrhyn Road campus, which incorporates lecture theatres, flexible teaching space and information technology suites as well as a "Knowledge Centre" for students to do coursework. The Business School acquired a new £26-million home in 2012, complete with atrium, modern teaching rooms and break-out spaces. A new learning resources centre is part of an £11-million improvement programme at the University's Knights Park campus, which includes the refurbishment of studio space, an upgraded reception and gallery area and external landscaping. There have been extensive upgrades of the library facilities on each campus, bringing together library, computing and multimedia facilities to encourage interactive and group learning. There are bookable study rooms with multimedia facilities and specially equipped spaces dedicated to meeting the needs of

---

River House
53–57 High Street
Kingston upon Thames
Surrey KT1 1LQ

0844 855 2177 (enquiries)
aps@kingston.ac.uk
www.kingston.ac.uk
www.kusu.co.uk
Affiliation: University Alliance

The Times and Sunday Times **Rankings**

Overall Ranking: **111** (101)

Student satisfaction:	=115	(76.2%)
Research quality:	=78	(3.3%)
Entry standards:	=75	(313)
Student–staff ratio:	87	(20.4)
Services & facilities/student:	97	(£1,183)
Expected completion rate:	=99	(80.1%)
Good honours:	97	(57.1%)
Graduate prospects:	=89	(57.3%)

disabled users. The main centres are open 24 hours a day during term-time weekdays and a high-tech self-issue system makes borrowing much quicker and easier.

Kingston is particularly strong on entrepreneurship: it has produced more graduate start-up companies than any other university for four years in a row. More than 200 companies got off the ground in 2011–12, creating the equivalent of 2,216 full-time jobs. The combined total of £30-million turnover was bettered by only one university. Approaching a third of the university's submission to the 2008 Research Assessment Exercise was rated world-leading or internationally excellent. The star performance was in history of art, architecture and design, where half of the submission was at least internationally excellent. In nursing, 15 per cent of the work reached the top level, and in business and management studies, the proportion was 10 per cent, making Kingston the highest-rated new university in the field. The Faculty of Health and Social Care Sciences (run jointly with St George's, University of London) now has more than 4,000 students and is about to see a further increase in enrolments in nursing and physiotherapy and a boost to its funding after winning two major NHS London contracts. Radiotherapists hone their clinical skills in a simulated cancer treatment room, while the Centre for Paramedic Science serves as a hub for course delivery and research projects. The Royal Marsden School of Cancer Nursing and Rehabilitation launched a new collaboration with the faculty in 2010.

Students like the university's location, although they complain about the high cost of living. A "one-stop shop" deals with student issues ranging from careers and accommodation to complaints and financial advice. There is also a new unit, thought to be unique in the UK, offering free mediation of disputes involving local people. Each session is conducted by a student, but supervised by staff from the university law school who are accredited mediators. More than £20 million has been spent on halls of residence and Kingston's sports facilities have improved. A new £2.65-million sports pavilion, designed to suit both able-bodied and disabled users, and an upgraded sports ground opened in 2010.

Undergraduate Fees and Bursaries

- » Fees for UK/EU students 2014–15 £9,000
  Foundation degree £4,600–£6,000
- » International student fees 2013–14 £10,750–£12,350
- » 682 NSP awards of £3,000 as mixture of fee waiver, accommodation discount and £1,000 cash in year 1.
- » For household income below £25K and not receiving NSP award, 750 Kingston scholarships of £1,000 in year 1.
- » Progression awards (£500–£1,500) in years 2 and 3 with conditions.
- » Check the university's website for the latest information.

Students

Undergraduates:	**18,580**	**(1,955)**
Postgraduates:	**2,570**	**(2,950)**
Mature students:	**27.4%**	
Overseas students:	**12.6%**	
Applications per place:	**6.3**	
From state-sector schools:	**95.4%**	
From working-class homes:	**40.0%**	
Satisfaction with students' union	**60%**	

For detailed information about sports facilities: www.kingston.ac.uk/sport.

Accommodation

Number of places and costs refer to 2013–14
University-provided places: 2,365; private hall: 214
Percentage catered: 0%
Self-catered costs: £103.25–£132.00 a week (university provided; 40 weeks); £191.00 and £244.00 (private hall; 50 weeks).
Offers accommodation to many first-years who make Kingston their firm choice.
International students: offered places if conditions met, subject to availability.
Contact: www.kingston.ac.uk/accommodation/

Lancaster University

Despite slipping out of the top ten in our league table last year, Lancaster is still comfortably the highest-placed university in the North-West of England. It was one of the few universities in England to increase its applications as £9,000 fees arrived. Having completed a £400-million makeover for its campus, Lancaster has been expanding its overseas activities in line with its ambition to be truly international. The campus hosts students from more than 100 countries, but there will soon be more graduating with the university's degrees in India, Malaysia and Pakistan than in Lancaster itself. The university has a campus near Delhi in partnership with an Indian group and offers dual degrees with COMSATS Institute of Information Technology in Pakistan. With the prospect of a new campus in the Guangdong province of China, where there are already joint degrees, the university is poised to become one of the first to have campuses in both India and China.

A £10-million building for the Lancaster Institute for the Contemporary Arts has brought together art, design and theatre studies with the university's public art gallery, concerts and theatre. A £20-millon sports centre opened in 2011.

Still a relatively small institution, Lancaster is rated among the leading universities in the world that are less than 50 years old. More than 60 per cent of its work was rated as world-leading or internationally excellent in the last Research Assessment Exercise. Physics was the star performer, with the best grades in the country, but there were good results in health studies, computer science, art and design, management and sociology. In an unusual move, the university has also acquired the London-based think tank, the Work Foundation.

A new 24-hour student learning space at the centre of the campus provides flexible learning environments and social space with up-to-date technology. Infolab 21, the £15-million centre of excellence in information communication technology, acts as a technology transfer and incubation facility and houses a training facility for high-tech businesses. Other recent developments include a leadership centre for the highly rated Management School and the establishment of the Lancaster University Confucius Institute as a hub for Chinese language teaching and culture. The Management School was *Times Higher Education* magazine's 2012 business school of the year.

Lancaster is another of the campus universities which has always championed a flexible degree structure. Most undergraduates can broaden their first-

---

Bailrigg
Lancaster LA1 4YW

01524 592028 (admissions)
contact via website
www.lancaster.ac.uk
www.lusu.co.uk
Affiliation: 1994 Group

The Times and Sunday Times **Rankings**
Overall Ranking: **=12** (12)

Student satisfaction:	=24	(83.8%)
Research quality:	12	(28.3%)
Entry standards:	=21	(439)
Student–staff ratio:	27	(15.4)
Services & facilities/student:	39	(£1,684)
Expected completion rate:	16	(94.7%)
Good honours:	35	(73%)
Graduate prospects:	31	(72.7%)

year studies by taking a second or third subject. The final choice of degree comes only at the end of that year. Combined degree programmes, with 200 courses to choose from, are especially popular. The degree portfolio now includes medicine, with the students registered jointly with the University of Liverpool and receiving a Liverpool degree. From this year, the students will be registered as Lancaster students as the university seeks permission from the GMC to award its own medical degrees. The university has established a new Department of Chemistry, which is offering an undergraduate degree in the subject, while another partnership with Liverpool has seen the opening of the £9.8-million Centre for Global Eco-Innovation. Other recent developments have included a research centre specialising in bipolar disorder and a new Centre for Organisational Health and Wellbeing.

Lancaster is more successful than most research universities in widening participation among under-represented groups. Nine out of ten undergraduates are state educated and almost a quarter come from the four lowest socio-economic classes. Future outreach activity will include summer schools for 600 sixth-formers and college students, masterclasses for 2,000 and mentoring for 250 students. The projected dropout rate of just over 5 per cent is lower than average for the subjects on offer.

The university won five awards in the 2012 National Student Housing Survey. Students join one of eight residential colleges on campus, which become the centre of most students' social life. Most house between 800 and 900 students in self-catering accommodation and each has its own bar and social facilities. Cartmel and Lonsdale colleges have transferred to the New Alexandra Park area of the campus with enhanced social facilities. The pioneering 800-room Eco Residence, which opened in 2008, has won an environmental award. Lancaster itself is a ten-minute bus ride away. Both the campus and city have been rated among the safest in the UK. Sports facilities are good and conveniently placed, and for the outdoor life, the Lake District is within easy reach. Road and rail communications are good, but Lancaster is inevitably more limited than larger university centres for off-campus nightlife.

Undergraduate Fees and Bursaries

- » Fees for UK/EU students 2014–15 £9,000
- » International student fees 2013–14 £12,640–£15,850
- » Around 600 NSP awards of £1,000 fee waiver, £1,000 cash, £1,000 accommodation discount, year 1; £1,000 cash in subsequent years.
- » For household income £25K–£42.6K, £1,000 cash a year.
- » Scholarship of £2,000 in year 1 for all those with A*A*A at A Level or equivalent.
- » Scholarship of £1,000 a year for those with household income below £42.6K and with A*AA at A Level or equivalent.

Students

Undergraduates:	**8,870**	**(365)**
Postgraduates:	**2,335**	**(1,510)**
Mature students:	**4.6%**	
Overseas students:	**21.1%**	
Applications per place:	**6.7**	
From state-sector schools:	**89.6%**	
From working-class homes:	**22.6%**	
Satisfaction with students' union	**71%**	

For detailed information about sports facilities:
http://sportscentre.lancs.ac.uk

Accommodation

Number of places and costs refer to 2013–14
University-provided places: 6,600 (plus about 1,050 places in university-managed houses)
Percentage catered: 5%
Catered costs: £122.08 (standard) – £157.78 (en suite) a week.
Self-catered costs: £82.25 (standard) – £140.35 (studio) a week.
All first years are normally accommodated; no formal guarantee for Insurance, Clearing and late applicants.
International students: as above.
Contact: accommodation@lancaster.ac.uk

University of Leeds

Only two universities attracted more applications than Leeds when the fees went up to £9,000. Although this still represented a substantial drop and the intake was 600 students down on the previous year, the university did better than most others. It had devoted one of the largest amounts of any university to student support, and will continue to do so in 2014, when up to a third of UK and EU undergraduates are expected to benefit from subsidies, which they can choose to take as fee waivers, bursaries or accommodation discounts. An unusually wide range of degree subjects gives applicants more than 550 undergraduate programmes. The university was one of only three last year to be commended by the Quality Assurance Agency for its enhancement of the student learning experience. A curriculum enhancement programme is intended to deliver significant improvements to degree courses in 2013, without altering the integration of teaching and research that the university regards as its greatest strength. There are opportunities for undergraduates to get involved in designing and directing their own piece of research in their third year.

A member of the Russell Group of research-led universities, Leeds occupies a 98-acre site within walking distance of the city centre. The university scaled back its most ambitious campus development plan, but is still spending heavily on new facilities that are designed to propel it into the top 50 universities in the world. It already features among the top 100 in the QS World University Rankings, and in the top 50 for history, English, education and earth sciences. By 2015–16 Leeds will have spent £157 million on new buildings and refurbishment. A new undergraduate library is due to open in September 2014. Recent developments have included a new £4.4-million home for the Institute of Communications Studies with 41 edit suites, TV and radio studios, newsroom and 60-seat cinema; a £12.5-million Energy Research building that contains a suite of advanced laboratories; and a £9.5-million refurbishment of the Leeds Dental Institute. The already large students' union, famous for its long bar and big-name rock concerts, has been extended to provide better services and more space for students to socialise. The union is the only one in the country to have won two gold standard awards in the Students' Union Evaluation Initiative.

The university is truly cosmopolitan, with over 5,000 international students from 145 countries. It has one of the largest Study Abroad programmes in the country, with nearly 200 options ranging from Spain to Singapore. Leeds is part of the Worldwide Universities Network, which brings together

Leeds
West Yorkshire LS2 9JT

0113 343 2336 (enquiries)
study@leeds.ac.uk
www.leeds.ac.uk
www.leedsuniversityunion.org.uk
Affiliation: Russell Group

The Times and Sunday Times Rankings
Overall Ranking: **=29** (30)

Student satisfaction:	=33	(83.2%)
Research quality:	=27	(22.7%)
Entry standards:	27	(428)
Student–staff ratio:	=42	(16.8)
Services & facilities/student:	51	(£1,496)
Expected completion rate:	=22	(93.2%)
Good honours:	16	(79.5%)
Graduate prospects:	=44	(69.2%)

18 research-led universities to collaborate on research and postgraduate programmes. More than 60 per cent of the university's submission was rated as world-leading or internationally excellent in the last Research Assessment Exercise. Electrical and electronic engineering produced the best results in the country, with social work and social policy, English, Italian, geography and nursing also highly rated. But teaching is not neglected: Leeds has been awarded more National Teaching Fellowships than any other university in England.

More than a quarter of the undergraduates attended independent schools and only a fifth come from working-class homes – both below average for the university's subjects and entry grades. The rise of Leeds as a shopping and clubbing centre has added to the attractions of a university which has long been one of the giants of the higher education system. Town–gown relations are generally good, although residents in Headingley, the main student area, have complained about the impact on their neighbourhood. The wider local community benefits from 2,000 student volunteers. A partnership document introduced in 2011 sets out students' rights and responsibilities.

The university's employability strategy encourages early career planning and offers regular engagement with employers and professional bodies. The Leeds for Life initiative helps students to identify opportunities such as work placements and volunteering to develop their skills. The Careers Centre, which won two awards in 2011, hosts some of the world's biggest employers at the university, as well as advising those who choose to set up on their own.

Leeds guarantees accommodation for all first-year undergraduates, international and exchange students and students with disabilities. Sports and social facilities are first rate, and Leeds teams regularly excel in competition. The university hosts one of six centres of cricketing excellence. The university has more playing field space than any other, while The Edge houses indoor facilities that include a 25-metre swimming pool and a huge fitness suite.

Undergraduate Fees and Bursaries

» Fees for UK/EU students 2014–15 £9,000
» International student fees 2013–14 £12,900–£16,200
  Medicine £20,000–£29,950
» For English students with household income of £4K or below, £5,000 fee waiver and £1,000 cash, year 1; £3,000 as fee waiver, cash or university accommodation in subsequent years; £4K–£25K, £3,000 package year 1; £2,500 ,years 2 and 3; £25K–£30K, £2,000 ,year 1; £1,500, years 2 and 3; £30K–£36K, £1,500, year 1; £1,000, years 2 and 3; £36K–£42.6K, £1,000 ,year 1; £500, years 2 and 3.
» Transition to HE Bursary of £1,000 in year 1 for students with household income below £25K.
» Check the university's website for the latest information.

Students		
Undergraduates:	**23,085**	**(1,235)**
Postgraduates:	**5,490**	**(2,695)**
Mature students:	**9.4%**	
Overseas students:	**9.3%**	
Applications per place:	**7.7**	
From state-sector schools:	**72.9%**	
From working-class homes:	**18.4%**	
Satisfaction with students' union	**90%**	

For detailed information about sports facilities:
www.leeds.ac.uk/sport

Accommodation

Number of places and costs refer to 2013–14
University-provided places: 7,900
Percentage catered: 23%
Catered costs: £83 (standard) – £182 (en suite) (39 weeks).
Self-catered costs: £78 (standard) – £153 (studio) a week (42 weeks).
Single first years are guaranteed a place provided conditions are met.
International students: as above
Contact: www.accommodation.leeds.ac.uk; accom@leeds.ac.uk

Leeds Metropolitan University

Leeds Met's senior management stirred up a hornet's nest in 2013 by announcing that the university had "outgrown" its Metropolitan name and suggesting three alternatives: Beckett, Headingley or Ridings. After consultation, and a hostile student reaction, the university decided to seek formal approval for "Leeds Beckett University". The proposal followed a 15 per cent decline in applications with the arrival of higher fees and a first-year intake 1,800 smaller than in 2011. The university is moving to £9,000 fees in 2014, having moved in stages from a starting point of £8,500. The extra income will enable Leeds Met to maintain a strong portfolio of scholarships and bursaries. There are awards for high achievers and for applicants from target schools and colleges, as well as the normal range of bursaries for students from low-income families.

Only just over half of all undergraduates are taking conventional full-time degrees, such is the popularity of sandwich and part-time courses. It is intended that all Leeds Met students should leave the university with three graduate attributes; to be enterprising, digitally literate and have a global outlook. All undergraduate courses have been redesigned with these qualities in mind and all include at least two weeks work-related learning a year.

Leeds Met has a longstanding reputation for widening participation in higher education: well over 90 per cent of undergraduates are state-educated and almost a third come from working-class homes. A quarter of the students come from the Yorkshire and Humberside region, and around one in five is 21 or over on entry. The university runs a wide range of summer schools, which benefit more than 24,000 young people per year. A Regional University Network of further education colleges, which stretches from Belfast to Glasgow, enables students to take Leeds Met courses locally.

However, the university's projected drop-out rate of nearly 17 per cent, whilst an improvement on some previous years, remains above the national average for its courses and entry qualifications.

There are two bases in Leeds: the City Campus, in the heart of the city centre, and the Headingley Campus, three miles away in the 100 acres of park and woodland of Beckett Park. The latter boasts outstanding sports facilities, including a new sports arena and multi-use sports pitches, which opened in 2012. The sports centre offers a variety of options for performance and participation sport, alongside the £2-million Carnegie Regional Tennis Centre, as well as teaching accommodation for education,

---

City Campus
Leeds
West Yorkshire LS1 3HE

0113 812 3113 (enquiries)
contact via website
www.leedsmet.ac.uk
www.leedsmetsu.co.uk
Affiliation: million+

The Times and Sunday Times **Rankings**
Overall Ranking: **103** (104)

Student satisfaction:	(79%)Research quality:
quality:	(2.0%)Entry standards:
standards:	(278)Student–staff ratio:
ratio:	(20.7)Services & facilities/student:
facilities/student:	(£1,073)Expected completion rate:
completion rate:	(80.2%)Good honours:
(57.5%)Graduate prospects:	
(60.3%)	

informatics, law and business. Over 7,000 students take part in some form of sporting activity, and there is a range of £2,000 sports scholarships. The Athletic Union hosts 32 clubs and university teams – especially those for women – are among the most successful in national competition. A season pass for both the Headingley campus and City Campus facilities costs around £100. In the first developments of their kind, a new stand was built at the Headingley rugby ground, with classrooms, coaching facilities and social space for use by the university and the two professional clubs, and a new pavilion at the adjacent Test and County Cricket ground has similar multi-use facilities.

The City Campus has seen a £100-million transformation over the past five years, with the opening of the award winning Rose Bowl and Broadcasting Place. The futuristic lecture theatre complex next to Leeds Civic Hall now houses the business school, while Broadcasting Place is home to the Faculty of Arts and Society. The former BBC building next door has reopened as Old Broadcasting House and hosts the Enterprise Office, which helps identify opportunities to generate commercial income and support bids for funding and contracts. A growing emphasis on educational technology is enhanced by 24-hour libraries, which have achieved the Customer Service Excellence standard for ten years in a row. They contain more than 800 computers and over 2,000 study spaces.

Relatively few academics were entered for the 2008 Research Assessment Exercise, but nearly a third of their work was judged to be world-leading or internationally excellent. Communication, cultural and media studies, sport, and library and information management produced the best results. Students are included on the committees that design and manage courses. As Leeds Met's reputation for applied research continues to grow, three new interdisciplinary research centres have recently been opened to provide a renewed focus for areas of research expertise.

Leeds Met is benefiting from the city's growing reputation for nightlife, but it is making its own contribution with a famously lively entertainments scene. With 4,500 bed spaces, those who accept places before Clearing are guaranteed university accommodation.

Undergraduate Fees and Bursaries

- » Fees for UK/EU students 2014–15 £9,000
- » International student fees 2013–14 £9,500
- » 776 NSP awards with priority criteria: £1,000 cash and £2,000 support services, year 1; £1,500 support services, years 2 and 3.
- » Leeds Met Bursary of £300 in year 1 for students coming from partner schools and colleges.
- » Range of other scholarships and bursaries available.
- » Check the university's website for the latest information.

Students

Undergraduates:	**19,075**	**(4,670)**
Postgraduates:	**1,850**	**(2,390)**
Mature students:	**20.1%**	
Overseas students:	**5.4%**	
Applications per place:	**6.3**	
From state-sector schools:	**93.1%**	
From working-class homes:	**32.5%**	
Satisfaction with students' union	**66%**	

For detailed information about sports facilities:
www.leedsmet.ac.uk/sport

Accommodation

Number of places and costs refer to 2013–14
University-provided places: 4,500
Percentage catered: 0%
Self-catered costs: £98 (single) –£160 (studio) a week (41–51 weeks).
First years with Conditional Firm or Unconditional Firm offers guaranteed accommodation.
International students: guaranteed accommodation if conditions are met.
Contact: www.leedsmet.ac.uk/accommodation

Leeds Trinity University

Leeds Trinity is one of two new Catholic universities, the only ones in the UK. The former university college welcomes students of all faiths and none, but does not hide its affiliation, proclaiming that its students are "provided with a sense of vocation, so that they may use their skills and knowledge to contribute to the betterment of society." There is a BA in Catholic studies, responding to the need for in-service theological education to degree level for people working for or with the Catholic Church. The university grew out of two Catholic teacher training colleges established in the 1960s, which merged in 1980. Education is still the biggest subject, but there are also departments of Media, Film and Culture; Journalism; Business, Management and Marketing; Psychology; and Sport, Health and Nutrition. Indeed, while many universities were scaling back their degree options in 2013, Leeds Trinity launched 18 new courses, including accelerated two-year degrees in education and sport, and tourism and leisure management. The two-year degrees will cost £9,000 a year in 2014, while the conventional courses will go up by £500 a year to £8,500.

The university's campus is 20 minutes north-west of Leeds city centre, in Horsforth. Millions of pounds have been spent in recent years to transform it into a modern campus village. The latest big development was the upgrading of the Media Centre, which is now fully digital for video and audio operations, and students are able to shoot in HD following the purchase of broadcast-quality portable cameras. A new range of computers and studio cameras have been installed to meet the demands of journalism and media production courses. The Centre for Journalism has also developed two additional multimedia newsrooms with easy access to studios, equipment and edit suites.

Leeds Trinity's Digital Campus project will see the investment of £1.2 million over three years to provide a seamless, resilient and flexible ICT environment. The new technology will also reduce the university's carbon footprint by using lower wattage computers that have much longer lifespan than the current PCs. Users will be able to access the system from off campus with no loss of functionality. Another modernisation scheme has seen the launch of a self-service system for borrowers at the library, which has doubled usage figures.

The Students' Union has been relocated to the main campus building, bringing it closer to the other student services. The existing Students' Union building will be transformed into a modern teaching and learning block, creating two new lecture theatres with capacity for 100 in

---

Brownberrie Lane
Horsforth, Leeds LS18 5HD

0113 283 7150 (enquiries)
enquiries@leedstrinity.ac.uk
www.leedstrinity.ac.uk
www.ltsu.co.uk
Affiliation: GuildHE,
　Cathedrals Group

The Times and Sunday Times Rankings
Overall Ranking: **104** (n/a)

Student satisfaction:	=52	(81.9%)
Research quality:	=100	(1.7%)
Entry standards:	=99	(286)
Student–staff ratio:	111	(23.3)
Services & facilities/student:	111	(£1,001)
Expected completion rate:	94	(80.6%)
Good honours:	116	(50.8%)
Graduate prospects:	=84	(57.9%)

tiered seating, and five large classrooms with capacity of 40. Extra social space for students and staff will be developed at the same time. The student bar and venue has been revamped and given a new location. Named "The Lounge" and opened in 2013, it has greatly expanded the social space, catering and bar facilities available on campus.

There have also been significant educational developments. The launch of the Centre for Children, Young People and Families, for example, was a response to the reorganisation of those services in central and local government. It offers new study opportunities through the development of external partnerships. The new university's stated aim is to be an "autonomous teaching-led research-informed institution providing higher education characterised by vocational excellence." Every course includes a work placement, with inherent benefits for graduate employment.

Applications dropped significantly when higher fees were introduced in 2012, but the eventual first-year intake was within 40 students of the 2011 figure. Nearly two-thirds of the students are female and three-quarters are school or college leavers, rather than mature students. Almost 60 per cent are the first in their family to attend university. Leeds Trinity exceeds all its national benchmarks for widening participation in higher education: more than 40 per cent of undergraduates come from working-class homes, while nearly 20 per cent are from areas with little tradition of sending students to university – one of the highest proportions in the country. However, the 14 per cent projected dropout rate is higher than the national average for Leeds Trinity's courses and entry qualifications.

There are still little more than 3,000 students, despite recent growth, and the new university was displaying high levels of student satisfaction well before its new status was conferred. Leeds Trinity provides 575 residential places, most of which are reserved for first-year students. They include the £6-million All Saints Court development, opened in 2010 with almost 200 en-suite bedrooms. Sports facilities are good and include a new 3G pitch. The city is one of the most popular with students, although the campus is not central.

Undergraduate Fees and Bursaries

» Fees for UK/EU students 2014–15: £8,500
Accelerated two-year degree £9,000
Foundation degree £2,250
» International student fees 2013–14: £9,300–£11,000
» Around 400 NSP awards of £3,000 in year 1 (full details to be confirmed).
» Range of other scholarships and bursaries available.
» Check the university's website for the latest information.

Students		
Undergraduates:	**2,590**	**(85)**
Postgraduates:	**170**	**(480)**
Mature students:	**1.8%**	
Overseas students:	**2.1%**	
Applications per place:	**4.7**	
From state-sector schools:	**97.3%**	
From working-class homes:	**42.3%**	
Satisfaction with students' union	**54%**	

For detailed information about sports facilities:
www.leedstrinity.ac.uk/services/TrinitySport/

Accommodation

Places and costs refer to 2013–14
University-provided places: 575
Percentage catered: 35%
Catered costs: £107–£115 a week (38 weeks).
Self-catered costs: £88–£113 a week (38 weeks).
Priority is given to first-year students.
International students: same as above.
Contact: accommodation@leedstrinity.ac.uk
www.leedstrinity.ac.uk/services/accommodation/Pages/default.aspx

University of Leicester

Leicester hit the headlines when its archaeologists discovered Richard III buried under a car park in the city. The subject is one of a number in which the university excels and which have been moving it up the top 20 in our league table. It is in the top ten for staffing levels and high spending on student facilities, as well as producing consistently high scores in the National Student Survey. The university has been trialling the use of social media to improve feedback in an attempt to increase satisfaction levels even more. Leicester has shown the scale of its ambitions with a £1-billion development plan. The Queen opened the £32-million library in 2008, and another £16 million has been spent more recently on an award-winning students' union.

Leicester was one of the universities to maintain the size of its undergraduate intake when the fees went up to £9,000 despite experiencing a sharp drop in applications. Although the university celebrated its 90th anniversary in 2011, fewer than 10,000 full-time undergraduates are based on its main campus, representing little more than half of the student population. But substantial postgraduate and distance learning programmes bring Leicester close to the size of other big city universities. The Vice-Chancellor, Professor Sir Robert Burgess has focused on strengthening research, and Leicester entered a much larger proportion of its academics than many of its peers in the 2008 Research Assessment Exercise. As a result of the large entry, less than half of the university's submission was considered world-leading or internationally excellent, but there was a big increase in research funding. The star performers were the nine entrants in museum studies, who produced the highest proportion of world-leading research in any subject at any UK university, with almost two-thirds of their work placed in that top category. The university is divided into four colleges, partly to encourage greater collaboration between academics from different subjects.

Leicester has the most socially diverse intake of any university in our top 20, aided by initiatives such as a summer school for local teenagers. An £8-million scholarship programme is designed to keep it that way, offsetting the impact of £9,000 undergraduate fees. Nearly nine out of ten undergraduates come from state schools and more than a quarter are from working-class homes. The 6 per cent projected dropout rate falls below the national average for the university's courses and entry grades.

Leicester was awarded national centres of excellence for teaching and learning in geography, genetics and physics. The university also has a long-established

---

University Road
Leicester LE1 7RH

0116 252 5281 (admissions)
admissions@le.ac.uk
www.le.ac.uk
http://leicesterunion.com
Affiliation: 1994 Group

The Times and Sunday Times **Rankings**
Overall Ranking: **14** (17)

Student satisfaction:	22	(84%)
Research quality:	=38	(20.0%)
Entry standards:	32	(413)
Student–staff ratio:	11	(12.9)
Services & facilities/student:	8	(£2,271)
Expected completion rate:	18	(93.7%)
Good honours:	23	(75.5%)
Graduate prospects:	35	(71.6%)

reputation in space science, with Europe's largest university-based space research facility, including the £52-million National Space Centre. The medical school, which allows graduates in the health and life sciences to qualify in four years, has among the most modern facilities in Britain, including a new £12.6-million cardiovascular research centre. The siting of a medically based interdisciplinary research centre at the university was another indication of strength. The genetics department, where DNA genetic fingerprinting was discovered, has helped make Leicester's academics among the most cited in Britain.

Clinical medicine is taught at the city's three hospitals, but all other teaching and much residential accommodation is concentrated in a leafy suburb a mile from the city centre. Its location, adjacent to one of Leicester's main parks, is popular with students. The new library has doubled the available space and brought the total number of workspaces to 1,500. The refurbished students' union has won numerous design awards and was named as the NUS students' union of the year in 2013, as well as previously achieving the top grade for good ethical and environmental practice. The union is the only one in the country to contain an O_2 Academy which has hosted gigs from the likes of Kasabian and Noah and the Whale.

Extensive residential accommodation includes a £21-million 600-bed en-suite development. The university has over 4,000 student bed spaces so first years are guaranteed a residential place. Many second- and third-year students also live in hall, although the majority choose to live in the reasonably priced private accommodation available nearby. The main sports facilities are conveniently located: in 2013–14, students will pay £115 a year to use them.

As a city, Leicester is not one of the most fashionable student destinations, but its ethnic diversity makes for a rich cultural experience. It is big enough to provide all the normal sports and entertainment opportunities, but also offers events such as the biggest Diwali celebrations outside India. The Demos Bohemian index rated Leicester the second most creative city in Britain behind London, and Birmingham is also easily accessible via public transport.

Undergraduate Fees and Bursaries

» Fees for UK/EU students 2014–15   £9,000
» International student fees 2013–14   £12,365–£15,815
  Medicine   £27,710
» NSP awards of £1,000 cash and £2,000 fee waiver, year 1;
  £1,000 cash, years 2 and 3.
» Academic scholarships of £1,000 fee waiver for those with
  specified A level (or equivalent) grades.
» Care leaver bursary of £2,000 a year; 100 awards of £1,000 in
  year 1 for students from local colleges; £1,000 cash each year
  for students from Realising Opportunities programme.

Students

Undergraduates:	**9,835**	**(1,260)**
Postgraduates:	**3,265**	**(2,695)**
Mature students:	**14.9%**	
Overseas students:	**20.0%**	
Applications per place:	**6.4**	
From state-sector schools:	**87.6%**	
From working-class homes:	**25.1%**	
Satisfaction with students' union	**77%**	

For detailed information about sports facilities: www.le.ac.uk/sports

Accommodation

Number of places and costs refer to 2013–14
University-provided places: 4,366
Percentage catered: 28%
Catered costs: £123.90–£220.50 a week (30 weeks).
Self-catered costs: £81.20–£167.30 (42 weeks).
First-year students are guaranteed accommodation if conditions are met.
International students: as above, with priority to those returning.
Contact: www.le.ac.uk/accommodation

University of Lincoln

Lincoln's meteoric rise up our league table has halted, at least temporarily, after two years in which the university made more progress than any other. It remains among the top eight post-1992 universities and close to the top 50 overall. The opening of an impressive purpose-built campus alongside a marina in the centre of Lincoln in 1996 brought about the most dramatic transformation of any university in recent times. Humberside University, as it had been, even gave its new location pride of place in its title. Five years later it went a step further, selling the previous headquarters campus in Hull and becoming the University of Lincoln. While not moving out of Hull entirely, the university has concentrated its activities there on a much smaller city-centre site and invested £140 million in its Brayford Pool campus in Lincoln.

The switch has paid undoubted dividends, helping to attract high-quality academics. The number of professors grew from eight to 87 in four years. Student applications have increased for most of the last decade, despite rising admission requirements. Even the introduction of £9,000 fees did not prevent applications from rising again in 2012, although the number of students taking up places dropped. New entrants were offered support packages worth up to £3,000. The most recent major addition to the campus is the £7-million Engineering Hub, opened in 2011 in collaboration with Siemens and emda, the UK's first purpose-built engineering school in 25 years. A new building for the School of Art and Design is due to open in September 2013 and the university has planning permission for considerable further development over the next ten years.

New science laboratories, sports facilities, an architecture school, a library in a converted warehouse and a students' union and entertainment venue in a former railway engine shed were previous developments. A £6-million performing arts centre contains a 450-seat theatre and three large studio spaces, while the Human Performance Centre is a regional facility for excellence in sport, coaching and exercise science. In addition, the Lincoln Business School has its own building and there is a thriving business incubation unit. A one-stop-shop provides students with careers advice, enhances their CVs, helps them to gain work experience and find jobs, as well as supporting graduates who are setting up their own businesses. The university expanded its graduate internship scheme and launched a new summer placement programme in 2011.

Lincoln initially concentrated on social sciences, but the university now has a much wider range of courses. The School

---

Brayford Pool
Lincoln LN6 7TS

01522 886644 (enquiries)
contact via website
www.lincoln.ac.uk
http://lincolnsu.com
Affiliation: University
Alliance

The Times and Sunday Times **Rankings**

Overall Ranking: **=57** (=52)

Student satisfaction:	**77**	(80.8%)
Research quality:	**=63**	(5.0%)
Entry standards:	**63**	(324)
Student–staff ratio:	**=72**	(19.4)
Services & facilities/student:	**80**	(£1,282)
Expected completion rate:	**47**	(87.4%)
Good honours:	**=79**	(60.7%)
Graduate prospects:	**48**	(68.4%)

of Architecture, for example, has over 400 students. Art and design is based in the city centre, while animal, biological and equine studies are at Riseholme Park, a 1,000-acre site ten minutes outside Lincoln. Riseholme was chosen as one of the training centres for equine events ahead of the 2012 Olympic Games. Only the School of Health and Social Care remains in Hull, following the transfer of art and design degree provision in the city to Hull College.

The university was determined to achieve a high-profile return in the Research Assessment Exercise in 2008 to match a sharp rise in its research income. Lincoln entered more of its academics for assessment than many institutions in its peer group and improved on previous results, with 28 per cent of its submission judged to be world-leading or internationally excellent. The result was a £2-million boost in research grants. Communication, cultural and media studies and computer science and informatics produced the highest grades. The university has also had successes in applied research and knowledge transfer, notably with the National Centre for Food Manufacturing, based in Holbeach, which specialises in the production of chilled foods.

All students take the Effective Learning Programme, which uses computer packages backed up by weekly seminars to develop study skills and produce a detailed portfolio of all their work. Some degrees can be taken as work-based programmes, with credit awarded for relevant aspects of the jobs. Lincoln was the first university to win a Charter Mark for exceptional service.

More than a third of the undergraduates come from working-class homes and the improved dropout rate of 10 per cent is below the average for the subjects on offer, given the entry standards. The city is adapting to its new student population with new bars and clubs, although the social scene there is not the prime draw for students. The campus now has more than 1,000 beds, while private developments close to the university now provide well over 2,000 further residential places.

Undergraduate Fees and Bursaries

» Fees for UK/EU students 2014–15 £9,000
» International student fees 2013–14 £11,130–£12,755
» For students with household income below £25K and in university accommodation, £1,000 cash and £2,000 accommodation discount (not in university accommodation, £3,000 support package), in year 1; £700 cash, years 2 and 3; household income £25K–£40K, £450 a year.
» Scholarships and bursaries for local students, sports, engineering and care leavers.
» Range of other scholarships and bursaries available.
» Check the university's website for the latest information.

Students

Undergraduates:	**9,210**	**(1,980)**
Postgraduates:	**650**	**(1,280)**
Mature students:	**16.8%**	
Overseas students:	**3.6%**	
Applications per place:	**4.4**	
From state-sector schools:	**96.5%**	
From working-class homes:	**33.6%**	
Satisfaction with students' union	**69%**	

For detailed information about sports facilities: www.lincoln.ac.uk/home/campuslife/sportsandsocieties

Accommodation

Number of places and costs refer to 2013–14
University-provided places: 1,037
Percentage catered: 0%
Self-catered costs: £105.00–£118.65 a week.
Student accommodation prioritised by distance within application date.
International students are given detailed information and assistance.
Contact: www.lincoln.ac.uk/accommodation

University of Liverpool

Liverpool is investing £600 million in its campus, as well as extending its reach beyond the university's home city. It already had a joint venture in China with Xi'an Jiaotong University, which will have 10,000 students by 2015, and now it has added a postgraduate site in the City of London for management courses. The 10-year development plan for the main campus has already provided new and upgraded teaching and research facilities, as well as improved leisure facilities and more student accommodation. New teaching laboratories for the sciences are said to be Europe's most advanced and the university is also spending £70 million on interdisciplinary research facilities for the health and life sciences that will bring together more than 600 scientists to focus on the major health challenges of the 21st century. The management school has been extended and the Guild of Students building refurbished. Other new developments include major improvements in student social space and a £4-million investment in sports facilities.

A major beneficiary of recent investment has been the university's library, which underwent a £17-million redevelopment in 2008 and now offers 24-hour access to computers. More than half of the work submitted for the last Research Assessment Exercise was judged to be world-leading or internationally excellent. Computer science, materials, architecture, English and history produced particularly good results. The university now focuses on interdisciplinary research wherever possible.

Liverpool had been attracting increased applications, but there was a sharp decline when £9,000 fees were introduced in 2012 and the undergraduate intake dropped by about 10 per cent. The university had committed more than 30 per cent of its additional fee income to support for students from lower-income backgrounds and enhanced measures to prevent students from dropping out. More than a quarter of new undergraduates qualify for a support package totalling £3,000 in their first year and £2,000 a year for the rest of their course. The 5 per cent projected dropout rate is significantly better than average for Liverpool's subjects and entry grades. Liverpool was among the first traditional universities to run access courses for adults without traditional qualifications. The proportion of undergraduates from working-class homes is among the highest in the Russell Group of leading research-based universities, although still less than the national average for the courses and entry qualifications.

Liverpool's Chinese initiative began in 2006 with the opening of a new university in the World Heritage City of Suzhou in

---

Liverpool L69 3BX

0151 794 5927 (enquiries)
contact via website
www.liv.ac.uk
www.lgos.org
Affiliation: Russell Group

Edinburgh
Belfast
LIVERPOOL
London
Cardiff

The Times and Sunday Times **Rankings**
Overall Ranking: **36** (29)

Student satisfaction:	=59	(81.5%)
Research quality:	=38	(20.0%)
Entry standards:	28	(420)
Student–staff ratio:	12	(13.3)
Services & facilities/student:	18	(£2,041)
Expected completion rate:	30	(91.7%)
Good honours:	36	(72.8%)
Graduate prospects:	36	(71.5%)

partnership with Xi'an Jiaotong University. Chinese students can complete the latter part of their studies in Liverpool, while Liverpool-based students are offered work experience at Suzhou Industrial Park, which is home to 84 "Fortune 500" companies. Since September 2011, students in electrical engineering and electronics, computer science and maths have been given the opportunity to spend a year studying in China. All staff and students across the university can take a course in Mandarin for £10. Liverpool is involved in further collaborations with universities in Chile, Mexico and Spain that will allow students to complete part of their degree at one or more of these institutions via a range of options such as projects or placements. Students will have access to a full range of support services while abroad.

Back in Liverpool, one of Europe's largest facilities for training dentists opened in 2007, marking the start of another big investment programme following the award of an additional 125 dental places from 2009. There has also been substantial investment in new educational technology. But by far the biggest spending programme, totalling some £250 million, is devoted to student accommodation. A 710-bedroom development, featuring shops and a restaurant, opened on the city-centre campus in 2012. The university's other accommodation is being refurbished and

another 1,500 study bedrooms are planned on the main campus. New residences will also be built at the Greenbank site, at suburban Mossley Hill, to provide a self-contained student village.

The Guild of Students is the centre of campus social activity. The university's indoor and outdoor sports facilities are undergoing a £4.5-million refurbishment programme and a new gym has opened at the Greenbank Halls site. A new 25-metre swimming pool is open to the public as well as students. The university has one of the largest careers resources centres in the UK and has recently introduced an innovative programme of "boot camps" giving new graduates opportunities for networking with employers while developing a range of employability skills. Over the next two years, more than £2 million will be invested in student and graduate internships, most of them paid and lasting for substantial periods.

Undergraduate Fees and Bursaries

- » Fees for UK/EU students 2014–15 £9,000
- » International student fees 2013–14 £11,862–£15,251
  Dentistry and medicine £23,108
- » Household income below £25K, £3,000 fee waiver/university services or £2,000 fee waiver/university services and £1,000 cash, year 1 for English students (£2,000 package for other UK students), £2,000 package for all students, other years (£1,000 for year abroad or sandwich year); £25K–£35K, £1,000 package a year (£500 for year abroad or sandwich year).

Students

Undergraduates:	**15,320**	**(2,130)**
Postgraduates:	**2,975**	**(1,455)**
Mature students:	**11.1%**	
Overseas students:	**15.6%**	
Applications per place:	**8.0**	
From state-sector schools:	**87.6%**	
From working-class homes:	**22.0%**	
Satisfaction with students' union	**55%**	

For detailed information about sports facilities:
www.liv.ac.uk/sports

Accommodation

Number of places and costs refer to 2013–14
University-provided places: 4,330
Percentage catered: 52%
Catered costs: £124.60–£183.05 a week.
Self-catered costs: £90.30–£141.40 a week.
First-year students are guaranteed accommodation if Liverpool is their first choice and requirements are met.
International students: as above.
Contact: accommodation@liverpool.ac.uk
www.liv.ac.uk/accommodation

Liverpool Hope University

Liverpool Hope continues to opt out of league tables after finishing at the bottom of our table on its only appearance in *The Times Good University Guide*. The university has improved some scores since then, but believes that the criteria used in league tables are biased in favour of wealthier institutions with a longer history. It insists that its objections "can't be summed up in one sentence". Hope had enjoyed big increases in applications before a substantial drop when the fees went up to £8,250 in 2012. They have since risen further to £9,000, which will remain the level for those starting full-time degrees in 2014. In addition to bursaries for students from low-income families, there will be scholarships for academic achievement and for national level involvement in sport, music, dance and drama.

Hope is a unique ecumenical institution formed from the merger of two Catholic and one Church of England teacher training colleges in 1980. A university since 2005, it describes itself as "teaching led, research informed and mission focused" and includes "taking faith seriously" among its five key values. The university opened its own joint Church of England and Roman Catholic academy in September 2011, replacing two comprehensive schools. There are also partnerships with the Royal Liverpool Philharmonic Orchestra, Liverpool Tate and the National Museums Liverpool to develop cultural programmes and new curricular areas such as art history and curating. The university has made Frank Cottrell Boyce, a scriptwriter for the opening ceremony in the 2012 Olympics, the first Professor of Reading in the UK.

Most students opt for combined subject degrees, choosing after the first year whether to give them equal weight or to go for a major/minor arrangement. Hope is moving away from modular degrees to an "integrated undergraduate curriculum" in order to give students a more rounded view of their subject. The university has increased its national recruitment profile, with nearly 60 per cent of students now coming from beyond Merseyside. Hope undergraduates can register for the Service and Leadership Award, which is credit-rated and runs alongside their degree work. Students can volunteer locally, within the region or internationally as part of Global Hope, the university's award winning overseas charity.

Nearly 30 per cent of the undergraduates are over 20 on entry and female students outnumber their male counterparts by more than two to one. Hope comfortably exceeds all the official benchmarks for widening participation in higher education. Almost all the undergraduates are state educated, approaching 40 per cent are from working-

Hope Park
Liverpool L16 9JD

0151 291 3111 (enquiries)
enquiry@hope.ac.uk
www.hope.ac.uk
www.hopesu.com
Affiliation: Cathedrals
Group

The Times and Sunday Times **Rankings**
Liverpool Hope blocked the release of data from the Higher Education Statistics Agency and so we cannot give any ranking information.

class families and almost one in five is from an area with little tradition of higher education – one of the highest proportions in England. The Network of Hope brings university courses to sixth-form colleges across the North West of England, in areas where there is limited higher education. Single Honours and Foundation degrees are taught in Bury and Blackburn. At just over 9 per cent, the projected dropout rate has improved but remains below average for the university's courses and entry qualifications.

The university is concentrated on two sites in Liverpool, and there is a residential outdoor education centre in Snowdonia, North Wales. The main campus – Hope Park – is three miles from the city centre in the suburb of Childwall, while the creative and performing arts are based at the more central Creative campus in Everton, where a new performance centre opened in 2010. It houses one of only three Steinway Schools in England, as well as practice rooms, recording spaces and a theatre. The £5-million main library, on the Hope campus, has 270,000 items and 700 study spaces, with electronic access from other sites. More than a quarter of the academics were entered for the 2008 Research Assessment Exercise – a higher proportion than at most comparable institutions. Theology was the top scorer, although a small amount of world-leading work was found in applied social sciences.

Other recent campus developments have included a Centre for Education and Enterprise, which supports local business as well as hosting the Faculty of Education. More than £1 million has been spent on a new food court and a dedicated library and reading room has opened on the Creative campus, with a Renaissance-style garden which includes an outdoor performance area. "Our Place", which opened in 2012, includes a pizza restaurant, a coffee area and bar, as well as a new auditorium where comedy nights, live music and other social events are held. Sports facilities have been improving and there is a range of residential accommodation, some of it provided by a private firm. Places are guaranteed for international students and first years who apply before Clearing.

Undergraduate Fees and Bursaries

» Fees for UK/EU students 2014–15   £9,000
» International student fees 2013–14   £9,000
» 160 NSP awards with priority criteria: £6,000 (£3,000 accommodation discount, year 1; £1,000 credit against university services, years 2 and 3; and £1,000 cash year 3).
» Range of other scholarships and bursaries available.
» Check the university's website for the latest information.

Students

Undergraduates:	**4,890**	**(875)**
Postgraduates:	**810**	**(1,175)**
From state-sector schools:	**98.9%**	
From working-class homes:	**38.2%**	
Satisfaction with students' union	**53%**	

For detailed information about sports facilities:
www.hope.ac.uk/hopeparksports

Accommodation

Number of places and costs refer to 2013–14
University-provided places: 1,178
Percentage catered: 0% (catering packages an optional extra)
Self-catered costs: £87 (shared); £105–£113 (en suite) a week.
First years are guaranteed accommodation if Liverpool Hope is their first choice and they apply before Clearing.
International students: rooms are available at specific locations, depending on course
Contact: www.hope.ac.uk/lifeathope/residentiallife;
accommodation@hope.ac.uk

Liverpool John Moores University (LJMU)

Liverpool John Moores (LJMU) is one of the risers in this year's league table, with increases in student satisfaction, degree classifications and especially entry standards moving it towards the university's goal of a place in the top 60 by 2017. However, the price for a 50-point rise in average entry points was 800 fewer first-year students than in the previous year. LJMU was among a minority of post-1992 universities charging undergraduate fees of £9,000 in 2012. It said the maximum fee was necessary to promise students a "distinctive, life-changing experience worth the financial commitment". With most of its peer group now also charging the maximum, the university will hope that its prizewinning World of Work (WoW) initiative will help to restore previous levels of enrolment. Work-related learning is included in every degree and all undergraduates are encouraged to become expert in eight transferable skills, applicable to a wide range of careers.

The programme has been shaped and steered by leading companies and business organisations. More than 150 local employers have been trained as WoW skills verifiers, working with LJMU to deliver graduate-entry-level interviews. In future, all students will have their skills verified through an employer-validated statement. The Centre for Entrepreneurship supports students and graduates who want to start up in business, become self-employed or work freelance, as well as working closely with programme teams to provide enterprise education through the curriculum.

Naming itself after a football pools millionaire set a pattern of innovation for LJMU. Early examples included the original student charter and the first degrees in sports science and criminal justice, as well as the first distance learning degree in astronomy. It has invested £180 million over the last ten years to transform its three campuses. Developments include the award-winning Art and Design Academy and the £25.5-million life sciences building, opened by Liverpool footballer and LJMU honorary fellow Steven Gerrard, where the world-class facilities include an indoor 70-metre running track and labs for testing cardiovascular ability, motor skills and biomechanics functions. A new £37.6-million student-centred building was opened in 2012, as a gateway to the Mount Pleasant campus and the city's Knowledge Quarter. It houses the Liverpool Screen School, the Faculty of Business and Law, and the university's new Professional Centre.

There is a learning resource centre in each of the three campuses and a state-of-the-art media centre that is open all

---

Roscoe Court
4 Rodney Street
Liverpool L1 2TZ

0151 231 5090 (course enquiries)
courses@ljmu.ac.uk (enquiries)
www.ljmu.ac.uk
www.liverpoolsu.com
Affiliation: University
 Alliance

The Times and Sunday Times Rankings

Overall Ranking: **83** (=93)

Student satisfaction:	**=61**	(81.4%)
Research quality:	**=76**	(3.7%)
Entry standards:	**=59**	(327)
Student–staff ratio:	**=100**	(21.6)
Services & facilities/student:	**89**	(£1,237)
Expected completion rate:	**=74**	(83.6%)
Good honours:	**51**	(68%)
Graduate prospects:	**95**	(55%)

hours. The university's Virtual Learning Environment enables students to access most teaching materials and a range of other support features online. Mainly concentrated in an area between Liverpool's two cathedrals, the university now has 24,000 students in the city and another 4,500 taking LJMU courses overseas. Arts and science courses occupy separate sites within easy reach of the city centre, with the IM Marsh campus three miles away for education and community studies. Nearly half of the students are drawn from the Merseyside area.

A growing research reputation is a source of particular pride. A third of the research assessed in 2008 was rated as world-leading or internationally excellent, with 12 of the 17 subject areas having some work in the top category. LJMU was among the top four of post-92 universities for electrical and electronic engineering, general engineering, sports-related studies, architecture and built environment, anthropology, physics, biological sciences, and computer sciences and informatics. A £1.6-million maritime centre features the UK's most advanced 360-degree ship-handling simulator and there is a sophisticated robotic telescope in La Palma, in the Canaries for the astronomers.

The university's efforts to extend access to higher education are successful: almost all the undergraduates are state-educated and 37 per cent are from working-class homes. Among the scholarships and bursaries introduced to offset the impact of higher fees are the John Lennon Imagine Awards, match-funded through a gift of £260,000 from Yoko Ono, which help students who have either been in local authority care or who are estranged from their parents. LJMU also has a wide range of disability support services and has been addressing concerns about its dropout rate which, at 10 per cent, is now better than the national average for the university's courses and entry grades. An assessment room is available for students with disabilities and requiring additional support to test out a range of furniture, equipment and technologies based on their own specific needs.

Student facilities have been improving. The university has partnerships with a range of private accommodation providers so that all new students are guaranteed accommodation if they require it.

Undergraduate Fees and Bursaries

» Fees for UK/EU students 2014–15 £9,000
STEM Foundation year £4,000
» International student fees 2013–14 £11,055–£12,040
» Over 1,000 NSP awards with priority criteria: £2,000 fee waiver/accommodation discount and £1,000 cash in year 1.
» For any student with household income below £25K, progression bursary of £500 a year cash.
» Further academic, sports and care leaver's awards including six Vice Chancellor's Scholarships of £10,000 a year.

Students

Undergraduates:	**17,230**	**(3,200)**
Postgraduates:	**1,680**	**(2,345)**
Mature students:	**19.7%**	
Overseas students:	**10.2%**	
Applications per place:	**5.6**	
From state-sector schools:	**96.6%**	
From working-class homes:	**37.2%**	
Satisfaction with students' union	**59%**	

For detailed information about sports facilities:
www.ljmu.ac.uk/sport

Accommodation

Number of places and costs refer to 2013–14

University-provided places: 3,200 plus 15,000 through Liverpool Student Homes.

Percentage catered: 0%

Self-catered costs: £78–£123 a week.

All new students are guaranteed a place in university housing, even if applying through Clearing.

International students: as above

Contact: accommodation@ljmu.ac.uk

www.ljmu.ac.uk/accommodation

University of London

The federal university is by far Britain's biggest conventional higher education institution, with more than 120,000 students. The majority study at colleges in the capital, but such is the global prestige of the university's degrees that over 50,000 students in 180 different countries take University of London International Programmes.

The university, which celebrated its 175th anniversary in 2011, consists of 18 self-governing colleges, the Institute in Paris and the School of Advanced Study, which comprises ten specialist institutes for research and postgraduate education (details at **www.sas.ac.uk**). The members include some of the most famous names in UK higher education, although Imperial College left in 2007. The university's students have access to joint residential accommodation, sporting facilities and the University of London Union, but most identify with their college.

Other prestigious colleges have considered following Imperial in going their own way and applied for their own degree-awarding powers to hold in reserve, but they remain bound together by the London degree. Reforms to the university's governance have given the colleges more autonomy and look to have staved off further departures for now.

The following colleges – some of which have dropped the word from their title to underline their university status – have separate entries in this chapter. Each also appears in the main university league table, with the exception of Birkbeck, whose overwhelmingly part-time provision does not lend itself to a full comparison on the measures used in our *Guide*.

» Birkbeck College
» Goldsmiths, University of London
» King's College London
» London School of Economics and Political Science
» Queen Mary, University of London
» Royal Holloway
» SOAS London
» University College London

Many of London's teaching hospitals have now merged with colleges of the university:

» King's College London now incorporates Guys and St Thomas's (the United Medical and Dental Schools of Guys and St Thomas's).
» Queen Mary now incorporates St Bartholomew's and the Royal London School of Medicine and Dentistry.
» University College London now incorporates the Royal Free Hospital Medical School and the Eastman Dental Hospital.

The School of Slavonic and Eastern European Studies and the School of Pharmacy are both now part of University College London.

Senate House
Malet Street
London WC1E 7HU

020 7862 8000
enquiries@london.ac.uk
www.london.ac.uk
www.ulu.co.uk

Edinburgh
Belfast
Cardiff
LONDON

Enquiries: to individual colleges, institutes or schools.

Nine colleges (and the Institute in Paris) do not have separate entries in the *Guide*. These are listed below, with postal, telephone and electronic contacts.

Courtauld Institute of Art
Somerset House, Strand
London WC2R 0RN
020 7848 2645 (admissions)
ugadmissions@courtauld.ac.uk
www.courtauld.ac.uk
155 undergraduates. History of art degree.
Undergraduate fee £9,000.

Heythrop College
Kensington Square, London W8 5HN
020 7795 6600 (switchboard)
admissions@heythrop.ac.uk
www.heythrop.ac.uk
570 undergraduates. Degrees in theology and philosophy.
Undergraduate fees £9,000.

Institute of Education
20 Bedford Way, London WC1H 0AL
020 7612 6000 (switchboard)
info@ioe.ac.uk
www. ioe.ac.uk
Mainly postgraduate education courses;
485 undergraduates.
Undergraduate fees £7,200–£9,000.

London Business School
Regent's Park, London NW1 4SA
020 7000 7000 (switchboard)
webenquiries@london.edu
www.london.edu
Postgraduate MBA and other courses.

London School of Hygiene and Tropical Medicine
Keppel Street, London WC1E 7HT
020 7299 4646 (admission enquiries)
registry@lshtm.ac.uk
www.lshtm.ac.uk
Postgraduate medical courses.

Royal Academy of Music
Marylebone Road, London NW1 5HT
020 7873 7393 (registry)
registry@ram.ac.uk
www.ram.ac.uk
325 undergraduates. Degrees in music.
Undergraduate fees £9,000.

Royal Central School of Speech and Drama
Eton Avenue , London NW3 3HY
020 7722 8183 (undergraduate admissions)
enquiries@cssd.ac.uk
www.cssd.ac.uk
615 undergraduates. Acting and theatre practice.
Undergraduate fees £9,000.

Royal Veterinary College
Royal College Street, London NW1 0TU
020 7468 5147 (undergraduate admissions)
enquiries@rvc.ac.uk
www. rvc.ac.uk
1,575 undergraduates. Degrees in veterinary medicine.
Undergraduate fees £9,000 (veterinary nursing £7,500)

St George's, University of London
Cranmer Terrace, London SW17 0RE
020 8725 2333 (admissions)
contact via website
www.sgul.ac.uk
4,410 undergraduates. Degrees in medicine.
Undergraduate fees £9,000;
Foundation degree £7,500–£8,000.

University of London Institute in Paris
9–11 rue de Constantine
75340 Paris Cedex 07, France
(+33) 1 44 11 73 83
french@ulip.lon.ac.uk
www.ulip.lon.ac.uk
Degrees offered in conjunction with Queen Mary and Royal Holloway colleges.

London Metropolitan University

London Met has endured a tumultuous year in which its very survival was questioned when it lost the right to recruit international students. Its intake dropped dramatically as some transferred to other universities or returned home, but the university has now won back its recruitment licence and become more stable. The university was already planning to reduce the numbers of new students entering in 2012 by cutting the number of courses from more than 550 to fewer than 200. Professor Malcolm Gillies, the Vice-Chancellor, said drastic action was necessary to tackle well-publicised financial difficulties and prepare for the new fees regime. However, even he probably was not bargaining for 43 per cent fewer entrants than in 2011. London Met charged the lowest fees of any university in England when the new regime came in and will do so again in 2014, when the average will be £7,268 a year. There is a range of different fees from £4,680 for a Foundation year to £9,000 for a few degrees.

London Met has always catered particularly for groups who are under-represented at traditional universities. It considered making some parts of the university alcohol-free in deference to the large number of Muslim students. More than a third of the students are Afro-Caribbean, and the proportion of mature students is among the highest in England. More than 48 per cent of the UK students come from working-class homes, far above the average for the courses and entry qualifications.

The course changes were part of a "radical overhaul of undergraduate education", which includes a move to year-long modules consisting of 30 weeks of timetabled teaching. Over a year, students will typically study four modules worth 30 credits each and receive a minimum of 60 teaching hours per module. The university expects first-year students to have 12 hours of teaching a week, giving more opportunity for development and guidance. Student support services, from admission to careers advice, have been remodelled and there is a particular emphasis on academic and pastoral counselling on entry and at other key points of courses. But the projected dropout rate of almost 27 per cent, although a slight improvement on last year, is now the highest in England.

The university administration has promised a "renewed focus on student satisfaction and the quality of student learning" following a succession of low scores in the National Student Survey. There has been increased investment in the campus, with more study zones and a £13.5-million refurbishment programme.

166–220 Holloway Road
London N7 8DB

020 7133 4200 (enquiries)
contact via website
www.londonmet.ac.uk
www.londonmetsu.org.uk
Affiliation: million+

The Times and Sunday Times **Rankings**
Overall Ranking: **121** (=116)

Student satisfaction:	**121**	(72.4%)
Research quality:	**=78**	(3.3%)
Entry standards:	**120**	(229)
Student–staff ratio:	**=102**	(21.7)
Services & facilities/student:	**121**	(£369)
Expected completion rate:	**117**	(72.2%)
Good honours:	**114**	(51.5%)
Graduate prospects:	**118**	(45.6%)

Among the latest additions is a newsroom for journalism students, which opened in 2012. A refurbished library on the Holloway Road site has more computers, informal learning spaces, technobooths and teaching rooms, as well as a café. There is also a new headquarters for the students' union on the site. At the same time, the university has been working hard to reduce its carbon footprint. A 12 per cent reduction led to the award of the Carbon Trust Standard in 2011.

Earlier developments saw four "business-related" departments join together to form the London Metropolitan Business School which, with 10,000 students, is one of Europe's largest. The £30-million science centre, features a "superlab" with 280 workstations, specialist laboratories for tissue culture research and microbiology, and a nuclear-magnetic resonance room. The biomedical sciences degree leads on to an MD course from the University of Health Studies in Antigua. The six-year programme is based in London and graduates will complete the United States Medical Licensing Examination, enabling them to practise in America.

Since its establishment from the merger of London Guildhall and North London universities in 2002, the level of UK applications to London Met has been uneven, but overseas enrolment has remained healthy. Only three universities recruit more students from the EU, and around 20 per cent of all London Met's undergraduates are from outside the UK, making the dispute over its recruitment practices even more crucial. The university's sites are centred on the City of London and the capital's Holloway Road, where there is a graduate school designed by Daniel Libeskind. London Met entered more academics than most former polytechnics in the 2008 Research Assessment Exercise, when almost a quarter of its work was placed in the top two categories. About half of the 21 subject areas contained some world-leading research, with architecture, media studies, education and social studies producing the best results.

Residential accommodation is limited, but many of London Met's students live at home. There are nine fitness centres, as well as other sports facilities. The competitive teams are successful and the social scene is lively, particularly in north London.

Undergraduate Fees and Bursaries

» Fees for UK/EU students 2014–15   £4,680–£9,000
    Foundation year   £4,680
    Foundation degree   £5,700
» International student fees 2013–14   £9,000
» 1,290 NSP awards of £2,000 fee waiver, £1,000 cash year 1.
» Range of other scholarships and bursaries available.
» Check the university's website for the latest information.

Students

Undergraduates:	14,460	(3,245)
Postgraduates:	2,855	(2,720)
Mature students:	48.1%	
Overseas students:	18.2%	
Applications per place:	5.3	
From state-sector schools:	97.0%	
From working-class homes:	47.8%	
Satisfaction with students' union	52%	

For detailed information about sports facilities:
www.londonmet.ac.uk/services/sport-and-recreation/

Accommodation

Number of places and costs refer to 2013–14
University-provided places: Students have access to accommodation in a wide range of halls of residences provided by specialist student accommodation providers.
Percentage catered: 0%
Self-catered costs: approximately £129–£320 a week.
The university cannot guarantee a place in halls.
All students have access to halls spaces.
International students: as above.
Contact: accommodation@londonmet.ac.uk

London School of Economics and Political Science (LSE)

The LSE is abandoning the gesture of setting fees for new undergraduates at £500 below the maximum allowable in England in 2014. With more applications per place than any other university, joining the majority of universities on £9,000 is unlikely to affect the intense competition for admission. Even in 2012, when demand dropped slightly, there were 11 applicants for every place and there were even more in 2013. Always one of the big names of British higher education, the LSE has a global reputation: it is one of the top two social science institutions in the world, according to the QS global rankings. Areas of study range more broadly than the School's name suggests, however. The 250 undergraduate courses range as far as law, management, mathematics and environmental policy. Only Cambridge recorded higher average scores than the LSE in the last Research Assessment Exercise, which saw almost 70 per cent of the work submitted rated world-leading or internationally excellent. Ninety-five per cent of the economics submission, 80 per cent in social policy and 75 per cent in law reached the top two categories.

Craig Calhoun, the American sociologist who chaired the US Social Science Research Council for more than a decade, took over as Director in 2012 after a difficult year for the LSE which saw the resignation of his predecessor over the School's links to the Gaddafi regime in Libya. Professor Calhoun is an active communicator with the students, especially through a monthly twitter forum. The school has a long history of political involvement, from its foundation by Beatrice and Sidney Webb, pioneers of the Fabian movement, to the 31 alumni who are MPs and 35 current members of the House of Lords. The tradition lives on, not only among the academics, but in a students' union which claims to be the only one in Britain to hold weekly general meetings at which every student may attend and vote.

The LSE has added 1,000 places in recent years – many of them for postgraduates – having seized the opportunity to tackle a longstanding shortage of teaching space by acquiring former Government buildings near the school's Aldwych headquarters. A student centre opens in late 2013, the school's first new building for more than 40 years. It will house the careers and accommodation services, as well as a multi-faith prayer centre. The campus has a cosmopolitan feel that derives from the highest proportion of overseas students at any publicly funded university. Only the much larger Manchester University has more applications from overseas. More than

Houghton Street
London WC2A 2AE

020 7955 7125 (admissions)
ug.admissions@lse.ac.uk
  (admissions)
www.lse.ac.uk
www.lsesu.com
Affiliation: Russell Group

The Times and Sunday Times **Rankings**

Overall Ranking: **3** (3)

Student satisfaction:	=75	(80.9%)
Research quality:	3	(38.7%)
Entry standards:	4	(542)
Student–staff ratio:	=2	(11.1)
Services & facilities/student:	4	(£2,464)
Expected completion rate:	=5	(97%)
Good honours:	11	(81.3%)
Graduate prospects:	=18	(77.1%)

30 past or present heads of state have either been students at, or taught at, the university, as have 16 Nobel prizewinners in economics, literature and peace – including George Bernard Shaw, Bertrand Russell, Friedrich von Hayek and Amartya Sen. The latest of them is Professor Christopher Pissarides, who shared the prize for economics in 2010.

Its international character not only gives the LSE global prestige but also an unusual degree of financial independence. Only an eighth of its income will come from the Higher Education Funding Council for England in 2014, although the LSE has still been affected by cuts in Government funding. Just under a third of British students are from independent schools – one of the highest ratios in the country. Efforts are being made to attract a broader intake with Saturday classes and summer schools. The LSE is one of 12 universities selected to deliver the Sutton Trust's Pathways to Law programme, for example, giving state school students from non-privileged backgrounds the opportunity to sample a specialised legal programme before choosing a degree. The LSE's projected dropout rate of 3 per cent is among the lowest at any university.

Improvements have been made to the campus over a number of years. A £30-million Norman Foster-designed redevelopment of the Lionel Robbins Building houses a much-improved library. The move was a welcome one since the number of books borrowed by LSE students is more than four times the national average, according to one survey. Routes between most of the buildings have been pedestrianised, in keeping with a commitment to green issues that has seen the School in the top echelons of the People and Planet Green League of universities' environmental performance for five years in a row.

Partying is not the prime attraction of the LSE for most applicants, who tend to be serious about their subject, but London's top nightspots are on the doorstep for those who can afford them. The 3,740 residential places for 9,000 full-time students offer a good chance of avoiding central London's notoriously high private sector rents; there are spaces in hall for all first year students who want them.

Undergraduate Fees and Bursaries

» Fees for UK/EU students 2014–15   £9,000
» International student fees 2013–14   £15,768
» For UK/EU students, annual bursary of £4,000 for those with household income below £18K decreasing in 5 bands to £750 for household income £40–£42.6K.
» Additional 110 NSP awards for household income £7K or less, £2,000 support and £1,000 cash, year 1; £1,500 fee waiver, years 2 and 3.
» Scholarships and bursaries available.
» Check the university's website for the latest information.

Students

Undergraduates:	**3,935**	**(80)**
Postgraduates:	**5,245**	**(550)**
Mature students:	**10.9%**	
Overseas students:	**44.6%**	
Applications per place:	**11.5**	
From state-sector schools:	**69.1%**	
From working-class homes:	**18.8%**	
Satisfaction with students' union	**56%**	

For detailed information about sports facilities:
www.lsesu.com/activities/ausports/

Accommodation

Number of places and costs refer to 2013–14
University-provided places: 3,740
Percentage catered: about 38%
Catered costs: from £98–£205 a week.
Self-catered costs: £89–£350 a week.
First-year undergraduates are guaranteed an offer of accommodation.
Policy for international students: same as above.
Contact: accommodation@lse.ac.uk
to apply online: www.lse.ac.uk/accommodation

London South Bank University (LSBU)

London South Bank (LSBU) came closer than most universities to withstanding the shock of higher fees, suffering only a small decline in enrolments in 2012. Its performance was all the more impressive since about half of the first-degree entrants are 21 or over, the group that has seen the biggest drop in applications nationally. Students are attracted by a carefully tailored programme of vocational courses that regularly produce the best-paid graduates of any post-1992 university. Fees for full-time degrees were pegged at £8,450 in the first two years of the new funding regime, but will rise to £9,000 in 2014. The university's Foundation degrees are taught at a number of partner colleges around London, where the fees will be £5,950, and its degrees are also taught at a network of overseas colleges that stretches from China to the Caribbean.

Three-quarters of the students are from the capital and more than half are drawn from ethnic minorities. Of about 18,000 undergraduates, 43 per cent study part-time and many are on sandwich courses. Fewer than half enter with traditional academic qualifications. The diversity of the intake is encouraged by initiatives such as the summer school for local people to upgrade their qualifications. The courses, some catering for mature students and others for younger students, start at the end of June and are limited to 15 hours a week so as not to affect students' benefit entitlement. South Bank has always given a high priority to widening participation in higher education. It won a London Education award for its work with non-traditional learners who have no family history or aspirations to apply to university. Diploma and degree courses run in parallel so that students can move up or down if they are better suited to another level of study. However, the official dropout rate has frequently been among the highest in the country – well above the average for LSBU's courses and entry qualifications – and the university has struggled in the National Student Survey. LSBU is targeting much of its fee income on measures to ensure that more students complete their courses in the expected time.

The university has invested over £50 million in modern teaching facilities in recent years, and developments costing another £38 million are planned. A new student centre opened in 2012, bringing the students' union and many support services together to make them more convenient and accessible. An Enterprise Centre will showcase the achievements of students and staff and provide start-up units for students who have created their own businesses. LBSU is one of the top universities for

---

103 Borough Road
London SE1 0AA

0800 923 8888 (course enquiries)
course.enquiry@lsbu.ac.uk
www.lsbu.ac.uk
www.londonsouthbanksu.
   com
Affiliation: none

The Times and Sunday Times **Rankings**
Overall Ranking: **118** (111)

Student satisfaction:	=111	(76.6%)
Research quality:	=88	(2.7%)
Entry standards:	115	(242)
Student–staff ratio:	114	(23.7)
Services & facilities/student:	103	(£1,110)
Expected completion rate:	112	(76.1%)
Good honours:	109	(53.5%)
Graduate prospects:	93	(56%)

"knowledge transfer partnerships" with firms and other outside organisations, its projects spanning construction, manufacturing, energy and environment, food, information technology, health and the creative industries.

Specialist facilities such as the Centre for Explosion and Fire Research carry the vocational theme through into research. Although the university entered only 87 academics for the 2008 Research Assessment Exercise, their average grades were among the best of the new universities. More than 40 per cent of the submission was rated as world-leading or internationally excellent, with social policy, engineering and communication, culture and media studies leading the way.

The main campus is in Southwark, near the Elephant and Castle, and not far from the South Bank arts complex. It includes the Centre for Efficient and Renewable Energy in Buildings, a unique teaching, research and demonstration resource for low carbon technologies, and the UK's first inner city green technology research centre. Some health students are based on the other side of London, in hospitals in Romford and Leytonstone, where there is a smaller satellite campus in Havering to supplement that in Southwark. The university now trains 40 per cent of London's nurses. It is ranked first for occupational therapy, second for mental

health nursing, adult nursing, diagnostic radiography, and therapeutic radiography in NHS London's quality assessments. Psychology degrees were revamped for 2012–13, making the university one of the first to adopt industry recommendations for an integrated curriculum that provides a deeper knowledge of the subject.

A new hall of residence means that the university now has residential places within ten minutes' walk of the main campus, but first year students cannot yet be guaranteed housing. Some of the capital's biggest attractions are on the doorstep of the main campus for those who can afford them. Sports facilities include a 40-station fitness suite, a free weights room, exercise classes and a sports injury clinic. The university provides a comprehensive sports scholarship scheme, and has the top men's and women's university basketball teams in London.

Undergraduate Fees and Bursaries

» Fees for UK/EU students 2014–15 £9,000
  Foundation degree £5,950
» International student fees 2013–14 £10,500
» Over 500 NSP awards with priority criteria: £1,000 cash and £2,000 university services, year 1; £2,000 in university services after progression to year 2.
» Progression bursary of £500 for those successful at July 2015 examination boards.
» Students with at least ABB at A level or equivalent: £3,000 a year (£1,000 cash, £2,000 university services).
» Sports and other scholarships and care leaver's bursaries.

Students

Undergraduates:	11,535	(6,740)
Postgraduates:	1,655	(3,420)
Mature students:	49.7%	
Overseas students:	6.5%	
Applications per place:	5.9	
From state-sector schools:	97.9%	
From working-class homes:	42.4%	
Satisfaction with students' union	54%	

For detailed information about sports facilities:
www.lsbu.ac.uk/sports

Accommodation

Number of places and costs refer to 2013–14
University-provided places: 1,400
Percentage catered: 0%
Self-catered costs: £109–£112 (standard) – £134 (en suite) a week.
First-year UK students are not guaranteed accommodation, but high priority is given to those who live outside the Greater London area.
International students: first years are guaranteed accommodation if conditions are met.
Contact: accommodation@lsbu.ac.uk

Loughborough University

Loughborough has become a regular fixture in or around our top 20 and suffered only a small decline in enrolments when the fees went up to £9,000 in 2012. The university remains best known for its successes on the sports field, but has enhanced its academic reputation in recent years, particularly in its other core areas of art, design and engineering. Loughborough was chosen as the official preparation camp headquarters for Team GB prior to the London 2012 Olympics. There were 90 athletes with Loughborough connections competing at the Olympic and Paralympic Games, winning a total of 13 medals. Lord Sebastian Coe, who chaired the organising committee for the Games and is himself a double gold medallist, is a Loughborough alumnus and now a Pro Chancellor of the university. In 2012 Loughborough was asked to host a £10-million National Sport and Exercise Medicine Centre of Excellence, one of three in the UK.

The university consistently registers among the best scores in the National Student Survey and also improved its performance in the 2008 Research Assessment Exercise. Although the results were patchy, more than half of the research in art and design was considered world-leading, and there were particularly good results in architecture and sport. The Office for Standards in Education also rates Loughborough in its top category for teacher training in physical education, design and science. Loughborough remains a major centre of engineering, with more than 2,800 students in a £20-million integrated engineering complex. The university hosts the £1-billion national Energy Technologies Institute, as part of a consortium with Birmingham and Nottingham universities, concentrating on low-carbon energy. Civil, aeronautical and automotive engineering are particularly strong. Loughborough is also taking the lead in a £5-million project to boost research, training and industry partnerships in the solar energy sector. The new SUPERSOLAR hub will see the creation of the UK's first standards lab for solar energy devices which will link research carried out in universities and industry.

The original 216-acre campus has benefited from a sustained development programme which included a large student union extension and a new business school, as well as the gradual refurbishment of residential accommodation. The first phase of a £68-million on-campus accommodation development has more than 5,000 rooms, with another 1,300 bedrooms to come in four new halls. Arts facilities are improving with the upgrading of the Cope Auditorium to serve the campus and local community. An £8-million building for Health, Exercise and Biosciences opened in 2010 and a new Design Centre, the first project in a wider masterplan for the East

Ashby Road
Loughborough
Leicestershire LE11 3TU

01509 223522 (admissions)
admissions@lboro.ac.uk
www.lboro.ac.uk
www.lufbra.net
Affiliation: 1994 Group

The Times and Sunday Times **Rankings**
Overall Ranking: **21** (16)

Student satisfaction:	=29	(83.6%)
Research quality:	=18	(24.7%)
Entry standards:	33	(411)
Student–staff ratio:	44	(16.9)
Services & facilities/student:	29	(£1,818)
Expected completion rate:	=19	(93.4%)
Good honours:	34	(73.3%)
Graduate prospects:	23	(75.4%)

Park area of the campus, opened its doors in October 2011.

The purchase of the adjacent Holywell Park site increased the size of the campus by 75 per cent. This will become the focus for research and collaboration with industry, including a £59-million BAE-sponsored Systems Engineering Innovation Centre. The university prides itself on a close relationship with industry, which accounts for its record haul of six Queen's Anniversary Prizes. In 2012 Loughborough was awarded over £2 million by the Engineering and Physical Sciences Research Council to enable companies to engage with the university's research projects at an early stage and benefit from the breakthroughs and knowledge they generate.

Most subjects are available either as three-year full-time or longer sandwich degrees, which include a year in industry. This has helped to give graduates an outstanding employment record, as well a dropout rate of only 6 per cent, which is particularly low for the subjects Loughborough offers. The university is a leader in the use of computer-assisted assessment, offering students the chance to gauge their own progress online. However, Loughborough misses all its access benchmarks: fewer than a quarter of the undergraduates are from working-class homes and just under 6 per cent are from areas of low participation in higher education. The university has promised up to £7 million in scholarships and bursaries worth £3,000 a year in accommodation discounts and other support to students from disadvantaged backgrounds.

The programme of sports scholarships is the largest in the university system. The campus boasts a 50-metre swimming pool, national academies for cricket and tennis, a gymnastics centre and a high-performance training centre for athletics. The university also boasts the UK's only centre for disability sport and has spent £15 million on its Sports Technology Institute. SportPark, a bespoke hub for some of the country's leading sports bodies, allows a variety of organisations to share best practice and innovation.

Social activity is concentrated on the students' union. The relatively small town of Loughborough, a mile away, is never going to be a clubber's paradise, but both Leicester and Nottingham are within easy reach.

Undergraduate Fees and Bursaries

» Fees for UK/EU students 2014–15 £9,000
» International student fees 2013–14 £13,250–£16,750
» For UK (excluding Welsh) students, household income below £18K, £3,000 package, years 1–3, £2,000 bursary and £5,000 fee waiver, year 4 Integrated Masters; £18K–£22K, £2,000 package, years 1–3; £2,000 bursary and £4,000 fee waiver year 4; £22K–£25K, £1,000 bursary, years 1–3; £1,000 bursary and £3,000 fee waiver, year 4; £25K–£32K, £500 bursary; enhanced terms for mature students.
» Scholarships of £9,000 over 3 years for those with at least ABB from low HE participation areas.

Students

Undergraduates:	**11,320**	**(385)**
Postgraduates:	**2,465**	**(1,850)**
Mature students:	**4.2%**	
Overseas students:	**10.9%**	
Applications per place:	**6.2**	
From state-sector schools:	**81.4%**	
From working-class homes:	**22.0%**	
Satisfaction with students' union	**88%**	

For detailed information about sports facilities:
http://loughboroughsport.com

Accommodation

Number of places and costs refer to 2013–14
University-provided places: 5,269
Percentage catered: 46%
Catered costs: £4,702.70 – £6,234.50 (39-week contract).
Self-catered costs: £3,131.70 – £5,670.60 (39-week contract).
Undergraduate first-year first-choice students are guaranteed accommodation if they apply prior to 1 August.
International students: guaranteed housing for two years.
Contact: SAC@lboro.ac.uk
http://accommodation.lboro.ac.uk

University of Manchester

Manchester has moved back into the top 30 in our league table and its international ranking is almost as high. With global league tables focusing mainly on research and the domestic variety designed with undergraduates in mind, the contrast suggests that research rather than teaching is Manchester's strength. But the university has made concerted efforts to improve the student experience and has seen the results in improved satisfaction ratings. Its aim is to be among the top 25 research universities in the world by 2020, but outstanding teaching is one of the three goals within that strategy. The university has set aside £20 million to attract top academics. The new recruits will join three Nobel prizewinners on the staff. Professors Andre Geim and Professor Konstantin Novoselov brought the all-time complement of laureates to 25 when they took the physics prize in 2010. Sir John Sulston, who chairs the Institute of Science, Ethics and Innovation, won the prize for physiology and medicine in 2002.

The merger with the neighbouring University of Manchester Institute of Science and Technology (UMIST) in 2004 created the biggest conventional university in the UK outside the federal University of London. A £400-million building and refurbishment programme, the largest ever in UK higher education has been completed and another £250 million of investment is planned by 2015. The £24-million "Learning Commons" building opened in 2012, the first phase providing more than 1,000 flexible learning spaces, high quality IT facilities, and a campus hub for student-centred activities and learning support services. The latest addition to its estate was close to the university's iconic Jodrell Bank telescope, in Cheshire, where Manchester will host the control centre for what will be the world's largest radio telescope. Manchester was among the top ten universities in the 2008 Research Assessment Exercise, with almost two-thirds of its submission considered world-leading or internationally excellent. There were particularly strong performances in cancer studies, nursing, biology, dentistry, engineering, sociology, development studies, Spanish, and music and drama.

Manchester attracted more applications than any university in the UK in 2012, despite experiencing a decline of almost 10 per cent as the fees went up. The university has been trying to broaden its intake, with a particular focus on increasing recruitment from the city and its surrounding area. But it is yet to reach the national average for its courses and entry qualifications for the recruitment of state-educated students or those from working-class homes. Manchester spends more on

---

Oxford Road
Manchester M13 9PL

0161 275 2077 (admissions)
ug-admissions@manchester.ac.uk
www.manchester.ac.uk
http://manchesterstudents
 union.com
Affiliation: Russell Group

Edinburgh
Belfast
MANCHESTER
London
Cardiff

The Times and Sunday Times Rankings

Overall Ranking: **26** (33)

Student satisfaction:	=70	(81.1%)
Research quality:	11	(28.7%)
Entry standards:	=16	(457)
Student–staff ratio:	=23	(14.8)
Services & facilities/student:	42	(£1,671)
Expected completion rate:	=19	(93.4%)
Good honours:	=37	(72%)
Graduate prospects:	32	(71.9%)

bursaries and fee waivers for students from poor families than any other member of the Russell Group of leading research-intensive universities – over £5 million a year.

UMIST's legacy was a strong reputation among academics and employers alike in its specialist areas of engineering, science and management. Surveys of employers frequently place Manchester among their favourite recruiting grounds, helping to produce an unrivalled network of industrial sponsorship. Employers have also rated Manchester's careers service the best at any university. The merger produced the largest engineering school in the UK, with a £20-million budget and 1,200 students. The first phase of a new chemical engineering facility, with a sophisticated industrial pilot plant, as well as teaching laboratories, opened in 2011.

A £39-million research centre dedicated to biomedical science opened in 2009, housing one of the largest complexes of its kind in Europe. A £60-million development will create a new hotel, conference venue, and executive education centre for Manchester Business School in the strategically important Oxford Road Corridor. The business school is among the strengths of the merged institution, as is the medical school, which was rewarded for impressive teaching ratings with extra places. A new teaching block helps to cater for 2,000 undergraduates following a problem-based curriculum. Google is helping to fund new research that could help blind people to find their way around the worldwide web.

The city's famed youth culture and the university's position at the heart of a huge student precinct help to ensure keen competition for places – and hence high entry standards – in most subjects. First-rate sports facilities have improved further since the city hosted the Commonwealth Games. Students get discount rates at the on-campus aquatics centre opened for the Games, for example. The university sports teams are also high achievers, ranking highly in the BUCS league. The city's reputation for violent crime has subsided, but the students' union runs late-night minibuses, self-defence classes, and regular safety campaigns.

Undergraduate Fees and Bursaries

» Fees for UK/EU students 2014–15 £9,000
» International student fees 2013–14 £13,000–£17,000
  Medicine £16,500–£30,000
» Household income below £25K, £1,000 cash, £2,000 fee waiver or accommodation discount, year 1; £3,000 cash or fee waiver (or mix of both) other years; £25K–£42.6K, £2,000 each year.
» Foundation year bursaries up to £5,000 package.
» Fee discounts and bursaries for year abroad or work sandwich.
» Other scholarships and bursaries available.
» Check the university's website for the latest information.

Students

Undergraduates:	**27,150**	**(1,005)**
Postgraduates:	**8,335**	**(4,190)**
Mature students:	**10.8%**	
Overseas students:	**21.1%**	
Applications per place:	**6.7**	
From state-sector schools:	**77.0%**	
From working-class homes:	**20.4%**	
Satisfaction with students' union	**71%**	

For detailed information about sports facilities:
www.sport.manchester.ac.uk

Accommodation

Number of places and costs refer to 2013–14
University-owned/managed places: 8,123
Percentage catered: approx 23%
Catered costs: £3,500–£6,681 (40 weeks).
Self-catered costs: £3,972–£5,985 (40 weeks).
First years are guaranteed housing provided conditions are met.
International non-EU students are guaranteed accommodation for the duration of their stay if conditions met.
Contact: accommodation@manchester.ac.uk
www.manchester.ac.uk/accommodation

Manchester Metropolitan University

Only three universities received more applications than Manchester Metropolitan (MMU) when the fees went up in 2012, but the total was still 16 per cent down on the previous year and the first-year intake dropped by more than 1,400. More than a sixth of the students are 21 or over on entry, the group most affected by the new fees regime. MMU had set lower fees than most of its competitors for the majority of degrees and froze its charges in 2013, but has opted for £9,000 for all subjects in 2014. In return, it will spend 27 per cent of the income from fees on access measures, including more than £11 million on bursaries for students from low-income families. There is a longstanding commitment to extending access to higher education: more than a third of the undergraduates come from working-class homes, many from areas of low participation in higher education. The projected dropout rate had improved in the latest survey but, at more than 20 per cent, remains significantly worse than average for the subjects and entry qualifications.

With some 36,000 students including part-timers, MMU is one of the largest universities in Britain. More than 1,000 courses are offered in over 70 subjects. But the giant institution boasts quality as well as quantity: academics are encouraged to take a three-year MA in teaching and more than a third of the work entered for the 2008 Research Assessment Exercise was rated as world-leading or internationally excellent. Education, English, and art and design produced the best results. The Poet Laureate, Professor Carol Ann Duffy, is Creative Director of the Writing School in the English department. The university is also proud of its record on green issues, finishing top of the People and Planet Green League of environmental performance in 2013.

The university has more professionally accredited courses than any other university and many courses involve work placements. Education courses have fared well in the Teaching Agency's performance indicators, especially for primary training. The university trains more teachers than any other and has launched a Centre for Urban Education to develop its expertise further. Some 800 trainees and other students taking contemporary arts and sports science are based at Crewe, 40 miles south of Manchester and now rebranded as MMU Cheshire. A former college campus at Alsager has been merged with the Crewe campus in an area now known as the University Quadrant. Some arts subjects moved there with the opening of a £6-million drama, music and dance centre,

---

All Saints Building
All Saints
Manchester M15 6BH

0161 247 2000 (general enquiries)
contact via website
www.mmu.ac.uk
www.mmunion.co.uk
Affiliation: University
   Alliance

The Times and Sunday Times **Rankings**
Overall Ranking: **89** (102)

Student satisfaction:	92	(79.3%)
Research quality:	=70	(4.3%)
Entry standards:	55	(333)
Student–staff ratio:	=68	(19.2)
Services & facilities/student:	106	(£1,083)
Expected completion rate:	92	(81%)
Good honours:	71	(61.8%)
Graduate prospects:	=87	(57.8%)

and there is a £30-million student village. The £10-million Sport Science Centre opened in 2010 and the Business School followed in 2012. Exercise and sport science students were the final group to make the six-mile move to Crewe, and now only sports facilities remain at Alsager.

The five sites in Manchester will soon be reduced to two linked campuses as part of a £350-million development programme. MMU will move out of Didsbury in the southern suburbs and create a £120-million "Campus for the Professions" in the city centre by September 2014. The Birley Fields campus will be one of the most environmentally sustainable in the UK, uniting the remaining provision for teachers with that for nurses, health and youth workers. The new site is close to the existing All Saints campus, on the university's border with Hulme and Moss Side. New science and engineering buildings at All Saints cost £42 million, while an impressive new £75-million business school headquarters next to the Mancunian Way opened in 2012. A new School of Art opened in 2013. Overseas links have expanded rapidly in recent years, with MMU offering exchange opportunities in Europe and further afield, as well as establishing teaching bases abroad. However, more than half of the students come from the Manchester area, easing the pressure on accommodation in a city of nearly 70,000 students. The university

plays an important role in the region's economy, not least because 70 per cent of graduates stay and work in the North West. MMU is currently employing 25 of its own graduates on paid internships for up to 12 months.

All first years who request accommodation can be housed, with priority for university-owned halls going to the disabled and those who live furthest from Manchester. The university's sports facilities are good and the city's attractions do no harm to recruitment levels, but much depends on where the course is based; students at Crewe can feel isolated. Some potential applicants are daunted by the sheer size of the university, but individual courses and sites usually provide a social circle.

Undergraduate Fees and Bursaries

» Fees for UK/EU students 2014–15 £9,000
Foundation year £3,500
» International student fees 2013–14 £10,000–£16,500
» For all students with household income below £25K, £3,000 support package, year 1; £1,000, year 2; £500, year 3.
» Other scholarships and bursaries available.
» Check the university's website for the latest information.

Students

Undergraduates:	25,275	(2,730)
Postgraduates:	2,525	(3,900)
Mature students:	16.7%	
Overseas students:	6.6%	
Applications per place:	6.5	
From state-sector schools:	95.0%	
From working-class homes:	34.4%	
Satisfaction with students' union	60%	

For detailed information about sports facilities: www.mmu.ac.uk/sport

Accommodation

Number of places and costs refer to 2013–14
University provided places: 3,530
Percentage catered: 3.9%
Catered costs: £106 a week.
Self-catered costs: Manchester £86–£118; Cheshire £70–£80 a week.
All new full-time students will be housed if applications are received by 15 August and requirements are met.
International students: as above.
Contact: www.mmu.ac.uk/accommodation/

Middlesex University

Middlesex has been spreading its wings well beyond its north London home base. Having opened campuses in Mauritius and Dubai, it is adding one in Malta in September 2013 after six years of offering business and computing degrees through one of the island's colleges. Middlesex will become the first overseas university on the island, where it expects to attract students from North Africa and the Middle East, as well as from Malta itself. More than 10,000 students are already taking the university's degrees outside the UK, while almost a fifth of the undergraduates studying in London also come from other countries. They include more than 1,000 from other parts of the EU, the legacy of a longstanding commitment to Europe.

With 40,000 students worldwide, Middlesex is one of the UK's largest universities. By September 2013, it will have spent more than £200 million concentrating most of its activities on the much-improved main campus in Hendon, while also developing space nearby and at the new Saracens rugby stadium at Allianz Park. The initial phases of development at Hendon saw the construction of a new library and the roofing over of the main quadrangle to provide social space. This was followed by a new building for science subjects and the opening of the Forum for student services and leisure facilities. The latest major addition, in 2011, was a new art, design and media building for 1,600 students described by the Greater London Authority as "world class design". The campus, which boasts one of the country's few Real Tennis courts, also houses the business school.

The developments have enabled the university to sell off most of the seven sites that used to straggle around the northern fringes of the capital. The last of them, once the university's headquarters in a stylish mansion at Trent Park, closed in 2012. Only the health students and nurses are based outside Hendon, in four London teaching hospitals and on a campus at Archway which is shared with the University College and Royal Free Hospital medical schools. There is also a joint degree in veterinary nursing run with the Royal Veterinary College.

In the first year of the new fees regime, Middlesex was said by the Office for Fair Access to have the second-highest average charges in England after allowing for all forms of student support. Prospective students seem not to have been deterred, however, as both applications and enrolments held up better than at most universities. This followed two big increases in applications in successive years, buoyed by changes in nursing and art and design. The university's growing

---

The Burroughs
London NW4 4BT

020 8411 5555 (enquiries)
contact via website
www.mdx.ac.uk
www.mdxsu.com
Affiliation: million+

The Times and Sunday Times Rankings
Overall Ranking: **94** (90)

Student satisfaction:	=86	(79.7%)
Research quality:	=63	(5.0%)
Entry standards:	112	(250)
Student–staff ratio:	110	(23)
Services & facilities/student:	6	(£2,333)
Expected completion rate:	110	(76.9%)
Good honours:	105	(55.3%)
Graduate prospects:	=109	(52.8%)

popularity coincided with a programme of reorganisation that introduced a new pattern of courses and more international recruitment. Middlesex also rationalised its schools to focus on its strengths in business, computing and the arts, registering particular successes with work-based courses, which drew praise from quality assessors. The university reports higher spending on student facilities than any institution outside the top five in the table and £1,000 per student higher than most of its peers.

The £9,000 fees will remain in 2014, but the university is devoting more of the income to bursaries and other measures intended to widen participation in higher education. About a third of the undergraduates are 21 or over on entry and half of the full-timers come from London. Almost all of the British students are from state schools, nearly 48 per cent of them from working-class homes. The projected dropout rate has improved considerably since last year's survey and, at 17 per cent, is now in line with the national average for the university's subjects and entry qualifications. The highly flexible course system allows students to start some courses in January if they prefer not to wait until autumn, and offers the option of an extra five-week session in the summer to try out new subjects or add to their credits. The introduction of year-long modules had

the benefit of instilling a deeper level of learning, allowing students to get to grips with a subject before assessment. Nine out of ten students take vocational courses. Media students, for example, benefit from a Skillset Academy. The business school is the biggest subject area, but almost half of the undergraduates are on multidisciplinary programmes.

There are nearly 1,000 residential places, with more to come in the next few years. Priority in their allocation is given to international students and other first years who live outside London. Sports facilities have been improving and now include a "fitness pod" at Hendon with a gym and multipurpose outdoor courts. The West End and London's other attractions are only a tube ride away.

Undergraduate Fees and Bursaries

» Fees for UK/EU students 2014–15 £9,000
» International student fees 2013–14 £10,400
» 641 NSP awards of £2,000 fee waiver and £1,000 cash for all years.
» Academic, sports and other scholarships available..
» Check the university's website for the latest information.

Students

Undergraduates:	**15,405**	**(2,960)**
Postgraduates:	**2,380**	**(2,795)**
Mature students:	**29.8%**	
Overseas students:	**19.9%**	
Applications per place:	**7.3**	
From state-sector schools:	**97.8%**	
From working-class homes:	**47.9%**	
Satisfaction with students' union	**63%**	

For detailed information about sports facilities:
www.mdx.ac.uk/sport

Accommodation

Number of places and costs refer to 2013–14
University-provided places: 940
Percentage catered: 0%
Self-catered costs: £115–£133 a week (40 weeks).
Full-year students have priority; residential restrictions apply.
International students are guaranteed a room provided they apply by the deadline.
Contact: accomm@mdx.ac.uk;
www.mdx.ac.uk/accommodation

Newcastle University

For four years in a row, Newcastle was named as the best university city in the UK and sixth-formers responded with increased applications. Even with the introduction of £9,000 fees in 2012, the numbers starting degree courses went up, albeit from a smaller pool of applicants. Now the university is aiming to raise its profile as a "world-class civic university" combining local engagement with growing international activity. The university is the senior partner in the futuristic Centre for Life, for example, a science village which has transformed a run-down area of the city centre. The latest overseas venture saw the opening of a new campus in Johor, Malaysia, for medicine and biomedical sciences. A second branch campus in Singapore offers degrees in engineering and naval architecture.

On its home campus, the university is spending £10 million a year upgrading its teaching and research facilities. The glass-fronted King's Gate building created a new "front door" to the university, as well as housing all the main student services and a visitor centre. New buildings have opened for music and medical sciences, and nearly 100 study bedrooms have been added. Science and engineering laboratories have been upgraded, disabled access improved and the students' union refurbished at a cost of £8 million. A new teaching and accommodation complex for international students opened in 2012 and the library facilities have been reorganised and extended. New learning and research space has been provided in the main Robinson Library and an off-campus "Research Reserve" opened with thousands of metres of additional shelving. The library provides extra help with academic writing styles and maths, and there is a separate centre offering free tuition in 50 languages.

Newcastle is popular with students from independent schools, who take more than 30 per cent of the places, but the university was among the first in the UK that made positive efforts to attract students from a broader range of backgrounds. As well as offering the normal range of bursaries, it leads the Realising Opportunities Scheme, which brings together a number of leading universities to promote fair access to higher education and social mobility. The scheme helps to raise aspirations and attainment among teenagers from socially and economically disadvantaged backgrounds, encouraging more than 1,500 of them to go to research-intensive universities in its first three years. The dropout rate, at only 4.4 per cent, is one of the lowest in the country.

The university's origins can be traced back to a school of medicine and surgery established in Newcastle in 1834, which later became part of Durham University before going its own way again in 1937. Its excellence

King's Gate
Newcastle upon Tyne
NE1 7RU

0191 208 3333 (enquiries)
contact via website
www.ncl.ac.uk
www.nusu.co.uk
Affiliation: Russell Group

The Times and Sunday Times **Rankings**
Overall Ranking: **=18** (23)

Student satisfaction:	=15	(84.6%)
Research quality:	=30	(21.7%)
Entry standards:	=23	(438)
Student–staff ratio:	26	(15.3)
Services & facilities/student:	37	(£1,724)
Expected completion rate:	15	(94.9%)
Good honours:	18	(78.3%)
Graduate prospects:	12	(79%)

in that area was confirmed by its selection as a national centre to disseminate best teaching practice in medicine. The Medical School now has a new partnership with Durham, with about a third of trainees spending their first two years at Durham's Stockton campus. Cancer research was the star performer in the latest Research Assessment Exercise, with 90 per cent of work considered world-leading or internationally excellent. Newcastle entered fewer academics than most Russell Group universities, but almost 60 per cent of its work reached the top two categories, with art and design, music, English, town planning and civil engineering all producing excellent results.

Recent additions to the portfolio of degrees have included food marketing and mechanical engineering with microsystems. Newcastle already had a number of unusual features for a traditional university, such as a fine art degree with intense competition for places. It also has a longstanding reputation for agriculture, which benefits from two farms in Northumberland. The award-winning NCL+ initiative encourages all students to develop employability skills through activities such as working as a student ambassador or writing for the university newspaper. On most courses, a career development module gives credit for work experience, volunteering or part-time employment.

The university has done better than most of its fellow members of the Russell Group in the National Student Survey and has also shown high levels of satisfaction among its overseas students in i-graduate's International Student Barometer. The campus occupies 50 acres close to the main shopping area, civic centre and Newcastle United's ground. The campus also hosts an expanded and refurbished independent theatre. Tyneside has plenty more culture to offer in the riverside Sage Gateshead music centre and the BALTIC Centre for Contemporary Art. The cost of living is reasonable and town–gown relations better than in many cities. Sport is a particular strength: a new £5.5-million sports centre supplements two older venues, which have been extensively refurbished. The main outdoor pitches are two miles away. Over £30,000 is awarded annually in sports bursaries for elite athletes.

Undergraduate Fees and Bursaries

» Fees for UK/EU students 2014–15   £9,000
» International student fees 2013–14   £11,500–£14,750
    Medicine and dentistry   £14,750–£27,305
» Household income below £25K, £2,000 fee waiver or accommodation discount, £1,000 cash year 1; £500 fee waiver and £1,500 cash, subsequent years; household income £25K–£35K £1,000 cash a year.
» Access scholarships, with conditions, of £500 cash a year.
» 20 Promise Scholarships of £4,500 fee waiver, £4,500 cash each year for students from deprived background.
» Check the university's website for the latest information.

Students		
Undergraduates:	**14,975**	**(65)**
Postgraduates:	**4,430**	**(1,580)**
Mature students:	**8.0%**	
Overseas students:	**16.7%**	
Applications per place:	**6.0**	
From state-sector schools:	**69.2%**	
From working-class homes:	**19.5%**	
Satisfaction with students' union	**78%**	

For detailed information about sports facilities: www.ncl.ac.uk/sport

Accommodation

Number of places and costs refer to 2013–14
University-provided places: 3,724
Percentage catered: 23%
Catered costs: £122.99 a week.
Self-catered costs: £75.88–£136.00 a week.
All single undergraduates are guaranteed a room in university-managed accommodation provided requirements are met. Local restrictions apply.
International students: as above.
Contact: web enquiry form at www.ncl.ac.uk/enquiries

Newman University

The new university, one of two Catholic foundations among the latest crop of institutions to be upgraded, takes its name from John Henry Newman, the author of *The Idea of the University* and a Catholic cardinal in the 19th century. His vision of a community of scholars guides the university, which was established in 1968 as a teacher training college, but now has a wider portfolio of degrees, mainly in the social sciences and humanities. Among the 18 subject areas are criminology, counselling, information technology and theology. The university's Catholic affiliation is stressed in its literature, but so is its commitment to be inclusive in its recruitment and subsequent activities. It says it is proud to welcome staff and students of all religions and backgrounds, adding that, "In line with Newman's view of a university we focus on a formative education, developing the whole student into independent thinkers who have the ability to question, evaluate and develop creative solutions to problems rather than just retain knowledge about their subject."

Based in Bartley Green, eight miles southwest of Birmingham city centre, the campus is in a quiet residential area with views over the Bartley Reservoir and the Worcestershire countryside beyond. The modern buildings are arranged around a series of inner quadrangles of lawns and trees. A £20-million development programme is now complete and includes an impressive new library and entrance building. The project has also added more lecture theatres, a research centre and a state-of-the-art sport performance suite. Community sports facilities have also been refurbished. Newman received one of eight national awards to bring about change in the strategic approach to technology in learning and teaching. The university's successful bid involves students producing their own online learning resources while learning about their subject, and in doing so also improving their digital literacy, as well as their graduate employment prospects. The project starts in September 2013 and is part of a larger initiative called "Newman in the Digital Age", which aims to improve students' digital literacy.

All full-time degrees include work placements, with students working with a wide range of employers including Aston Villa Football Club, Capital FM and Warwick Castle. There are also opportunities to gain work experience abroad and undergraduates can opt to study at a partner university in Europe or further afield to broaden their horizons and boost their CVs. The degree options include sustainability and ethics in business, early childhood education and care, sports coaching science and combined honours

---

Genners Lane
Bartley Green
Birmingham B32 3NT

0121 476 1181 (admissions)
admissions@newman.ac.uk
www.newman.ac.uk
www.newmansu.org
Affiliation: GuildHE,
 Cathedrals Group

The Times and Sunday Times **Rankings**
Overall Ranking: **=73** (n/a)

Student satisfaction:	**=12**	(85.4%)
Research quality:	**=115**	(0.3%)
Entry standards:	**=82**	(307)
Student–staff ratio:	**=59**	(18.4)
Services & facilities/student:	**90**	(£1,235)
Expected completion rate:	**108**	(78.3%)
Good honours:	**99**	(56.8%)
Graduate prospects:	**=79**	(60%)

in maths or chemistry in association with Aston University. There is also a range of part-time courses and Foundation degrees, some of which are taught at a local further education college. Many of the courses are recognised by professional bodies such as the Chartered Management Institute and British Psychological Society.

Newman has done well over a number of years in the National Student Survey. Three-quarters of the 2,800 undergraduates are female, almost all of them state-educated. More than 40 per cent come from working-class homes – only two universities in England have a higher proportion – while 20 per cent come from an area of low participation in higher education, also in the top three in the country. Applications dropped by almost 1,000 and there was a 19 per cent fall in the numbers enrolling when fees of £8,400 were introduced in 2012, before the award of university status was announced. Having increased the fees for degree courses by £300 in 2013, Newman will join the majority of universities on £9,000 in 2014. Much of the additional income will go on bursaries and scholarships based on academic achievement worth between £2,000 and £10,000 over three years.

Psychology, education, sport and the early years are the university's main research areas. Fewer than a dozen academics were entered for the last Research Assessment Exercise (RAE), when a quarter of the submission in education was considered "internationally excellent". A specialist research centre for Children, Young People and Families will form the backbone of the university's entry in the successor to the RAE.

Halls of residence provide single study-bedrooms for 225 students, close to the teaching areas and library. First-year students are given priority in their allocation, but those coming through Clearing may have to live off campus. The newly refurbished fitness suite and performance room have improved sports facilities that already included an artificial sports pitch, sports hall, gymnasium and squash courts. Birmingham city centre, with its abundance of cultural venues and student-oriented nightlife, is about 20 minutes away.

Undergraduate Fees and Bursaries

» Fees for UK/EU students 2014–15: £9,000
  Foundation degree £7,500
» International student fees 2013–14: £8,900
» 117 NSP awards of £1,000 cash and £2,000 university services and/or fee waiver in year 1; £1,500 university services or fee waiver in years 2 and 3; priority to care leavers, carers, students from low achieving schools.
» Academic achievement and progression scholarships from £2,000 to £10,000 over three years, subject to conditions.
» Other scholarships and bursaries available.
» Check the university's website for the latest information.

Students

Undergraduates:	**1,785**	**(840)**
Postgraduates:	**305**	**(220)**
Mature students:	**28.7%**	
Overseas students:	**1.3%**	
Applications per place:	**5.8**	
From state-sector schools:	**98.9%**	
From working-class homes:	**44.6%**	
Satisfaction with students' union	**67%**	

For detailed information about sports facilities:
www.newman.ac.uk/sport

Accommodation

Places and costs refer to 2013–14
University-provided places: 225
Percentage catered: 0%
Self-catered costs: £3,233.00 (standard single) for academic year.
Priority, but no guarantee, is given to new first-year students.
International students: guaranteed housing.
Contact: www.newman.ac.uk/accommodation/500

University of Northampton

Northampton has managed the biggest rise in our league table this year, leaping 40 places thanks to big improvements in nearly all of the eight indicators. Its stated aim is to be the number one university in the UK for social enterprise by 2015 and to make this its distinctive offer to students. The university intends that all degree courses should include some aspect of social enterprise, whether as a work placement, volunteering or building sustainable social and economic partnerships which would, in turn, be supported by the university. Podiatry, occupational therapy and events management degree programmes are already developing new social enterprises allowing students to earn money while they work and learn. The Ashoka global network of social entrepreneurs named Northampton as the first "Changemaker Campus" in the UK in 2013.

Although it was awarded university status only in 2005, Northampton can trace its history back to the 13th century. Henry III dissolved the original version, allegedly because his bishops thought it posed a threat to Oxford. The modern university originated in an amalgamation of the town's colleges of education, nursing, technology and art. It has a particular focus on training for public services in the region, with students combining their studies with work placements in the community. The police and criminal justice studies Foundation degree, for example, is delivered for Northamptonshire Police Authority and has been designed to prepare students for a career in policing or the criminal justice system.

A raft of new courses in leather technology, midwifery, nursing, and health and social care helped Northampton to two years of record increases in applications before £8,500 fees were introduced in 2012. Although this brought a sharp drop in the number of applicants, the university still achieved a small increase in undergraduate enrolments. Fees for degree courses will rise to £9,000 in 2014, while Foundation degrees will go up to £7,250. Overall student numbers are now up to around 14,000, more than 1,000 of whom are from outside the EU.

Business is the university's most popular area, but teacher training and health subjects are not far behind – the university is the region's largest provider of teachers and healthcare professionals. Northampton was close to the bottom of the ranking for the 2008 Research Assessment Exercise, although there was some world-leading research in four of the ten subject areas, with history producing by far the best results. There are now 11 research centres, focusing on everything from contemporary

---

Park Campus
Boughton Green Road
Northampton NN2 7AL

0800 358 2232 (courses freephone)
study@northampton.ac.uk
www.northampton.ac.uk
www.northampton
union.com
Affiliation: none

The Times and Sunday Times **Rankings**
Overall Ranking: **59** (99)

Student satisfaction:	28	(83.7%)
Research quality:	=106	(1.3%)
Entry standards:	90	(299)
Student–staff ratio:	=79	(20)
Services & facilities/student:	17	(£2,053)
Expected completion rate:	=84	(81.9%)
Good honours:	76	(61%)
Graduate prospects:	=84	(57.9%)

fiction to anomalous psychological processes and transitional economics in China.

The university is planning a new Waterside Campus, at a cost of more than £330 million, but it will not be open before 2018 at the earliest. In the meantime, there are two sites: Park Campus on the edge of Northampton and the smaller, but more central, Avenue Campus. They are linked by a regular and free weekday bus service. Park Campus is set in 80 acres of open green parkland, with accommodation, a sports hall, students' union centre and nightclub. Two of the main buildings have been refurbished and expanded as part of an £80-million programme of improvements. The Business School, which benefited from a £1.7-million extension in 2011, is also on the campus.

Avenue Campus, the centre for art, design, science and technology, and the performing arts, hosts frequent theatre performances and exhibitions in its own art gallery. A £13-million investment saw the conversion of an adjacent Grade II listed former school into a technology and research centre with NVision and a 3D immersive technology and visualisation facility. Another university-backed development is the iCon building in Daventry, which opened at the end of 2011. The facility will offer a base for a diverse range of innovative, green businesses.

Northampton takes its mission to widen participation in higher education seriously: almost all the undergraduates attended state schools or colleges and more than a third come from working class homes. At 15 per cent, the projected dropout rate matches the national average for the university's courses and entry qualifications.

There are 1,700 residential places and 475 more are due to become available in the centre of Northampton by the end of 2013. Sports enthusiasts are well catered for, with rugby union, football, first-class cricket and the Silverstone motor circuit on the doorstep. The university has added a £100,000 gym to its sports facilities, which include a sports hall and outdoor pitches on the Park Campus. The town has a number of student-oriented bars, but the two campuses' union bars remain the hub of the social scene. Both London and Birmingham are only an hour away by train.

Undergraduate Fees and Bursaries

» Fees for UK/EU students 2014–15   £9,000
   Foundation degree   £7,250
» International student fees 2013–14   £9,750–£10,750
» 873 NSP awards of £1,000 cash and £2,000 fee waiver or accommodation discount in year 1, with priority given to those with the lowest residual household income.
» Household income below £25K, £1,000 bursary each year; £25K–£42.6K, £500 a year.
» Other scholarships and bursaries available.
» Check the university's website for the latest information.

Students

Undergraduates:	**9,280**	**(2,945)**
Postgraduates:	**810**	**(1,570)**
Mature students:	**26.3%**	
Overseas students:	**8.7%**	
Applications per place:	**5.5**	
From state-sector schools:	**96.9%**	
From working-class homes:	**36.2%**	
Satisfaction with students' union	**69%**	

For information about sports facilities:
www.northampton.ac.uk/study/campus-facilities/sports-facilities

Accommodation

Number of places and costs refer to 2013–14
University-provided places: 1,699
Percentage catered: 0%
Self-catered costs: £58 (small twin) – £115 (en-suite single) a week (42-week contract).
New first years have priority, on first come, first served basis, provided requirements are met. Local restrictions apply.
International students: As above.
Contact: www.northampton.ac.uk/study/accommodation/

Northumbria University

Northumbria is one of the leading post-1992 universities in *The Times and Sunday Times* league table, with an ambitious goal to break into the top quarter as a "new type of excellent university". It is the largest university in the North East of England and has seen the demand for places almost double in five years. Expansion came to at least a temporary end in 2012, when the introduction of £8,500 fees brought a drop of more than 500 in the number of first-year undergraduates. Fees for new and continuing students will rise to £9,000 in 2014, although there will be bursaries and accommodation discounts of up to £4,000 a year for students from the poorest homes and academic scholarships worth up to £2,000. Free one-day taster courses run throughout the year to give prospective students an idea of what studying at Northumbria would be like. More than 30 per cent of the undergraduates are from the four lowest socio-economic classes, but the university has managed to bring the projected dropout rate below 10 per cent – lower than the national average for its courses and entry grades.

Northumbria has invested £160 million in its impressive city centre campus, where the award-winning City Campus East development is linked to the original main campus by an iconic footbridge spanning Newcastle's central motorway. A recent expansion to the University Library has added 100 IT spaces, more social learning and informal space, a zone fitted with Smart boards and a dedicated Language Zone. The £7-million renovation of the students' union produced immediate results as Northumbria won the 2011 NUS Students' Union of the Year award. Most subjects are based in the city centre, with health, education and community programmes located at the Coach Lane campus less than two miles away, where £18 million has been spent upgrading facilities. Coach Lane has a learning resources centre, new sports facilities and a clinical skills centre, where students can learn in simulated hospital environments. Northumbria's pre-registration nursing programmes were the first in the country to receive accreditation from the Royal College of Nursing.

Three-quarters of students are from the North East, but numbers drawn from other parts of the UK have been rising year on year. There are also 3,500 international students on campus and a similar number taking courses overseas. The university is promising to increase the number of academics, as part of an £18-million staffing plan. Nine of the current staff have won National Teaching Fellowships. More than 550 employers sponsor undergraduate programmes and accreditation comes

Ellison Terrace
Newcastle upon Tyne
NE1 8ST

0191 243 7420 (admissions)
er.admissions@northumbria..ac.uk
www.northumbria.ac.uk
http://mynsu.northumbria.
  ac.uk
Affiliation: University
  Alliance

The Times and Sunday Times Rankings

Overall Ranking: **62** (58)

Student satisfaction:	=68	(81.2%)
Research quality:	=88	(2.7%)
Entry standards:	58	(331)
Student–staff ratio:	=46	(17.1)
Services & facilities/student:	=58	(£1,429)
Expected completion rate:	=48	(87.2%)
Good honours:	87	(59.3%)
Graduate prospects:	69	(61.8%)

from almost 50 professional bodies. This is one of the highest rates in the UK, enabling a high proportion of students to leave with professionally certified qualifications. Teacher education is a strength: Northumbria is one of only 17 universities rated outstanding by Ofsted. But Northumbria's best-known feature is its School of Design, which has a satellite campus in London. Its academics produced some of the university's best results in the last Research Assessment Exercise. The university entered a comparatively low proportion of its academics overall, but more than a third of its submission was considered world-leading or internationally excellent. Architecture and the built environment, general engineering and nursing and midwifery were other high scorers. Northumbria intends to double its capacity in research and enterprise over the next five years.

Northumbria is one of the leading universities for sport and continually ranks in the top 20 of the British Universities and Colleges Sport (BUCS) league table. An investment of over £40 million has been made in facilities and staff over recent years. A £30-million sports centre includes a swimming pool with an adjustable floor, multiple laboratories and a climbing wall, and there is a 3,000-seater indoor arena for professional sport and other events. There is also a generous Sport Scholarship scheme that supports talented student athletes financially throughout their degree programme.

Most first years are offered places in university accommodation. Two large residential developments with en-suite rooms opened in 2011, and almost 1,000 new bedrooms will be available in 2014 with the opening of new student accommodation in nearby Gateshead as a core element of the regeneration of the town centre. Designed with students in mind, the development is based in the heart of a thriving town centre filled with shops, restaurants and cultural attractions. It will boast landscaped walkways, fitness facilities and a multi-use games area as well as offering stunning views across the Tyneside skyline. There is a plentiful supply of privately rented flats and houses in Newcastle, a location that frequently wins awards as the best student city in the UK.

Undergraduate Fees and Bursaries

» Fees for UK/EU students 2014–15 £9,000
» International student fees 2013–14 £10,700–£12,700
» Household income below £16K, £4,000 cash or, if in university accommodation, £2,000 cash and £2,000 accommodation discount; £16K–£25K, £3,000 cash or £2,000 cash and £1,000 accommodation discount; £25K–£40K, £1,000 cash.
» Award of £2,000 for those with at least ABB at A Level or equivalent, continued in years 2 and 3 based on academic achievement.
» Check the university's website for the latest information.

Students

Undergraduates:	**18,925**	**(5,310)**
Postgraduates:	**2,520**	**(2,550)**
Mature students:	**15.9%**	
Overseas students:	**9.1%**	
Applications per place:	**4.7**	
From state-sector schools:	**90.1%**	
From working-class homes:	**29.7%**	
Satisfaction with students' union	**72%**	

For detailed information about sports facilities:
www.nusportcentral.com

Accommodation

Number of places and costs refer to 2013–14
University-provided places: 4,500
Percentage catered: 6%
Catered costs: £127.75 a week.
Self-catered costs: £86.80 (single) – £110 (en suite); £169.00 (studio) a week.
First years who need accommodation can be offered rooms.
International students: first years are guaranteed accommodation if requirements met.
Contact: rc.accommodation@northumbria.ac.uk

Norwich University of the Arts (NUA)

NUA was one of a dozen new universities created when the minimum size for universities was reduced from 4,000 to 1,000 students in 2012. It does not appear in *The Times and Sunday Times* league table because its courses do not cover the broad range of subjects needed for meaningful comparisons to be made with less specialist universities, but it has a powerful reputation in its field. Unlike the other arts universities, NUA makes a virtue of focusing entirely on the arts, design and media, rather than venturing into business or the humanities and social sciences. There are only 11 BA degrees, including one in architecture and others in graphic communication, and film and moving image production. As a university college, before its new status had been announced, Norwich succeeded in attracting more students in 2012 than it had before the fees went up. The new university restricted fees for degree courses to £8,600 this year, but will be joining most of the sector in charging the maximum £9,000 in 2014. Only Year 0, or Foundation, courses will cost less, at £4,000.

NUA traces its history back to 1845, when the Norwich School of Design was established by the artists and followers of the Norwich School of Painters, the only provincial British group with an international reputation for landscape painting. Former tutors include Lucian Freud, Michael Andrews and Lesley Davenport. The campus consists of seven buildings in the pedestrianised centre of Norwich, from the 13th-century Garth, which is now the photography centre, to the Monastery Media Lab and St Georges, where the traditional high ceilings and huge windows make it an ideal setting for Fine Art. The university's public art gallery enables students to showcase their work and gain experience curating and organising exhibitions, while the library houses the largest specialist art, design and media collection in the eastern region, including 34,000 books, subscriptions to over 400 journals, over 800 DVDs and an extensive bank of electronic resources. NUA has invested significantly in hardware and software that is professionally relevant and suitable for its diverse range of academic requirements. IT resources can be accessed in the workshops, library, computer-teaching rooms, seminar rooms, and at numerous terminals available throughout the campus. NUA has its own art materials shop, open daily, which sells a wide range of basic and specialist art supplies at discounted prices.

Norwich produced higher levels of overall satisfaction than the other specialist arts universities in the 2013 National

Francis House
3-7 Redwell Street
Norwich NR2 4SN

01603 610561 (enquiries)
info@nua.ac.uk
www.nua.ac.uk
www.nua.ac.uk/study/
   support/studentsunion
Affiliation: none

The Times Rankings
Norwich University of the Arts does not appear in the league table this year because its courses do not cover the broad range of subjects needed for meaningful comparisons to be made with less specialist institutions.

Student Survey, registering a big increase on previous scores and placing it among the top 50 of all universities. Its projected dropout rate is only 5 per cent, less than half the national average for its courses and entry qualifications. Individual studio space is provided for all full-time students in the faculties of art and design, while students in the media faculty have access to digital media workstations. Workshops for everything from digital video editing to laser cutting provide specialised resources and are staffed by experienced professionals, including graduates and practising artists.

The university still has under 2,000 students, 57 per cent of whom are female. More than a third of the undergraduates come from working-class homes. Applications in art and design are judged primarily on the quality of students' portfolios, but minimum entry requirements for every course are published on the university's website. Most courses include units of self-managed learning and exploration that allow students to concentrate on areas of particular interest and develop as learners. Agreements with tutors focus on personal study and help students negotiate individual pathways through their courses. More than a third of the work submitted to the last Research Assessment Exercise was judged to be world-leading or internationally excellent.

There are only 165 places in the three housing complexes managed by the new university. Almost half of them are in the one university-owned block of four and 12-bedroomed units, while the two privately owned sites also group students together in self-catering houses. Priority for residential places is given to international students and first years living furthest away from the university. NUA does not have its own sports facilities, but its students have access to the University of East Anglia's Sportspark, which boasts an Olympic-sized swimming pool, climbing walls, martial arts clubs and classes, badminton, squash and tennis courts and a running track. The campus is located in Norwich's city-centre cultural quarter, a ten-minute walk from the railway station. The timber-beamed NUA Bar has regular social events including performances, DJs, bands, themed parties and exhibitions. The city is attractive and popular with students, as well as being safer than most university centres.

Undergraduate Fees and Bursaries

» Fees for UK/EU students 2014–15: £9,000
  Foundation year (Year 0) £4,000
» International student fees 2013–14: £11,400
» 142 NSP awards, with eligibility criteria, of £2,000 fee waiver and £1,000 towards accommodation or maintenance in year 1 only; eligible to university bursary (see below) from year 2.
» University bursary for those with household income below £25K (and not receiving an NSP award), £1,000 cash a year; household income £25K–£42.6K, £500 a year.

Students		
Undergraduates:	**1,550**	**(0)**
Postgraduates:	**30**	**(55)**
Mature students:	**14.3%**	
Overseas students:	**3.6%**	
Applications per place:	**3.5**	
From state-sector schools:	**97.8%**	
From working-class homes:	**35.5%**	
Satisfaction with students' union	**74%**	

For detailed information about sports facilities: www.nua.ac.uk/study/support/studentsunion

Accommodation

Number of places and costs refer to 2013–14
University-provided places: 165
Percentage catered: 0%
Self-catered costs: £95–£136 a week (46 weeks)
First years cannot be guaranteed housing. Distance restrictions apply.
International students: as above
Contact: accommodation@nua.ac.uk;
www.nua.ac.uk/study/accommodation

University of Nottingham

Nottingham has added "United Kingdom, China, Malaysia" to its branding to underline the international nature of the university. It is the nearest Britain has to a truly global university, with campuses in China and Malaysia modelled on a headquarters that is among the most attractive in Britain. A second Chinese venture has been launched in Shanghai, where undergraduates will begin their courses before transferring to Nottingham. A member of the Russell Group, Nottingham is in the top 75 in the QS World University Rankings and one of the most popular universities in the UK in terms of applications. It bucked the national trend in 2012 when both applications and enrolments were maintained at record levels despite the introduction of £9,000 fees. Seen as a prime alternative to Oxbridge, the university still attracts more than seven applicants for each of its 42,000 places.

Nottingham has shown its strength in research with two Nobel prizes since the millennium for work carried out at the university. Professor Sir Peter Mansfield, who won the medicine prize for research leading to the development of the MRI scanner, has spent almost all his academic career there. The university further underlined its status by winning a £12-million grant from GlaxoSmithKline to establish a centre of excellence in sustainable chemistry. Almost 60 per cent of a big submission to the last Research Assessment Exercise was judged to be world-leading or internationally excellent, with pharmacy and Spanish, Portuguese and Latin American studies producing the best results in the UK, and chemistry and physics the second-best.

The original University Park campus has won ten consecutive Green Flag awards for its 330 acres of parkland and was named as the most sustainable campus in the world by the UI Greenmetric in 2013. A £50-million building programme for the next two years includes the extension and refurbishment of the specialist library for engineering and science, which will double in size. A new £20-million eco-friendly hotel has already opened on the campus. A mile away is the 30-acre Jubilee campus, where futuristic buildings cluster around an artificial lake and house the schools of management and finance, computer science and education, as well as 750 residential places. It will house the new chemistry centre and has seen the opening of new sports facilities, research laboratories, teaching space and student accommodation. The Queen's Medical School is also close to University Park, although its graduate-entry outpost is in Derby. The biosciences and the new veterinary school are at Sutton Bonington,

---

University Park
Nottingham NG7 2RD

0115 951 5559 (enquiries)
undergraduate-enquiries@
    nottingham.ac.uk
www.nottingham.ac.uk
www.su.nottingham.ac.uk
Affiliation: Russell Group

The Times and Sunday Times **Rankings**

Overall Ranking: **23** (20)

Student satisfaction:	=52	(81.9%)
Research quality:	=21	(24.0%)
Entry standards:	=21	(439)
Student–staff ratio:	16	(14)
Services & facilities/student:	32	(£1,795)
Expected completion rate:	17	(94%)
Good honours:	22	(76.5%)
Graduate prospects:	20	(77%)

12 miles south of the city in a rural setting. The latest development there is the construction of a new £9-million Amenities Building, which will include a 500-seat dining hall, student common rooms and staff lounge, as well as a graduate centre, faith room and Student Guild Service.

Nottingham has longstanding links with the Far East, which provides the majority of its 8,000 overseas students in the UK. The two branch campuses outside Kuala Lumpur, in Malaysia, and at Ningbo, in China, now host another 8,000 students. The purpose-built campuses have echoes of Nottingham's distinctive clock tower. All students have the opportunity to move between the three countries. The latest venture is collaboration with the East China University of Science and Technology, where the Shanghai Nottingham Advanced Academy will be based. It will deliver joint courses that include periods of study in Nottingham UK, with teaching and research at undergraduate, postgraduate and doctoral levels.

The university has succeeded in broadening its UK intake, but still has more independent school students and fewer from working-class homes than the national average for the subjects it offers. Summer schools and master classes provide support for teenagers from backgrounds without a history of progressing to selective universities and the university is to join the Sutton Trust's Pathways to Law access programme. Once in, students tend to stay the course – the 4 per cent dropout rate is among the best in the country. The university has also stepped up its efforts to give students the best possible chance in the jobs market. The Nottingham Advantage Award offers extra-curricular modules, as well as providing scores of internships for graduates, who enjoy lifetime access to the careers service.

The two main campuses in Nottingham are within three miles of the city centre, which has a good selection of student-friendly clubs. However, halls of residence and the students' union tend to be the centre of social life for students. New bars, café facilities and a nightclub were included in a £1-million makeover of student facilities. Sports provision is excellent. A £1.6-million sports pavilion opened in 2010 at the university's playing fields adjoining the main campus.

Undergraduate Fees and Bursaries

- » Fees for UK/EU students 2014–15   £9,000
- » International student fees 2013–14   £12,830–£16,510
  Medicine   £17,400–£30,240
  Veterinary medicine   £16,510–£24,470
- » NSP awards for household income below £20K, £1,000 cash, £2,000 fee waiver/accommodation discount year 1; following years as below.
- » Household income below £15K, £3,000 cash a year; then sliding scale to £42.6K, £2,000–£750 a year. Additional £1,000 cash bursary a year if certain conditions met.

Students

Undergraduates:	**23,515**	**(1,620)**
Postgraduates:	**7,715**	**(2,780)**
Mature students:	**9.5%**	
Overseas students:	**16.4%**	
Applications per place:	**7.3**	
From state-sector schools:	**72.4%**	
From working-class homes:	**18.6%**	
Satisfaction with students' union	**75%**	

For detailed information about sports facilities: www.nottingham.ac.uk/sport

Accommodation

Number of places and costs refer to 2013–14
University-provided places: 7,500
Percentage catered: 50%
Catered costs: £119.39 (twin)–£193.32 (en suite) a week (31 weeks).
Self-catered costs: £93.24–£164.96 a week (44 weeks).
First years are guaranteed accommodation if conditions are met.
International undergraduates: as above.
Contact: www.nottingham.ac.uk/accommodation

Nottingham Trent University

Nottingham Trent (NTU) has spent £350 million in ten years recruiting new staff and upgrading its three campuses, the latest tranche going on a new students' union building on the main City site. The development includes over 500 student bedrooms and follows the regeneration of two listed buildings and the construction of a central court linking them. Other projects have added new lecture theatres, restaurants, student services areas and laboratories. The Boots Library and the art and design facilities on the City site have been upgraded, while the Clifton Campus, five miles away, has a new "superlab" for 200 science students. At the same time, £20 million has been spent on a new animal unit and veterinary nursing centre at the Brackenhurst campus, 14 miles outside Nottingham, where an eco-friendly library is nearing completion.

NTU has reversed a two-year decline in our league table, climbing 17 places this year to regain its position among the top dozen modern universities. But applications were down by almost 17 per cent when fees of £8,500 were introduced in 2012 and 500 fewer first-year students enrolled than in the previous year. Like most other universities that have been charging less than the maximum, NTU is raising its fees in 2014 so that all degree courses will cost £9,000 a year. The university expects 2,000 undergraduates to qualify for financial support, although this will be mainly through fee waivers rather than cash bursaries.

There are more than 26,000 students, 4,500 of whom are postgraduates and 4,500 part-time. International undergraduates make up more than 5 per cent of the student body in Nottingham and its partner colleges in the UK, while another 7,000 are studying overseas. Almost a third of the undergraduates come from working-class homes and over 93 per cent attended state schools or colleges. The projected dropout rate has improved and, at less than 12 per cent, practically matches the national average for the university's courses and entry grades. Best known for fashion and other creative arts, the university also boasts one of the UK's biggest law schools, offering legal practice courses for both solicitors and barristers, as well as degrees. A three-year LLB (Hons) Law and Legal Practice course integrates an LLB law degree with the solicitors' Legal Practice Course. Other recent academic developments include a number of sponsored degrees offered by the business school, where the students work full-time for a company whilst studying for their degree. Students have their fees paid by the sponsoring company and also receive a salary. A new management and finance

Burton Street
Nottingham NG1 4BU

0115 848 4200 (admissions)
contact via website
www.ntu.ac.uk
www.trentstudents.org
Affiliation: University
   Alliance

The Times and Sunday Times Rankings
Overall Ranking: **61** (=78)

Student satisfaction:	**=61**	(81.4%)
Research quality:	**=70**	(4.3%)
Entry standards:	**=66**	(321)
Student–staff ratio:	**=79**	(20)
Services & facilities/student:	**56**	(£1,468)
Expected completion rate:	**=58**	(86.2%)
Good honours:	**=62**	(63%)
Graduate prospects:	**=70**	(61.7%)

degree gives students a degree and CIMA qualification in four years instead of the usual seven, also with fees and salary paid by a company.

An extensive research programme attracted a £7.65-million donation – thought to be the largest to a post-1992 university – to advance the university's work in cancer diagnosis and therapy. A new conference centre, opened in 2010, will also help to boost income and investment. The university held its own in the last Research Assessment Exercise, although it entered fewer academics than some of the other leading new universities. More than a third of its submission was rated world-leading or internationally excellent, with communication, culture and media studies, social policy, engineering and biomedical sciences producing the best results.

Art and design, architecture, law, business and the social sciences are taught on the main campus, while science and technology, education, and the humanities are based at Clifton, which has seen the addition of six new blocks of high-quality student accommodation that will form part of a student village. The university runs a bus service linking Clifton and the city. The Brackenhurst campus is devoted to animal, rural and environmental studies. It includes one of the region's best-equipped equestrian centres, with a purpose-built indoor riding area. Another 300 residential places were added there in 2006, following a £3-million renewal of the teaching facilities. With private providers adding to the university's residential stock of more than 4,000 beds, all first years and overseas students can be housed.

NTU has a strong sporting reputation and always fares well in the BUCS leagues. The new Lee Westwood Sports Centre, opened by the golfer himself, is on the Clifton campus and boasts an array of top facilities, including sports halls, studios, fitness suites and a nutrition training centre. NTU alumni include England rugby player Nick Easter and Great Britain hockey players Crista Cullen, Adam Dixon and Alistair Wilson. Social life varies between campuses, but all have access to the city's lively cultural and clubbing scene. A late-night bus service links the main campuses and the city's new tram system serves the university.

Undergraduate Fees and Bursaries

» Fees for UK/EU students 2014–15   £9,000
    Foundation degree   £6,750
» International student fees 2013–14   £11,100–£11,600
» Around 1,700 NSP awards of £2,700 fee waiver and £300 cash in year 1. Students eligible for NTU Scholarship from year 2.
» NTU Scholarship for students with household income less than £25K, fee waiver of £1,300 and £300 cash a year.
» Range of other scholarships and bursaries available.
» Check the university's website for the latest information.

Students

Undergraduates:	**20,585**	**(2,195)**
Postgraduates:	**2,700**	**(2,455)**
Mature students:	**12.7%**	
Overseas students:	**5.1%**	
Applications per place:	**5.6**	
From state-sector schools:	**93.3%**	
From working-class homes:	**32.3%**	
Satisfaction with students' union	**70%**	

For detailed information about sports facilities: www.ntu.ac.uk/sport

Accommodation

Number of places and costs refer to 2013–14
University-provided places: 4,200
Percentage catered: 0%
Self-catered costs: £81.83–£147.70 (44–51 weeks).
First years and new students are guaranteed accommodation if conditions are met.
International students: guaranteed if conditions are met.
Contact: www.ntu.ac.uk/accommodation
accommodation@ntu.ac.uk; 0115 848 2894

The Open University (OU)

The Open University (OU) is a model for open and distance learning institutions around the world and has now become the platform for the UK's first venture into massive open online courses (MOOCs). The university already offers curriculum resources free via its OpenLearn website. Now it is to host Futurelearn, a consortium of leading universities and cultural organisations such as the British Museum and the British Council, offering higher education courses of varying lengths, also free of charge. MOOCs have taken off in the United States, where universities like Stanford and Harvard have invested heavily in the concept. Some see them as a threat to traditional university education. For the OU, however, its own 473 undergraduate modules and other higher education courses will remain its top priority. With some 250,000 students, it is already one of the largest universities in the world and more than twice the size of any in the UK.

The OU has ranked at or very near the top for student satisfaction in every National Student Survey since 2005. But it does not appear in *The Times and Sunday Times* league table because the absence of on-campus undergraduates makes the OU unsuitable for comparison with other universities on some of the measures used.

Undergraduate fees of £5,124 a year for the equivalent of full-time study (120 credits) by distance learning will be the cheapest at any university in 2013–14. The average age of new undergraduates is 31, but the demand from school leavers has grown to the point where more than a quarter are under 25 years old. Over 60 per cent of undergraduates are female and most live in the UK, but there are now 16,000 students outside the country. The OU offers special support for disabled students and currently has around 17,000 students with disabilities.

The university's headquarters are at Milton Keynes, Buckinghamshire, but it has 350 study centres and regional centres in each of its 13 regions around the UK, as well as offices and exam centres in other countries. The open access principle that was a cornerstone of its foundation remains in place: no formal qualifications are required to study on most undergraduate programmes. Four out of ten undergraduates come with less than two A levels or their equivalent, while seven out of ten remain in full-time or part-time employment while studying. But the OU provides financial support for those from poor backgrounds and expanded its efforts when the fees went up in 2012 with a new programme called Access to Success.

Almost 7,000 part-time associate lecturers (tutors) guide students through degrees. The OU's "Supported Open

---

Walton Hall

Milton Keynes MK7 6AA

0845 300 6090 (enquiries)
contact via website
www.open.ac.uk
www.open.ac.uk/ousa
Affiliation: University
  Alliance

Edinburgh
Belfast
MILTON KEYNES
Cardiff
London

The Times and Sunday Times Rankings

The available data do not match the data used to rank the other full-time universities, so the Open University could not be included in the league table this year.

Learning" system allows students to work where they choose – at home, in the workplace or at a library or study centre. They can study full-time or part-time, at a pace to suit their circumstances. They have contact with fellow students at tutorials, day schools or through online conferencing and electronic forums, social networks and informal study groups. An increasing amount of material is delivered online, and can be accessed on mobile devices as well as computers. OU learning materials are the result of years of experience and research into how to teach at undergraduate level, and are also used by other institutions.

Gone are the late-night BBC television programmes that were the mainstay of teaching until 2006. The OU now produces mainstream television and radio programming aimed at bringing learning to a wider audience. The university also leads the universities placing material on the iTunes U site and was one of the first in the world to make e-books available there. The 1,200 full-time academics have a proud research record: more than half of the work submitted for the last Research Assessment Exercise was regarded as world-leading or internationally excellent. Art and design, computer science, geography and sociology produced the best results. The OU employs more than 500 people engaged in research and there are over 1,300 research students.

The OU covers all the main academic disciplines, and its business school produces more MBAs than the rest of the UK's business schools put together, as well as offering Honours and Foundation degrees. In addition to degrees in a named subject, the OU also awards "Open" Bachelor degrees, where the syllabus is designed by the students through combining a number of modules. The OU has strong links to business and industry, and offers a range of professional and vocational qualifications. Assessment is by both continual assessment and examination or, for some modules, a major assignment. Except in fast-moving areas such as computing, there is no limit on the time taken to complete a degree.

Undergraduate Fees and Bursaries

» Fees vary depending upon the type of course, on where you live and the number of credits you plan to study. In England a course of 120 credits of study (a year's full-time study) is £5,124, which can be covered by a tuition fee loan. In Scotland, Wales and Northern Ireland, a course of 120 credits is £1,510–£2,815, and there may be government assistance in paying the fee.

» For international students, a course of 120 credits is £5,124.

» The costs of all courses are given in the OU prospectus: **www3.open.ac.uk/study/undergraduate/index.htm**

» Various forms of financial help are available. Details are given at: **www3.open.ac.uk/study/undergraduate/qualifications/ways-to-pay**

Students

Undergraduates:	15	(188,905)
Postgraduates:	285	(12,065)
Overseas students:	0.1%	

Satisfaction with students' union	61%

For detailed information about sports facilities:
www.open.ac.uk/ouclub/main/grounds-and-facilities

Accommodation

As the courses provided are part time, the university does not provide accommodation.

Contact: www3.open.ac.uk/contact/faq.aspx?t=S&cat=1-1SOVWF

University of Oxford

Oxford has slipped off the top of our league table for the first time in more than ten years, but remains almost inseparable from Cambridge in terms of points and overall reputation. This year's scores could hardly be closer and the two ancient rivals remain close to repeating the dead-heat they experienced in the first edition of this *Guide* 20 years ago. Both are head and shoulders above the other institutions in *The Times and Sunday Times* table and in the view of most experts. Oxford is the oldest and probably the most famous university in the English-speaking world. It is also among the top six universities in the world, according to the QS and *Times Higher Education* world rankings. By its own high standards, however, Oxford has been slipping on the important measure of graduate prospects, although it still outscores Cambridge on staffing, degree classifications and spending on student facilities.

The introduction of £9,000 fees had predictably little impact on the demand for places. There were still fewer than six applicants to the place – a much more favourable ratio than at some other leading universities – but 99 per cent of successful candidates achieve at least three As at A level, or their equivalent. Some subjects now demand two A* grades and

another A at A level. The university is still struggling to broaden its intake and shake off allegations of social elitism. The long-term growth in demand for places is due, at least partly, to more systematic attempts to get the message through to teenagers that Oxford is open to all who can meet the exacting entrance requirements. Student visits to comprehensive schools have been supplemented by summer schools, recruitment fairs and colleges' own initiatives, as well as tireless public statements of intent by the university. For all the university's efforts to shed its *Brideshead Revisited* stereotype, however, official figures still show more than 40 per cent of Oxford's students coming from independent schools – the largest proportion at any university. Just one student in nine comes from a working-class home, despite the introduction of generous financial support that will be extended in 2014. The university expects 15 per cent of its undergraduates to receive some support, with fee waivers bringing the effective rate for students from the poorest homes down to £3,500 in their first year and £6,000 subsequently. In addition, there will be bursaries of between £500 and £3,300 for students whose parental income is less than £42,600, funded partly by Europe's biggest-ever donation for student support.

Applications must be made by mid October – a month earlier if you wish to be

---

University Offices
Wellington Square
Oxford OX1 2JD

01865 288000 (admissions)
contact via website
www.ox.ac.uk
www.ousu.org
Affiliation: Russell Group

The Times and Sunday Times **Rankings**

Overall Ranking: **2** (1)

Student satisfaction:	=9	(85.9%)
Research quality:	2	(44.3%)
Entry standards:	2	(583)
Student–staff ratio:	=2	(11.1)
Services & facilities/student:	1	(£3,490)
Expected completion rate:	2	(98.4%)
Good honours:	1	(90.9%)
Graduate prospects:	=13	(78.3%)

interviewed overseas. There are written tests for some subjects and you may be asked to submit samples of work. Selection is in the hands of the 30 undergraduate colleges, which vary considerably in their approach to this issue and others. Sound advice on academic strengths and social factors is essential for applicants to give themselves the best chance of winning a place and finding a setting in which they can thrive. A minority of candidates opt to go straight into the admissions pool without expressing a preference for a particular college. The choice is particularly important for arts and social science students, whose world-famous individual or small group tuition is based in college. Science and technology are taught mainly in central facilities. All subjects operate on eight-week terms and assess students entirely on final examinations – a system some find too pressurised. Nevertheless, Oxford remains one of the top universities for student satisfaction.

The development of a new campus on the site of the Radcliffe Infirmary represents the first fruit of the Oxford Thinking fundraising campaign, which passed its £1.25-billion target in 2012. Oxford's biggest capital development for more than a century will provide more student accommodation for neighbouring Somerville College, a new Mathematical Institute building and a new building for the humanities. In the Science Area, existing buildings will be refurbished and modernised. Among the many current projects is an £11-million Middle East Centre, due to open in 2014.

There was never much doubt about the strength of Oxford's research, but the 2008 Research Assessment Exercise found more than 70 per cent of it to be world-leading or internationally excellent. Oxford entered more academics for assessment than any other university – twice as many as some research-based universities of similar size. There were good results in all areas, but the university was pre-eminent in several medical specialisms, as well as statistics, development studies, education and French. Oxford also attracts the largest amount of research income among UK universities.

Undergraduate Fees and Bursaries

- » Fees for UK/EU students 2014–15   £9,000
- » International student fees 2013–14   £13,860–£20,405
       Medicine   £15,910–£27,550
       College fees   £6,465
- » UK/EU students (excluding Welsh students) with household income below £16K, £5,500 fee waiver, year 1; £3,000, other years; £16K–£20K, fee waiver £2,000 a year; £20K–£25K, fee waiver £1,000 a year.
- » UK/EU students with household income below £16K, a bursary of £4,300, year 1; £3,300 other years; £16K–£42.6K, bursary on sliding scale £3,500–£1,000 year 1; £3,000–£500, other years.
- » 100 Moritz–Heyman scholarships for students with household income below £16K and other conditions: £5,500 cash a year and £5,500 fee waiver a year.

Students

Undergraduates:	**11,490**	**(5,180)**
Postgraduates:	**7,270**	**(1,655)**
Mature students:	**3.9%**	
Overseas students:	**12.7%**	
Applications per place:	**5.5**	
From state-sector schools:	**57.7%**	
From working-class homes:	**11.0%**	
Satisfaction with students' union	**36%**	

For detailed information about sports facilities:
www.sport.ox.ac.uk

Accommodation

See chapter 13 for information about individual colleges.

Oxford Brookes University

Oxford Brookes has moved back into the top 50 in our league table, with only one post-1992 university above it. Even after a boom year for applications in 2011 and the subsequent introduction of £9,000 fees for degree courses, the demand for places barely dropped in 2012, when there were more than seven applicants per place. Fees for Foundation degrees taught at partner colleges will remain at £6,000 in 2014. The university's location has always been an advantage in student recruitment, but the quality of provision is the real draw. Ofsted rates the primary teacher training as outstanding, for example, and the university's departments feature near the top of *The Times and Sunday Times* rankings for several subjects. Brookes was awarded national centres for hospitality, leisure and tourism, and the teaching of business and undergraduate research, as well as one for teacher training in partnership with Westminster University.

The university is particularly popular with independent schools, which provide over a quarter of the undergraduates – by far the highest proportion among the new universities and twice the national average for the university's subjects and entry grades. However, the proportion from working-class homes, at 41 per cent, is also considerably ahead of the official benchmark. Brookes has been trying to attract more students from state schools and has targeted areas in Oxfordshire and the wider region, as well as offering a range of bursaries for those from low-income families. The projected dropout rate of less than 9 per cent is better than the university's benchmark.

Grades in the last Research Assessment Exercise showed improvement, with more than a third of the work judged to be world-leading or internationally excellent. History, which made headlines in 2001 with a higher grade than its world-renowned neighbour, again produced the best results, but there were good performances, too, in history of art and computer science.

As a polytechnic, Brookes pioneered the modular degree system that has swept British higher education. After more than 20 years' experience, the scheme has now trimmed the 2,000 modules it once offered, but undergraduates can pair subjects as diverse as history and biology, or catering management and environmental management. Each subject has compulsory modules in the first year and a list of others that are acceptable later. Students are encouraged to take advantage of a range of placement and exchange opportunities as well as subjects outside their main area of study, such as additional language modules. The university is proud of its Brookes Virtual integrated e-learning network and has been chosen to pilot a national e-learning project to use

---

Headington Campus
Gypsy Lane
Oxford OX3 0BP

01865 484848 (enquiries)
query@brookes.ac.uk
www.brookes.ac.uk
www.brookesunion.org.uk
Affiliation: University
  Alliance

The Times and Sunday Times **Rankings**

Overall Ranking: **50** (=52)

Student satisfaction:	**=43**	(82.2%)
Research quality:	**60**	(5.7%)
Entry standards:	**49**	(352)
Student–staff ratio:	**50**	(17.3)
Services & facilities/student:	**62**	(£1,387)
Expected completion rate:	**40**	(89.4%)
Good honours:	**47**	(68.9%)
Graduate prospects:	**62**	(63.6%)

new technologies and redesigned courses to expand the reach of education and lifelong learning. A partnership with the Association of Chartered Certified Accountants already has more than 200,000 students worldwide registered for a Brookes BSc in Applied Accounting.

The extra income from fees will help to speed up planned developments on the Headington, Wheatley and Harcourt Hill campuses over the next few years. Some £132 million is being invested in an impressive new library and teaching building that is due to open at the original Gipsy Lane site, at Headington, by early 2014. This will provide social learning space that allows students to work together and engage with careers guidance, volunteering opportunities and student support services. Maths and engineering have now joined computing and business five miles away at Wheatley. A new engineering building supports the university's status as a Government-designated regional centre for motorsport and high performance engineering. The Harcourt Hill campus, at Botley, focuses on teacher education, human development and learning. A fourth site, in Swindon, where Brookes is also opening a university technical college, focuses on adult nursing, operating department practice and a range of continuing professional development courses. The Ferndale Campus is unique in having its own osteopathic training clinic on site.

Oxford Brookes was in the top ten in the People and Planet Green league of 2013, the sixth successive year that has featured in the top category of the environmental assessments. A 25-metre swimming pool and 9-hole golf course have been added to the already impressive sports facilities. The gym and climbing centre have been refurbished. Representative teams have a good record, with the rowers particularly successful, winning medals at three consecutive Olympic games, and the cricketers now combining with Oxford University to take on county teams. The Boat Club, one of the leaders among UK universities, opened a new £600,000 boathouse in 2013. The students' union runs one of the biggest entertainment venues in Oxford, a city that can be expensive, but which offers enough to satisfy most students.

Undergraduate Fees and Bursaries

» Fees for UK/EU students 2014–15 £9,000
  Foundation degrees at partner colleges £6,000
  Bachelor degrees at partner colleges £7,000
» International student fees 2013–14 £11,400–£13,150
» For UK students with household income below £10K: £2,000 cash, £2,000 accommodation discount and £1,000 fee waiver; £10K–£15K, £1,500 cash, £2,000 accommodation discount and £1,000 fee waiver; £15K–£25K, £1,000 cash and £1,500 accommodation discount; accommodation discount in year 1 only, cash and fee waiver for each year of study.
» Community scholarships of £1,000 in year 1 for local students.
» Check the university's website for the latest information.

Students

Undergraduates:	11,700	(2,465)
Postgraduates:	1,840	(2,425)
Mature students:	22.5%	
Overseas students:	15.2%	
Applications per place:	7.4	
From state-sector schools:	71.0%	
From working-class homes:	41.3%	
Satisfaction with students' union	37%	

For detailed information about sports facilities:
www.brookes.ac.uk/sport

Accommodation

Number of places and costs refer to 2013–14
University-provided places: 4,600
Percentage catered: 3%
Catered cost: £136 a week (38 weeks).
Self-catered cost: £100–£152 (38 weeks).
All accommodation is allocated to first year who select Oxford Brookes as Firm choice through UCAS and meet all deadlines for application.
International students: as above.
Contact: accomm@brookes.ac.uk

University of Plymouth

Plymouth has become the only post-1992 university with its own medical school after dissolving its partnership with Exeter University in the management of the former Peninsula College of Medicine and Dentistry. The new school will be small, with an annual entry of only 86 students, but Plymouth has kept all 64 of Peninsula's places in dentistry. As part of the plans, Plymouth has already invested £25 million to further medical and health research in the South West. The university is the largest provider of nursing, midwifery and health professional education and training in the region. Plymouth is one of the UK's largest universities with more than 30,000 students. The Vice-Chancellor, Professor Wendy Purcell, who graduated from the university in the 1980s, has declared a mission to make it the top "enterprise university". It was awarded a Queen's Anniversary Prize for Higher and Further Education in 2012 and was the first university to be awarded Regional Growth Fund money to promote economic development. The university was chosen to lead the national Social Enterprise University Enterprise Network and is home to one of the country's top 10 business incubation facilities – part of its managed portfolio of £100-million worth of incubation and innovation assets.

Over £200 million has been spent on the main city campus. The library was extended and upgraded and the students' union refurbished, while a £35-million arts complex opened in 2007. Two new buildings, housing the Faculty of Health and the Faculty of Education and Society, were opened in 2008 and include sports facilities and clinical skills laboratories as well as teaching space. Plymouth has also opened a £1-million Immersive Vision Theatre, thought to be the first of its kind at a UK university, which gives the feeling of being "in", rather than just observing, different types of image. In 2012, the Duke of Edinburgh opened the university's £19-million Marine Building, which contains the country's most advanced wave tanks, a navigation centre with ship simulator, and business incubation space for companies in the marine renewables sector. A £7-million centre for performing arts is scheduled to open in 2013. The university's commitment to sustainability was also recognised through its ranking as the second greenest university in the People and Planet league.

The university is a partner in the Combined Universities in Cornwall, which is boosting further and higher education in the county. Plymouth has established a unique relationship with its 18 partner colleges, which have become a faculty of the university, sharing £3.5 million in capital investment. They spread from Cornwall

---

Drake Circus
Plymouth
Devon PL4 8AA
01752 585858 (enquiries)
contact via website
www.plymouth.ac.uk
www.upsu.com
Affiliation: University
    Alliance

to Somerset, taking in Jersey, and have 10,000 students taking university courses. The intake reflects Plymouth's position as the working-class hub of the South West, with almost 95 per cent of students state-educated and nearly a third from the poorest social classes. The projected dropout rate of less than 10 per cent is below average for the courses and entry grades. Some 12,000 students undertake work-based learning or placements with employability skills embedded throughout the curriculum from day one, while the new Plymouth Award recognises extra-curricular achievements. However, there was a big drop in both applications and enrolments when £9,000 fees arrived in 2012.

Plymouth was chosen to house no fewer than four national teaching centres – in health and social care placements, experiential learning in environmental and natural sciences, institutional partnerships, and education for sustainable development – all of which have now been brought into the university's core activities. No university has exceeded the 16 National Teaching Fellowships won by its academics. Plymouth entered by far the largest number of academics of any post-1992 university in the latest research assessments – twice the proportion entered by some of its peer group. More than a third of the submission was rated world-leading or internationally excellent. Computer science produced by

far the best results, but civil engineering, geography and environmental science, and art and design also did well.

A 1,300-bed student village costing £15 million, has greatly improved the university's residential stock, and another 800 places should be available in 2014. With excellent and recently upgraded facilities for water sports as well as an £850,000 fitness centre, the sports facilities have improved, while a range of sports scholarships and bursaries support high-fliers. The university has a partnership with Plymouth Albion Rugby Club to promote and support sport in the city and it invested £2.5 million in the new £45-million Plymouth Life Centre. Students can benefit from exclusive sessions at the international-standard swimming and fitness facility, which includes an Olympic-size swimming pool. Plymouth is the only university in the UK to have its own diving and water sports centre.

Undergraduate Fees and Bursaries

» Fees for UK/EU students 2014–15 £9,000
   Foundation year £7,500
   Partner colleges £5,960–£7,500
» International student fees 2013–14 £10,750
   Medicine £16,750–£31,000
» 1,094 NSP awards: £1,000 cash and £2,000 university services in year 1; priority given to local students and mature students. Partner colleges offer their own NSP awards.
» Care leaver and sports bursaries.

Students

Undergraduates:	**21,625**	**(5,315)**
Postgraduates:	**1,895**	**(2,265)**
Mature students:	**21.5%**	
Overseas students:	**7.3%**	
Applications per place:	**4.5**	
From state-sector schools:	**93.4%**	
From working-class homes:	**30.1%**	
Satisfaction with students' union	**81%**	

For detailed information about sports facilities:
www1.plymouth.ac.uk/getactive/Pages/default.aspx

Accommodation

Number of places and costs refer to 2013–14
University-provided places: 2,500
Percentage catered: 0%
Self-catered costs: £87.95–£145.00 a week (40–51 weeks).
First years are not guaranteed university provided accommodation.
International students: overseas students have priority for allocation.
Contact: accommodation@plymouth.ac.uk
www.plymouth.ac.uk/accommodation

University of Portsmouth

Portsmouth is among the top six post-1992 universities in our league table after improved scores across the board produced another rise this year. Only one of its peers had more satisfied students in the 2013 National Student Survey. The university did well to maintain the size of its intake when the fees went up in 2012, despite a substantial drop in applications. It charged £8,500 for degree courses then, but will join the trend for £9,000 fees in 2014. Much of the extra income will go on measures to attract and retain a broader range of students. A threshold of £25,000 family income to qualify for full bursaries and fee waivers is more generous than at most universities, and there will be extra awards for modern languages – one of the university's strengths and an area of national decline. Portsmouth has one of the largest language departments in the country, teaching six languages to degree level and offering free language courses to all students. About 1,000 Portsmouth students go abroad for part of their course, and at least as many come from the continent.

The university also has a growing reputation in health subjects. The £9-million Dental Academy, which opened in 2010, trains student dentists in their final year at King's College London in a team-based primary care setting with other professionals complementary to dentistry. More than 600 radiographers, paramedics, medical technologists, pharmacists, clinicians and social workers graduate each year. Specialist research centres include one for molecular design and the UK's first Brain Tumour Research Centre of Excellence, as well the Institute of Biomedical and Biomolecular Sciences and the Institute of Cosmology and Gravitation. Forty per cent of the work submitted for the last Research Assessment Exercise was considered world-leading or internationally excellent. Portsmouth was in the top ten for allied health professions and studies, applied mathematics and European studies. The university is an official centre of teaching and research about the EU.

The main city-centre Guildhall campus has undergone extensive redevelopment. A new £14-million building is due to open before the end of 2013, giving the Faculty of Creative and Cultural Industries more space for teaching, learning and exhibition facilities. Earlier developments included the prize-winning green library complex and the aluminium-clad St Michael's Building, where £750,000 has been spent recently to refurbish laboratories. The business school is housed in a £12-million building on the main campus. Other recent developments include a sports science building with laboratories, a swimming flume and two accredited climatic chambers, as well as a £1.1-million nursery

University House
Winston Churchill Avenue
Portsmouth
Hampshire PO1 2UP

023 9284 8484
info.centre@port.ac.uk
www.port.ac.uk
www.upsu.net
Affiliation: University
   Alliance

for the children of students and staff.

Many courses have direct input from business and the professions, a high proportion leading to professional accreditation. Wherever possible, students are given opportunities for hands-on practice in their chosen career. Simulated learning environments include a mock court room, a journalism newsroom, a health simulation suite, a £1-million model pharmacy and a "forensic house" where criminologists work on simulated crime scenes. Teaching in all subjects is concentrated on the Guildhall campus, with most residential accommodation nearby. A £6.5-million student centre caters for the multicultural population of the university with alcohol-free areas and an international students' bar. There is also a new social learning space, with café, wireless internet and learning spaces for individuals and groups. Modernised sport, exercise and fitness facilities include gyms, dance studios and a sports hall.

Portsmouth has a larger working-class population than most cities in the south of England. Three undergraduates in ten come from the four lowest socio-economic groups, although this is still below the national average for the university's subjects and entry qualifications. Efforts to broaden the intake further include an award-winning membership club that introduces teenagers to higher education through workshops,

holiday courses and access to university facilities. The projected dropout rate has improved considerably and, at less than 10 per cent, is now significantly lower than the university's benchmark.

Many students live in Southsea, which has a vibrant social scene and quirky shops. In recent years the city has seen considerable regeneration, including the retail and entertainment complex at Gunwharf, dominated by the 170-metre landmark Spinnaker Tower. The cost of living is not as high as at many southern universities, and the sea is close at hand. University-allocated accommodation is offered to around two-thirds of new first years who apply, and assistance is offered to those who want to find accommodation in the private rented sector, including house-hunting events, online resources and regular drop-in advice sessions.

Undergraduate Fees and Bursaries

» Fees for UK/EU students 2014–15   £9,000
  Courses at partner colleges   £6,000
» International student fees 2013–14   £10,500–£11,900
» English students with household income below £25K, £1,000 cash and fee waiver or £2,000 accommodation discount, year 1; £1,060 cash, years 2–4; £25K–£32K, £1,000 cash, year 1; £1,060, years 2–4; £32K–£42.6K, £500, year 1; £530 years 2–4.
» English students with household income below £25K, modern foreign language bursary of £2,000 as cash or fee waiver each year of study.
» Check the university's website for the latest information.

Students

Undergraduates:	**17,300**	**(2,380)**
Postgraduates:	**1,800**	**(2,220)**
Mature students:	**14.8%**	
Overseas students:	**13.5%**	
Applications per place:	**5.4**	
From state-sector schools:	**94.6%**	
From working-class homes:	**29.9%**	
Satisfaction with students' union	**77%**	

For detailed information about sports facilities:
www.port.ac.uk/sport

Accommodation

Number of places and costs refer to 2013–14
University-provided places: around 3,000
Percentage catered: 25%
Catered costs: £96–£123 a week (37 weeks).
Self-catered costs:£79–£125 a week (37 weeks).
Majority of first years offered university accommodation.
International, Channel Island and Isle of Man students guaranteed university accommodation subject to terms and conditions.
Contact: Student.housing@port.ac.uk
www.port.ac.uk/studentlife/accommodation/

Queen Margaret University

Scotland's first new university of the 21st century has enjoyed four successive years of growth in the demand for places. While the absence of tuition fees for Scottish students has obviously helped, this is far from the whole story since half of the students are from outside Scotland. A quarter come from outside the European Union, many studying in their home countries. Queen Margaret opened the first UK university campus in Singapore, a joint venture with the East Asia Institute of Management, which already taught Queen Margaret degree courses. Other international programmes run in Nepal, Egypt, Saudi Arabia, Greece and Switzerland.

For the majority of students, however, the major attraction is the gleaming, modern campus in the seaside town of Musselburgh, to the southeast of Edinburgh, where QMU moved when it was awarded university status in 2007. The "campus in the park", as it has been dubbed, was designed in consultation with students, and is one of the most environmentally sustainable in the UK, exceeding current standards. The campus has won a string of awards and the university has made sustainability a top priority, in the curriculum as well as in the way it operates.

Named after Saint Margaret, the 11th-century Queen of Scotland, the institution dates back to 1875 and was originally a school of cookery for women. The college had been awarding its own degrees for 15 years before it became a university. There are more than 6,000 students at all levels, three-quarters of them female. The university has established three flagship areas as a focus for future investment and development: health and rehabilitation, sustainable business, and culture and creativity. It promises "inter-professional" teaching and research to encourage the professions to work better together.

Restructuring of the performing arts courses consolidated four drama degrees into one interdisciplinary programme, under the title of drama and performance. The university no longer offers conservatoire training, but the new degree draws together the university's recognised strengths in acting, screen work, community theatre, contemporary performance and playwriting to reflect the current needs of a changing profession. QMU also offers a degree in costume design, the only one of its kind in Scotland. Another new development saw the university go back to its roots with a partnership with the Edinburgh New Town Cookery School, run by a former graduate of QMU, to hone the practical skills of students on the international hospitality management degree. The

---

Queen Margaret University
  Drive
Musselburgh EH21 6UU

0131 474 0000
contact via website
www.qmu.ac.uk
www.qmusu.org.uk
Affiliation: none

EDINBURGH
Belfast
London
Cardiff

The Times and Sunday Times **Rankings**
Overall Ranking: **=71** (83)

Student satisfaction:	=96	(78.7%)
Research quality:	=78	(3.3%)
Entry standards:	=56	(332)
Student–staff ratio:	=88	(20.5)
Services & facilities/student:	72	(£1,339)
Expected completion rate:	95	(80.4%)
Good honours:	33	(73.4%)
Graduate prospects:	=41	(69.7%)

university has also introduced a new associate degree programme, delivered with Edinburgh College, with 60 places in events management, international tourism and hospitality management. The students will have full access to all university facilities and may even live in QMU accommodation.

Health is an area of particular strength: QMU has the broadest range of courses in Scotland, from dietetics, podiatry and audiology, to art therapy, music therapy and health psychology. The university has an international reputation for its work in speech sciences, and launched a new CASL (Clinical Audiology, Speech and Language) Research Centre in 2011. Courses in international health attract students from all over the world and there programmes in Angola, Guatemala, Uganda, Ethiopia, Gambia, India and Cuba.

All has not been plain sailing for the new university, however. Only one university had a lower average score in the 2008 Research Assessment Exercise, and Queen Margaret has struggled with debts, although it has since reported a surplus a year ahead of the target date. The projected dropout rate of less than 14 per cent has been improving, but is still higher than average for the university's courses and entry qualifications. More than three undergraduates in ten come from working-class homes and around a quarter are 21 or over on entry.

An impressive learning resource centre, parts of which are open 24 hours a day, offers a variety of study spaces. Specialist laboratories and clinics are well equipped. The nursing simulation lab, for example, is set out exactly like a hospital ward, helping to instil students with the confidence to move on easily to a work placement or career in the NHS or private practice. There are also specially equipped rooms for podiatry, radiography, occupational therapy, physiotherapy and art therapy.

The campus is located next to Musselburgh train station, from where Edinburgh city centre is only a six-minute journey. There is also a frequent bus service from the campus to the city centre. There are 800 residential places on the campus, about 300 of them larger, premier rooms with double beds. Other features include a students' union building, indoor and outdoor sports facilities, a variety of catering outlets and landscaped gardens with a range of environmental features.

Undergraduate Fees and Bursaries

» Fees for Scottish and EU students 2013–14   No fee
» Fees for Non-Scottish UK (RUK) students 2013–14   £6,750
» Fees for international students 2013–14   £10,170–£12,090
» For RUK students (2013–14), annual bursaries: household income up to £20K, £2,000 cash; sliding scale to £42.6K, £1,500–£500.
» Range of other scholarships and bursaries available.
» Check the university's website for the latest information.

Students

Undergraduates:	2,780	(705)
Postgraduates:	490	(1,275)
Mature students:	24.4%	
Overseas students:	17.4%	
Applications per place:	6.0	
From state-sector schools:	93.6%	
From working-class homes:	31.6%	
Satisfaction with students' union	52%	

For detailed information about sports facilities: www.qmu.ac.uk/sports

Accommodation

Number of places and costs refer to 2013–14
University-provided places: 800
Percentage catered: 0%
Self-catered costs: £97–£114 a week (40 or 50 week contract).
First years are guaranteed accommodation. Residential and age restrictions apply.
International students: guaranteed housing.
Contact: accommodation@qmu.ac.uk
www.qmu.ac.uk/accommodation/

Queen Mary, University of London

Queen Mary (QM) surprised many observers by joining the Russell Group of leading research universities in 2012. But, with a big medical school contributing to a high volume of research, it fitted the profile of the group better than some of the other new entrants. QM is aiming to be among the top ten universities in the UK by 2015, although has set its own criteria, which give more weight to research than is the case in *The Times and Sunday Times* league table, where it remains outside the top 30. Applications have risen at the rate of 7 per cent a year for most of the last decade. Although the demand for places dropped when £9,000 fees were introduced, it bounced back impressively in 2013, when applications increased by more than 20 per cent. There has been particular success in attracting overseas students, who make full use of a unit specialising in English as a foreign language and now account for about one in six of the 18,000 students.

Queen Mary's self-contained campus in the newly fashionable East End of London is the most extensive in the capital. Some £250 million has been spent over the last 15 years on new facilities and strengthening the academic staff. The main campus includes a state-of-the-art learning resource centre with 24-hour access and an award-winning student village with 2,000 en-suite rooms. An arts quarter contains research and teaching facilities, as well as a conference centre. The £20-million Arts2 building, featuring a drama studio and lecture theatre was opened by the Princess Royal in 2012. There is even room for the second-oldest cemetery in England, the Nuevo Jewish burial ground dating from the 18th century. The modern setting is a far cry from the People's Palace, which first used the site to bring education to the Victorian masses, but there is still a community programme as well as conventional teaching and research. The arts-based Westfield College and scientific Queen Mary came together in 1989. The sale of Westfield's Hampstead base released the necessary capital to begin to modernise the Mile End Road campus. Now the historic People's Palace building, which is still QM's most recognisable feature, has been restored to host cultural events for the institution and the local community.

The university's Barts and the London School of Medicine and Dentistry is based in nearby Whitechapel, in the £44-million Blizard Building. Next door is the new BioEnterprise Innovation Centre for science companies. The Centre of the Cell is also located on the Whitechapel campus, the first such interactive facility to be based within a working medical school

---

Mile End Road
London E1 4NS

020 7882 5511 (admissions)
admissions@qmul.ac.uk
www.qmul.ac.uk
www.qmsu.org
Affiliation: Russell Group

The Times and Sunday Times **Rankings**

Overall Ranking: **37** (38)

Student satisfaction:	**=64**	(81.3%)
Research quality:	**=25**	(23.0%)
Entry standards:	**31**	(417)
Student–staff ratio:	**9**	(12.2)
Services & facilities/student:	**26**	(£1,914)
Expected completion rate:	**41**	(89%)
Good honours:	**50**	(68.1%)
Graduate prospects:	**=41**	(69.7%)

research laboratory to give young people a glimpse of how scientists operate. Grades improved spectacularly in the last Research Assessment Exercise, when almost two thirds of the work submitted was rated world-leading or internationally excellent. Linguistics, geography and drama produced the best results in their fields, with dentistry, English and several medical specialisms in the top five, propelling Queen Mary into the top 25 UK universities for research. Queen Mary is best known for its strength in the humanities, where it boasts a clutch of high-profile academics. But the medical school was rated in the top 30 in the world in 2011 and QM is also leading a national initiative to boost the number of maths graduates.

Results in the National Student Survey have been consistently good and improved again in 2013, when overall satisfaction reached 89 per cent. Most lectures are filmed and made available through the Virtual Learning Environment to allow students to go back over parts that they may not have understood. The majority of undergraduates take at least one course in departments other than their own. Interdisciplinary study has always been encouraged: for example, medics can choose selected modules in English and drama. Queen Mary has the highest proportion of undergraduates from working-class homes in the Russell Group – almost a third. Many come from London's ethnic minority groups,

although QM also attracts students from 150 countries outside the UK. There is a flourishing exchange programme, which includes universities in the USA and Japan, as well as Europe, while more than 2,000 students are in Beijing taking joint degrees from QM and the Beijing University of Posts and Telecommunications.

Social life centres on the campus, which features a refurbished students' union with a new bar and a subsidised health and fitness centre, which has helped improve the sports facilities. Students welcome the relatively low prices (for the capital) in east London, and their proximity to the lively youth culture of Spitalfields, Shoreditch and Brick Lane.

Undergraduate Fees and Bursaries

- » Fees for UK/EU students 2014–15 £9.000
- » International student fees 2013–14 £12,750–£15,500
  Medicine £19,400–£29,600
- » Household income below £25K; £1,500 cash a year; £25K–£42.6K, £1,200 a year.
- » 762 NSP awards, linked to UCAS tariff points, of £1,500 fee waiver, £1,000 cash and £500 university services in year 1 only; then bursary as above.
- » Other academic and targeted scholarships available.
- » Check the university's website for the latest information.

Students

Undergraduates:	11,195	(5)
Postgraduates:	2,720	(940)
Mature students:	14.9%	
Overseas students:	20.8%	
Applications per place:	6.7	
From state-sector schools:	83.7%	
From working-class homes:	32.5%	
Satisfaction with students' union	68%	

For detailed information about sports facilities: www.qmsu.org/sportandfitness/

Accommodation

Number of places and costs refer to 2013–14
University-provided places: 2,376
Percentage catered: 5%
Catered costs: £170 upwards a week.
Self-catered costs: £115–£155 a week.
First years giving Queen Mary as first choice get priority, if terms and conditions are met. Residential restrictions apply.
International students given priority if conditions are met.
Contact: residences@qmul.ac.uk

Queen's University, Belfast

Queen's is Northern Ireland's premier university, with graduates in senior leadership positions in 80 of the province's top 100 companies. A member of the Russell Group of leading UK research institutions, it is in the top 200 in the QS World University Rankings and has set about recruiting scores of high-calibre academics, partly in order to move towards the top 100 over the next few years. Its international profile is such that it is a favourite destination for American Fulbright Scholars, while it is also among the top ten universities in Europe for the number of students who go on work placements abroad as part of the Erasmus scheme. Queen's is moving steadily up our league table, following its best-ever performance in the National Student Survey, which places it in the top 20 for overall student satisfaction. Both applications and enrolments increased significantly in 2012, despite fees of £9,000 for British students from outside Northern Ireland.

Over the past ten years, Queen's has invested £350 million in its campus, and plans to spend another £300 million over the next decade. The biggest current development is a £175-million Institute of Health Sciences, part of which is already open. Completed projects include the £50-million McClay Library, which has become a big hit with students, the award-winning £45-million Elms Student Village, a Student Guidance Centre and a new Postgraduate and International Student Centre. The students' union has had a £9-million refurbishment and now includes Enterprise SU, an area for students to improve their enterprise and employability skills. Queen's offers Degree Plus – a qualification providing official recognition of extra-curricular activities and achievements to help graduates in the job market. Skills development is embedded in all the university's programmes to enhance student employability. Key elements include opportunities for work-related learning, engagement with employers and/or alumni and careers workshops. David Gibson, from the Management School, who pioneered the model, was named the world's top enterprise educator by the United States Association of Small Business and Entrepreneurship. A tangible example of this accent on employability was the opening of the first derivatives trading room in the Management School.

Strictly non-denominational teaching is enshrined in a charter which has guaranteed student representation and equal rights for women since 1908. Queen's was one of four university colleges for the whole of Ireland in the nineteenth century, and still draws students from all over the island. Overseas numbers have been boosted by a variety

---

University Road
Belfast BT7 1NN

028 9097 3838 (admissions)
admissions@qub.ac.uk
www.qub.ac.uk
www.qubsu.org
Affiliation: Russell Group

The Times and Sunday Times **Rankings**
Overall Ranking: **=29** (35)

Student satisfaction:	=12	(85.4%)
Research quality:	40	(18.7%)
Entry standards:	40	(388)
Student–staff ratio:	=30	(15.6)
Services & facilities/student:	30	(£1,816)
Expected completion rate:	29	(91.9%)
Good honours:	39	(71.7%)
Graduate prospects:	26	(74.8%)

of agreements with universities in India, Malaysia, China and the USA. However, the majority of students still come from Northern Ireland and Queen's suffers in the comparison of entry grades in league table like ours because relatively few sixth-formers in the Province take four A-levels.

Students are encouraged to take language programmes from a "virtual" language laboratory, which provides online tuition from any computer in the university. IT facilities are good: Queen's was the first institution to meet the national target of providing at least one computer workstation for every five undergraduate students. Support for students has been enhanced by the establishment of new mentoring schemes involving students and alumni. An unusually large proportion of graduates go on to further study, which does Queen's no harm in the employment stakes. The last Research Assessment Exercise showed some progress, with more than half of the university's submission rated as world-leading or internationally excellent, and Queen's is ranked in the UK's top ten in 11 subject areas. Music, English and anthropology produced the highest grades and all branches of engineering were placed in the top ten in their respective disciplines.

The city centre is not short of nightlife, but the social scene is still concentrated on the students' union and the surrounding area. Sports facilities, which include a university cottage in the Mourne mountains, were further improved with the completion of a £20-million programme of investment. The university's new facility at Upper Malone features an arena pitch which can host football, rugby or Gaelic sport, with a further 14 pitches on the same site. A spectator stand adjoins the new clubhouse and there are more than 20 changing rooms, as well as a strength and conditioning suite, conference and hospitality facilities, and a 3km recreational trim trail.

The university district is among the most attractive in Belfast, and is one of the city's main cultural and recreational areas. The university's highly successful international arts festival runs each autumn, and the university boasts the only full-time university cinema in the UK, as well as an art gallery and theatre, all of which are open to students and the wider community alike.

Undergraduate Fees and Bursaries

» Fees for Northern Irish/EU students 2013–14   £3,575
» Fees for English, Scottish, Welsh (RUK) students   £9,000
» International student fees 2013–14   £11,500–£14,750
    Medicine   £15,225–£28,720
    Dentistry   £23,322
» The top 50 NI students on STEM course, year 1 scholarship of £1,000.
» RUK students (excluding medicine, dentistry and pharmacy) with at least AAB at A-Level or equivalent, fee waiver of £2,500 a year; with ABB or equivalent, £1,750 fee waiver a year; with offer grades, £1,250 fee waiver a year.

Students

Undergraduates:	**13,765**	**(4,100)**
Postgraduates:	**2,835**	**(2,290)**
Mature students:	**13.6%**	
Overseas students:	**5.0%**	
Applications per place:	**5.5**	
From state-sector schools:	**97.5%**	
From working-class homes:	**31.3%**	
Satisfaction with students' union	**80%**	

For detailed information about sports facilities:
www.queenssport.com

Accommodation

Number of places and costs refer to 2013–14
University-provided places: around 2,000
Percentage catered: 0%
Self-catered costs: £71.89–£102.50 a week.
First-year students are guaranteed accommodation if conditions are met.
International students: as above.
Contact: accommodation@qub.ac.uk
www.stayatqueens.com

University of Reading

Reading bucked the national trend with 11 per cent growth in the demand for places when £9,000 fees were introduced in 2012 and managed almost another 5 per cent increase in 2013. With nearly seven applications for every place, the competition for admission has never been as great. Applications from British students continued to grow in 2013, but the biggest increase was 35 per cent from international applicants. Many will have been attracted by Reading's new venture in Malaysia. The first undergraduates will begin courses on a temporary site at Johor Baru, close to Singapore, in 2014. The university's stylish new campus will open at the Iksandar Education City, on the southern tip of Malaysia, in 2015.

In recent years, Reading has invested over £400 million in new teaching and research facilities on its hometown campus, opened two new halls of residence and improved catering outlets and other student facilities. The £17-million Hopkins Building added laboratories and teaching space for pharmacy and cardiovascular research, and there is a new world-class Chemical Analysis Facility. The £11-million Minghella Building for film, theatre and TV opened in the spring of 2011, while a separate Enterprise Centre brings together academic expertise with local and international technology-based businesses.

With 17,000 students, Reading is one of the medium-sized campus universities that have demonstrated their appeal through the National Student Survey. Consistently in or near the top 20, it again satisfied almost 90 per cent of its final-year undergraduates in the 2013 results. The university also did well in the last Research Assessment Exercise, despite entering a much higher proportion of its academics than many of its peers. More than half of their work was considered world-leading or internationally excellent, with archaeology and art and design doing particularly well. There are international centres of research excellence in areas such as food security, agriculture, biological and physical sciences, meteorology, and European histories and cultures.

There are three main sites within Reading, including the original 320-acre parkland site, and the university also owns 2,000 acres of farmland at nearby Sonning and Shinfield, where the renowned Centre for Dairy Research (CEDAR) is located. To these has been added the former Henley Management College, which became the university's business school in 2008. The college's attractive site, on the banks of the river at Henley-on-Thames, houses postgraduate and executive programmes, while undergraduates are taught in the £35-million business school on the main

Whiteknights
PO Box 217
Reading RG6 6AH

0118 378 8618/9
student.recruitment@
    reading.ac.uk
www.reading.ac.uk
www.rusu.co.uk
Affiliation: none

The Times and Sunday Times **Rankings**
Overall Ranking: **35** (=24)

Student satisfaction:	**=41**	(82.3%)
Research quality:	**=27**	(22.7%)
Entry standards:	**42**	(378)
Student–staff ratio:	**=30**	(15.6)
Services & facilities/student:	**53**	(£1,484)
Expected completion rate:	**38**	(90.4%)
Good honours:	**26**	(74.6%)
Graduate prospects:	**=44**	(69.2%)

Whiteknights campus.

Reading was the only university established between the two world wars, having been Oxford's extension college for the first part of the last century, but the attractive main campus now has a modern feel. A multimillion-pound student services building provides a one-stop shop for student support and welfare, and sports facilities have been extended. Water sports are a strong focus, with off-campus boathouses on the Thames and a sailing and canoeing club nearby. Representative teams have a good record in inter-university competitions and the campus was chosen as a pre-Olympics training camp for basketball and fencing. The university's location, a bus ride away from Heathrow Airport, and an international reputation in key areas for developing countries have always ensured a healthy flow of overseas students. About one undergraduate in six is from an independent school and just under a quarter come from working-class homes, below average for the university's subjects and entry qualifications.

All undergraduates take career management skills modules that contribute five credits towards their degree classification. The online system, which has 200 web pages of advice, exercises and information, has been bought by 30 other universities and colleges. Sessions are delivered jointly by academics and careers advisors, with input from alumni and leading employers. Reading's recent graduate employment figures have been good and the university is hoping to improve them further by providing placement opportunities for all students, regardless of degree.

The town may not be the most fashionable, but it has plenty of nightlife and an award-winning shopping centre. It also offers temporary and part-time employment opportunities for students. London is easily accessible by train, but the cost of living is on a par with the capital. The university has spent £200 million on new student accommodation and there are plans for a private company to redevelop some of the older stock. The large students' union was refurbished in 2007, improving and extending its popular main venue. The union has been voted among the best in Britain, and has won numerous awards, including Best Bar None status for encouraging safe drinking. Students who live in town can make use of the free night bus service to take them back into Reading.

Undergraduate Fees and Bursaries

» Fees for UK/EU students 2014–15 £9,000
» International student fees 2013–14 £12,600–£15,000
» 700 NSP awards of £3,000 variable package in year 1, £1,000 in other years (eligibility assessed each year)
» Foundation degree fee waivers of 50 per cent for selected courses.
» Other academic and targeted scholarships available.

Students

Undergraduates:	**8,825**	**(115)**
Postgraduates:	**2,625**	**(1,945)**
Mature students:	**7.5%**	
Overseas students:	**14.2%**	
Applications per place:	**7.2**	
From state-sector schools:	**83.4%**	
From working-class homes:	**24.3%**	
Satisfaction with students' union	**80%**	

For detailed information about sports facilities: www.sport.reading.ac.uk

Accommodation

Number of places and costs refer to 2013–14
University-provided places: about 4,300
Percentage catered: 20%
Catered costs: £122.78–£167.58 (40 weeks, catering during terms).
Self-catered costs: £99.89–£149.59 (40–51 weeks).
First-year undergraduate students are guaranteed a place if conditions are met.
International students: guaranteed if conditions are met.
Contact: www.reading.ac.uk/accommodation

Robert Gordon University

Robert Gordon University (RGU) has slipped from being the top post-1992 university in our league table this year, but it remains in the top five. Overall student satisfaction remains well above average for the university's courses and entry qualifications, but graduate employment is its strongest suit. RGU regularly features among the top 20 universities on this measure. Close links with the North Sea oil and gas industries help in this respect, but work placements lasting up to a year that have become the norm on all the university's courses take much of the credit. With nursing and health sciences now accounting for a large share of the places, RGU gives itself the soubriquet of the Professional University. The creative industries are a growth area and there is a full portfolio of courses in business, design and engineering. Flexible programmes, with credit accumulation and transfer, make for easy movement in and out of the university for an often mobile local workforce.

Named after an eighteenth-century philanthropist, RGU currently has two sites around the city. The historic Schoolhill site adjoins Aberdeen Art Gallery in the city centre, while Garthdee, where the majority of undergraduates are taught, is located at the south side of the city, overlooking the River Dee. The university is planning to relocate all teaching to the Garthdee campus, which is in the midst of a £170-million development programme. A striking new green glass library tower has become a landmark at the heart of the campus. New facilities for Engineering, Computing, Pharmacy and Life Sciences faculties opened in 2013, while those for Art, Architecture and the Built Environment are planned for Phase 2 of the project. Other developments in recent years have included additional specialist facilities for the Faculty of Health and Social Care. The Aberdeen Business School, designed by Norman Foster, is already being upgraded with new teaching and student learning spaces and an open plan area with IT access, group study areas, exhibition and seminar space.

Robert Gordon University has a pedigree in education that goes back 250 years. The university now offers about 150 degrees. Students from the city's two universities mix easily, and there is healthy academic rivalry in some areas, despite the obvious differences. There are also partnerships with Aberdeen and Banff and Buchan colleges, which have become associate colleges of the university to encourage progression from school, to further and then higher education. Almost a third of RGU's submission in the last Research Assessment Exercise was considered world-leading or internationally

---

Schoolhill
Aberdeen AB10 1FR

01224 262728 (enquiries)
ugoffice@rgu.ac.uk
www.rgu.ac.uk
www.rguunion.co.uk
Affiliation: none

ABERDEEN
Edinburgh
Belfast
London
Cardiff

The Times and Sunday Times **Rankings**
Overall Ranking: **=52** (51)

Student satisfaction:	=64	(81.3%)
Research quality:	=61	(5.3%)
Entry standards:	50	(350)
Student–staff ratio:	77	(19.7)
Services & facilities/student:	92	(£1,216)
Expected completion rate:	=84	(81.9%)
Good honours:	=67	(62.5%)
Graduate prospects:	7	(81.8%)

excellent, with library and information management the star performer. Three research institutes have since been launched to focus on the university's strengths in business and information; innovation, design and sustainability; and health and welfare.

Like many modern universities, Robert Gordon recruits most of its students locally, nearly 60 per cent of them female. However, overseas student numbers have been growing sharply and the overall demand for places has been more consistent than at most universities north of the border. Both applications and enrolments increased in 2012, following even stronger growth in the previous year. Efforts to extend access beyond the normal higher education catchment have produced a diverse student population, with three in ten undergraduates coming from working-class homes and 93 per cent coming from state schools or colleges. The dropout rate has improved and at little more than 11 per cent, matches the UK average for RGU's subjects and entry qualifications.

The university has a strong focus on new technology. An award-winning virtual campus was launched with an online course in e-business for postgraduates. It also enables management undergraduates to receive course materials via an intranet, and other degree and short courses are available. The new Moodle system is used across Robert Gordon courses for both on-campus and distance learning students, providing teaching, notes, online forums for discussion and electronic submission options.

Aberdeen is a long way to go for English students, but train and air links are excellent, and the city regularly features in the top ten for quality of life. A £12-million sports and leisure centre opened at the university in 2005, providing a centre of excellence for the region in hockey, as well as a 25-metre swimming pool, three gyms, a climbing wall and bouldering room, a café bar, three exercise studios and a large sports hall. Sports scholarships are available to budding athletes, with Olympic swimmer Hannah Miley amongst the recipients. Although accommodation can be expensive in the private sector, low prices in the students' union partially compensate, and there are enough residential places to guarantee housing to first years from outside the local area.

Undergraduate Fees and Bursaries

» Fees for Scottish and EU students 2013–14   No fee
» Fees for Non-Scottish UK (RUK) students 2013–14
    £5,000–£6,750
   Pharmacy   £8,500
» Fees for international students 2013–14   £9,900–£12,000
» Academic and targeted scholarships available.
» Check the university's website for the latest information.

Students

Undergraduates:	**7,030**	**(1,585)**
Postgraduates:	**1,850**	**(2,230)**
Mature students:	**21.8%**	
Overseas students:	**11.4%**	
Applications per place:	**5.2**	
From state-sector schools:	**93.4%**	
From working-class homes:	**30.9%**	
Satisfaction with students' union	**70%**	

For detailed information about sports facilities:
www.rgu.ac.uk/rgusport

Accommodation

Number of places and costs refer to 2013–14
University-provided places: 1,563
Percentage catered: 0%
Self-catered costs: £92 (single) – £175.00 (flat) a week.
All first-year students are eligible to apply for student accommodation. Residential restrictions apply.
International students: given priority for accommodation.
Contact: accommodation@rgu.ac.uk
www.rgu.ac.uk/living/accommodation

Roehampton University

Roehampton will be one of a dozen universities – and the only one in London - charging less than £9,000 for all its degree courses in 2014. At £8,750 a year, it will not be a big discount, but since the introduction of the new fee regime in 2012, Roehampton has been transparent about its own costs and the amount that would be spent on undergraduate education. There was a sharp drop in applications when the fees went up to £8,000, but the numbers accepting a place were only 200 down on the previous year. Now there is an additional attraction on the 54-acre campus in south-west London, with a Swiss hospitality management college opening a branch campus there. The Glion Institute of Higher Education will offer undergraduate and postgraduate programmes in hospitality in its first venture outside Switzerland. The university has also gone into partnership with Laureate, Glion's owners, to offer courses online, beginning a suite of Masters degrees in business and management.

Roehampton has been fully independent since 2004, after four years in a federation with Surrey University. There have been record intakes despite rising entry requirements. Roehampton has a proud and distinguished history dating back to the 1840s, its colleges having been among the first in the country to open higher education to women. Today the university has diversified into business, the arts and humanities, social sciences and the human and life sciences, while maintaining its historic strength in education, which still accounts for a quarter of the students. The university has embraced the new School Direct system of school-based teacher training, operating in partnership with schools as well as running its own postgraduate and undergraduate training programmes. Successes in the last Research Assessment Exercise, when Roehampton entered a much higher proportion of its academics than most of its peer group, added to the university's reputation. A third of the submission was judged to be world-leading or internationally excellent, with the university producing the best results in the country for dance and biological anthropology, and doing well in drama, theatre and performance studies, English literature and education.

Roehampton is a collegiate university with four distinctive colleges, which still maintain some of the traditional ethos of their religious foundations: the Anglican Whitelands, the Roman Catholic Digby Stuart, the Methodist Southlands, and the Froebel, which follows the humanist teachings of Frederick Froebel. Students need not follow any of these denominations to enrol in the colleges. The university also

---

Erasmus House
Roehampton Lane
London SW15 5PU

020 8392 3232 (enquiries)
enquiries@roehampton.ac.uk
www.roehampton.ac.uk
www.roehampton
  student.com
Affiliations: Cathedrals
  Group

has a Jewish resource centre and Muslim prayer rooms. All four colleges are based on a single campus, with stunning parkland and lakes, on or adjacent to Roehampton Lane. It is the first Living Landscape University in London, having joined the Beverley Brook Living Landscape, which neighbours and extends onto the campus. The scheme will provide opportunities for students to learn practical conservation, as well as teamwork and leadership skills.

Whitelands is based in Parkstead House, the 18th-century mansion overlooking Richmond Park, which also houses the School of Human and Life Sciences. The buildings have been refurbished with IT facilities, student accommodation, laboratories and teaching space. The colleges all have their own bars and other leisure facilities, although they are open to all members of the university. Recent capital projects include a £4-million facility for the School of Arts and a new national centre of excellence for teaching on citizenship education, human rights and social justice. There is a fully functioning newsroom for journalism and media students.

The Quality Assurance Agency complimented Roehampton on the accessibility of academic staff to students and the positive ways in which they responded to student needs. One example has been the provision of enhanced sports facilities on campus, with a new gym, two football pitches, running track and a multi-use games area. The sport performance and rehabilitation centre provides state-of-the-art laboratory facilities and performance coaching. The university is a high-performance centre for British fencing and sitting volleyball.

More than 95 per cent of undergraduates were educated in state schools and 37 per cent come from working-class homes. The projected dropout rate improved dramatically in the last two years. At only 6.5 per cent, it is less than half the national average for Roehampton's courses and entry grades.

Most first years who want a hall place are offered one, with priority going to those living furthest away. While rents are not cheap for those who prefer the private sector, students like the proximity of central London and the lively and attractive suburbs around Roehampton.

Undergraduate Fees and Bursaries

» Fees for UK/EU students 2014–15   £8,250
    Foundation degree   £7,500
» International student fees 2013–14   £10,950
» 249 NSP awards based on best UCAS tariff scores: £3,000, year 1; £1,500, years 2 and 3, mainly as fee waiver; 33 NSP awards of £2,500 fee waiver and £500 cash in year 1 only.
» For those with at least ABB at A level or equivalent, subject to conditions, £2,000 a year scholarship.
» For male primary education students with household income below £25K, £1,000 bursary each year.

Students

Undergraduates:	**6,175**	**(600)**
Postgraduates:	**1,320**	**(1,155)**
Mature students:	**23.1%**	
Overseas students:	**7.4%**	
Applications per place:	**3.5**	
From state-sector schools:	**95.4%**	
From working-class homes:	**37.4%**	
Satisfaction with students' union	**72%**	

For detailed information about sports facilities: www.roehampton.ac.uk/Sport-Roehampton

Accommodation

Number of places and costs refer to 2013–14
University-provided places: 1,500
Percentage catered: 0%
Self-catered costs: £100.45–£114.10 (standard) – £129.50 (en suite) a week.
First years are given priority if conditions met. Local restrictions apply.
International students: guaranteed for first year
Contact: accommodation@roehampton.ac.uk or tel: 020 8392 3166

Royal Agricultural University

After 168 years as the Royal Agricultural College, which every monarch since Queen Victoria has visited, the RAU was awarded university status in 2013. With only 1,100 students, it was not eligible for its new title until the criteria changed in 2012 and it is now the smallest publicly-funded university in the UK. The new university enjoys a global reputation but does not appear in our main league table because, with only six degree subjects, it does not offer the broad spread of courses necessary for a meaningful comparison with less specialist universities. However, the RAU does offer degrees in business management, and real estate and land management, as well as its portfolio of agricultural courses on an attractive campus close to Cirencester, in the Cotswolds.

The RAU was the first agricultural college in the English-speaking world when it was established in 1845 on the initiative of the Fairford and Cirencester Farmers' Club, which was concerned at the lack of government support for education, particularly in relation to agriculture. As the Royal Agricultural College, it launched its first degree in 1984 and was fully independent until 2001, when it began to receive state funding.

The institution embarked on its biggest-ever campus development programme in the run-up to university status. A new teaching block has opened with seven well-equipped teaching rooms; a biomass heating system has been installed as part of the university's green agenda, but also as a teaching resource; a postgraduate study centre has been added; a new accommodation block has opened with 50 en-suite rooms. There are two university farms, both close to the campus, covering a total of 1,200 acres. Coates Manor Farm focuses on arable farming, while Harnhill Farm, which was bought in 2009, is an example of an integrated livestock and cropping system. In addition, there is an equestrian centre providing a stabling and livery facility, and students also have access to a large dairy complex. All are run as commercial enterprises and students learn from their physical and financial data.

Perhaps not surprisingly in view of the range of subjects on offer, the university is one of the few in the UK that has a majority of male students. Almost nine out of ten undergraduates are school or college leavers, rather than mature students, and there is a small contingent of international students, who pay the same fees as their British and European counterparts. Those have been set at £9,000 since 2012, when the number of new undergraduates dropped despite a rise in applications. As the Royal Agricultural College, the institution always had a reputation for attracting well-heeled

---

Stroud Road
Cirencester
Gloucestershire GL7 6JS

01285 889912 (admissions enquiry)
admissions@rac.ac.uk
www.rac.ac.uk
http://rac.ac.uk/student-life/
leisure/student-union
Affiliation: none

The Times Rankings
The Royal Agricultural University does not appear in our main league table this year because its courses do not cover the broad range of subjects needed for meaningful comparisons to be made with less specialist institutions.

students: the 43 per cent of undergraduates from independent schools is higher than at Oxford or Cambridge. But 41 per cent come from the four poorest socio-economic groups – also one of the largest proportions in the UK – contributing to a unique student population, in which perhaps only one in five does not fall into either category.

All business, equine and agriculture courses include a 20-week work placement. There is an extensive network of student placement sponsors in the UK and overseas, and part-time work is available both in the university and in nearby Cirencester. On campus, there is a well-stocked library and computer suites, as well as specialist laboratories. The virtual learning environment ensures that all teaching materials are available online 24 hours a day. However, there was a substantial drop in student satisfaction in the 2013 National Student Survey. Although 84 per cent of final-year undergraduates declared themselves satisfied overall with their course, this represented a drop of three percentage points at a time when satisfaction was rising nationally. Scores in the NSS are one of the factors holding the university back in our agriculture table, together with relatively low grades in the last Research Assessment Exercise. Fewer than ten academics were entered and only 15 per cent of the work submitted was considered internationally excellent.

There are eight halls of residence on campus for undergraduates with enough rooms for most first-years to be offered a place. However, there is no guarantee and rooms are allocated in a first-come-first-served basis. Private rentals are available in Cirencester and the surrounding area. Sport plays an important part in student life and, in addition to the normal range, there are clubs for polo, clay pigeon shooting, beagling and team chasing (a cross-country equestrian sport). The campus is the centre of social activities, including four balls each year, which the university claims are amongst the country's finest. There are ample opportunities to explore the Cotswold countryside and London is only 90 minutes away by train.

Undergraduate Fees and Bursaries

» Fees for UK/EU students 2014–15: £9,000
» International student fees 2013–14: £9,000
» At least 31 NSP awards for disadvantaged students of minimum £3,000 a year fee and/or accommodation waiver, based on academic achievement.
» For those with household income below £25K from disadvantaged background but not in receipt of an NSP, £1,000–£3,000 a year fee or accommodation waiver.
» For those with household income £25K–42.6K in financial need, £1,500 fee and/or accommodation waiver in year 1.
» Skills bursarie80.5 of £250 in years 1 and 2 to enhance the development of personal and professional skills.
» Academic scholarships, internships and bursaries for student-led projects also available.

Students

Undergraduates:	**940**	**(30)**
Postgraduates:	**205**	**(15)**
Mature students:	**9.0%**	
Overseas students:	**9.3%**	
Applications per place:	**2.8**	
From state-sector schools:	**54.5%**	
From working-class homes:	**40.7%**	
Satisfaction with students' union	**58%**	

For detailed information about sports facilities:
www.rau.ac.uk/student-life/leisure/sports-clubs

Accommodation

Number of places and costs refer to 2013–14
University-provided places: 284
Percentage catered: 20%
Catered costs: £129 (en-suite twin) – £210 (en-suite single) a week; £102 (en-suite twin) – £183 en-suite single) a week for dinner, bed & breakfast
Self-catered costs: £125 (en-suite single) a week.
First years cannot be guaranteed accommodation.
International students: as above
Contact: www.rau.ac.uk/student-life/living/accommodation

Royal Holloway, University of London

Royal Holloway has spent £5 million refurbishing the 600 student rooms in perhaps the most distinctive university building in Britain. The Founder's Building, which also houses teaching and exhibition space, is modelled on a French chateau and was opened by Queen Victoria. It is the centrepiece of the University of London's "campus in the country", 135 acres of woodland between Windsor Castle and Heathrow, which was the Olympic village for the rowing teams in the 2012 Games. More than £100 million was been spent on the campus over five years, resulting in an impressive range of new and refurbished academic and social facilities.

Other recent projects have included extensions to the School of Management and the main library, as well as new student residences, which have been praised for their comfort and eco-friendly features. A new student services centre opened in 2013, following the £1.2-million refurbishment of the students' union in the previous year. The restoration and extension of the listed building that houses the drama and theatre department was also completed in 2013, with an auditorium seating around 175 people on two levels, rehearsal space and a foyer. Work has begun on the final phase of redevelopment of a huge Victorian boiler house to create a multipurpose cultural space that is due to open in September 2014.

Both Bedford College and Royal Holloway, which amalgamated to form the existing college in 1985, were founded for women only, their legacy commemorated in the Bedford Centre for the History of Women. However, the gender balance in the student population is now roughly equal and, although still best known for the arts, Royal Holloway has a broad portfolio of subjects, including a science Foundation year for those wishing to change academic direction. There are now a record 9,000 full-time students, and both applications and enrolments held up in 2012, against the national trend, when £9,000 fees arrived. The programme of student support includes £1 million for postgraduates so that students who graduate with large debts are not deterred from continuing their studies. The extra fee income will also go towards an expansion of the academic staff and better student services.

The three faculties have been reorganised to encourage an inter-disciplinary approach to teaching and research. A separate Faculty of Management and Economics has been created, while humanities subjects have been brought together with the arts in a new Arts and Social Science Faculty. There is no change

---

University of London
Egham
Surrey TW20 OEX

01784 414944 (admissions)
contact via website
www.rhul.ac.uk
www.su.rhul.ac.uk
Affiliation: 1994 Group

The Times and Sunday Times **Rankings**
Overall Ranking: **28** (27)

Student satisfaction:	=43	(82.2%)
Research quality:	15	(27.7%)
Entry standards:	35	(400)
Student–staff ratio:	=33	(16.2)
Services & facilities/student:	57	(£1,457)
Expected completion rate:	=22	(93.2%)
Good honours:	29	(73.7%)
Graduate prospects:	=58	(63.9%)

to the third Faculty of Science. Of the work entered for the 2008 Research Assessment Exercise, 60 per cent was rated world-leading or internationally excellent, cementing Royal Holloway's place among the top 25 research universities. Music was ranked top in the UK, with 90 per cent of its research in the top two categories, while biology, drama, earth sciences, economics, geography, German, media arts and psychology were all in the top 10 in their fields. Royal Holloway has been named an Academic Centre of Excellence in Cyber Security Research by the UK Government – one of only eight such awards nationwide.

Royal Holloway draws a fifth of its undergraduates from independent schools, although the proportion coming from working-class homes has been rising. The ethnic mix is above average and the projected dropout rate of 6 per cent is below the official benchmark. The new Royal Holloway Passport is intended to enhance graduates' employability. The scheme recognises the additional skills that students gain from many extracurricular activities and which future graduate employers greatly value. An Advanced Skills Programme, covering information technology, communication skills and foreign languages, further encourages breadth of study. The university offers a number of e-degrees and promotes numerous opportunities to study abroad, building on the international flavour of the campus and its links with institutions such as New York, Sydney and Yale universities.

Nearly 3,000 students live in halls of residence. The college's green belt location at Egham, Surrey, ensures that social life is concentrated on the active students' union. However, the centre of London is only 35 minutes away by rail for those determined to seek the high life. Sports facilities are good and have been upgraded recently – Royal Holloway claims to be "the University of London's best sporting college". It has had considerable success with its "student talented athlete award scheme" (STARS). Students enjoy an active cultural scene, and a thriving Community Action programme involves over 1,000 students volunteering with various local organisations and charities. Many students come from London and the Home Counties, and go home at the weekend, but the lively students' union puts on entertainment and activities seven days a week.

Undergraduate Fees and Bursaries

» Fees for UK/EU students 2014–15 £9,000
» International student fees 2013–14 £12,600–£14,250
» For all English students with household income below £25K, £2,000 fee waiver and/or university services and £1,000 cash, year 1; £2,000 package, other years; £25K–£30K, £1,000 cash; £30K–£42.6K, £750 cash.
» Care leavers provided with free year-round university accommodation for duration of study.

Students

Undergraduates:	**6,825**	**(530)**
Postgraduates:	**2,035**	**(475)**
Mature students:	**9.8%**	
Overseas students:	**25.0%**	
Applications per place:	**5.9**	
From state-sector schools:	**79.9%**	
From working-class homes:	**25.7%**	
Satisfaction with students' union	**60%**	

For detailed information about sports facilities:
www.rhul.ac.uk/sports

Accommodation

Number of places and costs refer to 2013–14
University-provided places: 2,979
Percentage catered: 37%
Catered costs: £83–£158 a week (30–38 weeks).
Self-catered costs: £118–£156 a week (30–38 weeks).
First years are guaranteed accommodation provided conditions are met.
International students: non-EU students guaranteed accommodation.
Contact: StudentAccommodation@rhul.ac.uk

University of St Andrews

Scotland's oldest university and the third oldest in the English-speaking world has been celebrating its 600th anniversary in 2013. It remains the leading Scottish university in our league table – a position it has occupied for the last eight years, thanks in large part to outstanding scores in the National Student Survey (NSS). There was another big rise in overall satisfaction in 2013. It is our Best Scottish University.

St Andrews has long been fashionable among a mainly middle-class clientele – students from independent schools take more than 40 per cent of the places – but its appeal is far wider than that, with nearly eight applicants chasing each place. International students from over 100 countries account for more than a third of the intake and give the university a cosmopolitan feel. Fee concessions and exchange schemes have boosted applications, particularly from the USA, which provides nearly a fifth of first-year students on its own. Along with Edinburgh, St Andrews has set the highest fees in the UK for undergraduates from England, Wales or Northern Ireland since 2012–13. It charges £9,000 a year for the full four years of a degree, although there are bursaries for students whose family income is below £42,600. Scots and other EU students continue to pay nothing. With almost 30 per cent of St Andrews students coming from south of the border, the new fees might have been expected to hit recruitment, but both applications and enrolments rose in 2012 and all available places were filled before Clearing began in 2013.

The town of St Andrews is steeped in history, as well as being the centre of the golfing world. The university at its heart accounts for nearly half of the 18,000 inhabitants. There are close cultural and social relations between town and gown. New students ("bejants" and "bejantines") acquire third or fourth-year "parents" to ease them into university life, and on Raisin Monday give their academic guardians a bottle of wine in return for a receipt in Latin, which can be written on anything. Another unusual feature is that all humanities students are awarded an MA rather than a BA. Many of the main buildings date from the 15th and 16th centuries, but sciences are taught at the modern North Haugh site a few streets away. Everything is within walking distance, but bicycles are common. Although small, St Andrews offers a wide range of courses. The university's reputation has always rested mainly on the humanities, which have a £1.3-million research centre. An £8-million headquarters for the School of International Relations opened in 2006, with Europe's first Centre for Syrian Studies, an

College Gate
St Andrews
Fife KY16 9AJ

01334 462150 (admissions)
student.recruitment@st-andrews.
    ac.uk (pre-recruitment)
www.st-andrews.ac.uk
www.yourunion.net
Affiliation: none

The Times and Sunday Times **Rankings**

Overall Ranking: **4** (6)

Student satisfaction:	=9	(85.9%)
Research quality:	=13	(28.0%)
Entry standards:	5	(524)
Student–staff ratio:	10	(12.6)
Services & facilities/student:	7	(£2,298)
Expected completion rate:	=7	(96.8%)
Good honours:	3	(88.8%)
Graduate prospects:	9	(X%)

Institute of Iranian Studies and a Centre for Peace and Conflict Studies. St Andrews has the largest mediaeval history department in Britain and has now added film studies and sustainable development. A full range of physical sciences is also on offer, with sophisticated lasers and the largest optical telescope in Britain.

A £45-million Medical and Biological Sciences Building opened in 2010, one of the first UK medical schools whose research facilities are fully integrated with the other sciences, offering an important new dimension to medical training and research. A £5-million Bio-medical Sciences Research complex, to lead the fight against superbugs and serious viral, bacterial and parasitic diseases, followed in 2011. The university is planning a Green Energy Centre and a Knowledge Exchange Centre for spin-out companies, new business and prototype testing on the site of the former paper mill five miles away at Guardbridge. Support for scholarships and medical research are among the first targets of a £100-million fundraising campaign launched by Prince William and his then fiancée, both St Andrews graduates, to mark the university's 600th anniversary. Nearly 60 per cent of the work submitted for the 2008 Research Assessment Exercise was rated as world-leading or internationally excellent. St Andrews was joint top in the UK for philosophy and top in Scotland for physics and astronomy, German, film studies, applied maths, French and psychology.

Students do not come to St Andrews for the nightclubs, but there is no shortage of parties in a tight-knit community. A £12-million extension and redevelopment of the Students' Association building has begun, but it will not be complete until the end of 2015. The sports facilities are excellent and more than half of all students live in halls. Self-catering accommodation for 920 students during term and three-star accommodation for golfers and other tourists in vacations was opened by Gordon Brown in 2007. Features such as the grass roof made it the first university residence to be awarded the Green Tourism Business Scheme's Gold Award. A further 250 residential places opened in 2010.

Undergraduate Fees and Bursaries

» Fees for Scottish and EU students 2013–14   No fee
» Fees for Non-Scottish UK (RUK) students 2013–14   £9,000
» Fees for international students 2013–14   £15,460
   Medical science   £23,540
» For Scottish students with household income below £42.6K, 50 academic bursaries of up to £2,000 a year. For all students, top 100 at the end of year 1, £5,000 scholarship.
» For RUK students (2013–14) with household income below £42.6K, bursary to top up student's official funding to £7,500 a year.
» Scholarships and bursaries are available.
» Check the university's website for the latest information.

Students

Undergraduates:	**6,600**	**(1,200)**
Postgraduates:	**1,640**	**(415)**
Mature students:	**2.5%**	
Overseas students:	**41.6%**	
Applications per place:	**8.4**	
From state-sector schools:	**58.7%**	
From working-class homes:	**13.0%**	
Satisfaction with students' union	**73%**	

For detailed information about sports facilities:
www.st-andrews.ac.uk/sport

Accommodation

Number of places and costs refer to 2013–14
University-provided places: 3,702
Percentage catered: 40%
Catered costs: £127–£209 a week (33 weeks).
Self-catered costs: £75–£189 a week (38 weeks).
Single first-year undergraduates are guaranteed accommodation if they apply by 30 June in year of entry.
Policy for international students: as above.
Contact: accommodation@st-andrews.ac.uk
www.st-andrews.ac.uk/admissions/Accommodation

University of St Mark and St John

Marjon, now the University of St Mark and St John, was already thriving in spite of the move to higher fees before its new title was announced. Both applications and enrolments were stable in 2012, against the national trend. Undergraduate fees, which were held at £7,995 for most subjects in 2013, will jump to £9,000 across the board in 2014. Only the 40 anticipated entrants to Marjon's Foundation degrees, taught at Exeter College, will pay less at just £5,250. Much of the extra income will go on bursaries for students from low-income families and outreach activities in the South West. The new university is among the top 20 in the country for the proportion of undergraduates from areas of low participation in higher education, but the projected dropout rate of 12 per cent is still better than the national average for its courses and entry qualifications.

Established in 1840 as a Church of England teacher training college in London, with the son of poet Samuel Taylor Coleridge as its first principal, Marjon describes itself as "arguably the third oldest Higher Education Institution in England." The College of St Mark and St John only moved to Plymouth in 1973. Following a period of affiliation to the University of Exeter, it was granted the power to award its own degrees in 2007 and achieved full university status in 2013. With fewer than 4,000 students, it was not eligible before this year's change in regulations, but now aims to create an "innovative model of a high-quality, smaller university". Professor Cara Aitchison has moved from the University of Edinburgh to become the first Vice-Chancellor.

Marjon is officially a Church of England Voluntary Institution, one of several religious foundations among the latest crop of universities. The attractive modern Chaplaincy Centre is at the heart of the campus, but there is less emphasis on religion in the new university's promotional material than at some of its counterparts. The new university lists sport at the top of its list of specialisms, followed by education, languages, journalism and the creative arts. A variety of two-year degrees have been introduced to supplement the traditional three-year model. But teacher training remains strong: Ofsted rates the primary training as outstanding.

There has been investment of £20 million in the campus buildings and sports facilities. The library underwent extensive refurbishment in 2011 to provide a new social learning space on the ground floor. The total book holdings are over 145,000 volumes and there is a rapidly

---

Derriford Road
Plymouth, Devon PL6 8BH

01752 636890 (admissions)
admissions@ucpmarjon.ac.uk
www.marjon.ac.uk
www.marjonsu.com
Affiliation: GuildHE;
    Cathedrals Group

The Times and Sunday Times **Rankings**

Overall Ranking: **=71** (n/a)

Student satisfaction:	**=4**	(86.3%)
Research quality:	**=115**	(0.3%)
Entry standards:	**=110**	(253)
Student–staff ratio:	**=88**	(20.5)
Services & facilities/student:	**=112**	(£954)
Expected completion rate:	**=48**	(87.2%)
Good honours:	**113**	(51.7%)
Graduate prospects:	**61**	(63.7%)

growing collection of e-books. The campus development programme has also seen a new sports centre, refurbished student housing and a new entrance and student centre. A new Journalism and Media Centre opened in 2013, conceived and designed by the lecturers. It includes an iPad teaching room, full iMac classroom, four iMac media editing suites, two of which act as a radio studio, and an editorial meeting room. The three BA programmes – journalism, sports journalism and media production – are strongly vocational, and the new centre is made available to commercial businesses.

The university occupies a large greenfield site on the outskirts of Plymouth. The green agenda extends to an on-campus duck pond and nature trail. The latest addition is an orchard planted with local varieties of apple tree, intended to celebrate the biodiversity of the campus. With around 3,500 students on a single campus, Marjon sells itself as small and friendly as well as safe, with small class sizes and an extensive social programme organised by an active students' union.

Sports facilities are extremely good: there is a 25-metre swimming pool, climbing wall and both grass and artificial pitches. The Ghanaian Olympic team used Marjon as its base for pre-Games training in 2012 and Plymouth Argyle footballers now use the university's training facilities such as the gym, sports therapy centre and sports science lab. A new Foundation degree in football coaching and development is also part of the collaboration with the football club and there are links, too, with Plymouth Albion Rugby Football Club.

On campus there are residential places for 456 students in 7 halls of residence and 38 village houses. Rents compare favourably with most universities and were not increased in 2013. Most first-year students from outside the locality are offered places. If none is available, students are offered accommodation with a homestay family until a room on campus becomes available. Those living on campus may only bring a car in exceptional circumstances. Plymouth is a lively city that students tend to enjoy. The city centre, with its £200-million shopping mall, is a short bus ride from the campus.

Undergraduate Fees and Bursaries

» Fees for UK/EU students 2014–15   £9,000
   Foundation degrees   £5,250–£9,000
» International student fees 2013–14   £9,400–£10,350
» 128 NSP awards with priority criteria: £3,000 package, year 1; £1,500 package, year 2.
» Academic scholarships and targeted bursaries available.
» Check the university's website for the latest information.

Students

Undergraduates:	2,180	(70)
Postgraduates:	205	(390)
Mature students:	3.8%	
Overseas students:	5.3%	
Applications per place:	4.2	
From state-sector schools:	96.7%	
From working-class homes:	38.7%	
Satisfaction with students' union	68%	

For detailed information about sports facilities: www.marjon.ac.uk/marjonsport/sportscentre/

Accommodation

Places and costs refer to 2013–14
University-provided places: 456
Percentage catered: 35%
Catered costs: £115–£130 (inclusive of dining-in-scheme).
Self-catered costs: £85 (small single) – £90 (standard single).
Priority is given to students with Unconditional offers, on a first come first served basis, and to disabled students.
International students: guaranteed campus or homestay housing.
Contact: accommodation@marjon.ac.uk; www.marjon.ac.uk/studentlife/universityapprovedaccommodation/

University of Salford

Salford will cease to offer courses in modern languages, linguistics and some areas of politics and contemporary history in 2014 because of "low levels of interest from applicants", focusing instead on its strengths in media, technology, science, engineering and health. Across the university, there was a 14 per cent drop in applications when the fees went up to an average of £8,330 in 2012 and it was left with more than 800 empty places. The demand for places had been buoyant over several years before the new fees regime, as the university benefited from carefully targeted courses and an emphasis on the university's location close to the centre of Manchester. Fees for all degree courses have now risen to £9,000, in common with the vast majority of universities.

Salford is in the middle of a £500-million 15-year capital programme. There are four campuses, three of them clustered around the River Irwell and within walking distance of Manchester city centre. The exception is the MediaCityUK development in Salford Quays – home to five BBC departments, where some 1,500 students on 39 courses will enjoy exceptional opportunities to work with media professionals using the latest equipment, studios and laboratories. There is also a £38-million Arts and Media Centre on the Adelphi Campus and a £22-million headquarters for the Faculty of Health and Social Care on a third site, with practice clinics, hospital ward facilities and a human performance laboratory. The landscaped main campus is a haven of lawns and shrubberies with its own railway station. University House, where students go for advice and support, has seen a £3-millon upgrade, while a 1960s teaching building has been remodelled and extended to accommodate six lecture theatres equipped with large screen displays, a series of learning and breakout spaces, plus a café. Nearby, a Gateway Building for the new merged School of Arts and Media is under construction.

The university set itself the goal of finishing in the top quarter of all universities in the league tables by 2017 – an extremely challenging target that will require a rise of more than 60 places in three years. It has been held back this year by a decline in National Student Survey scores that left Salford among the bottom dozen universities for overall student satisfaction. However, Salford does well on the Government's access measures: more than 45 per cent of the undergraduates come from working-class homes and there is a high proportion from areas sending few students to higher education. The projected dropout rate has fluctuated, but a dramatic improvement in the latest figures took it

---

The Crescent
Salford
Greater Manchester
M5 4WT

0161 295 3306 (admissions)
ugadmissions@salford.ac.uk
www.salford.ac.uk
www.salfordstudents.com
Affiliation: University
   Alliance

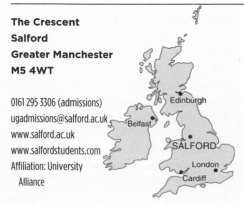

The Times and Sunday Times **Rankings**
Overall Ranking: **98** (=91)

Student satisfaction:	113	(76.5%)
Research quality:	56	(9.3%)
Entry standards:	89	(300)
Student–staff ratio:	52	(17.6)
Services & facilities/student:	94	(£1,202)
Expected completion rate:	82	(82.4%)
Good honours:	=74	(61.4%)
Graduate prospects:	=79	(60%)

back below 15 per cent, better than the national average for the subjects and students' qualifications.

The university's growing involvement in health has seen the establishment of a national centre for prosthetics and orthotics, and Salford has a high reputation for the treatment of sports injuries. The School of Nursing and Midwifery, which received outstanding ratings from its regulatory body, runs Europe's first nursing course for deaf students. There is also a BA in journalism and war studies – the only undergraduate degree in the UK to combine the two disciplines. Engineering is the university's traditional strength, attracting many of the 3,000 overseas students. The university opened the world's first Energy House in 2011 – a full-size traditional terraced house built in a laboratory for students, researchers and industry to study domestic energy consumption. Two-thirds of all courses offer work placements, half of them abroad and almost all counting towards degree classifications. The university has partnerships which provide research and work experience with the BBC, Adobe and Carnegie Mellon University, in Pittsburgh, among others.

The Enterprise Academy scheme was commended by the EU after it helped 32 student businesses become established. Students are offered training in entrepreneurship and business skills, as well as a business mentor, while an innovative scheme also provides professional training and work experience for unemployed and under-employed graduates. Salford led the way in formally recognising interaction with business and industry as of equal importance to teaching and research. The university entered a relatively low proportion of its academics for the 2008 Research Assessment Exercise, but still had among the lowest grades of the pre-1992 universities. Architecture and business produced the best results. The university has since established nine interdisciplinary research centres and a graduate school.

There are 2,400 residential places within ten minutes' walk of the main campus, owned either by the university or a partner organisation. By the end of 2015, there will be more than 1,300 bedrooms on a student village with communal areas including a cinema, gym, TV and games room, group study lounges and a launderette.

Undergraduate Fees and Bursaries

» Fees for UK/EU students 2014–15 £9,000
  Foundation year £5,500
» International student fees 2013–14 £10,870–£12,540
» For Greater Manchester residents with household income below £25K, £3,000 package, year 1; £1,000 package, years 2 and 3.
» For students with at least ABB at A Level or equivalent, £2,000 cash scholarship in year 1.

Students

Undergraduates:	**15,105**	**(2,090)**
Postgraduates:	**2,050**	**(2,505)**
Mature students:	**36.2%**	
Overseas students:	**12.1%**	
Applications per place:	**5.3**	
From state-sector schools:	**97.8%**	
From working-class homes:	**45.2%**	
Satisfaction with students' union	**61%**	

For detailed information about sports facilities:
www.sport.salford.ac.uk

Accommodation

Number of places and costs refer to 2013–14
University-provided places: 1,309 plus 1,930 managed by specialist providers
Percentage catered: 0%
Self-catered costs: £66.01 (standard) – £91.07 (en suite).
First years are guaranteed accommodation (terms and conditions apply).
International students: as above.
Contact: www.accommodation.salford.ac.uk/

University of Sheffield

Sheffield is back in the top 20 of our league table, with buoyant levels of student satisfaction and the most popular students' union in the country. Applications were up by 17 per cent in 2013, following a sharp drop in 2012, when the introduction of £9,000 fees left about 500 places unfilled. Sheffield is in the top 75 universities in the world, according to the QS rankings, and attracts more than 5,000 students from outside the European Union. Its UK students are more diverse than those in most other Russell Group universities: more than 80 per cent of the undergraduates come from state schools or colleges and almost one in five comes from a working-class home. The projected dropout rate is less than 5 per cent.

Academic buildings are concentrated in an area about a mile from the city centre on the affluent west side of Sheffield, with most university flats and halls of residence only a little further into the suburbs. The main university precinct now stretches into an almost unbroken mile-long "campus". There has been sustained investment in new buildings and facilities over recent years – notably the conversion of the former Jessop Hospital into a new centre for the arts and humanities. Recent developments have seen the renovation of the original University Library and the refurbishment of the Arts Tower, still the tallest university building in the country after more than 40 years. The university is expanding the highly rated Faculty of Engineering, which has 4,000 students, with new teaching laboratories and a Graduate School that is due to open by the end of 2013. An £81-million engineering building is due to open in 2016. Sheffield is the lead institution for systems engineering, smart materials and stem-cell technology in a research network of European, American and Chinese universities. There is a separate technology park centred on an advanced manufacturing research centre, in which Boeing is the senior partner.

The students' union has been extended for the second time in three years, creating more facilities for students and staff in time for the start of the 2013–14 academic year. In both years in which unions have been assessed in the National Student Survey, it has satisfied at least 94 per cent of its members and finished top of a table in which the average was less than 70 per cent. Two modern student villages and a high-tech library and learning centre add to the student experience. The £23-million Information Commons, opened in 2007, operates 24 hours a day, providing 1,300 study spaces and 500 computers linked to the campus network, as well as 110,000 books and periodicals. A new employability strategy includes two internship schemes

Western Bank
Sheffield S10 2TN

0114 222 8030 (enquiries)
http://ask.sheffield.ac.uk
www.sheffield.ac.uk
www.shef.ac.uk/union
Affiliation: Russell Group

The Times and Sunday Times **Rankings**

Overall Ranking: **=18** (21)

Student satisfaction:	=15	(84.6%)
Research quality:	16	(27.3%)
Entry standards:	20	(442)
Student–staff ratio:	=28	(15.5)
Services & facilities/student:	48	(£1,574)
Expected completion rate:	12	(95.3%)
Good honours:	21	(77.5%)
Graduate prospects:	34	(71.7%)

offering 75 placements within the university.

Sheffield academics performed well in the last Research Assessment Exercise, when more than 60 per cent of their work was judged to be world-leading or internationally excellent. Politics and information studies achieved the best results in the country, while town planning, philosophy, Russian, architecture, and mechanical and aeronautical engineering were near the top for their fields. Former Home Secretary David Blunkett is a visiting professor in the Politics Department, where he was an undergraduate, helping to establish the world's first Centre for the Public Understanding of Politics. The growing School of Management, which is one of 57 in the world to receive accreditation from all three leading agencies, moved into new premises in 2013, following an £11-million refurbishment of the former School of Law.

Residential accommodation is plentiful, with most of the 5,880 university-owned rooms within walking distance of lectures. Private housing is reasonably priced in student areas that are close to the university.

First-years from outside Sheffield are guaranteed accommodation. The Endcliffe Village caters for about 3,500 students in a mix of refurbished Victorian houses and new flats, while the Ranmoor Village has over 1,000 students in en-suite self-catering apartments including some family apartments and studios. The excellent sports facilities close to the main university precinct include five floodlit synthetic pitches, a large fitness centre with more than 150 pieces of equipment, swimming pool with sauna and steam rooms, sports hall, a fitness studio, multipurpose activity room, four squash courts and a bouldering wall. The 45 acres of grass playing fields for rugby, football and cricket are a bus ride away. Sheffield has one of the biggest programmes of internal leagues at any university.

A famously lively social scene is based on the students' union, but also takes full advantage of the city's burgeoning club life. Town–gown relations are much better than in most major university centres and the latest crime statistics identify Sheffield as the safest big city in England.

Undergraduate Fees and Bursaries

» Fees for UK/EU students 2014–15	£9,000
» International student fees 2013–14	£12,760–£16,640
Medicine	£30,080

» Around 360 NSP awards for students from economically deprived areas, £6,000 or £9,000 fee waiver or funding packages for year 1. Further NSP awards for care leavers, adult learners and local students achieving ABB at A level (or equivalent).

» Cash bursaries on sliding scale of £1,400–£500 for UK students with household income up to £42K.

» Other scholarships and bursaries available.

Students

Undergraduates:	**17,275**	**(1,275)**
Postgraduates:	**5,425**	**(1,985)**
Mature students:	**6.9%**	
Overseas students:	**16.1%**	
Applications per place:	**6.7**	
From state-sector schools:	**83.7%**	
From working-class homes:	**17.8%**	
Satisfaction with students' union	**93%**	

For detailed information about sports facilities:
www.sport-sheffield.com

Accommodation

Number of places and costs refer to 2013–14
University-provided places: 5,879
Percentage catered: 8%
Catered costs: £5,574,24 – £6,106.38 (42 weeks; 31 weeks of catering).
Self-catered costs: £4,021.92 – £7,268.52 (42–51 weeks).
First years are guaranteed accommodation if conditions are met.
International students: as above.
Contact: accommodationoffice@sheffield.ac.uk
www.sheffield.ac.uk/accommodation

Sheffield Hallam University

Sheffield Hallam was among the top six universities in England in terms of the volume of applications, when its fees went up to £8,300 in 2012. But this still represented a 17 per cent drop and the numbers finally accepting places through UCAS fell by more than 700 compared with the previous year. Like many other universities, Hallam has moved to £9,000 fees in 2013 and will charge the same next year. The university is mid-way through a £95-million development plan for its campuses, following heavy investment in buildings and new staff over the last ten years. The focus of current activity is the Collegiate Campus, in a leafy inner suburb of Sheffield, where improvements costing £25 million will be complete by the end of 2014. A new social centre has opened there and a £14-million development has allowed the Faculty of Health and Wellbeing to almost double in size, as extra provision was made for nursing, radiotherapy, physiotherapy and social work. The Centre for Sport and Exercise Science, with its £6-million research facility is one of the largest of its kind in Europe, with more than 2,000 students. The faculty is the biggest provider of health and social care training in the UK and offers the widest range of sports courses.

Previous developments focused mainly on the main campus in the heart of the city centre, near the railway station. The main learning centre was refurbished and all the departments in the arts, computing, engineering and sciences were brought together for the first time, placing them in the heart of Sheffield's cultural industries quarter. The university had already launched the Sheffield Business School in 2009, bringing together business, finance, management and languages, with the university's specialisms of facilities management, food and nutrition, tourism, hospitality and events management. Business and management courses, which account for easily the biggest share of places, have their own city-centre headquarters, as does the students' union, which took over the spectacular but ill-fated National Centre for Popular Music.

The university currently exceeds most of its access benchmarks, although the share of undergraduate places going to working-class entrants is slightly below average for the courses and entry qualifications, at less than a third. The projected dropout rate of 10 per cent beats the benchmark set for the university. Scores in the National Student Survey improved slightly in 2013, but still left the university below the national average for student satisfaction. It did better in the latest International Student Barometer, where its overseas students

City Campus
Howard Street
Sheffield S1 1WB

0114 225 5555 (enquiries)
enquiries@shu.ac.uk
www.shu.ac.uk
www.hallamunion.org
Affiliation: University
   Alliance

The Times and Sunday Times **Rankings**
Overall Ranking: **=77** (=73)

Student satisfaction:	90	(79.6%)
Research quality:	=73	(4.0%)
Entry standards:	=69	(316)
Student–staff ratio:	=79	(20)
Services & facilities/student:	64	(£1,376)
Expected completion rate:	=56	(86.5%)
Good honours:	61	(63.1%)
Graduate prospects:	=87	(57.8%)

proved to be the most satisfied in the UK with their learning experience and especially pleased with the standard of learning technology, laboratories and learning spaces. The university has a growing international dimension as well as bringing students to Sheffield: it celebrated its 5,000th Malaysian graduate in 2010 and has an office in India.

Hallam traces its origins in art and design back to the 1840s and celebrated the centenary of education and teacher training in 2005. It is now one of the largest of the new universities, with more than 36,000 students, including high proportions of part-time and mature students, and more than 1,000 taught on franchised courses in further education colleges. Business and industry are closely involved in the development hundreds of courses, with almost half of the students taking sandwich course placements with employers. More than 200 "specialist flexible courses" mix part-time study, distance learning and work-based learning. The university claims to have the largest number of students at any university taking courses that include work placements of a year, and it offers a full fee waiver for that year out.

A "virtual campus" offers students email accounts and cheap equipment to access the growing volume of online courses, assignments and discussion groups provided by the university, even when they are at home or on work placements.

Unlike many big post-1992 universities, Hallam now guarantees accommodation for first years, although the large local intake means that many live at home. Transport in the city is excellent, with both well-run bus and tram services. Sports facilities are supplemented by those provided by the city for the World Student Games. The impressive swimming complex, for example, is on the university's doorstep. Enthusiasm for sport produced the largest number of student volunteers for the 2012 Olympics at any UK university.

Undergraduate Fees and Bursaries

» Fees for UK/EU students 2014–15 £9,000
» International student fees 2013–14 £10,680–£11,880
» 1,774 NSP awards of £1,500 fee waiver, £1,000 cash, £500 for university services or additional fee waiver in year 1.
» For those who meet NSP criteria but do not gain an award, £3,000 package, year 1.
» Students with household income £25K–£49K from associated local schools and colleges, £300 cash in year 1.
» Scholarships and bursaries are available.
» Check the university's website for the latest information.

Students

Undergraduates:	22,705	(5,705)
Postgraduates:	3,225	(5,525)
Mature students:	16.8%	
Overseas students:	7.7%	
Applications per place:	5.6	
From state-sector schools:	95.7%	
From working-class homes:	32.1%	
Satisfaction with students' union	58%	

For detailed information about sports facilities: www.shu.ac.uk/sport/active/

Accommodation

Number of places and costs refer to 2013–14
University-provided places: 4,961
Percentage catered: 0%
Self-catered costs: £80.00 (single standard) – £200.00 (large double self-contained flat) for 42–44 weeks.
All first years offered university allocated accommodation or private housing.
International students: as above, providing conditions are met.
Contact: www.shu.ac.uk/accommodation

SOAS, University of London

The only higher education institution in the UK specialising in the study of Africa, Asia and the Middle East has dropped its full title (School of Oriental and African Studies) and started promoting itself as SOAS, University of London. The school has a global reputation in subjects relating to two-thirds of the world's population. The library is one of just five National Research Libraries in the country, holding 1.5 million volumes, periodicals and audio-visual materials in 400 languages, and attracts scholars from around the world. SOAS is having to contend with a national decline in applications to study non-European languages, but enrolments went up in 2012 in spite of a decline in applications with the prospect of £9,000 fees.

There are 5,600 students on campus, plus over 3,000 studying distance learning programmes. They come from more than 130 countries, but two-thirds are from Britain and the rest of the EU – and the proportion is higher still among the undergraduates. Independent school candidates account for a quarter of the British entrants to degree courses, while the same proportion come from working-class homes. The school has almost doubled its investment in student support with the switch to higher fees, as well as increasing its outreach activities, which include summer schools, masterclasses and academic buddying.

Results in the National Student Survey have been better than for most London-based institutions. Overall satisfaction increased sharply in 2013, propelling SOAS up the table on this measure with scores well above the national average. More than 40 per cent of degree programmes offer the opportunity to spend a year at one of the school's many partner universities in Africa or Asia. The projected dropout rate has fluctuated over recent years. At just under 13 per cent in the latest statistics, it was significantly better than the UK average for SOAS's subjects and entry qualifications.

SOAS has a much wider portfolio of courses than its name would suggest, offering more than 400 degree combinations and 100 postgraduate programmes. Degrees are available in familiar subjects such as law, music, history and the social sciences, but with a different emphasis. There is also a more limited portfolio of Foundation programmes and language courses. Approximately 45 per cent of undergraduates take a language as part of their degree and the school has now introduced a Language Entitlement programme which offers one term of a non-accredited SOAS Language Centre course free of charge. SOAS was chosen to house a national teaching centre for languages

Thornhaugh Street
Russell Square
London WC1H 0XG

020 7898 4034 (student recruitment)
study@soas.ac.uk
www.soas.ac.uk
http://soasunion.org
Affiliation: 1994 Group

The Times and Sunday Times Rankings
Overall Ranking: **24** (31)

Student satisfaction:	=86	(79.7%)
Research quality:	=30	(21.7%)
Entry standards:	25	(437)
Student–staff ratio:	8	(11.8)
Services & facilities/student:	27	(£1,895)
Expected completion rate:	=53	(87.1%)
Good honours:	=12	(80.6%)
Graduate prospects:	54	(66.8%)

and won a Queen's Anniversary Prize for the excellence, breadth and depth of its language teaching in 2010. The £6.5-million Library Transformation Project has added more language laboratories, music studios, discussion and research rooms, gallery space and other facilities. SOAS is in the top 80 in the QS World Rankings for the arts and humanities, and has been strengthening its academic staff in a variety of disciplines as it approaches its centenary in 2016.

The numbers taking distance learning courses, mainly outside the UK, have grown considerably. The transfer of University of London postgraduate programmes previously taught by Imperial College has made SOAS one of the world's largest providers of distance learning at this level. Postgraduates are attracted by a research record which saw more than half of the work submitted for the last Research Assessment Exercise rated world-leading or internationally excellent. SOAS was ranked top in the UK for Asian studies and did well in anthropology, politics, history and music.

SOAS is located at the heart of the University of London in Bloomsbury. There is a second campus less than a mile away and adjacent to two student residences, providing student-orientated facilities such as a Learning Resource Centre and an internet café. The centrepiece of the main campus is an airy, modern building with gallery space as well as teaching accommodation, a gift from the Sultan of Brunei. There is no separate students' union building, although the students do have their own recently refurbished bar, social space and catering facilities. The well-equipped and under-used University of London Union is close at hand, with swimming pool, gym and bars. The West End is also on the doorstep.

Nearly 1,000 residential places are available within 15 minutes' walk of the school. Another 101 places are available in flats at the second campus. However, the school has few of its own sports facilities and the outdoor pitches are remote, with no time set aside from lectures. Students tend to be highly committed and often politically active – not surprising since many will return to positions of influence in developing countries – and the variety of cultures makes for lively debate.

Undergraduate Fees and Bursaries

» Fees for UK/EU students 2014–15 £9,000
» International student fees 2013–14 £14,590
» For students from low participation neighbourhoods, 30 awards: £2,500 fee waiver and £2,000 cash a year; for academic achievers with household income below £25K, 90 awards of £3,000 package a year.
» 90 NSP awards, year 1, for those on courses leading to a profession, £2,000 fee waiver, £1,000 cash.
» 40 partner college bursaries of £500 in year 1 for mature students.
» Scholarships and bursaries are available.

Students

Undergraduates:	**2,935**	**(35)**
Postgraduates:	**1,885**	**(545)**
Mature students:	**23.2%**	
Overseas students:	**39.3%**	
Applications per place:	**4.4**	
From state-sector schools:	**74.5%**	
From working-class homes:	**25.9%**	
Satisfaction with students' union	**72%**	

For detailed information about sports facilities:
http://soasunion.org/sports-and-societies/

Accommodation

Number of places and costs refer to 2013–14
University-provided places: 770 (Sanctuary Management Services); 170 (intercollegiate)
Percentage catered: 18%
Catered costs: £108.50–£276.50 a week.
Self-catered costs: £143.43–£249.20 a week.
Priority given to first years on first come basis. Residential restrictions apply.
International students: as above, although they are a high priority.
Contact: student@sanctuary-housing.co.uk

University of South Wales

The merger of Glamorgan and Newport universities finally came about in 2012 after several years of on/off negotiations and no little political intervention. The partners were already working together on the Universities Heads of the Valleys Institute, developing adults' skills in the former mining area. The new University of South Wales is one of the ten largest universities in the UK with over 33,000 students across five campuses. However, it does not appear in any of our tables because the university is not releasing data for rankings this year while the amalgamation takes effect.

South Wales intends to combine the breadth of provision with the widest possible access to education. Both partners had proud records in attracting students from poor backgrounds. The new university will offer a full range of qualifications, from Foundation degrees to PhDs. The courses include the full range of science and engineering subjects, from aircraft engineering and mathematics to computing and surveying. The university is also an experienced provider of teacher training.

About half of the students are full-time undergraduates and two-thirds are 21 or over. There is a focus on employability and simulated learning to ensure that students learn how their future profession works in real life. There are partnerships with industry leaders and major employers, from British Airways to the National Health Service. Teaching facilities include the university's own aircraft, moot court room, TV studios, stock exchange trading room, hospital wards, and scenes-of-crime house. Sport students train and play on facilities used by Olympic athletes and the All Blacks.

The university is a significant player in the arts, with an internationally acclaimed film school, industry-standard animation facilities, one of the UK's oldest photography schools and a strong reputation for theatre design, as well as the national music and drama conservatoire. The main research strengths are in applied projects, and it is a member of the St David's Day Group, which brings together all of the Principality's universities to focus on research and innovation.

Both Glamorgan and Newport suffered falls of about 20 per cent in the number of students enrolling in 2012, even though less than a quarter were required to pay the higher fees introduced in England. Two of the former Glamorgan campuses are 10 miles outside Cardiff, near Pontypridd, while the third is in the city itself. Around £28 million is being spent on improvements, more than half of it on an expansion of the university's campus in the heart of Cardiff. The £35-million ATRiuM building houses the Cardiff School of Creative and

Pontypridd CF37 1DL

08456 76 77 78 (enquiries)
enquiries@southwales.ac.uk
www.southwales.ac.uk
www.uswsu.com
Affiliation: University
 Alliance

The Times and Sunday Times **Rankings**
The University of South Wales blocked the release of data from the Higher Education Statistics Agency and so we cannot give any ranking information.

Cultural Industries, which was formed from an earlier merger with the Royal Welsh College of Music and Drama. It was part of a £130-million investment in new facilities. Recent developments include a £15-million expansion of facilities for health, science and sport, as well as new halls of residence. There has also been a new home for the Law School on the Treforest campus and new laboratories at nearby Glyntaff.

Amenities on the Treforest campus have been developing, with a modern recreation centre and a new students' union. The sports facilities were good enough for Glamorgan to have been awarded the 2001 British University Games and have continued to improve: a £4-million sports park opened in 2011. The university also hosts one of six centres of excellence in cricket. Glamorgan has been successful in student competitions, especially in rugby, and offers a number of sports bursaries for students with international potential.

Newport's £35-million City Campus opened in 2011 and won an award from the Royal Institute of British Architects for its striking design. It is at the heart of Newport's new Cultural Quarter, designed to attract inward investment and strengthen the local economy. Newport was rated the top university in Wales for enterprise education by the Knowledge Exploitation Fund for three years in a row, helping more than 70 new start-up businesses. Newport is also well-known for photography and film, hosting the International Film School Wales, whose graduates include double-BAFTA winner Asif Kapadia, and Justin Kerrigan, director of the cult movie *Human Traffic*.

The Caerleon Campus, a few miles from Newport, caters for humanities, education, health and social sciences and photography. There is a student village of 661 self-catered study bedrooms and the Wales International Study Centre opened on the campus in 2008. A well-equipped sports centre has transformed facilities. The city of Newport is undergoing a £2-billion regeneration programme and has plenty of clubs and entertainment venues, but students in search of serious cultural or clubbing activity gravitate to nearby Cardiff.

Undergraduate Fees and Bursaries

» Fees for UK/EU students for 2014–15   £8,250–£9,000
    Foundation degree   £6,750
    Welsh Assembly non-means-tested grant to pay fees above £3,575 (2013–14) for Welsh students.
» International student fees 2013–14   £9,950–£11,000
» Centenary Bursary of £1,500 university accommodation discount (Treforest, Caerleon and Cardiff) for those paying full fees. Not available to those receiving Welsh Government tuition fee grant..
» Flying Start scholarship of £750 and an iPad in year 1 for students with at least 320 UCAS points.
» 5 Welsh-medium scholarships of £1,000 a year for students studying at least one module in Welsh.
» Further general bursaries and scholarships.

Students

Undergraduates:	**16,675**	**(8,725)**
Postgraduates:	**2,815**	**(2,960)**

Student numbers obtained by combining Glamorgan and Newport figures for 2011–12. It is not possible to give combined figures for the other measures usually shown here.

For detailed information about sports facilities:
http://sport.southwales.ac.uk

Accommodation

Number of places and costs refer to 2013–14
University-provided places: 1,867
Percentage catered: 0% but catering package available.
Self-catered accommodation: £79 (standard) – £115.50 (premium) a week (40 weeks); £155.00 (studio flat, 42 weeks).
First-year students are offered accommodation. Local restrictions apply.
International students are guaranteed housing.
Contact: accom@southwales.ac.uk (Cardiff, Glyntaff & Treforest)
accommodation@southwales.ac.uk (Newport & Caerleon)

Southampton University

Southampton was left with almost 700 empty places when the fees went up in 2012, but the Vice-Chancellor, Professor Don Nutbeam, predicted that enrolments would be back to their previous level, or better, in 2013. The university had promised "ground-breaking" reforms to its teaching and student support in exchange for £9,000 fees, with a more flexible curriculum and an academic adviser for every student to guide their independent learning and progress. Before the new fees regime, the demand for places had grown steadily over several years, reflecting substantial investment in campus facilities and good results in the National Student Survey. The university is now in the final phase of a £250-million programme to upgrade its sites in Southampton and Winchester, having also opened a campus in Malaysia dedicated to mechanical engineering in 2012. The new campus is close to Singapore at the Iksandar Education City development, in the south of Malaysia, where undergraduates will study for two years before finishing their degree in Southampton.

Engineering was one of Southampton's strengths in the last Research Assessment Exercise, when the university finished among the top 20 in the country. More than 60 per cent of its submission was considered world-leading or internationally excellent, with good grades coming in medicine, music, sociology and social policy, computer science and nursing. Southampton is in the top 100 universities in the world, according to the QS World University Rankings and the proportion of income derived from research is among the highest in Britain. With Sir Tim Berners-Lee, inventor of the Worldwide Web, a professor in the School of Electronics and Computer Science, Southampton was a natural choice as one of the Government's eight Academic Centres of Excellence in Cyber Security Research. The university was awarded a Queen's Anniversary Prize for Higher and Further Education for its research in performance sports engineering in 2011. Over a 1,000 elite athletes, including Sir Chris Hoy, were helped in their Olympic preparation by the university's aerodynamics research and wind tunnel complex.

Although the percentages of students from working-class homes and areas with little tradition of university education are lower than the national average for Southampton's entry requirements and subjects, the statistics agency considers this largely a matter of location. The university exceeds its benchmark for the number of entrants from state schools and for the proportion of students who have a disability. Students act as ambassadors, associates and mentors in local schools and colleges, as

---

University Road
Southampton SO17 1BJ

023 8059 2421 (enquiries)
admissns@southampton.ac.uk
www.southampton.ac.uk
www.susu.org
Affiliation: Russell Group

Edinburgh
Belfast
Cardiff   London
SOUTHAMPTON

The Times and Sunday Times **Rankings**

Overall Ranking: **20** (=18)

Student satisfaction:	=54	(81.8%)
Research quality:	=25	(23.0%)
Entry standards:	=23	(438)
Student–staff ratio:	14	(13.7)
Services & facilities/student:	24	(£1,930)
Expected completion rate:	21	(93.3%)
Good honours:	20	(77.6%)
Graduate prospects:	25	(75.2%)

part of the university's efforts to broaden its intake. There are more than 5,000 international students and a network of overseas partnerships. From 2013, medical students will be able to take part of their course in Europe, for example, and there are joint degrees in graphic design and fashion design with Dalian Polytechnic University, in China. The Centre for Contemporary China links Southampton with a number of leading Chinese universities.

Most courses are taught at the main Highfield campus, which is in an attractive green location two miles from the city centre. The students' union has been refurbished and a purpose-built student services centre added to bring together learning support and other advisory facilities. The library has been greatly extended and new social learning space, designed by students for students, opened in 2011 as part of the innovative "Create your Campus" competition, which gives students the opportunity to influence the development of their learning environment. The striking £55-million Mountbatten Building for electronics and computer science and the Optoelectronics Research Centre and the £50-million Life Sciences Building are recent additions.

The university has four sites in Southampton. The National Oceanography Centre Southampton is based in the city's revitalised dock area. A £50-million joint project with the Natural Environment Research Council, it is considered Europe's finest. The Avenue campus, near the main site, is home to most of the humanities departments. Clinical medicine is based at Southampton General Hospital, where a new medical research centre is funded by the National Institute for Health Research to develop new treatments for respiratory diseases. Winchester School of Art, which has been part of the university since 1996, has also enjoyed significant recent investment in new facilities. The arts are well represented in Southampton, too, with three nationally renowned arts centres: the Turner Sims concert hall, the Nuffield Theatre and the John Hansard Gallery, all based at Highfield.

Sports facilities are first class, with an indoor sports complex next to the students' union. The outdoor sports complex has grass and synthetic pitches. Student housing is plentiful and first years are guaranteed an offer of accommodation.

Undergraduate Fees and Bursaries

» Fees for UK/EU students 2014–15   £9,000
» International student fees 2013–14   £12,420–£15,250
   Medicine   £29,450
» For English students with household income below £16K, £3,000 package each year; household income £16K–£25K, £2,000 package each year; household income £25K–£30K, £1,000 package each year.
» Around 300 bursaries of £1,000 a year for students from Hampshire and Isle of Wight or from the Access to Southampton programme.

Students

Undergraduates:	**16,000**	**(805)**
Postgraduates:	**5,415**	**(1,910)**
Mature students:	**15.2%**	
Overseas students:	**14.7%**	
Applications per place:	**7.7**	
From state-sector schools:	**83.7%**	
From working-class homes:	**19.2%**	
Satisfaction with students' union	**74%**	

For detailed information about sports facilities:
www.southampton.ac.uk/sportandwellbeing/

Accommodation

Number of places and costs refer to 2013–14
University-provided places: more than 5,000
Percentage catered: 10%
Catered costs: £115.15–£160.58 a week.
Self-catered costs: £77.28–£154.98 a week (self-contained flat).
All full-time first years are guaranteed an offer of accommodation. Conditions apply.
International students: All non-EU students are guaranteed accommodation. Conditions apply.
Contact: www.southampton.ac.uk/accommodation

Southampton Solent University

Southampton Solent is raising its fees by almost £1,000 in 2014, following the overwhelming trend among universities in England to charge the maximum £9,000 for all degree courses. Its current charges are among the lowest in the country and it was one of the few universities to meet its recruitment targets in 2012, albeit from a much-reduced pool of applicants. But the university has decided to change its approach, putting more of its income from fees into bursaries and outreach activities to encourage wider participation in higher education. More than a third of the undergraduates already come from working-class homes – considerably more than the national average for the university's subjects and entry qualifications – and 96 per cent are state-educated.

The largest of the nine universities created in 2005, Southampton Solent also has the broadest range of programmes, stretching from Foundation courses to doctorates. Over 12,000 higher education students embrace civil and mechanical engineering, as well as media, arts and business, with a separate maritime centre capitalising on the coastal location. The subject mix may be one reason that the former Southampton Institute is now one of the few universities with a majority of male students. Solent recruits mainly in London and the south of England, a quarter of the students coming from Hampshire, but about 1,500 come from outside the UK. The rebranded Solent Curriculum plays to the university's strengths in "skills focused" courses. There is a strong representation of "non-traditional" disciplines, such as yacht and powercraft design, computer and video games, and comedy writing and performance. A Graduate Enterprise Centre provides advice and rent-free offices for those hoping to start their own businesses, while an internship scheme provides places for 100 recent graduates.

Solent is held back in *The Times and Sunday Times* league table by poor scores in the National Student Survey, where it was in the bottom five for overall satisfaction in 2013. But the projected dropout rate has improved for six years in a row. Before the switch to higher fees, applications had practically doubled in five years and more were making Solent their first-choice university. Demand for places remains strong in marine-based courses, which benefit from an internationally renowned training and research facility for the shipping and offshore oil industries. The university is higher education's premier yachting institution, with a world champion student team that has won the national

---

East Park Terrace
Southampton SO14 0YN

023 8031 9000 (main switchboard)
ask@solent.ac.uk
www.solent.ac.uk
www.solentsu.co.uk
Affiliation: GuildHE

The Times and Sunday Times **Rankings**
Overall Ranking: **114** (113)

Student satisfaction:	118	(74.9%)
Research quality:	=112	(0.7%)
Entry standards:	102	(282)
Student–staff ratio:	=88	(20.5)
Services & facilities/student:	=87	(£1,243)
Expected completion rate:	111	(76.7%)
Good honours:	91	(58.8%)
Graduate prospects:	117	(48.5%)

championships four times in six years. Three new boats support courses at the purpose-built Watersports Centre, where some activities are targeted towards disadvantaged young people.

The main campus has few architectural pretensions, but is conveniently based in the city centre within walking distance of the station. The university has spent more than £25 million on improvements since 2008 and is planning to invest another £45 million over the next 20 years. New teaching and learning facilities will open in 2015 on land adjoining the main campus. Other recent developments include a £2.7-million ship handling centre, a new city centre site for the Southampton School of Art and Design, and new football facilities that are used by the city's Premier League team. The Lawrie McMenemy Centre for Football Research is helping to cement the university's reputation for academic study of the sport and, having assumed responsibility for sport development in the city, Solent has also become the country's largest provider of coaching education. A new School of Health, Exercise and Social Science was launched in 2013 to encourage collaboration in health and exercise science, social work and psychology.

Solent entered fewer academics for the 2008 Research Assessment Exercise than any university in England – fewer than one in ten of those eligible. But two of the three areas in which it made a submission contained some world-leading research, with art and design achieving much the best results. Creative Arts and Society courses now attract almost as many students as the consistently popular business school. There are new music studios with an industry-standard recording complex, as well as a performance space and dance studio. The Centre for Professional Development in Broadcasting and Multimedia Production includes an online editing suite, digital television studio and gallery, for use by undergraduates as well as community groups and professionals.

Students like the university's location, close to the city centre's shopping area and growing complement of bars and nightclubs. There are more than 2,300 hall places, most of which are allocated to first years. There is the usual range of sports facilities, with a sports hall and fitness suite on campus and outdoor pitches, tennis and netball courts four miles away.

Undergraduate Fees and Bursaries

- » Fees for UK/EU students 2014–15 £9,000
- » International student fees 2013–14 £9,785–£10,815
- » NSP awards of £1,000 cash, £2,000 accommodation discount or fee waiver, year 1; £500 cash, years 2 and 3.
- » Combined complete fee waiver and cash award for Foundation year students with household income below £25K, primarily for local students from low participation areas.

Students

Undergraduates:	10,275	(1,590)
Postgraduates:	315	(350)
Mature students:	21.5%	
Overseas students:	13.1%	
Applications per place:	3.7	
From state-sector schools:	96.2%	
From working-class homes:	34.2%	
Satisfaction with students' union	55%	

For detailed information about sports facilities:
www.solent.ac.uk/sport

Accommodation

Number of places and costs refer to 2013–14
University-provided places: 2,340.
Percentage catered: 0%
Self-catered costs: £89.95–£119.98 a week (41 weeks).
First years are allocated 90% of rooms.
International students: some accommodation is set aside.
Contact: Accommodation@solent.ac.uk
www.solent.ac.uk/accommodation/accommodation_home.aspx

Staffordshire University

Prompted partly by its decline in league tables, Staffordshire has reviewed its academic portfolio and invested in new facilities. Both will take time to have an impact – the university has fallen out of the top 100 this year – but there was a small increase in overall student satisfaction in 2013. The review has resulted in a reorganisation of the four faculties and the relocation of the university's engineering provision from the Stafford campus to Stoke. This follows the opening of a new £30-million science block on the Stoke campus in 2012 and is intended to produce a focal point to help drive up the numbers of young people in the region opting to study science, maths and engineering subjects, where career prospects are good. Staffordshire is at the heart of Stoke's University Quarter project, which is designed to transform the South Sheldon area as well as encouraging greater participation in higher education.

Staffordshire will be one of just 13 universities to charge less than £9,000 for its conventional degrees in 2014. Only the two-year accelerated degrees will have the maximum fee, while the normal three-year courses will cost £8,620. The university enjoyed a 25 per cent increase in applications in the year before the fees went up. Although there was a sharp decline in 2012, the numbers actually enrolling fell only marginally and remained higher than in previous years. The university has made a commitment to students and employers through the Staffordshire Graduate programme to ensure that, alongside their academic learning, all students are equipped with employability skills.

The university's two main sites, in Stoke-on-Trent and 16 miles away in Stafford, both have modern halls of residence, sports centres and lively students' union venues. Some £12 million is being invested in the Stoke campus to create a more attractive study environment with dedicated student spaces, exhibition areas, cafes and landscaping. There is a 25-acre nature reserve – part of the university's sustained green commitment – as well as a business village offering affordable business space for start-up companies. The Stafford campus, where the Octagon Centre was once among the largest university computing facilities in Europe, is home to the School of Computing and the university's highly-ranked nursing and midwifery courses. It is also the base for teacher training programmes that have been rated as "outstanding" in the last four Ofsted inspections and placed Staffordshire fourth among university providers in the 2012 ranking of teacher training.

A third site in Lichfield houses an integrated further and higher education

College Road
Stoke-on-Trent ST4 2DE

01782 294400 (admissions)
enquiries@staffs.ac.uk
www.staffs.ac.uk
www.staffsunion.com
Affiliation: million+

The Times and Sunday Times Rankings		
Overall Ranking: **108** (100)		
Student satisfaction:	=82	(80.3%)
Research quality:	=108	(1.0%)
Entry standards:	109	(254)
Student–staff ratio:	86	(20.3)
Services & facilities/student:	=85	(£1,249)
Expected completion rate:	106	(78.8%)
Good honours:	=101	(56.3%)
Graduate prospects:	98	(54.5%)

centre, developed in partnership with South Staffordshire College, as well as 26 business start-up units. There are also more than 9,000 students taking Staffordshire courses outside the UK, almost half of them located around the Pacific Rim. They now make up more than a third of the university's intake, in addition to a growing cohort of international students on the university's UK campuses. Staffordshire entered only a small proportion of its academics for the last Research Assessment Exercise. Three of the ten subject areas had some world-leading research, with general engineering and education producing the best results. Applied research has led to the development of new products in markets as diverse as medical technology and recycling.

The university is a pioneer of two-year fast-track degrees, which are now offered in accounting and finance, computing science, business, English and law. There already was an extensive portfolio of two-year Foundation degrees, largely taught by the university's UK partners, which include the National Design Academy. With almost all of its undergraduates state-educated and four in ten coming from working-class homes Staffordshire exceeds all the benchmarks for the breadth of its intake. There is good provision for students with disabilities and one undergraduate in five comes from areas with little participation in higher education, one of the biggest proportions in the country. The downside is dropout rate, which was projected at more than 20 per cent in the latest survey, well above the national average for the university's courses and entry qualifications.

Stoke is not the liveliest city of its size, but the University Quarter is attracting more social and leisure facilities. The campus is within easy reach of the city centre and has a buzzing students' union. Stafford is the more attractive setting and offers the best chance of a residential place, but the town is quiet and the campus is a mile and a half outside it. Sports facilities are good, especially in Stafford, where there is a modern £1.4-million sports centre and all-weather pitches. Good coaching has helped attract some outstanding athletes, who have access to a sports performance centre to help with training schedules, psychological support and dietary assessments.

Undergraduate Fees and Bursaries

» Fees for UK/EU students 2014–15 — £8,620
  Courses at partner colleges — £4,250–£5,995
  Two-year fast-track degrees — £9,000
» International student fees 2013–14 — £9,875
» 557 NSP awards of £2,500 university services and £500 cash, year 1; £1,250 university services and £250 cash, years 2 and 3; 183 NSP awards of £2,000 university services and £1,000 cash in year 1 only. Awards prioritised for low-income households from deprived areas.
» Check the university's website for the latest information.

Students

Undergraduates:	**10,895**	**(7,355)**
Postgraduates:	**1,035**	**(2,480)**
Mature students:	**31.3%**	
Overseas students:	**4.7%**	
Applications per place:	**4.7**	
From state-sector schools:	**97.3%**	
From working-class homes:	**39.4%**	
Satisfaction with students' union	**71%**	

For detailed information about sports facilities:
www.staffs.ac.uk/teamstaffs

Accommodation

Number of places and costs refer to 2013–14
University-provided places: 1,072 (Stoke); 605 (Stafford)
Percentage catered: 0%
Self-catered accommodation: £80–£108 a week (36 weeks).
First years have priority, if conditions are met.
International students: have priority, if conditions are met.
Contact: Accommodation_stoke@staffs.ac.uk
Accommodation_stafford@staffs.ac.uk
www.staffs.ac.uk/courses_and_study/student_services/accommodation/

University of Stirling

Stirling took a record number of students in 2012, increasing its intake by no less than 40 per cent. There was scope to do so since the university had the largest number of applications per place of any in the UK in the previous year – more than a dozen – and a spacious main campus capable of considerable expansion. The demand for places had risen by more than 50 per cent in two years, although there was actually a small decline in applications in 2012. Applicants are attracted by the spectacular setting and community feel of a university with only 12,300 students, although Stirling did not score as well as some small campus institutions in the 2013 National Student Survey. Overall student satisfaction was just above the average for Scotland.

The main campus nestles at the foot of the Ochil hills on the shores of a loch in a 330-acre estate, although the university stresses that it is easily accessed from Edinburgh and Glasgow airports. Stirling is particularly well provided for sports facilities, having been designated Scotland's University for Sporting Excellence in 2008. The campus is home to national swimming and tennis centres, as well as a golf course and a football academy. The university runs an international sports scholarship programme and manages Winning Students, the national sport scholarship programme for students in colleges and universities across Scotland. There are two other campuses: one for nurses and midwives in the modern Centre for Health Science, in Inverness, and a Western Isles campus, located in Stornoway, where the teaching accommodation is an integral part of the Western Isles Hospital.

Stirling was the British pioneer of the semester system, which has now become so popular throughout higher education. The academic year is divided into two blocks of 15 weeks with short mid-semester breaks. Students have the option of starting courses in February, rather than September, and can choose subjects from across all seven Schools. Degrees are built up of credits accumulated through modules taken and awarded each semester, rather than at the end of the academic year. Undergraduates can switch the whole direction of their studies, in consultation with their academic adviser, as their interests develop. They can also speed up their progress on a Summer Academic Programme, which squeezes a full semester's teaching into July and August. Full-time students are not allowed to use the programme to reduce the length of their course, but part-timers can use it to make rapid progress. The university's projected dropout rate of less than 10 per cent is better than the UK average for its courses and entry qualifications.

Stirling Campus
Stirling FK9 4LA

01786 467044 (admissions)
admissions@stir.ac.uk
www.stir.ac.uk
www.stirlingstudentsunion.com
Affiliation: none

STIRLING
Edinburgh
Belfast
London
Cardiff

The Times and Sunday Times Rankings
Overall Ranking: **51** (50)

Student satisfaction:	=82	(80.3%)
Research quality:	49	(13.7%)
Entry standards:	43	(374)
Student–staff ratio:	=56	(18.3)
Services & facilities/student:	73	(£1,335)
Expected completion rate:	89	(81.3%)
Good honours:	=62	(63%)
Graduate prospects:	63	(63.5%)

The intake is surprisingly diverse, with nearly 95 per cent of undergraduates state-educated and almost 30 per cent coming from working-class homes. Two-thirds are from Scotland, but the remainder come from more than 100 different countries. International exchanges are common, with many of Stirling's students going to American, Asian and European universities each year, while 175 Study Abroad or exchange students come in the opposite direction.

The university has nominated five "core areas" for teaching and research: health and well-being, culture and society, environment, enterprise and economy, and sport. In the last Research Assessment Exercise, Stirling produced the best results in Scotland in film and media, nursing and midwifery, education and sport. Other good grades came in philosophy, social policy and social work, aquaculture and economics. Facilities on campus include a recently modernised library and more than 700 computers for student use, many available 24 hours a day. The sports facilities, which include a 50-metre pool and a golf centre with indoor facilities and a synthetic putting green, are used for teaching and research, as well as for training by elite athletes and recreation for the university community. Sports study students benefit from sports scholarships available in golf, swimming, disability swimming, tennis, triathlon and football.

The first phase of a £38-million expansion of student accommodation was completed in time for the new academic year, with the second and third phases due be ready in 2014 and 2015. Students appreciate the individual attention that a small campus university can offer, although some find the atmosphere claustrophobic. Stirling is not the top choice of night-clubbers, but the students' union won "Best Bar None" status for three years in a row and there is a lively social scene. The MacRobert Arts Centre offers a full programme of cultural activities, while the surrounding countryside offers its own attractions for walkers and climbers. The campus has been described by police as one of the safest in Britain, but a community policeman is based there and available to students for extra advice.

Undergraduate Fees and Bursaries

» Fees for Scottish and EU students 2013–14   No fee
» Fees for Non-Scottish UK (RUK) students 2013–14   £6,750
» Fees for international students 2013–14   £10,750–£12,900
» For RUK students (2013–14) with at least AAB in one sitting at A Level or equivalent, £1,000–£2,000 cash each year.
» A range of sports scholarships for all students.
» Check the university's website for the latest information.

Students

Undergraduates:	**6,700**	**(1,125)**
Postgraduates:	**2,230**	**(1,065)**
Mature students:	**18.6%**	
Overseas students:	**8.0%**	
Applications per place:	**8.8**	
From state-sector schools:	**94.6%**	
From working-class homes:	**27.9%**	
Satisfaction with students' union	**58%**	

For detailed information about sports facilities: www.stir.ac.uk/sport-at-stirling/

Accommodation

Number of places and costs refer to 2013–14
University-provided places: 3,000
Percentage catered: 0%
Self-catered costs: £72–£115 (single); £140 (studio flat) a week (38 weeks).
All first years are guaranteed suitable housing arranged by the university.
International students: as above.
Contact: Accommodation@stir.ac.uk; www.stir.ac.uk/campus-life/accommodation/

University of Strathclyde

Strathclyde was named as *Times Higher Education* magazine's 2012 University of the Year, recognised for its dedication to working with industry, which the judges said put a modern slant on its 18th-century founder's vision of a "place of useful learning". The university promises courses that are both innovative and relevant to employers' needs – hence product design and innovation, energy systems or international business with modern languages. It has set itself the target of becoming one of the world's leading technological universities, and the Vice-Chancellor, Professor Jim McDonald, has called for improvements in research to achieve this goal. The university has invested £89 million in a new Technology and Innovation Centre that will open in 2014, bringing academic and industrial researchers together, with financial support from government, industry and Europe. Strathclyde has also been chosen as the European partner for South Korea's global research and commercialisation programme and as the UK headquarters of Fraunhofer Gesellschaft, Europe's largest contract research organisation.

Business and law were the main successes in the last Research Assessment Exercise, when almost 60 per cent of the university's submission was rated as world-leading or internationally excellent. Pharmacy and some branches of engineering also achieved good results. The business school, rated among the top 40 in Europe by *The Financial Times*, is normally considered Strathclyde's greatest strength. It is among the largest in Europe and one of only 55 in the world to be "triple accredited" by the main international bodies. The school has opened its own branch campus near Delhi. The engineering faculty is the largest in Scotland and home to the biggest university electrical power engineering and energy research grouping in Europe.

With nearly 22,000 students, including part-timers, Strathclyde is the third-largest university in Scotland but its numbers swell to more than 60,000 when short courses and distance learning programmes are included. Applications dropped in 2012, when most Scottish universities were enjoying increased demand for places, but it still managed a small increase in enrolments. Mature students account for an eighth of the places. The university has endorsed an international movement to establish "Age-Friendly" universities. Strathclyde's Learning in Later Life programme has established itself as one of Scotland's most successful routes to education for older people, while the Centre for Lifelong Learning has been one of the foremost providers of education to people in later life for some four decades.

---

16 Richmond Street
Glasgow G1 1XQ

0141 548 2762 (prospectus)
contact via website
www.strath.ac.uk
www.strathstudents.com
Affiliation: none

GLASGOW
Edinburgh
Belfast
London
Cardiff

The Times and Sunday Times **Rankings**
Overall Ranking: **42** (=36)

Student satisfaction:	85	(79.9%)
Research quality:	44	(16.7%)
Entry standards:	15	(465)
Student–staff ratio:	=56	(18.3)
Services & facilities/student:	44	(£1,639)
Expected completion rate:	76	(83.5%)
Good honours:	24	(75.1%)
Graduate prospects:	28	(74.3%)

Strathclyde actively promotes wider access, comfortably exceeding the UK average for state-educated students. The projected dropout rate had fallen below 10 per cent in the latest survey, although this is still higher than average for the university's subjects and entry qualifications.

Strathclyde, which has taken to adding Glasgow to its name, continues with its ambitious £350-million development programme. The Jordanhill campus has closed and all courses are now taught on the city-centre John Anderson campus. The integrated campus places the Faculty of Humanities and Social Sciences at the heart of the university and is enabling staff to work more closely with colleagues in research, teaching and partners in collaborative ventures. The developments feature new and improved teaching areas, study space and facilities for students tailored to their specific subjects. Space has been created for a Confucius classroom, part of the Confucius Institute for Scotland's Schools, which opened at the university earlier this year and supports the teaching of Chinese language and culture. The Strathclyde Institute of Pharmacy and Biomedical Sciences, a centre for excellence in drug discovery and development research, opened in 2011. In addition, the Advanced Forming Research Centre, a research partnership with international engineering firms, has opened near Glasgow Airport.

The university's normally high scores in the National Student Survey slipped in 2013, when overall satisfaction was down by 3 percentage points, although Strathclyde still matched the average for Scotland. There is a student village on the main campus with 1,400 places, all with network access. Another 500 residential places are nearby in the Merchant City. The ten-floor union building attracts students from all over Glasgow. There are numerous cultural and political clubs and societies, plus over 40 sporting clubs and university teams. Strathclyde was the only training venue in Scotland for the London 2012 Olympics, hosting the men's football team from Spain and the women's equivalent from the USA. Proximity to Glasgow's vibrant and celebrated music scene is a plus, and for those with more sophisticated tastes, there are numerous theatres and arts organisations, as well as standout museums such as the Kelvingrove Gallery, one of Scotland's top attractions.

Undergraduate Fees and Bursaries

» Fees for Scottish and EU students 2013–14   No fee
» Fees for Non-Scottish UK (RUK) students 2013–14   £9,000 (capped at £27,000 for any course)
» Fees for international students 2013–14   £10,500–£15,600
» For RUK students (2013–14), annual bursaries for household income below £20K, £4,250; sliding scale to £42.6K, £2,500–£1,000; year 1 bursary of £1,000 for those in university accommodation; those with at least AAB at A Level or equivalent, £1,000 cash for each year of study.

Students

Undergraduates:	**11,540**	**(2,525)**
Postgraduates:	**3,240**	**(2,450)**
Mature students:	**12.7%**	
Overseas students:	**8.2%**	
Applications per place:	**6.2**	
From state-sector schools:	**90.8%**	
From working-class homes:	**23.7%**	
Satisfaction with students' union	**73%**	

For detailed information about sports facilities: www.strath.ac.uk/sport

Accommodation

Number of places and costs refer to 2012–13
University-provided places: 1,838
Percentage catered: 0%
Self-catered costs: £72–£112 a week.
First years are offered accommodation if they live further than 25 miles from the university.
International students: as above.
Contact: student.accommodation@strath.ac.uk
www.strath.ac.uk/accommodation/

University of Sunderland

Sunderland will again offer some of the lowest fees in England, having held the cost of laboratory-based science degrees at £8,500 for the third year in succession. With classroom-based degrees costing £7,800, the average for all courses after all forms of student support will be held to £7,390. The university is spending £1.36 million to provide all UK undergraduates with free public transport throughout Tyne and Wear, or a £500 discount against university rents. Sunderland sees transport costs as a key barrier to study, especially in its local communities, which are the lifeblood of the university. It has a proud record of attracting students from groups that are under-represented in higher education. More than a quarter come from areas of low participation – the highest proportion at any university and double the national average for Sunderland's courses and entry qualifications – while 41 per cent are from working-class homes. A pioneering access scheme offers places to mature students without A levels, as long as they reach the required levels of literacy, numeracy and other basic skills. The Learning North East initiative even offers free taster courses to take at home. However, nothing could prevent applications and enrolments dropping by more than 10 per cent in 2012.

Sunderland has also suffered a big fall in the latest edition of our league table, partly because it has not managed to keep pace with improvements in student satisfaction and completion rates elsewhere in the university system. But provision for disabled students is excellent, with award-winning information issued to those with disabilities, trained support staff in the libraries and in every academic school, and special modules to help dyslexics. The main campus also houses the North East Regional Assessment Centre, which assesses the learning support requirements of students with disabilities and specific learning difficulties. There is special provision at the five halls of residence.

The university now has three campuses, two in Sunderland and one in London, near Canary Wharf, which offers business, tourism and nursing degrees, as well as postgraduate programmes, for up to 3,000 students. Within Sunderland, the university has spent £130 million on its original campus in the city centre and an award-winning 24-acre site on the banks of the River Wear. The Sir Tom Cowie campus, at St Peter's, is built around a 7th-century abbey described as one of Britain's first universities and incorporates a working heritage centre for the glass industry. It houses the business school and the faculties of applied sciences, law, and arts, design and media. A glass and ceramics design

---

City Campus
Chester Road
Sunderland SR1 3SD

0191 515 3000 (course helpline)
student.helpline@
sunderland.ac.uk
www.sunderland.ac.uk
www.sunderlandsu.co.uk
Affiliation: million+

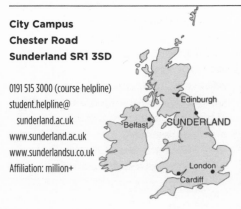

The Times and Sunday Times Rankings

Overall Ranking: **=96** (77)

Student satisfaction:	**=61**	(81.4%)
Research quality:	**=67**	(4.7%)
Entry standards:	**107**	(272)
Student–staff ratio:	**45**	(17)
Services & facilities/student:	**69**	(£1,355)
Expected completion rate:	**107**	(78.4%)
Good honours:	**111**	(52.6%)
Graduate prospects:	**116**	(49.6%)

degree maintains a Sunderland tradition, while teaching and research in automotive design and manufacture serve the region's modern industrial base. The large pharmacy department is another strength and the well-equipped Faculty of Applied Sciences is one of the largest in the UK, with over 4,000 students. The redevelopment of the original City Campus is well underway, after the opening of the £12-million CitySpace sports and social space and the new Sciences Complex and Quad. A £12-million student village is now fully open. The campus also boasts an outdoor performance area, a design centre, and the Gateway, a one-stop-shop for student services.

Sunderland now has more than 17,000 students, including 1,000 from outside the European Union. Many take work placements with the multinational companies that have been attracted to the North East and now have links with the university. The Institute for Automotive and Manufacturing Advanced Practice has a team of 40 researchers and consultants working with local businesses, while nearby Nissan played an important role in designing a course in automotive product development. The media centre provides students with excellent television and video production facilities, including the former Blue Peter studio, which has been transported from the former BBC Television Centre. The popular media courses now include magazine, fashion and sports journalism. The LLB degree includes space law, the first module of its kind in the UK. Sunderland had only moderate success in the 2008 Research Assessment Exercise, although more than half of the 16 subject areas contained at least some world-leading work. Communication, cultural and media studies produced by the far best grades, but history and English also did well.

Sunderland itself is fiercely proud of its identity and has the advantage of a coastal location. The leisure facilities are better than one might imagine: the city has the North East's only Olympic-sized swimming pool and dry ski slope, as well as Europe's biggest climbing wall and a theatre showing West End productions. Those in search of more cultural events or serious nightlife head for Newcastle, which is less than half an hour away by Metro.

Undergraduate Fees and Bursaries

» Fees for UK/EU students 2014–15   £7,800–£8,500
    Foundation degrees   £7,000
» International student fees 2013–14   £9,000
» 456 NSP awards with priority criteria: £2,000 fee waiver and £1,000 cash in year 1.
» For all first-year students, £500 towards local transport costs or campus accommodation.
» For those with ABB at A level or equivalent, £2,000 fee waiver for all years.
» Fee waiver of £1,200 a year for students on Foundation degrees at partner colleges.

Students

Undergraduates:	**9,220**	**(5,405)**
Postgraduates:	**1,800**	**(955)**
Mature students:	**22.5%**	
Overseas students:	**15.6%**	
Applications per place:	**5.3**	
From state-sector schools:	**97.7%**	
From working-class homes:	**40.9%**	
Satisfaction with students' union	**61%**	

For detailed information about sports facilities:
www.unisportsunderland.com

Accommodation

Number of places and costs refer to 2013–14

University provided places: 1,468 beds in Halls, 548 (The Forge).

Percentage catered: 0%

Self-catered costs: £2,720 (standard room;) – £3,599 (en suite) for 40 weeks. Option to purchase catering vouchers.

New first years are guaranteed accommodation in accordance with the university's allocation policy.

International students: as above.

Contact: www.sunderland.ac.uk/residentialservices

University of Surrey

Student satisfaction has been growing by leaps and bounds at Surrey, contributing to a continuing and impressive rise in our league table. Overall satisfaction has increased by 10 percentage points in three years, standing at 92 per cent in the 2013 National Student Survey and placing Surrey in the top ten on this measure. The university has been among the most innovative in the UK in recent years, reducing its dependence on state funding even before the introduction of £9,000 fees, developing a new campus in Guildford and launching a joint venture in China. Now it is planning a veterinary school, which will be only the second new foundation in half a century. The demand for places doubled in six years, despite sharply increasing entry standards. Both applications and enrolments dropped by more than 15 per cent – well above the national average –when the fees went up, but demand recovered strongly in 2013.

The university has remained true to its technological history with large numbers taking engineering and science subjects, but it has other strengths in business and the sector-leading School of Hospitality and Tourism Management. Surrey has incorporated the Guildford School of Acting and opened the £4.5-million Ivy Arts Centre in 2011, with a 200-seat theatre and workshops. Undergraduates in most subjects undertake work placements of one year, or several shorter periods, often abroad. As a result, most degrees last four years. The format and the subject balance combine to keep Surrey at or near the top of the graduate employment league, and the dropout rate is low. All students are encouraged to take a free course in a European language alongside their degree, in a programme known as the Global Graduate Award. Over 92 per cent of Surrey undergraduates are state educated and nearly 28 per cent are from working class backgrounds.

International activities have been increasing. Surrey has one of the largest proportions of overseas students at any university – more than a fifth – and is a member of the University Global Partnership Network (UGPN) involving North Carolina State University and the Universidad de Sao Paulo in Brazil. The biggest development has seen the opening of a campus in Dalian, China with the Dongbei University of Finance and Economics. More than half of the work submitted for the last Research Assessment Exercise was considered world-leading or internationally excellent. Electrical and electronic engineering was ranked second in the country, while health and medical sciences, sociology and general engineering were in the top 10 in their fields. More

---

Guildford
Surrey GU2 7XH

0800 980 3200 (enquiries)
ug-enquiries@surrey.ac.uk
www.surrey.ac.uk
www.ussu.co.uk
Affiliation: none

The Times and Sunday Times **Rankings**
Overall Ranking: **=12** (26)

Student satisfaction:	=6	(86.2%)
Research quality:	=35	(20.3%)
Entry standards:	=29	(418)
Student–staff ratio:	40	(16.6)
Services & facilities/student:	15	(£2,121)
Expected completion rate:	26	(92.7%)
Good honours:	25	(74.7%)
Graduate prospects:	22	(75.6%)

recently, Surrey's chemical engineering received two awards for innovation and excellence from the Institution of Chemical Engineers and the university has secured £35-million funding for a 5G communication research centre. The proportion of its research income coming from private business and industry has grown to about 70 per cent in little over a decade. The Surrey Research Park is one of only three science parks still owned, funded and managed by the university.

The compact campus is a ten-minute walk from the centre of Guildford. Many of the buildings date from the late 1960s, but the newly refurbished and extended library and learning centre, and the gleaming Duke of Kent Building, which houses the growing health and medical provision, offer a striking contrast. The campus includes two lakes, playing fields and enough residential accommodation to enable all first years to live in. A new online network will allow students to work virtually with others on their courses through group work, discussions and blogs, as well as allowing lecturers to set coursework and interact virtually with students. The Manor Park campus, now well established adjacent to the university's Stag Hill headquarters, provides over 1,500 new residential places for students and staff, as well as a new reception building with café, bar and lounge areas. The impressive Surrey Sports Park,

with extensive indoor and outdoor facilities, opened in 2010. Surrey's new veterinary school will be based on the Manor Park campus and open in 2014 with an emphasis on research, veterinary pathology and livestock medicine. It will be only the eighth school in the UK. The aim is to produce vets who are equally employable as clinicians, scientists or researchers.

The main campus is the centre of social life, and has seen recent improvements to leisure facilities including new dining and social areas. Guildford has plenty of retail, cultural and recreational facilities and the proximity of London (35 minutes by train) is an attraction to many students, although it also helps account for the high cost of living.

Undergraduate Fees and Bursaries

» Fees for UK/EU students 2014–15 £9,000
» International student fees 2013–14 £12,130–£15,160
» Household income below £25K, £3,000 campus accommodation discount (if off campus £2,000 fee waiver and £1,000 cash), year 1; £1,000 fee waiver and £1,000 cash, year 2; £2,000 fee waiver and £1,000 cash, other years; £25K–£30K, £1,500 campus accommodation discount (if off campus £1,000 fee waiver and £500 cash), year 1; £500 fee waiver and £500 cash, year 2; £1,000 fee waiver and £500 cash, other years.
» Scholarship of £3,000 cash in year 1 for those with A*AA at A level or equivalent.
» Sports and other scholarships available.
» Check the university's website for the latest information.

Students

Undergraduates:	**9,600**	**(1,095)**
Postgraduates:	**2,880**	**(1,480)**
Mature students:	**19.2%**	
Overseas students:	**21.1%**	
Applications per place:	**7.4**	
From state-sector schools:	**92.6%**	
From working-class homes:	**27.4%**	
Satisfaction with students' union	**81%**	

For detailed information about sports facilities:
www.surreysportspark.co.uk

Accommodation

Number of places and costs refer to 2013–14
University-provided places: 5,063
Percentage catered: 0%
Self-catered costs: £65–£148 a week.
All first years are guaranteed a place.
International non-EU students are guaranteed accommodation for the standard duration of their course. Remaining places are allocated to final year students.
Contact: www.surrey.ac.uk/Accommodatio

University of Sussex

Sussex has dropped 14 places and out of the top 30 in our league table after a second successive fall, due mainly to declines in student satisfaction and graduate employment prospects. But it was one of the few universities to attract more students when the fees went up to £9,000 in 2012 and it remains a popular choice. The campus, four miles from the centre of Brighton, now serves a record 13,000 students, 9,500 of them undergraduates. The university has now completed a £100-million campus development plan, refurbishing Sir Basil Spence's original buildings and adding new ones. A striking new £29-million academic building offers a mix of lecture theatres, study and teaching space, and a social centre. The Gardner Centre will be brought back to life during the 2013–14 academic year as an interdisciplinary arts hub for the university and the wider community, named after the university's former Chancellor, Lord Attenborough. The library, which has undergone a £6-million redevelopment and introduced 24-hour opening during term-time, has seen a 50 per cent increase in use. An investment of £1.5-million in IT developments has doubled the number of computers available to students and installed Wi-Fi in all the student residences.

The interdisciplinary approach that has always been Sussex's trademark has been re-examined and adapted for the 21st century. Arts and social science students take the biggest share of places, but the life sciences are not far behind. The School of Business, Management and Economics, which opened in 2009, offers a portfolio of undergraduate and postgraduate business and management programmes. Dedicated student social space is being created in each of the university's 12 schools to encourage staff and students to engage both academically and socially. Sussex has reviewed all its courses since the switch to higher fees and has become a late covert to the semester system. The university believes that two 12-week teaching periods with a mid-year assessment period will improve the way students learn and are assessed. Student support includes a work-study programme to help students earn money, funded work placements and three years' aftercare for graduates to help them into a career. The Sussex Plus programme documents and credits students' extra-curricular skills, while a new initiative, Startup Sussex, supports students' creative business ideas and social projects.

Relations with neighbouring Brighton University are good. The two institutions opened a joint medical school in 2003 and recorded another 10 per cent increase in applications for courses beginning in 2012. The Brighton and Sussex Medical School is split between the Royal Sussex County

---

Sussex House
Brighton BN1 9RH

01273 876787 (enquiries)
ug.enquiries@sussex.ac.uk
www.sussex.ac.uk
www.bsms.ac.uk
www.sussexstudent.com
Affiliation: 1994 Group

The Times and Sunday Times **Rankings**
Overall Ranking: **32** (=18)

Student satisfaction:	=43	(82.2%)
Research quality:	17	(25.7%)
Entry standards:	34	(407)
Student–staff ratio:	=46	(17.1)
Services & facilities/student:	36	(£1,729)
Expected completion rate:	=27	(92.4%)
Good honours:	=14	(79.6%)
Graduate prospects:	99	(54.4%)

Hospital and the two universities' Falmer campuses. Sussex generates more than a third of its income from private sources, largely in research contracts. Its reputation was enhanced by good results in the last Research Assessment Exercise, when almost 60 per cent of an unusually large submission was rated as world-leading or internationally excellent. The first fruits of a £50-million fundraising campaign have seen the opening of major research centres on adoption, corruption, Middle East studies and consciousness science.

Sussex is committed to taking candidates with no family tradition of higher education and has much larger numbers of mature students than most of its peer group of institutions. The proportion of working-class students is lower than the national average for the university's subjects and entry grades, but this is attributed to the university's south coast location. The projected dropout rate remains at just below 8 per cent – lower than the university's benchmark. Sussex has always attracted overseas students in large numbers and has seen big increases recently. The university has performed consistently well in the International Student Barometer, which gauges overseas students' satisfaction. Together with first years, they are guaranteed a place in university-managed accommodation that has been expanded and upgraded in recent years. A new residential complex in 2011 brought the number of

residential places to 4,500 and another 1,000 will become available in 2013. The university's plans for the future include a major housing development to replace old East Slope accommodation, as well as the construction of a new biomedical sciences building to complement the highly rated Genome Research Centre.

The campus is located within the newly created South Downs National Park, with excellent transport links into town. There is no shortage of social events on campus and Brighton has plenty to offer. Sports facilities were good enough to house pre-Olympic training. Sports scholarships are available to outstanding athletes, including four reserved for basketball and hockey players. Sussex has also opened a new purpose-built childcare facility for 100 pre-school children of students and staff.

Undergraduate Fees and Bursaries

» Fees for UK/EU students 2013–14 £9,000
» International student fees 2013–14 £13,000–£16,200
 Medicine £24,860
» Students with household income below £42.6K, £1,000 cash a year plus, in year 1 and Foundation year only, £2,000 fee waiver or accommodation discount.
» Check the university's website for the latest information.

Students

Undergraduates:	9,310	(35)
Postgraduates:	2,830	(955)
Mature students:	12.9%	
Overseas students:	18.7%	
Applications per place:	5.9	
From state-sector schools:	85.2%	
From working-class homes:	20.2%	
Satisfaction with students' union	67%	

For detailed information about sports facilities:
www.sussex.ac.uk/sport/

Accommodation

Number of places and costs refer to 2013–14
University-provided places: 4,591
Percentage catered: 0%
Self-catered costs: £81.60–£137,40 (single) a week. Some shared rooms available.
First-year students are guaranteed accommodation if conditions are met.
International students: given priority providing conditions are met.
Contact: housing@sussex.ac.uk
www.sussex.ac.uk/study/ug/location/accommodation

Swansea University

Swansea was the UK's first campus university when it opened in 1920. But the Singleton campus is now the smallest main site at any pre-1992 university, and with more than 14,000 students and rapidly increasing research activities, the university has begun to outgrow its scenic surroundings overlooking the sea on the outskirts of Wales's second city. Undergraduates will still be taught on the main campus, which has a prime position at the gateway to the Gower Peninsula, the UK's first Area of Outstanding Natural Beauty. But work has begun on a new campus for science and innovation, six miles away. The university will use its new site to focus on research and interaction with technology companies and will ultimately provide accommodation for 2,000 students there, as well as retail facilities. The new development will be ready in 2015, relieving pressure on the main campus and allowing for new developments there. It has already seen the opening of a £1.2-million facility in the university library to house the Richard Burton archives. Other recent additions have included the £4.3-million Digital Technium Building, which houses the media and communication studies department. A second Institute of Life Sciences building and a Centre for NanoHealth, based within

it, opened in 2011 at a combined cost of more than £50 million.

Swansea is back in our top 50 after a rise in this year's league table and has seen an 18 per cent increase in applications for courses beginning in 2013. There were declines close to the national average in both applications and enrolments, when £9,000 fees arrived for UK students from outside Wales. But the current year has seen rising demand for places in 13 of the 15 subject groups offered at the university. This included a 15 per cent increase in languages at a time of falling demand elsewhere, as well as a 64 per cent increase in maths and computer science and engineering. Most of those who take up places seem to enjoy their time at Swansea: overall satisfaction is higher than in most universities in Wales, although only on the average for the whole UK. Swansea became independent of the University of Wales in 2007. There are now about 350 degree courses in the modular scheme, and undergraduates are encouraged to stray outside their specialist area in their first year.

The most important academic development of recent years came with the opening of the School of Medicine and the subsequent development of a full four-year graduate entry medical degree, launched in 2009. Previous entrants spent half of their course in Cardiff, but the new degree is linked to a new NHS University Health

---

Singleton Park
Swansea SA2 8PP

01792 295111 (enquiries)
admissions@swansea.ac.uk
www.swansea.ac.uk
www.swansea-union.co.uk
Affiliation: none

The Times and Sunday Times **Rankings**
Overall Ranking: **47** (=52)

Student satisfaction:	=86	(79.7%)
Research quality:	=45	(16.0%)
Entry standards:	45	(360)
Student–staff ratio:	32	(16.1)
Services & facilities/student:	55	(£1,477)
Expected completion rate:	45	(88.2%)
Good honours:	60	(63.8%)
Graduate prospects:	17	(77.5%)

Board and the Institute of Life Sciences. The institute is home to Blue C, one of the few supercomputers in the world dedicated to life science research. In addition, the physics department is involved with CERN's Large Hadron Collider.

The university has links to more than 100 partner institutions worldwide and offers many degrees that include opportunities to study abroad. Popular study abroad summer programmes allow students to experience living and studying in India, China and the USA. The university has won more than £100 million in European funding for projects such as Graduate Opportunities Wales, which steers students towards small firms through industrial placements and vacation jobs. Closer to home, the department of adult and community education teaches mature students in locations throughout the Valleys and elsewhere in South Wales. Compacts with the region's schools encourage students in areas of economic disadvantage to aspire to higher education.

Swansea makes a particular effort to cater for disabled students, whose needs are coordinated through a £250,000 assessment and training centre. Nine out of ten undergraduates come from state schools and colleges, but fewer than a quarter come from working-class homes – significantly less that the UK average for the university's subjects and entry grades. However, the projected dropout rate of 7 per cent is better than Swansea's benchmark figure.

The 1,900 computers available for student use represent one of the best ratios at any university. In the past few years Swansea opened two new halls of residence that take the total number of residential places to more than 3,000. The sports facilities in the £20-million Sports Village include an athletics track, grass and all-weather pitches, squash and tennis courts plus the indoor athletics training centre and gym. The 50-metre pool is the Wales National Pool and one of only five facilities in the UK to be awarded Intensive Training Centre status. The campus is the focal point of most students' leisure activities, but the city has a good range of leisure facilities.

Undergraduate Fees and Bursaries

» Fees for UK/EU students 2014–15 £9,000 with Welsh Assembly paying fees above £3,575 (2013–14) for Welsh students.
» International student fees 2013–14 £10,500–£13,500
» For those with household income up to £30K, retention cash bursary of £1,000–£3,000 over 3 years and a priority subject cash bursary of £500 a year.
» Award of £1,500 in years 1 and 2 for those with AAA at A level or equivalent; £1,000 in years 1 and 2 for AAB or equivalent.
» Sports scholarships and care leaver's bursaries available.
» Check the university's website for the latest information.

Students

Undergraduates:	**10,505**	**(1,850)**
Postgraduates:	**1,815**	**(600)**
Mature students:	**20.8%**	
Overseas students:	**9.6%**	
Applications per place:	**4.1**	
From state-sector schools:	**89.1%**	
From working-class homes:	**24.6%**	
Satisfaction with students' union	**74%**	

For detailed information about sports facilities: www.swansea.ac.uk/sport/

Accommodation

Number of places and costs refer to 2013–14
University-provided places: about 3,500
Percentage catered: 5%
Catered costs: £111.50–£116.50 a week.
Self-catered costs: £80 (standard) – £118 (en suite) a week.
First-year students holding a firm offer are guaranteed accommodation if conditions are met.
International students: offered up to 3 years.
Contact: www.swansea.ac.uk/accommodation/
accommodation@swansea.ac.uk

Teesside University

Teesside will charge the lowest fees of any university in England in 2014, having decided not to raise the top rate from £8,450. This will apply to laboratory-based degrees in science and engineering and also to design, journalism and other animation and multimedia courses. The remaining classroom-based programmes, including law, business and psychology, will still cost less than £8,000. When the new fees regime arrived in 2012, Professor Graham Henderson, the Vice-Chancellor, said that for many students, the university's package of grants, scholarships, loans and other support measures would make higher education more accessible and affordable. There was a sharp drop in applications when the new fees came in but, unlike most other universities, Teesside actually increased its enrolment. Scores in the National Student Survey had been improving, but that came to at least a temporary halt in 2013 when overall satisfaction slipped slightly, against the national trend. However, the students' union was rated among the top ten in the country, 17 percentage points ahead of the national average.

There are more than 25,000 under-graduates, nearly half of them taking part-time courses below degree level. Almost two-thirds of the students are from the North East and around a third of the full-time undergraduates are 21 or over on entry. There are strong partnerships with five further education colleges in the Tees Valley, each having a separate centre offering the university's Foundation degrees and other courses, and a £13-million campus in Darlington. But there has also been rapid growth in the number of international students coming to Teesside. The university has featured consistently among the leaders in the International Student Barometer, which measures satisfaction among overseas students. The university has always recruited from a wide range of backgrounds. It is in the top ten for the proportion of UK undergraduates coming from working-class homes – nearly 43 per cent – and the 24 per cent share of places going to students from areas of low participation in higher education is almost twice the national average for Teesside's courses and entry qualifications. The projected dropout rate continues to improve and is now well ahead of the university's benchmark, at less than 13 per cent.

Some £135 million has been spent in recent years on the main campus in the centre of Middlesbrough. A £17-million sport and health sciences building, with dentistry training and hydrotherapy pool, opened in 2010. The library was refurbished for the 2012–13 academic year, adding social and interactive spaces, group learning areas and a café. Computer provision is generous, with

---

7 Borough Road
Middlesbrough TS1 3BA

01642 218121 (switchboard)
enquiries@tees.ac.uk
www.tees.ac.uk
www.tees-su.org.uk
Affiliation: University
  Alliance

The Times and Sunday Times **Rankings**

Overall Ranking: **93** (87)

Student satisfaction:	38	(83%)
Research quality:	=100	(1.7%)
Entry standards:	=66	(321)
Student–staff ratio:	83	(20.1)
Services & facilities/student:	91	(£1,233)
Expected completion rate:	=102	(79.1%)
Good honours:	=103	(56%)
Graduate prospects:	100	(54.1%)

2,700 workstations for student use. Other recent developments include a centre for creative technologies for computing, media and design, where specialist facilities include a new digital sound and TV studio. But the flagship project has been DigitalCity Innovation, the university's centre for digital excellence and entrepreneurship. Some 430 new businesses and 600 jobs have been created by the new centre and by graduate enterprise, leading Dr Vince Cable, Secretary of State for Business, Innovation and Skills, to describe Teesside as "Britain's best university for working with business". The university was awarded the £1-million maximum to support further collaboration with business and industry.

The 11,000 health students are by far the largest group in the university, but Teesside is also strong in niche markets such as computer games design and animation, sport and exercise, and forensic science. Teesside supports the career development of its graduates for a minimum of two years after graduation and is expanding paid work placements as part of a student's course. The Get Ahead scheme provides three-month paid internships and training for graduates, as well as helping to provide summer placements for second-year students.

Computer science and history produced the best results in the last Research Assessment Exercise. Only a small proportion of Teesside's academics were entered for assessment, but 30 per cent of their research was considered world-leading or internationally excellent. Five research-led institutes will focus on digital innovation, health, culture, social science and technology.

Middlesbrough has more nightlife than sceptics might imagine, and the booming student population has attracted new pubs, cafés and student-orientated shops in and around the Southfield Road area. The university has also forged a new partnership with the nationally renowned Middlesbrough Institute of Modern Art – mima – in the centre of town. The cost of living is another attraction: both university rents those in the private sector are reasonable. Sports facilities include a newly refurbished gym on campus and a water sports centre on the River Tees. The university supports elite athletes with a package of support that includes bursaries, training and access to the latest sport science techniques.

Undergraduate Fees and Bursaries

» Fees for UK/EU students 2014–15	£7,950–£8,450
Year 4 of MEng degree	£4,450
Foundation degree	£5,750
» International student fees 2013–14	£10,450
» 975 NSP awards with priority for those with lowest household income, £3,000 fee waiver in year 1 only.	
» Check the university's website for the latest information.	

Students

Undergraduates:	9,620	(15,075)
Postgraduates:	1,180	(2,100)
Mature students:	30.9%	
Overseas students:	5.1%	
Applications per place:	3.9	
From state-sector schools:	98.5%	
From working-class homes:	42.8%	
Satisfaction with students' union	83%	

For detailed information about sports facilities:
www.tees.ac.uk/sport

Accommodation

Number of places and costs refer to 2013–14
University-provided places: 1,149
Percentage catered: 0%
Self-catered costs: £55.95–£95.80 a week (residences, 40 weeks);
£62–£66 a week (managed housing, 40 weeks)
First years are guaranteed a place if conditions are met.
International students: guaranteed accommodation if conditions met.
Contact: 01642 342255; accommodation@tees.ac.uk;
www.tees.ac.uk/accommodation

Trinity St David, University of Wales (UWTSD)

Two mergers in two years created the University of Wales Trinity Saint David and brought in the former Swansea Metropolitan University. Now a third one has been agreed, adding one of the largest further education colleges in Wales to the network, in the shape of Coleg Sir Gar, in Carmarthenshire. The new institution describes itself as a "dual sector university" since it will now offer courses from A level to postgraduate degrees to more than 25,000 students, half of them on Sir Gar's five campuses in south-west Wales. The university does not appear in any of our league tables, however, having chosen not to release data this year. Swansea Metropolitan boycotted league tables throughout its brief existence as an independent university, and the new institution felt that a partial assessment might mislead prospective students. The old Trinity Saint David finished just outside the bottom ten last year and was in the bottom four for overall satisfaction in the 2013 National Student Survey.

Even without Sir Gar, the university offered students the choice of a rural or urban experience – from the green campuses of Lampeter and Carmarthen to the urban surroundings of Swansea Metropolitan. There is also a new London campus for international students, offering business, management and IT degrees. The university markets itself as both old and new since in the whole of England and Wales, only Oxford and Cambridge were awarding degrees before St David's College, Lampeter. The college went on to become the smallest publicly funded university in Europe before merging with Trinity University College, 23 miles away in Carmarthen. Swansea is as far away again and will continue to have its own UCAS code for applications.

The UWTSD Lampeter Campus (formerly University of Wales, Lampeter) has continued to make a virtue of its size by stressing its friendly atmosphere and intimate teaching style. It remains a small, rural community that suits students who seek a close-knit campus experience. Based on an ancient castle and modelled on an Oxbridge college, St David's College was established to provide a liberal arts education. The original quadrangle remains but there have been significant changes in recent few years, notably the introduction of such subjects as anthropology, archaeology, Chinese, classics and philosophy, as well as education as a minor and combined subject with a range of humanities programmes for prospective teachers. There is a strong research culture on the campus as

---

UWTSD

Carmarthen Campus
Carmarthen SA31 3EP
01267 676767

Lampeter Campus
Ceredigion SA48 7ED
01570 422351

Swansea Campus
Mount Pleasant
Swansea SA1 6ED
01792 481000

www.trinitysaintdavid.ac.uk
www.tsd.ac.uk
www.smu.ac.uk
www.tsdsu.co.uk
Affiliation: Cathedrals Group

well as unique resources, including an archaeological dig site at nearby Strata Florida and a collection of medieval manuscripts housed within the Roderic Bowen Library and Archives.

The Carmarthen Campus was established in 1848 to train teachers. It has a long history of teacher training and has developed a reputation for education-related programmes including early childhood, social inclusion, and youth and community work. In addition, the university offers a range of programmes in the creative and performing arts, as well a growing portfolio within the School of Sport, Health and Outdoor Education, which makes use of the natural resources of west Wales, supplemented with expeditions around the UK and to extreme climates in various parts of the world.

The Swansea Campus has retained its own website under its old name, with UWTSD as a subsidiary heading. It began life as a college of art in 1853, subsequently joined by education and technical colleges. Based in the centre of Wales's second city, Swansea Met became a university only in 2008 and had expanded to about 6,000 students before becoming part of UWTSD. Its automotive engineering courses – especially those focused on motorsport – are its best-known feature, but there has been strong demand for places on a variety of vocationally oriented courses. The campus surpasses all its benchmarks for widening participation in higher education, but the 25 per cent projected dropout rate is by far the highest in Wales.

There has been recent investment across all of the university's campuses. In Swansea, there is a new building for the Business School and a refurbished centre for the Institute of Sustainable Design. In Lampeter, a new hub has opened for student services and the sports facilities were extended in 2013, while Carmarthen has seen refurbishment of student accommodation and the opening of a new art building. The London campus opened in 2012 in a new building overlooking the Regent's Canal, close to St Pancras Station. The university has a focus on future employment and has introduced the TSD+ Employability Award to run alongside academic programmes, with work placement schemes and internships to provide opportunities for students to build core skills to improve their future career prospects.

Undergraduate Fees and Bursaries

» Fees for UK/EU students 2013–14: £7,500 with Welsh Assembly paying fees above £3,575 for Welsh students.
» International student fees 2013–14 £9,576–£10,000
» Scholarships and bursaries available, organised by campus.
» Check the university's website for the latest information.

Students

| Undergraduates: | **3,080** | **(2,065)** |
| Postgraduates: | **435** | **(560)** |

Student numbers obtained by combining Trinity St David and Swansea Metropolitan figures for 2011–12. It is not possible to give combined figures for the other measures usually shown here.

Accommodation

Number of places and costs refer to 2013–14
L refers to Lampeter, CM to Carmarthen, S to Swansea
University-provided places: 500 (L), 512 (CM), 350 (S)
Percentage catered: 0% (L), 44% (CM); 0% (S)
Catered costs: £109 a week; meals for 5 days (L & CM).
Self-catered costs: £53.00–£87.50 (L & S); £86.50 (CM) a week.
First years can normally be placed in university accommodation.
International students: guaranteed housing for first year.
Contact: www.tsd.ac.uk/en/accommodation; www.smu.ac.uk/index.php/potential-students/accommodation/for-students

University of Ulster

Ulster is only just outside the top ten universities for the volume of applications it attracts and was one of the few also to register a significant increase in enrolments in 2012, when new fee arrangements were brought in. Most students were from Northern Ireland and paying less than £3,500, while fees for students from other parts of the UK were £6,000. It is planning for further expansion, initially at the Magee campus in Derry-Londonderry, but also at a £250-million campus for 15,000 students that is about to be built in Belfast's Cathedral Quarter. The new campus will open in 2018, extending the current Belfast site, when courses will be transferred from Jordanstown, seven miles outside the city. The main Jordanstown building, which dates from Ulster's days as a polytechnic, is nearing the end of its use, but will remain the location for courses starting in 2014 in business and management, the built environment, computing and engineering, health and sport sciences, and social sciences. The fourth campus, at Coleraine on Northern Ireland's north coast, focuses on environmental and life sciences, humanities, modern languages and tourism management. A Confucius Institute opened there in 2012 to foster academic, cultural, economic and social ties between the university and China. Coleraine is home to the £11-million Centre for Biosciences, whose academics produced the most highly rated work in the last Research Assessment Exercise, achieving grades that were among the top three in the UK. There were other top-three performances in Celtic Studies and nursing and midwifery, and almost half of the university's whole submission was considered world-leading or internationally excellent.

Ulster has over 25,000 students, including almost 9,000 part-timers. All undergraduates complete their studies on a single campus, each of which has well-equipped library and computer facilities. Belfast concentrates on art and design, architecture and hospitality, while Magee has a focus on the creative and performing arts, nursing and social work, computing, business and management, and social sciences. The campus has been a central hub for the programme of events associated with Derry-Londonderry as the UK's first City of Culture in 2013, hosting an international conference on music, a festival of creative and performing arts, and a history symposium. Student numbers at Magee are expected to grow, following the signing of an option agreement with the City Council, which will see the university almost double its footprint in the city. There will be growth in computer science, engineering and creative technologies.

Jordanstown has seen £20 million invested in the sports facilities, including

---

Cromore Road
Coleraine
Co. Londonderry
BT52 1SA

028 701 23456
  (switchboard)
enquiry via website
www.ulster.ac.uk
www.uusu.org
Affiliation: none

The Times and Sunday Times Rankings

Overall Ranking: **=73** (=65)

Student satisfaction:	**31**	(83.4%)
Research quality:	**=52**	(11.0%)
Entry standards:	**101**	(284)
Student–staff ratio:	**=61**	(18.6)
Services & facilities/student:	**=58**	(£1,429)
Expected completion rate:	**=77**	(83.1%)
Good honours:	**=81**	(60.3%)
Graduate prospects:	**115**	(50.7%)

outdoor and indoor sprint tracks, sports science and sports medicine facilities. They will be further upgraded to house the Sports Institute of Northern Ireland and continue to host training by Northern Ireland's leading sportsmen and sportswomen. The university's specialist engineering facilities will also remain at Jordanstown, serving FireSERT, which is one of only eight fire training facilities in the world. The rest of the campus will be given over to housing, shared between students and the local community. Another development in 2012 saw the university's first graduation ceremony in London, conferring awards in business, computing and engineering from courses delivered in partnership with the QA Business School at their branch campuses in London and Birmingham. Ulster also has a growing number of international students – about 2,400 from 80 different countries. The eLearning at Ulster programme provides an alternative mode of study, offering courses online to students all over the world.

The university has committed itself to becoming the leading provider of "professional education for professional life". One aim is for an increasing number of degrees to provide placement opportunities and professional accreditation. The majority of courses now include a year-long work placement. The 2013 National Student Survey showed increased levels of satisfaction, with 88 per cent of final-year undergraduates satisfied overall.

Nearly 100 per cent of undergraduates are from state schools and 46 per cent come from working class backgrounds – among the highest levels at any UK university. Ulster is adding to its portfolio of programmes to widen participation in higher education with a £360,000 project to engage some of Coleraine's most disadvantaged communities. The university runs workshops in primary schools, as well as organising a range of activities to encourage secondary pupils to try a degree. Its award-winning sports outreach programme has been particularly successful. The projected dropout rate has been improving but, at 15 per cent, remains higher than the UK average for Ulster's subjects and entry qualifications.

Accommodation is guaranteed for all first-years students on all four campuses and the students' union is also active at every location. The social life inevitably varies depending on location.

Undergraduate Fees and Bursaries

» Fees for NI/EU students 2013–14	£3,575
» Fees for English, Scottish and Welsh students	£6,000
» International student fees 2013–14	£9,805
» Range of scholarships and bursaries available.	
» Check the university's website for the latest information.	

Students

Undergraduates:	**16,300**	**(4,440)**
Postgraduates:	**2,265**	**(3,555)**
Mature students:	**23.4%**	
Overseas students:	**14.4%**	
Applications per place:	**6.1**	
From state-sector schools:	**99.9%**	
From working-class homes:	**45.9%**	
Satisfaction with students' union	**59%**	

For detailed information about sports facilities: www.sportsulster.com

Accommodation

Number of places and costs refer to 2013–14
University-provided places: 2,425 over three campuses.
Percentage catered: 0%
Self-catered costs: average £68 (standard) – £97 (en suite) a week (37 weeks).
First-year students are guaranteed accommodation if conditions are met.
International students: same as above.
Contact: accommodation@ulster.ac.uk
www.accommodation.ulster.ac.uk/

University College London

While the demand for places at most universities dropped when the fees went up to £9,000, UCL increased the number of new undergraduates it enrolled by more than 20 per cent. The college seized the opportunity to fill nearly 800 more places when restrictions were lifted on the recruitment candidates with top grades at A level. The expansion demonstrated the pulling power of UCL, which had been attracting almost ten applications for every place, and also represented a change of direction since it had been expected to take more postgraduates and fewer undergraduates over the coming years.

UCL remains in the top ten in our league table, but does even better (fourth) in the QS World University Rankings, which place more weight on its strength in research. In the last Research Assessment Exercise, two-thirds of its submission was judged to be world-leading or internationally excellent. The top scorers were economics, with 95 per cent of its work rated in the top two categories, and computer science and informatics, immunology and infection, environmental sciences and history of art, all of which had at least 80 per cent at this level. Architecture, chemical engineering, cancer studies, law, philosophy and psychology also produced outstanding results.

Already comfortably the largest of the University of London's colleges, UCL can award its own degrees and has more than 700 professors – the largest number in Britain. It includes several specialist schools and institutes, the School of Pharmacy being the latest to join, in 2012. There is also a new "strategic partnership" with the university's Institute of Education, which falls short of a merger. UCL's medical school, with 11 associated teaching hospitals, is now a large and formidable unit. Its credentials were strengthened still further with the announcement that UCL will be a founding partner in the new Francis Crick Institute (formerly UK Centre for Medical Research and Innovation) that will open in 2015, next to St Pancras Station. The centre will undertake cutting-edge research to advance understanding of health and disease. The various acquisitions mean that there are now outposts in several parts of central and north London, as well as an archaeology and conservation campus in Qatar, but the main activity remains centred on the original impressive Bloomsbury site. UCL is pioneering the idea of education for global citizenship, ensuring students are given opportunity and encouragement to explore academic ideas from different cultural perspectives and to work on problems of international importance, as well as contributing to their local community and the university's social and cultural life.

Gower Street

London WC1E 6BT

020 7679 2000 (main switchboard)

contact via website

www.ucl.ac.uk

www.uclu.org

Affiliation: Russell Group

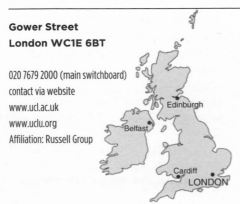

The Times and Sunday Times Rankings

Overall Ranking: **9** (7)

Student satisfaction:	98	(78.5%)
Research quality:	=4	(33.0%)
Entry standards:	6	(511)
Student–staff ratio:	1	(10.2)
Services & facilities/student:	9	(£2,225)
Expected completion rate:	9	(96.7%)
Good honours:	5	(84.2%)
Graduate prospects:	10	(79.8%)

UCL's excellence is built on a history of pioneering subjects that have become commonplace in higher education: modern languages, geography and fine arts among them. Since 2012, there has been a new requirement for a foreign language GCSE at grade C or above, although students are allowed to reach this standard during their degree if they have not taken a language at school. UCL has done better than most London institutions in the National Student Survey, although overall satisfaction dropped slightly in 2013, when the national trend was upwards. All first-year students are helped to make the academic and social adjustment to university life through UCL's Transition Programme, which includes a variety of activities such as peer mentoring and workshops. There is a commitment to teaching in small groups, especially in the second and subsequent years of degree courses. The projected dropout rate of only 3.4 per cent is among the lowest in the country.

UCL is conscious of its traditions as a college founded to expand access to higher education, but the 35 per cent share of places going to independent school students is one of the highest in Britain. About one undergraduate in six has a working-class background. Concerted attempts are being made to broaden the intake with summer schools for state-school students, outreach activities and campus-based programmes.

The focus is mainly but not exclusively on schools in London and the South East. UCL sponsors an academy, which it sees as part of its contribution to the local community.

The academic pace can be frantic but, close to the West End and with its own theatre and recreational facilities, there is no shortage of leisure options. Students also have access to the University of London's underused central students' union facilities in Bloomsbury. Residential accommodation is plentiful and of a good standard. Indoor sports and fitness facilities are close at hand, but the main outdoor pitches, though good enough to attract professional football clubs, are a (free) coach ride away in Hertfordshire. Hockey players have access to Astroturf pitches at the Old Cranleighans ground, in Thames Ditton.

Undergraduate Fees and Bursaries

» Fees for UK/EU students 2014–15   £9,000
» International student fees 2013–14   £14,750–£19,500
     Medicine   £29,000
» For all UK/EU students with household income below £12K, £1,000 cash and £5,000 fee waiver or UCL accommodation discount, year 1; following years £2,000 cash; household income £12K–£25K, £1,000 cash and £2,500 fee waiver or UCL accommodation discount, year 1; following years £2,000 cash; £25K–42.6K, £1,000 cash each year.
» Range of departmental and academic scholarships.
» Check the university's website for the latest information.

Students

Undergraduates:	**12,635**	**(860)**
Postgraduates:	**8,915**	**(3,115)**
Mature students:	**7.3%**	
Overseas students:	**35.6%**	
Applications per place:	**7.7**	
From state-sector schools:	**64.7%**	
From working-class homes:	**16.3%**	
Satisfaction with students' union	**68%**	

For detailed information about sports facilities:
http://uclu.org/services/active-uclu

Accommodation

Number of places and costs refer to 2013–14
University-provided places: 4,545 (including 819 intercollegiate places)
Percentage catered: 30%
Catered costs: £130.90 (single) – £230.30 (en-suite) a week.
Self-catered costs: £101.50 (twin) – £213.50 a week (en-suite single) (39 weeks).
First years are guaranteed accommodation if conditions are met.
International students: as above.
Contact: www.ucl.ac.uk/prospective-students/accommodation

University of Warwick

The most successful of the 1960s "new" universities, Warwick has never been out of the top ten in *The Times* league table and is near the top 50 in the QS World University Rankings. The university has global ambitions and has expanded a portfolio of international activities that includes a base in Venice, a close partnership with Monash University in Australia, and a programme for gifted teenagers around the world. Warwick is also the only European institution to be involved in the Center for Urban Science and Progress, a consortium of leading universities established in New York.

The university has reconfigured its research around its "Global Research Priorities" programme, which brings together expertise from different subjects to focus on key areas of international significance. Current themes include energy, connecting cultures, food security, global governance, individual behaviour and innovative manufacturing. The university does not neglect its locality, however. Its mission statement stresses community links and the extension of access to higher and continuing education. There is a smaller proportion of independent school students than at most Russell Group universities – around a quarter – although this does not translate into large numbers of working-class undergraduates. The university has one of the lowest dropout rates in Britain at little more than 4 per cent. Warwick is charging £9,000 undergraduate fees for 2013–14, but students from the poorest backgrounds will receive up to half of that amount in fee waivers and bursaries. There was a surprisingly large drop in applications – 10 per cent – in the first year of higher fees, but the university still filled nearly as many places as in 2011.

Almost two-thirds of the work submitted for the 2008 Research Assessment Exercise was considered world-leading or internationally excellent, placing Warwick among the top ten UK universities. Film and television studies, and horticultural research achieved two of the top scores for any subject at any university, while pure maths, French and Italian were in the top three. There were particularly high grades, too, for economics, applied maths, and theatre, performance and cultural studies. Opposition from the students' union meant Warwick was a late starter in the National Student Survey, but is now achieving better scores than many other universities with similar subjects and entry scores. Languages, history and archaeology have been especially popular with the final-year students who complete the survey.

The university has invested shrewdly in business, science and engineering and

---

Coventry CV4 7AL

024 7652 3723 (admissions)
ugadmissions@warwick.ac.uk
www.warwick.ac.uk
www.warwicksu.com
Affiliation: Russell Group

Edinburgh
Belfast
COVENTRY
Cardiff
London

The Times and Sunday Times **Rankings**
Overall Ranking: **10** (8)

Student satisfaction:	=59	(81.5%)
Research quality:	=9	(29.0%)
Entry standards:	8	(506)
Student–staff ratio:	19	(14.3)
Services & facilities/student:	14	(£2,122)
Expected completion rate:	11	(95.7%)
Good honours:	=14	(79.6%)
Graduate prospects:	=13	(78.3%)

there is now a thriving graduate entry medical school, with more than 2,000 students. Warwick is also one of the few leading universities to embrace two-year Foundation degrees, running courses in childhood, education and society; health and social policy; and social studies.

Warwick's financial investment programme is set to continue to 2015 with another £150 million being spent on campus infrastructure. A second significant extension to students' union facilities opened in 2010. A new Centre for Mechanochemical Cell Biology followed in April 2012 as part of the Medical School campus. The centre is part of the Science City Research Alliance, a strategic partnership of Birmingham and Warwick universities, focusing on advanced materials, energy futures and translational medicine. The last year has also seen the opening of a newly refurbished £1.5-million undergraduate chemistry laboratory and the first phase of a £1.54-million refurbishment of the library. A new almost £1-million interactive teaching facility in the university's School of Life Sciences is nicknamed "The Orchard" as it is filled with 120 iMac computers, alongside state of the art interactive audio visual systems.

Also recently completed is an analytical science research facility for the physics and chemistry departments. A £12.5-million building houses a digital laboratory for manufacturing and engineering research, and a clinical trials unit. The university recently announced that a £92-million National Automotive Innovation Campus (NAIC) is to be established at the university and which will work closely with Warwick Manufacturing Group. NAIC will be part-funded by the Government through the UK Research Partnership Investment Fund as well as by Jaguar Land Rover and Tata Motors European Technical Centre.

Warwick added further study spaces in its Rootes Grid early in 2013 and created a dedicated off-campus study facility for students living in nearby Leamington Spa. The 750-acre campus is three miles south of Coventry and three times as far from Warwick. University accommodation is plentiful, and all first years can be accommodated on campus. The sports facilities are both extensive and conveniently placed – the main Sports Centre and Gym completed an extensive refit in February 2013.

Undergraduate Fees and Bursaries

» Fees for UK/EU students 2013–14 £9,000
2+2 Foundation degree £6,000
» International student fees 2013–14 £14,420–£18,390
Medicine (graduate entry) £16,840–£29,340
» English students from state schools, household income below £25K, £3,000 package a year; £25K–£36K, £1,000 cash a year; £36K–£42.6K, £500 a year.
» Range of other scholarships available.

Students

Undergraduates:	**12,490**	**(4,535)**
Postgraduates:	**5,695**	**(4,725)**
Mature students:	**7.2%**	
Overseas students:	**22.9%**	
Applications per place:	**7.4**	
From state-sector schools:	**73.3%**	
From working-class homes:	**18.6%**	
Satisfaction with students' union	**76%**	

For detailed information about sports facilities:
http://warwicksport.warwick.ac.uk

Accommodation

Number of places and costs refer to 2013–14
University-provided places: 6,272 (on campus); 1,900 (head leasing)
Percentage catered: 0%
Self-catered costs: £79–£153 a week (30, 39 and 50 week contracts).
Warwick Accommodation plans to accommodate all first years in campus accommodation (terms and conditions apply).
International students: as above.
Contact: www.warwick.ac.uk/accommodation

University of West London

Like other universities to have changed their names in recent years, West London's decision to dispose of the tarnished title of Thames Valley University paid instant dividends with a healthy rise in applications, although they did not translate into increased enrolments in the first year of higher fees.

Professor Peter John, the Vice-Chancellor, said students recognised that the university had entered a "new dawn" and they were attracted by a guaranteed work placement, in-study financial support and a strong probability of getting a job once they graduate. Standard fees for 2012–13 were among the lowest in England, at £7,500, but have gone up by £1,000 for 2014–15. Some degrees will cost £9,000 a year.

Helped particularly by changes in nursing education, which accounts for about a quarter of the places, there had already been big increases in the demand for places for two years before the change of title. The university's new name reflects a new, narrower geographical focus. Having tried the expansion route with little success, it is concentrating most activities on the university's original home in Ealing, where the main building has been refurbished and major redevelopment is planned. Among the additions planned are nine residential units and a house. The work is designed to improve the external appearance of the site as well as improving the internal facilities.

The Slough campus has closed. Its 1,000 full-time students, two-thirds of whom are on pre-registration nursing courses, have moved to the Reading campus, leaving just part-time business courses and some post-registration nursing at a different site in Slough. The restructuring will not alter the aim to become the country's leading university for employer engagement, with an accent on the creative industries and entrepreneurship.

The Reading campus, known as the Berkshire hub, is within walking distance of the mainline station and focuses entirely on nursing and midwifery. The Ealing campus has a more traditional university feel and has already had almost £10 million spent on it. The landmark Paragon Building in Brentford, not far from the Ealing campus, will remain the headquarters of one of the largest healthcare faculties in Britain with top quality ratings for nursing and midwifery. The site contains 850 residential places, as well as teaching facilities.

Amid the reconstruction, new Honours degrees have been launched in areas such as video production, 3D design, entrepreneurship, computing and information systems. The portfolio of two-year Foundation degrees is growing, with employers such as Compaq, Ealing

---

St Mary's Road
Ealing
London W5 5RF

0800 036 8888 (admissions)
courses@uwl.ac.uk
www.uwl.ac.uk
www.uwlsu.com
Affiliation: million+

Studios and the Savoy Hotel Group helping to provide courses. Some are run in conjunction with Stratford-upon-Avon College – one of several partner institutions.

The university scores highly for its spending on student facilities and its student satisfaction ratings have been improving, but it still finds itself towards the bottom of the National Student Survey. However, the School of Hospitality and Tourism is recognised by the Académie Culinaire de France for its culinary arts programmes, while the London College of Music, which is part of the university, has some of the longest-established music technology courses in the country.

West London improved its ratings considerably in the 2008 Research Assessment Exercise, but entered only a small proportion of its academics. Only nursing and midwifery was judged to have world-leading research. A policy of open access puts the university at a disadvantage on some measures in our ranking, contributing particularly to high dropout rates. Whilst hardly low, the latest official projected dropout rate of less than 20 per cent represents an improvement of more than a third in a single year. Including part-timers, three-quarters of the students are over 24, and about 60 per cent are female. More than 40 per cent of the undergraduates come from working-class homes. The university is also very ethnically

diverse with only four in ten undergraduates of white, UK origin.

The town-centre sites in Ealing and Brentford are linked by a free bus service. The busy Ealing base is within easy reach of central London without the metropolitan hassle that students encounter at some institutions in the capital. Almost half of the students are from London or Berkshire, and there is an unexpectedly large contingent of international students. Residential accommodation is growing and the Paragon building, in Brentford, won *Building* magazine's Major Housing Project of the Year award. However, students who rely on private housing find the cost of living high. There is a football ground and cricket pitch close to the Ealing campus, but otherwise sports facilities are limited.

Undergraduate Fees and Bursaries

» Fees for UK/EU students 2014–15   £8,500–£9,000
» International student fees 2013–14   £9,350
» 750 NSP awards with priority criteria: £2,000 fee waiver and £1,000 credit for study costs in year 1.
» £100 credit for learning materials for all new students.
» Range of other scholarships available.
» Check the university's website for the latest information.

Students

Undergraduates:	**7,670**	**(3,330)**
Postgraduates:	**685**	**(720)**
Mature students:	**39.3%**	
Overseas students:	**18.1%**	
Applications per place:	**6.9**	
From state-sector schools:	**97.7%**	
From working-class homes:	**40.1%**	
Satisfaction with students' union	**59%**	

For detailed information about sports facilities: www.uwlsu.com

Accommodation

Number of places and costs refer to 2013–14
University-provided places: 839
Percentage catered: 0%
Self-catered costs: from £136.70 (en suite) – £185.60 (studio) a week (incl. utilities and internet).
First years are allocated housing on a first come, first served basis.
International students: same as above.
Contact: onestopshop@uwl.ac.uk
www.uwl.ac.uk/students/student_life/Accommodation.jsp

University of the West of England, Bristol (UWE)

The University of the West of England, Bristol (UWE) may soon become the first higher education institution to share its campus with a Football League club. Plans for the Frenchay Campus include a new students' union building, and planning approval has been given for a 20,000-seat stadium with Bristol Rovers. Both schemes are part of a £250-million extension and development of its main campus, which will eventually see some outlying sites close. UWE is the largest provider of higher education in the South West of England and is one of the most popular post-1992 universities, both in terms of total applications and the proportion who subsequently choose to study there. But its applications dropped by more than 13 per cent in 2012 as fees for degree courses climbed to £9,000.

The university has sometimes found itself in trouble for missing its benchmarks for widening access to higher education, but it has broadened its intake considerably in recent years. The proportion of independent school entrants has dropped to less than 9 per cent, while the share of places going to students from working-class homes is around 30 per cent, and they have surpassed their target for entries from students living in areas less likely to enter higher education. The dropout rate has been coming down significantly; the latest projection is only just above the national average for the university's subjects and entry qualifications.

UWE boasts one of the largest networks of student representatives in the country, supported by a comprehensive programme of training and personal development. The Graduate Development Programme helps new students settle in and supports them throughout their studies. Personal tutoring helps signpost the many development opportunities for students and they benefit from some 100 clubs and societies.

More than half of the students come from the West Country and there are close links with business and industry. These provide guest lecturers, professors involved in practice, and thousands of part-time jobs and work placements for students, as well as helping to ensure that the curriculum is up-to-date and relevant. Recent links include CERN in Geneva, Hewlett Packard and the BBC, joining about 1,000 smaller organisations.

A tradition of vocational education regularly helps the university to a healthy graduate employment record. Law received a commendation from the Legal Practice Board and the degree in architecture and planning won a similar accolade from the Royal Town Planning Institute for bringing

---

Frenchay Campus
Coldharbour Lane
Bristol BS16 1QY

0117 32 83333 (switchboard)
contact via website
www.uwe.ac.uk
www.uwesu.org
Affiliation: University
  Alliance

Edinburgh
Belfast
Cardiff London
BRISTOL

The Times and Sunday Times Rankings
Overall Ranking: **60** (62)

Student satisfaction:	=75	(80.9%)
Research quality:	=67	(4.7%)
Entry standards:	65	(322)
Student–staff ratio:	=102	(21.7)
Services & facilities/student:	50	(£1,548)
Expected completion rate:	=68	(84.7%)
Good honours:	44	(69.6%)
Graduate prospects:	50	(68%)

together the two disciplines in one joint-honours course giving dual professional qualifications. UWE is one of just four universities recognised by the Forensic Science Society for the quality of courses in the subject. It has some 85 undergraduate and postgraduate courses with professional accreditation. Only two new universities entered more academics than UWE in the 2008 Research Assessment Exercise. More than a third of the work was judged to be world-leading or internationally excellent. Physiotherapy and other health subjects, media studies and general engineering produced the best results.

For the moment, there are four sites in Bristol itself, mainly around the north of the city. Only Bower Ashton, which has new TV and radio studios and edit suites for its art, media and design students, is in the south. The main campus at Frenchay, four miles out of the city centre, has already doubled in size and is to expand again after the purchase of adjoining land. The UK's largest robotic laboratory was opened in 2012 and on the campus there is the biggest exhibition and conference centre in the South West, allowing it to stage major careers fairs for its students and enhance links with employers. The St Matthias campus is to close, and its social sciences and humanities courses transfer to Frenchay over the next two years. Glenside campus is home to midwifery, nursing, occupational therapy, physiotherapy and radiography.

A network of 15 colleges stretches into Somerset and Wiltshire, offering UWE programmes. Hartpury College, near Gloucester, is an associate faculty of the university, specialising in agriculture, equine studies and other land-based courses, and there are university centres near hospitals in Gloucester and Bath that concentrate on nursing and allied health professions.

Bristol is a hugely popular student centre: an attractive and lively city, but not cheap. University accommodation has become more plentiful in recent years, with over 4,000 places available, including nearly 2,000 in a new £80-million student village on the Frenchay campus. Sports facilities were a bone of contention for students, but a sports complex opened in 2006. It was chosen as a pre-Olympics training site for badminton, fencing, table tennis, indoor volleyball and wrestling.

Undergraduate Fees and Bursaries

» Fees for UK/EU students 2014–15 £9,000
Foundation degrees at partner colleges £6,000–£7,500
» International student fees 2013–14 £10,750
» 711 NSP awards of £1,000 cash and £2,000 university services, year 1; £1,000 university services thereafter.
» 500 bursaries and progression bursaries of £500 to students on low income not receiving NSP awards.
» Check the university's website for the latest information.

Students

Undergraduates:	**20,430**	**(3,975)**
Postgraduates:	**1,540**	**(4,445)**
Mature students:	**24.5%**	
Overseas students:	**7.7%**	
Applications per place:	**4.5**	
From state-sector schools:	**91.0%**	
From working-class homes:	**28.8%**	
Satisfaction with students' union	**67%**	

Information about sports facilities: www1.uwe.ac.uk/aboutus/departmentsandservices/professionalservices/centreforsport

Accommodation

Number of places and costs refer to 2013–14
University-provided places: about 4,000
Percentage catered: 0%
Self-catered costs: £3,821–£6,825 (40 or 45 weeks).
First-year students are guaranteed housing in university-approved accommodation provided requirements are met.
International students are offered accommodation where possible.
Contact: accommodation@uwe.ac.uk

University of the West of Scotland (UWS)

A new £81-million campus at Ayr represents the latest stage in the development of Scotland's largest modern university. Created from the merger of Paisley University and Bell College, in Hamilton, the University of the West of Scotland (UWS) has been enjoying booming demand for its courses. Having registered the biggest increases in applications at any UK university for two years in succession, it managed another 8.5 per cent increase at degree level in 2012. These successes have come in an area of low participation in higher education is impressive and at a time when the number of 18-year-old Scots is falling. Growth has been fuelled mainly by the move to an all-graduate nursing profession – the School of Health, Nursing and Midwifery is the largest north of the border – but degrees in subjects such as computer animation, commercial music, computer games technology, sports studies and music technology have all been popular.

Research grades improved in the last assessments, although UWS made only a small submission. A quarter of the work was rated as world-leading or internationally excellent, with biomedical sciences and social policy and social work producing the best results. The university returned to *The Times* league table two years ago after blocking the release of data until all the statistics related to the new institution.

UWS has continued its parent institutions' strong record in attracting under-represented groups onto courses. Hundreds of youngsters aged 14 and 15 attend the "University Experience" to sample a week of student life. Almost all UWS's students are state educated and 40 per cent are from working-class homes, but the projected dropout rate of more than 30 per cent is the highest in the UK. That is more than twice the benchmark set according to the subject mix and entry qualifications.

The university's four bases are in Ayr, Dumfries, Hamilton and Paisley. Among the first developments were the £5.5-million library and student support services in Dumfries, a £2-million engineering centre at Hamilton and a £1-million employment centre for students across all campuses, which has its hub at the Paisley campus. The Ayr campus opened last September for around 3,500 students and includes an energy-efficient teaching building and new student residences.

The university continues to implement its £200-million improvement plan on the four campuses, which are within reach of nearly 40 per cent of Scots. UWS is bringing more students into Paisley town centre

---

Paisley Campus
Paisley
Renfrewshire PA1 2BE

0800 027 1000 (enquiries)
uni-direct@uws.ac.uk
contact via website
www.uws.ac.uk
www.sauws.org.uk
Affiliation: million+

The Times and Sunday Times **Rankings**
Overall Ranking: **117** (109)

Student satisfaction:	=101	(78.2%)
Research quality:	=67	(4.7%)
Entry standards:	=97	(288)
Student–staff ratio:	=102	(21.7)
Services & facilities/student:	84	(£1,256)
Expected completion rate:	120	(65.8%)
Good honours:	=103	(56%)
Graduate prospects:	92	(56.5%)

with the completion of a £17.6-million student accommodation development. The investment includes the refurbishment of some 160 university-owned flats, as well as the construction of a new £13.2-million student with 336 bed spaces, divided into flats for six students, each with large en-suite bedrooms and with a shared kitchen and lounge.

Over £9 million was invested in student facilities in Paisley in the early years of UWS. The main campus, 20 acres in the town centre, has also benefited from a new library and learning resource centre, a £5-million students' union building, and recently upgraded indoor and outdoor sports facilities. The Dumfries campus, operated in partnership with Glasgow University, has over 500 students. The Hamilton campus contains teaching facilities, a students' union, an upgraded leisure centre and some accommodation. The Centre for Engineering Excellence is the newest addition.

Paisley is Scotland's largest town, while Hamilton ranks fifth. Both draw a high proportion of the students from the local area, many on part-time courses. Numbers at Paisley have grown particularly rapidly in recent years and there are around 1,400 international students, thanks to a growing number of Chinese and Indian nationals and long-established links with over 50 EU institutions.

Courses are strongly vocational, with business, multimedia and health subjects by far the most popular choices. There are close links with business and industry and all students are offered hands-on computer training. Paisley was the first UK university to be approved by Microsoft, Macromedia and Cisco, and has the status of Microsoft Academic Professional Development Centre. A games development laboratory, supported by Sony, is part of a £300,000 package of investment in multimedia and games facilities.

Paisley pioneered credit transfer in Scotland, including credit for non-academic achievement, and the modular course system covers day, evening and weekend classes. Most students either take sandwich degrees or have work placements built into their courses, earning an average of £10,000 in the process, but the impact on graduate employment has not been as great as elsewhere.

Undergraduate Fees and Bursaries

» Fees for Scottish and EU students 2013–14   No fee
» Fees for Non-Scottish UK-domiciled students 2013–14   £7,250
» Fees for international students 2013–14   £10,000–£10,500
» For RUK students (2013–14) receiving maintenance grant, £500 bursary and £500 university accommodation discount in year 1.
» Check the university's website for the latest information.

Students

Undergraduates:	**9,720**	**(3,580)**
Postgraduates:	**820**	**(730)**
Mature students:	**44.5%**	
Overseas students:	**3.8%**	
Applications per place:	**3.5**	
From state-sector schools:	**98.3%**	
From working-class homes:	**40.0%**	
Satisfaction with students' union	**64%**	

For detailed information about sports facilities:
www.uws.ac.uk/study-at-uws/life-at-uws/sports-and-social/

Accommodation

Number of places and costs refer to 2013–14
University-provided places: 927 (571 at Paisley; 200 at Ayr; 156 at Hamilton)
Percentage catered: 0%
Self-catered costs: £82 (Hamilton) – £106–£137 (other campuses) a week.
First-year students have priority (conditions apply).
International students: single students guaranteed accommodation if conditions are met and applications received by 27 July.
Contact: placetostay@uws.ac.uk; www.uws.ac.uk/accommodation

University of Westminster

Westminster was one of many universities to be left with empty places in the first year of higher fees – the numbers recruited through UCAS were 12 per cent down on 2011 – but this has not halted its ambitious plans for the future. The university, which has been celebrating its 175th anniversary in 2013, has continued to invest heavily in its buildings and facilities, with major refurbishment taking place at three of its campuses. The £20-million project at the Marylebone Campus was completed in the autumn of 2012, providing a new social and learning hub for the Faculty of Architecture and the Built Environment and Westminster Business School. Significant progress has also been made on the £38-million redevelopment of the Harrow site, home to the highly rated Faculty of Media, Arts and Design. Students there are already benefiting from new library and resource centres, and bigger open spaces and better natural light for the fashion and fine art learning areas. The project, to be completed by 2014, will eventually include spaces for a gallery and catwalk, flexible performance areas, a café, reception and multimedia newsroom. Major refurbishment work at the Regent Campus will be completed in 2013, while the School of Life Sciences has recently invested £2 million in modernising its laboratories.

The demand for places at Westminster rose by more than 25 per cent in two years before the switch to £9,000 fees for all degree courses. The university promised that almost three-quarters of UK degree students would receive partial fee waivers. A new undergraduate academic model promotes deeper learning through year-long modules and weaves work-related skills into degree programmes. Theory and practice are integrated wherever possible and connections made between subjects. Undergraduates are also given research opportunities.

The university has won a £1.5-million Heritage Lottery Fund grant to restore the historically important Regent Street Cinema housed within the Regent Campus, considered to be the birthplace of British cinema. The headquarters building, near the BBC's Broadcasting House, houses social sciences, humanities and languages. Westminster offers one of the widest ranges of language teaching of any British university and partners the School of Oriental and African Studies in leading the Routes into Languages programme to encourage more people to learn a language. The West End sites provide the perfect catchment area for part-time undergraduates, who account for over a fifth of some 16,000 undergraduate places.

However, by no means all of

309 Regent Street
London W1B 2UW

020 7915 5511 (enquiries)
course-enquiries@
westminster.ac.uk
www.westminster.ac.uk
www.uwsu.com
Affiliation: none

The Times and Sunday Times **Rankings**

Overall Ranking: **=106** (=95)

Student satisfaction:	**117**	(76%)
Research quality:	**=63**	(5.0%)
Entry standards:	**=59**	(327)
Student–staff ratio:	**93**	(20.8)
Services & facilities/student:	**77**	(£1,292)
Expected completion rate:	**93**	(80.9%)
Good honours:	**=81**	(60.3%)
Graduate prospects:	**=102**	(53.7%)

Westminster's students are Londoners. Over 5,000 come from overseas – among the most at any post-1992 university – and Westminster also has the largest number of ethnic minority students in Britain. The university's courses taught in nine overseas countries, from Sri Lanka to Uzbekistan, a characteristic which won the university a Queen's Award for Enterprise.

Westminster hit the headlines in the 2008 Research Assessment Exercise, when it was rated top in the UK for media studies with one of the highest proportions of world-leading research (60 per cent) in any subject. More than a third of all the work submitted by the university was rated in the top two categories, resulting a doubling of Westminster's research grants. Art and design, architecture and biomedical sciences all achieved good grades. The university has since been chosen to head a €1-million European research project to explore the relationship between scarcity and creativity in the built environment. Accolades for its teaching include fashionista.com ranking its fashion design degree second in the UK, and in the top 10 worldwide.

More than four out of ten undergraduates are from working-class homes – a much higher proportion than the national average for the subjects offered. The university also exceeds its benchmark for the admission of students from state schools and colleges, although those from lower participation neighbourhoods are under-represented. The projected dropout rate improved in the latest survey and, at less than 16 per cent, is better than the university's benchmark.

Westminster has added considerably to its stock of residential accommodation in recent years. The latest development saw the opening of a student village for first-years close to Wembley Stadium and Wembley Park tube station, with speedy links to all the university's campuses. The university had already added a £6-million block of halls in Harrow and refurbished its Marylebone halls, but there is no way round the capital's inflated housing market at some stage. The Harrow campus is lively socially, but those based on the other campuses tend to be spread around the capital. Sports facilities are also dispersed, with playing fields and a boathouse in Chiswick, west London. Smoke Radio, Westminster's student radio station, has won several awards and has now spawned Smoke Television.

Undergraduate Fees and Bursaries

» Fees for UK/EU students 2014–15   £9,000
» International student fees 2013–14   £11,370
» Fee waivers given on a course-by-course basis to local students.
» 618 NSP awards of £3,000 support package in year 1 and £3,000 package split over following years.
» Westminster Scholarship of £2,000 fee waiver. Other scholarships available.
» Check the university's website for the latest information.

Students

Undergraduates:	**12,980**	**(3,685)**
Postgraduates:	**2,480**	**(2,360)**
Mature students:	**21.7%**	
Overseas students:	**20.6%**	
Applications per place:	**5.5**	
From state-sector schools:	**94.6%**	
From working-class homes:	**44.0%**	
Satisfaction with students' union	**54%**	

Information about sports facilities: www.westminster.ac.uk/study/current-students/support-and-facilities/sport-and-leisure

Accommodation

Number of places and costs refer to 2013–14
University-provided places: 1,750
Percentage catered: 0%
Self-catered costs: £98–£191 a week (36–51 week contracts).
First-year students have priority for 1,000 rooms. Residential restrictions apply.
International students: as above.
Contact: studentaccommodation@westminster.ac.uk
www.westminster.ac.uk/housing

University of Winchester

Winchester has jumped 18 places this year and is now among the top ten post-1992 universities. It was among the minority of institutions to see an increase in the number of students it recruited as the fees went up in 2012. There had been a small decline in applications, but the university was one of those to be allocated extra places as institutions with average fees below £7,500 after allowing for student support. The university stresses its "human scale", with only 6,400 students and an emphasis on providing a supportive community. The approach appears to have struck a chord: applications have been healthy and Winchester has often been among the top 30 universities for student satisfaction.

The university traces its history as an Anglican foundation back to 1840 and has occupied its King Alfred campus since 1862. The compact site is on a wooded hillside overlooking the cathedral city, a ten-minute walk away, with views of the surrounding countryside. Known as King Alfred's College until 2004, the university is still best-known for teacher training, which accounts for about a third of the places. Ofsted rates the teacher training courses as outstanding. It is one of the largest providers of primary school training in England, but courses on the main campus also span business, arts, humanities, health and social care, and social sciences. Degrees range from choreography and dance, through social work, business, accounting, law, media and teacher training to modern liberal arts. The university is involved in a national initiative to promote social entrepreneurship and already offers support to graduates who wish to start their own businesses.

Winchester improved on already respectable grades in the 2008 Research Assessment Exercise, when it was ranked second among the new universities in history, with over half of its submission considered world-leading or internationally excellent. Overall, more than a third of the university's work reached the top two categories, and there was some world-leading research in four of the six subject areas.

The university is particularly proud of its low dropout rate, which improved again in the latest projections, dropping below 10 per cent for the first time and remaining below the national average for Winchester's courses and entry qualifications. Nearly 96 per cent of the British students are state-educated and three in ten are from working-class homes, and there are about 150 overseas students from a range of countries. Winchester students can take advantage of exchange schemes with American universities in New York, Maine, Oregon and Wisconsin, as well as with universities in Japan.

Winchester
Hampshire SO22 4NR

01962 827234 (enquiries)
course.enquiries@winchester.ac.uk
www.winchester.ac.uk
www.winchester
  students.co.uk
Affiliations: Cathedrals Group,
  GuildHE

The Times and Sunday Times **Rankings**

Overall Ranking: **=57** (=75)

Student satisfaction:	=24	(83.8%)
Research quality:	=73	(4.0%)
Entry standards:	=82	(307)
Student–staff ratio:	53	(17.7)
Services & facilities/student:	108	(£1,069)
Expected completion rate:	42	(88.9%)
Good honours:	=62	(63%)
Graduate prospects:	=107	(53%)

The main campus is well equipped, with its theatrical performance spaces, sports hall and fitness suite now supplemented by the £3.5-million Winchester Sports Stadium. Open to local people as well as students, the stadium has an Olympic standard 400-metre eight-lane athletics track with supporting facilities for field events and also a floodlit all-weather pitch. There are six performing arts studios in a new building that opened in 2010 on the King Alfred campus, offering the latest technology for student productions. A new Learning and Teaching Building on the King Alfred campus has significantly improved the facilities for lectures and independent study. The low-energy building has a number of eco-friendly features which helped win an award from the Royal Institute of British Architects in 2013. Winchester also registered a big rise in the People and Planet green league table, moving into the top 40 universities for sustainability.

The award-winning University Centre transformed the students' union, adding a nightclub, cinema, catering facilities, a bookshop and a supermarket at a cost of £9 million. A "learning café" creates an informal working space with networked PCs and wireless internet access. An award-winning extension to the library made room for 200,000 books, 450 study spaces and 150 computers. The students' union achieved one of the best ratings in the 2013 National Student Survey and the university is one the few to have appointed its own ombudsman to handle complaints.

A £12-million student village, a short walk from the main campus, provides more than 700 residential places. The business school is also located on the West Downs campus. A second village, with en-suite rooms arranged in cluster flats, opened in 2010, and another new student village is due to be complete in time for the 2014–15 academic year. Winchester guarantees campus accommodation to first year full-time undergraduates, overseas students and students with medical needs as long they apply by the deadline. Students value the close-knit atmosphere and find the city is livelier than its staid image might suggest, with a number of bars catering to their tastes. Southampton is not far for those who hanker after the attractions of a bigger city, and London is only an hour away by train.

Undergraduate Fees and Bursaries

» Fees for UK/EU students 2014–15   £8,500
     Foundation degree in childhood studies   £4,200
» International student fees 2013–14   £9,775
» 234 NSP awards linked to academic performance: £3,000 fee waiver, year 1; £1,500 fee waiver, years 2 and 3.
» All students with household income below £25K, £500 fee waiver and £750 cash each year.
» Academic, sport and music scholarships available.
» Check the university's website for the latest information.

Students

Undergraduates:	**4,705**	**(695)**
Postgraduates:	**210**	**(715)**
Mature students:	**14.6%**	
Overseas students:	**7.2%**	
Applications per place:	**4.8**	
From state-sector schools:	**95.8%**	
From working-class homes:	**30.4%**	
Satisfaction with students' union	**83%**	

For detailed information about sports facilities:
www.winchester.ac.uk/campuscitylife/Sportsfacilities

Accommodation

Number of places and costs refer to 2013–14
University-provided places: 1,220 on campus; 212 off campus
Percentage catered: 15%
Catered costs: £4,083.38 (term-time only).
Self-catered costs: £2,903.60 – £4,998.00 (37–40 weeks).
First years are guaranteed accommodation if conditions are met.
International students: non EU, as above.
Contact: housing@winchester.ac.uk

University of Wolverhampton

Wolverhampton has set the most eye-catching fees for 2014–15, saving future graduates a total of £300 compared to the costs incurred at most universities by charging £8,900 a year for all degrees. The university is in the throes of a £45-million redevelopment of its City Campus. Work has started on a £21-million Science Centre, which will see well-equipped laboratories, teaching and meeting rooms ready by the end of 2014. A new £11-million building is also planned for the Business School near the Molineux football ground on the City Campus North. Student facilities have been improved with the redevelopment of the Students' Union on the City Campus and the opening of a new union bar on the Walsall Campus.

The university is one of five that refuses to allow the Higher Education Statistics Agency to release data on their performance for league tables. Just outside the top 100 on its last appearance in our table, its student satisfaction and dropout rates have improved since then, and it might have finished higher this time. A statement on the university's website says that tables such as ours disadvantage universities like Wolverhampton and do not represent a fair picture of their strengths. As a result, it is missing from both the main ranking and all the subject tables.

Wolverhampton's success in widening participation in higher education is such that it is one of only two universities in the UK where just over half of the undergraduates come from working-class homes. Almost all the students are from state schools and nearly one in five comes from an area of low participation. The university draws two-thirds of its 23,000 students from the West Midlands, although it has a growing contingent from overseas. A third of the places are filled by mature students and about the same proportion come from the region's ethnic minorities. Big outreach programmes take courses into the workplace. Both applications and enrolments were relatively stable when the fees went up to £8,500 in 2012.

The three West Midland campuses each have their own learning centres and are linked by a free bus service. The original site is in Wolverhampton city centre, while sport and performance, education and part of the School of Health and Wellbeing are based in Walsall. A purpose-built campus at Telford in Shropshire focuses on business and engineering in a county with no higher education institution of its own. A branch campus in Mauritius opened in 2012, offering law degrees and an MA in education.

Wolverhampton has been investing

Wulfruna Street
Wolverhampton WV1 1LY

01902 321000 (enquiries)
enquiries@wlv.ac.uk
www.wlv.ac.uk
www.wolvesunion.org
Affiliation: million+

Edinburgh
Belfast
WOLVERHAMPTON
Cardiff
London

The Times and Sunday Times **Rankings**
Wolverhampton blocked the release of data from the Higher Education Statistics Agency and so we cannot give any ranking information.

heavily in its "New Horizons" infrastructure programme. At Telford the £7-million e-Innovation Centre has won awards for the support it offers to e-businesses. A 350-bed student village and sports facilities, including a Sports Science and Medicine Centre which was used to train Olympic contenders, opened on the Walsall Campus. In 2011, the Performance Hub, the university's centre for performing arts, opened on the same campus. The £15-million facility has exceptional facilities for music, dance and drama. Wolverhampton was the third university in the UK to be awarded All-Steinway School Status.

The university pioneered interactive multimedia communication degrees, as well as offering one of the first degrees in British sign language and one of the first in virtual reality design and manufacturing. It was the first university to be registered under the British Standards for the quality of its all-round provision. Wolverhampton stresses innovation and enterprise in its work with students and businesses, encouraging student start-up companies and leading a project to develop student placements for those who wish to become entrepreneurs. The Flying Start Programme for Sports Business was the first of its kind in the UK, providing specialist workshops. Teacher training courses are rated highly by Ofsted, and Wolverhampton academics have been awarded six National Teaching Fellowships by the Higher Education Academy. Overall satisfaction improved sharply in the 2013 National Student Survey, although the university was still only just in the top 100.

Research is mainly applied, serving the needs of business and industry, as well as underpinning teaching at all levels. The university was ranked fourth in the UK for statistical cybermetrics and sixth for computational linguistics in the last Research Assessment Exercise. A relatively low proportion of the academics were entered for assessment, but 30 per cent of their research was considered world-leading or internationally excellent. As part of its commitment to research, the university has set aside £6 million to finance new projects.

Social facilities vary between sites. Wolverhampton has a growing nightlife and the university has been voted the friendliest in the West Midlands. The cost of living is reasonable and Birmingham is only a metro tram ride away.

Undergraduate Fees and Bursaries

» Fees for UK/EU students 2014–15   £8,900
    Foundation degree   £7,325
    Foundation degree at partner colleges   up to £6,000
» International student fees 2013–14   £10,420
» 420 NSP awards of £3,000 support package.
» 725 NSP awards with priority criteria: £1,000 fee waiver, £1,000 cash bursary and £1,000 accommodation discount or additional fee waiver, year 1; £1,000 fee waiver, years 2 and 3.

Students

Undergraduates:	**12,745**	**(4,935)**
Postgraduates:	**1,570**	**(2,255)**
From state-sector schools:	**98.8%**	
From working-class homes:	**51.3%**	
Satisfaction with students' union	**66%**	

For detailed information about sports facilities:
www.wlv.ac.uk/sport

Accommodation

Number of places and costs refer to 2013–14
University-provided places: 1,603
Percentage catered: 0%
Self-catered costs: £2,590 – £3,589 (37 weeks).
First-year students are offered accommodation provided requirements are met. Residential restrictions apply.
International students: same as above.
Contact: accommodationservices@wlv.ac.uk

University of Worcester

Worcester has carried out the most ambitious development plans of any of the new universities created since 2005 and has been rewarded with strong demand for places at time when rival institutions have been suffering. A second campus in the heart of the city opened in 2010 and a spectacular library and history centre – the first joint public and university library in Britain – was opened by the Queen in July 2012. The library team has since won a national award for delivering the project. The university has also invested in a state-of-the-art indoor sporting arena for the city, one of only two specialist sports venues in the UK designed specifically for wheelchair athletes as well as the able-bodied.

The university will be one of two charging a mere £100 less than the maximum £9,000 fee for all undergraduate degrees in 2014. The university has been one of the fastest growing in Britain and was one of the few to see increases in degree applications both when the new tuition fees were introduced and again in 2013. Business courses have been particularly popular and there have been big increases, too, in physical education, sports studies, forensic science, marketing, pre-hospital and emergency care, journalism, social work and advertising. An emphasis on employability

in the curriculum was commended in an audit by the Quality Assurance Agency in 2011.

First as a post-war emergency teacher training college and later as a university college, the institution has always been the only provider of higher education in Herefordshire and Worcestershire. The university remains strong in education and also in nursing and midwifery. It received the best possible inspection report from the Nursing and Midwifery Council and was ranked number one in England for its nursing degree in the 2012 National Student Survey. Worcester is the partner university for the National Childbirth Trust and delivers all of the UK's antenatal training. The university also received one of the best Ofsted reports in the country for its teacher training, scoring "outstanding" in all sections for primary and "outstanding overall" for secondary. The six academic departments also cover applied sciences, geography and archaeology, a business school and arts, humanities and social sciences.

The 23 academics entered for the 2008 Research Assessment Exercise (RAE) represented the smallest contingent from any university in England, but Worcester plans to enter around 100 academics for the successor to the RAE in 2013. Only English had any world-leading research in 2008, although there are pockets of excellence

---

Henwick Grove
Worcester WR2 6AJ

01905 855111 (admissions)
admissions@worc.ac.uk
www.worc.ac.uk
www.worcsu.com
Affiliation: GuildHE

The Times and Sunday Times **Rankings**
Overall Ranking: **102** (=93)

Student satisfaction:	93	(79.2%)
Research quality:	=115	(0.3%)
Entry standards:	103	(281)
Student–staff ratio:	113	(23.6)
Services & facilities/student:	109	(£1,026)
Expected completion rate:	62	(85.9%)
Good honours:	78	(60.8%)
Graduate prospects:	60	(63.8%)

such as the Association for Dementia Studies and the National Pollen and Aerobiology Research Unit, which produces all of Britain's pollen forecasts.

More than a third of the undergraduates come from working-class homes. The projected dropout rate has improved significantly to around 10 per cent – better than average for Worcester's subjects and entry standards. The university has three campuses less than a mile from each other and all close to the city centre. A fourth campus, a short distance from the others, is currently under development. The City Campus occupies the historic buildings of the former Worcester Royal Infirmary. It includes teaching, residential and conference facilities and is the site of Worcester Business School. The Hive, neighbouring the City Campus holds the new library and history centre, which brings together many services from Worcestershire County Council, including archaeology and history, with those of the university.

The St John's campus occupies a parkland site 15 minutes' walk from the city centre. It includes science facilities; the National Pollen and Aerobiology Research Unit; the digital arts centre and drama studio, and a modern Astroturf pitch. The Riverside campus, mostly for sport performance, includes the new 2,000-seat Worcester Arena, which is part of the 2012 Olympic and Paralympic legacy. Sport plays an important part in university life. A mobile 3D motion analysis laboratory has been used by the England and Wales Cricket Board. Sports scholarships are offered in partnership with Worcestershire County Cricket Club, Worcester Wolves Basketball Club and Worcester Hockey Club. The university's commitment to disability sports extends to the UK's first Disability Sport degree.

Worcester has surpassed benchmarks for widening participation of students from working class backgrounds, assisted by long-established projects working with primary schools. The university has excellent links with local businesses and runs an extensive learn-while-you-earn programme. A number of local partner colleges offer Worcester courses, as well as less conventional study centres such as hospices and specialist national organisations. The cathedral city is not large, but is safer than many university locations.

Undergraduate Fees and Bursaries

» Fees for UK/EU students 2014–15	£8,900
Foundation degrees at partner colleges	£6,200
» International student fees 2013–14	£10,600
» Around 738 NSP awards of £2,000 fee waiver and £1,000 cash in year 1 with priority to those with lowest household income.	
» For all students receiving partial maintenance grant, £2,000 fee waiver in year 1.	
» Award of £1,000 cash in year 1 for those with ABB at A level or equivalent. Around 150 £1,000 cash scholarships for academic achievement after year 1 and year 2.	

Students

Undergraduates:	**7,240**	**(1,735)**
Postgraduates:	**550**	**(1,170)**
Mature students:	**20.4%**	
Overseas students:	**7.2%**	
Applications per place:	**4.8**	
From state-sector schools:	**97.0%**	
From working-class homes:	**34.5%**	
Satisfaction with students' union	**67%**	

For detailed information about sports facilities:
www.worcsu.com/sports_activities/

Accommodation

Number of places and costs refer to 2013–14

University-provided places: 973 university-owned; 282 university-managed.

Percentage catered: 0%

Self-catered costs: £84–£137 a week.

First-year students are guaranteed accommodation, on a first come, first served basis, if conditions are met.

International students are accommodated if conditions are met.

Contact: accommodation@worc.ac.uk

University of York

York was one of four universities to join the Russell Group of leading research institutions in 2012 and has since been ranked seventh in the world by *Times Higher Education* among universities under 50 years old. It will be a short-lived distinction since the university has been celebrating its 50th anniversary in 2013, but York is competing successfully against institutions of all ages. The university remains close to the top ten in *The Times and Sunday Times* league table and has been growing in popularity with prospective students. The demand for places was unaffected by the introduction of fees of £9,000 in 2012–13.

York decided ten years ago that it was too small to maximise its research capability, play a leading role in the economy of the region and satisfy the growing demand for its places. In an audacious move for a highly selective university, it has opened a second campus to accommodate up to 50 per cent more students and strengthen its research. A new residential college for 600 students and buildings for computer science, law, management, and theatre, film and television have already opened on the Heslington East site. The campus expansion will take 10 to 15 years to complete and will eventually contain housing for an additional 3,300 students, as well as more academic buildings, sports facilities and a performing arts and community complex. A £21-million "hub" for the campus expansion opened in 2010 and a second residential college was completed in 2012. A £20-million refurbishment of the university library was also completed in 2012 and a £16.5-million redevelopment of the department of chemistry is taking shape to provide new research and undergraduate laboratories.

The expansion has allowed York to introduce new subjects. The first intake of undergraduates in law and in writing, directing and performance in theatre, film and television graduated in 2011. Medicine was introduced in 2003 in partnership with Hull University. York also runs its own nursing and midwifery programmes. The university believes that, with more than six applicants for every place, other departments can grow at the same time as retaining or achieving a place in the top ten for their subject.

The university has done well in all years of the National Student Survey, both in its own right and at the medical school, which is assessed separately. Entrance requirements are high and the dropout rate of less than 5 per cent is among the lowest in the country. The university is getting closer to meeting its benchmark for having pupils from working class backgrounds and those from areas less likely to enter higher

---

Heslington
York YO10 5DD

01904 324000 (admissions)
ug-admissions@york.ac.uk
www.york.ac.uk
www.hyms.ac.uk
www.yusu.org
Affiliation: Russell Group

The Times and Sunday Times **Rankings**
Overall Ranking: **11** (13)

Student satisfaction:	21	(84.1%)
Research quality:	=9	(29.0%)
Entry standards:	=16	(457)
Student–staff ratio:	=28	(15.5)
Services & facilities/student:	20	(£1,996)
Expected completion rate:	=13	(95.1%)
Good honours:	19	(78.1%)
Graduate prospects:	29	(73.9%)

education. Every student has a supervisor responsible for their academic and personal welfare, and undergraduates are entitled to a course of free language tuition and have access to a Mathematics Study Skills Centre. Undergraduates can also take the York Award, comprising a range of courses, work placements and voluntary activities which aim to prepare students for the world of work. Over 600 students work as volunteer teaching assistants in local schools. The development of alumni professional networks in banking law and finance, creative industries, science and technology and third sector/government enable students to connect with senior alumni and gain access to mentoring, career advice and internships.

York was among the top ten institutions in the 2008 Research Assessment Exercise, when more than 60 per cent of the work submitted was judged to be world-leading or internationally excellent. The university was ranked top in the UK for English and health services research, joint top for sociology, and among the leaders for linguistics, and nursing and midwifery. Nearly 30 per cent of the full-time students are postgraduates.

The original campus occupies 200 acres of landscaped parkland, a mile outside the historic city centre. Students join one of eight colleges, which mix academic and social roles. Most departments have their headquarters in one of the colleges, but the student community is a deliberate mixture of disciplines, years and sexes. Nursing apart, only archaeology and medieval studies are located off campus, sharing a medieval building in the centre of the city.

Social life on campus is lively. There are television and radio stations, as well as several student newspapers and magazines. Sports facilities are good, and include a 50-station fitness suite, four sports halls and dance studio. The £9-million York Sports Village opened on campus in 2012, featuring a 25-metre pool, learner pool, 100-station gym, full-size 3G pitch and three further five-a-side pitches. Cultural events abound on campus and in the city, which is also famous for a high concentration of pubs and its music scene. The free Festival of Ideas brings world-class speakers to the campus and includes a lively student fringe festival.

Undergraduate Fees and Bursaries

» Fees for UK/EU students 2014–15 £9,000
» International student fees 2012–13 £13,580–£17,650
  Medicine £24,680
» For all UK students with household income up to £15K, £1,000 fee waiver and £3,500 accommodation discount, year 1; £2,000 fee waiver or bursary in other years; £15K–£25K, £3,500 package, year 1; £2,000, other years; £25K–£30K, £1,500 accommodation discount, year 1, £1,000 package, other years; £30K–£35K, £500 accommodation discount, year 1, £500 package other years.
» Enhanced fee waiver of £7,500–£8,500 for Foundation year.
» Separate support scheme for HYMS.

Students

Undergraduates:	**11,150**	**(1,015)**
Postgraduates:	**4,260**	**(980)**
Mature students:	**9.6%**	
Overseas students:	**13.9%**	
Applications per place:	**6.3**	
From state-sector schools:	**77.3%**	
From working-class homes:	**18.6%**	
Satisfaction with students' union	**62%**	

For detailed information about sports facilities:
www.york.ac.uk/study/student-life/sport/

Accommodation

Number of places and costs refer to 2013–14
University-provided places: 5,159
Percentage catered: 14%
Catered costs: £121.03–£150.64 a week
Self-catered costs: £99.05–£127.33 a week.
First-year undergraduates are provided with accommodation if terms and conditions are met.
International students: as above.
Contact: accommodation@york.ac.uk
www.york.ac.uk/accommodation

York St John University

York St John bucked the national trend in the first year of higher fees and attracted 11 per cent more applicants – one of the biggest increases at any university. As a result, it was able to take another 150 students at a time when many of its counterparts were left with empty places. The university's popularity continued a well-established trend: undergraduate applications have risen by almost 60 per cent since 2008, with growth in the arts, business, theology, education, health and life sciences. York St John is up 16 places in our league table and also broke into the top ten of *Times Higher Education*'s student experience poll in 2013. Professor David Fleming, the Vice-Chancellor, said the university had invested in the quality of its teaching and the campus environment, as well as offering a strong package of fee waivers and student support.

One of the four universities designated in 2006, York St John is a Church of England foundation that dates back almost 170 years. The eight-acre site faces York Minster across the city walls and is a five-minute walk from the city centre. Now serving over 6,000 students, the campus has seen £91 million of development in recent years and more is planned. The Fountains Learning Centre, which provides a striking entrance to the university, has just undergone a £1.1-million refurbishment programme. It now has 530 computer workstations, multimedia group-work facilities, 24-hour access to enhanced self-service facilities and an enlarged book stock, as well an internet café and lecture theatre. Nearby, the prize-winning De Grey Court, which cost £15.5 million and serves the health and life sciences, links the university quarter with the city centre.

York Diocesan Training School opened in 1841 with one pupil on the register, in whose honour the current (and recently refurbished) students' union is named. Divided between York and Ripon for most of its existence, the institution diversified beyond teacher training in the 1980s and decided at the start of this decade to concentrate all its teaching on York. The university's mission statement says its provision is "shaped" by the York St John's church foundation, although it welcomes students of all beliefs. Education and theology remains the biggest faculty, with 1,700 students taking programmes in teacher education, education studies, and theology and religious studies. Health and life sciences are not far behind in terms of size, with 1,600 full-time students and 200 part-timers studying courses such as physiotherapy and occupational therapy, as well as psychology and sport. The York St John Business School, launched in

---

New Mayor's Walk
York YO31 7EX

01904 876598 (information hotline)
admissions@yorksj.ac.uk
www.yorksj.ac.uk
www.ysjsu.com
Affiliations: Cathedrals
  Group, GuildHE

The Times and Sunday Times **Rankings**
Overall Ranking: **=64** (80)

Student satisfaction:	**19**	(84.3%)
Research quality:	**=108**	(1.0)
Entry standards:	**88**	(301)
Student–staff ratio:	**94**	(20.9)
Services & facilities/student:	**99**	(£1158)
Expected completion rate:	**44**	(88.6%)
Good honours:	**73**	(61.5%)
Graduate prospects:	**=70**	(61.7%)

May 2008, engages with a range of local and regional small- to medium-sized enterprises, as well as offering the normal range of undergraduate and postgraduate courses. The university has launched a number of successful enterprise initiatives. Its latest venture, the Phoenix Centre, a business incubation facility, supports both the university's graduates and new local businesses.

The Faculty of Arts, which was formed in 2001, has been one of the main points of expansion, especially in degree programmes such as film and television, media and American studies. The university was awarded a national centre for excellence in creativity, based on its work in English and theatre studies, although funding for such programmes has now ceased. Another music technology suite has been added and performance spaces include two dedicated TV studios, digital non-linear edit suites, digital imaging equipment and equipment for sound manipulation.

Drama, dance and performing arts was the most successful field in the 2008 Research Assessment Exercise and the only one to contain world-leading research. Student satisfaction has been on a rising trend over several years. Seven out of ten students are female – one of the highest proportions at any university. Almost 95 per cent of them attended state schools or colleges, while 29 per cent are from working-class homes. The projected dropout rate of just over 5 per cent maintains the impressive improvement of recent years and is well below the national average for the university's courses and entry qualifications.

Relatively high numbers of local mature students ease the pressure on residential accommodation. As a result, first years who want to live in university-owned accommodation are now guaranteed places. The Foss Building houses a sports hall, climbing wall, basketball, netball, indoor football and cricket nets. The university recently acquired a 57-acre site 15 minutes' walk from campus, where it has made huge improvements to the sports facilities with cricket, rugby and football pitches, tennis and netball courts, and a six-lane athletics track. York is popular as a student city with a growing range of clubs as well as, supposedly, a pub for every day of the year.

Undergraduate Fees and Bursaries

» Fees for UK/EU students 2014–15 £9,000
  Foundation degrees in education & theology £3,500
» International student fees 2013–14 £9,000–£11,500
» For UK/EU students, fee waivers based on household income: below £10K, £3,000 a year; £10K–£20K, £2,000 a year; £20K–£42.6K, £1,000 a year.
» In addition 395 NSP awards with priority criteria: £3,000 fee waiver in year 1.
» 150 Entry Scholarship for students with ABB at A Level or equivalent, £2,000 fee waiver and £1,000 cash, targeted at under-represented groups.

Students

Undergraduates:	**3,940**	**(1,190)**
Postgraduates:	**285**	**(555)**
Mature students:	**11.1%**	
Overseas students:	**4.1%**	
Applications per place:	**5.9**	
From state-sector schools:	**93.8%**	
From working-class homes:	**29.0%**	
Satisfaction with students' union	**74%**	

For detailed information about sports facilities:
www.yorksj.ac.uk/ysjactive

Accommodation

Number of places and costs refer to 2013–14
University-provided places: 1,850
Percentage catered: 8.5%
Catered costs: £135–£158 (semi-catered) a week for 33 weeks.
Self-catered costs: £72–£118 a week; £147–£154 (studio) for 44–48 weeks.
First years choosing university as first choice are guaranteed accommodation. Residential and age restrictions apply.
International students: guaranteed housing.
Contact: accommodation@yorksj.ac.uk

Additional Institutions of Higher Education

This listing gives contact details for other degree-awarding higher education institutions not mentioned elsewhere within the book. All the institutions listed below offer degree courses, some providing a wide range of courses while others are specialist colleges with a small intake. Those marked * are members of GuildHE (**www.guildhe. ac.uk**). The list includes private institutions. Fees are given for UK/EU undergraduates for a single year of study.

BPP University
BPP House, Aldine Place,
142-4 Uxbridge Road, London W12 8AW
Campuses in Abingdon, Birmingham,
Bristol, Cambridge, Leeds, London,
Manchester, Newcastle, Swindon
0845 077 5566   www.bpp.com
Fees 2013–14: £6,000

Conservatoire for Dance and Drama
(Comprised of Bristol Old Vic Theatre School, Central School of Ballet, Circus Space, London Academy of Music and Dramatic Art, London Contemporary Dance School, Northern School of Contemporary Dance, Rambert School of Ballet and Contemporary Dance, Royal Academy of Dramatic Art.)
Tavistock House, Tavistock Square
London WC1H 9JJ
020 7387 5101   www.cdd.ac.uk
Fees 2014–15: £9,000

Glasgow School of Art
167 Renfrew Street, Glasgow G3 6RQ
0141 353 4500   www.gsa.ac.uk
Fees 2013–14: Scotland/EU, no fee
RUK £9,000

Guildhall School of Music and Drama
Silk Street, Barbican, London EC2Y 8DT
020 7628 2571   www.gsmd.ac.uk
Fees 2014–15: £9,000

ifs University College
8th floor, Peninsular House,
36 Monument Street, London EC3R 8LJ
New campus opening late 2013:
8 Lovat Lane, London EC3R 8DW
01227 829499   www.ifslearning.ac.uk
Fees 2013–14: £6,000

The University of Law
Birmingham, Bristol, Chester, Guildford,
Leeds (2014), London (Bloomsbury and Moorgate), Manchester, York.
0800 289997   www.law.ac.uk
Fees 2014–15: £9,000 (two-year course)
                    £6,000 (three-year course)

Leeds College of Art*
Blenheim Walk, Leeds LS2 9AQ
0113 202 8000   www.leeds-art.ac.uk
Fees 2014–15: £9,000

Liverpool Institute for Performing Arts*
Mount Street, Liverpool L1 9HF
0151 330 3000   www.lipa.ac.uk
Fees 2014–15: £9,000

New College of the Humanities
19 Bedford Square, London WC1B 3HH
020 7367 4550   www.nchum.org
Fees 2013–14: £18,800 (including exam fees)

Ravensbourne*
6 Penrose Way, London SE10 0EW
020 3040 3500   www.ravensbourne.ac.uk
Fees 2014–153: £8,750–£8,850

Regent's University London*
Inner Circle, Regent's Park,
London NW1 4NS
020 7487 7700   www.regents.ac.uk
Fees 2013–14: £14,200

Rose Bruford College of Theatre and Performance*
Lamorbey Park, Burnt Oak Lane,
Sidcup, Kent DA15 9DF
020 8308 2600   http://bruford.ac.uk
Fees 2014–15: £9,000

Royal College of Music
Prince Consort Road, London SW7 2BS
020 7591 4300   www.rcm.ac.uk
Fees 2014–15: £9,000

Royal Conservatoire of Scotland
100 Renfrew Street, Glasgow G2 3DB
0141 332 4101   www.rcs.ac.uk
Fees 2013–14: Scotland/EU, no fee;
RUK £9,000

Royal Northern College of Music
124 Oxford Road, Manchester M13 9RD
0161 907 5200   www.rncm.ac.uk
Fees 2014–15: £9,000

Royal Welsh College of Music and Drama
Castle Grounds, Cathays Park,
Cardiff CF10 3ER
029 2034 2854   www.rwcmd.ac.uk
Fees 2014–15: £9,000

St Mary's University College*
Waldegrave Road, Strawberry Hill
Twickenham TW1 4SX
020 8240 4000   www.smuc.ac.uk
Fees 2014–15: £9,000

St Mary's University College*
191 Falls Road, Belfast BT12 6FE
028 9032 7678   www.stmarys-belfast.ac.uk
Fees 2013–14: £3,465; RUK £9,000

Scotland's Rural College
Campuses at Aberdeen, Ayr, Broxburn,
Cupar, Dumfries, Edinburgh
0800 269543   www.sruc.ac.uk
Fees 2013–14: Scotland/EU, no fee; RUK
£5,600

Stranmillis University College
Stranmillis Road, Belfast BT9 5DY
028 9038 1271   www.stran.ac.uk
Fees 2013–14: £3,465; RUK £9,000

Trinity Laban Conservatoire of Music and Dance
Music Faculty: King Charles Court
Old Royal Naval College,
Greenwich, London SE10 9JF
020 8305 4444
Dance Faculty: Laban Building, Creekside
London SE8 3DZ
020 8305 9400   www.trinitylaban.ac.uk
Fees 2014–15: £9,000

University Campus Suffolk
Waterfront Building, Neptune Quay
Ipswich IP4 1QJ
Other campuses at Bury St Edmunds,
Lowestoft, Otley, Great Yarmouth
01473 338000   www.ucs.ac.uk
Fees 2014–15: £8,500

Writtle College*
Chelmsford, Essex CM1 3RR
01245 424200   www.writtle.ac.uk
Fees 2014–15: £9,000

Index